PIMLICO

90

# THE FALL OF BERLIN

Anthony Read and David Fisher had extremely successful careers in television as writers and producers before embarking on their collaboration as authors. Their best-selling books include *Operation Lucy, Colonel Z, The Deadly Embrace* and *Kristallnacht* for which they were awarded the H. H. Wingate Prize in 1989.

*By the same authors*

Operation Lucy
Colonel Z
The Deadly Embrace
Kristallnacht

*By Anthony Read (with Ray Bearse)*

Conspirator: Churchill, Roosevelt and Tyler Kent, Spy

# THE FALL
# OF BERLIN

ANTHONY READ
and
DAVID FISHER

PIMLICO

PIMLICO

20 Vauxhall Bridge Road, London SW1V 2SA

London Melbourne Sydney Auckland Johannesburg
and agencies throughout the world

First published by Hutchinson Radius 1992
Pimlico edition 1993
Reprinted 1993, 1995, 1998

© Anthony Read and David Fisher 1992

The right of Anthony Read and David Fisher to be
identified as the authors of this work has been asserted by
them in accordance with the Copyright, Designs and
Patents Act, 1988.

Printed and bound in Great Britain by
Mackays of Chatham PLC, Chatham, Kent

ISBN 0-7126-5797-5

# CONTENTS

# LIST OF MAPS

# ABBREVIATIONS

GKO:    (Soviet) State Defence Committee

NKVD:    (Soviet) State Security Service

NSV:    *Nationalsozialistische Volkswohlfahrt* – Nazi Welfare Service

OKH:    *Oberkommando des Heeres* – (German) Army High Command

OKW:    *Oberkommando der Wehrmacht* – (German) Supreme Command of the armed forces

OSS:    (US) Office of Strategic Services

RLB:    *Reichsluftschutzbund* – Reich Air Protection League

RSHA:    *Reichssicherheitshauptamt* – Reich Security Head Office

SA:    *Sturmabteilung* – Hitler's brownshirted shock troops

SD:    *Sicherheitsdienst* – SS Security Service

SHAEF:    Supreme Headquarters Allied Expeditionary Force

SHD:    *Sicherheits- und Hilfsdienst* – Security and Aid Service

SS:    *Schutzstaffel* – Nazi Police and Military Organization

# ACKNOWLEDGEMENTS

W E MUST express our thanks to all those who helped us with our research through interviews and correspondence, sharing their personal experiences with us and allowing us to tell their stories in this book. A full list appears elsewhere, and it would be invidious to single any of them out for special mention here. We are particularly grateful, however, to Herr Hans von Herwarth and Frau Elisabeth von Herwarth, for giving us so many valuable introductions, opening so many doors again, as they have done in the past, and to Dr Walter Schmid and his late wife, Eva, for their hospitality, encouragement and support.

We would also like to express our thanks to Walter Lassally, Hans-Jürgen Röber and Rudi Friedl for their help as guides, translators and interpreters, and to our publishers and editors, Starling Lawrence and Donald Lamm in New York, and Neil Belton in London, for keeping us firmly on the right path when we were tempted to stray.

We are grateful, too, for guidance and encouragement from Professor John Erickson, from Michael Bloch, Inge Haag and Frederick Kendall.

We could not have completed – or even begun – this book without the assistance of various librarians, libraries and institutions. We offer our special thanks to the Imperial War Museum, the London Library, the Goethe Institute in London, Berkshire Public Libraries at Maidenhead and Slough, Norfolk Public Library at Diss, and Suffolk Public Library at Eye, the Public Record Office at Kew, and the Soviet news agency Novosti. In Germany, we received particularly valuable help from the Berlin Information Centre, the Gedankstätte Deutscher Widerstand, the Bundesarchiv in Koblenz and the Militärarchiv in Freiburg.

We gratefully acknowledge the following publishers and copyright holders for permission to use quotations from the books listed.

Cassell PLC: *The Testament of Adolf Hitler.*
Chatto and Windus Limited: *The Berlin Diaries of Marie 'Missie' Vassiltchikov*, and *The Naked Years* by Marianne MacKinnon.
Harcourt Brace Jovanovich Inc: *A Woman in Berlin.*

HarperCollins Publishers: *Memoirs* by Field Marshal Viscount Montgomery; *Letters to Freya* by Helmuth James von Moltke.

Hodder and Stoughton Limited and W. W. Norton & Company: *The Fringes of Power* by Sir John Colville.

Novosti Press Agency Publishing House: *The Final Assault* by Vladimir Abyzov.

Peters, Fraser & Dunlop: *The Goebbels Diaries* edited by Hugh Trevor-Roper.

R. Piper GmbH & Co: *Berlin im zweiten Weltkrieg* by Hans Dieter Schäfer.

Suhrkamp Verlag and Henry Holt and Company: *Berlin Underground (Der Schattenmann)* by Ruth Andreas-Friedrich.

Viking Books: *The Berlin Raids* by Martin Middlebrook.

VSA Verlag: *Arbeiten für den Krieg* by Barbara Kasper, Lothar Schuster and Christof Watkinson.

Weidenfeld and Nicolson Limited and Macmillan New York: *Inside The Third Reich* by Albert Speer; *While Berlin Burns* by Hans-Georg von Studnitz.

Finally, as always, we are eternally grateful to our wives, Rosemary Read and Barbara Fisher, for their support and above all for their patience and forbearance during the long process of research and writing.

# DEDICATION

To the memory of Eva-Liselotte Schmid, a dear friend whose vitality, wit and warm hospitality sustained us on so many visits to Germany

Greater Berlin

Frohnau

Wittenau

Reinickendorf

Tegel

Spandau

R. Panke

Pankow

Weissensee

Wedding

Moabit

BERLIN

Mitte

Tiergarten

Lichtenberg

Hohenschönhausen

Marzahn

Köpenick

Kreuzberg

Neukölln

Teltow Kanal

R. Spree

Charlottenburg

Wilmers-
dorf

Schöne-
berg

Steglitz

Lichterfelde

R. Havel

Grunewald

Gatow

Zehlenhdorf

Havel

Wannsee

Teltow Kanal

Havel Kanal

Potsdam

miles

kms

0      5

0      5

# Central Berlin 1945

Weissensee

Prenzlauer Berg

Wedding

Moabit

Tiergarten

Friedrichshain

Neukölln

Kreuzberg

Wilmersdorf

ELBINGER STR

LANDSBERGER

flak tower

ALLEE

FRANKFURTER STRASSE

Andreas Platz

GREIFSWALDER STR

PRENZLAUER ALLEE

DANZIGER STR

SCHONHAUSER ALLEE

STRASSE

LOTHRINGER STR

Alexander Platz

ALEXANDER STR

MARKUS STR

ANDREAS STR

KOPERNICKER STRASSE

SKALITZER STR

Schlesische Gate

R. Spree

Landwehr Canal

BRUNNEN STRASSE

flak tower

Humboldthain

STRASSE

ORANIENBURGER STR

Museum Island

Lustgarten

DEN LINDEN

KONIG STR

DRESDENER

ORANIEN STR

Moritz Platz

STR

URBAN STR

HASENHEIDE

MULLER STRASSE

Spandau Canal

FENN STR

INVALIDEN

Oranienburger Gate

REINHARDT STR

FRIEDRICH STR

Reichstag

Brandenburg Gate

WILHELM

Stadtmitte

LEIPZIGER STR

KOCH STR

STRASSE

GITSCHINER

Halle Gate

GNEISENAU STR

PREBURGER STR

Post-Stadion

BISMARK STR

Königs Platz

CHAUSSEE

Chancellery

BELLEVUE ALLEE

Anhalter Station

STRESEMANN STR

Viktoria Park

Berlin-

West Hafen

BEUSSEL STRASSE

TURM STR

HUTTEN STR

R. Spree

Bellevue

ALT. MOABIT

CHARLOTTENBURGER

Tiergarten

TIERGARTEN STR

Zoo

LÜTZOW STR

BULOW STR

POTSDAMER STR

YORKSTRASSE

HOHENZOLLERN DAMM

BISMARK STR

BERLINER STR

flak tower

KANT STRASSE

BUDAPESTER STR

Lützow Platz

KURFURSTEN STR

KLEIST STR

NURNBERGER STR

KURFURSTEN DAMM

GRUNEWALD STR

mile

0    1

**From the Vistula to the Oder**

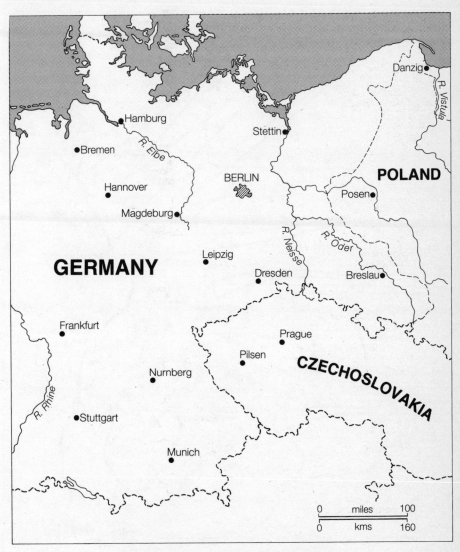

**From the Rhine to the Vistula**

**Operation Berlin; The Soviet Plan of Attack**

# PART ONE

# So much glory, and so much shame

# 1

IT WAS an extraordinary sight – General Hermann Göring, prime minister of Prussia, president of the German Reichstag, minister for air, commander-in-chief of the Luftwaffe, creator of the Gestapo and second only to Hitler himself in the Nazi hierarchy, sitting 'wreathed in smiles and orders and decorations' astride a carousel horse in a Tyrolean-style carnival. Round and round he rode, backed by merry fairground music, waving gaily to hundreds of applauding guests. Looking like an overweight Bacchus in his white dress uniform, he presented a jovial and unthreatening image, a benign new face for the Third Reich.

Göring's display of bonhomie on that chilly evening in August 1936 was part of a careful campaign. The reign of terror inflicted by the Nazis on Germany in general and Berlin in particular had suddenly been relaxed. Even the persecution of the Jews was eased, and thousands of political prisoners had been released from the concentration camps. To the world's wishful thinkers, it seemed the regime was stabilizing at last: that it had no further need of the excesses that had marred its first three years. To the more hopeful citizens of Berlin, it seemed to signal the possibility of a return to the frenetic glamour of the 'golden Twenties', when their city had been the artistic centre of Europe.

Hitler, ably assisted by his minister of public enlightenment and propaganda, Dr Joseph Goebbels, had simply embarked on one of the biggest whitewashing operations of all time. The city had been put on its best behaviour. No one was discriminated against because of race, religion or colour. Visitors flocked in from all over the world, and stayed to marvel at a city that had been reborn in three short years. Berlin was staging the 11th Olympic Games.

IT HAD not been Hitler's idea to stage the 1936 Olympics in Berlin – he had inherited the arrangement when he came to power. In fact, having previously denounced the whole Olympic movement as an invention of Jews and freemasons, he had been inclined to cancel the games out of hand. A frantic

3

German Olympic Committee eventually managed to persuade him that the games could have some political value, but he remained lukewarm.

It was the Olympic stadium that finally sparked his interest: as always, he simply couldn't resist an opportunity for grandiose construction. With little or no government funding, the Olympic Committee planned to refurbish a stadium built for the 1916 Olympiad, which had never taken place because of the First World War. But when Hitler inspected this stadium in the Grunewald woods to the west of the city centre, he declared it was too small, too insignificant. It should be not merely reconstructed but replaced completely with something worthy of his new Reich. 'The proper solution of the problem,' he boasted later, 'demanded thinking on a grand scale.' Convinced that only he was capable of thinking grandly enough, he envisaged a totally new sports complex, bigger and more impressive than anything built for previous Olympiads. Suddenly, his enthusiasm was fired. The Berlin Olympics would be a symbol to the entire world of Germany's resurgence, a showcase for Nazi supremacy.

From the very first, every aspect of the games had a dual purpose. After the Olympics were over, the main arena would stage propaganda displays designed to increase party and patriotic fervour, particularly amongst the young. The Olympic village built to house male athletes in a wooded valley at Döberitz, nine miles to the west, would become new barracks for the army. But for Hitler, the most valuable area of the whole complex was what came to be known as the May Field, a huge expanse of some 130,000 square yards of turf, with low tiers of seats on two sides. This was to provide the dramatic setting for future Nazi party rallies – until then there had been no suitable space for them in Berlin.

More immediately, construction work provided jobs for the unemployed: when the Nazis came to power, one in four of all Berlin males was on welfare. Building the new complex was a huge task – the demolition of the old stadium alone took nearly a year – and much of the work was done by hand in order to use the maximum number of men: some 2,600, most of whom had previously been out of a job, were soon working flat out round the clock.

Inevitably, costs sky-rocketed, but Hitler, typically, did not care. At a time when Germany desperately needed hard currency, the Olympics were guaranteed to draw in thousands of free-spending visitors from abroad. 'I can still see the faces of my colleagues,' he recalled nine years later, 'when I said that I proposed to make a preliminary grant of 28 million marks for the construction of the Berlin Stadium! In actual fact, the stadium cost us 77 million marks – but it brought in over half a billion marks in foreign currency!'

In the city itself, Hitler decided to 'improve' the eight-mile-long east–west route from the Alexanderplatz to the new Olympic complex. This was to become a great *via triumphalis* not just for sporting heroes but also for

German armies returning victorious from war, a highway broad enough for troops to march twelve abreast down each carriageway. Fifty-foot-high, green-painted flagpoles shot up along it like weeds. People who lived on the route found they were eligible for special grants to cover exterior redecoration.

As a result of the road widening, many well-loved old buildings had to go. Worse was to come. While building Unter den Linden station as part of a new north–south S-Bahn line, the authorities committed the ultimate sacrilege. They not only dug up the central promenade, scarring part of the Linden for well over a year with ugly piles of sandy soil, but they also cut down many of the famous lime trees that gave the avenue its name.

Berliners were extremely superstitious about their linden trees. They believed the words of a favourite old song by Walter Kollo, which had become the city's unofficial anthem: 'As long as the old trees still bloom on Unter den Linden, nothing can defeat us – Berlin will stay Berlin.' As the trees came down, the whisper went round: 'No more lime trees in Unter den Linden . . . presently there will be no more Berlin.'

Disturbed by the popular reaction, the city authorities hastily attempted to make good the damage, replacing the desecrated trees with several hundred four-year-old 16-foot American lime saplings. Staked, sprayed, protected with railings, the new trees were neatly planted at intervals of 25 feet, interspersed between new Biedermeier-style street lamps. Since the lamps were tall and ornate, the saplings looked weedy and stunted by comparison. Berliners were not slow to give the avenue a new name: 'Unter die Lanterne'.

# 2

THE MAIN problem facing the Nazis in 1936 was to sanitize the country before foreign visitors began arriving. This meant, among other things, taking down all the anti-Semitic signs, the 'Jews Out' and 'Jews Not Wanted Here' notices in shops and at the entrances to towns and villages. All the crude slogans that had been painted on walls not only in Berlin but all over Germany had to be temporarily erased. Julius Streicher's Jew-baiting tabloid *Die Stürmer* – 'the only paper Hitler reads from A to Z' – was put into cold storage for the duration of the games, vanishing from its swastika-decorated brown display cases on practically every street corne. of the city. Other newspapers were instructed to tone down their virulent anti-Semitism. The works of writers like Heinrich Heine and Marcel Proust, whose books had been burned three years earlier in front of the university, suddenly reappeared in Berlin's bookshops.

Under the Nuremberg Laws promulgated in 1935, Jews were not permitted to fly the swastika flag. The law said nothing about the Olympic flag, however, and Jewish stores in the west end of Berlin – normally conspicuous because of their rows of empty flagpoles – carried whole rows of Olympic banners throughout August. Unfortunately, this defiance was counter-productive in the long term, helping to disguise the extent of anti-Semitism in the Reich by failing to draw attention to flagless buildings.

The cover-up was completed by the fact that there were even two Jewish athletes in the German team: Gretel Bergmann, a talented high jumper then living in England, and Helene Meyer, a half-Jewish fencer who had won a gold medal at the 1928 Olympics. She, too, was resident abroad, in California. Their selection had been forced on Hitler by the International Olympic Committee, which had threatened to remove the games from Berlin if Jewish athletes were denied the opportunity of representing their country.

One of the most tragic consequences of the whitewash was that thousands of German Jews, who should have know better, were themselves taken in. As the anti-Semitic laws were eased, many Jews relaxed their efforts to flee the country, convinced that the worst was over. They believed the propaganda because they wanted to believe it; the reality was more than they could bear.

Klaus Scheurenberg, then an eleven-year-old schoolboy living in Reinickendorf, recalls how his father, Paul, refused to contemplate the truth of their situation. Paul Scheurenberg, whose family had lived in Germany since 1280, was a department store salesman, who had been fired by the Hermann Tietz store in January 1936, the last victim of the store's compulsory Aryanization. He now eked out a living with occasional temporary work in one of the few surviving Jewish-owned stores, such as N. Israel, R. & S. Moses, and Tuchhaus Hansa. But he continued to believe that he and his family would not be harmed by the Nazis. After all, he told his son, as well as having a family background of 650 years in the country, he was a German hero: he had won an Iron Cross in the First World War. In 1935 he had even received a new medal from Hitler, the Frontkampfer Cross, plus a certificate signed by the Führer himself addressing him as 'Dear Comrade Scheurenberg' – at that time, the party had not yet eliminated Jews from the list of medal holders. The Olympic truce in 1936 convinced him that there were better times ahead.

Inge Deutschkron was the fourteen-year-old daughter of an assimilated Jewish family. Her father had been dismissed from his post as a senior high school teacher not because of his race but because he was a social democrat. Now he had been sacked again from a private school, this time because he was Jewish. Yet he refused to contemplate leaving the country, even when he was offered a job in Australia, because he still thought of himself as a good civil servant, 'who could not just run away'. Some Jews, Inge recalls, even returned to live in Germany at that time, because they couldn't adapt to conditions in other countries. One of her uncles had managed to get into Palestine, but was so put off by the peculiarities of the people there, and by 'so much dirtiness', that he chose to go back to Nazi Berlin.

SWEEPING the Jewish problem under the carpet was desirable, but not vital – anti-Semitism, after all, was a worldwide phenomenon. A more essential part of the Nazis' window dressing was that Berlin should be seen to be a Christian, God-fearing city. There should be no visible sign of the repression of the churches, or of the Nazis' determination to bring them totally under government control. To help promote this image, Hans Kerrl, Reich minister for church affairs, arranged for a huge marquee to be erected near the Olympic stadium. In it, Reich church services would be conducted, with tame ministers preaching about Christ and Adolf Hitler in the same breath. At least, that was Kerrl's plan. But some of the ministers had other ideas. Among them was Pastor Dietrich Bonhoeffer, of the evangelical Confessing Church.

Big, moon-faced and bespectacled, with thinning fair hair, the thirty-year-old Bonhoeffer did not cut an impressive figure at first sight. He looked more like a country butcher than a charismatic preacher recognized as one of the most brilliant and controversial Protestant theologians of his day. Bonhoeffer had been a thorn in the flesh of the Nazi regime from its beginning, falling foul of the Gestapo as early as 1933. He had consistently attacked the anti-Semitic legislation, quoting Luther in pointing out that the Apostles had all been Jews, and that without their courage in the face of persecution in bringing the word of Christ to the Gentiles, the Germans would not have become Christians.

On 6 June 1936, Bonhoeffer and a group of fellow ministers delivered a memorandum to the Reich chancellery which they hoped would provide a basis for discussion with Hitler. It covered such matters as the 'de-Christianization' of schools, universities and colleges, criticized the ideology of anti-Semitism, objected to the manipulation of the Reichstag elections, the existence of concentration camps, the legal non-accountability of the Gestapo, and so on. Hitler had ignored the document, but nearly seven weeks later its contents were printed word for word in the Swiss German newspaper, the *Basler Nachrichten*.

The publication caused an uproar. No one would admit to authorizing it. The Lutheran Council publicly dissociated itself from the document. One councillor, Gauleiter Holtz, even declared that the authors were guilty of high treason. Three of Bonhoeffer's friends wound up in Sachsenhausen concentration camp, joining hundreds of other ministers who had been arrested in May. One of them, Friedrich Weissler, who was Jewish, died there six days after his arrest, as a result of savage beatings.

However much they may have hated him, however, the Nazis could not afford to ignore Bonhoeffer, who was one of the most popular preachers in Germany. But when he was invited to preach in Kerrl's marquee, he refused, saying he would not lend his name to Nazi propaganda. Nor would he permit his photograph to appear on the official publicity handout, knowing that this, too, would give a bogus seal of approval to a regime he loathed.

In the end, fellow ministers of the Confessing Church persuaded Bonhoeffer to join them in a series of half-hour theological lectures, not in the marquee, but in St Paul's church, well away from the stadium. Such was the reputation of Bonhoeffer and the other ministers that night after night the enormous building was packed and overflow meetings had to be held in another large church. The official report in the government-approved paper *Die Christliche Welt* was disapproving: 'This state of affairs must cause great alarm among those concerned with the future of the Evangelical Church,' it warned.

Bonhoeffer himself came across a more direct threat to the Confessing Church, on printed cards he found in a Berlin bookshop, bearing a sinister piece of doggerel:

> After the end of the Olympiade,
> We'll beat the CC to marmalade,
> Then we'll chuck out the Jew,
> The CC will end too.

But rebels like Dietrich Bonhoeffer were only a tiny minority. Swept up in the excitement of the great event, most of the people of Berlin were happy to play along with Hitler's great deception. 'Today, no other city is so filled with the Olympic spirit as the capital of the Reich,' ten-year-old Marianne Gärtner's headmaster told her and her friends before their school broke up for the games. Unaware of any conflict with the true Olympic spirit, he went on: 'Berlin and its people are not only waiting to show off their accomplishments, but to demonstrate to the world that Germany has left the Treaty of Versailles behind, and with it its national inferiority.' He ended by making it clear that even little children had a part to play: 'And now, girls, off you go. Let the world see what happy, healthy maidens you are! Heil Hitler!'

So by the time the foreign visitors arrived, Berlin presented a different picture from the reality of only a few weeks before. The visitors saw no persecution of Jews, no repression of churches, no brutal imprisonment of dissidents. They saw instead a model country full of blonde, broad-beamed, dirndl-skirted fräuleins and helpful, smiling Hitler Youths, a country which, they were told, had been rescued from anarchy by Adolf Hitler. In short, they saw what they were supposed to see – and in the main they believed it.

# 3

ON FRIDAY, 31 July 1936, the day before the Olympics were due to open, Berliners in their thousands took to the streets to admire their city. And well they might. To little Marianne Gärtner, Berlin 'seemed to click its heels and salute its guests. . . . Happy crowds sauntered along the broad boulevards where generous flower displays lent grey, stuccoed façades and monumental Third Reich edifices a cheerful touch. There was a holiday atmosphere about the city, a festive mood which not even the sight of massed uniforms could dispel. . . . For two weeks, the world had come to Berlin; for two weeks the world seemed to have shrunk to a few square kilometres.'

The Unter den Linden and all the roads leading to it were jammed with cars. People overflowed the pavements – the police later estimated that 1.2 million visitors had come to the city for the games. Street entertainers, banned for three years, were back in business. Officially imposed closing hours were suspended. Jazz, condemned by the Nazis as 'degenerate nigger music', made a low-key reappearance in some of the clubs. Teddy Stauffer and his Original Teddies swung at the Delphi Palast.

With so many visitors – the international press corps alone numbered over 1,500 – Berlin's hotels were soon filled, and even the best restaurants were forced to turn away customers in droves. Tea time at the exclusive Hotel Adlon, near the Brandenburg Gate on the corner of Pariser Platz and Wilhelmstrasse, normally the resort of diplomats and the German aristocracy, now sounded like the waiting room in the Tower of Babel, with everyone talking at the tops of their voice in almost every language known to man.

Music blared from loudspeakers installed along the entire length of the *via triumphalis*, from the Lustgarten in the east, along the Unter den Linden, beneath the Brandenburg Gate, which was festooned with green garlands and swastika flags, along the Charlottenburger Chaussee, through the Tiergarten, along Bismarckstrasse and Kaiserdamm, up the wide Heerstrasse between clipped hedges and double files of sycamores, right out to the stadium. Every night during the games they played Viennese waltzes, military marches and jolly drinking songs, interspersed with official announcements, as though Berlin were just one huge holiday camp.

# 4

THROUGHOUT July the weather in Berlin had been perfect – warm, bright and dry. But on the evening of Friday, 31 July, the skies began to cloud over and Saturday, 1 August, the day of the opening, dawned overcast and grey, with the threat of rain. Soon it began to drizzle. But the crowds already gathering in the streets refused to be downhearted. Nothing was going to dampen their spirits.

As always with the Nazis, there were mass demonstrations – beginning with 100,000 schoolchildren dancing, running and performing gymnastics on playing fields all over Berlin from 8 to 10 am. Members of the International Olympic Committee visited one field. At 11 am it was the turn of the armed forces: special army, navy and air force units, along with foreign students and youth organizations, marched down the Unter den Linden from the Brandenburg Gate to provide a guard for a wreath-laying ceremony at the war memorial, performed by Count Henri de Baillet-Latour, president of the IOC, and Dr Theodore Lewald, the head of the German Olympic Committee.

The morning ended with the brownshirted Hitler Youth and white-clad Bund Deutsches Mädchen, 28,000 young people in all, parading before the Old Museum on the square known as the Lustgarten, the site of an exotic garden laid down by Princess Louise, wife of the Great Elector of Prussia, in the seventeenth century, but turned into a parade ground by Hitler in 1935. At exactly 12.58 pm, Goebbels ended the patriotic speeches with the cry 'Holy flame, burn, burn, and never go out!' Punctually to the second, the flame appeared, as the runner carrying the Olympic torch arrived, ran up to the brazier that stood on an altar before the rostrum, and ignited its contents with the torch. It was then guarded by the Hitler Youth until 3 pm.

AT THE stadium, those fortunate enough to have tickets took their places early after lunch. While they waited, they were kept entertained by selections from Wagner and Liszt, played by the newly created Olympic Symphony Orchestra, recruited from the personnel of several other orchestras, including the entire Berlin Philharmonic. In the crowd were many distinguished foreign visitors, among them several princes and a clutch of maharajas.

With so many exotic foreigners, the staff of the VIP box were not surprised when a distinguished-looking couple, a man and a woman in their late twenties and early thirties, presented themselves at the door. When asked for their tickets, they replied at length in a totally unknown language. The attendant called one of the official interpreters, who, after trying several languages, was forced to admit defeat. He called another interpreter, who had a different range of tongues. When he gave up, a third was called. In all, seventeen interpreters failed to establish the nationality of the visitors, who were by now growing visibly annoyed. Finally, to prevent what threatened to become an international incident, they were allowed into the box, and seats were found for them just behind the Führer.

No one took much notice of them – no one except General Walter von Reichenau, one of the most ardent Nazis in the officer corps, who almost had a fit when he saw them there as he joined Hitler. Reichenau recognized the woman as his sister-in-law, Maria Countess von Maltzan, and her husband, Walter Hillbring, a Berlin cabaret artist. Unable to afford tickets, they had decided to gatecrash the ceremony. 'We were quite good with each other,' Maria von Maltzan laughs as she recalls the general's reaction. 'I just sort of winked my eye and he said nothing. In the evening he asked, "How did you get in?" I said, "Quite easy. With a new language that we invented, paying not a penny!"'

It was an exploit typical of Maria von Maltzan, a striking and unconventional young woman with a powerful personality, who later became known – quite erroneously – as 'the Red Countess'. The daughter of an ancient Silesian family, she was utterly unimpressed by authority, especially that wielded by men such as the Nazi leaders, whom she regarded as little more than despicable worms.

EXACTLY ON the stroke of 3, Hitler's cavalcade, five big, black Mercedes tourers, left the old chancellery building on Voss-strasse, drove north up Wilhelmstrasse to the Unter den Linden and turned left to cross Pariserplatz and pass through the centre of the Brandenburg Gate. Hitler stood upright beside the driver of the leading car, gripping the windshield with his left hand while he saluted the hysterical crowds with his right arm held almost horizontally before him.

At the same time, the runner carrying the Olympic torch set off from the Lustgarten, followed by twelve others wearing white or black strip. In strict V-formation like migrating geese, they ran steadily across the broad bridge over the Spree and then along the Unter den Linden.

The members of the IOC had been driven out to the stadium already, to greet Hitler on his arrival. Decked out in gold chains of office and wearing frock coats and top hats, they looked like refugees from the smart magazines. As they passed along the route, the Berlin crowd grumbled noisily, as is the way with Berlin crowds, that they had not stood in the rain for well over two hours, 'driving their knees up into their bellies', just to watch a *verdammte* fashion show!

By the time Hitler's Mercedes pulled up by the bell tower, the drizzle had stopped. A guard of honour drawn from all three services, plus members of the International and German Olympic committees and athletes of the fifty-one competing countries, stood waiting to greet him. As he entered the stadium, a small brown-clad figure leading a procession of notables, sixty trumpeters raised their instruments and blew a specially composed fanfare. The crowd rose deliriously to its feet.

Proceeding across the arena, Hitler paused to receive a bouquet from a little girl wearing a chaplet of flowers on her head. She was Gudrun Diem, five-year-old daughter of Carl Diem, secretary of the German Olympic Committee. Always good with children, the Führer bent, cupped the child's face in his hands in the gesture familiar to him, and, smiling, spoke to her gently as though the two of them were quite alone. Above the cheering of the crowd, the orchestra burst into Wagner's March of Homage.

Slowly at first, the great Olympic bell with its inscription '*Ich rufe die Jugend der Welt*' ('I summon the youth of the world'), began to toll. As if in answer to its summons, the athletes in their national teams began marching into the arena through the marathon gate.

The opening ceremony followed its conventional course of salutes, speeches, fanfares, oaths, the lighting of the flame and the release of 3,000 doves – flying away, Emerson Bainbridge of the *Blackshirt* claimed, 'to distant lands to dispel the lies and hatred bred by international Jewry'. But there was one more custom to be observed before athletes and spectators could disperse. It had nothing to do with the Olympic movement but was inescapable in Nazi Germany: the singing of the 'Horst Wessel Song'. Later that evening Hitler returned to the Olympic stadium for a spectacular pageant involving a cast of over 10,000 young people. Virtually every one of them was as excited and awe-struck as Marianne Gärtner, whose eyes kept straying over to the grandstand, 'Where I know the Führer is watching – is watching me!'

# 5

THROUGHOUT the games, Hitler continued to visit the stadium as often as affairs of state permitted. His arrival was greeted with the raising of the Nazi and Olympic flags at opposite corners of the government box and the sudden roar of the loyal German crowd, ritually crying 'Sieg Heil! Sieg Heil!' no matter what race was under way, no matter who was winning. He became passionately involved, leaning eagerly over the rail during races, eyes popping with excitement. When the flag of the winning nation was run up the flagpole, he was always first on his feet, whoever had won. But when the winner was German, his delight was unmistakable. Diplomatic correspondent Bella Fromm observed that when a German won he went into 'an orgiastic frenzy of shrieks, clappings and contortions. He behaved like a madman, jumping from his seat and roaring when the swastika was hoisted, or when Japanese or Finns won a victory. Other champions left him cold and personally offended at their victories over their Nordic contestants.'

Above the stadium for the duration of the games, buzzing gently like a huge, silver bumble bee, floated the *Hindenburg*, the latest and finest of the Zeppelins. Its presence was the symbol of Hitler's determination to squeeze every drop of propaganda value out of the Olympics. Often described as a flying hotel, with a crew of forty and a grand piano in its lounge, the *Hindenburg* held the Blue Riband for the fastest crossing of the Atlantic. Now, however, it carried Heinz von Jaworsky, one of Germany's top cameramen, just back from filming the progress of the sacred flame all the way from Greece to Berlin.

Like Goebbels, Hitler was a film buff, and fully aware of the medium's vast potential. What better way could there be of showing off the achievements of his new Germany to the whole world than this now universal medium, in which one extraordinary image could be worth a thousand words of laboured prose? So, he had commissioned a film of the games to be made by his favourite director, Leni Riefenstahl, who became a familiar figure during all the great events, in her long white coat and big white felt hat, busily urging on her crews.

Riefenstahl, a thirty-four-year-old ex-ballet dancer turned actress, had starred in and finally directed a series of popular mountaineering pictures in the 1920s and early 1930s. Hitler greatly admired her work and made her the top film executive of the Nazi Party. She had proved her worth by directing a brilliant propaganda epic, *Triumph des Willens* (*Triumph of the Will*), about the 1934 Nuremberg rally.

For the new project, Hitler decreed that money was no object. Despite Goebbels's intense personal jealousy – it is said he even tried to prevent Riefenstahl setting foot in the stadium – finance was provided through his Propaganda Ministry, and the director was given all the resources she needed: no fewer than forty-one cameramen are listed on the credits. She was given absolute authority over all filming in the stadium: any outside photographer or cameraman who impeded her crews, or who was anywhere Riefenstahl thought he should not be, was swiftly approached by an attendant, who handed him a pink slip. The message was brief and to the point: 'Remove yourself immediately from where you are now. Riefenstahl!' Receipt of two such slips in one day meant permanent removal of the offender, by force if necessary.

Hitler's decision to commission Riefenstahl proved to be inspired. In her masterpiece, *Olympia*, he got more than his money's worth: it was undoubtedly the greatest movie ever made about Olympic sport, and a permanent memorial to the glory that was Berlin in 1936.

## 6

FOR THE whole of the Olympics, Berlin remained perpetually *en fête*. Göring's jovial carousel ride took place during an evening garden party in the grounds of his Air Ministry – only one of many spectacular celebrations in the city during the games. The members of the International Olympic Committee needed iron constitutions to keep up with the endless flow of rich food and German wines and, of course, speeches, speeches and more speeches. They were entertained to luncheons and dinners by the mayor and city of Berlin, by the Reich sports leader, Dr Hans von Tschammer und Osten, and numerous others, including Hitler himself. They dined in state in the White Room of the old Imperial Palace, in the House of German Fliers, in the Golden Gallery of Charlottenburg Palace, aboard warships in Kiel harbour.

Hitler's dinner for 150 guests on Wednesday, 12 August, was the most select formal occasion of the games. But the most keenly anticipated events in the social calendar were the parties given by the most senior Nazi paladins, Göring and Goebbels. The two men were not only political rivals, but also bitter personal enemies: they could be relied upon to compete in the extravagance of their celebrations, just as they competed for favour with Hitler.

There could be little doubt who was favourite to win the present competition. Goebbels was never popular with Berliners, who saw him as a deformed, upstart Rhinelander, on the make in their city. Göring, who came from the minor aristocracy of Prussia though he had been brought up mainly in Bavaria, was known almost affectionately as 'Der Dicke' (Fatso) or 'Unser Hermann' (our Hermann), while Goebbels was usually referred to merely as 'Der Krüppel' (the cripple).

Göring was a genuine war hero, a world war fighter ace, decorated with the coveted 'Blue Max', Germany's highest decoration for valour. Goebbels had no such distinction, having been barred from military service by his short left leg, the result of an operation for osteomyelitis at the age of seven. Berliners admired Göring's gusto, the fact that he made no bones about enjoying the good things of life, and that as long as he was the centre of attention he did not seem to mind making a fool of himself. They believed he really did have a sense of humour – a dangerous assumption to make of any politician. There was even a story that he would pay five marks to anyone bringing him new jokes about himself, which he was said to write down in a book kept permanently on his desk.

Goebbels, looking like something out of a tale by E.T.A. Hoffmann, with his small, sinister figure and obvious limp, was incapable of arousing such a warm response. Berliners were mildly amused by the stories of his randiness. Some were no doubt envious of his reputation for asserting his *droit de seigneur* over young actresses, but their jokes about him were touched with more than a little malice.

'When Goebbels dies,' went one such quip, 'they're going to have to take his mouth out and shoot it, or the corpse will never stop talking.' Another concerned the buxom golden angel on top of the Siegessäule, the Victory Column. Weighing over 30 tons, the angel is described by Berliners as the heaviest woman in the city – and the cheapest, because it only costs one mark to visit her. When Hitler decided to have the column moved from its original position in front of the Reichstag building to the Grosser Stern, a circle in the centre of the Charlottenburger Chaussee in the Tiergarten (where it still stands today), he had the column made considerably taller. 'Why did they have to put the angel up higher?' asked the city wags. Answer: 'So that Goebbels couldn't get up her skirts!'

The Berlin Olympics ended on the evening of Sunday, 16 August, with a ceremony that was every bit as impressive as the opening, complete with rockets, gun salutes, the tolling of the great bell, fanfares from massed trumpeters, the singing of hymns and anthems, and powerful searchlights reaching up to form a tent of light over the stadium in the style perfected at the Nuremberg rallies. No one was aware of any irony when the IOC president bid the nations reassemble for the 1940 Olympics in Tokyo.

The games had been a huge success for Germany, whose athletes had topped the medal table with 33 golds, followed by the USA with 24, Hungary with 10 and Great Britain and Austria with 4 each. But the most important result for the Nazis was the triumph of their propaganda. 'Every one of you,' Goebbels had told the party in advance, 'must be a host. The future of the Reich will depend on the impression that is left on our guests.'

The party had gone out of its way to please foreign businessmen, particularly the Americans, and had succeeded brilliantly. When William Shirer interviewed a group of his fellow countrymen, they told him they were 'favourably impressed by the Nazi "set-up"'. Asked what they thought about, for instance, the Nazi suppression of churches, they replied that Göring had convinced them this was all a figment invented by US correspondents, all of whom were anti-Nazi. 'He assured us,' one business-man told Shirer, 'that there was no truth in what you fellows write about persecution of religion over here.'

Shirer became so concerned at the false image American businessmen were gaining that he invited Douglas Miller, US commercial attaché in Berlin and one of the best-informed men in the embassy, to give a talk to a group of American visitors one lunchtime. But Miller got nowhere: 'The genial tycoons told *him* what the situation in Nazi Germany was. They liked it, they said. The streets were clean and peaceful. Law and Order. No strikes, no trouble-making unions. No agitators. No Commies.'

Hitler could hardly have asked for more.

# 7

T HE YEAR of the Olympic Games marked the high point of Nazi Berlin. In fact, in many ways it was the high point of the city's entire history. Hitler's regime may have been a brutal dictatorship, but that was hardly anything new. The Hohenzollern dynasty, after all, had ruled as an absolute monarch for 477 years, dealing with the city and its people entirely as it pleased. Right through to November 1918 both Reichstag and city council were little more than talking shops: the elected members discussed, but the Kaiser decided. The habit of submitting to the whims of a despot had become deeply ingrained in Berliners over many generations. They had learned to live with autocracy, to cope with the existence of a secret police and its spies and informers, and to make their political protests as black jokes rather than public demonstrations, long before Hitler came to power.

In a history of over 700 years, Berlin had experienced barely fourteen years of democracy. And in those years, between 1919 and 1933, the city had suffered revolution and counter-revolution, street battles, political murder, hyper-inflation, soaring unemployment, moral depravity, and a complete breakdown in the established social order.

For those who had the money, the looks and the energy, the Twenties had been golden years. Berlin had suddenly become the artistic centre of the world and its high life one continuous wild party. But for hundreds of thousands of others, those years brought nothing but misery and despair. And the frenetic gaiety evaporated into a terrible morning after in the great crash of 1929. Chaos returned, a fearful reminder of the anarchy that had reigned in the years immediately after the war.

In 1931 and 1932 the threat of civil war between Nazis and the forces of the right on one side, and socialists and communists on the other, cast its giant shadow over Germany as a whole and Berlin in particular. In just six weeks before the elections in July 1932, there were 461 pitched battles on the streets. Over 200 people were killed, mostly Nazis and communists; hundreds more were wounded. And when the Nazis took power in 1933 the violence escalated still further: terror had become government policy.

BY THE time of the Olympics, however, the streets were clean and safe. Unemployment had almost disappeared. In the space of only two years industrial production had doubled. Internationally, too, Hitler had scored a series of striking successes. The shame of Versailles had been dispelled with the ending of reparations and the beginning of rearmament. The Saar had been returned from French occupation, and no one in France or Britain had raised a finger to stop the remilitarization of the Rhineland. To the man in the street, Hitler had brought prosperity, national rehabilitation and the return of German pride. And if these had been achieved at a certain cost, what did it matter?

In fact, it mattered a great deal to thousands of Berliners – Christians like Dietrich Bonhoeffer, conservative thinkers like Albrecht Haushofer, Jews like the Scheurenbergs, bloody-minded aristocrats like Maria von Maltzan, senior officers like General Ludwig Beck, chief of the general staff, who were disgusted by the regime's coarse behaviour. It mattered to the thousands of left-wing political activists who had been harassed and beaten up and thrown into concentration camps.

It mattered to all those workers in districts like Wedding, who for generations had given the city its nickname of 'Red Berlin': in every single election since the very first in 1849, the citizens of Berlin had voted overwhelmingly for the liberals, social democrats and communists. While the rest of Germany was making the Nazis the largest party in the Reichstag in 1932, almost three out of four Berliners voted against them. Even in March 1933, with brownshirt squads on the streets and their political opponents outlawed and locked up, the Nazis could only raise less than a third of the Berlin votes.

# 8

ALTHOUGH Berlin was the capital of Prussia, its people never considered themselves Prussians, but a quite separate breed. In many ways they were right, for the modern Berliner was the product of a unique mixture of races and nationalities which had poured into the city in wave after wave since 1640.

There were Dutch builders and farmers and engineers, Jewish business-men and bankers and thinkers, French Huguenots, other Protestant refugees from Poland, Italy and the southern German states, soldiers from Switzerland and Sweden, Jacobite rebels from Scotland, and, finally, poor immigrants from all over Eastern Europe. Above all, in the nineteenth and early twentieth centuries there had been a great flood of migrants from the neighbouring province of Silesia, themselves a strange racial mixture, half German, half Slav, as different from the Prussians as the Scots or Irish are from the English. It has long been a standing joke that every true Berliner is a Silesian. Ask any Berliner where his or her family comes from, and there is a good chance that the answer, accompanied by a broad grin, will be 'Silesia – of course!'

But whatever their roots, the people of Berlin were inordinately proud of their city. They were proud of its immaculate cleanliness – there was never any litter to be seen, even after a big parade. They were proud of the fact that although it was laced with waterways and lakes there were no mosquitoes, and that unlike most major cities, it had very few rats, either. They were proud of its size: the whole of the industrial Ruhr valley would fit comfortably inside its boundaries. And they were proud of the amount of open space it contained: forests, lakes, rivers and parks accounted for over 135 of its 339 square miles.

The western half of Berlin in particular was blessed with mile after mile of woodland and water. Within the north-western city boundaries, herds of deer and even wild boar roamed free among the birches, beeches and horse chestnuts of the forests of Tegel, Falkenhagen and Spandau. Further south, the Grunewald – literally, the greenwood – brought the country almost to the end of the Kurfürstendamm. The Grunewald also fringed the sparkling waters of the seven-mile-long Havel lake, which was crowded every weekend and holiday with pleasure boats. At Wannsee, at the southern end of the Havel, elegant waterside promenades, exclusive clinics and a smart lido with a sandy bathing beach – the biggest inland beach in Europe – created a permanent resort atmosphere.

Even the more industrial eastern half of the city, where thousands of workers were crammed into huge, ageing apartment blocks, was well served with parks. There was water here, too, with canals and the rivers Spree and Dahme broadening into elongated lakes. These waterways were busy with industrial and commercial traffic, but they were still used for recreation.

Central Berlin was never beautiful, but it was always imposing. There were, in fact, two centres, one on either side of the Tiergarten, that stretch of sandy Prussian heathland some two miles long by one mile wide that still survived, only partially tamed, in the heart of the city. Each side had its own, distinct character.

To the east, beyond the Brandenburg Gate topped with the four-horse chariot of the goddess of victory, the old 'official' centre lay around the Unter den Linden. This magnificent avenue, a mile long by 200 yards wide, with 1,000 lime or linden trees planted four abreast, had been created in 1670 by Dorothea of Holstein, wife of the Elector Friedrich Wilhelm, as an attractive approach to the new suburb of Dorotheenstadt, which she was building outside the then city walls. In the 1930s it was no longer a rural ride, but a fine city boulevard where Berliners liked to promenade on summer evenings, past exclusive shops, bustling pavement cafés, luxury hotels, the headquarters of banks and business corporations, and the monumental buildings of earlier times.

Its rulers, the Electors, Kings and finally Emperors, had changed Berlin in a little over 250 years from a remote provincial town of 6,000 inhabitants into an imperial capital of 4.5 million. The memorials to that progress were ranged along the length of the Linden: the baroque Zeughaus, or Arsenal, its yellow stucco exterior decorated with ornate carvings and fine sculptures; the austere, columned guardhouse, the Neue Wache, which had become the national war memorial housing Germany's tomb of the unknown soldier; the stately palace originally built for Frederick the Great's brother, Prince Heinrich, which had been home to the university since its foundation in 1815; opposite the university, Opernplatz, a square created by Frederick the Great around his magnificent State Opera House, flanked by St Hedwig's Catholic cathedral, its domed design based on the Roman Pantheon, two more royal palaces, and the Prussian state library with its elegant classical façade. Two blocks to the south, on the square known as the Gendarmenmarkt, stood the grey stone bulk of the old National Theatre, framed between a matching pair of cathedrals, the French and the German, both with tall domed towers.

On either side of the Linden, successive rulers had built new streets and districts during the seventeenth and eighteenth centuries. Running south from Pariserplatz, the great parade square immediately in front of the Brandenburg Gate, the most important of these streets was Wilhelmstrasse. In Wilhelmstrasse and Wilhelmplatz, the square through which it ran, were the chancellery, the old presidential place, the Foreign Ministry, the ministries of Justice, Economics, Finance, Transport, Food and Agriculture, Air, and Propaganda, plus the regional headquarters of the SA, the *Sturmabteilung*, Hitler's brownshirted shock troops, and the British embassy. Most other ministries and offices were in the adjoining streets, so that the quarter as a whole came to be known quite simply as 'the Wilhelmstrasse'.

On the other side of Pariserplatz, alongside the Brandenburg Gate, stood the Reichstag, a monument to the continuing failure of parliamentary government in Germany. Completed in 1894, it was a square, stone structure, its roofline heavy with statuary, a turret at each corner, a neo-baroque squared dome at its centre, and a pediment supported by six Corinthian columns framing the entrance. At the time of the Olympics, however, the burned-out Reichstag was little more than a blackened skeleton at Hitler's feast.

19

Halfway along, the Linden was bisected by Friedrichstrasse, a bustling street of hotels, stores and cafés originally used by troops of the Berlin garrison – who at times had made up over 25 per cent of the city's entire population – to march south to their main parade ground at Tempelhof. Friedrichstrasse, by Hitler's time, had become the slightly seedy entertainments centre of old Berlin, as the smarter clientele of its earlier days had moved westwards.

At the eastern end of the Linden the original city centre was marked by a cluster of heavy stone buildings on the island in the River Spree where the first settlers, a group of fishermen, had built their simple huts. The old imperial palace, a massive building of considerable grandeur if little grace, was surrounded by several museums housing a remarkable collection of antique treasures and works of art. The finest building among them, facing the palace across the paved expanse of the old Lustgarten, was the Old Museum, a severely classical masterpiece by Berlin's greatest architect, Karl Friedrich Schinkel, who transformed the face of the city during his period as royal building master from 1815 until his death in 1841. Most of his buildings were still standing in the 1930s, shaping the physical character of 'official' Berlin. Between the palace and the museum was the Berlin cathedral, completed just before the First World War, another domed neo-baroque structure.

The ancient heart of the city lay to the east of Museum Island, where several old churches stood on narrow medieval streets around the Alexanderplatz, the city's less glamorous shopping centre. Here the department stores for the most part catered for the needs of less affluent Berliners, though the very first, N. Israel, founded in 1815, still prided itself on serving its traditional clientele of army families, the solid bourgeoisie, and old landowners of the Brandenburg district. Towering over the square was the nineteenth-century 'Red Town Hall' – named after the colour of its bricks, though it could just as well have applied to the politics of every administration that had occupied it from Bismarck's time until Hitler's.

Alexanderplatz had been Berlin's original business centre, but fashionable life had long since moved away, down the Linden and across the Tiergarten, to the new west end which mushroomed at the end of the nineteenth century around the Kaiser Wilhelm memorial church. Built in 1891 to commemorate the first Kaiser of a united Germany, the big church stood stiffly amid swirling traffic on an island site at the junction of five broad shopping streets. Opposite, in the south-west corner of the Tiergarten, was the zoo, its bright red, pagoda-like entrance supported by two giant statues of Indian elephants.

The smartest of all the new streets was the Kurfürstendamm. Barely forty years old at the time of the Olympics, it had until the 1890s been an open road where army officers exercised their horses each morning between the Tiergarten and the woods of the Grunewald. Now it was a boulevard to rival the Linden, with smart shops that equalled those of Bond Street or Fifth

Avenue. Their luxury goods were displayed in elegant glass cabinets on the broad, tree-shaded pavements. Fashionable *pâtisseries*, cafés and restaurants were filled with the smart and the chic. After dark, night clubs and cabarets competed with palatial movie theatres to provide entertainment for those who could afford it, while the ladies who sauntered along the pavements were the most expensive whores in Berlin.

The architectural style of the west end was in marked contrast to that of the older city across the Tiergarten. The traditional Prussian restraint of Schinkel and his predecessors was here replaced by a bombastic exuberance often known as 'Reich braggadocio style'. Vast, stuccoed office and apartment blocks were festooned with heavy-handed decoration, every doorway and balcony supported by muscular caryatids or straining Atlases. But whatever their aesthetic faults, they were solidly built and strong.

In the second half of the nineteenth century, when Berlin had exploded in the space of two or three decades from a medium-sized royal residence that could not even build its own steam engines to the biggest and most powerful industrial city in Europe, there had been a huge influx of workers. To house the new millions, speculators and industrialists had thrown up thousands of the notorious *Mietskasernen* ('rental barracks') in the industrial areas like Moabit, Wedding, Kreuzberg and Neukölln, which ringed the city centre on the north, south and east.

These monstrosities, unique to Berlin, were huge tenement buildings, usually covering all four sides of an entire city block in an unbroken hollow square. The interior of each block was filled in with a honeycomb of more apartments built in a series of square courts or wells, stretching back as many as six deep, with a single access from the street through a dark tunnel of archways. In many of the inner courts, small workshops and factories were crammed in alongside communal privies, adding to the general noise and dirt. Each block housed hundreds of families, with shared kitchens and inadequate drainage, perfect incubators for disease – and for political extremism. Berliners, characteristically, took a perverse pride in claiming they had the worst industrial slums in Europe.

In the 1930s the older industrial districts were still filled with *Mietskasernen*: street after street, block after block of five-storey slabs, each housing thousands of people in dismal gloom. The inhabitants found some escape in the hundreds of *Kneipen*, little bars that were to be found on just about every street corner, dispensing humour, *Weissbier*, the distinctive local 'white beer', and mounds of Berlin food – sausages and potatoes and sauerkraut, hams and smoked pork cutlets.

On summer evenings or at weekends they swarmed to their 'colonies' of *Schrebergärten*, allotments on the edge of the central districts, each with its highly individual summerhouse set on a few square yards of land that could be cultivated for food or flowers and lawn. These little gardens are a feature of most German cities, but they were started in Berlin – by Dr Daniel Schreber, in the 1870s – and nowhere was their development brought to such a peak as in the dozens of colonies in and around Berlin.

Some workers had managed to escape completely from the squalor of the inner city slums. From the late nineteenth century onwards, the more enlightened industrial employers in Berlin, companies such as the electrical giant Siemens and the Borsig heavy engineering works, had moved out from the city centre and started building bright new factories surrounded by bright new suburbs to house their workers.

In the 1920s their efforts were joined by the newly formed municipal authority for Greater Berlin. Young architects were commissioned to design and build modern housing developments, mostly through public-utility enterprises. Boldly and imaginatively planned, these included large estates of low-rise houses and flats, set amid immaculate gardens, lawns and parks, which still look modern today. The 135,000 new homes built during the decade gave a whole new look to the suburbs surrounding the old city: clean-cut, simple, restrained.

The wealthy commissioned the same men to design single homes for them in the leafy surroundings of the Grunewald, resulting in many remarkable examples of modern domestic architecture. In the public sphere, the overblown style of the Wilhelmine era was replaced with the simple lines of buildings such as the new broadcasting centre and Tempelhof airport, and the glass and steel structures of Walter Gropius, Mies van der Rohe and Eric Mendelsohn. These men and their associates – most of them teachers or alumni of the Bauhaus school of arts and crafts – revolutionized architecture and industrial design. Their creed that 'form follows function' created a powerful and distinctive style of clean lines and uncluttered façades. They put Berlin at the forefront of modern design in the Twenties and early Thirties, before Hitler forced a return to pomposity.

# 9

B ERLINERS' metropolitan contempt for provincials naturally extended to Hitler, an Austrian politician based in Bavaria. Until 1930, most of them still thought of him as a small-time beerhall rabble rouser who had launched a ludicrous attempt at a national coup – in Munich of all places – in November 1923. The marchers he had led, alongside the First World War military leader General Erich Ludendorff, had been routed by a few rounds from a police machine gun. What sort of a revolution was that?

Hitler returned their contempt, with interest. He had not set foot in Berlin until October 1916, when he was already twenty-seven years old and recovering from a leg wound. He took an instant dislike to the city, which turned to a lasting hatred in January 1918 when its munitions workers went on strike, demanding an end to the war. 'What was the army fighting for,' he demanded bitterly, 'if the homeland itself no longer wanted victory?'

Hitler's attitude to Berlin before he came to power was reflected in his newspaper, the *Völkischer Beobachter* ('People's Observer'), which was published, of course, in Munich. A virulent diatribe in July 1928 denounced the capital as 'a melting pot of everything that is evil – prostitutes, drinking houses, cinemas, Marxism, Jews, strippers, Negroes dancing, and all the vile offshoots of so-called "modern art".'

Hitler never owned a private residence in the city – until he became chancellor his Berlin base was a suite in the Kaiserhof Hotel. His homes remained in the south: a nine-roomed apartment on the second floor of 16 Regentenplatz, Munich, and his alpine retreat, the Berghof, near Berchtesgaden. Throughout his entire rule, he rarely spent more than a few days at a time in Berlin, always escaping at the first opportunity.

# 10

THE NAZI assault on Berlin was led not by Hitler but by Joseph Goebbels, whom he sent there as Gauleiter of Greater Berlin, the supreme party chief for the area, in 1926. The twenty-eight-year-old Rhinelander, a doctor of philosophy in literature from Heidelberg university, took over a moribund and divided local party, whose members were more interested in fighting each other than the communists and socialists. Goebbels himself later claimed there were only 300 members; he was probably exaggerating – he usually did – but there were certainly less than 1,000. Party headquarters was in a dingy building at 109 Potsdamerstrasse, which he described as 'a kind of dirty cellar, we called it the opium den . . . It had only artificial light. On entering, one hit an atmosphere that was thick with cigar, cigarette and pipe smoke. Doing solid, systematic work there was unthinkable. Unholy confusion reigned. Any real organization was practically non-existent. The financial position was hopeless.'

Realizing that his only hope of winning political power was not with reasoned argument, but with clubs, bricks and broken bottles on the streets, Goebbels deliberately provoked bloody confrontation with the communists.

He set the brownshirted stormtroopers of the SA to fight pitched battles with the communist Red Banner Fighters, and sent them to the fashionable streets of the west end to beat up 'bold, presumptuous and arrogant' Jews.

Goebbels had never before shown any great antipathy for Jews. Before taking up his post he had been engaged to a half-Jewish girl, and had had no compunction in applying (unsuccessfully) for jobs as a writer on Jewish-owned publications. But he was a revolutionary looking for a cause, a prophet looking for a messiah, and Hitler happened to come along at the right time. He had once embraced Marxism, but now turned his talents to promoting National Socialism. Whatever happened, the Nazis had to be headline news. 'Let them curse us, libel us, battle and beat us up,' he cried, 'but let them talk about us!'

To ensure that the party got headlines, and the sort of headlines he wanted, he started his own newspaper, *Der Angriff* ('The Attack'), in July 1927, first as a weekly, later converting it to daily publication. After an initial disaster, he quickly learned to change his literary style to the coarse language of the gutter, so that not even the meanest intelligence could find the paper too intellectual. Convinced that martyrs make the best headlines of all, he celebrated every wounded SA man in the pages of *Der Angriff*, and made as much as he could of every bruise and every stab wound they bore. When an SA man was killed, his fledgling propaganda machine really went to town.

Goebbels's greatest coup came when a young SA agitator called Horst Wessel was shot by a communist pimp at the beginning of 1930. Wessel took six weeks to die, during which time Goebbels publicized every aspect of his condition, turning the young thug into 'a socialist Christ who had chosen to live amongst those who scorned and spat upon him'. The funeral was spectacular. The communists obliged by covering the cemetery walls with crude graffiti and even stoning the mourners at the graveside. The bloody brawl that followed was a gift to Goebbels, who had declared: 'We must beat the shit out of the murderers!' In his account of the battle, he wrote that he had had a vision of the dead Horst Wessel 'raising his weary hand and beckoning into the shimmering distance: Forward over the graves! At the end of the road lies Germany!'

There was one final bonus from the death of Horst Wessel. He had submitted to *Der Angriff* a lyric to be sung to a melody from a communist songbook, which itself had been adapted from a Salvation Army hymn. The main refrain ran:

> *Die Fahne Hoch! Die Reihe dicht geschlossen!*
> *SA marschiert mit ruhig festem Schritt.*
> *Bald flattern Hitlers Fahnen über alle Strassen!*

> The flags held high! The ranks stand firm together!
> The SA marches with steady, resolute tread.
> Soon Hitler's flags will fly over every street!

It was hardly poetry, but Goebbels published it, and turned it into a party anthem. Three years later, to the disgust of all non-Nazis, it was to become a national hymn.

WHEN THE Nazis won ten seats in the Reichstag on 20 May 1928, Goebbels was given one of them. It brought him a salary of 750 marks a month, immunity from prosecution, and greater political prominence. His star was rising fast. His finest moment of all came on 30 January 1933, when he staged the great victory parade to mark Hitler's appointment as chancellor.

At Goebbels's instruction, every SS and SA man in the city put on his uniform and turned out to do his duty. For hour after hour, Nazi supporters tramped through the Brandenburg Gate in massed columns, shoulder to shoulder, sixteen abreast, to the thunder of drums and the blare of military bands, roaring out the 'Horst Wessel Song' and other fighting anthems.

Crowds of supporters who had been flocking into the city centre all day packed windows and pavements. Young men perched in the branches of trees, boys 'hung from the iron railings like bunches of grapes'. The Adlon and other hotels along the route had to lock their doors; every room was packed full.

Goebbels's reward was confirmation of his position as one of Hitler's top three lieutenants. He was also perhaps the closest thing the Führer had to a friend in the upper reaches of the party. Hitler regularly visited his home for tea or dinner, and even stayed with him at his villa on Schwanenwerder, a near-island on the Havel just above Wannsee, when there was building work going on at the chancellery.

# 11

ON THE evening of 27 February 1933 Hitler was dining *en famille* with Joseph and Magda Goebbels in their Berlin apartment on the Reichskanzlerplatz near the old Olympic stadium. Halfway through dinner, Hitler was informed by telephone that the Reichstag was on fire. Looking out and seeing the reflections of the flames in the sky above the Tiergarten, he immediately cried 'It's the communists!' He and Goebbels set off at once for the blazing Reichstag. When they arrived, they found Hermann Göring, immense in a camel-hair coat and with his soft brown hat turned up at the front, already inside the building giving orders – the first of which, characteristically, had been 'Save the tapestries!' The valuable Gobelin tapestries, which were his personal property, were handed out to safety before anything else was touched. Göring, who had been president of the Reichstag since the end of August 1932, was now living in the old Prussian presidential palace, which was connected to the building by an underground tunnel. He had been the first person on the scene after the alarm was raised.

Like Hitler, Göring was quick to apportion blame. 'This is the start of a communist uprising!' he yelled even before the arsonist was caught and dragged from the flaming building. 'Not a moment must be lost!'

'Now we'll show them!' Hitler interrupted. 'Anyone who stands in our way will be mown down. The German people have been soft too long. Every communist must be shot. All communist deputies must be hanged this very night. All friends of the communists must be locked up – and that goes for the social democrats and the Reichsbanner as well!'

In fact, the fire had been organized by Göring and Goebbels. The arsonist, a simple-minded young Dutch communist named Marinus van der Lubbe, had been picked up a few days earlier after unsuccessfully trying to set fire to the old royal palace and two other government buildings. These first attempts were hopelessly amateur and inadequate, but when it came to the Reichstag, he had clearly been given expert help. Forensic evidence showed that the fire that engulfed it so quickly had been started in various parts of the building, with such large quantities of chemicals and petrol that one man could not have carried them in, or ignited them simultaneously. Poor van der Lubbe was eventually beheaded, after a prolonged imprisonment and a show trial.

Hitler's first comment on arriving at the blazing Reichstag had been: 'Good riddance to the old shack.' The 'old shack' was, of course, hardly ancient, being exactly forty years old – but he put its burning to excellent use. Within a few hours he had persuaded the semi-senile President Hindenburg to declare a state of emergency and to suspend all civil rights, giving the chancellor virtually unlimited authority. Coming just one week before the new national elections which Hitler needed to confirm and consolidate his power, this gave him *carte blanche* to suppress his opponents and win a free run for the Nazis.

Four thousand leading communists were seized by the SA, along with a great many social democrats and liberals, including Reichstag members who were constitutionally immune from arrest. Even then, Hitler only just managed to scrape home with the support of Franz von Papen's Nationalist Party, and had to lock up large numbers of opposition deputies in order to gain the two-thirds majority required to pass an enabling act giving him dictatorial power 'to end the distress of people and state'.

The Reichstag was now destroyed both physically and politically. It would never again play any important role. It seemed appropriate that the new assembly should meet in the ornate Kroll Opera House facing the burnt-out hulk across Königsplatz – a suitably theatrical setting where its members were reduced to applauding the performances of Hitler and singing the Nazi anthems under the baton of Hermann Göring. Berliners soon took to describing it as 'Germany's most expensive choral group'.

Even with most of his opponents suppressed, terror squads on the streets and thousands of voters imprisoned, the Nazis had only managed to raise 31 per cent of the Berlin votes during the national elections. And in new local elections a week later they received fewer votes than the outlawed communists and the harassed social democrats, winning only 86 of the 225 seats. Two days later, the Prussian state government was dissolved by presidential decree, and both state and city were brought under direct Reich control, ruled by a Reich commissioner.

# 12

ONCE HITLER had been confirmed in power, Nazi thugs rampaging through the streets of Berlin had official blessing. Truckloads of stormtroopers broke into homes, businesses and bars all over the city, dragging their victims away to the first 'wild' concentration camps, mostly disused warehouses and factories, where they beat, tortured and in many cases murdered them.

On 9 March, Goebbels let loose the SA strong-arm squads on the city's 160,000 Jews. Working in groups of between five and thirty men, they toured the streets without fear of interference, pouncing on any Jews they encountered and beating them senseless. Over the following days and weeks the attacks intensified.

Siegbert Kindemann, a baker's apprentice, was taken to SA headquarters. Before the Nazis came to power he had been attacked by SA thugs, who had been arrested, charged and convicted. Now they took their revenge, and beat him to death. Before they threw his body on to the street from an upstairs window, they took their daggers and carved a large swastika into his chest. This time there were no arrests, and no convictions.

As individual attacks mounted, the Nazi assault on the Jews, which was to have such an enormous effect on the life of Berlin, was acknowledged as government policy. On 1 April the party organized a nationwide boycott of Jewish businesses, stores, cafés, restaurants, lawyers and doctors, setting the pattern for the future. SA men daubed the Star of David on Jewish shopfronts, along with the word *Jude* (Jew), swastikas, and slogans such as 'Jews Out!', 'Perish Judah!' and 'Go to Palestine!' Lists were distributed detailing every Jewish business, and committees were formed to coordinate the boycott and control other forms of Jew baiting. Following party orders, notices were posted in the streets giving the names of those who continued to buy from Jewish stores, 'pointing out to the miscreant members of the nation the shamefulness of their deeds, making them aware of the shame to which they would be subjected if they were proceeded against publicly'.

Party members were warned that they must constantly remind their friends and neighbours not to buy from Jews, and that they must break off friendships with anyone who did. 'It must go so far,' the order stated, 'that no German will speak to a Jew if it is not absolutely necessary, and this must be particularly pointed out.'

There were demands for the removal of all Jewish students from German schools and colleges: a new law laid down that they were to be treated as foreigners. On 7 April Hitler issued a decree for the dismissal – euphemistically described as 'retirement' – of all civil servants 'who were not of Aryan descent'. The division of the population into 'Aryan' and 'non-Aryan' had begun, a division that was to be formalized by the Nuremberg Laws of September 1935, and refined into grades depending on the proportion of parents and grandparents who were Jewish. The descendants of the philosopher Moses Mendelssohn and all the other distinguished Jews who had contributed so much to the life and development of Berlin were entering their long, dark nightmare.

ON 10 MAY 1933, it rained in Berlin. Albert Klein, then a young Jewish journalist, still shudders when he remembers how he found himself tangled up in a torchlight procession in the Linden that night. It was made up not of stormtroopers but of thousands of students. They gathered in Opernplatz, between the university and the State Opera house, and the national library. Awaiting them in the centre of the square was a massive pile of 20,000 books, collected during the day by students and stormtroopers from libraries and bookshops all over Berlin on the orders of Dr Goebbels. They were doused with petrol and set on fire with the marchers' torches, while students and stormtroopers danced round the flames under the stony gaze of the statues of the scientist Wilhelm von Humboldt and his brother Alexander, the great naturalist and explorer, who had founded the university in 1809.

As each new bundle was thrown into the flames, the name of the author was called out, to be greeted with shouts of derision. At midnight, Goebbels arrived by car to announce that 'the phoenix of a new spirit' would arise from the ashes. Then he headed back to his ministry, leaving the dwindling crowd to grow more and more sodden. Klein made his way home, physically sickened by what he had witnessed outside one of the world's great centres of intellectual endeavour.

The book burning was not one of the Nazis' best organized spectacles, but, perhaps more effectively than anything else, it revealed that a new barbarism had been unleashed on Germany. Following it, the great exodus of creative talent began.

The dead hand of state censorship, after a temporary absence during the Twenties, was back, wielded with a fanatical zeal by Joseph Goebbels. The Bauhaus was closed down; its architects and designers left for exile in the USA, Britain or the Soviet Union. The music of Jewish composers, like Mendelssohn and Mahler, was banned. Jazz and swing – described by Goebbels as 'the impudent swamp flowers of Negroid pandemonium' – were officially frowned upon and eventually banned.

With the departure of so many of the best directors, writers and actors, the Berlin theatre lost both its edge and its audience. The greatest Nazi theatrical success before the war was a heavy-handed farce, *Krack um Iolanthe*, the heroine of which was a sow. Hitler saw the production several times, and described it as 'epoch-making'.

Control of the press, radio and films also came under Goebbels's direction. To him, these media were simply tools for disseminating propaganda. Truth was never a consideration, unless it could be made to serve his ends. Party functionaries were appointed to supervise all newspaper offices, where the editors were informed they were now salaried employees of the party. In 1928 Berlin had 147 independent daily and weekly newspapers. By the spring of 1933, it had none.

By summer it had no political parties either, other than the Nazis. The communist party, of course, had already been outlawed after the Reichstag fire. Shortly after the March elections, the Nazis had attacked the social democrats, confiscating their offices and all their property, and forbidding meetings. The right-wing nationalists, supposedly the Nazis' partners in the coalition that had given Hitler power, were next to go, followed by the small People's Party. The Catholic Centre Party and the Bavarian People's Party dissolved themselves. A new law in July 1933 banned all parties other than the Nazis, and abolished their uniformed, quasi-military offshoots such as the Stahlhelm and the Reichsbanner, which were in effect private armies attached to each party.

The only private army now left in Germany was the Nazis' *Sturmabteilung*, the brownshirted SA. To drive home the message that no opposition would be tolerated, they had staged another large-scale terror raid in Köpenick that June, seizing well over 500 communists, social democrats and trades unionists and dragging them off to local SA barracks, the former Reichsbanner water-sports centre and the local prison, where they were tortured and beaten. Ninety-one of them were murdered, their mutilated corpses sewn into sacks and thrown into the River Dahme.

Now that he had total power, protected by his personal guard, the *Schutzstaffel* ('Protection Squad') or SS, and with his new secret police, the Gestapo, to control subversion, Hitler no longer needed the stormtroopers.

Indeed, as a paramilitary force several times larger than the army, they could pose a threat to his position. Their leader, Ernst Röhm, had become the only man in Germany capable of successfully opposing him. On 30 June 1934, in a swift and deadly operation that has gone down in history as 'the night of the long knives', that threat was removed.

While Hitler flew to Munich to arrest Röhm personally, Göring took charge of the purge in Berlin. SS and Gestapo death squads grabbed SA leaders and took them to Gestapo headquarters in Albrechtstrasse or to the former cadet school in Lichterfelde, now an SS barracks, where they were lined up in batches in front of firing squads. During twenty-four hours, the order to fire was given over 100 times.

Throughout the Reich, at least 1,000 people were murdered that night. By no means all of them were SA officers, for the party took advantage of the opportunity to settle old scores. Hitler's predecessor as chancellor, General Schleicher, who had blocked his accession to power in 1932, was among the victims, gunned down in his own home along with his young wife. The decapitated SA had been brought back firmly under party control. President Hindenburg and the generals congratulated Hitler on removing the threat of revolution.

'If anyone reproaches me and asks why I did not resort to the regular courts of justice,' Hitler told the Reichstag on 13 July, 'then all I can say is this: in this hour I was responsible for the fate of the German people. Everyone must know for all future time that if he raises his hand to strike the state, then certain death is his lot.'

Two weeks later, Hindenburg died. Hitler declared himself president as well as chancellor. He also assumed the title of supreme commander of the armed forces, and followed the example of Kaiser Wilhelm II by demanding a personal oath from all officers and men:

> I swear by God this sacred oath, that I will render unconditional obedience to Adolf Hitler, the Führer of the German Reich and people, supreme commander of the armed forces, and will be ready as a brave soldier to risk my life at any time for this oath.

The ill-fated German republic was finally over. The fifteen-year experiment with democratic government had been replaced by yet another absolute ruler, in a new empire, the Third Reich.

DURING the next two years the Nazis continued to tighten the screw on their opponents. With the SA brought to heel the brutality was less visible, but it was still there. The important difference was that it had been legalized. Those who transgressed were visited not by the strong-arm thugs of the SA but by the Gestapo, the state secret police, founded by the supposedly avuncular Göring. They were 'tried' in the new 'People's Court', a tribunal drawn from party members and headed by a rabid Nazi, chief judge Roland Freisler. And the beatings they received were not carried out in the public gaze, on the streets, but in the privacy of the Gestapo cellars in Prinz Albrechtstrasse, or the concentration camps in various parts of the Reich. For Berlin, the local camp was Sachsenhausen, a former SA barracks at Oranienburg, eighteen miles north-west of the city.

Everyone knew of the existence of the camps, but hardly anybody spoke of them. And when prisoners were released during the general relaxation of the regime in preparation for the Olympic Games, most people simply breathed a sigh of relief and willed themselves to believe that the improvements would be permanent.

# 13

THE EUPHORIA surrounding the Games lasted well into the next year – until the Nazis started clamping down again on the Protestant churches. Throughout 1937 a stream of new restrictions made it increasingly difficult for the churches to operate – it became illegal to take collections, to hold services anywhere but in registered church premises, to make proclamations, to circulate duplicated notices or letters. Dietrich Bonhoeffer got around this by heading every copy of his own circulars 'personal letter' and signing each of them by hand. By the summer, the number of pastors and church members arrested was growing at an alarming rate.

On 1 July Bonhoeffer and his friend Eberhard Bethge arrived at the house of Pastor Martin Niemöller, the leader of their wing of the Confessing Church, to talk to him about the latest arrests. But they found that Niemöller had just been taken away by the Gestapo. As they were speaking to his wife about it, they saw a line of black Mercedes cars drawing up outside. A Gestapo man already in place foiled their attempt to slip out of the back door, and they were held under house arrest while the Gestapo agents spent seven hours meticulously searching every inch of the place. Bonhoeffer was part comforted and part alarmed to see his mother driving past the house at regular intervals during the day. She had somehow got word of what had happened, and was determined to keep an eye on things until her son was released and allowed to return home.

During the rest of the year another 807 pastors or leading laymen were rounded up. Bonhoeffer's seminary near Stettin was closed down on 28 September, on the orders of Heinrich Himmler. Forewarned by a telephone call, Bonhoeffer and his students had already gone by the time the Gestapo arrived. Bonhoeffer headed for Berlin, to protest to the authorities. It was in vain, of course. He wrote to all his students, giving them advice on what they should do, then found himself another post as assistant minister in a small market town deep in what was known as Further Prussia.

The following January he was in Berlin attending a routine meeting of officers of the Confessing Church when the Gestapo burst into the room and arrested everyone. They had expected to find an illegal session of the seminary in progress. When they discovered their mistake, they released their prisoners, but imposed restrictions on their future movements: those who lived in Berlin were banned from leaving it, those who lived in the country were not allowed to enter the city.

The Bonhoeffers, however, were a prolific as well as a distinguished family – Dietrich was one of eight children and his father, Karl, was professor of psychiatry and neurology at Berlin university. They were either related to or professionally associated with some of the most influential people in Germany, and by pulling the right strings Karl managed to get the ban on his son eased. Dietrich would be allowed to come and go as he pleased, as long as he did not try to work in the city.

In February, Dietrich's brother-in-law, Hans von Dohnanyi, introduced him to four men who were to play a major part in his future life: General Ludwig Beck, chief of staff of the OKW, the supreme command of the armed forces, Admiral Wilhelm Canaris, head of the Abwehr (German military intelligence), Colonel Hans Oster, Canaris's chief of staff, and Dr Karl Stack, chief of the army's legal department. These four men were the leading figures in the principal opposition group against Hitler. Dohnanyi had been an active member of the group since 1933, when he had started compiling a detailed record of all the crimes of the Nazi regime, for a future indictment.

Hans von Dohnanyi, son of the Hungarian composer, was a brilliant and charming lawyer who had married Dietrich Bonhoeffer's elder sister, Christine, in 1925. In 1929 he had become personal assistant to the minister of state for justice, and stayed on in the post when Hitler came to power. When he continued to refuse party membership, he was denounced by Freisler and was forced out of the ministry, taking up a position as a judge advocate in the Supreme Court in Leipzig. A year later he transferred to the Abwehr, to work on Oster's staff.

Dohnanyi and the four officers tried to persuade Bonhoeffer to become an active member of the conspiracy, but he was not yet ready. Everything in his upbringing and religion resisted the idea of conspiring to overthrow the government. People of his background were traditionally loyal and staunchly patriotic. They were not afraid to protest at something they felt to be wrong, but they drew the line at revolution. For the moment, therefore, the resistance would have to proceed without him. But the idea had been planted in his mind, and had taken root.

# 14

IN 1938 BERLIN celebrated along with the rest of the Reich when Hitler brought Austria back into the German empire after an enforced absence of sixty-seven years. Austria was a more than willing bride, and it was by no means a shotgun wedding for the Germans, either. For Berlin, there was the added satisfaction of seeing its old imperial rival, Vienna, in a subservient role. But when Hitler turned his attention to the Sudetenland and was clearly eager to gobble up the rest of Czechoslovakia, the enthusiasm of the Berliners, like most Germans, was severely muted. When mobilized troops drove through the Brandenburg Gate and passed along the Wilhelmstrasse to be reviewed by the Führer before departing towards the Czech frontier, the pavements were empty. Far from cheering their soldiers on to glory, as they had done in 1914 and 1870, most people turned their backs and hurried away.

Most anti-Nazis thought Hitler had finally shot his bolt. The international community *must* see the truth now. The great powers *must* finally unite against him. At last it would be possible to overthrow him and put an end to his vile regime. General Beck and his fellow conspirators prepared themselves to seize power at the right moment: when Hitler had been humiliated by the world leaders, the German people would be happy to see him removed.

Unfortunately, the right moment never came. Instead of warning Hitler that they would not tolerate any attempt to seize the Sudetenland, prime ministers Daladier of France and Chamberlain of Great Britain flew to confer with him on his own ground in the Nazi party headquarters in Munich. There they capitulated shamefully, appeasing him by agreeing to his demands. Hitler emerged once again as a conquering hero. Berlin went wild with joy, a joy compounded of relief at the news of peace, and pride in a bloodless victory over the Allies.

33

# 15

I F THE Berliners had been lulled by the Munich triumph, they were in for a savage awakening six weeks later. On 9–10 November the volcano of anti-Semitism, dormant since the Olympics, suddenly erupted again in the so-called *Kristallnacht* pogrom. Supposedly in 'revenge' for the murder of a German diplomat in Paris by a distraught seventeen-year-old Jew, nation-wide action by the SA was initiated by Goebbels from Munich, where Hitler and his party henchmen were celebrating the anniversary of the failed *putsch* of 1923. The pogrom took place in every town and city in the Reich, but inevitably the biggest and best organized action was in Berlin.

Since 1933, the racial background of every citizen in the Reich had been ascertained and registered. Every Jewish home or business was listed, so before the stormtroopers were sent to wreck them, Count von Helldorf, the police president, gave them detailed instructions on where to go. Police squads isolated Jewish buildings, cut telephone wires, and switched off electricity and gas supplies to Jewish shops. At 2 am, they gave the signal for the 'spontaneous' action to start.

By dawn, nine of the twelve synagogues in Berlin were ablaze. Outside the biggest, just off the Kurfürstendamm in Fasanenstrasse, Davidson, the reader of the synagogue, appealed to the captain of a fire crew who were watching the blaze with professional interest, begging him to turn on his hoses. The man refused. It was against orders. 'We've come to protect the building next door,' he explained.

With daylight, the mobs swarmed down the Linden, the Kurfürstendamm and Tauentzienstrasse, smashing plate-glass windows, hauling out furs, jewellery, furniture, silver – but only from Jewish-owned businesses. Already the death toll was mounting: Jews were beaten mercilessly, leapt from upper-storey windows, or were trapped in flames. There were undoubtedly many Berliners who revelled in the awful carnage, gloating at the misfortunes of the Jews they despised or hated. Middle-class women were seen holding up their children to watch the fun, clapping their hands and screaming with glee. Most people, however, like the inhabitants of all the other towns and cities throughout the Reich, simply looked away in horror and shame.

Hans Werner Lobeck watched stormtroopers emerging from the wreck-age of a Jewish-Hungarian restaurant, the Czardas on Kurfürstendamm, near the still smouldering synagogue on Fasanenstrasse. They were carrying dozens of bottles of Tokay wine, which they tried to give to 'some of the old Berliners' who were watching. 'A shudder went through the crowd, and it fell back,' Lobeck said. 'The people dispersed, leaving the SA men alone on the sidewalk.'

For many Berliners, their disapproval had nothing to do with race, only with civilized standards of behaviour. Kate Freyhan, a teacher in a Jewish girls' primary school, found her corner shop full of people watching children throwing cobblestones through the windows of the synagogue on the opposite side of the street. The young woman who owned the shop was indignant: it was disgraceful, the police just standing there and doing nothing. 'After all,' she declared, 'it is private property.'

WHEN THE immediate violence was over, adult Jewish men under the age of sixty were rounded up and transported to Sachsenhausen, where they were beaten, tortured, starved and held for weeks or in some cases months. The arrests were carried out in a calm, well-ordered way; the police and Gestapo were instructed not to harm the men.

But once they arrived at the camp it became a different story. The London *News Chronicle* printed an eye-witness report on the reception given to a group of sixty-two Berlin Jews, including two rabbis. At the gate they were handed over by their police escort to SS camp guards, who forced them to run a gauntlet of sharpened spades, whips and clubs. The police turned away, unable to bear the sight, or the sound of their cries. As the men were beaten, they fell to the ground; as they fell, they were beaten again. The orgy of violence lasted half an hour. When it was over, the witness reported, 'twelve of the sixty-two were dead, their skulls smashed. The others were all unconscious. The eyes of some had been knocked out, their faces flattened and shapeless.'

The men rounded up after *Kristallnacht* were supposed to be hostages, to be held in safe keeping as a guarantee of good behaviour by the Jewish community. But of the 30,000 who were taken from all over the Reich, almost 2,500 died in the camps.

The trauma of that night and day of violence has remained with Berlin ever since. But it did not mark the end of anti-Semitism, nor even its climax, only the beginning of a terrible new phase. Within days, Göring decreed that the Jews must make good all the damage caused, and pay an 'atonement fine' of one billion marks. The programme of 'Aryanization' of Jewish businesses was stepped up, with new regulations on 28 November for the winding up and dissolution of all Jewish enterprises.

That same day, regulations were introduced banning German or stateless Jews from many parts of the capital. Those unfortunate enough to live in a forbidden area would need a police permit to cross the boundary – and from

1 July 1939, they were warned, there would be no more permits. In any case, there were ominous new plans for Jews to be forced to sell their homes in fashionable districts, and move into controlled Jewish quarters. The movement ban covered most of central Berlin, including government offices and embassies, which made it more difficult than ever to get exit visas. As an added touch, Jews were forbidden to own cars. They were also banned from all places of entertainment or recreation.

Even the most ardently patriotic Jews now realized that there was no future for them in Germany. But as 1938 ended it was becoming more and more difficult to find somewhere to go. People like Maria von Maltzan, the young countess who had gobbledy-gooked her way into the Olympic stadium, did what they could to help. Her two-roomed apartment on the ground floor of a converted store in Detmolderstrasse, near the rail yards on the southern edge of Wilmersdorf, became a centre for helping Jewish refugees. 'It was ideal for me,' she says, 'because I could put up Jewish friends and acquaintances there very discreetly. People who wanted to get out of Germany and who were afraid to spend the last days before the journey in their own homes, where they could be attacked.'

Even with the help of people like Maria, there were still countless tragedies. The husband of one of her close friends, Lulu Hirsekorn, paid a man a large sum of money to smuggle him and a group of other fugitives across the frontier into Holland. The man took the money, then betrayed them to the Gestapo. Hirsekorn was picked up, held in the Gestapo prison, then thrown into Oranienburg concentration camp. On Lulu's birthday in March 1939, two SS men appeared on her doorstep with a small package. 'This is from your husband,' they told her. Overjoyed to receive what she thought must be a present, she tore open the wrappings. She found herself holding an urn containing his ashes.

# 16

FOR BERLIN, the great event of January 1939 was the opening, two days early, of the new Reich chancellery running from Wilhelmplatz along the entire length of Voss-strasse. For the past year, the whole government quarter around Wilhelmstrasse had been dominated by frantic building work. For civil servants in the ministries there was no escape from the construction traffic jamming the streets, or the racket of drills, hammers and cranes as 4,500 men slaved day and night on the task of completing the enormous project in less than a year. In the event, they finished with forty-eight hours to spare.

Hitler had described the old chancellery, formerly the eighteenth-century Radziwill palace, as being 'only fit for a soap company'. 'I need grand halls and salons,' he had told Speer, 'which will make an impression on people, especially the smaller dignitaries.' With the new chancellery – the last great public building to be erected in old Berlin – Speer had done him proud.

Everything about the new building was on a grand scale. The Voss-strasse frontage stretched for a quarter of a mile of yellow stucco and grey stone. Huge square columns framed the main entrance, where visitors drove through great double gates into an enormous court of honour. An outside staircase led them into a reception room: from there they passed through double doors almost 17 feet high and flanked by gilded bronze and stone eagles, each clutching a swastika in its claws, and on into a large hall with floor and walls clad in gold and grey mosaic tiles. From this Mosaic Hall, a flight of steps led up to a circular chamber with a high domed ceiling, and from there the visitor passed into a gallery lined with red marble pillars. At 480 feet long, the Marble Gallery was twice the length of the Hall of Mirrors in Versailles, a fact that gave Hitler particular pleasure. Beyond this was a great hall for state receptions. The whole concourse of rooms through which a visitor had to tramp from the Voss-strasse entrance until he arrived at Hitler's reception area stretched over 725 feet of rich materials and colours.

But there was one significant part of the building that remained unadorned, its bare concrete walls never seen by visitors: in the cellars, Speer had installed a reinforced concrete air-raid shelter.

HITLER's dreams of military glory involved Berlin at every level. As well as being the administrative centre of the new German empire, Berlin was also the powerhouse of the nation's war effort, the greatest industrial and commercial city on the continent of Europe. It housed an enormous garrison, with more than ninety military headquarters, barracks and depots, as well as the ministries of all three armed services and their combined high command. With twelve main lines converging on it from all directions, it was the hub of the rail network for Germany and indeed the whole of northern Europe, a network vital to Hitler for the rapid movement of troops and material as well as for trade. The internal waterways, which had been developed continuously since the time of the Great Elector, consolidated the city's position at the heart of the northern canal and river system, connecting Berlin's two inland harbours with the city's satellite industrial region in the Ruhr, and with the ports of Hamburg and Stettin on the North Sea and the Baltic.

More than half of Germany's entire electrical industry was located in Berlin. As well as the giant Siemens plant just to the west of the central area, there were also ten AEG (German General Electric) plants making a wide

37

range of products including radio components, insulators and generating equipment. Telefunken made radio and telecommunications equipment at Tempelhof, just south of the city centre, Lorenz was at Zehlendorf in the south-west, and Bosch just beyond it at Kleinmachnow.

At Spandau, in the west of the city, the Alkett factory produced tanks, self-propelled guns, and half of the Wehrmacht's field artillery. Auto-Union factories at Spandau and Halensee, on the western end of the Kurfürsten-damm, also produced tanks, while the engines to drive them were built in the Maybach factory at Tempelhof. Rheinmetall-Borsig, in its new factory town in the north-west of the city, made heavy artillery as well as its more traditional lines in locomotives and rolling stock, and DIW and the DWM plant at Wittenau in the north of the city both produced small arms, mortars and ammunition.

As a centre for the production of ball bearings, Berlin ranked third in Germany, and it also played an important role in aircraft production: the Heinkel works at Oranienburg was busy turning out heavy bombers, while the Henschel works produced Junkers bombers as well as Henschel attack aircraft. The Dornier, Flettner and Focke-Wulf companies all had factories in the city making components or assembling parts of aircraft. In Reinickendorf was the Argus works, where the engines for the V1 flying bombs would later be made, and to the south at Genshagen was the largest Daimler-Benz aero-engine plant in Germany.


IN THE spring of 1939, tension was mounting over Poland's rejection of German claims to Danzig, the ancient Hansa seaport that had been made a free city by the Treaty of Versailles. But Hitler was not yet ready to tackle the Poles. On 15 March his troops marched unopposed into the remainder of Czechoslovakia, to be greeted with stunned silence by a population betrayed both by its own government and by Britain and France. A week later, he personally led another army into the Baltic port of Memel, to reclaim territory that had been sliced from East Prussia in 1919 and given to Lithuania.

With every newspaper, magazine, newsreel and radio broadcast pumping out only what they were given by Goebbels's propaganda ministry, even normally sceptical Berliners could not help but be impressed with Hitler's achievements. But for anyone who still doubted – and there were many in the capital who did – the Nazis staged a gigantic show in honour of his fiftieth birthday on 20 April. Celebrations started the night before, when Hitler drove with Albert Speer along the length of the newly completed East–West Axis – basically the *via triumphalis* of the Olympics, with further widening at various points. As Hitler officially declared it open, bands played the traditional Badenweiler March and fireworks lit up the sky with an enormous swastika.

At midnight, a choir from the SS Life Guards sang in the courtyard of the chancellery, while Hitler inspected the hundreds of presents laid out for him. These included a scale model of the vast triumphal arch he planned for the city, and dozens of model ships, aircraft and other military paraphernalia which he seized upon like a small boy.

Next morning, Berlin awoke to the sounds of military units arriving from all over Germany for the grand birthday parade. Six army divisions, 40,000 men with 600 tanks, armoured personnel carriers, and countless artillery pieces, rolled past the dais for four solid hours. Overhead flew wave after wave of bombers, fighters, and the new Stuka dive bombers. The spectators cheered and applauded the show.

But some onlookers were not so enthusiastic. 'An advance showing of the National Socialist war potential,' Ruth Andreas-Friedrich, a divorced thirty-seven-year-old journalist, commented in her diary. 'Again, masses of people line the streets,' she went on. 'In front, a row of stormtroopers holds them back; behind them are German Girls' League and Hitler Youth. The stormtroopers make a game of blocking the little girls' view with their broad backs. "Just put your heads between our legs," they suggest with a smirk. The smirk that goes with the suggestion is not a nice one. Nor is the smirk with which forty out of a hundred girls accept it.'

But these troops were not just for display. Before the parade started, Hitler received his three commanders-in-chief, Göring, Brauchitsch and Raeder, together with the chief of staff of the OKW, the supreme command of the armed forces, in his study. He told them he intended to go to war that year.

ONE BERLINER who was not around to watch Hitler's parade was Inge Deutschkron's father. As the massed ranks of steel-helmeted troopers goose-stepped through the Brandenburg Gate he was sitting, forlorn but full of hope, on a train heading for the North Sea coast, and the boat to England. He had managed to contact relatives who had been living in England for two generations, who were prepared to take one member of the family. They could not afford more: they had to deposit a large sum of money with the British government for each refugee they sponsored, as a guarantee that if he or she couldn't find work, they would not be a burden on the state. There was no chance of refugees being able to support themselves without work, since they were allowed to take only ten marks out of Germany.

On the evening of 19 April Herr Deutschkron climbed aboard a train at the Zoo station, to become one of 50,000 German Jews who found refuge in Britain during 1939.

# 17

IN AUGUST, the message Hitler had given to his commanders in secret on his birthday was made clear to everyone. With the newspapers screaming of Polish provocations and threats, trying to persuade the German people that it was their country that was about to be invaded, general mobilization was ordered on 15 August.

The first quarter of a million reservists were called up for duty on the western front, just in case the French should decide to do anything stupid. The army general staff began moving out of Berlin's Bendlerstrasse to wartime headquarters in Zossen, some 25 miles south of the city. The railways were alerted to prepare for the immense task of moving men and equipment to the Polish border. And the pocket battleships *Graf Spee* and *Deutschland*, together with twenty-one U-boats, were made ready to sail for battle stations in the Atlantic astride British shipping routes.

The big worry for the Germans was that the First World War alliance between Britain, France and Russia would be repeated, forcing them once again to fight a two-front war, surrounded by enemies. The Soviet Union appeared to be the key to the whole thing. Without the Soviets, the British would surely not intervene, and without the British, the French would certainly not fight. Hitler would be free to wage his 'Silesian War', as he liked to describe the campaign he was planning against Poland, without interference.

On Tuesday, 22 August, that worry was removed. Berliners awoke to the news that their government was about to sign a non-aggression pact with the Soviet Union. In streets and homes, on buses and street cars, subways and trains, citizens read the news with relief. Stalin, once the arch-enemy of the Nazis, had given them *carte blanche* to deal with the troublesome Poles. Hitler had done it again – he was about to deliver yet another bloodless victory.

WEDNESDAY, 23 August, was hot and close in Berlin. The humid conditions did not help the taut nerves of those waiting for confirmation that Ribbentrop and Soviet prime minister Molotov had actually signed the pact, that Stalin had not changed his mind, that nothing had gone wrong. It finally came at about 2 am on Thursday morning.

Germany was now blockade proof. With a back door open for the import of food and raw materials from the Soviet Union, there was no way the British navy could strangle the Reich as it had done during the First World War. And Britain and France would surely not go to war over Poland now. Hitler, it seemed, had outmanoeuvred everyone.

The crowds in the streets of Berlin that day were as cheerful, good-humoured and noisy as if they had won the national lottery. No doubt they felt as though they had. The cafés along the Linden and the Ku'damm were filled to overflowing with Berliners celebrating peace for their time. They joked and played pranks on each other, greeted friends and acquaintances with 'Heil Stalin' instead of the usual obligatory 'Heil Hitler'. Some young men even rang the doorbell of the Soviet embassy in the Linden, shouted 'Heil Moscow!', then ran off like naughty schoolboys, roaring with laughter. And in at least one mid-town *Bierstube* the band struck up the 'Internationale', bringing the entire clientele to its feet as though they had played 'Deutschland über Alles'. There would be no great war, everyone said you could bet on it. Indeed, many people did just that. So confident were some diplomats at the Foreign Office in the Wilhelmstrasse that they were offering odds of twenty to one on peace, in bottles of champagne.

But while the revellers on the Ku'damm were celebrating peace, Berlin's preparations for war continued unchecked. Unending streams of German bombers flew eastwards over the city all day. Luftwaffe personnel continued installing anti-aircraft guns in squares, parks, sports fields, any open space throughout the city. Even the red hard courts of the august Rot-Weiss (Red-White) Lawn Tennis Club, which boasted Göring, Ribbentrop and former chancellor Papen among its members, began sprouting guns. The club had been practically taken over by the military: the floor of the ballroom in the clubhouse was covered with hay to provide bedding for recruits, and camp kitchens erected behind the building were 'seasoning the air with the aroma of potato, carrot, and suggestion-of-pork stew'. In spite of all this activity, however, keen tennis players still managed to get in a game or two.

BERLINERS sobered up fast when the news came that Britain and France were showing signs of standing firm on Poland: both countries were starting to mobilize. When they heard on Friday the 25th that Hitler had cancelled the speech he was due to give that Sunday at Tannenberg, the scene of Hindenburg's great victory over the Russians in the First World War, the people knew there was something seriously wrong.

Suddenly, the streets were full of marching men instead of partygoers. Some were even veterans of 1914–18. A stream of vehicles, including commandeered furniture vans and grocery trucks, rattled eastwards down the broad boulevards carrying troops and equipment. Overhead, flights of Stukas and Messerschmitts headed for airfields close to the Polish frontier. This time, unlike 1914, there were no cheering crowds. The cafés were empty. No one sang patriotic songs. No one threw flowers. The glum faces of the Berliners reflected their anxiety.

On the radio, Hitler's deputy, Rudolf Hess, spoke openly of war. 'If it comes,' he warned, 'it will be terrible.' The newspapers were now filled with stories of Polish atrocities against Germans living in Poland and Danzig. In screaming headlines, the *12-Uhr Blatt* accused the Poles of firing on three unarmed German passenger aeroplanes, and of torching German farmhouses in the Polish Corridor between East Prussia and the rest of Germany – 'that strip of flesh torn from the body of Germany', as Hitler called it. GERMAN FAMILIES FLEE, the *Berliner Zeitung* proclaimed, accusing the Poles of massing troops on the German border. The Nazi Party's own *Völkischer Beobachter* continued to whip up war hysteria on 27 August with the headlines: WHOLE OF POLAND IN WAR FEVER! 1,500,000 MEN MOBILIZED! NON-STOP TROOP MOVEMENT TOWARDS THE FRONTIER! CHAOS IN UPPER SILESIA! To drive home the seriousness of the situation, German radio played continuous martial music, broken only by occasional announcements.

The Germans, of course, had been mobilized for the past two weeks, though the papers said nothing about this. Now, it was announced that what was called 'the organization of all measures for eventualities' had come into force. Berliners discovered that long-distance and international telephone services had been cut off, and that they could no longer leave the city by train or air. The whole national transport system was now under military control. Only foreigners or those whose journeys were of national importance were allowed to travel.

Signs of impending doom continued to mount with each passing day. It was announced that Hitler had now cancelled the next Nuremberg rally, billed as the great party congress of peace, which was to have been the biggest ever Nazi event, attended by over a million party members. (In fact, Hitler had given the order two weeks earlier, but it had not been made public at the time.) Most ominous of all, on Sunday, 28 August, a hot and glorious day when half of Berlin had made its way to the beach at Wannsee to brown in the sun and take their minds off the international situation, policemen began knocking on doors and handing out ration cards. As of Monday, people were informed, they would need the cards to buy food, soap, shoes, textiles, and even coal.


HITLER HAD only returned to Berlin from his mountain retreat near Berchtesgaden on the 24th. He had not been seen in public since. He did not appear on the balcony of the chancellery to greet the diminishing crowds who came for support and solace. But on Monday the 28th he summoned Reichstag deputies to a meeting at 5.30 pm. They found themselves facing a man who looked, according to General Franz Halder, the OKW chief of staff, 'exhausted, haggard . . . preoccupied', and who 'in a croaking voice' delivered a speech designed to warn them of the real possibility of war, and at the same time to allay their fears. Yet even this tame audience of party hacks and toadies could raise little enthusiasm for what he had to say. The applause, as Halder noted, came on cue, but was thin.

As the week wore on, uncertainty remained. The British ambassador, Sir Nevile Henderson, shuttled to and fro between the embassy and the chancellery, and even between Berlin and London, as diplomatic efforts to avert the catastrophe of war became more and more frantic. The French ambassador, Robert Coulondre, brought desperate messages from prime minister Daladier, and at one stage treated Hitler to an impassioned speech on his own behalf, lasting forty minutes. Unofficial envoys, like Birger Dahlerus, a Swedish businessman with strong British connections, joined in the search for peace. But the ordinary citizens of Berlin knew nothing of this.

By 30 August they were talking openly of their dissatisfaction. 'How can a country go into a major war with a population so dead against it?' William Shirer asked in his diary. 'People also kicking against being kept in the dark. A German said to me last night: "We know nothing. Why don't they tell us what's up?" '

# 18

ON THURSDAY, 31 August, there was a full-scale practice air-raid alert in the city. The long, undulating wail of the sirens soon cleared the streets. All traffic stopped as drivers and passengers joined pedestrians scurrying into cellars and basements marked out as shelters. Diners in restaurants were herded into back rooms and kept there for an hour and a half, until the all-clear sounded. They were warned that in a real raid they would have to take refuge in the cellars. All the street lights were turned off. People at home had to close their windows, which they had already covered with black paper – if they had been able to find any. Every piece of dark-coloured paper in the shops had been snapped up in the past few days.

On almost every roof, soldiers with binoculars kept watch on planes flying overhead – though since this was a rehearsal, the only planes they could see were from the Luftwaffe. The streets below them were empty and still as death within a few minutes. Kerbstones and crossings, which boys of the Hitler Youth had been busy daubing with white luminous paint, glowed eerily in the dark. The only living souls – apart from horses tied to lamp posts while their drivers took shelter – were grim-faced policemen, their gas masks held at the ready. For all the alleged fear of poison gas, only a few thousand masks for civilian use were ever manufactured. And despite all the propaganda photographs of mothers and babes in arms wearing special masks, most of them were issued to officials like the police – unlike Britain, where every single member of the population was given one.

AFTER THE appalling results of raids by the German Condor Legion in the Spanish civil war and Japanese attacks on Chinese cities like Shanghai, everybody expected any modern war to start with aerial bombardment. So in addition to holding practice drills, providing air-raid shelters for the general population was a top priority in Berlin's preparations. Unfortunately, there was a grave shortage of skilled building workers: those who had not been called up were engaged on official projects. So the authorities decided to make ordinary citizens responsible for constructing shelters in the cellars of their own buildings. Supervision was no problem: every building already had its own party *Hausleiter* (house leader) keeping an eye on the tenants and reporting their activities to the authorities.

Officials from the Air Ministry inspected each cellar for suitability, and advised on construction. The tenants were then expected to start digging. It was a massive undertaking, involving a great many unlikely people in hard physical labour. The workforce in the block near the Kurfürstendamm where *Life* correspondent William Bayles lived, for example, included an internationally known scholar and lecturer, an operatic tenor, a ballerina from the State Opera, and a lady's maid, in addition to Bayles himself and, of course, the house leader and his wife.

Their first task was to create an emergency exit for use if the usual entrance to the cellar became blocked by rubble. This involved enlarging the rear window, so that it could be used as a door leading into a back court, and then to sandbag the approach to it, to protect against bomb splinters or pieces of flying debris.

With a sledgehammer and crowbar, Bayles set to work to make a hole 'large enough for the portliest Berliner to squeeze through'. The ballet dancer, the house leader's wife and the maid shovelled sand into sacks, which they had been collecting or making for some time. The men lifted them and put them into position. It was a back-breaking task. The sandbag wall had to be five feet high and three feet thick, which meant that several hundred bags, each weighing about a hundred pounds, had to be filled, carried and lifted into position.

Inside, the cellar was furnished with wooden benches, chairs and a table. It was also equipped with a fire extinguisher, pails of water, several lanterns, pickaxes, and spades. In one corner the house leader placed a small wooden beer keg with one end removed and a toilet seat attached, declaring proudly

44

that he did not know another shelter in the neighbourhood that had its own toilet. There was no screen around it, so it was in full view of the other residents. Bayles asked the ballet dancer if she would use it. She shrugged. 'Why not?' An older Berliner among them was highly amused by the whole thing. 'I think that when bombs begin to drop around this building,' he chuckled, 'no one will need the toilet.'

<hr>

# 19

<hr>

FRIDAY, 1 September, dawned grey and sultry. Clouds hung low over the capital. At 5.11 am, in the vastness of his new chancellery study, Hitler signed the document that made Germany officially at war with Poland. It was purely academic. German bombers had begun their attack forty minutes earlier.

The people received the news with numb apathy, going about their business as though nothing had happened. Few bothered to buy the news extras that hit the streets at breakfast time. Only along the East–West Axis, where Luftwaffe crews were setting up five big anti-aircraft guns to protect Hitler when he addressed the Reichstag at 10 am, was there any reaction.

Hitler looked worn and harried when he was driven to the Kroll Opera House, wearing a new light grey uniform adorned only with the swastika and the Iron Cross he had won in 1918. His speech was an extraordinary performance; he was like a man driven by some mystical necessity, mimicking some Wagnerian hero confronting his personal demons: 'I made proposal after proposal . . . I made an offer to them some time ago . . . only I myself could have made such an offer . . . I proposed a solution on the basis of direct negotiations. For two long days I have been waiting . . . I am now determined to talk the same language to Poland that Poland has been talking to us . . . I myself am today, and will be from now on, nothing but a soldier of the German Reich; just as I fought in the last war, so I shall fight now. I shall not take off this uniform until we have achieved victory . . .' 'I', 'I', 'I', like the tolling of a bell: no fewer than seventy-eight times. It was the speech of a megalomaniac.

THAT NIGHT, the general blackout in Berlin was not a rehearsal. The first proper air-raid alert came at 7 pm. A rumour swept through the city that seventy Polish bombers were approaching. In fact, two Polish aircraft had managed to get as far as the city, but they did no damage and were themselves unharmed. All the same, everyone dashed for cover.

William Bayles took refuge in the shelter he and his fellow tenants had completed only that afternoon. His companions noticeably failed to demonstrate the kind of *esprit de corps* and enthusiasm for the war that the party expected. One elderly woman began to cry. A brownshirted man who, Bayles noted, had not helped with the construction work, ordered her to shut up. But she was past taking any notice of him. 'It really is unbearable when you think that we must go through all that again, just because . . .' she blurted out, then stopped. Everyone looked at the brownshirt. 'Am I to understand that you are critical of the Führer's decisions?' he demanded. The woman subsided into a stifled silence, while her husband nervously babbled that anything the Führer did was right and that his wife had not meant it that way. 'Then let her keep her mouth shut,' retorted the Nazi.

It may have been a reaction to the strain of their first real alert, but when the all-clear had sounded and people emerged from their cellars, many seemed determined to have a last fling before the shutters finally came down. Suddenly the cafés, restaurants and beerhalls were packed with people drinking for all they were worth.

That night, a new decree had been issued, forbidding anyone from listening to foreign broadcasts. From then on, anyone caught listening to the BBC from London – which many Berliners had depended on since 1933 as their only reliable source of news – faced the executioner's axe.

ON SATURDAY, 2 September, the Berlin railway stations were jammed with military personnel on their way to join their units, and with hordes of small German children with blue tags around their necks giving their names and home addresses, who were being evacuated to the safety of the countryside, away from the expected bombing.

Foreigners who had waited too long before leaving flocked to the Stettiner station, which was now their only way out – international connections had been cut to all countries apart from those in the north. The US embassy had reserved two coaches for American citizens on a train for Copenhagen. The train was packed. Passengers sat on their suitcases. They doubled or tripled up on the seats. Late arrivals, frantic to escape, stuffed their baggage in through open windows, then had themselves pushed through by friends or onlookers.

Outside, Berliners enjoyed the last of the Indian summer, strolling through the sunlit streets as they did every weekend. But there were few smiling faces. Everyone was waiting anxiously to see what Britain and France would do.

The waiting ended next day, Sunday, 3 September, when the Berlin radio station interrupted an orchestral concert from Hamburg. For those who were not at home clustered anxiously around their radio sets, there were loudspeakers fixed to lamp posts in many Berlin streets, so that everyone could hear the news first-hand. Shortly after noon, Liszt's *Hungarian Rhapsody* was suddenly faded and a man's voice said: 'Achtung! Achtung! In a few minutes we shall be making an important announcement.' Ten minutes later came the news that Britain had declared herself at war with Germany.

The people in the streets, even the small crowd of about 250 gathered in front of the chancellery, listened in silence, shocked to find that Hitler had led them into what would undoubtedly be another world war. Four hours later their fears were confirmed when they learned that France, too, had declared war.

The correspondent of the *Saturday Evening Post*, John McCutcheon Raleigh, rushed to get the reaction of the Ministry of Propaganda, but the clerk on the desk asked him if he had any news. 'You are at war with France and England,' Raleigh told him. The man turned white. 'Gott!' he exclaimed. 'Gott in Himmel!' He walked to the director's office, 'feeling his way carefully, as someone might after a motor accident.'

In their apartment at 167/8 Uhlandstrasse, Inge Deutschkron and her mother sat in tears. Friendly neighbours tried to comfort them, but it was little use. The interminable formalities of immigration and emigration had dragged on too long. Now it was too late: they were trapped in Berlin, along with 80,000 other Jews.

THERE WAS no war fever in Berlin, no excitement, not even any hatred for the French and British enemies. As always, though, the city was soon alive with rumours, most of them absurdly optimistic. Papen, it was said, was already in Paris negotiating a separate peace with the French government; German and French soldiers facing each other across the Rhine were already fraternizing and refusing to fight; the Soviet Union had delivered an ultimatum to Britain, threatening to join Germany in the war. On a more pessimistic note, it was said that Saarbrücken, for example, had been shelled by French guns and was now in ruins.

The party faithful, however, would have no truck with such defeatist talk at a time when Germany was about to avenge the betrayals of 1918. When Himmler made a stirring speech to the SS, he concluded by topping Lord Nelson's message to the British fleet at Trafalgar: 'Hitler expects every man to do *more* than his duty! God commands and Heil Hitler!'

# PART TWO

# *Put out the flags*

# 1

WITH HIS campaign in Poland under way, Hitler could hardly wait to get out of Berlin. At 9 pm on Sunday, 3 September 1939, barely five hours after learning that both Britain and France had declared war on Germany, his special train *Amerika* pulled out of the Anhalter station, heading east. Completed only days before, the train consisted of a steam engine and fifteen cars, protected at front and rear by banks of 2-centimetre quick-firing anti-aircraft guns mounted on flat cars, manned by a crew of twenty-six. Hitler's own Pullman car, number 10206, was in the centre, along with his press chief's car, a communications centre with a 700-watt short-wave radio transmitter, a kitchen car and a bath car.

*Amerika* was the first of a long series of Führer headquarters which Hitler would occupy for most of the war, preferring the cramped and inconvenient accommodation of rail cars and damp concrete bunkers to the luxury of his new chancellery. Over the next five and a half years his visits to the capital were always temporary affairs, kept as short as possible. As far as he was concerned, Berlin could go hang.

For the first week of the war, everything went like a German dream. After only five days the Polish army had been cut to shreds, while the Germans had lost only 150 killed and 700 wounded. By the sixth day, the Polish government had fled from Warsaw to Brest-Litovsk. Two days later, on 8 September, the German 4th Panzer Division smashed its way into the suburbs of the Polish capital, and Ribbentrop was urging Stalin to move in and take possession of the eastern half of Poland – his pay-off for signing the Nazi–Soviet Pact. But then things began to go wrong.

The Poles rallied, defending their capital with defiant valour and driving the invaders back. In other parts of the country, too, the Poles fought back desperately. The government called on all citizens to defend their country with any means they could devise. No quarter was to be asked or given. They urged women to destroy tanks by pouring petrol over them and setting them alight. Against such tactics, it was soon clear that the Panzers, which had been so effective charging across the plains, were not suited to street fighting. Hitler ordered his commanders to pull their men back, leaving the artillery and the Luftwaffe to bombard Warsaw into submission.

By 23 September the German high command could announce: 'The Polish army of a million men has been defeated, captured or routed. . . . Only fractions of individual groups were able to avoid immediate destruction by fleeing into the swamps of eastern Poland.' Yet still Warsaw held out. For another four days it endured non-stop bombing and shelling, a salutary reminder to the world's military commanders that even with the most modern weapons, capturing a large city is a dangerous, difficult and bloody undertaking.

GOEBBELS chose to play down the Poles' brave resistance. 'Was there a war at all?' mocked the Berlin daily, *12-Uhr Blatt*. Many families were only too well aware that there had been. Official casualty figures were 10,572 Germans killed, 30,322 wounded and 3,400 missing. Whole pages of the newspapers were filled with obituary notices for sons, husbands, loved ones, who had died 'for Führer and Fatherland'.

2

IT MAY have been the bitter reminder of what war could mean that led the normally sceptical Berliners to be taken in by the rumours that swept through the city on Tuesday, 10 October. 'Have you heard the news?' they asked each other eagerly. The 'news' was that the government in London had fallen. Prime Minister Chamberlain and the arch anti-Nazi Winston Churchill, then first lord of the Admiralty, had resigned. King George VI had abdicated in favour of the Duke of Windsor, the former Edward VIII. The Allies were asking for an eighteen-day armistice, so that peace talks could begin.

There seemed no reason to doubt that the rumour was true. For all their brave words, the Allies had not fired a shot against Germany in the west. Even when RAF bombers had appeared over Berlin during the night of 1 October they had dropped only leaflets, not a single bomb. Britain and France had declared war on behalf of Poland – but Poland had ceased to exist. So what point could there be in their going on?

Without waiting for official confirmation, people started celebrating. Anyone who had not heard the news was soon told. Taxi and bus drivers shouted it to their passengers. Postmen on their morning rounds knocked on every door to announce it. The operators on the Berlin telephone exchange called up subscribers to tell them, '*Der Krieg ist aus!*', 'The war is over!' Market women threw their cabbages in the air, overturned their stalls and headed for the nearest *Kneipe* to celebrate with schnapps. In Wilmersdorf, a butcher was so carried away that he sold his entire stock of meat and sausages without taking a single coupon, believing ration cards were already a thing of the past. A fancy *pâtisserie* on the Kurfürstendamm gave away the day's supply of bread and pastries. A father, anxious to share the good news with his soldier son, went to his local post office to buy an armed forces *Feldpost* card, which did not need a stamp. The counter clerk told him there was no longer a free postal service for the armed forces, and he would have to pay like everyone else. Another father, who had two sons and a son-in-law in the army, was so elated that he spent his entire month's wages on a party for everyone in his office.

The evening papers claimed that the rumours had been spread by the British Secret Service. In fact, they were started by the 'Freedom Station', an illegal radio transmitter run by a group of anti-Nazis moving constantly from place to place to keep one step ahead of the Gestapo. The official Berlin radio station had announced that because of engineering work it would not be broadcasting that day until 12.30 pm. Promptly at 6 am, its normal start time, the Freedom Station used the same wavelength to broadcast what purported to be an official news item about the immediate prospect of peace. It did not seem to matter that the signal was underpowered and much of the message was indistinct – it was the news that people wanted to hear, and they were more than eager to believe it.

Goebbels claimed that the station was financed and directed by the British, but on 10 October 1939 it succeeded in pulling off a propaganda coup that was wholly *Berlinisch*: a cheeky, mischievous, but essentially harmless act of defiance against an all-powerful authority.

## 3

'YOU MAY call me Meier,' Göring boasted at the beginning of the war, 'if one single enemy plane ever enters German airspace!' Other Nazi leaders wisely failed to share his optimism – they made sure the blackout and other air-raid precautions were rigorously enforced throughout Germany. Not a light was to be seen anywhere in Berlin after dark. The few cars that risked the streets travelled at a snail's pace, their drivers straining to see by the narrow beam cast through a slit in the black felt covering each headlight. The white double-decker buses lumbered slowly through the blackout, head-lamps similarly hooded and their interiors lit by a ghostly blue light that made the passengers look like zombies. The only bright sparks in the blackness were the blinding blue flashes from an occasional tramcar.

Piles of rubble dug out of cellars during their transformation into air-raid shelters made the streets hazardous at night. People sporting slings, bandages and other badges of the blackout after tripping over them were a common sight. Yet the police were quick to pounce on anyone lighting so much as a match in the street, and cafés, restaurants and shops that stayed open after dark had to hang large curtains lined with leather or leatherette inside their doors to prevent light spilling out when anyone entered or left.

Electric torches were allowed, as long as the glass was covered with red or blue paper, but there was an acute shortage of torches, bulbs and batteries. So people had to find other ways of getting around safely. Some used white-painted sticks and tapped their way as though they were blind. Others announced their presence with loud honking noises, like children in pedal cars. Luminous buttons on coats were popular: keen party members arranged them in the shape of a swastika, others created designs that were altogether more imaginative and less decorous.

The blackout brought even greater risks than usual to the street whores – who naturally covered their torches with red paper, shining them on their legs by way of advertisement – as groups of soldiers on leave took advantage of the darkness to grab women and gang-rape them. During the first eighteen months of the war there were thirty-five reported cases of rape in Berlin, most of them involving prostitutes. No one can guess how many other attacks went unreported.

Berlin had never had a very high level of street crime – the pitched battles and political violence of the late Twenties and early Thirties were a separate phenomenon. But the darkness brought a string of bloody sex murders and a sharp increase in such offences as bag-snatching.

WHILE THE blackout was a nuisance for most Berliners, food rationing was much worse. In fact, there was no need for rationing at that stage of the war – the German government had stockpiled huge reserves of food, and supplies were still plentiful. But they were determined to get the country on to a real war footing as soon as possible, and imposed a spartan diet from the start, at a level they knew they could sustain over a long period. Unfortunately, the system was so unwieldy that Berliners joked that even those who managed to survive the war would be driven mad trying to figure it out.

Each person received seven different ration cards every month, each a different colour: blue for meat; yellow for fats, cheese and other dairy products; white for sugar, jam and marmalade; green for eggs; orange for bread; pink for flour, rice, cereals, tea and coffee substitutes (ersatz coffee was made from roasted barley and acorns, and was known colloquially as 'nigger sweat'); purple for confectionery, nuts and fruit. As always, there were compensations for the wealthy: shellfish was one of the few things not rationed, so those who could afford to eat out in expensive restaurants gorged themselves on lobster, crab and oysters.

Berliners complained loudly over the amounts they were entitled to each month. But in spite of the moaning, most people did get more than enough to eat in the early years of the war – though the situation deteriorated later. It has been estimated that 40 per cent of the German population were better fed then than they had ever been in peacetime. But there was one group of people who received considerably less: Jews had separate cards, giving them only a fraction of the quantities available to Aryans. They were also forbidden to shop at normal hours, and had to wait until the end of the day, when stocks were usually exhausted.

Food rationing gave rise to the usual crop of Berlin political jokes. One concerned Mahatma Gandhi: 'Question: What's the difference between India and Germany? Answer: In India one man starves for millions; in Germany millions starve for one man.' But the jokes, though more bitter than ever, were no longer told as openly as in the past. The Nazis were not renowned for their sense of humour, so stories had to be whispered among trusted friends after a careful look over each shoulder to see who else might be listening, a movement that became known as the *Berliner Blick*, the Berlin glance.

As the war continued and the apparatus of terror tightened its grip, expression of dissent became more and more dangerous. There had never been any shortage of paid informers in Berlin, but in wartime many ordinary Germans saw it as their patriotic duty to denounce anyone who had the temerity to question the regime. Anything that could be construed as defeatist talk – and that included irreverent jokes – was regarded as treason, and could lead to prison, a concentration camp, or even death.

CLOTHES rationing was introduced on 16 November 1939, with annual cards worth a set number of points. In 1940, the card was worth 150 points, sufficient for the replacement of ordinary items such as shirts and underwear.

But perhaps the greatest problem for German housewives was soap. Rationing allowed only five 50-gram tablets of *einheit* ('standard') toilet soap every four months, the equivalent of about two ounces per month for each person. Roughly half the size of a prewar bar, and a nasty greyish-green colour, *einheit* soap contained pumice or some scouring agent which made it feel harsh and gritty. It made no lather, but left a thick scum floating on the water. The general opinion was that it was capable of removing the skin from the hands of anyone who washed too enthusiastically.

Toothpaste was in equally short supply and of equally poor quality. Toilet paper also fell victim to the *einheit* philosophy – the official toilet roll was the colour and consistency of brown wrapping paper, and was so rough it could have been used for sanding down woodwork. Fortunately, when the British air raids began, the RAF dropped great quantities of flimsy leaflets, which were soon pressed into service. And according to Berliners, the only reason for the continuing popularity of the Nazi party newspaper, the *Völkischer Beobachter*, was its usefulness in the bathroom.

The general lack of soap was most noticeable on the S- or U-Bahn, particularly in the rush hour, when the combination of unwashed clothes and unwashed bodies in a confined space could prove quite overpowering. The stench increased still more after 5 January 1940, when a new decree banned all baths, except on Saturdays and Sundays.

PETROL WAS even more severely rationed, and special laws governing the use of cars were passed daily. As fewer and fewer motor vehicles appeared on the streets, their places were taken by horse-drawn wagons. Diplomats rode to their ministries and embassies on bicycles. Polish prisoners were used to haul overloaded carts. The 'For Sale' columns in the local newspapers were filled with advertisements offering cars at give-away prices, but with no petrol available, who would buy? Petrol was as valuable as cash, and a man with a petrol ration book was rich indeed.

As the war progressed, buses, taxis and those private cars still permitted to run were forced to convert from petrol to compressed gas, a by-product of the synthetic fuel programme for producing oil from coal. Some buses and vans operated on methane gas made from refuse, and many private cars on wood gas, with a stove in the car or on a small trailer towed behind.

The number of taxis was rapidly reduced until there were little more than 100 still operating in the whole of Berlin. Apart from emergencies, and certain specified purposes such as journeys to and from railway stations with heavy luggage, their use was restricted to carrying government officials and invalids.

SMOKERS and drinkers suffered as a result of the shortages. Cigars were almost unobtainable, cigarettes were not only scarce but almost unsmokable, and pipe tobacco was said to taste like 'poor-grade mattress filling'. All were strictly rationed. But for many Germans the most painful shortages were those of wine and beer, aggravated by increased consumption as worried Berliners sought solace in drink. The grapes still grew and the wine was still made, but there was no transport to bring it to Berlin. As for the beer, that staple of Berlin life, complaints about watering were widespread. The amount of grain allowed for brewing was restricted, so the only way to satisfy the increasing demand was dilution.

*

THE MISERY was lightened a little by a surprising relic of life in the Twenties – the cabarets. Several of those resurrected at the time of the Olympics had somehow managed to survive. Of course, the behaviour was not so outrageous as it had been during the 'golden' years: both male and female transvestism were sternly discouraged, and homosexuals were persecuted as badly as Jews, gypsies and Jehovah's Witnesses. Nor was the humour as fierce or as anti-establishment. But all the same, the cabarets provided Berliners with an important escape valve, offering sly, disrespectful comment on their rulers and the conduct of the war. Their shows were hugely popular, and the songs and jokes spread immediately throughout the Reich.

Berlin's favourite comedian was Werner Finck. In his show on New Year's Day in 1940, he obliquely voiced the gloom that many Berliners felt. 'Last year,' he complained to his audience, 'brought me twelve months. I hope this one won't bring me quite so many.'

# 4

FRED LAABS was an athletic twelve-year-old living in Greifswalderstrasse, in the working-class district of Prenzlauerberg, to the north-east of the city centre. He was in a rowing club, and had well-developed muscles for his age, so his teacher picked him, along with three or four of his classmates, for civil defence training with the SHD, the *Sicherheits- und Hilfsdienst* (Security and Aid Service). They were ordered to report in the afternoon to a bunker in a backyard off Kastanianallee. It looked like a lock-up garage, but that didn't stop young Fred and his pals feeling very important, especially when they were kitted out with overalls, steel helmets and boots.

The training began with exercises, then moved on to practising rescue and salvage operations. The boys were taught how to fight fires, and deal with incendiary bombs. Inside the backyard bunker were a number of small cells, which were filled with artificial smoke, where they were trained to work in gas masks, taking them off and putting them on again in the dark. 'Of course,' says Fred, 'there were always adults around, elderly men taking care that we didn't hurt ourselves.'

For Fred and his friends, training was a wonderful game and the bunker a splendid playground. So, too, were the shallow, narrow trenches that were dug in Berlin's parks and open spaces to offer protection against fragmentation bombs – until 1941 there were no purpose-built public shelters in the city.

After about a year of training, at the age of thirteen Fred was attached to the local SHD office as a runner. The SHD was organized along the same lines as the police force – it came under the overall control of the police president – with a network of offices staffed by a few full-time officers, who wore blue-grey uniforms with black piping. Part-timers got no uniforms apart from their overalls, but were issued with armbands. In his early days, Fred had little to do. Sometimes there were papers to be taken to another unit, but most of his two-hour spells of duty were spent simply hanging around waiting for orders, or occasionally typing something.

In this relaxed, almost casual atmosphere, Fred saw his first British plane – a single reconnaissance aircraft flying across a clear blue sky above the city. To his surprise, there was no response from the air defences, not even a warning siren. Life continued as usual, disturbed only by a brief mention in the radio news that one enemy plane had intruded on Berlin airspace.

CIVILIAN air-raid protection at street and home level was controlled by the *Reichsluftschutzbund*, RLB for short, the Reich Air Protection League, whose organization mirrored that of the Nazi party right down to wardens responsible for individual buildings. The equivalent of Britain's ARP (Air Raid Precautions), the RLB had been founded by Göring in April 1933 – the Nazi leaders had been thinking of war from the moment they took power. Ten years later, civilian membership had grown to 22 million, trained and organized by 75,000 full-time paid officials.

In March 1940 the RLB authorities ordered property owners to provide additional exits from their cellar shelters. They were told to cut through the walls of their cellars into those next door, to make an escape route for people trapped when their own building was hit. The holes were lightly filled with a single layer of bricks that could be easily broken down again in an emergency. Eventually, all the cellars in entire city blocks were interconnected, so that people could make their way from one end to the other if necessary.

At rooftop level, the RLB had timber partitions between the lofts of adjacent buildings taken out, to improve access for firefighting. The remaining wooden beams, rafters and laths were sprayed with lime or carbide mud, which could delay the spread of fire for twenty to thirty minutes, theoretically giving time for flames to be extinguished before they had a chance to take hold.

While all these precautions were being taken, there was no let-up in racial discrimination: Jews were banned from sharing cellars with Germans. In some cases they were allowed a small room next to the main part of the cellar where the 'Aryans' sheltered, but more often – where a cellar had only one room – they would have to take refuge in the entrance hall on the ground floor, next to or under the stairs. This offered some protection against bombs landing on the roof, but would usually be completely exposed to blast and splinters from the street.

# 5

A T PRECISELY 5.20 am German summer time on 9 April, the German ministers in Norway and Denmark handed over notes informing their host foreign ministers that their countries were being taken under German protection for the duration of the war. This 'protection' involved immediate occupation of both countries – in their own best interests, of course. They were asked to 'respond with understanding to the German action, and to offer no resistance to it'. Any resistance, they were told, could only lead to bloodshed, since the Germans would be forced to crush it.

The Danes, aware that their flat little country was completely defence-less, could only submit and watch helplessly as German troops on bicycles and horseback rode in, supported by guns and tanks. A few brave souls tried to stem the invasion, but they were soon dealt with. By lunchtime it was all over, at a cost to the Germans of just twenty men.

The Norwegians proved much more difficult. They started by sinking Germany's latest heavy cruiser, the *Blücher*, as it approached Oslo carrying Gestapo officials and administrators on their way to arrest and replace the Norwegian government. A thousand men were killed when the ship blew up and capsized.

In spite of the presence of British ships, the Germans still managed to occupy every one of Norway's most important towns and cities during the morning. The valiant efforts of the shore batteries on Oslo Fjord in driving off the German invasion fleet had been in vain, for the city's airfield had been left unprotected. By noon, eight companies of infantry had landed, and 1,500 men were formed up behind a military band to march ceremonially into the centre of the capital.

At 5.30 pm, General von Falkenhorst, commander of the invasion force, reported to Hitler: 'Denmark and Norway occupied . . . as instructed.' That evening, in the chancellery in Berlin, Hitler and his entourage sat down to a celebratory dinner.

THE CELEBRATIONS were slightly premature. Next day, the Royal Navy struck back at Narvik, where ten German destroyers and five troop transports had landed 2,000 mountain troops with little opposition. Despite a blinding snowstorm on 10 April, five British destroyers managed to penetrate the fjord at dawn high water, 4 am, and attacked the German vessels. Three days later they were joined by the First World War battleship *Warspite*, and more destroyers. All the German ships were sunk – thus accounting for no less than half the total destroyer strength of the German navy and crippling it for the rest of the war.

Hitler was devastated by this news. When he heard that British troops had actually landed near both Narvik and Trondheim, his nerve cracked and he started to panic. 'The hysteria is frightful,' General Alfred Jodl, chief of the OKW operations staff, wrote in his diary.

As more British, French and Polish troops landed, Hitler continued to dither and despair. But instead of losing faith and deserting him, his senior generals worked hard to stiffen his resolve. Jodl stood over him as he pored over maps spread on the red marble table top in his chancellery study, seeking ways of evacuating his troops. Rapping the table with his knuckles until they showed white, Jodl lectured him sharply: 'My Führer, in every war there are times when the supreme commander must keep his nerve.' Hitler pulled himself together and carefully asked, 'What would you advise?' Jodl presented him with an order he had already drafted telling the commander in Narvik, Major-General Eduard Dietl, to hold out for as long as possible. Hitler signed it without demur.

Hitler's fears were unfounded. The Allied attempts to dislodge him from Norway were a catalogue of bungling inefficiency, beset by confusion and indecision. The troops they sent were mostly inexperienced and poorly equipped. Even the French Alpine Chasseurs, who should have been ideally suited to Norwegian conditions, had no bindings for their skis. By 9 June, it was all over. Hitler, his confidence restored, called the campaign 'not only bold, but one of the sauciest undertakings in the history of modern warfare'.

## 6

HITLER HAD left Berlin again on the evening of 9 May – he had been there since 26 March, one of his longest ever stays – and as dawn broke on the 10th he was installing himself and his commanders in a new field head-quarters, codenamed *Felsennest* ('Rocky Eyrie'), a converted anti-aircraft site blasted out of a wooded mountain top near Münstereifel, 45 kilometres by road from the Belgian border. Even as he inspected the bare concrete bunker that was to be his home for the next few weeks, its furnishings minimal, its soundproofing so poor that OKW chief General Keitel, who had the next-door cell, would be able to hear him turning the pages of a newspaper, the air was filled with the roar of aero engines. Wave after wave of Luftwaffe bombers, fighters and troop carriers swept overhead, on their way to attack airfields in Belgium, Holland and northern France.

Colonel Hans Oster, the resistance leader in the Abwehr, had personally warned the Dutch of the attack. But for some reason, both they and the Allies had chosen to ignore his information. When the bombers struck and German paratroops landed and the tanks roared across the frontier, the defenders were caught napping. Hitler had, amazingly, achieved the vital element of surprise once again: it was soon clear that he was about to score a quick and easy victory. The Dutch government and royal family fled to England, where on 10 May Winston Churchill had at last replaced Chamberlain as prime minister. On 14 May the last Dutch resistance was ended after the Luftwaffe blasted the defenceless city of Rotterdam in what was then the most brutal and devastating air raid in European history, killing 980 people and destroying 20,000 buildings.

THE OCCUPATION of Holland was important, but the real key to Hitler's plan lay in Belgium. The fortifications of the Maginot Line sealed off the whole Franco-German frontier, stretching from Switzerland to the Belgian border. This meant that the only way the Germans could invade France without suffering terrible casualties was by going round the Maginot Line, through neutral Belgium. And this was precisely what Hitler now did.

In the First World War the Germans had also attacked through Belgium, following what was known as the Schlieffen Plan, making a great sweep across Belgium to the coast, then turning south and advancing on north-west France on a broad front. Assuming Hitler was repeating history, the British and French rushed their armies north to meet the threat head on. But Hitler and Panzer General Erich von Manstein had other plans. The main thrust of their attack on France was to be through the mountains and forests of the Ardennes, avoiding the Maginot line altogether and bursting directly into north-east France at Sedan. Believing this route to be impassable for tanks, the French had left it virtually unguarded.

The German army planners had allowed nine days for the Panzers to reach the French frontier at the River Meuse. General Heinz Guderian, 'Hurrying Heinz', the brilliant commander of the XIX Panzer Corps occupying the left flank of the attack, said he could do it in four. In the event, he did it in two. At 1500 hours on Monday, 13 May, the first German soldiers crossed the Meuse and established a bridgehead. At dawn next day, Guderian's tanks began pouring across. By 15 May his way was clear and he swept on across France, ignoring orders to halt first from his Army Group A commander, Colonel-General Gerd von Runstedt, and then from Hitler himself, who had once again temporarily lost his nerve, unable to believe his good fortune.

For mile after mile, Guderian's tanks sped on, still unopposed, racing towards the coast over open roads, sweeping 'like a sharp scythe' as Churchill put it, behind the Allied armies. When they ran short of fuel, they simply helped themselves to more at roadside filling stations. From time to time, some even stopped for their crews to milk cows in the fields. The other divisions in Army Group A – the most northerly led by the recently appointed General Erwin Rommel, who had previously only commanded Hitler's bodyguard – also powered their way west.

On 20 May Guderian reached the Channel coast near Abbeville. Along with the French First Army, the entire British Expeditionary Force – a quarter of a million men with virtually all of Britain's modern weapons and equipment – was caught in a vast trap. On 26 May the British began evacuating as many of their own and the French troops as they could from the beaches of Dunkirk.

# 7

O N 14 JUNE German troops entered Paris, emulating Bismarck's victory parade after the Franco-Prussian war in 1871 by marching past the Arc de Triomphe and down the Champs-Elysées. Three days later, the campaign in the west was over as France sued for peace. It had taken the Wehrmacht only ten astonishing weeks to conquer the whole of western Europe apart from the British Isles. France's formal surrender was signed on 22 June, and by 27 June German troops reached the Spanish border, to put the entire Atlantic coast from the North Cape to the Pyrenees in Hitler's hands.

The news of the great battles which Hitler declared would decide the fate of the Reich for the next 1,000 years was received in the city with phlegmatic calm bordering on total indifference. Berliners obeyed the orders to put out flags for each victory, but without any great enthusiasm. 'Put out the flags; take in the flags. Every window, every gable, every tower, all a sea of swastika flags,' Ruth Andreas-Friedrich wrote in her diary. 'If there is a gap in the red wall of pennants, the block supervisor appears and calls the culprit to account. Two hours' grace to buy flags. Anyone who hasn't put out flags by that time is taken away.' Few people even bothered to buy the noon editions of the papers carrying the news, and hardly any gathered outside the chancellery hoping to hear the Führer speak. If anything, Berliners appeared to be more concerned by the ban on dancing and the early closing times imposed on cafés by an order announced on Sunday, 12 May.

But the calm evaporated about a month later, when a division of local infantry, looking suntanned and healthy, returned from France to be demobilized. The troops celebrated their victory in the old Prussian style with a triumphal march through the Brandenburg Gate, where the salute was taken by Goebbels and the commander of the Berlin garrison from a reviewing stand outside the French embassy on Pariserplatz. They marched on up the Linden, between buildings draped with huge red and white pennants. Cheering crowds jammed the pavements and showered them with clouds of confetti. Children broke through the police cordon to present little bouquets of flowers. A dozen military bands played martial music. The war, it seemed, was over.

FOR SOME of those in Berlin who opposed Hitler, the war was only just beginning. The news from France deeply affected Count Helmuth James von Moltke, a great-great-nephew of the field marshal whose armies had crushed France in 1870 and cleared the way for Bismarck to unite Germany under Prussian rule. The thirty-three-year-old Moltke, a tall, thin man with dark eyes and a lantern jaw, was a serious intellectual and a committed Lutheran. He had an English mother, whose father had been chief justice of South Africa, and besides his German law qualifications had been called to the Bar in London's Inner Temple. Associates described him as having the sharpest legal mind they had ever encountered.

At the beginning of the war he had joined the foreign division of the Abwehr, as legal adviser to the OKW. There, of course, he found himself working alongside the anti-Nazi conspirators. He was clearly in sympathy with their motives, but could not bring himself to join them, since his high-minded beliefs would not allow him to contemplate assassinating Hitler, or indeed any act of force. On 17 June, however, as the German nation rejoiced at the victory over France, he decided the time had come to do something more positive. While still abjuring violence, he wrote to several of his friends asking them to join him in an organized group dedicated to the creation of a new Germany after the overthrow of Hitler. The first members of the group, which the Gestapo later labelled the 'Kreisau Circle' after Moltke's country seat in Silesia where they held many of their meetings, included some of the most illustrious names from Prussian history: besides Moltke himself, there were Count Peter Yorck von Wartenburg, a descendant of the general who had freed Berlin from Napoleon in 1812, and Count Horst von Einsiedel, who was a descendant of Bismarck. All were happy to accept Moltke as their leader.

THE 17TH of June 1940 was a decisive day for Dietrich Bonhoeffer, too. He heard of the fall of France while sitting in an open-air café on the waterfront at

Memel in East Prussia, with his friend and former student, Eberhard Bethge. They were chatting idly in the sun when the café's loudspeakers boomed out a fanfare of trumpets – the usual signal for a special announcement –followed by the news that France had capitulated. The other customers in the café could scarcely contain themselves. They leapt to their feet. Some stood on chairs. Everyone cheered. They raised their arms in the Hitler salute. They sang 'Deutschland, Deutschland, über alles' and the 'Horst Wessel Song'.

Bethge remained seated, but was astonished to see Bonhoeffer on his feet, arm raised and joining in the singing like a good Nazi. 'Raise your arm!' he hissed at Bethge. 'Are you crazy?' It was at that point, Bethge believed, that Dietrich Bonhoeffer began his double life.

After another brush with the Gestapo near Königsberg, Bonhoeffer returned to Berlin to tell Hans von Dohnanyi that he was now eager to take an active part in the conspiracy against Hitler. Dohnanyi and Hans Oster – now promoted to major-general – came up with the idea of employing him in the Abwehr, not as a fully-fledged agent, but as an unpaid assistant. The Abwehr often used Jews and communists for undercover work, so why not a pastor of the Confessing Church?

# 8

To most Berliners, unaware of the conspiracies against Hitler, the summer of 1940 marked a high spot that would remain unmatched for fifty years. For a while, it seemed almost too good to be true. Not only were the troops returning victorious from the west after suffering remarkably light casualties, but they were also laden down with booty in the shape of goods they had bought in the conquered lands. The German government had fixed a rate of exchange against the French and Belgian francs and other currencies that priced the Reichsmark at many times its real value. As a result, the German soldier with his small monthly pay at last had access to foreign luxuries he could never normally hope to afford.

Soldiers coming home on leave staggered under the weight of boxes, baskets and suitcases packed to bursting with good things, the like of which their wives and girlfriends had never seen before. Charwomen and factory girls began wearing silk stockings from the boulevard Haussmann; men who had served in Norway returned home burdened down with luxurious silver fox furs. Suddenly Berlin smelt sweet again, for along with the silks and elegant furs, soldiers also brought back bottles of French perfume and boxes of expensive toilet soap from Paris. Drenched in clouds of Mon Plaisir and Chanel No. 5, the city smelt like an expensive brothel.

Ordinary Berlin street-corner *Kneipen*, where only weak beer and dubious so-called liqueurs had been available, now displayed shelves of Armagnac, Martell and Courvoisier cognac. At bourgeois dinner parties Berliners served the best French champagne and thought nothing of it, while they carved thick slices from whole smoked hams, or doled out large helpings of pâté de foie gras.

All this was encouraged by the Nazi authorities. These were the spoils of war, the fruits of victory: enjoy them now. There would be other victories and more plunder; there was still much of the world left to conquer. It was bribery, of course, calculated to keep the soldiers and their folks back home happy and contented, and for the time being, it succeeded.

# 9

STILL RIDING high on the wave of victory, Hitler issued orders on 2 July for Operation Sea Lion, the invasion of Britain. A great fleet of barges from the rivers and canals of Germany, France, Belgium and Holland was assembled on the French coast, ready to carry his troops to final victory over the obstinate British. After the hammering it had taken during the Norwegian campaign, however, the German navy was not strong enough to protect this armada against the Royal Navy and the RAF. Before it could set sail across the English Channel, Göring's Luftwaffe would have to destroy the RAF and achieve total air supremacy.

Göring accepted the challenge with glee, and began preparing three aerial armies. On 8 August Hitler sent a signal to all Luftwaffe units: 'Operation Eagle: Within a short period you will wipe the British air force from the sky! Heil Hitler.' On 15 August, the day after Göring had been promoted to the newly created rank of Reichsmarschall, Operation Eagle opened with 1,786 sorties against British airfields. But the British were ready for them, fighting back with determined ferocity. By the end of the first day, the Luftwaffe had lost 75 aircraft, while downing only 32 of the RAF's 700 fighters. It was a pattern that was to be repeated every day during the next five weeks, as the skies over southern and eastern England became the setting for an epic aerial conflict. The Battle of Britain had begun.

*

ON SATURDAY, 24 August 1940, the Luftwaffe began attacking RAF bases in the London area. At the same time, ten German bombers were sent to attack oil storage installations at Thameshaven, some twenty-five miles downriver from central London. But their navigation was faulty: somehow they managed to drop their bombs right in the heart of the City of London, destroying many historic buildings including the Christopher Wren church of St Giles, Cripplegate.

Over a month earlier, Winston Churchill had told his secretary of state for air, Sir Archibald Sinclair, that if the Germans bombed London, 'it seems very important to be able to return the compliment the next day upon Berlin'. He had asked for confirmation that this was possible. Sinclair had replied that it was certainly possible, given twenty-four hours' notice. In fact, he added, after 2 August the whole of Britain's bomber force could be sent to Berlin at only twelve hours' notice, and would be able to drop 65–70 tons of bombs every night for a week, rising to 150 tons on alternate nights. The German bombers had hardly left London in the early hours of 25 August before the order to retaliate was given.

That night, 103 aircraft took off to bomb Germany, 89 of them heading for Berlin. They were all obsolescent twin-engined aircraft: Hampdens, Wellingtons and a few Whitleys, with cruising speeds of between 155 and 165 mph. Each was capable of carrying a full bomb load of 4,000 to 4,500 lbs, but even with reduced loads, they were stretched to their limit. Unlike the German bombers, which were operating over comparatively short distances from airfields in France and the Low Countries, accompanied by fighter escorts, British aircraft faced an unprotected round trip to Berlin of 1,160 miles. Only during the long nights of winter could they hope to get there and back under cover of darkness. Nevertheless, the very fact that they could strike at the heart of the Reich would have an enormous psychological impact both in Germany and at home.

Because of persistent cloud and a lack of sophisticated navigation equipment, only 29 bombers actually reached Berlin – over a 580-mile outward trip, the 20 mph cross wind they encountered could blow a bomber off course by as much as 66 miles. When they got there, they found the city masked by thick cloud, which made accurate bombing impossible. Fortunately it also prevented the German searchlights picking up the aircraft, and the flak gunners could only fire wildly in the direction of the engine noise as planes flew over them.

According to the German newspaper reports, which Goebbels limited to his six-line official communiqué, the only bombs that fell within the city limits were a handful of incendiaries which destroyed a wooden summer-house in the northern suburb of Rosenthal, slightly injuring two people. Certainly, most of the bombs landed in the countryside to the south of the city, some of them on one of the large municipal farms. The joke swiftly went round Berlin: 'Now the Tommies are trying to starve us out!' But many people plainly heard bombs exploding in the city centre, and next day three streets were roped off to keep people from seeing the damage. In addition to 22 tons of bombs, many with delayed-action fuses, the British planes also dropped leaflets, telling Berliners that 'the war which Hitler started will go on, and it will last as long as Hitler does'.

The first British raid had not been a success, and on the return trip the planes met strong head winds that increased the hazards. Three were shot down on the way home and another three ran out of fuel and ditched in the sea. But the next day, Churchill demanded more. When he heard that the RAF's target for that night was to be Leipzig rather than Berlin, he telephoned the chief of the air staff and told him: 'Now that they have begun to molest the capital, I want you to hit them hard – and Berlin is the place to hit them.'

THEY HIT Berlin again on the night of 28–9 August, and thirty-eight more times between then and the end of October. Although there were some casualties, the harm they caused was not really serious, since relatively few aircraft were involved. 'If the damage doesn't get any worse in the future,' commented Ruth Andreas-Friedrich, whose home in Steglitz was three and a half miles due south of the Zoo, 'we needn't worry too seriously about this particular spectre of war. After each raid the populace turns out, curious and sensation hungry, to view the so-called damage. They gape at a burned attic here, a few paving stones dug up there, a half-collapsed house over yonder. In general they don't take things too hard; they make it a point of pride to show themselves stoics, and are gradually getting used to sleeping the night in the basement.'

ON 4 SEPTEMBER, after the fourth British raid, Hitler made a surprise appearance at the launch of that year's winter relief campaign. Ranting against the 'cowardly RAF', he promised he would 'answer' the British raids 'night for night', and that for every two or three or four thousand kilograms of bombs dropped on Germany, 'we will in one night drop 150-, 230-, 300-, or 400,000 kilograms'. His audience, mostly women nurses and social workers, applauded so hysterically that he had to wait before continuing: 'When they declare that they will increase their attacks on our cities, then we will raze *their* cities to the ground!'

Berliners were not told that their planes were actually bombing London until 7 September, when the RAF had improved its accuracy enough to hit two railway stations and a rubber factory. The OKW then issued a statement saying: 'The enemy again attacked the German capital last night, causing some damage to persons and to property as a result of his indiscriminate bombing of non-military targets in the centre of the city. The German air force, as a reprisal, has therefore begun to attack London with strong forces.'

That night, 625 German bombers unleashed a massive bombardment on London, the start of the 'Blitz' proper. From then until 13 November between 150 and 300 Luftwaffe bombers dropped at least 100 tons of high explosives on the British capital almost every night. They also dropped about a million incendiary bombs. Buckingham Palace and St Paul's Cathedral were both hit on 11 September. Six days later, 10,000 Londoners were killed or injured in a single raid.

THAT SAME day, 17 September, the exhausted British fighter pilots waited in vain for the order to scramble. All day, the blue sky remained empty – for the first time in nearly five weeks no German raiders appeared. The Luftwaffe had admitted defeat in the Battle of Britain after Churchill's legendary 'Few' in their Spitfires, Hurricanes and Defiants had shot down 1,733 German planes for the loss of 915 British aircraft. Hitler postponed Operation Sea Lion 'indefinitely'.

With its airfields intact, the RAF kept up attacks on Berlin throughout the rest of the year. In September and October British bombers hit railway yards north of the Stettiner and Lehrter stations, and marshalling yards at Charlottenburg, Rummelsburg and Schöneberg, power stations at Moabit and Wilmersdorf, gas works, Bahrenfeld airfield, and a whole range of industrial installations, including the BMW aero engine factory, Siemens cable works, and the Viktoria chemical works.

Twice they just missed the S-bahn line running east–west through the centre of Berlin, which carried long-distance passenger trains as well as the bulk of the suburban commuter traffic. Even though there had been no direct hits on the line, thousands of morning commuters coming in from the north-eastern suburbs had to get off their trains at three different places where debris was still being cleared from the track, to be ferried on buses to where they could board other trains.

Some raids lasted so long that the Ministry of Education ordered that 'in cases where the air raids continue after midnight, grade schools will remain closed the following morning, in order to allow children to catch up on their sleep'.

'We shall pay the English gentlemen back, with interest,' Goebbels vowed. But by then Berliners were growing cynical about the stories of Luftwaffe 'reprisals'. If the reprisals were so fierce, they asked, how come the RAF were still dropping bombs on them? Berliners buying their evening newspapers, priced at ten pfennigs, took to asking for 'ten pfennigs' worth of reprisals'. They did not believe what they read, and they certainly did not believe what they heard over the radio. They also had a grudging admiration for the RAF flyers: when the American air attaché in Berlin sent back reports in October on the raids, he said the population had praised the boldness, courage and determination of the RAF crews. And in contrast to Goebbels's repeated statements about indiscriminate bombing, he said Berliners believed the planes were obviously searching out specific targets, undeterred by the flak.

The Berliners generally managed to retain their cynical sense of humour. With their penchant for attaching irreverent labels to monuments and buildings, they renamed Göring's Air Ministry the 'Meier Ministry'. A favourite story of the time arose from the advice given by the head of the Berlin Air Protection Service for people to go to bed early and get at least a couple of hours' sleep before the raids started, so that no matter how heavy a raid was, they would at least have had some sleep and would be ready for work in the morning. Berliners joked that this meant they could divide people going into a shelter into three types. Those who greeted the others in the shelter with a 'Good morning' had followed the official advice. Those who greeted them with a 'Good evening' had not yet had any sleep. But those who greeted everyone with a Nazi salute and a 'Heil Hitler' had *always* been asleep.

THE RAIDS brought an additional hardship for many Berlin Jews. At the start of the war there had still been some 23,000 apartments in Berlin either owned or occupied by Jews. Albert Speer had been steadily taking them over, mainly to accommodate non-Jewish tenants who had lost their homes in his urban renewal schemes. As British bombs made more and more people homeless, Speer stepped up his seizure of Jewish-owned apartments to rehouse them. He also needed to find accommodation for the capital's growing army of civil servants and officials – larger and more luxurious homes in the more fashionable districts were especially sought after by leading party members.

Paul Scheurenberg, the First World War hero who had been lulled into a false sense of security by a new medal from Hitler in 1935, was still in Berlin with his family. He had realized his mistake too late. Since losing his job as a department store salesman, he had administered a Jewish community house. When he took it over in 1937, it was bursting at the seams with sixty inhabitants. By 1940 there were 240 living in the same space, and the numbers were still rising. The pressure was increased by the fact that Berlin's Jewish population was growing every day, as more and more Jews from other parts of Germany left the small towns and villages where they felt isolated and exposed, to seek the anonymity of the big city and the comfort of being with their fellows. More than half of all the Jews in Germany were now living in Berlin.

Under-fed, overcrowded, and deprived of the right to pursue any profession or business, most Berlin Jews were directed into compulsory labour in armaments factories or other essential war work. In general, they were highly valued for their skills, intelligence and industry, and so enjoyed a certain amount of protection for the first two years of the war, avoiding the fate of Jews in other parts of Europe. Although they were heavily persecuted, the policy of extermination had not yet begun and they were not thrown into concentration camps simply for being Jewish. There was one scare in October 1940, when several hundred Berlin Jews were rounded up and shipped off to Poland, but this appeared to be an isolated incident.

# 10

THE BOMBING campaign was still raging when Vyacheslav Molotov, premier and foreign minister of the Soviet Union, arrived in Berlin on Tuesday, 12 November, for discussions with Hitler and Ribbentrop. Relations between the countries had become strained since the heady days of the signing of the Nazi–Soviet Pact and the partition of Poland. Germany still needed Soviet oil, grain, minerals and other raw materials, which were pouring in from the east to sustain the Reich and its ability to wage war. But the supply of German arms and machinery promised in return had been spasmodic at best, and Stalin was growing increasingly dissatisfied.

Molotov's visit was to prove enormously significant to the future of Berlin, for it represented the last chance of averting war with the Soviet Union. Hitler was already preparing his plans for an attack, to win *Lebensraum* for his people on the great, fertile plains of the east. There was, however, just a chance that Stalin would be prepared to make him an offer, to buy him off. But Molotov proved obdurate, insisting that Germany fulfil her existing obligations under the pact. Far from trying to placate Hitler, he argued with him and even lectured him severely – a new and unwelcome experience for the Führer.

At the end of three hours of talk, Hitler was pleased to find an excuse to call a halt for the night. It was already dark outside, he pointed out, rising from his armchair. 'I fear we must break off this discussion,' he went on. 'Otherwise we shall be caught by the air-raid warning.'

But there was no raid that night, and the magnificent reception laid on by Ribbentrop at the Kaiserhof Hotel, just along the Wilhelmstrasse from the Foreign Ministry, went ahead without interruption. Next night, however, when the Soviets returned the compliment with a dinner at their embassy on the Linden, the RAF arrived in the middle of the speeches. 'We had heard of the conference beforehand,' Churchill wrote later, 'and though not invited to join the discussions did not wish to be entirely left out of the proceedings.' The embassy did not have its own shelter, so Ribbentrop, Molotov and their staffs adjourned to the shelter in Ribbentrop's residence, just around the corner.

At 9.45 pm, to an accompaniment of anti-aircraft guns and exploding bombs, Ribbentrop began his final attempt to stave off the rupture in German–Soviet relations. Once again, as he had done in previous discussions during the two-day visit, he attempted to redirect Soviet ambitions away from Europe and towards the Indian Ocean. The USSR, he urged, should concentrate its efforts on the dismemberment of the British empire. The British, he declared, were finished, the end was only a matter of time.

Molotov was not impressed. 'If that is so,' he asked, 'then why are we in this shelter, and whose are those bombs that are falling?'

Next morning, 14 November, Molotov and most of his advisers left the Anhalter station at 11 am, exactly forty-eight hours after their arrival. The only leading Nazi there to see them off was Ribbentrop. For Hitler, and for Berlin, the die was now cast – the Führer had decided to attack the Soviet Union in 1941, whatever it might cost. The principal target for the Luftwaffe that night was not London but the city of Coventry: 449 German bombers dropped 503 tons of high explosive and as many as 30,000 incendiaries. It was total, indiscriminate bombing, flattening the centre of the city, destroying the ancient cathedral and 75 per cent of the residential districts, demolishing or damaging some 60,000 buildings, killing 554 people and injuring 865. It sickened and enraged the people of Britain, strengthening their determination to give as good as they got through raids on German cities.

# 11

WITH CHRISTMAS approaching, the Berlin papers announced on 19 December that there would be a special rations allotment for the festive season. Until 9 March, in fact, everyone would be able to buy three times the normal weekly ration of eight ounces each of beans, lentils and peas. Extra sugar and marmalade were also available until 12 March, as well as further allowances of cinnamon and cloves to flavour home-made Christmas cakes – but no extra eggs, flour or butter to make them with. The newspapers, instead, printed recipes telling women how to bake cakes with no eggs and almost no fat. The extras were small, but still welcome to people whose diet was becoming increasingly monotonous.

There were plenty of Christmas trees, but none in squares and other public places. The traditional Christmas market in the Lustgarten was held, and was as rowdy as ever, but few shops bothered with special window displays, since it was dark by 4 pm and lights were, of course, forbidden under the blackout regulations.

For children, there was a special Christmas allotment of sweets and cakes – almost half a pound of chocolates or half a pound of sugar candy, plus a quarter-pound of cakes for each child. The toys in the shops were mostly leftovers from the previous year and mostly war games featuring, inevitably, bombers, U-boats, tanks and guns. There were soldier suits for boys, and nurses' uniforms and dolls for girls. Toy soldiers were no longer made of lead but of wood and plastic.

On Christmas Day itself, which fell on a Wednesday, Goebbels gave a short speech to the police at a parade at the Brandenburg Gate, thanking them for their 'service, protection and help'. In the evening he visited a flak battery at Teltow, on the city's south-eastern boundary. 'First, I inspect the battery's position with Colonel-General Weise,' he wrote in his diary. 'An imposing sight. Here is our protection. Then a very atmospheric Christmas party in the barracks. Wonderful music. I thank the flak briefly for providing our shield and protection. And then hand out an absolute mountain of gifts. I feel most at ease with such simple people.'

Goebbels did not record what the 'wonderful music' was, but it almost certainly included special arrangements of traditional carols, such as the Nazi version of 'Silent Night':

> Silent night, holy night,
> All is calm, all is bright.
> Only the chancellor stays on guard
> Germany's future to watch and to ward,
> Guiding our nation aright.
>
> Silent night, holy night,
> All is calm, all is bright.
> Adolf Hitler is Germany's star
> Showing greatness and glory afar
> Bringing us Germans the might.

For many Berlin families the Christmas celebrations were marred by the absence of their children. The authorities had begun their compulsory evacuation from the city at the end of October, shipping some 60,000 young Berliners to the safety of the eastern provinces. Now a further exodus was in progress, with seventy-five special trains to transport an additional 30,000 youngsters under the age of fourteen to safety.

At first, the evacuations did not go well – many mothers objected to having their children forcibly removed, even though it was for their own safety. Goebbels confided to his diary that it had been clumsily handled and had created enormous discontent: 'I had expressly ordered that the process should be carried out without compulsion. I summon the ten Berlin Kreisleiters [local district leaders] and read them the riot act. They are to warn the local party branches immediately and bring order back into the situation . . . I hope things will work out, even so.'

Things did work out. The pressure on the local authorities eased, for there were no more RAF raids on Berlin until March 1941. The British needed to reassess their effectiveness in view of the problems of navigation and accuracy associated with night bombing. Meanwhile, other targets took greater priority for Bomber Command. During the last four and a half months of 1940 there had been thirty raids on the city; in the whole of 1941, there were to be only seventeen.

## 12

M OST OF the raids in 1941 came in the six weeks following 12 March, when British bombers devastated the heart of the Linden, hitting the state library, the old royal palace, and many other buildings for several blocks on either side. The State Opera House was gutted. Its massive exterior walls were left standing, but direct hits by some thirty incendiary bombs created an inferno that reduced the auditorium to a mess of burnt timbers and twisted girders. The great golden eagle of the kaisers, which had been mounted on red velvet hangings behind the old imperial box, was discovered by sightseers next morning, lying charred, discoloured and sodden under the ruins.

After the first raid in March, Goebbels, in his capacity as Gauleiter, had a visit from Berlin's police chief, Count Wolf von Helldorf, a man who had made a fortune before the war by confiscating the passports of wealthy Jews who were desperate to get out of the country, then selling them back to them at prices around 250,000 Reichsmarks. Helldorf was worried about Berlin's ability to withstand really heavy bombing. There were, he said, simply not enough adequate public shelters. Goebbels had always regarded the police chief as a pessimist, and listened impatiently. 'What London can put up with,' he told him, 'Berlin will also have to bear.'

Fortunately, after April Berlin did not have to bear much more until the autumn: the RAF was ordered to concentrate on attacking the bases of the U-boats and long-range Focke-Wulf Kondor bombers that were having such an effect on British merchant shipping, threatening the country's lifeline. For several months, British bombers were directed against targets such as Kiel, Hamburg, Bremen and Bordeaux, giving Berlin a much-needed respite.

# 13

ONE MAN who missed most of the bombing in the spring of 1941 was Dietrich Bonhoeffer, who started his active life as an Abwehr agent with a trip to Switzerland on 24 February. Travelling on a permit issued by the Foreign Office, he spent about a month there, renewing and re-establishing his international church contacts and helping to set up what was to be known as 'Operation 7'. The seven referred to seven Jewish friends of Admiral Canaris, who were to be got out of Germany into Switzerland posing as Abwehr agents, with the help of the Swiss Reformed Church among others. Later, Hans von Dohnanyi decided to add his own Jewish friends, increasing the total to about fifteen.

The whole process took a year to arrange. It was not only the RSHA (Heydrich's Reich Security Head Office) that was suspicious. The Swiss authorities were reluctant to get involved in anything that might compromise their neutrality. Other members of the Abwehr who were not in on the secret had to be persuaded that it was all above board. And the Jews themselves were understandably nervous – two refused to go if it meant working for the Abwehr, and were only convinced with the greatest difficulty that it was merely a ploy to get them safely out of the country. Bonhoeffer had to return to Geneva in August and September to keep things going there. In the end Operation 7 succeeded only because Canaris intervened personally at the highest level.

# 14

Gerald Rahusen was a schoolboy living in Frohnau on the northern edge of Berlin, with his mother, a determined anti-Nazi who had been born in Odessa, where her German grandfather had gone to make his fortune. Although they had various Jewish connections and lived permanently in Berlin, they were Dutch citizens, and this enabled them to remain unmolested throughout the war. One day in 1941 Gerald and a schoolfriend were cycling across the heathland near the River Havel when they suddenly came across a strange plywood and canvas 'town'. Built in the open country, it was fitted with oil lamps to give a dim glow at night as though from inadequately blacked-out buildings, to tempt enemy aircraft to drop their bombs there. 'Next to it was the steel works at Hennigsdorf,' Gerald recalls, 'and they wanted to protect this from bombs, so they put this false affair next to it. But as far as I know, not a single bomb was ever dropped there.'

Gerald Rahusen's decoy was one of many efforts in and around the city to confuse British flyers. Berlin was a navigator's and bomb aimer's delight, with the broad expanse of the East–West Axis running in a straight line from the Havel to the Spree, pointing like an arrow to its heart. On a dark night, with a low cloud base and heavy anti-aircraft fire, it was not always so simple, but even then a pilot would only have to pick up one or two unmistakable landmarks and he would have a pretty good idea of his position.

The Germans did everything they could to frustrate Allied aircraft, going to elaborate lengths to disguise the city. They erected dummy buildings in the Adolf Hitler Platz along the Kaiserdamm and in other open spaces in and near the centre. They strung a canopy of camouflage netting, laced with strips of green cloth and false fir tree tops, on fifteen-foot poles along the whole length of the Charlottenburger Chaussee from the Brandenburg Gate through the Tiergarten, to hide the long stretch of concrete. Even the lamp posts were dressed up as fir trees. For local motorists and pedestrians, it was like passing through 'an enormous, overgrown, green circus marquee'. At the centre of the avenue, the Siegessäule, the Victory Column, was draped in netting from head to foot. The buxom goddess on top was stripped of her gold leaf and painted a dull brown.

Many individual building and installations were also camouflaged. The Deutschland Halle, for example, the giant exhibition hall just off the East–West Axis near Broadcasting House at the beginning of the Kaiserdamm, which was used during the war for storing grain, was covered in painted netting so that from the air it looked like a park with paths running through it. And the nearby Lietzensee was also covered with netting to stop it reflecting the moon like a mirror. The lake was planted with covered scaffolding structures intended to look like buildings on a housing estate. Later in the war, when the RAF began using radar to locate their targets, Berlin's lakes were studded with cross-shaped sheets of metal to reflect the signal back again – without them, the lakes appeared as black holes on radar screens.

Elsewhere in and around the city there were even more ambitious deceptions, including no fewer than five dummy cities.

On a more central site just to the east of the Spree, beyond Ostkreuz S-Bahn station, vacant lots were covered with dummy triumphal arches and replicas of government buildings, designed to trick raiders into thinking they were over the Wilhelmstrasse. From the ground they may have looked like a badly designed film set, but in the darkness, from the bomb aimer's nacelle of an aircraft under attack, they could easily pass as genuine parts of Berlin.

To complete the illusion, on most dummy sites there were huge piles of brushwood fitted with electric ignition devices ready to be fired by soldiers in near-bombproof concrete dugouts immediately after bombs were dropped, to simulate burning buildings. The Berliners, however, did not place too much faith in their decoy sites – there was a persistent story that some British bombers peeled off from the main line of attack to drop wooden bombs on at least one of them.

Mobile flak and searchlight batteries played their part in the deception tactics by moving from place to place in order to confuse pilots. Normally, aircraft approaching from the west were greeted with a heavy flak barrage as they reached the Grunewald forest on the west of the city. Sometimes, however, the guns were moved, and planes were allowed to fly right over the western suburbs and the centre of the city without being fired on or meeting the usual searchlight batteries until they reached the eastern suburbs. The aim was to persuade raiders that the centre of Berlin was about twenty miles further east. German broadcasting stations hurriedly went off the air as soon as British planes approached, fearful that RAF navigators would use their signals as radio beacons.

# 15

'F LAK' IS short for *Fliegerabwehrkannonen*, anti-aircraft guns, though Allied aircrew used the expression for the shells they fired: 'The flak was so thick you could get out and walk on it,' as one USAF Flying Fortress bombardier remarked of the Berlin air defences later in the war.

German flak guns ranged from quick-firing 20 mm (¾-inch) automatic cannon, belt-fed like machine guns and mounted in pairs or fours, through 37 mm, 88 mm and 105 mm guns, right up to heavy 128 mm (5-inch) artillery pieces capable of firing 57 lb high explosive shells to a height of 45,000 feet, over eight miles, well above the ceiling of any wartime bomber. At a pre-set height, the shells exploded into clouds of shrapnel that could instantly turn the wing of a bomber into something resembling a sieve.

During the first two years of the war, Berliners tended to regard the flak defences of their city as a joke: 'Hermann's sleeping battalions' they called them – Hermann, of course, being Göring, who, as commander-in-chief of the Luftwaffe, was responsible for protecting the city. But during 1941 the situation changed dramatically. By the end of that year Berlin positively bristled with searchlights and flak batteries arranged in concentric rings around the city.

The outer searchlight belt was sixty miles in diameter, the flak area forty miles across. The searchlights not only picked out individual aircraft in a cone of light to provide a target for the guns, but also hoped to blind the bomb aimer so that he would be unable to find his aiming points. Hitler even had the bizarre idea of mounting mirrors in such a way that enemy pilots would be blinded by the reflections of the searchlights, too. He envisaged the day when every village in Germany would have its own searchlight and flak battery.

There were many fortified gun emplacements throughout the city, including one at the Red-White Tennis Club, and individual guns mounted on top of buildings such as the IG Farben headquarters in Pariserplatz. But after 1941 Berlin's inner defences were dominated by three massive flak towers built during that year: in the Zoological Gardens near the Kaiser Wilhelm memorial church; in Humboldthain park due north of the Unter den Linden; and in Friedrichshain park east of Alexanderplatz.

Designed by Albert Speer's office in the heavy *Ordensburgen* (literally 'order castles') style, the towers were intended to remind people of medieval fortresses. Part of the Nazi romantic fantasy, they were a throw-back to the

German dream of the times when heroic Teutonic knights rode out to conquer and subdue the pagan Slavonic hordes. But above all, the towers were meant to look impressive because they were to be the first buildings for Hitler's new city of Germania, which was to replace Berlin after the war.

The flak towers were bomb-proof and shell-proof, modern Crusader castles with walls of reinforced concrete more than eight feet thick, their deep-cut window slits shielded by solid steel shutters. They were 120 feet or more in height, and descended to as many as six levels below ground. With their own water and electricity supplies and their own hospitals, they were kept stocked with enough food and ammunition to sustain a twelve-month siege.

On top of each tower, projecting above the trees of the surrounding park, eight 128 mm guns were mounted in pairs – 'double-barrelled', Hitler called them, 'the most beautiful weapons yet fashioned'. Each pair was operated by a team of twenty-one gunners under the command of a non-commissioned officer. They were capable of firing a salvo every 90 seconds, eight shells set to explode simultaneously at a given height and in a planned pattern, creating a killing area, known as a 'window', 260 yards across. Any plane caught in the window was doomed.

Just below roof level, four more gun positions housed twelve multi-barrelled 20 mm quick-firing 'pompoms' and 37 mm cannon to give protection against attack by low-flying aircraft. 'When the guns start firing, the earth trembles, and even in our flat the noise is ear-splitting,' commented Missie Vassiltchikov, who lived near the Zoo.

The Zoo tower was the biggest of the three: at 132 feet tall it was the equivalent of a thirteen-storey building. It had five levels above ground: the top, immediately beneath the gun platforms, contained the barracks for the 100 gunners; the fourth a 95-bed hospital, fully staffed and equipped, complete with two operating theatres; the third was a secure warehouse containing the treasures from Berlin's art galleries and museums. The two lower levels formed an air-raid shelter for 15,000 members of the public, as well as kitchens, storerooms and emergency quarters for the staff of the Deutschlandsender national broadcasting station. Below ground were the power generators, air-conditioning units and other service equipment, plus the magazines for ammunition, which was carried to the guns by elevators that rattled upwards through the building, adding to the almost unbearable noise during a raid.

The Humboldthain tower, though slightly smaller, could provide refuge for even more Berliners, as its lower floors were connected to one of the deepest stations on the U-Bahn system, Gesundbrunnen; 21,000 people could shelter there during raids.

Alongside each flak tower stood a slightly smaller communications and radar control tower, with giant Würzburg and smaller Freya radar dishes on its roof. These towers, too, were protected by cannon. From the Zoo communications tower, Luftwaffe controllers directed the air defence of the city, issuing orders to all Berlin's flak and searchlight units. Beside the radar dishes was an observation turret like a small penthouse, large enough to hold at least a dozen people, from which party notables could watch the progress of a raid.

'From the flak tower, the raids on Berlin were an unforgettable sight,' wrote Albert Speer, who became Reich minister for munitions and construction in February 1942,

> and I had constantly to remind myself of the cruel reality in order not to be completely entranced by the scene: the illuminations of the parachute flares, which the Berliners called 'Christmas trees', followed by flashes of explosions which were caught by the clouds of smoke, the innumerable probing searchlights, the excitement when a plane was caught and tried to escape the cone of light, the brief flaming torch when it was hit. No doubt about it, this apocalypse provided a magnificent spectacle.

# 16

WITH THE lull in the bombing in 1941, and everything quiet in the occupied lands both to the east and west, Berliners could concentrate for a while on the remaining pleasures of life in the capital city. For Goebbels, as both Gauleiter of Berlin and minister of propaganda and public enlightenment, there were delicate decisions to be made – should he, for instance, allow semi-nude shows at the Frasquita club? Should he allow public dancing to continue in clubs and dance halls, or ban it, as the Kaiser had done during the First World War? He decided to follow tradition, and forbid it while German troops were fighting – as they were at that time in North Africa. Rommel had landed in Tripoli on 12 February with the two Panzer divisions of the Afrika Korps and the 90th Light Division, to bolster up the Italians, who were being severely battered by the British Eighth Army.

In spite of Goebbels's sudden burst of puritanism, there were still clubs where hostesses were available to sit and drink with male customers, who were often party officials or diplomats. One, the Golden Horseshoe, even boasted a black hostess, said to be the only black woman in the city. The club's other main attraction was a small circus ring, round which lady customers could ride on horseback. The purpose of this was to show off the ladies' legs – with clothes rationing, skirts were getting shorter and shorter as girls were forced to trim their worn hems. For 50 pfennigs a man could enjoy watching a slow, discreet trot around the ring. An extra 25 persuaded the horse to break into a more revealing canter.

One of the most popular haunts was Walterchen der Seelensorger ('Little Walter the carer for souls'), a small, working-class dance hall near the Stettiner railway station. The main entertainment consisted of a kind of public lonely hearts club, with Walterchen himself playing Cupid and introducing elderly and middle-aged customers with a view to matrimony, or at the very least companionship. Walterchen's sign was unmistakable: a big red heart, transfixed by an arrow.

Those traditional sources of entertainment and relaxation for ordinary Berliners, beerhalls like Die Neue Welt, were closed for much of the time, owing to the shortage of beer. It had been found that watered-down beer did not keep, so although the strength was slightly increased again, supplies had to be reduced. To help cope with this, it was announced, on 1 May 1941, that beer could only be sold between 11.30 am and 3 pm, and from 7 pm to 10 pm – a hardship that caused much grumbling in Berlin, but which, ironically, was very similar to the peacetime licensing hours for pubs in Britain. Even with restricted hours, however, supplies regularly ran out. And when Die Neue Welt was open, it could not have been the most convivial place, since Gestapo men were given to roaming around inside, demanding to see customers' identity cards.

For the more urbane, there were still clubs like the Jockey Bar, with pictures of American film stars on the wall, including Leslie Howard – actually a Hungarian-born naturalized Briton – who was then broadcasting regularly for the BBC. The orchestra played American dance music in modern tempo for what was apparently a sophisticated crowd, but of course no one was allowed to dance to it.

There was no shortage of theatrical entertainment, and theatres were packed every night. But although they were doing good business, the management of the big Berlin variety theatres, like the Scala or the Wintergarten, had a harder and harder job filling the bill. At one time, the Scala had relied entirely on foreign artists, with a Spanish month, an American month, and so on. But now many foreign performers were either unacceptable or were no longer prepared to face the horrors of wartime travel, not to mention the bombs. And audiences would only put up with just so many juggling or acrobatic acts.

Many musicians had fled, yet Berlin still remained a great centre for music. Despite a considerably reduced repertoire, the Berlin Philharmonic flourished under Wilhelm Furtwängler, its musical director since 1922, who continued to conduct throughout the Nazi era. Hitler disapproved of Furtwängler's uncompromising defence of Jewish musicians in the orchestra, but tolerated him because of his masterly interpretations of Wagner. Furtwängler's junior, Herbert von Karajan, was more popular with Hitler – he was perhaps even better at interpreting Wagner, particularly the operas, and had no compunction about joining the Nazi Party.

After the damage to the State Opera House, the regular season continued at the German Opera House. The only real problem was that not every Berliner wanted a diet of almost unrelieved Wagner, and many other composers were barred either because their native countries were now enemies of the Reich, or because they were Jewish or had Jewish connections. Even Mozart was restricted, since *The Marriage of Figaro, Don Giovanni* and *Così fan tutte* had libretti by Lorenzo da Ponte, a baptized Jew, and *The Magic Flute* had a masonic theme.

Films were not as popular as they should have been, largely because Goebbels still insisted that the studios churn out war epics. In 1941 the cinemas were showing a steady stream of historical movies with a message, like the viciously anti-Semitic *Jud Süss*, or war films with such unimaginative titles as *Bomber Wing Lützow* or *Stukas*. The result was that the Ufa-Palast on the Kurfürstendamm, showing *Bomber Wing Lützow* would be half empty, while the Gloria-Palast fifty yards down the street would be packed with people watching a second-rate little comedy, *Der Gasmann*, starring a small, cheeky comic called Heinz Rühmann. Goebbels despised these films for their low artistic value, but Göring was said to have laughed himself sick at Rühmann's antics.

# 17

BERLINERS were cynically amused on 13 May when news was released that Hitler's deputy führer, Rudolf Hess, had flown to Britain on a half-baked personal peace mission. Hess had done a bunk, they said – so what? They had always regarded him as quite mad, and now the Berlin humorists had a field day. 'The 1,000-year Reich,' ran one joke, 'has now become the 100-year Reich. One zero has gone.' Another story envisaged Churchill interrogating Hess on his arrival: 'Churchill: So you are the madman? Hess: No, only his deputy.'

Hess was rapidly transformed into a non-person: it was as if he had never existed. By 14 May all postcards of him had been withdrawn from Berlin's shops and news-stands. The *Völkischer Beobachter* declared that Hess 'had been in poor health for many years and latterly had increasing recourse to hypnotists, astrologers and so on. The extent to which these people are responsible for the mental confusion that led him to his present step has still to be clarified.'

Apart from Hitler's natural anger, the real concern over both Hess and the astrologers lay in what they might reveal. The massive build-up of German forces for Operation Barbarossa, the invasion of the Soviet Union, had been in progress for some time, cloaked by intense secrecy and an elaborate deception operation. Anything that might jeopardize this had to be dealt with promptly and efficiently. Hess could be aware of the plans for Barbarossa, and would probably tell the British – indeed, this seemed almost certainly to be the main reason for his flight. And the British might well tell the Soviets. By declaring that he was both mad and under the influence of fortune tellers, the Nazi leadership hoped to destroy any credibility Hess might have had with the British. In fact, they need not have worried. The British were bemused by Hess's strange behaviour and simply locked him up until the end of the war, and in any case he proved to know nothing of Barbarossa.


MOST GERMAN astrologers were agreed that there would be a conjunction of the heavenly bodies in April–May 1941 that would be particularly baleful for Hitler. Prophecy is a dangerous business, and never more so than when predictions prove accurate – people start asking whether the information may have come from somewhere other than the stars. In addition, talk of bad luck for Hitler at that time was hardly likely to raise the spirits of the German people. Clearly, the prophets had to be dealt with.

On 6 June, the day after Hitler agreed the final timetable for the attack on the Soviet Union, Hess's former deputy Martin Bormann issued a decree to all Gauleiters – including Goebbels – ordering them to bear down not merely on 'astrologers, fortune tellers and other swindlers', but also on the churches. Goebbels complied enthusiastically, taking it upon himself to add clairvoyants, magnetopaths, Rudolf Steiner's Anthroposophists (a breakaway group from the theosophical movement) and others to the list. 'We have finally put an end to these fraudulent operations,' he crowed in his diary. 'Oddly enough, not a single clairvoyant predicted that he would be arrested. A poor advertisement for their profession.'

The astrologers' prediction of problems for Hitler during April and May had proved true, however. Barbarossa had originally been set to begin on 15 May but a *coup d'état* in Yugoslavia at the end of March had upset the plans. The new Yugoslav government, under the young King Peter, refused to allow the German army to pass unhindered through the country to kick the British out of Greece and clear Hitler's southern flank for the invasion of the Soviet Union, so Barbarossa had to be postponed until June while he smashed Yugoslavia first, before attacking Greece and occupying Bulgaria and Romania. The delay, which lasted five weeks, was to prove fatal.


THE BUILD-UP to Barbarossa, which continued from February through May, was so enormous it was impossible to conceal from the people of Berlin.

Despite a great deception campaign which somehow managed to fool Stalin, everybody knew that the city's factories had been frantically turning out tanks, guns, munitions and aircraft for months, and that almost all had been transported in one direction. Between February and May 1941 nearly 20,000 special trains had shipped over 3 million men and their equipment to the east – and inevitably most of those trains either started from or passed through Berlin.

As the time for the start grew nearer, so Berlin became a ferment of rumours. Many were deliberately started by Goebbels's Propaganda Ministry as part of the deception plan to counter any suggestion of an attack on the Soviet Union. One rumour was that Stalin himself was coming to Berlin to negotiate personally with Hitler. Suddenly everyone in the city was talking about it. Ruth Andreas-Friedrich was told about it by her milkman. 'Two hundred women had been put to work sewing flags,' he said. A neighbour she met on the stairs confirmed the news, adding that he had heard Stalin was arriving 'by special armoured train'. Official backing for the rumour was strengthened when instructions were given to the management of the Schloss Bellevue guest house to prepare for a visit by Soviet dignitaries, and the Anhalter railway station was closed to the public at the beginning of June while elaborate decorations involving red flags and a huge, illuminated red star were tried out.

To divert attention to imaginary preparations for an attack in the west against Britain, handbooks were printed on the British way of life, dummy ministries were set up in Berlin to take charge of a conquered Britain, and there was intensive and ill-conceived air reconnaissance of possible landing sites there. In Berlin cafés and restaurants, paratroop and Panzer officers ostentatiously smoked Dutch cigars and talked about the pleasures of living in France, and word was 'allowed' to trickle around the capital of large forces being assembled in the Channel ports.

Despite all the deceptive gossip buzzing around the city, however, Berlin's more intelligent and worldly-wise observers were not fooled. The Soviet Union remained at the front of their minds as summer approached. Ruth Andreas-Friedrich's suspicions were confirmed by a man from the Foreign Office 'who seemed to have victory in his hip pocket'. The invasion would begin next Saturday, 21 June, he told her, continuing: 'On 15 October our victorious armies will be on a line from Astrakhan to Archangel.' When she questioned whether the Russians would give in so easily, her arguments were brushed aside.

# 18

JUNE 1941 had been mostly warm and sunny in Berlin, and Saturday, 21 June, was no exception. As the day wore on, it became increasingly hot and humid. By lunchtime, thousands of Berliners had left the city centre to sunbathe or swim at Wannsee or Nikolassee, or to relax in the parks around Potsdam. Among them were most of the staff of the Soviet embassy. Valentin Berezhkov, who had accompanied Molotov as an interpreter, was now first secretary at the embassy. He was left almost alone in the gloomy old palace on the Linden that Saturday, trying to fix an urgent meeting between Ambassador Dekanozov and Ribbentrop to discuss the critical state of German–Soviet relations.

Berezhkov, a handsome young man with a mop of dark hair, found it impossible to contact Ribbentrop, or State Secretary Ernst von Weizsäcker. At midday he did manage to speak to the head of the Foreign Ministry's political department, Ernst Woermann, but Woermann could only say that no one was available because they all seemed to be at a conference in the Reich chancellery. Berezhkov kept trying, ringing the Wilhelmstrasse every half-hour throughout the day, but without success.

Shortly before 2 am next morning, Erich Sommer, a Russian language interpreter with the protocol department of the Foreign Office, was woken up by his mother in their west end flat. Frau Sommer stood by her son's bedside holding the telephone. 'An urgent call from the department,' she whispered. At the other end of the line was Sommer's boss, Dr Hans Strack. 'You will be picked up in about fifteen minutes by an official car,' Strack told him. He was to wear his dress uniform, complete with belt – 'full warpaint' as they called it in the office.

Sommer scrambled out of bed and dressed hurriedly, trying to gather his wits – he had had less than an hour's sleep before the telephone call. He just had time to swallow a pep pill and a gulp of hot coffee to wake himself before the car arrived. His mother handed him his black cap, with the Reich eagle on its high front. She squeezed his hand, knowing intuitively what the call meant. 'God bless you, and keep us all,' she murmured as he left to be driven swiftly across Wittenbergplatz and through the deserted streets in the official black Mercedes, up to the green-painted front door of 76 Wilhelmstrasse.

Showing his pass at the porter's lodge, Sommer noticed that the entrance leading from the street directly to Bismarck's old room, with its two stone sphinxes guarding the doorway, was open. This entrance was used only on special occasions. Inside, to his surprise, the Biedermeier chandeliers were ablaze with lights. The gaudy red carpet on the shallow stairway seemed more vivid than ever, reminding him of freshly spilled blood.

Sommer hurried into his ground-floor office, where Strack greeted him with a serious face, shaking his hand solemnly. Speaking slowly and emphatically, he told him: 'We are about to declare war on the Russians. Please telephone the Soviet embassy.'

Valentin Berezhkov was still at his desk when the telephone rang. He picked it up immediately. Sommer, his throat tightening with nerves, informed him that Reichsminister von Ribbentrop wished to see the Soviet ambassador in his office in half an hour's time. An official car would be at the embassy to collect him in fifteen minutes. Berezhkov caught his breath before he replied, his voice shaking, that the ambassador would be ready.

Dawn was breaking beyond the domes of the old royal palace and the cathedral as the Mercedes sped back down the Linden carrying Ambassador Dekanozov and Berezhkov the short distance to the Foreign Office. Sommer and Strack sat uncomfortably on the jump seats, facing them. As they turned left into the Wilhelmstrasse, the first light from the east caught the Brandenburg Gate, turning the great stone pillars to gold. Dekanozov leaned forward.

'It promises to be a glorious day,' he said.

Sommer translated for Strack. 'We hope so, Mr Ambassador,' he replied.

At that moment, 500 miles to the east, 3.2 million men were pouring across the Soviet frontier in the greatest invasion of all time. Few of them realized that they were sowing the wind – or that it would be Berlin that would reap the whirlwind.

CORRESPONDENTS in Berlin were called to the Foreign Office for a special press conference at 6 am. Even as they arrived, the loudspeakers on the streets were already booming out the Führer's message: 'People of Germany! National Socialists! The hour has now come. Oppressed by great cares, doomed to months of silence, I can at last speak frankly . . .'. Between them, he said, the Soviet Union and Britain were planning to crush Germany with aid supplied by the USA. 'I therefore decided today to lay the fate and future of the German Reich in the hands of our soldiers. May Almighty God help us in this fight.'

At the press conference Ribbentrop read a prepared statement repeating in slightly different words what Hitler had said. Both statements were later broadcast all over Europe. As the correspondents left, the first extra editions of the papers, each as usual no more than a single sheet, were being bought as soon as they were delivered to the news-stands. 'War Front from North Cape to Black Sea Bringing the Moscow Traitors to Reckoning. Two-Faced Jewish

Bolshevik Rulers in the Kremlin Lengthen the War for the Benefit of England,' trumpeted the *Völkischer Beobachter*. The other papers, if less wordy, were equally bellicose.

On his way to the press conference, *New York Times* correspondent Howard K. Smith noticed a slogan painted on a building in the Kalckreuth-strasse near the Roma restaurant, the hang-out for the Italian press corps, just off Kleiststrasse. *Rotfront Siegt!* (Red Front Victorious!), it read. On his way home two hours later he saw that it had been painted out, presumably by the special police 'paint squad', which had the job of keeping Berlin free of anti-Nazi slogans. Next day, the message was back, but this time it took the police several hours to get around to erasing it – they had hundreds of other slogans all over Berlin to deal with. What surprised Smith was that the slogans he saw were in the west end, rather than in working-class districts. He reported seeing similar slogans in Lietzenbürgerstrasse and by the Zoo. Clearly, red Berlin still survived beneath the surface.

The Nazi authorities contributed their own form of graffiti a few days after the start of Barbarossa. A sign over the newly vacated Soviet embassy read 'Closed for Fumigation'. It brought a brief grin to the faces of many Berliners who enjoyed that kind of humour, but that was about all. Soon the euphoria of the initial war news from the east began leaking away.

THE SOVIETS began trying to bomb Berlin on 8 August, when five Ilyushin Il–4 aircraft took off from Estonia. Two were shot down before they reached the city; two more failed to find it; the survivor dropped its light bomb load on rail tracks on the outskirts. Four more Soviet raids were almost as ineffectual. After 5 September, when Estonia fell to the Germans, there were to be no more until almost the end of the war, since the Soviets had no planes with the range to reach Berlin.

ORDINARY LIFE in Berlin went on pretty much as usual. There was championship football at the Olympic stadium with players on special release from the forces, and Berliners turned out in the sun in their thousands to watch international dinghy sailing on the Spree. They sat in cafés and strolled the Linden as before. But they were uneasy. There was a scent of disaster in the air, a feeling that calamity lay just around the corner.

Curiously, one of the things that depressed them was Goebbels's propaganda, which was as well prepared and well executed as the Wehrmacht's campaign – too well, as it turned out. People did not want their news organized into neat, sanitized packages of information, given out with fanfares every few days. The routine German victory twice a week made them uneasy. Initially, of course, those on the right were delighted by the invasion of the Soviet Union. They had never really understood the need for the Nazi–

Soviet Pact in the first place – to them, Bolshevism had been the enemy since 1918. 'At last,' they said, 'we are fighting the real enemy.' But before long even their exuberance had faded.

It was clear after the immediate successes that the German army, like Napoleon's 130 years before, was becoming bogged down in the vastness of Russia. 'The enemy has proved himself harder than the one we fought in the west,' declared the *Frankfurter Zeitung*. Even the party's own newspaper was constrained to admit that 'we are dealing with the most difficult enemy we have met so far.' 'The fight,' acknowledged the *Völkischer Beobachter*, 'has been bloody and bitter.' Indeed it had: during the first six weeks the Germans had lost 30,000 dead. More and more of the obituary notices in the newspapers omitted the customary 'For Führer' from their heading and simply stated 'For the Fatherland'. It was a small protest, but a heartfelt one.

BY 1 SEPTEMBER, five weeks later than the Nazis had predicted for a total Soviet defeat, the German army was besieging Odessa in the south and Leningrad in the north, but their forces were still 150 miles from Moscow. And then, on Friday, 12 September, came the first early warning signs of the Russian winter. Softly, out of a dove-grey sky, snow began to fall, all along the front from Leningrad to Odessa. The snow did not stick – the seasonal rainstorms which followed, the *rasputitsa*, caused more immediate disruption to the Germans' progress, turning the land into a sea of mud – but it was an ominous sign.

What brought the reality of war home to the Berliners was something they had not noticed before – the sight of maimed and wounded soldiers on the streets. The Polish and French campaigns had brought relatively few casualties – US correspondent Joseph Harsch, who left Germany before Barbarossa, estimated that he had never seen more than a dozen wounded men on the street in his whole time in the city. But suddenly, they were everywhere. Young men with their arms in slings, walking with crutches or canes, or without an arm or leg, were to be seen on every block. Previously, there had been few women in mourning, but they, too, were now commonplace. More and more people seemed to be wearing black.

The Berlin transport authorities recognized the changed situation in their own way. A mere eight weeks after the invasion new signs were being fixed in trains, trams and buses, informing travellers that end seats were reserved for cripples and those wounded in the war.

HELMUTH VON MOLTKE wrote to his wife, Freya, on 26 August: 'The news from the east is terrible again. Our losses are obviously very, very heavy. But that could be borne if we were not burdened with hecatombs of corpses. Again and again one hears that in transports of prisoners or Jews only 20 per cent arrive, that there is starvation in the prisoner-of-war camps, that typhoid and all the other deficiency epidemics have broken out, that our own people are breaking down from exhaustion. What will happen when the nation as a whole realizes that this war is lost, and lost differently from the last one?'

A few days later, he was staggered by a report that landed on his desk complaining that dumdum bullets found on captured Russian soldiers were in breach of international law. The head of the Institute for Forensic Medicine, Colonel Dr Gerhart Panning, had prepared a scientific study proving the effects of the bullets by using them in a large-scale experimental execution of Jews, noting the results when they were fired into the head, chest, abdomen and limbs. This careful study, Panning shamelessly explained, proved the violation of international law 'without a doubt'.

Every contact with such depravity served to reinforce Moltke's conviction that it was vital for Germany to be totally and comprehensively defeated. Only then, he believed, could the country be purged sufficiently for a new beginning to be made. The anti-Hitler generals had missed their opportunity, and now it was too late. 'Every day costs 6,000 German and 15,000 Russian dead and wounded,' he wrote to Freya. 'Every hour costs 250 Germans and 625 Russians, every minute 4 Germans and 10 Russians. That's a terrible price which must now be paid for [the generals'] inactivity and hesitation.'

# 19

YOUNG Klaus Scheurenberg had a job with a timber company manufacturing and installing rail ties, wood-block road surfaces and heavy-duty flooring. Their products were vital to tank factories, bridges and flak emplacements – every anti-aircraft gun in Berlin was mounted on baulks of timber, since concrete broke up after only a couple of rounds had been fired. When he was working the day shift, Klaus made the hour-long journey to the factory in Niederschönhausen on the same train every morning, leaving at 5.20 am. He always shared the same car with the same travelling companions, their bleary faces showing their lack of sleep, especially after air-raid alarms.

Klaus had a regular seat on a cross-bench between a burly bricklayer who spent the journey reading the *Berliner Zeitung*, and a man who was trying to keep up appearances from better days: he always wore a collar and tie with his frayed suit, and tried to look like a gentleman. On the opposite side sat a young man – Klaus thought he was an Italian gigolo – who grinned at him and had once given him a cigarette. A plump middle-aged woman with blonde hair and chubby cheeks stood by the door. She never sat down and got out after five stations. They all knew each other, and always greeted the young Klaus with 'Guten Morgen' or the familiar Berlinisch 'Morjn!'

On Friday, 19 September 1941, two days short of his sixteenth birthday, Klaus left home at the usual time, but with a heavy heart. He felt horribly ashamed, and kept to the shadows as he walked to the station, trying to hold the bag containing his breakfast across his chest, to hide the yellow Star of David on his coat. 'I was in a fever,' he says. 'I felt naked.'

A new regulation had come into effect that morning, ordering all Jews to wear the cloth star, firmly sewn on to their clothes at all times. Covering or concealing the star in any way was strictly forbidden. Along with this came other restrictions. One was that they had to obtain police permission before they could leave the district in which they lived. Another forbade their using public transport except, as a special concession, to travel to and from work, and then they were not permitted to sit down. Others banned them from buying clothes, smoking tobacco, using public telephones, keeping pets, having their hair cut by an Aryan barber, or owning any electrical appliances, record players, typewriters or bicycles.

The star, with the word *Jude* (Jew) written across the centre in Hebrew-style letters, was about the size of a man's hand, but to Klaus Scheurenberg it seemed to weigh a ton. At the station, the fat old man who always waited for the train with him, but then rode in a different car, looked at him desperately, beads of sweat standing out on his brow – he, too, was wearing a star.

When the train arrived, Klaus automatically boarded his usual car. Nervously he whispered 'Morjn!' His travelling companions looked up, considered for a moment, then loudly replied in a chorus. 'Morjn!' Then, as always, there was silence – it was too early for conversation. Klaus remained standing by the door, next to the plump woman. Suddenly the voice of the bricklayer boomed out, over-loud: 'Why don't you sit down, then? Your place is here.' The others looked on, and nodded.

'I can't sit down,' Klaus replied in his best Berlinisch. 'It is forbidden.'

'Oh, *Quatsch* [rubbish]!' the bricklayer shouted. 'Sit down.' The others nodded agreement. Klaus sat, nervously, on the edge of the seat. The 'gigolo' leaned over and gave him a cigarette. The 'gentleman' lit it for him. 'For a couple of seconds,' Klaus remembers, 'there was a conspiracy – no, humanity.'

Sadly, the conspiracy did not last. Other people in the car looked on with hostility, showing their disapproval. Klaus's friends grew apprehensive – were there informers watching? At the next station they all made their excuses and got out, completing their journey in the next car. Embarrassed and no doubt ashamed of their cowardice, they never travelled in the same car with him again.

Generally speaking, Klaus Scheurenberg recalls, the reaction of most Berliners to the stars was positive. 'Only occasionally would someone spit at us, shove us around, beat us up. Every Jew with a star experienced this. But you rose above it. You washed off the spit, cleaned yourself up, came to terms with it.' And there were many examples of humanity to counterbalance the evil – albeit usually a little furtive and careful.

Klaus's sister Lisa was a beautiful young woman who knew how to dress elegantly and with chic. And she could make something out of nothing. Lisa walked along Elsässerstrasse, where the family lived, elegant as ever, her head held high, wearing her star. If she was frightened, she didn't show it. Across the street from the Jewish house was a brothel, whose madam knew the Scheurenbergs by sight. As Lisa walked along, she came out of the house, crossed the street and barged into her, saying very loudly, 'Watch where you're going, greasy Jew!' At the same moment, with a broad wink, she shoved a parcel under Lisa's arm. It turned out to be full of the choicest delicacies – Wurst, chocolate, silk stockings, cigarettes. 'Such people, themselves living on the edge of society, had the most understanding and sympathy,' Klaus recalls. 'This woman, who never spoke to us, never came into our house, regularly slipped us something, then disappeared before we could thank her.'

MANY YOUNGER Jews defied the order to wear the star, leaving if off to go out during the evenings into forbidden areas and flouting the curfew – Jews were not allowed out of their homes after 8 pm in winter and 9 pm in summer. It was dangerous. Anyone caught was liable to be arrested, beaten up, and thrown into a concentration camp. But for brave, frustrated youngsters the excitement was worth the risk. Klaus Scheurenberg had a special shirt, made from white nettle fibre, with a detachable breast pocket to cover the star. He and his friends regularly went into the west end, or to swimming baths, or simply into parks, but took care not to let their nervous parents know what they were up to.

THE NEW regulations and restrictions on Jews caused problems for Bonhoeffer and Dohnanyi in their efforts to get people out to Switzerland through Operation 7. After a great deal of difficulty, they had finally got approval for a passport to be issued to one of their group, Charlotte Friedenthal, a Jewish Christian who had been a member of the governing body of the Confessing Church for some years. She was ordered to go to the Gestapo office in the Alexanderplatz to collect it. Naturally, she would have to appear at the 'Alex' wearing her star – but while she was wearing it she could not use any public transport from Dahlem. Nor could she go to the Swiss consulate to get her visa, since it was in Fürst-Bismarckstrasse, a street forbidden to Jews. Fortunately the weather was warm, and she was able to carry her coat, with its sewn-on star, rolled up under her arm on the S-Bahn, putting it on when she reached the Alexanderplatz, and rolling it up again when she had safely collected her passport.

On the train to the Swiss frontier, the coat served as a seat cushion until they had passed Weil, the last German station, when she put it on, to the horror of the Aryan passengers who had unwittingly shared the compartment with her. There was a moment's panic when officials at the frontier took all her papers away, but they returned them after a few minutes. She stepped on to the platform in Basle, to be greeted by Hans Bernd Gisevius, the regular Abwehr courier to Switzerland and one of the conspirators. Smiling at her nervousness, he pointed at her coat. 'You don't have to wear the star here,' he gently reassured her.

20

A CONCENTRATED drive by Albert Speer during August 1941 had produced a further 5,000 apartments for his rehousing programme. At the end of September, he warned the Jewish community leaders who had to find new homes for those who had been evicted that he would shortly begin a further 'resettlement'. But this time, the resettlement took a different form. On 15 October, as darkness fell, two Gestapo men arrived at each apartment to be vacated and ordered the family to pack one suitcase with essentials. They took them to the remains of the synagogue on Levetzowstrasse, still in ruins since it was burned down during *Kristallnacht*. There they were kept for three days before being marched in a long procession through the city to the railway station at Grunewald. Young children and the sick were driven in trucks. On 18 October, the first train left, carrying 1,000 Jews to be dumped in the working ghetto of Lodz, in eastern Poland. Over the next ten weeks, another twenty-five trains followed, carrying Berlin Jews to Lodz and other ghettos in Minsk, the capital of Belorussia, Kaunas, at that time the capital of Lithuania, Riga, capital of Latvia, and Smolensk, in Russia.

Many Jews did their best to avoid the SS by spending their nights away from home, staying with Aryan friends. 'If you aren't at home, they go away,' Ruth Andreas-Friedrich's friend Margot Rosenthal told her. 'Everything's all right if you aren't at home.' But on Friday, 5 December, she failed to turn up at Andreas-Friedrich's flat. On Christmas Eve, a letter arrived from her. She was in the ghetto at Landshut, in Bavaria. 'Send us something to eat, we are starving,' she wrote. 'Don't forget me. I cry all day.'

*

AT THE beginning of 1942 there were still 40,000 Jews in Berlin, most of whom were saved from deportation by their jobs in war industries. But on 20 January a conference in a villa at Wannsee under the direction of Reinhard Heydrich – postponed for three weeks due to America's entry into the war, which had closed the final escape route for Jews still hoping to emigrate – set out the plan for the 'final solution' of the Jewish problem. The remaining Jews throughout Nazi-occupied Europe, including the Reich itself, were to be exterminated in special death camps to be built in the east. The technique that would be used to dispose of them had been perfected over the preceding two years, when more than 50,000 mentally deficient or incurably sick Germans had been gassed to death in rooms designed as public showers. Jews working in munitions factories would be systematically replaced by foreign workers from the occupied territories. Berlin would at last become *Judenfrei*.

By the middle of the year, those remaining were in great danger of being starved to death, as rations were cut once more. For the general population, this meant further reductions in meat, lard and butter. For Jews, the meagre rations of meat, eggs and smoked foods were withdrawn altogether. Even their vegetable allocation was virtually non-existent, allowing a family perhaps two turnips a week. Those groups of Aryans who had devoted themselves to helping the Jews had to work harder than ever to collect enough coupons to feed their Jewish protégés.


FROM FEBRUARY 1942, Maria von Maltzan was hiding a permanent lodger in her Detmolderstrasse apartment: her Jewish lover, Hans Hirschel. Hans disappeared from the apartment he shared with his mother by faking suicide, leaving a note saying he could not go on living in Nazi Germany and was drowning himself in the Wannsee. He and Maria gambled successfully that the police would not feel inclined to start dragging the lake and river for the body of yet another Jewish suicide.

Hans was not allowed to know where she disappeared to so often during dark nights, while he stayed locked in her flat. Since 1940 she had played an active role in a resistance ring run by the Swedish church in Berlin, getting both Jews and political dissidents out of Germany to Sweden. On dark nights, she would shepherd small groups of escapers through the woods north of Berlin to secret spots where they could be slipped aboard freight trains and hidden in crates of furniture bound for Stockholm or Gothenburg.

It was dangerous work, and Maria had several narrow escapes. On one occasion she eluded the police who were closing in on her during an air raid by joining the firefighters trying to save a factory that had been hit by bombs. When the flames were finally out, she persuaded the fire chief to give her a signed note certifying that she had spent the night helping them, and with this she got past the patrols and returned home, blackened, bedraggled and weary.

Hans and Maria were in constant fear of betrayal or discovery. Their biggest danger was that one of the fugitives who spent a few days and nights with them before moving on to the next safe house might prove to be a traitor, or might talk after being captured and tortured. Their closest shave came when the Gestapo arrived one day accusing Maria of sheltering Jews. Neighbours had reported seeing them enter and leave. One, a young woman, had been picked up. Standing before a life-sized portrait of her aristocratic father in full imperial uniform, Maria drew on her considerable reserves of hauteur. Yes, she condescended, from time to time she had indeed given a home for a few nights to people who had been bombed out of their own places and had nowhere to go. And yes, the young woman in question had stayed with her for two weeks. But she was not Jewish. Maria had seen her papers, and they were all quite in order. In fact, of course, she had done more than look at the woman's papers – she and her organization had printed them.

The Gestapo men grudgingly accepted her explanation, but still insisted on searching the flat. Hans, during all this, was hidden inside a large ottoman, with an ornately carved mahogany wood base. Inevitably, the Gestapo men tried to open it. They failed, for Hans had fastened it securely with a catch on the underside of the lid. They demanded that Maria open it. She claimed that she could not, and had not been able to discover how to since she had bought it three weeks before. The officer persisted, clearly suspicious. Finally, in desperation, Maria declared: 'If you don't believe me, you'll have to take your gun out and shoot through the couch. But I warn you that you'll be responsible for paying for new upholstery, and for any repairs that are necessary – and I want that in writing before you do anything.' The men hesitated, then left.

A few minutes later, while she was still calming down a terrified Hans, the doorbell rang again. Fearing the worst, she bundled Hans back into his hiding place and went to the door. It was two Jewish fugitives, seeking shelter. For once, Maria did not take them in, but warned them that the flat was under observation and sent them on their way to another hideout.

Since Hans had no income and no food ration cards, Maria had to support them both with her earnings as a veterinarian, supplemented by black market trading in vegetables given to her by grateful farmers and cattle breeders. She even managed to have Hans's baby, persuading a homosexual Swedish diplomat to pose as the child's father. Sadly, the child was born prematurely, and died in hospital the same night, when an air raid cut off the electricity supply to its incubator.

# 21

THE YEAR 1942 had started with German supremacy unquestioned from the Atlantic to the Black Sea, from the icy Arctic to the deserts of North Africa. There had been setbacks in the Soviet Union, but these could be put down to the weather and the toughness of their Slav opponents. The ground recovered by the Red Army during the winter and early spring would be recaptured in the great offensive planned for the summer. The RAF raids on Berlin and other cities, though they had caused a fair amount of damage and a number of deaths, had not been an unqualified success: in many ways it was still possible to regard them as an irritant rather than a disaster. But then, things began to go wrong.

On 28 March, the RAF introduced the new technique of saturation bombing to destroy the ancient city of Lübeck. On 30–31 May they applied it to a bigger target, the city of Cologne, using an incredible total of 1,080 bombers to drop some 2,000 tons of high explosives in ninety minutes, turning the city into a raging inferno. The well-developed shelter system kept the number killed to fewer than 500, with 5,000 injured, but 45,000 people were left homeless as 600 acres of the city were devastated.

Göring refused to believe the figures. 'It's impossible!' he screamed. 'That many bombs cannot be dropped in a single night!' Churchill, however, promised that the raid was but a herald of what Germany would receive in the future, and further massive raids on Bremen, Hamburg, Düsseldorf and Osnabrück bore out his words. The Berliners received news of these raids with trepidation, knowing that sooner or later they would have to face the same treatment. It was not a cheerful prospect.

With fewer air raids on the city during 1941 and none at all in the early part of 1942, many of the children who had been evacuated during the autumn of 1940 had returned to their families. Now, a new programme had to be started to move them out again, under the supervision of members of the Hitler Youth not much older than themselves.

Klaus Ziegler, the son of a minor official with the military administration in Paris, was drafted to help with the evacuation of Berlin children to the safety of occupied Czechoslovakia – what was then known as 'the Protectorate'. At the age of sixteen, he was put in charge of entire trains of up to 1,000 evacuees. Although there were Red Cross nurses and welfare workers aboard, Klaus was ultimately responsible for looking after the children, including hundreds of homesick eight- or nine-year-olds, crying for their mothers. Usually the sexes were segregated, with boys and girls travelling on separate trains. But Klaus recalls one mixed transport: some of the girls were aged fourteen or fifteen, and very sexually aware. Trying to keep them under control was a considerable problem on a journey of more than two days and nights.

The evacuations were well organized, Klaus recalls. The children had labels fixed to their clothes, giving their names and home address. Each child was allowed to take whatever could be fitted into one suitcase or rucksack. Other essentials, such as schoolbooks, were sent on later by post. There were usually between 500 and 1,000 children per train, 64 in each coach. Food was provided at stations along the route, together with any medical attention that might be needed. Unlike Britain, where evacuees from the big cities were accommodated with individual families in their homes, the children were mostly billeted in hotels, castles or schools. Klaus had to see them safely installed, then leave next day to supervise the return of the train to Berlin.

YOUNG PEOPLE like Klaus Ziegler were central to the Nazi philosophy as the heirs of the thousand-year Reich. The Nazis exploited their youthful aggressiveness and sense of dedication, and rewarded them for loyalty and keenness: the young had much to thank them for – camps, holidays, jobs, education, and, of course, uniforms. Any boy who did well in the Hitler Youth could expect to be guaranteed a place in high school regardless of his academic record.

Many foreign observers believed that young Nazis were a greater threat than their elders – 'more dangerous than a cholera epidemic' was how one correspondent described them. Tom Macleod, a British prisoner of war made to work in a gang repairing and maintaining rail tracks in Berlin, had the truth of this brought home to him in a particularly vivid way. As his squad was marched to work each morning, a sympathetic German couple often slipped him a scrap of paper with news from BBC broadcasts, a gesture that he and his companions greatly appreciated. One morning, however, they arrived outside the station to find the couple being stood against a wall, and were forced to watch as they were summarily executed. Turning away in horror, Macleod saw the couple's young son on the opposite side of the square, being rewarded with a Nazi medal for betraying his parents.

# 22

ON 10 APRIL 1942, Dietrich Bonhoeffer was sent by the Abwehr to visit Norway, accompanied by none other than Helmuth von Moltke. The official reason for their trip was to study the battle between the Nazi puppet government of Vidkun Quisling and the Norwegian Lutheran church, and to see how it might affect the German occupation.

The two envoys spent their time secretly encouraging the Norwegian churchmen in their resistance. Bonhoeffer urged them to be prepared to go to any lengths in their struggle, even as far as martyrdom. For him, the affair aroused painful memories of the time when he had tried to organize a protest movement in the German Protestant churches in 1933, and had failed to gain any sizeable support.

During their time together, Bonhoeffer and Moltke naturally discussed the problems of overthrowing Hitler. Ironically, it was Bonhoeffer, the ordained minister of God, who argued that the Führer must be got rid of by any possible means, including assassination. Moltke remained unconvinced, still rejecting the idea of violence, but he invited Bonhoeffer to Kreisau in four weeks' time, 'to meet some like-minded friends'.

In four weeks' time, however, Bonhoeffer was on a visit to Sweden, where his old friend Bishop George Bell was a member of a British cultural mission, along with Kenneth Clark, the art historian, and T. S. Eliot, the poet. On Whit Sunday, the two churchmen met in Bell's room at the Manfred Björquist evangelical academy in the small town of Sigtuna.

Bell was especially pleased to see Bonhoeffer, not only as a dear friend, but also because he needed his advice. A few days earlier he had been approached in Stockholm by a Dr Hans Schönfeld, a minister of the official German church. Schönfeld, who had appeared very nervous, had handed him a remarkable document, containing a detailed breakdown of the entire German resistance movement, plus a plan to eliminate Hitler, Göring, Goebbels, Himmler, and all the Nazi leadership, and form a new German government. The document also contained proposals for a postwar Federation of European States, and suggestions on how to deal with the threat of communism posed by the Soviet Union. But before there could be any *coup d'état* in Germany, the Wehrmacht leaders had to be assured that the Allies would agree to treat with the new government, once Hitler and his minions were dead.

It was a startling proposition, but also very worrying. The bishop had no means of knowing how serious it was, or even if it was some Nazi plot to discredit him. The very fact that Dr Schönfeld was a member of the official German church made him doubly suspicious. What did Bonhoeffer think? Could he vouch for Schönfeld?

Bonhoeffer could vouch for Schönfeld, though he said he had known nothing of his mission. He could also verify the provenance of the document, which had originated with the resistance group in the Foreign Office that included Adam von Trott, Hans-Bernd von Haeften – who also belonged to Moltke's circle – and Dr Eugen Gerstenmaier, of the foreign affairs office of the Evangelical Church.

Bonhoeffer, of course, had come to speak to Bell on behalf of the Abwehr group that he represented. When asked for names, he gave the bishop a list that included General Beck, Colonel-General Kurt von Hammerstein, Carl Goerdeler, former government minister and mayor of Leipzig, and the trade unionists Jacob Kaiser and Wilhelm Leuschner. Beck and Goerdeler, he said, would head the new government. Like Schönfeld, Bonhoeffer begged Bell to pass on to the British government the pleas of the resistance groups for support.

Presuming that the British government would be only too delighted to support any German group that could overthrow Hitler and bring the war to an end, Dr Bell returned to London, and duly passed on the messages. On 30 June he succeeded in getting a meeting with the foreign secretary, Anthony Eden, who promised to study the documents. He also took copies to John Winant, the US ambassador in London, for the US government. Both governments rejected the appeals out of hand.

# 23

'ONE THING is certain,' physician Dr Walter Seitz declared to Ruth Andreas-Friedrich on Saturday, 1 August. 'The day of the lone wolves is over. The strong man is not mightiest alone now. We've got to form a shock troop – all over Berlin, in every neighbourhood, we've got to have our own people. Sworn allies that we can rely on absolutely.'

The friends set about enlarging their group, trying to bring in specialists in everything they needed. They found a printer who could make perfectly forged identity documents, passes and ration cards, an electrician who could sabotage cables so effectively that it was almost impossible to repair them.

They took the name 'Uncle Emil' – after an imaginary character they invented to cover telephone conversations, using questions about his health and progress as a coded way of passing information.

They also began making contact with other anti-Nazi groups. On 11 October, they held a meeting in the home of Hans Peters, a lawyer who was then a major on the Luftwaffe general staff. It was a distinguished gathering, bringing together what Andreas-Friedrich described as 'a collection of the most varied opinions'. One opinion, however, was common to them all: the only sure way of getting rid of the Nazis was for Germany to lose the war.

One person at the meeting made a particular impression on Andreas-Friedrich: a serious-looking man who sat quietly in an armchair, watching everyone closely and saying little. He took only a small part in the excited discussions, just occasionally nodding agreement or giving gentle encouragement.

'Who is that man?' she asked Peters after he had left ahead of everyone else.

'Moltke,' Peters told her. 'He'll be heard from one of these days. There are big groups behind him, from right to left. He's working for Canaris.'

The impression made by Moltke was a lasting one. Over the following weeks and months, Andreas-Friedrich and her friends maintained respectful contact with him as they went about their clandestine work. He was by no means a man of action, but they became convinced that he was the one who possessed the moral courage to lead Germany back out of darkness, when the right day came.

# 24

THE DAY of Germany's deliverance suddenly seemed much closer in the last quarter of 1942, as the Wehrmacht suffered its first major defeats since the Battle of Britain. In the Atlantic, new British radar equipment and the extension of aerial patrols began to turn the tide: in October, for the first time, the Allies sank more U-boats than Germany launched.

In North Africa, too, there was nothing but bad news for Hitler. On 5 November, Montgomery's British Eighth Army, which included Australian, New Zealand, South African, Indian, Greek and Free French troops, completed the rout of Rommel's Germans and Italians at El Alamein. Three days later, American and British troops landed in Morocco and Algeria.

In the east, the great summer offensive that had swept the Germans forward through the Crimea and the Caucasus ground to a halt at Stalingrad, a major military objective which controlled the Soviet Union's main north–south supply lines along the Volga river.

For both Hitler and Stalin, the city of Stalingrad held an almost mystical significance. Originally known as Tsaritsyn, it had been held for the Reds in the Russian civil war of 1918 by Voroshilov, Budenny and Stalin. All three claimed credit for the victory, but when Stalin assumed absolute power he rewrote the history books to give himself all the honour, renamed the city and turned its defence into a Soviet military legend. Along with Leningrad, which was itself under siege, Stalingrad was one of the two 'holy cities' of Soviet Russia. If Hitler could capture it, he believed, he would destroy Stalin.

The German Sixth Army, commanded by Field Marshal Friedrich von Paulus, reached Stalingrad and the Volga on 23 August. On 13 September, Paulus launched a major offensive to capture the city, which quickly developed into a savage battle through streets, houses and factories. For two months the two sides fought with guns, grenades, bayonets, knives and even sharpened shovels.

At first it seemed the Germans must prevail. But the city was held by the Soviet Sixty-second Army under a new young general, Vassili Chuikov, whose tactical flair was matched by an almost unbreakable nerve. Even when his front was reduced to a few hundred yards, with entire divisions reduced to barely 500 men, his determination never flagged. Nor did that of the men under his command, men like Sergeant Pavlov of the 13th Guards Division, who crammed sixty soldiers with rifles, mortars, heavy machine guns and anti-tank weapons into a four-storey house and held it against every assault for an incredible fifty-eight days. Or the eighteen survivors in 138th Divisional HQ, who took on seventy German tommy-gunners in hand-to-hand fighting and successfully beat them off.

While Chuikov, at his last gasp and almost out of ammunition, held the Germans locked in the carnage of the city, General Georgi Zhukov was preparing for battle on a grand scale. Zhukov, the Red Army's most brilliant strategist, had been appointed deputy supreme commander under Stalin at the end of August, and had immediately flown from Moscow to take personal control of the Stalingrad front. For weeks he had struggled to build up his forces. Then, on 19 November, in temperatures as low as −30° centigrade, he launched his counter-attack, Operation Uranus, smashing through the German armies around the city and their Italian, Romanian and Hungarian allies in a huge pincer movement. Within four days, he had completed the encirclement of the entire German Sixth Army, trapping 260,000 men. Hitler's long drive to the east was over.

# PART THREE

# *Target Berlin*

# 1

B Y THE beginning of 1943 Berlin had enjoyed fourteen months free from air raids, apart from an ineffectual Soviet attack on 30 August 1942, and a daylight sortie by a single RAF Mosquito fighter-bomber on 19 September. Despite the horrifying reports of continuing raids on other parts of Germany, the city's anti-aircraft defences, like most of its people, had grown complacent. So, when 201 RAF bombers suddenly struck on the night of 16 January, the Berliners were taken completely by surprise. Wing Commander Leonard Cheshire, a future winner of the VC who was on his sixth visit to Berlin, reported seeing only one small searchlight, and described the flak as 'negligible'. Only one aircraft failed to make it home.

The bombers killed 198 people, including 53 prisoners of war – 52 of them French – and five foreign workers. But 10,000 others, who had crowded into the Deutschlandhalle in Wilmersdorf to watch the annual circus, had a miraculous escape. A stick of incendiary bombs landed directly on the hall, completely gutting it, but the police and fire service managed to evacuate everyone safely, along with the circus animals. Twenty-one people were slightly injured in the crush, but not a single life was lost.

The following night, the British struck again, with 187 planes. For the first time ever, a war correspondent flew with them. The BBC's Richard Dimbleby flew in a Lancaster piloted by Wing Commander Guy Gibson, another future VC for the 'Dambusters' raids, recording his impressions directly on to disc for broadcast on his return. It was a risky assignment – the anti-aircraft gunners had been severely jolted by their failure of the night before, and this time they were on the alert. Together with the nightfighters along the bombers' route, they shot down twenty-two RAF aircraft, a devastating success rate.

Goebbels airily claimed that not a single building had been destroyed during the second raid. But Ursula von Kardorff, a journalist with the Ullstein Press, watching the raid from the balcony of her apartment, did not agree. 'Suddenly an absolutely hellish noise sent me flying down to the cellar quicker than I had ever run in my life,' she recorded in her diary. 'A bomb had obliterated two houses in Zähringstrasse.'

It was the second time that day that the realities of war had been brought home to Kardorff. On her way to work that morning by S-Bahn, she had passed a troop train bound for the east. 'I suddenly realized,' she wrote, 'that every revolution of the wheels was taking those soldiers closer to death. Painted in white letters on the engine were the words, "Wheels must turn for victory." For death, too.'

ALTHOUGH THE new raids were not the mass attacks Berlin had been fearing ever since the 1,000-bomber raid on Cologne, they were an ominous reminder of what was likely to come. Churchill had pressed for more raids on the German capital, following demands from Stalin. But Air Marshal Sir Arthur 'Bomber' Harris, who had taken over Bomber Command on 22 February 1942, had been determined to wait until he had built up sufficient strength for the giant raids he planned to inflict on the German capital. 'Berlin is a city of four million inhabitants, which is five times as big as Cologne,' he wrote in response to the prime minister's persistent questioning, 'and 1,000 heavy bombers would not be too many if we are to inflict serious and impressive damage on it. The attack should be sustained. One isolated attack would do more harm than good. . . .'

During 1942, a whole new generation of heavy bombers had been brought into service – Stirlings, Halifaxes, and above all the superb Lancasters, four-engined aircraft with a longer range and higher ceilings than the old Wellingtons and Hampdens. They were also capable of much greater bomb loads. On the first raids of the new campaign, many of the aircraft were carrying 8,000 lb bombs, the heaviest yet dropped on Berlin.

They were also equipped with on-board radar equipment, $H_2S$, which displayed a map-like picture of the ground below the aircraft. $H_2S$ at that time was still fairly rudimentary and not entirely reliable, but it was a great improvement on previous aids to navigation and bomb aiming. It also destroyed the effectiveness of the German deception sites and much of their camouflage. Despite the formidable flak towers, Berlin was suddenly vulnerable again.

# 2

U LRICH VON HASSELL was shattered. 'If the Josefs [his nickname for the indecisive generals] intended to delay their intervention till it was quite clear that the corporal is leading us into the abyss, that dream has come true,' he wrote in his diary at the end of January 1943. Hassell, a former diplomat who had been forcibly retired when Ribbentrop took over the Foreign Office in 1938, was one of many who yearned for a return to the old ways of imperial rule. He was also a prominent member of the anti-Hitler conspirators, one of the main links between Moltke's and Beck's groups.

The news that so disturbed Hassell was the statement made by President Franklin D. Roosevelt in Casablanca, French Morocco, after a ten-day conference with Prime Minister Winston Churchill and their chiefs of staff among the date palms and bougainvillea. Morocco had been liberated only eight weeks earlier. 'Peace can come to the world only by the total elimination of German and Japanese war power,' Roosevelt announced at the joint press conference on 24 January. 'The elimination of German, Japanese, and Italian war power means the unconditional surrender by Germany, Italy and Japan.' Churchill endorsed the president's message, pledging that the Allies would apply 'design, purpose and unconquerable will to enforce unconditional surrender upon the criminals who have plunged the world into war'.

Unconditional surrender meant that the British and American governments would refuse to listen to any pleas from the German resistance. Nor would they offer them any support or encouragement in their plans to replace the Nazi regime. Hassell and his friends were on their own.

THE OTHER vital decision taken at Casablanca was when and where the Allies would open a second front in Europe. Stalin was demanding action, but their forces were not yet ready for Overlord, the proposed cross-Channel invasion of France. As an alternative, Churchill persuaded Roosevelt – against the advice of his military advisers – to agree to an invasion of continental Europe through Sicily and Italy, codenamed Husky. The British prime minister was already concerned with the communist threat to the postwar world. He had hopes that Husky might somehow be extended into an invasion through the Balkans, 'the soft underbelly of the Axis', which would forestall the advance of Soviet troops into central Europe.

An attack in the south, however, could not draw off enough German strength to relieve the pressure on the eastern front. The Soviets would still be facing the main German military presence alone. To avoid any danger of Stalin coming to separate terms with Hitler, the western Allies had to convince him of their good faith, while they were preparing for Overlord. They were, of course, already providing considerable quantities of material aid in aircraft and equipment. But they could also support Soviet efforts in the field by using their air power to cripple the German armaments industry.

This suited the British and American air chiefs, Air Chief Marshal Sir Charles Portal and General Ira Eaker, who had gone to Casablanca determined to get just such orders. They did not waste any time. On 21 January 1943, Portal instructed Bomber Harris that his primary objective would be 'the progressive destruction and dislocation of the German military, industrial and economic system, and the undermining of the morale of the German people to a point where their capacity for armed resistance is fatally weakened'.

Priority targets included U-boat construction yards and bases; the German aircraft industry; the whole enemy transportation system; oil plants and other targets important to the German war industry – and Berlin. The city, said the directive, 'should be attacked when conditions are suitable for the attainment of specially valuable results unfavourable to the morale of the enemy or favourable to that of Russia'.

The Allied intention to attack the German capital did not remain a secret for long. Soon, newspapers on both sides of the Atlantic were jubilantly trumpeting the news: 'BERLIN NEXT!'

## 3

THROUGHOUT the whole of January 1943 the war news had been bad for Germany. All along the eastern front, from the Baltic to the Black Sea, the Soviets had begun grinding forward in massive offensives. The people of Berlin, like Germans everywhere, followed the death throes of Paulus's doomed Sixth Army with helpless anguish as Zhukov steadily tightened the garotte around Stalingrad. It seemed almost an irrelevance when the British captured Tripoli on 23 January.

On 30 January the RAF marked the tenth anniversary of Hitler's accession with new shocks for Berlin. At twelve noon, Hitler began a broadcast speech to the nation. As he started a sharp attack on England, the sirens howled, and within minutes flights of Mosquitoes were roaring low over the rooftops in the city's first full-scale raid in daylight. Everyone dashed to the shelters, confused and terrified by this new departure. Helmuth Grossmann, a journalist who lived in the city during most of the war, found his shelter full of Germans cursing their Führer: 'He should cut out those provocative speeches,' they grumbled. 'Just look what they bring!'

Among the buildings destroyed in the raid was Rosenberg's Ministry for the East. As with many other bomb sites, a large swastika flag was planted among the ruins, together with a banner proclaiming: 'Führer, we march with you to final victory!' Neither the Berliners nor the RAF were impressed. Next day – celebrated in Berlin as Luftwaffe Day – the Mosquitoes came back twice, their attacks coinciding neatly and deliberately with the start of broadcasts by Göring and Goebbels.

The De Havilland Mosquito, with twin Rolls-Royce Merlin engines and a plywood airframe, was a remarkable aircraft. It was as fast and manoeuvrable as a fighter, with a top speed of over 400 mph – a generation of British schoolboys, brought up on the legend of the Spitfire's invincibility, were staggered when a Mosquito took the world air speed record from it. Although it was a small aircraft, it could carry almost as many bombs as the American B-17 'Flying Fortress' – a single 4,000 lb high-explosive blockbuster 'cookie', or a load of incendiaries, either of which it could plant on target with great accuracy. And because it could fly fast and low in loose formation, unlike the lumbering heavy bombers, a flight of Mosquitoes was extremely difficult to detect or intercept, adding the element of surprise to the other hazards testing the Berliners' overstretched nerves.

As THE Mosquitoes struck for the second and third times on 31 January, the news arrived that the drawn-out agony of Stalingrad was over. Paulus had finally surrendered. Two hundred thousand German troops had died in the long battle. Ninety thousand were now taken prisoner, among them twenty-four generals. It was a bitter blow to German pride. On 3 February, Goebbels ordered three days of national remembrance: all places of entertainment and all luxury restaurants were closed, and all traffic was halted for one minute's silence on the first and last days.

THE BERLINERS reacted to the renewed bombing, and even the disastrous news from Stalingrad, with their usual black humour. One example tells of two men meeting in the street. One complains to the other: 'Isn't the news terrible? I'm afraid we're going to lose the war.' 'Yes, I know,' replies the other, 'but *when*?'

Goebbels, who knew his Berliners and frequently despaired of them, reacted strongly to what he considered their defeatism. He launched a poster campaign based on two typical Berlin characters, Herr Bramsig, who was tall and melancholy, and Frau Knöterich, who was plump and jolly. The two were always in trouble with the police because they were scandalmongers, because they gossiped, and above all because they passed on bits of news picked up from the *Soldatensender*, the 'black' British radio station. But the campaign does not seem to have had any noticeable effect on the Berliners, who went on moaning, regardless.

The Berliners saw Propaganda Ministry posters as an opportunity for striking back. One poster – echoing the famous British slogans of the time, 'Walls have ears' and 'Careless talk costs lives' – showed a worker with a goose's head and the caption '*Schäm dich Schwätzer – Feind hort mit – Schweigen is Pflicht*', 'Shame on you, bigmouth – the enemy is listening – silence is your duty'. Such posters were plastered all over the S- and U-Bahn stations, frequently with the word 'enemy' scratched out and the initials 'SS' substituted. Another poster showed an obviously Aryan soldier chatting to a friend in a bar, while nearby sat a sinister man in horn-rimmed glasses trying to listen to their conversation. The caption read 'Careful what you say – who is the third person?' The jokers substituted 'Himmler' for 'who'.

# 4

IN MID-FEBRUARY, new posters appeared on walls and on the cylindrical Litfass columns throughout the city. The picture showed the German people, led by an angry giant, his face contorted with rage, marching out of their homes and workplaces to defend the Reich. With out-thrust jaws and set brows, they advanced, farmers with scythes across their shoulders, smiths carrying hammers, artists, businessmen, and engineers with clenched fists. 'TOTAL WAR!' the slogan above them read. A second slogan pasted and painted on walls and windows all over Berlin went one further than the one that Ursula von Kardorff had seen painted on a troop train: 'Wheels must turn *only* for victory.'

'Total war' was Goebbels's concept. Outlined in a decree issued to all Reichsleiters, Gauleiters and army headquarters on 15 February, it demanded complete mobilization of resources for military purposes. That same day he made a speech at Düsseldorf entitled 'Do You Want Total War?' He repeated it three days later to a specially selected audience of the party faithful at the Sportpalast in Berlin, and it was broadcast on national radio. All was to be sacrificed to the war effort, and anyone who did anything to detract from it would lose his or her head.

EARLY IN the morning of Saturday, 27 February, Leon König, a young Jew still employed as a skilled worker making armaments with Deutsche Waffen- und Munitionsfabrik at Wittenau in north Berlin, made his way to the Tiergarten S-Bahn station as usual to catch the train to work. On the platform he met a French worker from his factory, a man called Raymond with whom he had become friendly. Raymond warned him not to go to the factory – he had heard that the Gestapo were planning to swoop on Berlin's remaining 15,000 Jewish armaments workers, to round them up for deportation. Leon went back to his flat and locked himself in.

All too soon, the truth of the warnings became vividly clear. At 6 am lines of army trucks with grey canvas covers began roaring through the streets, escorted by armed SS men. They stopped at factory gates, in front of private houses and apartment blocks, to load up with human cargo. Men, women and children were herded and penned like animals destined for the stockyard. As more and more were dragged from their homes they had to be forced into the overcrowded trucks with blows from rifle butts.

Next evening, Leon was alone in his flat when the doorbell rang. He kept quiet as a mouse until he heard the unknown visitor going back down the stairs. Peeping out of the window from behind the curtains, he saw Raymond, already heading for the street corner. He rushed out and managed to catch him, and they hurried back inside together.

'What happened at the factory?' Leon asked.

'You were lucky, *mon petit*,' came the reply. 'All the Israelites were arrested at 9 o'clock yesterday morning. The SS came with their trucks, nearly fifty of them, and took all the Jews, men and women, from their workplaces. You alone escaped. That's what I came to tell you. Don't stay in this flat – they could be here at any moment.'

THE FINAL round-up had begun. In six weeks, the whole of Germany was to be *Judenrein*, 'Jew purified'. Day after day, week after week, trains of cattle trucks pulled out of Berlin, heading east for the gas chambers and ovens of the extermination camps. The whole operation was run with a deadly bureau- cratic efficiency. The transports ran strictly to schedule. The paperwork was immaculate. If a consignment was for 1,000 Jews, then there would be 1,000 Jews on board the train – not 1,001, never 999, but exactly 1,000.

There was, however, a hitch in the Nazi plan, brought about by one of the most unusual incidents of the whole era. During the initial round-up, some 6,000 Jewish men who were partners in mixed marriages were segregated from the others, and taken to a building in the Rosenstrasse, not far from SS headquarters in Burgstrasse. On the Sunday morning, their non-Jewish wives got together and set out to find them. They descended on Rosenstrasse, and crowded round the building where their husbands were being held. There they stood, refusing to leave, shouting and screaming for their men, hour after hour, throughout the day and the night and into the next day.

Worried SS leaders gathered in Burgstrasse, not knowing what to do. They had never been faced with such a situation. Would they have to machine-gun 6,000 German women? It seemed the only way out, apart from releasing the prisoners. All night the arguments raged, until at noon on the Monday a decision was reached: all men married to a non-Jewish wife could return home. 'Privileged persons,' the official announcement said, 'are to be incorporated in the national community.' 6,000 Jewish men had been given a precious breathing space. But both Jewish men and women involved in mixed marriages were aware that they were still in danger.


INGE DEUTSCHKRON and her mother had already been underground for a month by the time of the great Gestapo swoop. One of their social democrat friends, Frau Gumz, the owner of a washing and ironing establishment in Charlottenburg, heard from a German soldier what was already happening to Jews in the east. She swore to Frau Deutschkron that she and her husband would not let her and Inge be deported, but would shelter and help them. On 15 January 1943 Inge and her mother left their furnished room in Bambergerstrasse for the last time, tore off their stars, and moved into the Gumz family laundry.

After a brief spell working for IG Farben, Inge had managed to find a job in a workshop for the blind, some distance away. The owner, a fanatical anti-Nazi called Otto Weidt, bought a set of papers and a work permit for her from a prostitute, so that for the time being she became legal. Unfortunately, the prostitute was arrested shortly afterwards, and as she was listed as being in prison, Inge could no longer use her identity. Without papers again, she could not work for Weidt.

Soon afterwards, Frau Gumz's neighbours began to take an unhealthy interest in her guests. Inge and Frau Deutschkron began moving from place to place. For a long time they slept behind the counter of a shop, into which they were smuggled every evening after closing time. They slept in a boat house, on the floor of a small flat, with other social democrat friends in north Berlin, with a friend, Lisa Holländer, whose husband had been murdered by the Nazis – moving on each time when neighbours became curious. When their funds ran out, leaving them nothing to buy black market food with, they managed to find jobs with sympathetic employers. Frau Deutschkron worked for a printer, a former communist who didn't want to know her true identity. Inge found a place in a friend's stationery and book shop. They survived through friends giving them food they could not really spare.

The continuing confidence of their friends never ceased to amaze Inge. 'This war can't last more than another four months,' was the constant refrain. Inge and Frau Deutschkron were more than happy to believe them, though they sometimes found it grotesque to see how many of them, who had husbands or sons fighting at the front, longed for Germany to lose the war, since they were convinced this was their only chance of getting rid of the Nazis.

KLAUS SCHEURENBERG and his parents survived for over two months after the final round-up began because of Herr Scheurenberg's role as administrator of one of the last remaining Jewish community houses – though the house itself had been cleared on 13 December by Gestapo squads brought in from the already *Judenrein* Vienna to show their Berlin colleagues how to work more quickly and efficiently.

Young Klaus, now approaching eighteen, continued to go out in the evenings without his star, enjoying forbidden pleasures with his half-Jewish or Aryan friends. With or without the star, such outings were dangerous. Without the star, he was liable to be stopped by civil or military police wanting to know why a young man of military age was not wearing a uniform. With the star, he was likely to be the target of racial attacks – once, he was spotted by a gang of Hitler Youth who chased him through the streets shouting 'Beat the Jew to death!' Fear gave him the strength and speed to give them the slip, but such encounters were always a hazard of life with the star.

By this time, Klaus had lost his job with the timber company, which had finally been declared *Judenfrei*. But he had managed to find another on the S-Bahn, maintaining the live conductor rails. It was a good job, with regular hours and no shift work – even though Klaus was expected to work on the high-voltage rail without the protection of the heavy rubber insulation mats provided for his Aryan colleagues.

On 7 May Klaus's luck finally seemed to have run out. The Scheurenberg family was rounded up and taken to the collection point in the Grosse Hamburgerstrasse. There, they were issued with numbers for Auschwitz. Even then, fortune suddenly smiled again. While they were waiting to be marched off, they were spotted by a man Klaus's father had known as a policeman in the criminal investigation branch, who had now been con-scripted into the Gestapo. When they told him where they were heading, he replied, 'There's no question of that. Wait here.' A few minutes later he returned, with new numbers and a new destination for them. He had persuaded the commandant to revoke the order sending them to Auschwitz, and direct them instead to Theresienstadt, a 'holding' camp in Bohemia – not a death camp but a Nazi showpiece designed to demonstrate to the International Red Cross how humanely they treated Jewish prisoners.

The chance encounter with the former policeman saved the lives of the Scheurenbergs: of the 1,000 people who were deported from Berlin that day, only five survived the war. Klaus and his parents were three of them.

GOEBBELS was furious that the lightning strikes of 27 February had failed to round up every remaining Jew, as he had planned:

> The scheduled arrest of all Jews on one day has proved to be a flash in the pan because of the short-sighted behaviour of industrialists who warned the Jews in time. We therefore failed to lay our hands on about 4,000. They are now wandering about Berlin without homes, are not registered with the police and are naturally quite a public danger. I have ordered the police, the Wehrmacht and the party to do everything possible to round up these Jews as quickly as possible.

Goebbels was wrong: there were more than 5,000 Jews in the city who had decided to go underground, becoming 'U-boats' in Berlin slang, to sit out the war. Somehow, despite the bombing, despite the informers, despite the activities of the Gestapo, most of them managed to outlive the Berlin Gauleiter and his master. Thousands of decent non-Jewish Berliners of all classes had found a way in which they could resist the worst evils of the Nazi regime: by harbouring, succouring and protecting its intended victims.

# 5

'TONIGHT YOU go to the Big City,' Air Marshal Harris signalled to his bomber crews on 1 March. 'You have an opportunity to light a fire in the belly of the enemy and burn his Black Heart out.'

The raid that followed was the heaviest Berlin had experienced until then: 302 aircraft took part, over half of them Lancasters, the rest Halifaxes and Stirlings. For the first time, the British planes were carrying mostly incendiaries, plus 4,000 lb and 8,000 lb high-explosive 'cookies'. Once again the attack was not concentrated on one particular area, but spread over 100 square miles. Wilmersdorf and the south-western suburbs suffered worst, with fires everywhere and the air sulphur yellow and filled with smoke. By coincidence, it was the day after the Nazis had begun the final round-up of the Jews. 'The English have avenged the monstrous deed with a shattering raid on

Berlin, the like of which has never been seen,' Ruth Andreas-Friedrich recorded in her diary.

When the raiders struck, Ulrich von Hassell was enjoying a leisurely meal after the theatre with Major Count Alfred von Waldersee and his wife at Borchardt's, a famous old restaurant in Französischestrasse which had survived Goebbels's cuts. 'But then hell broke loose!' he noted. 'Very soon the neighbouring building began to burn, soldiers were called out of the shelter for rescue work, sparks rained down on the courtyard and ashes began to drift everywhere.'

Hassell and his friends seem to have been less appalled by the raid than by having to share a shelter with a group of jolly young women telephone operators. 'They began to behave badly,' he complained, 'and in spite of everything sang indecent songs, etcetera. Finally, when the firing died down somewhat, Waldersee and I seized our wives and walked through the centre of the city, where fires were blazing in many places.' St Hedwig's cathedral was burning fiercely, one of five churches gutted that night, and in Friedrich-strasse between the Halle gate and the Linden Hassell counted some thirty roof fires. Terrified people staggered through the streets hauling their belongings and household goods in bundles and bags, stumbling over shrapnel and rubble.

Finding they could not get to the U-Bahn, the Hassells and Waldersees headed home on foot through the Tiergarten, walking on the wooded side of the road where the going was easier. They discovered next day that the route they had chosen was littered with unexploded bombs.


FOR YOUNG Fred Laabs, the renewed raids brought a marked change in his part-time civil defence service. After an uneventful year as a runner, hanging around the SHD offices for a couple of hours each evening waiting for something to do, he suddenly found himself on the active strength of his local squad. He had to stay at the base every night, from 8 pm until breakfast, sleeping in a double-decker bunk bed, his steel helmet, gas mask, uniform, boots and other kit at the ready. His mother was furious, and complained loudly to the officer in charge that it was dreadful in such dangerous times to separate children of school age from their mothers, especially when the husbands and fathers were away at the front. But her protests were in vain.

Fred's first action came in March. In the middle of the night, one of the officers rushed into the room where the squad of eleven boys and four adults were sleeping. 'Alarm!' he yelled. Still half asleep, they scrambled into their clothes and tumbled out of the room, piling into a van in the yard. The building they were assigned to had suffered a direct hit from a high-explosive bomb. It had been razed to the ground, the rubble falling not into the street but into the rear courtyard and into the cellar where the inhabitants had been sheltering.

The fire service was already there. Fred heard the fire chief say they needed slim guys. They picked out three boys: Fred was one of them. Supported by a rope under his armpits, he was lowered through the cellar window, a flashlight in his hand, to see if there was any sign of life. For Fred, the sight facing him was the worst thing he had ever seen in his young life. The cellar roof had collapsed under the weight of rubble, burying all those sheltering there. He saw a leg here, an arm there, a head sticking out of the mess, blood and guts everywhere. There was no hope of anyone being alive.

The boys were hauled out again, and stood watching helplessly as men started clearing stones and timbers, knowing full well that it was useless. It was almost dawn when they were sent home to get ready for school – only on very rare occasions would the civil defence officers tell their teachers they were too exhausted to attend lessons.

THE EXTENT of the damage that night was enormous. At Tempelhof, 20 acres of the railway repair shops were destroyed. Elsewhere, 20 factories were badly damaged, and 875 buildings, mostly domestic dwellings, were reduced to rubble. The Pragerplatz, half a mile south of the Zoo, was completely flattened, the Foreign Office press office was destroyed, and there was considerable damage all along the Linden. Over 700 people were killed and 64,909 made homeless.

GOEBBELS had never doubted the resilience of 'his' Berliners and their ability to withstand bombing on the scale they were now suffering. In spite of the great devastation, he claimed, it would be wrong to imagine that Berliners would collapse under such raids, and that crowds of protesters would gather in the Wilhelmplatz. 'People are unbelievably long-suffering, and as long as they can still live they will choose any ordeal rather than death,' he told a press conference. 'I regard it as my task to train the people in the coming months to be tough.'

What Goebbels did not mention to the journalists, though no doubt many of them were already aware of the fact, was that he at least was going to be safe. In the garden of his official residence in Hermann–Göring–Strasse (how that address must have irked him!) a private shelter was being built at a cost of 350,000 RM. The architect complained that the material being used would have been sufficient to build 300 working-class homes.

UNTIL the spring of 1943 Berlin had not really looked like a city that had been heavily bombed. Although there had been a great deal of damage, it was spread over a wide area, and the repair services had worked with extraordinary speed and efficiency – often, it must be said, with the help of foreign workers and prisoners of war. Much of the damage was made good within a matter of weeks. Where this was not possible, properties would be boarded up and the boards plastered with notices announcing that the building was in the hands of a contractor. It did not fool the Berliners, but they could shrug their shoulders and ignore what they could not see: out of sight, out of mind.

By 1943 cosmetic effects were becoming more and more difficult to achieve. Whole streets sometimes had to be permanently closed off, yet great efforts were made to remove the piles of broken glass and rubble. But after the March raids Berlin began to look as ravaged and pock-marked as an elderly whore.

By some miracle, much of the city's tram system was still working. It passed through districts that had become vast fields of rubble, where nothing stirred except when the occasional gust of wind raised swirls of dust from the empty ruins. Passengers crowded to the windows to stare out at burnt-out vehicles and row after row of hollow-eyed house fronts. None of them uttered a word of anger or horror. They didn't even exchange glances; they just stared, in silence.

# 6

MORALE IN the city reached a new low in 1943, not simply because of the destruction but also because of the shortages. For the first time, Berliners became increasingly angry about the presence in their midst of foreigners who seemed to have more food and luxuries than anyone else, and who were generally better housed. The fact that they received these things in parcels sent in from abroad – parcels on which they were forced to pay heavy duties – did nothing to make them any more popular with the natives.

Many well-dressed foreigners were attacked, diplomats' cars had their tyres slashed, and anyone carrying a parcel from another country attracted angry stares. At the same time, food-related crime was on the increase – there were even cases of people being murdered for their ration cards by half-starved workers.

But food was in some ways the least of people's problems: the most intractable was housing. For those lucky enough to have an apartment that was not wanted by someone from the SS or the military or some other organization with enough influence to have them evicted, life was simple. All they had to worry about was the bombs.

Every air raid increased the number of homeless. After the March raids, the city authorities made every householder complete a form declaring the number of rooms in the house or apartment and the number of people living there. The rule was no more than one room per person: anyone with a spare room could be forced to take a lodger.

Naturally, some householders tried to cheat, listing the names of dead relatives or members of the family who were in the armed services. But the authorities were on to all the tricks. Householders were told that if they refused to take in lodgers, they would not be rehoused themselves if they were bombed out. If that threat was not enough, there were severe penalties under the law. 'Crime against the community spirit' was a serious offence which could lead to a period in a concentration camp, or worse. This often worked in favour of foreigners, since most householders preferred to let a room to a foreigner who could pay well rather than to a bombed-out, destitute Berlin family – yet another reason for Berliners to hate foreigners.

Some Berliners found other solutions. Helga Dolinski's family was bombed out twice in Friedrichshain, a couple of miles east of the city centre. Her father had a little general store, so when their building was hit they lost both their home and their business. Undaunted, he opened up another shop, only to lose that, too. Realizing that they were too close to the centre for safety, they moved out to live in their summer-house in Köpenick, on the south-east outskirts of the city.

Helga left school that spring, and started work in April as an apprentice bookkeeper in the offices of Deuta-Werke in Kreuzberg. The name Deuta was an abbreviation for Deutsche Tachometerwerke ('German Speedometer Works'), but during the war the company was manufacturing armaments components. The move to Köpenick did not worry her, since the U-Bahn station just around the corner was on a direct line to Kreuzberg, where the station was only a few minutes' walk from the factory gates.

The Dolinskis were fortunate to live on a line that remained largely undamaged for most of the war. For many people forced to move out from the centre, disruption caused by bomb damage meant they were spending more and more of their free time on travel. Where once few Berliners had taken more than three-quarters of an hour to get to work, two or three hours each way was now commonplace. Tempers were not improved by a compulsory increase in working hours: most people were now forced to work a 54-hour week – ten hours a day for five days, plus a half-day on Saturday.

# 7

PROFESSOR Karl Bonhoeffer, Dietrich's father, had been forced out of his job as director of the psychiatric clinic at Berlin's Charité hospital in 1938, but as a doctor he was still entitled to use a car. On 7 March 1943 Dietrich's disciple Eberhard Bethge used it to drive Hans von Dohnanyi to catch a night train to East Prussia. From there he would fly on to join Canaris, Oster and Colonel Lahousen at the headquarters of Army Group Centre in Smolensk, which the Führer was to visit for a conference on Saturday, 13 March. Dohnanyi's suitcase was unusually heavy: among the clothes and personal effects were two British limpet mines. These came from Abwehr stocks of material captured from resistance groups in occupied Europe, supplied by the British Special Operations Executive (SOE) for use against the Germans. Now, they were to be used by Germans against Hitler.

The need to get rid of Hitler was becoming more urgent every day, with each fresh military setback. The conspirators' plans for a new government and command system were ready. Everything was in place politically. The visit to Smolensk was the perfect opportunity. Major-General Henning von Tresckow, Field Marshal von Kluge's operations chief, and his adjutant, Lieutenant Fabian von Schlabrendorff – a cousin of Dietrich Bonhoeffer's fiancée, Maria – were entrusted with the assassination, which was given the code name Operation Flash.

Dohnanyi's bombs were chosen as the best method. An unexplained explosion in mid-air over Russia would be clean and certain, and had the added advantage that the army's honour would not be impugned. Dohnanyi delivered the explosives, known as 'clams', which were fitted with a delayed-action fuse activated by an acid capsule. He instructed Tresckow and Schlabrendorff on how to use them, then flew back to Berlin to await the result with Bonhoeffer and his other partners.

On the day, Tresckow asked a member of Hitler's entourage, Colonel Heinz Brandt, if he would take two bottles of brandy to his friend Major-General Helmuth Stieff back at Hitler's HQ. It was, he explained, payment of a bet he had had with Stieff – a private matter. He would send his aide, Lieutenant Schlabrendorff, out to the plane with them immediately before take-off. Brandt agreed readily. Schlabrendorff duly drove out to the plane and handed over the package as Hitler boarded, breaking the fuse capsule as he did so. Set for a thirty-minute delay, the bomb should have exploded while the plane was over Minsk. Two hours later, however, a routine message was received saying Hitler had landed safely at Rastenburg, in East Prussia.

Back in Smolensk, Tresckow and his fellow conspirators, anxiously waiting to pass the signal to Berlin and Zossen for the coup to start, were aghast. Clearly the bomb had failed, and the parcel was now lying, intact, in Hitler's headquarters, where it could be opened at any moment. Tresckow immediately put through a call to Colonel Brandt, telling him that there had been a mix-up and the wrong bottles had been sent. Fortunately, he said, Schlabrendorff had to come to Rastenburg next day on military business. He would bring the good stuff with him, and collect the other.

The replacement cost Tresckow two bottles of the finest brandy. Schlabrendorff, however, had the nerve-racking task not only of collecting the bomb, but also of dismantling it in his sleeping compartment on the night train to Berlin. When he did so, he could find no obvious reason why it had not exploded – the fuse appeared to have worked perfectly but the detonator cap had simply failed to fire. The explanation was probably that the cabin temperature in the aircraft had been sub-zero, due to a fault in the heating system, and this had affected the detonator.

But the would-be assassins did not give up immediately. They still had the two clams, and Tresckow saw a second opportunity in an exhibition of captured Soviet armaments that was to be opened by Hitler on 21 March, Heroes' Memorial Day, in the Zeughaus on the Unter den Linden. One of his officers, Colonel Freiherr Rudolf von Gersdorff, was head of the section that had prepared the exhibition. He therefore had good reason to visit it, and could plant the bomb to explode during Hitler's speech.

Gersdorff travelled to Berlin on 20 March, but when he looked around the area where the Führer was to speak, he realized there was nowhere he could put the bomb. Security was so tight that the only way he could be certain of killing Hitler would be to carry the bombs in his own coat pockets, set off the fuse, then position himself alongside the Führer and blow himself up with him. The shortest time for the chemical fuse was approximately ten minutes, which meant an agonizing wait, but there was no time to devise another method. Hitler was scheduled to take exactly ten minutes to walk around the exhibits before leaving the building to lay a wreath on the war memorial.

On Sunday, 21 March, Hans Dohnanyi and Dietrich Bonhoeffer sat with the rest of the family in the house of Dietrich's sister Ursula and her husband Rüdiger Schleicher in Marienburger-allee on the north-eastern edge of the Grunewald. They were rehearsing *Lobe den Herrn*, a cantata by Walcha, which they were to perform at a family party on 31 March to celebrate Professor Bonhoeffer's seventy-fifth birthday.

Outside, Dohnanyi's official car stood waiting to take him and Dietrich Bonhoeffer to Abwehr headquarters as soon as news came through of Hitler's death. While they played and sang, they waited for the telephone in the next room to ring. But the call never came. Hitler had arrived at the Zeughaus exactly on schedule. As he entered the building, Gersdorff broke the acid phial, and moved into position near him. But then, to everyone's astonishment, the Führer broke into a gallop, rushed through the exhibition and was outside in two minutes flat. Gersdorff was left to make a dash for the nearest cloakroom where he managed to extricate the fuse and flush it down the lavatory before it could detonate the bomb.

THE BONHOEFFER birthday party went ahead on 31 March, complete with the cantata as planned. But at noon five days later, when Dietrich tried to phone the Dohnanyis at their home at Sakrow an unknown man answered. Dietrich realized at once that the worst had happened: Hans and Christine had been arrested.

He knew he must be next on the list, but he did not panic. Running was out of the question: the Gestapo would simply take other members of the family in his place. Calmly, he went next door, to the Schleichers' house, and asked Ursula to cook him a large meal – he reckoned he would not be getting much to eat for some time. While she was cooking, he returned to his parents' house and went through his papers, destroying anything that might be incriminating in any way. Then he returned to the Schleichers', ate his meal, and waited. At 4 pm his father came to tell him two men had arrived and wanted to see him. They drove him away in a black Mercedes, to Tegel prison. The Dohnanyis were locked up elsewhere: Christine in Charlottenburg prison, and Hans in the military officers' prison in Lehrterstrasse, Moabit.

In fact, the arrests had nothing to do with the assassination attempts, or the anti-Hitler conspiracy. Bonhoeffer, the Dohnanyis and another Abwehr agent called Josef Müller who was taken at the same time, were simply victims of the rivalry between the Abwehr and the SS's Reich Security Head Office the RSHA. The RSHA had uncovered evidence of irregular currency deals involved with Operation 7, the scheme to get Jews into Switzerland, and had seized on this to discredit Canaris and advance Himmler's aim of taking over the Abwehr.

But with Dohnanyi, Bonhoeffer and Müller in prison and Hans Oster suspended from duty under house arrest, the heart of the conspiracy was disrupted. At the same time, General Beck was taken seriously ill and was out of action for several months, while another senior plotter, General Kurt von Hammerstein, died. It would be several months before the conspiracy could consider mounting another coup attempt.

# 8

For five months after the March 1943 raids Berlin was spared heavy attacks. RAF Bomber Command turned its energies to industrial targets nearer home in the Battle of the Ruhr, during which the Lancasters of Guy Gibson's 617 Squadron breached the Möhne and Eder dams with their famous 'bouncing bombs'.

Between the end of March and late August, there were twelve Mosquito raids on the capital. Only a handful of aircraft was involved each time, never more than twelve. But their unpredictable lightning attacks kept up the pressure on Berlin while Harris continued to prepare for an all-out assault on the city.

Pressure was increased almost unbearably by news of raids on other cities, and by terrifying new developments. On 24 July 2,600 bombers of the RAF and the US 8th Air Force began a sustained attack on Hamburg. For ten days, they bombed the city round the clock, the Americans by day, the British by night. They dropped some 9,000 tons of bombs, including nearly 1.5 million incendiaries. The death and destruction caused were almost incalculable: according to Hamburg Civil Defence officials, 'Exact figures could not be obtained out of a layer of human ashes.' But the city's police president calculated that at least 41,800 people were killed instantly, and 37,439 were injured. Over a million people were left homeless. For the first time, most of the damage was caused by phosphorus bombs, their deadly contents pouring down walls and along streets in a flaming lava flow, creating fire storms that frazzled objects and people alike, and sucked the very air out of their lungs.

Missie Vassiltchikov was told that thousands of little children were found wandering the streets after the raid, calling for their parents. 'The mothers are presumed dead,' she wrote, 'the fathers are at the front, so nobody can identify them. The NSV seems to be taking things in hand, but the difficulties are enormous.' For days, German trains were filled with refugees from Hamburg, in charred clothes and bandages smelling of smoke.

In the early hours of Sunday, 1 August, the RAF flew over Berlin and dropped not bombs but leaflets, calling on all women and children to leave the city at once. They had done the same thing immediately before the onslaught on Hamburg, so the implication for Berlin was ominous. Next morning, Geobbels ordered the evacuation of all remaining children and adults not engaged in war work. Something like 1.5 million people left the city, though many returned after a while, preferring, like true metropolitans, to face sudden death in the city rather than slow death by boredom in the countryside.

# 9

THE REPORTS from Hamburg were not the only bad news for Germany that summer. To the German navy, May became known as 'Black May': during the month a total of 41 U-boats, one-third of all those on station, were sunk by the Royal Navy and the RAF. The battle of the Atlantic was over. Conceding defeat, Grand Admiral Dönitz ordered all U-boats to pull out of the North Atlantic and reposition themselves south of the Azores.

On 12 May came news of the final surrender by General Jürgen von Arnim of all Axis forces in North Africa. They had been driven back relentlessly by Montgomery's British Eighth Army across 1,500 miles of desert from El Alamein to Tunis, where the British First Army and the US II Corps helped complete the job: 328,243 Germans and Italians were taken prisoner.

In June the US 8th Air Force began massive daylight raids on the Ruhr and other industrial centres, and on 9 and 10 July the US Seventh and British Eighth armies began landing on Sicily. The battle for Sicily lasted until 17 August, when the last remaining German troops were captured, leaving the Allies poised to invade the mainland of Europe through southern Italy. In the meantime, on 25 July, the Italians had overthrown their dictator, Benito Mussolini, Hitler's most faithful ally, and were clearly preparing to defect from the Axis.

But for the people of Berlin, the most disquieting news came not from the south or the west, but from almost exactly 1,000 miles due east of the city. For the whole of July, the German and Soviet armies had been locked in the greatest tank battle of all time, the battle of the Kursk salient. Some 4,000 Soviet and 3,000 German tanks and self-propelled guns, nearly a million German soldiers and over a million Soviets had hammered at each other across a terrain more heavily sown with mines than any other battlefield in history.

The battle had swung first one way and then the other, but by the beginning of August it was clear that the Wehrmacht had suffered its greatest ever defeat. Stalingrad had been traumatic: Kurst was disastrous. It was without doubt the single most important battle of the war, the decisive turning point on the eastern front. Although the Germans lost only 20,000 men at Kursk, compared with some 290,000 at Stalingrad, what counted was that the strength of the Panzers had been broken. However hard the bomb-battered German factories worked, German armour could never regain its numerical superiority over a Red Army backed by an arms industry that was only now getting into its awesome stride behind the Ural mountains, out of the reach of the Luftwaffe. The new Kirov tank factory at Chelyabinsk alone had sixty-four production lines turning out T34s round the clock, using power from a giant, purpose-built generating station fuelled with coal from mines recently sunk in Kazakhstan. By the end of the war, Soviet factories would have turned out over 40,000 T34s alone, more than twice as many as Germany's entire production of all types.

While Hitler and his generals counted the appalling cost of their failure, the Red Army was poised to begin rolling inexorably forward, smashing its way across 1,000 miles of devastation to its ultimate target: Berlin.

# 10

THE HEAVY bombers returned to Berlin with a vengeance on the night of Monday, 23 August 1943, when a total of 727 Lancasters, Stirlings and Halifaxes, plus a scattering of Mosquitoes acting as pathfinders, attacked the city. As they approached, they found themselves facing a new threat: Berlin was now defended by nightfighters as well as its formidable flak batteries. Until then, German fighters had kept away from the cities, where they were just as vulnerable to flak as were the British bombers. They had operated only along the routes from the coast, guided to their targets by ground-based radar. Once a nightfighter was close enough to pick up a bomber on its own airborne radar, it could go in for the kill.

Since the whole system depended on radar, it had collapsed when the Allies developed jamming devices earlier that summer. The most spectacular of these was codenamed Window, in which thousands of strips of tinfoil were scattered from bombers, breaking up their radar echo and effectively blinding German radar. Not only did Window completely hide the bombers, it also removed the nightfighters from their controllers' screens, making it impossible to direct them. RAF losses dropped dramatically.

To counter Window, Major Hajo Herrmann, an ex-bomber pilot who had never flown a fighter in his life, came up with a risky but effective tactic which he christened *Wilde Sau*, 'Wild Boar'. This involved committing fighters to a wild free-for-all in the skies over Berlin and other cities, where their pilots could rely on visual contact to find and attack enemy bombers caught in searchlight beams or the light of flares, or silhouetted against the glow of burning buildings on the ground. Because they were not relying on radar, conventional nightfighters with crews of two or three – a gunner and radar operator as well as the pilot – could be supplemented by faster, more manoeuvrable, single-seater aircraft. They aimed to catch the raiders in the middle of their bombing runs, when they were at their most vulnerable. Unable to manoeuvre or change course until their bomb bays were empty, they provided relatively easy targets for daring young Luftwaffe pilots.

Wild Boar tactics relied on the absolute cooperation of all flak commanders, who had to restrict the altitude at which their shells were set to explode. In theory, fighters could engage the enemy above that altitude without fear of being shot down by their own flak batteries. In reality, things never worked out quite so neatly. Sometimes gunners failed to observe the rules, or shells failed to explode below the prescribed height; sometimes fighter pilots seeking a kill ignored the limits of the flak-free zone and risked diving into the inferno below.

But until German scientists could come up with a better way of overcoming Allied radar jamming, Wild Boar tactics were the order of the day, in spite of a desperate shortage of both aircraft and pilots. Even when the nightfighters were at their peak, they rarely had more than 350 planes ready for action throughout Germany at any one time. On a good night, they could guarantee to mount only 200 to 250 sorties against enemy bombers – and this at a time when Bomber Harris was able to commit a thousand or more aircraft to a single target.

Erhard Milch, the dominant figure in German aircraft production until 1944, saw as early as 1943 that the only role now open to the Luftwaffe was a defensive one. What was needed was more fighters, not bombers – which cost nine times more to build in labour and resources. But when the British heavy bombers really began inflicting serious damage on German cities, Hitler demanded that the Luftwaffe retaliate in kind. Since they did not possess a heavy bomber equivalent to the Lancaster or the Boeing B-17, a great deal of time and effort was wasted in trying to design and build one, at the expense of fighter production.

Trained aircrew were just as scarce. By 1943 pilots with only 150 hours' flying time and less than adequate training in the skills of nightfighting were being hurled into the action. Not surprisingly, nightfighter losses were heavy, but they were mostly caused by taking off and landing in the dark, rather than by enemy action.

'The so-called nightfighter training unit at Ingolstadt was useless,' complained one young pilot, Leutnant (Second Lieutenant) Günther Wolf. 'I was only there for one week, making eleven short daylight flights, a few mock combats, but mostly flying around just for fun – not one night flight, not one radar training flight. My first operation came when the RAF attacked Berlin on 23 August.'

Another young pilot getting his first taste of Wild Boar action over Berlin that night was Leutnant Heinz Rökker. 'It was the first time I had seen a German city being attacked,' he recalled. 'We could see the flak and the markers and the city burning. Then I saw my first bomber, above me, the first four-engined bomber I had ever seen.' Going in for the attack, he 'pressed the button and gave him what we called *die Feuergarbe*, "a bundle of fire", both cannons and all four machine guns. I saw my shots hitting the right wing and fuselage, and the wing caught fire at once. He continued to burn and started to lose height, then he suddenly fell away to the left.'

Fourteen minutes later, Rökker shot down another bomber, then went in search of more prey. 'I flew right over the centre of the target then and could see the shapes of the bombers over the burning city, but I couldn't reach them – they were always too far away. I tried diving on them but I never caught one because, by the time I reached their level, they were no longer visible against the ground fires but were hidden in the dark ahead of me.'

BY NO means all the nightfighter crews were beginners like Wolf and Rökker. *Unteroffiziers* (Sergeants) Frank and Schierholz, pilot and radar operator respectively of a Junkers 88, were a highly experienced partnership with 118 missions together. They were reluctant to try the new tactics, and were determined to approach the forthcoming battle with great caution. When they were directly over Berlin, they spotted a Stirling and dived on it from above, the first time they had ever attacked in that way. They set it on fire, but when it went into a dive did not follow it down as they would normally have done – they had no intention of being caught by the flak. They got a second bomber, a Halifax, shortly afterwards, and again did not follow it down to deliver the *coup de grâce*. As they watched, they had the unnerving experience of seeing the crippled aircraft hit again by the flak. They fired on three more bombers, but were driven off by the guns of other RAF aircraft.

Although their first experience of Wild Boar tactics was undoubtedly a success, Frank and Schierholz preferred their earlier role as *Einzelkämpfer* ('lone warriors'). They did not like being mixed up with 'this mass of other aircraft'; it was all 'too hectic'. Leutnant Peter Spoden, the young and relatively inexperienced pilot of a Messerschmitt 110, had never seen so many aircraft at one time before: 'There must have been thirty or forty of them. Some were nightfighters, but the majority were four-engined bombers. Most of the planes seemed to be flying south to north, but the tracer was going in every direction.' In addition, there were hundreds of searchlights, their blinding light enough to disorientate any pilot. It was, said Spoden, 'the most intensive night battle of the war I ever saw, a terrible inferno.'

*

RUTH ANDREAS-FRIEDRICH had been sheltering in the cellar with her lover, the orchestral conductor Leo Borchard, and her eighteen-year-old actress daughter Karin, who had just moved in with them. They were terrified by the noise, confusion and blast as bombs fell all round them. When the all-clear sounded and the dust and smoke began to clear, Ruth discovered Karin lying on a mattress, blue-lipped and trembling. Her pulse was wildly erratic, racing, slowing, stopping. Borchard diagnosed smoke poisoning. The only medicine or heart stimulant they could find were a couple of lumps of sugar, but these seemed to help, and Karin quickly recovered.

They emerged from the cellar to find the house in ruins and on fire above their heads, the curtains bellying at the windows like blazing sails. For the rest of the night, they concentrated on trying to put out the fires and salvaging what they could. In the morning they packed up the bare essentials of their belongings and set out for the Anhalter station. Like thousands of other Berliners, they wanted to get away from the city, away from the bombs.

Although it should have been light, smoke from burning buildings blacked out the sun, making the streets dark as night as they joined the torrent of fugitives rolling past the Gestapo headquarters on Prinz–Albrecht–Strasse. A great crowd stood like a wall before the locked gate of the station, being allowed through in trickles as trains arrived.

After hours of waiting, Ruth and her companions at last managed to get on to the platform. There was more pushing and shoving from behind as people struggled and fought to get on board the train. At last it pulled out, its carriages packed like cans of sardines with sooty, greasy, shocked survivors. Normally, the trip to the country took about forty minutes; this time it took seven hours. At 9 pm, almost crying with exhaustion, they sank into the clammy feather beds of a remote village inn.


HANS-GEORG VON STUDNITZ, a press officer with the Foreign Office, used an official car to drive an elderly friend to the safety of Kerzendorf, a village to the south-west of Berlin. On their journey they got a good view of some of the damage. 'In Steglitz, Friedenau, Lichterfelde and Marienfelde we came upon places through which it was impossible to pass by car,' he noted in his diary. 'Craters filled with water, heaps of rubble, firehoses, pioneers, firemen and convoys of lorries blocked the streets, where thousands of those rendered homeless were searching the ruins, trying to rescue some of their possessions, or were squatting on the pavements and being fed from field kitchens.'

Although the raid had been over for eighteen hours, fires were still ablaze everywhere. Burnt-out tramcars and buses jammed the streets. Tram lines had been destroyed, trees blown down or shattered, their leaves and branches torn off. All that remained of one block of houses was a solitary blackened chimney, sticking up like a finger. On the edge of the city, herds of cattle wandered untended among the ruins.

Next morning, Studnitz drove back into Berlin, passing the burnt-out works of Henschel and Siemens in Tempelhof. 'The attack,' he said, 'had been plunged into the heart of Berlin, like a knife into a cake, and had sliced out a great triangle, the apex of which stretched as far as the Zoo station.' The last bomb fell in the Hardenbergstrasse, destroying the local military head-quarters, blowing the roof off the High School of Music and smashing every window in the vicinity.

THE RESCUE services were at full stretch during and after the raid, often hampered by the fact that they had few special vehicles. The armed services in front-line areas had priority for new trucks, vans, cars and motorcycles, so civil defence had to rely on their cast-offs or requisitioned private vehicles. And as more and more of the city's remaining active men were drafted to the eastern front, the proportion of elderly, semi-invalids and youngsters in the service increased. Boys like Fred Laabs were seasoned veterans by now, but still retained their youthful idealism.

'It wasn't the Fascist ideology that made us boys so enthusiastic about being members of the civil defence,' Fred recalls. 'I think it was more the kind of feeling of being helpful to other people, saving lives and all that.'

After the raid, Fred was at an apartment building that had been sliced in half. The half that survived included the staircase, and on the third floor there was a birdcage hanging on the wall, with a budgerigar still in it, hopping to and fro. An old woman came up to him. 'Oh, please young man,' she pleaded, 'fetch me that budgie from up there. He is the joy of my old age.' Without thinking of the danger that the stairs could collapse at any moment, plunging him to his death, Fred climbed up and rescued the bird.

For their hard and dangerous efforts, the boys were rewarded with extra food coupons, and occasionally received bread, sausage or fruit from some friendly donor, possibly a neighbouring military unit. But they suffered from the chaotic administration of their service, not really knowing who was responsible for them, or who had the right to give them orders. Even in action there was often chaos, with heated arguments between officers of the fire service, the Red Cross and the civil defence. More than once, Fred saw a fire chief and a civil defence officer fighting each other with bare fists in front of a burning, bombed house.

In spite of the destruction they had caused, the RAF did not regard the raid of 23–4 August as one of their successes. Their casualties were the heaviest ever sustained in one night: sixty-two aircraft, including one Lancaster that blew up on the ground in a bomb-loading accident. The Luftwaffe, on the other hand, could regard their night's work as eminently satisfactory. They had lost nine nightfighters, but only four aircrew. The new Wild Boar tactics were judged to have been a triumph.

*

THE RAF were back on 25 August, and again on 31 August and 3 September, but with fewer aircraft each time – the success of the flak and the nightfighters was steadily reducing the number of planes available to Air Marshal Harris. When they arrived over the 'Big City' on 31 August the bomber crews received another shock. Major Hajo Herrmann, the inventor of Wild Boar, had had another ingenious idea. He had loaded a number of Junkers 88 bombers with flares, and sent them to track the raiders from the Dutch coast. As they reached Berlin, the Ju 88s began to drop their flares, lighting up the British planes as sitting targets for nightfighters and flak.

'It was like running naked through a busy railway station, hoping no one would see you,' said one British pilot. Another spoke of the psychological effect of the flares and the sheer terror they inspired: the crews, he said, felt that the Germans 'knew exactly where we were at all times and were only allowing us to go on in the hope that the flak would get us. But we didn't know which second would be our last when we had served their purpose of marking the route of the coming attack.'

John Colville, formerly one of Churchill's private secretaries, who had escaped from Downing Street to become a fighter pilot, watched Lancasters and Halifaxes taking off for Berlin from an airfield near Cambridge. 'I stood outside a hangar and watched one three-ton lorry after another debouch a hundred or more young men, who walked silently and unsmiling to their allotted aircraft,' he wrote. 'Accustomed as I had already become to the gaiety and laughter of fighter pilots, I was distressed by the tense bearing and drawn faces of the bomber crews. At that time . . . some eighty-three per cent were failing to complete unscathed their tours of thirty operations. Of courage they had plenty, but there was nothing but lip-biting gloom registered on those faces.'

# 11

THE DISRUPTION caused by the raids to life in Berlin continued long after the fires had been extinguished. After each heavy raid, posters appeared all over the affected parts of the city, warning of unexploded bombs. This meant more work for the Luftwaffe's explosives squads, the *Sprengkommandos*, whose *Feuerwerkers* – armourers and bomb disposal experts – were responsible for clearing bombs from civilian sites.

To support the experts, labourers were needed to dig out the bombs. These men were conscripted from among the inmates of prisons and concentration camps, and were usually criminals or political prisoners, who could earn remission of their sentences by 'volunteering'. The *Feuerwerkers* themselves much preferred to employ political prisoners, because they were more reliable than criminals. The prisoners became part of the unit, sharing the same rations – if nothing else, they were well fed. Towards the end of the war, German soldiers undergoing punishment were also used as labourers. Inevitably, casualties were high; many prisoners did not survive to enjoy their remission.

In the early days, before the bombing became really heavy, disposal teams usually either blew up unexploded bombs where they had landed, or waited three days before trying to make them safe. In practice, this meant that if a bomb landed in a built-up area it would be destroyed as soon as possible. However, as more and more bombs fell, the Propaganda Ministry had second thoughts. Geobbels issued instructions that bombs were not to be exploded *in situ*, since this not only caused additional damage to surrounding property, but was also bad for morale.

Once a bomb had been uncovered, the labourers were called off and the officer or *Oberfeuerwerker* was left alone to get on with things. A bomb disposal man needed to have an encyclopedic knowledge of every type of British fuse, or his chances of survival were minimal. There was so much that could go wrong: no one could tell, for instance, when the fuse of a time bomb was set to detonate. As the *Hamburger Fremdenblatt* put it, 'there is no certainty as to why the bomb has not exploded, or whether it is going to explode at all and if so, when. Many hours' work are frequently necessary before one can approach the bomb. During this time, the delayed-action fuse runs on – how soon it will run out no one knows.' Other hazards included anti-handling devices. The British No. 845 anti-disturbance battery-operated fuse, for example, had a mercury tilt switch, in which a tiny globule of mercury was used to complete an electrical circuit, detonating the bomb if it was moved.

Once a bomb was defused, it was usually cut in half for transport to a bomb cemetery, where the explosive could be steamed out at leisure. The resulting emulsion of water and explosive was then filtered through hessian, and burned.

At every stage, things could go disastrously wrong. It is not surprising that large numbers of *Feuerwerkers* were killed, particularly after 1943.

# 12

THROUGH THE late summer and autumn of 1943, the Germans suffered a run of defeats. In the east, the Soviets steadily drove the Wehrmacht back in all sectors, to regain some of their major cities – Kharkov on 23 August, Smolensk on 25 September, Kiev, capital of the Ukraine, on 6 November. The Germans fought back, but all they could do was slow down the Soviet advance.

In the south, meanwhile, the British Eighth Army landed at Reggio di Calabria, on the toe of mainland Italy, on 3 September, after a secret armistice ended the Italian participation in the war as a member of the Axis. Six days later, the US Fifth Army landed south of Salerno to begin the main Allied attack. On 13 October, by which time the Allies had fought their way to within 100 miles of Rome, Italy formally joined the Allies as a 'co-belligerent' and declared war on Germany. 'By this act,' the Italian premier, Marshal Badoglio, told General Eisenhower, 'all ties with the dreadful past are broken and my government will be proud to march with you on to the inevitable victory.' By mid-November the Allies were busily preparing for a major assault on the German Winter Line, almost halfway up the leg of Italy.

On Monday, 22 November, Churchill and Roosevelt met again, this time in Cairo for a four-day conference. The Chinese Nationalist leader, Generalissimo Chiang Kai-shek, joined them to discuss operations in the Far East. But for the two Western leaders one of the main purposes of the meeting was to prepare themselves for their encounter with Stalin in Tehran the following Sunday, the first time the 'big three' would all sit down together. Undoubtedly, Stalin would once again be pressing for an early invasion of mainland Europe. He would also be demanding more evidence of commitment to support Soviet efforts by inflicting damage on Nazi Germany. This time, however, the Allies should have no difficulty in convincing him: the RAF had already started the Battle of Berlin.

# 13

Bomber Harris's Battle of Berlin began in earnest on Thursday, 18 November 1943, with a mass raid by 411 Lancasters, accompanied by four Mosquitoes carrying decoy flares. Harris was convinced that if the RAF could destroy Berlin, Germany would collapse and the war would be won without the need for further fighting on land. 'Berlin will be bombed until the heart of Nazi Germany ceases to beat,' he declared.

But the battle was by no means one sided. While the bombers might inflict grievous harm on the city, with an area of 339 square miles it was simply too big for anyone to destroy from the air alone. Certainly, Bomber Command could pound its centre to dust, but in the face of Berlin's formidable defences even this would require Harris to accept a level of casualties that could not be sustained either in men or machines. If losses rose above 4 per cent, then it became unlikely that any bomber crew would complete its tour of twenty-five to thirty missions unscathed. Since November 1942, losses had averaged just over 6 per cent.

In an attempt to reduce the toll taken by flak and nightfighters, Harris decided on a change of tactics. His bombers were at their most vulnerable while they were over the target. If he could shorten that time, by increasing the number of bombers over the target simultaneously, the flak would have less time to shoot at them, and the nightfighters less time to scramble. During the 1,000-bomber raid on Cologne, Bomber Command had experimented with twelve aircraft per minute over the target. In later raids they had increased the number to sixteen. Now, Harris was prepared to send no fewer than twenty-seven bombers a minute over Berlin, despite the obvious dangers of aircraft colliding or being hit by bombs from those flying above them.

For the people of Berlin, this meant that the raids changed from an hour of drawn-out agony into a few minutes of sheer, concentrated terror. On 18 November, the raiders were over the centre of the city for a mere sixteen minutes, but in that time they dropped 1,593 tons of bombs, the heaviest pounding Berlin had experienced.

'They won't be coming tonight,' Helmuth Grossmann told his wife on Monday, 22 November. 'The weather's so bad that we'll have some peace.' Most Berliners were saying much the same, for experience had taught them that the RAF liked clear nights, when they could see their targets, not murky, heavily clouded skies, with drizzle filling the air as it was that night. Frau Grossmann was staying with her mother in Wilmersdorf, while their own flat was awaiting repairs after being damaged in the March raid. Helmuth still slept there, to keep an eye on their belongings.

Confident that there would be no alarm, Grossmann's wife went to the cinema with a woman friend, while he was dining with a business colleague at a restaurant in Charlottenburg. The waiter echoed his thoughts when he said 'If they haven't come by 7.30, they won't be coming tonight,' as he took the order and clipped the ration coupons. Like everyone else in the restaurant, Grossmann found his eyes constantly drifting to the clock on the wall, as the hands moved steadily closer to the magic time. He was lifting his spoon to his mouth as the minute hand finally touched the half-hour – and at that precise moment, the sirens started up.

Grossmann was convinced it would be nothing more than a harassing raid – probably another lightning attack by Mosquitoes – but he joined the other diners seeking the safety of the Zoo flak bunker, rather than heading for home as he usually did. He had never been inside the great concrete fortress, and was curious to see what it was like. Inside, soldiers directed the flow of people up broad staircases to the different floors. In the dark niches at the corners, youngsters stood embracing and even making love. Adults who tried to complain to the authorities about these immoral goings on were warned to mind their own business – the young were privileged people in the Third Reich, whose leaders were anxious to encourage any increase in the birthrate, no matter how it was achieved.

Grossmann was directed to the second floor, but found there were already no seats left on the rows of benches set out like church pews. He had to stand against a wall, watching people doing needlework, reading, or simply clutching attaché cases containing their valuables. The immensely thick walls and ceilings gave a sense of security, muffling all the sounds of the approaching raid. Even so, the increasing thunder told them this was something more than a nuisance attack.

MISSIE VASSILTCHIKOV and her father had just taken shelter in the half-basement kitchen of their house when they heard the approaching aircraft. 'They flew very low and the barking of the flak was suddenly drowned by a very different sound – that of exploding bombs, first far away, then closer and closer, until it seemed as if they were falling on top of us. At every crash the house shook. The air pressure was dreadful and the noise deafening. For the first time I understood what the expression *Bombenteppich* ['bomb carpet'] means – the Allies call it "saturation" bombing. At one point there was a shower of broken glass and all three doors of the basement flew into the room, torn off their hinges. We pressed them back into place and leaned against them to try to keep them shut.'


ALBERT SPEER, Reich minister of munitions since February 1942 and in charge of all war production since July 1943, had been finishing a meeting in his private office when the sirens sounded. He did not dash for the shelter, but drove at top speed to watch the raid from the flak tower's observation platform. But he had scarcely reached the top of the tower when he had to take shelter inside; bombs falling nearby were so close that they were shaking the stout concrete walls. Injured anti-aircraft gunners crowded down the stairs behind him: the blast had smashed many of them against the sides of their turrets. For twenty minutes explosion followed explosion.


INSIDE THE flak tower, Helmuth Grossmann and his fellow shelterers clung to the rough grey walls as two particularly heavy blasts, one immediately after the other, shook the massive building to its foundations. Cement dust from the walls filled the air. Somewhere there was a loud, metallic crash, and the lights went out, like the batting of an eyelid. There was a deathly silence, until the guns opened up again. People started to rouse themselves, speaking to each other in low tones. Someone produced a flashlight, someone else a candle. Taking advantage of the darkness, someone lit a forbidden cigarette – but the guards noticed immediately, and ordered the sinner to put it out. A woman fainted; her companions called for water. Then it was quiet again. Conversations sank to whispers as everyone listened, waiting tensely. Another loud bang shook the building, followed by the sound of splitting timber.

'My God! That was a hit!' someone cried.

'Must be a damn fine attack,' said a dry voice from the shadows.

A girl's voice came from the darkness: 'Well, are you or aren't you?' Immediately, half a dozen male voices volunteered their services.

After what seemed like an eternity, Grossmann struck a match to look at his watch. Five minutes had passed.

'Oh, God. Oh, God,' another woman's voice whimpered in the dark. 'My old parents are all alone in the house . . . if nothing's happened to them . . .'. Grossmann thought of his wife, his throat tightening as he imagined worse horrors than Goya had ever painted. All he could do was wait, and hope.


As THE raiders left, Speer ventured out on to the platform again. Looking towards his ministry, he could see it was 'one gigantic conflagration'. He tumbled out of the flak tower, found his car undamaged, and drove over there at once. A few secretaries, looking like Amazons in their steel helmets, were dashing through the ruins trying to save files. Where Speer's private office had been, he found nothing but a huge bomb crater.

THE RAID was over by 8.30 pm, but the devastation continued long after the planes had left. They had dropped 2,501 tons of bombs, over half of them incendiaries. Eighty miles from the city on their way home, the RAF airmen could still see the fires they had started.

The Vassiltchikovs were called out of their cellar before the all-clear sounded by an unknown naval officer, who warned them that the wind had risen and the fires were spreading. This, the officer explained, was only the beginning; the greatest danger would come in a few hours' time, when the fire storm really got going. Already the smoke was making it difficult to breathe. Their maid, Maria, gave each of them a towel soaked in water, which they held over their mouths and noses.

Back in the house, the telephone was, amazingly, still working for incoming calls – Missie's friend Gottfried von Bismarck rang from Potsdam, anxious to know how they were – but there was no electricity, gas or water. Groping their way around with candles and torches, they were thankful that they had had time earlier to fill every bath tub, sink, basin or bucket with water, to use against fire. It soon looked as though they would need every drop.

'The wind had increased alarmingly,' Missie wrote in her diary, 'roaring like a gale at sea. When we looked out of the window we could see a steady shower of sparks raining down on our and the neighbouring houses and all the time the air was getting thicker and hotter, while the smoke billowed in through the gaping window frames.'

WHEN AT last the all-clear sounded, Helmuth Grossmann left the shelter with the crowd, making painfully slow progress as they groped their way down staircases and along corridors. In the entrance lobby, the doors had been blown in by the blast. Thick smoke poured in from the park, making everyone choke and cough. Outside, trees, shrubs, grass and buildings were burning. The Zoo station had not been hit, but almost all the buildings surrounding it had been. The Kaiser Wilhelm memorial church blazed fiercely. The Ufa-Palast cinema was a heap of ruins. Buildings on Joachim-stalerstrasse and the Ku'damm were in flames. Suddenly, time bombs started to explode nearby. People panicked and raced back to the flak tower, crushing into the lobby against those still trying to get out.

Grossmann started out for home, to find his wife and mother-in-law. He ran through the curtain of black smoke to the Kaiserallee, a handkerchief pressed over his mouth, his hat pulled down over his eyes, clutching his coat tight around him. Splinters of glass crunched beneath his feet at every step. A hot wind blew showers of sparks from burning buildings on to him as he stumbled over fallen street-car cables, torn-up trees and broken branches. Pausing to catch his breath, he saw that an old couple dragging a suitcase had stopped on the corner opposite, in front of a blazing store. Helplessly he watched as the parapet of the building started to break away and fall, as though in a slow-motion film, directly towards them, just as they began moving forward again. As the wall crashed to the ground they disappeared in a great cloud of dust and debris, before Grossmann could shout a warning. But as the dust cleared he saw them shuffling away, unharmed, seemingly unaware of their escape.

Grossmann hurried on through the smoke and the sparks. He heard someone shout 'You're burning! Beat it out!' but had gone another ten yards before he realized they meant him. In Pragerplatz he found his own building destroyed. A fire engine drove slowly through the rubble on the street. Behind it ran a woman, screaming madly: 'Come to me! You can still put it out! Please, please, please come! Come to my place!' The fire engine disappeared round the corner. No one took any notice of the woman, still pathetically waving her handkerchief after it, as she fell over a brick and lay in the street, weeping. Suddenly, the sirens started wailing again. The woman scrambled to her feet and ran away, like a hunted animal. Grossmann ignored the people hurrying back to the flak tower shelter, and continued on his way.

When he reached his mother-in-law's street, Grossmann found there was barely a building that was not ablaze. The noise was terrible, crackling and splintering everywhere, smaller explosions from inside the houses, tiles, bricks, beams, radio aerials, crashing down from the roofs and walls. The house was still standing, but the roof and top floor were on fire. There was no sign of his wife or anyone else, either on the street or in their flat, where the door swung open and the wind carried a continuous steam of sparks in through one broken window, across the room and out the other side.

Grossmann dashed down the stairs to the cellar. His wife and her mother were there, unhurt, in the process of carrying their belongings down from the flat. They had tried to put out the fires in the roof and upper floors, lugging buckets and cans up from the cellar until the water supply had failed. Now they were rescuing what they could, in the hope that something might survive in the cellar.

As Grossmann was talking to the two women, the burning staircase collapsed above them. They were trapped in a cellar that was rapidly filling with dense smoke. Residents staggered around, bumping into each other, barely able to see who was who. Some sat on their chairs or plank beds, too stunned to move. Others soaked blankets, scarves and handkerchiefs in what remaining water they could find in buckets or basins, to give some protection from smoke and flying sparks.

Grossmann helped smash an emergency exit through the thin wall into the next house. Soon, everyone was clambering through the hole, ready to repeat the operation on the next wall, and then the next, tunnelling beneath one blazing building after another towards the end of the street. Old people had to be helped along, babies and children lifted through each hole, cases and bags heaved through, until they reached the end of the line and were able to climb out to the surface.

The fire storm had grown worse. Grossmann's two women didn't believe they could get through to their goal, the nearby U-Bahn station. Defeated, their strength exhausted, they sat on their suitcases. Fortunately, a male neighbour helped support them and carried their suitcases as they forced themselves to stagger on. At the station they found that a section of track had been put out of action, but a train stood at the platform. They clambered aboard and collapsed, thankful to have found somewhere to rest at last.

Once he had regained his strength, Grossmann stowed their suitcases on the station platform and set off back to the flat, to see if anything more could be salvaged. The fire storm was raging more fiercely than ever, booming, crackling and howling – Missie Vassiltchikov described the noise outside her house as like the roar of an express train going through a tunnel. Grossmann kept to the middle of the wide streets, but even so he was in constant danger from falling masonry and collapsing façades. He heard a great bang behind him and turned to see the whole four-storey front of an apartment building falling right across the street, in a huge pile of bricks, beams and twisted ironwork.

Two or three times he struggled back into the flat to fill cases and bags, hauling them down to the U-Bahn station and then returning for more. As he was approaching for the last time, the building suddenly collapsed before his eyes. A tobacconist's kiosk spilled its contents across the street. Grossmann picked up a few cigarettes and stuffed them into his pockets. Cigarettes were as good as money: a fellow victim passed round his bottle of cognac for everyone to take a fortifying swig in exchange for one.

An aid point had been set up in a nearby cinema, run by women volunteers of the NSV (Nazi Welfare Service) and the Frauenschaft (Women's League) and now that they had no hope of salvaging any more possessions, Grossmann, his wife and mother-in-law took turns to go there. At least one of them had to stay behind to keep an eye on their suitcases – stealing and looting had become commonplace during the confusion that followed raids, in spite of the imposition of the death penalty for anyone caught and convicted. The women who ran the aid centres did a magnificent job, often in the face of great personal danger. During every raid they had to get together crockery and equipment, find suitable premises and set themselves up to start making a non-stop supply of real coffee and fresh Leberwurst sandwiches right through the night. These were handed out free of charge and without ration coupons to anyone who came along.

✻

HANS-GEORG VON STUDNITZ and his wife had spent a long weekend with friends in Pomerania and so missed the raid. But they arrived back in Berlin in the early hours of Tuesday morning. Their train had been able to get no closer than Bernau, some ten miles from the outskirts of the city, and their S-Bahn train only got as far as Pankow-Schönhausen before it, too, was forced to halt. Leaving their luggage in an emergency dressing station which was busy with a constant flow of injured people, they set out on foot to trudge the three miles to the Alexanderplatz. Still laden with gifts from their friends, they must have made a bizarre sight: the tall, elegant Studnitz, every inch the well-dressed boulevardier, was carrying a live turkey – their Christmas dinner – while his wife nursed a dachshund puppy, a gift for their small daughter.

After walking for an hour through clouds of acrid smoke, they gave up. 'The air was so polluted with the smell of burning and with the fumes of escaping gas, the darkness was so impenetrable and the torrents of rain so fierce, that our strength began to fail us,' Studnitz wrote in his diary. 'Our progress was further barred by uprooted trees, broken telegraph poles, torn high-tension cables, craters, and mounds of rubble and broken glass. All the time the wind kept on tearing window-frames, slates and gutters from the destroyed buildings and hurling them into the street.'

At 4 am, seeing a light, they found themselves in a pub among a crowd of newspaper women, gathered to collect the morning papers for delivery. It was an oasis of sanity and order in the midst of chaos: a group of Berlin women carrying on their normal trade, refusing to allow the bombs or the British to intimidate them. After resting for an hour, Studnitz and his wife, still carrying the turkey and puppy, were led by one of the women past rows of smouldering shops and offices, through flames, smoke and showers of sparks, to the Rosenthalerplatz U-Bahn station. The platform was crowded with bewildered people clutching whatever they had been able to salvage from their homes. Eventually they managed to squeeze aboard a train to Alexanderplatz.

The S-Bahn was still out of action in the centre of town, so they had to walk the rest of the way home to Händelallee just beyond the Victory Column in the Tiergarten. They emerged from the station into Alexanderplatz to find all the department stores that surrounded it burning fiercely. The rest of their journey was equally traumatic. The royal palace was ablaze, with 'gigantic tongues of flames' shooting skyward from one wing. The Zeughaus, the university, St Hedwig's cathedral and the state library had all been reduced to ashes. From the Unter den Linden dense clouds of smoke obliterated the view into Friedrichstrasse and the Wilhelmstrasse. In the Pariserplatz the head-quarters of IG Farben was burning, while the French embassy, the adjoining mansions and the corner houses built by Schinkel flanking the Brandenburg Gate 'displayed the beautiful profile of their architecture against a back-ground of flickering flame'.

The Tiergarten looked like a First World War battlefield, its trees reduced to jagged stumps. Along the Charlottenburger Chaussee a mass of dazed people picked their way through torn camouflage netting and the wreckage of burnt-out cars and lorries. The angel of victory still stood on her column in the Grosser Stern, but surrounded by an artificial lake created by burst water mains.

In Händelallee they found that their house was one of only three of the street's thirty-three houses still standing. But even as they watched, it burst into flames. Through a window they saw their empire chandelier, like a six-armed torch, swinging backwards and forwards then plunging through the floors and ceilings to the cellar below. They thought they had lost everything – food, clothes, furniture and 300 bottles of fine wine. But, in the dim light of dawn, they found Klara, their cook, at the corner of the Tiergarten, with a pile of linen and clothes which she had rescued from the inferno.

A little later, they witnessed an extraordinary sight when their neighbours came up out of their cellars, reacting with 'almost bacchantic frenzy' to the realization that they had all survived. 'Surrounded by the still burning ruins,' Studnitz recorded, 'they danced together, embraced one another and indulged in quite indescribably orgiastic scenes.'

MORNING BROUGHT little relief to the city. Helmuth Grossmann, who had made his way back to the site of his own flat in Charlottenburg during the night, just in case there was anything left, trudged back to his wife in the first light of day. The flat had been completely demolished. But he had found a working telephone and had called friends in the northern suburbs, who offered to accommodate him and his family.

As he walked back to Wilmersdorf, the scenes of destruction did not look quite as bad as they had seemed in darkness. Many buildings were still burning. Here and there, walls continued to collapse, often without warning. From time to time came the dull thump of an unexploded bomb being detonated by the *Feuerwerkers*, often bringing down more walls. Fire-fighters, police and salvage crews were still at work among the ruins, digging for survivors beneath the rubble, every so often calling for silence as they used listening equipment to detect any faint knocking, sliding oxygen hoses into cavities to help those who were still alive to breathe.

In some places, the digging went on for several days. The woman who owned the greengrocer's used by the Grossmanns was trapped in her cellar when an aerial mine exploded right by her home. She had been knocked unconscious, and came round in total darkness, lying amid the rubble. She heard whimpering and gurgling, then the unmistakable sound of someone's death rattle close by. When she tried to sit up she hit her head on the beam that had fallen across her, saving her life. As the realization of what had happened dawned, she cried out in fear and distress – only to choke on the dust in her throat.

She became aware that she was still clutching her purse. She opened it, found a box of matches and struck one. The flame was weak, but it was enough to reveal that the ceiling had collapsed, leaving a small cavity in which she lay. Alongside her, a head was sticking out from a heap of debris, the dead eyes wide open, the mouth clamped shut, the face veiled with white dust. A little further away, another body lay with its abdomen burst open. In the silence, she could hear water gurgling somewhere. The fear of drowning made her scream out in terror, crying for help. Then, more rationally, she got hold of a broken tile and began banging it systematically on the beam above her.

She did not know how long she went on knocking. But when she was beginning to fear that she would never be found, she was rewarded by the sound of scraping shovels, and hauled out to safety. She had been lucky: several corpses were dug out of the ruins, but three of her fellow residents were never found. Their bodies had been blown to pieces by the force of the explosion.

# 14

FROM THE RAF's point of view, the raid of 22 November had been their first real success. Of the total of 764 planes that had taken off for Berlin, only 26 had been lost over enemy territory. Even with an additional 6 written off as a result of crashes and accidents back in England, the losses amounted to only 3.4 per cent. Against this, 3,000 buildings had been destroyed or damaged and 175,000 people made homeless. An estimated 2,000 had been killed, 500 of them in one large public shelter in the basement of the Joachimstal school in Wilmersdorf when a 4,000 lb 'cookie' fell by the entrance; 105 people were crushed to death when they panicked trying to get down the steps to the shelter in a disused railway tunnel by the Neukölln gas works.

Next night, Harris sent 383 aircraft – nearly 100 of those that had flown in the previous night's raid could not be made serviceable in time. They did not need marker flares this time – many streets were lit up by the glare of fires still burning from the night before. The bomb aimers could hardly miss their targets.

Katharina Heinroth, a scientific journalist and wife of the director of the Aquarium, sat out the raid with her husband in the Aquarium cellar. Climbing out at the all-clear, she was horrified. The Aquarium itself was hardly damaged, but the rest of the Zoo had been hit several times, and most of the animal houses were burning fiercely. So, too, were most of the apartment buildings alongside the Zoo in Budapeststrasse. Heinroth raced to the Zoo bunker, to fetch the inhabitants of Budapesterstrasse, who regularly took refuge there. But as soon as they saw the scale of the inferno, most of them shrank back into the bunker again, too terrified to venture out.

As she dashed back to help at the blazing animal houses, Heinroth suddenly saw tongues of flame appear from the roof of her own home. All through the night, she worked alongside the firefighters. They saved her house, but the rest of the Zoo presented a hopeless task. Thousands of incendiaries and phosphorus bombs had done their worst, completely destroying fifteen animal houses, the administration buildings and the residence of Zoo director Lutz Heck. Every single one of the other animal houses was heavily damaged. In the ruins of the ornate Indian temple that had been the elephant house lay the mangled bodies of seven dead elephants. A rhinoceros lying alongside them seemed unmarked, but it, too, was dead – the blast had burst its lungs. In the antelope house, Heinroth found eighteen dead animals, including two giraffes. Two gorillas and fifteen smaller apes lay dead in the ape house. Throughout the entire Zoo, the story was the same.

Inevitably, Berlin being Berlin, rumours began to circulate almost immediately of man-eating lions and tigers wandering the streets until they were hunted down and shot. According to Missie Vassiltchikov, two crocodiles were caught as they were trying to slip into the River Spree. Hans-Georg von Studnitz also noted the crocodile story in his diary, with an added tale of a sweet-toothed tiger, which was said to have made its way into the ruins of the Café Josty, gobbled up a piece of *Bienenstich* pastry (a cake covered in grated almonds and sugar) – and promptly died.

The truth was that the lions and tigers had all suffocated and burned in their cages. A few antelope, deer and small apes did escape into the Zoo gardens, where they were soon rounded up, and a few exotic birds flew out through holes in the roofs, but the only potentially dangerous animal to escape was a wolf, which turned out to be a timid, frightened creature. It was found by Katharina Heinroth's husband hiding in a corner behind their front door, and gave itself up willingly.

AMONG THE casualties that night was Hans von Dohnanyi, victim of the first direct hit on the Lehrterstrasse prison when an incendiary bomb landed right in his cell. He was found with his speech and vision impaired, suffering from a brain embolism. Dohnanyi had been ill for some time – he had developed a serious inflammation of the veins in both legs – but the chief investigator, Judge Advocate Dr Manfred Roeder, had refused to allow him a consultation with Ferdinand Sauerbruch, the leading surgeon at the Charité hospital. Now, while Roeder could not be contacted amid the confusion after the raid, Dohnanyi's friends got him transferred to Sauerbruch's clinic, where he stayed until 22 January 1944. While at the Charité, he was certified unfit for trial, and so was safe for the moment. He was even able to receive visitors – in strict violation of Roeder's orders – including his brothers-in-law, Klaus Bonhoeffer and Rüdiger Schleicher, who were now part of the inner circle of the reorganized conspiracy.

The raid of 23 November gave Bonhoeffer and Dohnanyi a further respite, since many important documents concerning the case were destroyed by fire. But it also thwarted another suicide assassination attempt. A young infantry captain, Freiherr Axel von dem Bussche, volunteered to model a new army greatcoat and assault pack which was to be shown to Hitler on 24 November. He intended to carry two bombs in his pockets, fitted with 4.5-second hand grenade fuses. He would trigger them, then grab and hold Hitler as they exploded, blowing them both up together. Unfortunately, the new uniforms were destroyed in the air raid, so the presentation was cancelled. He was prepared to try again a month later, with replaced uniforms, but at the last minute Hitler decided to leave for Christmas at the Berghof. Bussche returned to his unit on the eastern front, where shortly afterwards he was seriously wounded, losing a leg.

# 15

Many Berliners felt the raid on 23 November had been even more awful than the bigger one the night before. Goebbels was inclined to agree, noting in his diary that the damage caused was equally extensive, with the inner city and the working-class suburbs getting the worst of it. He blamed Göring's Luftwaffe entirely, with some justification. The bombers had had an almost free run over the city: the nightfighters were scrambled too late to intercept most of the force, but the flak had still been forbidden to fire above their fixed altitude.

The ground and air defences were still not properly coordinated three days later, on Friday, 26 November, when the RAF struck yet again with 443 Lancasters. The Heinroths took shelter as usual in the Aquarium cellar, where they listened to the big crocodiles, joining in the noise of the flak barrage, which they apparently took to be the calls of some immense creature. But this was to be the last time they answered the guns. Suddenly there was an enormous crash. The walls shook, plaster and shelving rained down, clouds of dust made breathing difficult. More explosions, smaller but still ear-splitting, followed. As soon as the immediate noise had subsided, the Heinroths rushed up the steps from the cellar. At the same moment, Zoo director Lutz Heck arrived through the heavy front doors, which had been burst open, allowing a torrent of water to gush out down the steps. The beams of their flashlights revealed a scene of utter chaos. An aerial mine had crashed through the glass roof of the three-storey building, and exploded in the middle of the 30-yard-long crocodile hall, shattering heavy glass cases and partitions and flinging the animals out into the passageways. Every other piece of glass in the building had been smashed, too – roof, fish tanks, display cases, windows – and pieces of concrete and stone from the domed entrance hall lay in a great heap of rubble. The artificial jungle river, one floor up, where fifteen-foot crocodiles and alligators could be viewed from beneath through thick plate glass, had poured down through gaping holes, bringing with it bamboos, palms, tree trunks, soil and mud. Most of the crocodiles had also crashed through to the ground, where they now lay, with blood pouring from their nostrils. Two or three were still alive, lashing their tails in agony. One had slid as far as the doors, but never made it outside.

Heck clambered through the ruins to the remains of the great glass fish tanks, where thousands of dead and dying fish flapped and writhed on the floor. A sheat fish – a giant catfish from the Havel – still gasped for breath. Although at over six feet it was as big as himself, he grabbed it and hauled it out of the building into a pond in the garden outside, where it could survive. Between them, Heck and the keepers rescued other native or cold-water fish in this way, though many were too badly injured by glass splinters to live. But for the tropical fish there was no hope.

Of the 2,000 animals that had not been evacuated earlier in the war, 750 were killed in the two raids. More died soon afterwards through the cold, the effects of shock and injury, or lack of water. Many found their way into the cooking pots of Berlin housewives, a welcome supplement to the increasingly sparse meat ration. Deer, antelope and buffalo were not particularly out of the ordinary for people whose peacetime diet included a great deal of game. But Berliners discovered to their surprise that some unusual dishes were extremely tasty. Crocodile tail, for instance, cooked slowly in large containers, was not unlike juicy fat chicken, while bear ham and sausages proved a particular delicacy for Heck and his colleagues. Less appetizing carcasses were cut up as food for other animals.

The seven dead elephants, each weighing between four and six tons, posed the biggest problem. Even with a veterinary team working full time to dig out and cut up the carcasses, the job took a week. The smell grew worse by the day, while men rattled around inside the giant ribcages as though working behind bars, often disappearing amid heaps of intestines as they hacked, sliced and sawed at their tasks. A small fleet of trucks carted the pieces to the Rüdnitz animal processing plant, where they were converted into pet mince, bone meal and soap.

# 16

Berlin's industries were hit hard during the November raids. In addition to the Alkett works, serious damage was caused to five factories of the Siemens electrical group, the Mauser weapons factory, DWM (German Weapons and Munitions Works), the Rheinmetall-Borsig plant which, among other things, manufactured cannons for nightfighters, the Dornier aircraft works which produced some of the nightfighters, the BMW engine works, and many other war industry plants. But, as always, the ability of Berlin's industries, helped by efficient salvage services, to recover from the bombing was extraordinary. They continued to produce war material in scarcely diminished quantities almost up to the end.

The British estimated that 25 per cent of the city had been flattened. Goebbels was happy to encourage them in this belief. 'I am not issuing any denial of the exaggerations,' he noted in his diary. 'The sooner the British believe there's no life in Berlin, the better for us.'

Berlin was not knocked out – but in the immediate aftermath of three massive raids in five days, it was reeling. The NSV welfare services did what they could, opening field kitchens in wrecked streets serving hot soup, strong coffee, and even cigarettes – none of which could be bought in the shops. But their scope was strictly limited. 'In the city there is no water, light, or gas, so far,' Moltke told his wife. 'There is no bread in town either and hardly any food at all. Soup kitchen food is said to be atrocious: cabbage and water without potatoes.' Berliners could not wash or shave, and they had to rely on candles or kerosene lamps to light their shelters. There was no heating, except from the fires that were still burning – many of them consuming the city's stocks of coal and lignite, its fuel for the rapidly approaching winter.

Despite the heroic efforts of the rail repair gangs, travelling remained a nightmare, with some S-Bahn lines and stations not yet opened and several main-line stations flattened, some of them never to open again. And with the telephone system still largely out of action, communications were almost impossible. For Goebbels, this was the most serious problem. He could only keep in touch with the outside world, or with his own officials in Berlin, by using messengers – old men and boys on bicycles, motor cycles, cars, or even on foot.

On 29 November Goebbels gave a stirring speech to a gathering of the Hitler Youth and their parents at the Titania Palace, a cinema in Steglitz. He was delighted with the reception they gave him. Afterwards, he toured Reinickendorf and Wedding. 'At the Gartenplatz [near the Humboldthain park] I took part in feeding the public,' he recorded in his diary. 'The men and women workers received me with an enthusiasm as unbelievable as it was indescribable.' A packing case was found for him to stand on and he was 'forced' to make yet another speech.

But Goebbels had no illusions about the real situation in Berlin, with devastation as far as the eye could see. 'Wedding itself is for the most part a shambles,' he confessed to his diary. 'The same is true of Reinickendorf.' He was genuinely amazed that people in the street were still so good humoured, that their spirits were still so high. He would have been even more amazed, no doubt, if he could have seen what Moltke saw that day: 'In one of the rubble heaps I passed there must have been a carnival shop. Children from 4 to 14 had taken possession; they had put on coloured caps, held little flags and lanterns, threw confetti, and pulled long paper streamers behind them, and in this get-up they marched through the ruins. An uncanny sight to see, an apocalyptic sight.'

As THE MOON waxed again, the raiders paused, as they did each month. It was too dangerous for lumbering, overburdened bombers, with no fighter escorts to protect them, to make the long journey from Britain to Berlin in the light of a full moon, when they could be seen almost as clearly as in daylight. During the lull, Berlin began counting the cost.

Because of the administrative problems, coupled with the difficulty of digging the bodies of many victims out of the ruins, it was not until January 1944 that casualty lists of those killed and injured in the last three raids in November were issued. They made grim reading. In all, 4,370 people had been killed, with Charlottenburg, Tiergarten and Wedding suffering the worst losses; 574 of the bodies were still buried under the mountains of rubble. Property damage was enormous. No fewer than 8,701 residential buildings – houses, tenements, apartment blocks – representing 104,613 individual dwellings, had been totally destroyed. Many more had been seriously damaged, but were either still habitable or at least repairable. 417,665 people had been made homeless, though 36,391 of these had either found other accommodation or had returned to what was left of their homes within a month.

Goebbels decided to evacuate as many people as he could. The first trains began to leave the city on 24 or 25 November. But in spite of all the hardships they faced, many refused to leave: they wanted to stay to keep an eye on their household goods, or to salvage what they could from where they could.

*

DURING THE November raids, Hitler's special train had been destroyed in a Berlin railway siding. The Führer was not in it at the time – as usual, he was nowhere near Berlin, but at *Wolfschanze*, (Wolf's Lair), his headquarters at Rastenburg in East Prussia. Perhaps feeling that his absence from Berlin might be misinterpreted, the Propaganda Ministry published a thought for the day, printed on a six-pfennig postcard, which read: 'The Führer's whole life is struggle, toil and care; we must all take part of this load off his shoulders, to the best of our abilities.'

Berliners reacted to this with doggerel of their own, circulated anonymously. There was, for instance, a verse for children to recite at bedtime, based on a traditional children's prayer, with the opening lines:

> Wearily I go to bed
> Bombs still falling round my head . . .

The most famous of these defeatist missives was a grace to be spoken at mealtimes, which ended with the lines:

> No butter with our eats
> Our pants have no seats
> Not even paper in the loo
> Yet, Führer – we follow you!

# 17

WHILE THE people of Berlin were trying to clear up after the November raids, momentous decisions about the conduct of the war were taken by the Allied leaders. Churchill, Roosevelt and Stalin conferred at Tehran from 28 November until 1 December. With the Red Army rolling steadily westwards, and the British and Americans battling their way up through Italy, they agreed it was time to begin active preparations for Overlord, the invasion of France and the beginning of the march on Germany from the west.

They talked, too, about what they might do with Germany after the war. Roosevelt and Stalin were in favour of splitting the country up into several smaller states, so that none of them would ever be strong enough to threaten the peace of Europe again. Churchill was less enthusiastic about this, but agreed that some means must be found to keep Germany weak; he favoured separating Prussia, and thus Berlin, from the rest of Germany, and perhaps turning the south German states into some form of Danube confederation. No one was sure if Stalin was joking when he said that at least 50,000 and possibly as many as 100,000 German officers would have to be liquidated – Churchill was deeply offended at the very idea of the political executions of soldiers who had fought for their country. But Stalin was certainly not joking when he said he would want 4 million German men for an indefinite period to rebuild Russia. His cold anger at what the Soviet people had had to endure left no doubt that he was intent on wreaking a bloody revenge.

# 18

A T THE END of December and beginning of January, the British bombers returned. 'The old year ended in horror; in horror the new year begins,' Ruth Andreas-Friedrich wrote on Monday, 3 January. 'Here we are without water, transportation or electricity. The telephone is dead, too, and we only learn by roundabout ways whether our friends who live at a distance are alive.'

Meanwhile, the survivors shifted rubble, nailed boards or carpet pieces over broken windows, tried to make do. 'Since the air attacks of last November, life has taken on a new pattern,' Hans-Georg von Studnitz noted. Everything had changed. Where once he and his wife used to eat at home or with friends, they were now forced to eat in restaurants. This was largely due to the rationing system whereby – just as in wartime Britain – everyone had to register for certain foods at specific shops. If the shop was destroyed, they had to re-register, but this took time and trouble, even when they could find a shop that was prepared to accept them. So, in the end, it was simpler for those who could afford it to eat out – provided they could find a restaurant that was still open.

Working life changed considerably after the start of the Battle of Berlin. While daylight Mosquito raids made life difficult – the Mosquito was fast and agile enough to be a match for most fighters, so was used to keep up the pressure with spasmodic and unexpected attacks – it was still the night raids that people feared most. Normal office hours were abolished. People worked right through the day so that they could leave at 4 pm in order to be home before the raids started. For those who still lived in the centre this was not too bad, but for people whose homes were further out, travel was becoming more and more of a problem. One of the secretaries who worked in the Foreign Office information department with Missie Vassiltchikov spent seven hours a day simply getting to and from the office, so was able to spend only an hour at work.

MOLTKE HAD kept himself busy during the last few weeks of 1943, both with his official work and with his interminable plans for the future of Germany after the war. He still spent all his spare time meeting his circle of friends for discussions of the finer points of the economy, international relations and political morality. In December he travelled to Istanbul, ostensibly on OKW and Abwehr business. In reality, he hoped to meet his old friend Alexander Kirk, former US chargé d'affaires in Berlin, to tell him personally of the state of the resistance in Germany, and of his plans for a new, anti-Nazi government. But Kirk was away from Istanbul, in Cairo, and the American ambassador refused to meet Moltke. He sent his military attaché to talk to him, but neither man could trust the other. Moltke refused to give away German military secrets. He gave the man a letter for Kirk, but it was never passed on.

Back in Berlin after Christmas, Moltke met a thirty-six-year-old army officer who made a deep impression on him. The man was Lieutenant-Colonel Count Claus Schenk von Stauffenberg, whose elder brother Berthold was already a member of Moltke's group. Claus Stauffenberg had been severely wounded in April 1943, when he drove into a British minefield during the North African campaign, losing an eye, his right hand and two fingers of his left hand. He was now employed as chief of staff to General Olbricht, head of the General Army Office and a member of the Beck–Goerdeler group of conspirators. Moltke thought Claus 'a good man, better than my Stauffi [Berthold], more manly and with more character'.

Claus Stauffenberg was a cousin of Moltke's closest collaborator, Peter Yorck, with whom he started political discussions. Moltke's assessment of him proved accurate – he started to take a very active role in planning a military coup against Hitler and the Nazis, and was largely responsible for winning Yorck over to the idea that Hitler had to be killed. There was little chance that he would ever persuade Moltke to abandon his high-minded rejection of such violence, but in any case, he was to have little opportunity.

Early in January, Moltke learned that a colleague, Otto Kiep, was under surveillance by the Gestapo and about to be arrested. Kiep, who had been sacked as consul-general in New York before the war for attending a reception in honour of Albert Einstein, was the victim of an *agent provocateur*, a Swiss doctor called Reckse, who worked for Professor Ferdinand Sauerbruch at the Charité hospital. Reckse had been at a tea party at Kiep's home, where he had encouraged those present to make anti-Hitler statements. He had then denounced them.

The Gestapo bided their time, tapping the telephones of all those who had been at the tea party and keeping them under observation. During four months of watching and listening, they widened the net to include seventy-four 'traitors'. Now they were preparing to arrest them. Moltke discovered this, and warned Kiep. But it was already too late. Kiep and his friends were arrested on 12 January, given summary trials and executed.

Inevitably, the Gestapo discovered Moltke's warning. Himmler was delighted at this new evidence of the unreliability of the Abwehr. On 19 January, he had Moltke arrested and held in 'protective custody', first in Gestapo headquarters in Prinz Albrechtstrasse, where he was interrogated but not tortured, and then in a prison alongside Ravensbruck concentration camp. On 13 February, Admiral Canaris was dismissed, and five days later the Abwehr was dissolved and brought directly under the control of Himmler's *Sicherheitsdienst*, the SD.

# 19

ON TUESDAY, 15 February, 891 aircraft set out from their bases in Britain, the biggest bomber force ever sent to Berlin. The raid lasted twenty-two minutes, during which 2,643 tons of bombs were dropped, over half of them incendiaries. German controllers ordered the fighters to stay clear, to give the flak a free hand. The new tactic was strikingly unsuccessful – despite their numbers, only three bombers were shot down.

Over 1,100 separate fires were started, and nearly 1,000 residential buildings destroyed. But casualties were remarkably light – Goebbels's mass evacuation scheme, added to the many who had moved out to surrounding villages from which they commuted each day, had reduced the population of the city by well over a million, most of them from the central districts that were the bombers' regular targets.

On Saturday, 4 March, the air battle took a new turn. Twenty-nine B-17 bombers of the US 8th Air Force arrived over Berlin in the middle of the day. The Americans had suspended daylight raids after a disastrous attack on the German ball bearing manufacturing centre of Schweinfurt on 15 October 1943, when sixty out of 288 B-17s were shot down by German fighters. Now, however, new long-range versions of the USAAF's most successful fighters – Mustangs, Lightnings and Thunderbolts – had been developed, capable of escorting the B-17s all the way to Berlin.

Any doubts about the meaning of the test run on 4 March were swept away two days later, when a force of 814 US Flying Fortresses and Liberators, supported by 644 newly developed long-range fighters, struck at 1.04 pm.

Because of low cloud, precision bombing was impossible. Few military or industrial targets were hit, though the road and rail network suffered further damage. But two precious hours of production was lost while workers took to the shelters, and Berlin faced up to the prospect of round-the-clock air raids.

The only fighter protection the city had was the nightfighters, most of them comparatively cumbersome twin-engined machines, burdened with radar and other equipment, and totally unsuited for combat with the US fighters. Together with the flak, they knocked out 69 US bombers and 11 fighters – the highest total ever. But it was at the cost of 66 German aircraft destroyed or damaged beyond repair, and 46 pilots killed or seriously wounded. The loss of so many pilots in a single day was a severe blow to the Luftwaffe, whose training schools were already overstretched and incapable of turning out enough new pilots to replace those being lost.

There were further daytime raids by the USAAF on 8, 9 and 20 March, and another large-scale night attack by over 800 RAF bombers on the 24th, before the Battle of Berlin was called off for the summer. The city was battered almost beyond recognition, but in spite of the massive damage inflicted on property and industry over four years of bombing, it still continued to function. Senior RAF officers had no doubt about the final outcome of the battle. Sir Ralph Cochrane, AOC of 5 Group, confessed later: 'Berlin won. It was just too tough a nut.'

# PART FOUR

# *In the vice*

# 1

B Y THE early part of 1944, Berliners' morale was close to breaking point. 'Alarms, alarms, and more alarms,' Ruth Andreas-Friedrich noted gloomily on Friday, 4 February. 'You hear nothing else, see nothing else, think nothing else. In the S-Bahn, on the streets, in shops and buses, everywhere the same scraps of conversation: "Completely bombed out . . . roof blown off, wall collapsed . . . windows out . . . doors out . . . bomb-damage certificate . . . lost everything".' To add to the feeling of doom, the news from the fronts was uniformly bad: while Berlin was being pounded from the air, the German armies were being battered in the field.

In Italy, the situation had deteriorated into a bloody stalemate. Helped by the hilly terrain and relative narrowness of the front, the Germans had halted the American and British armies, but couldn't drive them back again. On 22 and 23 January, when Allied troops landed in force at Anzio, south of Rome, the German commanders' swift reaction prevented a breakout from the beachhead, but the two sides remained locked in savage combat for four long months.

There was deadlock, too, in central Italy, most notably around Monte Cassino, where from mid-January onwards German troops in the hilltop Benedictine monastery fought off every attempt to dislodge them. Soldiers from fifteen Allied nations were involved in the four-month battle, which claimed 20,000 dead and 100,000 wounded before Poles of the 3rd Carpathian Division raised their banner – hastily sewn together from pieces of a Red Cross flag and dozens of soldiers' handkerchiefs – over the ruins.

On the eastern front, the war was a catalogue of death and disaster, as the Soviet juggernaut ground forward. On New Year's Eve, the Red Army captured Zhitomir, and three days later crossed the pre-war Polish frontier. On 27 January the German grip on the besieged city of Leningrad was finally broken after nearly 900 days. During the first seventeen days of February, twenty-five German divisions were annihilated in the Ukraine. On 15 March the Red Army crossed the River Bug, which had formed part of the start line for Operation Barbarossa back in 1941. After two and three-quarter years of savage fighting, the German army was back where it began. On 18 March, as

Soviet troops reached the Romanian border, the Hungarian government deserted Hitler. He had to order the Wehrmacht to occupy Hungary immediately, to prevent the Red Army rolling through it unopposed into Austria.

At the end of 1943 the German order of battle had included thirteen armies, four of them Panzers. By April 1944 there were barely nine: four had been totally destroyed, and a fifth, the Seventeenth Army in the Crimea, was on the verge of annihilation. Only one full Panzer army remained, with a second desperately refitting in Galicia. The winter campaign had inflicted almost a million casualties on the German armies and their allies. By 12 May they had lost another 110,000 men in the Crimea.

# 2

As the Red Army reoccupied more and more territory, its officers and men were shocked by the sheer scale of the destruction and carnage wrought by almost three years of war. When the Germans invaded in 1941, Stalin had ordered his people to leave them nothing, and Russians, Belorussians and Ukrainians had destroyed everything possible as they retreated. Now that the Germans were themselves retreating, they compounded the devastation by conducting a scorched earth policy of their own. They set fire to those villages that still stood. They even torched their own dugouts. 'We burned everything, to the last board,' one German soldier, Helmut Pabst, recalled. He and his men rode out on horseback through the conflagration, shielding their faces from the rain of sparks, and thankful for the huge pall of smoke that rose above them, concealing them from attacks by enemy aircraft.

Bryansk, about 120 miles north of Kharkov, was one of many towns set on fire by the Germans before they fled. Helmut Pabst recalled 'racing through the white heat of dying streets', with burning houses on all sides and old birch trees flaring like torches. He rode through a forest of rigid, angular chimney stacks, the colour of Brussels lace above the black carpet of charred wood and ash.

When Soviet troops bludgeoned their way into Kiev on 5 November 1943 they found destruction on a scale hard to comprehend. Kiev, named after the Slavic hero Prince Kii, and capital of the early feudal state of Kievan Rus in the tenth and eleventh centuries until it was captured by the Mongols, had been one of the most beautiful and historic cities in the Soviet Union.

More than 6,000 buildings and 1,000 factories had been plundered or destroyed by the Germans. They had killed 200,000 civilians and sent a further 100,000 to slave labour camps. The liberators found a city with a population one-fifth of its pre-war size – a mere 80,000 survivors. And not far from Kiev they found Babi Yar, where more than 100,000 Jews had been killed.

But it was Leningrad that saw the greatest loss of life of any Soviet city during the war – or of any city anywhere in modern times. During the siege, ten times as many people died as were killed by the atomic bomb dropped on Hiroshima. The precise figure will never be known. At least 1.1 million men, women and children lie buried in mass graves in two of the city's cemeteries, but many thousands more were buried elsewhere, or never found a grave.

In the countryside, all over Russia and the Ukraine, wherever the Germans had been, whole villages had vanished off the face of the earth, almost without trace. Everywhere, forest, steppe and marsh were rapidly reclaiming their own. Only the occasional fence post or overgrown vegetable plot, standing out amidst the surrounding vegetation, gave any sign that people had ever lived there.

Such sights and experiences fuelled the anger of millions of Red Army soldiers, hardening their determination to avenge their dead countrymen. But hundreds of thousands more were conditioned to seek revenge for their own suffering: men who had been prisoners of the Germans had ample motivation to go on fighting them. Guy Sajer, a Frenchman from Alsace who served with the SS Gross Deutschland Division on the eastern front, recalls that Soviet prisoners who had been wounded but were designated fit for work were normally used to bury the dead after a battle. Sometimes they were caught stealing from the corpses, taking wedding rings and other pieces of jewellery – though more often they were probably going over the bodies looking for something to eat. 'The rations we gave them were absurd,' says Sajer. 'For example, one three-quart mess tin of weak soup for four prisoners every twenty-four hours. On some days, they were given nothing but water.'

Nevertheless, any prisoners suspected of robbing the dead were killed immediately. An officer would either simply shoot them on the spot without asking questions, or pass them on to a couple of toughs to be dealt with. Once, Sajer saw three Russians handed over for execution. Their hands were tied to a gate, while one of the executioners stuck a grenade into the pocket of one man's coat, pulled the pin and ran for cover. The three prisoners screamed for mercy until their guts were blown out.

A Hungarian tank commander reported waking up one morning and hearing what he took to be thousands of dogs howling in the distance. When he asked his orderly where the noise was coming from, he was told there were about 80,000 Soviet prisoners nearby. 'They're moaning because they're starving,' the orderly said. It has been estimated that about 3 million Soviet prisoners of war died while in German hands.

Both sides on the eastern front treated their prisoners appallingly – Soviet partisans, in particular, were guilty of dreadful savagery. Guy Sajer records finding the bodies of murdered and mutilated comrades – men who had been tied up and left naked in temperatures of −30°, men with their genitals cut off, and so on. But it was the Soviet survivors, not the Germans, who were freed to seek retribution. Whenever the advancing Red Army liberated its own men from prison camps, they fed and clothed them, then armed those who were fit enough and sent them back into the fray, usually in the second echelon to 'mop up' behind the main attack. They followed in constantly swelling numbers, an army of brutalized, half-crazed men advancing on Germany with vengeance in their hearts.

# 3

ON SUNDAY, 16 January, as the battle for Monte Cassino was just beginning and the Red Army was pouring into Poland, General Dwight David Eisenhower arrived in London, having landed at Prestwick the previous day after flying in from Washington via the Azores. There were no fanfares to greet him. Indeed, he was all but invisible: his train from Scotland edged slowly into Euston station in a classic London fog, so thick that two men had to walk in front of his car to guide it to his headquarters at 20 Grosvenor Square. The general and his aides even got temporarily lost while crossing from the kerb to the front door.

It was, nevertheless, a momentous arrival, for Eisenhower was taking up his appointment as supreme commander of the Allied Expeditionary Force, to lead all ground, sea and air forces for Overlord. The cross-Channel invasion of Europe was set for 1 June.

On that same foggy Sunday morning, Sir William Strang, a senior official at the Foreign Office, tabled British proposals for the occupation and administration of a defeated Germany. On 12 January, Stalin had written to Churchill about the day 'when we all arrive in Berlin', prompting the British prime minister to urge his officials to move more quickly in drawing up the lines dividing Germany between the three Allies – at that time, there was no intention to give the French a separate zone.

It was important to the West to obtain an agreement with the Soviet Union to divide Germany into three zones of more or less equal population, and it was important to obtain it soon. Although the British and Americans were now actively preparing for the invasion, it was conceivable that

Germany might collapse before they even set foot in France, or that the invasion would be unsuccessful. Certainly, it seemed quite likely that the Red Army might get to the Rhine before the Allies. In any of these events, the Soviets would be left to take complete control of the country. Churchill was determined that there should be a legal obligation for them to pull back to the east, come what may.

Stalin raised no arguments with the British proposals. The only real disagreements were between Britain and the United States, when Roosevelt tried to insist on America occupying the north-western zone rather than the south, since he feared having US lines of supply from the coast controlled by either Britain or France. But the proposed zones followed the positions of the Allied armies on the ground – US forces were based in south-western England, nearest to America, and would therefore invade France on the right and enter Germany to the south of the British. Any change was impracticable, and the US president was persuaded to drop his objections. However the dividing lines were drawn, Berlin would be deep inside the Soviet zone. So Berlin, too, was to be divided into zones or sectors. The city was to be carved up between the conquerors, long before any of them came anywhere near it.

# 4

YOUNG Fred Laabs left school at the end of 1943, which meant he also stopped working as an auxiliary with the civil defence. He had already witnessed more horrors during the raids than most people experience in a lifetime, but he still had the ambitions and hopes of any normal sixteen-year-old boy. More than anything, he wanted to be a car mechanic, and with the desperate shortage of labour in Berlin, he had no difficulty finding a job. In January 1944 he started an apprenticeship with Wieczorek Brothers, a Mercedes-Benz garage at 19 Schiffbauerdamm, close to Friedrichstrasse S-Bahn station.

Since they serviced mostly government-owned Mercedes cars, the management of the garage was 100 per cent pro-Nazi. Fred was dismayed to find that the foreman insisted on greeting everybody with the Hitler salute, something his former colleagues in the civil defence had long ago stopped worrying about. When he entered the workshop one day with an ordinary 'Good morning' instead of 'Heil Hitler', the foreman hit him across the face. 'You'd better learn that here we greet each other with the Hitler salute!' he snapped.

One of the other workers immediately leapt at the foreman. 'If you do that to the boy again – ' he warned. But the foreman cut him short with a threat.

The man who had intervened was a Dutchman, one of four foreign mechanics, two Dutch and two Belgian, who worked in the garage. Germans such as Fred were forbidden to speak to them or to have any contact with them except on strictly work-related matters. Needless to say, they soon found ways around the ban. The workshop was small, and many of the large government cars had to be parked outside, on the pavement. When they wanted to talk, Fred and the Dutchmen would exchange a secret signal, then pretend they had work to do outside. Lying on their backs under a car in the street, they would discuss the war. It was there that one of his Dutch friends told Fred that Germany was bound to lose. Fred didn't know whether or not to believe him: brought up surrounded by Nazi propaganda, he had never really considered defeat as a possibility. It still seemed unthinkable, but he was impressed by the man's seriousness, and it raised doubts in his young mind, perhaps for the first time.


HELGA DOLINSKI, still commuting from the family summer-house in Köpenick to her job as an apprentice bookkeeper with Deuta Werke in Kreuzberg, also came into contact with foreign workers. There were nearly 100 French and Ukrainian labourers in her factory. The Ukrainians were mostly employed as messengers and labourers, and lived communally in backyard flats not far from the factory. The French worked permanently on night shift, sleeping during the day on two-tier wooden bunk beds in a partitioned-off corner of the factory hall. Inevitably, some tension arose between the two groups – the French pointing out that the Ukrainians were not forced labourers but genuine volunteers, who had welcomed Hitler's troops as liberators from Stalin's dictatorship.


LISA DEYHLE, a young woman who was constantly under suspicion by the Gestapo, having spent eight years as a governess in England before the war, lived in Dahlem with her three-year-old son, Peter. The grounds surrounding the apartment house were tended by a French worker, who lived in a hut in one corner of the garden. Whenever she appeared at her window, he would sing 'Parlez-moi d'amour', though without ever looking up at her. He, at least, seemed reasonably contented with his lot, still managing to assert his Frenchness in his own way.

For most foreign workers in Berlin, however, life was not so pleasant. As the war entered its fifth year, with the German armed forces losing men in an unstemmable haemorrhage, more and more foreigners were needed to fill the gaps in the city's workforce. By March 1944 there were some 5 million foreign workers in Germany, over 800,000 of them in the city, from some twenty-six different countries, releasing an equivalent number of German men to fight on the eastern and Italian fronts.

Foreign workers were divided into four main categories. First were the 'volunteers', mostly from western and northern Europe, who were free to live out of barracks and move around the city as they pleased during their time off. Next came the forced labourers from all over western Europe, followed by the *Ostarbeiter*, workers conscripted from Eastern Europe in general and from Poland in particular – over half of all civilian foreign workers in Germany were Poles, who wore the letter 'P' sewn on to their clothes. These workers were confined to barracks and camps, from which they were marched to and from work each day.

At the bottom of the heap were Soviet prisoners of war, who were kept strictly segregated. Non-officer prisoners from other countries were made to work, but in jobs that were not directly connected with the German war effort, in accordance with the Geneva Convention. Soviet prisoners enjoyed no such protection. They were given the heaviest, dirtiest and most dangerous tasks in the armaments industry – at Borsig, for example, they were used mainly in the foundry – where they were literally worked to death.

Irma Diehn, a Berliner who worked in the Borsig machine shop at Tegel, saw them for the first time during an air raid. While the German and foreign workers were led to the deep underground shelter, the prisoners were taken to the upper level, which offered considerably less protection. 'They were in miserable shape,' she recalls, 'far worse than the foreign workers in our hall. It was winter, it was cold, and they wore such threadbare clothing.'

Irma and her friend Frau Meyer used to enjoy talking to the foreign workers in their section. Such contacts were dangerous – Irma was warned by one of the Dutchmen that a German machinist was about to denounce her for striking up a friendship with the leader of the Polish women, Maria Czerniewski, a former newspaper editor and wife of a resistance leader who had escaped to Switzerland. A denunciation could have been fatal – Irma would have been dragged before the People's Court, and might well have been beheaded for her crime, or at the least sent to a concentration camp.

Contact with workers from Western Europe was frowned upon and discouraged, but contact with Poles and Russians was strictly forbidden. German workers were issued with leaflets instructing them to 'keep a clear distance from the Poles', reminding them that the mixing of Polish and German blood was a racial crime, that those who treated them like Germans were 'putting their own fellow countrymen on the same level as alien races', and that 'it is a fact established by experience that any soft treatment weakens their will to work.'

'Be proud of your supremacy!' the leaflet exhorted. 'Poles have not been brought to Germany to enjoy a better life here than in the primitive conditions of their own homeland, but to compensate through their work for the immeasurable damage the Polish state has done to the German people. You must not treat the Poles dishonourably, but let there be no doubt that you are the masters in your own country.'

THE GREATEST danger to the Reich from contacts between German and foreign workers was not from racial defilement but from exposure to the truth. For ordinary Germans who had been shielded from the outside world by Nazi propaganda, it came as a great shock to be told other versions of events, and this could have a disastrous effect on morale.

Sixteen-year-old apprentice Rudolf Gehrig and his mates flirted warily with the attractive Polish girls imported into their workshop, sometimes giving them small presents, such as finger rings made from chromium tubes. Once such relations had been established, it became more and more difficult for them to think of the Poles as an inferior species. But it was a group of young male workers from Russia who really shook Rudolf's belief in the Nazi racial teachings.

Rudolf and half a dozen of his German apprentice friends used to go swimming in the company's river port in their spare time. So, too, did a group of four or five young Russian *Ostarbeiter*. At first, the two groups kept well apart, but day by day the distance between them shrank – first twenty yards, then ten, and then almost, but never quite, side by side. Although they talked and soon got to know each other's names, they always took care to remain in distinct groups, so that no one passing by could accuse them of mixing together.

Gradually, they learned a few words of each other's languages. The Russian boys taught the Germans how to catch freshwater crabs from under the stones on the river bank, and how to cook and eat them, something they had never done before. As confidence grew, the Russians told them about their own country. Where they came from, they said, there was a wonderful lake, much larger and more beautiful than the Tegelsee in which they now swam. This simple fact was a disturbing revelation to the German boys, brought up and educated in Hitler's Reich. They had always been taught that Russia consisted of nothing but desolate swamps and miserable villages, and now these Russian boys were saying that the countryside was more beautiful than their own.

'We felt very embarrassed,' Rudolf says. 'We had thought that we were the master race. Then these people came who we had been told were subhuman, and we suddenly realized that they were human beings just like us, human beings you could talk to, and who had the same zest for living as we did.'

*

IRMA DIEHN found the young Dutchmen in her section equally disturbing. Jaap Knegtmans and Jo van Amelrooij had been students at the College of Economics in Amsterdam before being forcibly conscripted for labour service in Germany, under threats not only of execution but also of reprisals against their families. 'They provoked us a great deal,' Irma Diehn recalls. 'One of them asked us why Russia had been attacked, and what was the meaning of this war. And he naturally told us things we had no idea about. When they told us this or that was done by the Germans, it was terribly awkward, because it was not our fault.'

Irma and her friends thought of themselves as loyal Germans, but did not feel part of the Nazi state. They had not been brought up that way at home. It came as a great shock to be told of the horrors the SS had inflicted on other countries, and to be asked if they approved of their actions. It came as an even greater shock to realize that all Germans were lumped together with the SS, and were blamed for what they had done.

Although they worked the same hours – 54 hours a week to begin with, rising to 72 hours as Germany's war situation became more desperate later in 1944 – foreign workers never achieved more than 60 per cent of the output of the Germans. In part, this was due to a general unwillingness, in part, to a lack of training. A few weeks after Jo van Amelrooij and Jaap Knegtmans started work in Borsig's western hall, notices were posted saying that production had fallen by 20 to 30 per cent since the Dutch students had arrived, with a warning that it had to be increased again.

The increases were made – but the quality of the work was another matter. Jo and Jaap were employed on machining the barrels for 128 mm anti-aircraft guns, cutting and grinding to tolerances of hundredths of a millimetre. It was a simple matter to grind away too much, so that the part was unusable, but as the inspectors got wise to this, the Dutchmen resorted to other tricks. The special H-shaped gauges to measure and check the finished parts could be dropped on the concrete floor to distort them imperceptibly. Failing this, it was possible to hit them with a hammer to achieve the same result. Either way, the parts checked against them would be useless and fit only for scrap.

Anyone suspected of deliberately spoiling parts faced a period in the Arbeits-Erziehungslager, the 'correction-through-work' camp. Borsig was a state within a state, and had its own private camp at Tegel. Dutch students who spent time in it came back to work as changed men, never saying a word about what had gone on there, and doing what they were told without question.

DESPITE ALL the small acts of sabotage, and the thousands of unskilled and badly trained workers, Berlin's factories still managed somehow to go on turning out guns, tanks, aircraft and other armaments right through till the

end. For every German worker who befriended the foreigners and did their best
to protect them, there were many others who followed the instructions of party
leaders, who were too proud to mix with their inferiors, and who were ready to
denounce anyone they thought was harming German interests. Although there
were so many unwilling workers, there were also thousands who still dreamed of
final victory, and who were prepared to work themselves into the ground to
produce the weapons and to patch up their factories after each air raid.

# 5

B Y THE spring of 1944, the shadow of fear hung over Berlin like a pall of
black smoke, seeping into every nook and cranny of everyday life. The
menace of the Red Army advancing steadily towards the city from the east
was heightened by terrible stories of Slav barbarism, actively fostered by Nazi
propaganda. The ceaseless air raids by the British and Americans continued to
grind away at people's nerves. But above all, Berliners lived in fear of 'them' –
no name was needed; everyone knew 'they' were the Gestapo.

As the war situation grew more desperate, efforts to root out what
the Nazis saw as subversion and defeatism grew ever more paranoid.
Increasingly, danger came not from bombing but from denunciation and the
summary condemnation of the People's Court. 'People disappear,' Ruth
Andreas- Friedrich wrote in her diary, 'and you don't know why. A friend is
in prison; but before you find out about it, he may be ten feet underground,
with his head between his feet.'

Decapitation by guillotine was the normal method of execution.
Commercial artist Oscar Fischer, who had been arrested on suspicion of
printing subversive leaflets, was held in prison for several months before
being released for lack of evidence. The other members of his group were
executed almost in front of his eyes, for his cell was opposite the execution
shed, a converted garage. From his window he watched condemned prisoners
brought out in batches. 'As a matter of delicacy' the men were not informed
that they were about to be executed until an hour before the time. They were
naked except for short drawers, shivering not from fear but from the cold as
they stood waiting for their names to be called. As each man went into the
shed, the next in line had to take off his drawers and place them, neatly folded,
on a pile, to save the textiles, and to save having to wash them. Each execution
took exactly two minutes.

*

ONE OF the more bizarre aspects of Nazi bureaucracy was that anyone who had the misfortune to be executed was expected to pay for the privilege. Pastor Alfons Wachsmann, a minister of the Evangelical Church at Greifswald, was condemned to death for opposing the regime, though the worst charges that could be brought against him were that he had listened to BBC radio broadcasts and that when the Germans were advancing in north Africa he had been heard to comment, 'We began by advancing in '14, too.'

Hans Peters, a distinguished lawyer, had known Wachsmann for years, and was so incensed when he heard of the sentence that he stormed off to see Dr Freisler, chief judge of the People's Court, personally, to plead for a reprieve. Freisler listened to him reasonably enough at first. 'Decent sort of fellow, this Wachsmann. A clever man, no doubt about it,' he began. Then, his face suddenly freezing into the familiar mask, he continued coldly: 'But an educated man who makes defeatist statements has been declared over and over again by the People's Court to deserve execution. Clemency is not my province. The Ministry of Justice makes those decisions.'

Wachsmann was guillotined on 21 February, and shortly afterwards an official contacted his sister and asked if she was prepared to pay the bill. When she enquired what would happen if she refused, she was told that her brother's estate would be seized. She agreed to pay. A few days later, by registered mail, she received an itemized account:

| | |
|---|---:|
| Board per day | 1.50 |
| Transport to Brandenburg Prison | 12.90 |
| Execution of sentence | 158.18 |
| Fee for death sentence | 300.00 |
| Postage | 1.84 |
| Postage for statement of costs | 0.42 |

Total RM 474.84

# 6

FRED LAABS's apprenticeship did not last long. In May 1944, now a young man of sixteen and nearly six feet tall, he was drafted for full-time service as a *Flakhelfer*, an anti-aircraft auxiliary. Fred was ordered to report to a training camp at Lankwitz, on the southern outskirts of Berlin, where he found himself treated exactly like a normal recruit to the armed forces. He was accommodated in barracks, with ten boys to a room, followed a normal military routine, and wore normal Luftwaffe uniform.

Initially, the boys were only supposed to carry out genuine auxiliary work in offices, telephone and telecommunications, fire control systems and so on. But early in 1943 Göring personally approved their deployment as gunners on lighter-calibre weapons like 2 cm and 3.7 cm quick-firing guns. It was not long before they were also crewing heavier guns, particularly the 8.8 cm gun, the standard German anti-aircraft weapon. This was hard work for fifteen- and sixteen-year-olds, for the shells – which had to be loaded manually several times a minute with the gun barrel almost vertical – weighed 32 lb each.

Because of an ability to see well in the dark, Fred was trained to operate searchlight laying gear, working the optical instrument that enabled the lights to lock on to an aircraft and follow its every move. When his training was finished, he was posted to a searchlight battery at Lützowplatz, along with eleven other boys of his age, to relieve adult troops. These soldiers, aged over forty, were being replaced at every anti-aircraft establishment in Berlin and sent to fight on the eastern front.

After that, only the flak towers were manned by fully trained Luftwaffe personnel, the cream of the service drafted in from all over the Reich. The other flak batteries around the city were crewed either by young *Flakhelfer* like Fred, or by the civilians of the *Heimatflak*, a kind of anti-aircraft Home Guard. Large factories and industrial complexes had their own batteries, crewed by factory employees: service was compulsory for everyone over the age of seventeen, and voluntary for those who were younger.

## 7

B Y THE end of April 1944 the Soviet general staff had worked out its master plan for a great new summer offensive. This involved feints on both wings of the 2,000-mile front, in the regions of the Baltic and the Ukraine. The main offensive would be a massive thrust in the centre, through Belorussia. The aim of this was to destroy the last great concentration of German military power, Army Group Centre, which was commanded by Field Marshal Ernst Busch. Once Army Group Centre was smashed, the Red Army would be poised to blast its way into Germany, straight to the gates of Berlin.

The offensive was intended to coincide with Overlord, the invasion of

France by the Western Allies. The heads of the American and British military missions in Moscow, Major-General John R. Deane and Lieutenant-General M.B. Burrows, informed General A.I. Antonov, deputy chief of the Soviet general staff, at the end of the first week in April that the invasion was now scheduled for 31 May, with a small margin on either side to allow for weather conditions. In the event, bad weather caused the invasion to be postponed for a week, but even then the Soviets were not ready. Problems with the rail system slowed deliveries of tanks, artillery, ammunition and fuel, while Marshals Vasilevsky and Zhukov – chief of the general staff and deputy to the supreme commander respectively – bombarded Stalin with midnight telephone calls begging him to lean on the transport commissar, Kaganovich, to speed things up.

AT 6.30 am on the morning of 6 June, two days after the US Fifth Army had entered Rome, Ruth Andreas-Friedrich was woken by a telephone call from Hans Peters, then serving as a major with the Luftwaffe general staff. 'Are you up?' he asked. 'Did you sleep well? Oh, by the way, I meant to tell you – the shipment got in. . . . That's right, by the morning train. Looks pretty good to me.'

Ruth deciphered frantically, trying to clear her head. In their private code, 'shipment' meant invasion. This was it – the Allies had landed.

Once dressed, she hurried out to the nearest newspaper kiosk for the morning paper. But the papers were late. At eight o'clock they had still not arrived, nor by nine, nor ten. The radio, too, was silent, with no news bulletins. At eleven, a delivery truck dumped bundles of papers at the corner of the street – but before they had even been untied, three policemen arrived to confiscate them. It was noon before Goebbels's Propaganda Ministry had decided what to tell people, and the reprinted papers could appear on the streets. 'Invasion by order of Moscow! Battle reports of the impact of German resistance,' they proclaimed. 'The long-awaited day of invasion has come. With the utmost confidence the German people look to their troops and their leadership, which are now in the decisive struggle of the war.'

The attack had begun during the hours of darkness, when three divisions of airborne troops, two American and one British, had landed by parachute and glider in the areas behind the Normandy beaches chosen for the seaborne landings. At dawn, five assault divisions – two American, two British, and one Canadian – had fought their way ashore through rough seas, supported by a vast array of air and sea power, 9,500 aircraft and 600 warships. It was the greatest amphibious operation in military history, and thanks to a hugely successful deception operation, it took the German defenders completely by surprise. By nightfall, Allied troops had established secure beachheads. Within twenty-four hours, 176,000 troops were ashore, with more following as quickly as they could be ferried across the Channel.

A week later, Hitler began unleashing his long-promised *Vergeltungs-waffen*, 'reprisal weapons', against Britain. The first, the V-1, was a flying bomb twenty-five feet long and carrying a one-ton high-explosive warhead, with stubby wings and a jet engine powered by petrol and compressed air. Because of its distinctive drone, the British people swiftly christened it the 'buzz-bomb' or 'doodlebug', but in spite of the joky name, the V-1 created considerable terror among the population of London. The unpredictability, and the awful silence between the engine cutting and the explosion upon impact were nerve-shattering. People who had cheerfully lived through the Blitz began leaving London in droves.

Eight thousand V-1s were launched at England; 2,300 reached London. Altogether, they were responsible for killing 5,479 people and injuring 15,934, damaging or destroying thousands of buildings, including schools, churches and hospitals as well as homes and businesses. But devastating as they were, the V-1s, and the V-2s that joined them in September – long-range rockets which were all the more frightening for arriving in almost total silence, plunging on London from a height of fifty miles – came too late to have any effect on the course of the war. If anything, their greatest value was as a propaganda tool for Goebbels to rally the German people with, a defiant gesture of revenge for the death and destruction rained down by the Allies on Berlin and other German cities.

# 8

COUNT CLAUS Schenk von Stauffenberg, the crippled war hero who had so impressed Helmuth von Moltke, was descended from a long line of military aristocrats. Although a devout Roman Catholic and, in his early years, a monarchist, he had welcomed the Nazis at first. Like many of his generation he had believed they might restore Germany's greatness. But as the true nature of the regime was revealed he had grown steadily more disillusioned. The breaking point came with *Kristallnacht* in 1938. After that, he was prepared to work against them.

In 1941, while he was in the east, engaged in recruiting Soviet prisoners of war for what was later to become the Russian Liberation Army, he met Major-General Henning von Tresckow and Fabian von Schlabrendorff. They recruited him into the conspiracy to overthrow Hitler. It seemed he would be unable to play much of a part in it when he was posted to Tunisia in 1942, but the terrible wounds he sustained there took him back to Germany.

Stauffenberg's injuries were so severe that he should have been invalided out of the army there and then, but he insisted that he was perfectly capable of carrying on as a staff officer. At the end of September 1943, more or less recovered, he was posted to Berlin as chief of staff to General Friedrich Olbricht, a prominent member of the conspiracy, who was head of the General Army Office.

Stauffenberg's single-minded determination and dynamic personality quickly breathed fresh life into the cabal, and by the end of the year he had become its unquestioned leader, dominating both the politicians and the generals. Throughout the first half of 1944, he set about organizing all the conspirators and preparing for a complete seizure of power. The key to this was the Reserve Army – it alone had the men and the weapons to take control. There was, in fact, already an official plan, approved by Hitler himself, for the Reserve Army to impose martial law in the event of a civil uprising or a rebellion by foreign workers. Codenamed 'Valkyrie', the plan was perfect for use by the conspirators, after they had disposed of the Führer.

The commander-in-chief of the Reserve Army was General Fritz Fromm, a man of huge physique but doubtful moral strength. The plotters knew that he was not unsympathetic to their cause, but they could not trust him to instigate anything. However, as the man in charge of army personnel matters, Olbricht had Stauffenberg promoted full colonel and appointed chief of staff to Fromm. In his new role, Stauffenberg was entitled to issue orders to the Reserve Army in Fromm's name, and would therefore be able to put Valkyrie into operation. What was more, as Fromm's chief of staff, Stauffenberg now had regular access to the Führer, and regular opportunities to kill him.

Because of his disabilities – he had lost his right hand and two fingers of his left – Stauffenberg could not use a pistol, so he decided that the best means of assassination would be a time bomb. Twice, on 11 and 15 July, he attended briefings with Hitler with a bomb in his briefcase. Twice, he aborted the operation – first because he had hoped to get Himmler and Göring at the same time, and Göring did not turn up, the second time because Hitler unexpectedly left the meeting early. Each time, the troops of the Reserve Army were already being marched from their barracks to take control of Berlin, and had to be turned around and marched back again. A third opportunity would come on 20 July, when Stauffenberg was to attend a staff conference with Hitler at Wolfsschanze, the Führer's field headquarters in East Prussia.

Hitler's briefings were often held in an underground concrete bunker. But that day the meeting was transferred to the *Gästerbaracke*, a wooden hut with tarpaper roof. Stauffenberg entered it at 12.37 pm, having activated the British-made fuse a few minutes earlier with a pair of pliers specially adapted so that he could use them with only three fingers. He put the briefcase containing the bomb on the floor beneath the heavy oak table, as close to Hitler as he could manage. Then, as previously arranged, he was called out to take a phone call from Berlin. While he was still speaking, at 12.42 pm, the bomb went off.

By that time, Stauffenberg was about 200 yards away, with another member of the conspiracy, General Erich Fellgiebel. They watched with a mixture of horror and satisfaction as the hut exploded in smoke and flame. Bodies and debris were flung through the open windows. Convinced that Hitler was dead, Stauffenberg left Fellgiebel to telephone Berlin with the signal to activate Valkyrie, while he and his ADC, Lieutenant Werner von Haeften, bluffed their way out of the compound and dashed to the airfield, where their Heinkel 111 plane was waiting.

They landed at Rangsdorf, forty-five minutes' drive from central Berlin, at 3.42 pm, to find that nothing had been done to put Valkyrie into action. Three vital hours had been lost. Although everyone involved in the plot had been warned the day before that 20 July was to be the day, none of the senior conspirators had even bothered to turn up at the army headquarters in Bendlerstrasse – Olbricht had actually gone out to celebrate the occasion with a half-bottle of wine over lunch.

Over the telephone from Rangsdorf, Stauffenberg told Olbricht what had happened at Wolfsschanze, and persuaded him to start issuing the orders for Valkyrie. Stauffenberg then leapt into a commandeered Luftwaffe car with Haeften, and headed for the Bendlerstrasse at full speed. By the time he arrived, Olbricht had learned that Hitler was not dead – indeed, at that moment he was calmly entertaining Mussolini to tea.

Another officer in the Führer conference – by an ironic coincidence it was Colonel Brandt, the man who had carried the 'bottles of brandy' in the attempt to blow up Hitler's aeroplane – had moved Stauffenberg's briefcase to the other side of a stout, solid oak table support. This had protected Hitler from the immediate effect of the explosion. The open windows and wooden construction of the *Gästerbaracke* had done the rest, the walls being blown outwards, lessening the blast. Brandt had been killed, Hitler had survived, apparently unharmed.


WHEN THEY learned of Hitler's survival, the conspirators panicked. Unfortunately for them, the Gauleiter of Berlin did not. Goebbels was in his office at the Propaganda Ministry, with Albert Speer and the economics minister, Walter Funk, when he received the telephone call from Führer headquarters informing him of the failed assassination attempt. Looking out of his window on to the Wilhelmplatz, he saw troops of the crack Guard Battalion Grossdeutschland in full combat gear taking up positions surrounding the ministry. He slipped a handful of poison capsules into his pocket, 'just in case', and sent for the commander of the battalion, Major Otto Remer.

Remer had been told by the commandant of the Berlin garrison, General

Paul von Hase, one of the principal conspirators, that Hitler had been assassinated and the SS were attempting a *putsch*. He was ordered to seal off the Wilhelmstrasse area and to arrest various ministers, including the propaganda minster. Remer was a loyal, non-political soldier, holding the highest decoration for bravery, and his duty was, he insisted, to obey the orders of his superior officer without question. When Goebbels reminded him of his oath of personal loyalty to the Führer, he replied that the Führer was dead.

'The Führer is alive!' Goebbels retorted. 'He's alive. I spoke to him myself a few minutes ago. An ambitious little clique of generals has begun this military *putsch*. A filthy trick. The filthiest trick in history.'

The silver-tongued Goebbels worked coolly to persuade Remer that destiny had afforded him a tremendous responsibility. As he wavered, the propaganda minster played his trump card.

'I am going to talk to the Führer now, and you can speak with him too. The Führer can give you orders that rescind your general's, can't he?'

Goebbels had a direct line to Hitler's headquarters, and within seconds the connection had been made and Hitler himself was on the phone. Remer snapped to attention on hearing the familiar voice, responding with a smart '*Jawohl, mein Führer!*' as Hitler promoted him to colonel on the spot and commanded him to crush the rebellion in Berlin. He was to obey only the orders of Goebbels, Himmler, who was now appointed commander of the Reserve Army in place of Fromm, and General Reinecke, who was being put in charge of all troops in the capital. Remer left Goebbels's office to switch his battalion over to the defence of the Nazi government, and to hunt down the ringleaders of the *putsch*.

At 6.30 pm, the powerful *Deutschlandsender* radio transmitter broadcast an announcement throughout Europe, saying that there had been an attempt on Hitler's life but that it and the coup had both failed. The plotters had omitted to take control of the radio stations, and the experienced Goebbels had instantly taken advantage of their mistake.

General Fromm, who had refused to go along with the plotters when he realized Hitler was still alive, had been locked up in his adjutant's office at the Bendlerstrasse for the past four hours. Now, in an effort to save his own skin, he broke out with the help of a group of loyal Nazis. There was a brief shoot-out, in which the only casualty was Stauffenberg, who was hit in his good arm. Eager to dispose of anyone who might reveal that he had known about the plot for several weeks but had said and done nothing to stop it, Fromm appointed himself supreme judge and jury, and condemned the ringleaders to immediate execution.

Beck was given the opportunity of taking the honourable way out by committing suicide, but he managed to bungle even that. 'Help the old gentleman!' Fromm ordered the guards after Beck had twice tried and failed to shoot himself in the head. He was unceremoniously dragged out for a sergeant to finish the job. Shortly after midnight, Stauffenberg, Olbricht, Haeften and Colonel Merz von Quernheim, Olbricht's chief of staff, were marched out into the courtyard and lined up against a wall. In the dim light from the hooded headlamps of a row of army vehicles, they faced a firing squad. Stauffenberg died proudly, standing straight and unbowed, crying 'Long live our sacred Germany!'

As the echo of the shots died away, Fromm ordered a teleprinter message to be transmitted immediately to Führer headquarters: 'Attempted *putsch* by irresponsible generals bloodily crushed. All ringleaders shot.' He marched across the yard to review the firing squad, then called for his car and headed for the gate. As he approached it, a white sports car screeched through it, driven by Albert Speer. Alongside him sat Colonel Remer.

'Finally, an honest German!' Fromm boomed. 'I've just had some criminals executed.'

Speer and Remer were not pleased. Dead men could not talk, could not provide names and details. Remer told the general to report at once to the Propaganda Ministry, where Goebbels and Himmler were already conducting an *ad hoc* inquiry. Fromm crammed his bulk into the car, and Speer drove him back to the Wilhelmplatz, for questioning over brandy and cigars.

SHORTLY BEFORE 1 am on Friday, 21 July, Hitler broadcast to the nation. The *Deutschlandsender* had been promising the speech since about 9 pm, but it had taken that long for a radio van to drive to Rastenburg from the East Prussian capital, Königsberg. Despite the late hour, constant announcements had kept the entire population sitting by their radio sets, waiting for living proof that the Führer had survived. At last, their patience was rewarded: after the usual fanfare of martial music, they heard that unmistakable voice telling them he was speaking to them 'first, so that you might know that I am unhurt and well, and second so that you may hear the details of a crime unparalleled in German history'.

A conspiracy to eliminate him had been hatched by 'a tiny clique of ambitious, irresponsible and at the same time stupid and criminal officers', he said. 'I was spared a fate which holds no terror for me, but would have had terrible consequences for the German people. I regard this as a sign that I should continue the task imposed upon me by Providence.' The criminals, he promised, would be ruthlessly exterminated.

SUDDENLY, THE Gestapo was everywhere, questioning everyone, searching homes and offices, hauling people off for interrogation. No one was safe. Among those arrested on 21 July was General Fromm – for all his bluster, shooting Stauffenberg, Olbricht and the others did him no good.

The collapse of the coup was total. The general staff was decimated as hundreds of officers were arrested, while others whose involvement could not be proved but who were considered unreliable were replaced. Many, including General Henning von Tresckow, Field Marshals Rommel and von Kluge, and General Eduard Wagner, first quartermaster-general of the army, committed suicide. The military governor of France, General Carl-Heinrich von Stülpnagel, tried to shoot himself in the head, but only succeeded in blowing out one eye and blinding the other.

To complete the humiliation of the German officer corps, Heinz Guderian, appointed chief of the general staff on 21 July, renewed its pledge of total allegiance to the Führer. The normal army salute was replaced with the Nazi raised arm. And on 29 July Guderian issued an order that:

> Every general staff officer must be a National Socialist officer-leader not only by his model attitude towards political indoctrination of younger commanders in accordance with the tenets of the Führer . . . I expect every general staff officer to declare himself immediately a convert or adherent to my views, and to make a public declaration to that effect. Anyone unable to do so should apply for transfer from the general staff.

Many of Missie Vassiltchikov's friends had been involved in the plot. One by one, they were picked up: Adam von Trott on 25 July, Peter Yorck, Moltke's closest friend, on 26 July, Gottfried von Bismarck on the 29th, and so it went on. At the time he was arrested, Bismarck actually had some of the explosive left over from making Stauffenberg's bomb hidden in the safe in his estate office at Potsdam. He managed to tell Princess Loremarie Schöneburg – Missie's best friend, who was visiting him just before the Gestapo came – and to slip her the key. She got to Potsdam very early the next morning and recovered two parcels wrapped in newspaper, each the size of a shoebox. Her problem then was how to dispose of them.

The park of Sanssouci, Frederick the Great's palace, was nearby and would, she thought, offer plenty of hiding places. So she climbed on to her bicycle and rode there, with one parcel balanced on the handlebars. On the way, she collided with a delivery boy, and fell off. The parcel crashed to the ground and Loremarie, terrified that it would explode, threw herself heroically on top of it. Since the plastic explosive had no detonator attached, it was perfectly safe, but princesses could hardly be expected to understand such matters. Still trembling, she carried it to a pond and threw it in. To her consternation it refused to sink, even though she kept pushing it to the bottom with a branch. In the end, she was forced to fish it out and bury it behind some bushes – at which point she looked up and realized that she was being observed by a man taking an early morning stroll.

Unable to face the prospect of repeating the operation, Loremarie buried the second parcel in a flowerbed back at the house. The episode may have bordered on the farcical, but it undoubtedly saved Bismarck's life: the Gestapo arrived shortly after the second parcel was buried, and took the house apart, searching for evidence. They found nothing.

HITLER HAD sworn that he would show no mercy to any of the conspirators, and those who found themselves in the Prinz–Albrecht–Strasse cellars of the Gestapo soon discovered this was no idle threat. Fabian von Schlabrendorff, who somehow survived the experience, soon realized that the object of the exercise was not primarily to extort a confession. What the Gestapo wanted was names, and they were prepared to use any means to extract them. Spikes were driven into Schlabrendorff's fingertips. His legs were encased in metal tubes lined with yet more spikes, which could be screwed slowly into the flesh. Meanwhile, his head was covered by a sort of metal helmet covered with a blanket to muffle his screams.

On 23 July, by pure chance, a series of diaries was discovered in the ruins of a bombed house, which incriminated Canaris and other senior officials. The former spy chief was arrested at once, and the Gestapo searchlight turned towards the Abwehr circle. For those already in prison, like Moltke, Dohnanyi and Bonhoeffer, it could only be a matter of time before proof of their involvement in the resistance movement was discovered.

AFTER THE first wild reaction, Himmler's men settled down to a deliberate and methodical investigation. Overall, the Gestapo made around 7,000 arrests over a period of several weeks. Yet few suspects attempted to flee. Danish journalist Paul von Stemann was astonished: 'Although they all knew that arrest meant torture and likely execution by hanging,' he wrote later, 'no one offered any resistance. Only a few went underground and tried to escape.' The Gestapo, he said, had no problems. 'They just sent a couple of men in a small car to someone's home or office and quietly collected their victim, who would invariably have a small bag ready with such essentials as would be useful in prison. Often, the Gestapo did not even go to this trouble, but would simply telephone the suspect and say they wished to see him next day at a given time at Gestapo headquarters . . . it was easier to gather their prey than it is for a shepherd to get his sheep into a pen. They didn't even need the help of a dog.'

There were a few exceptions, among them the family of the late Baron Kurt von Hammerstein, one-time army chief of staff and general of the infantry who remained an active anti-Nazi until his death in April 1943. His sons, Kunrat and Ludwig, both army officers, went underground, Kunrat in Cologne and Ludwig in Berlin, where he found refuge in the back room of the Kerp family's pharmacy in the working-class district of Kreuzberg. The Gestapo seem not to have thought of searching for an aristocrat in such a lowly area. The Gestapo had both brothers on its list of suspects. When they couldn't find them, they arrested their brother Franz, their two sisters and their mother, charging them with aiding and abetting.

Frau Maria von Hammerstein was a formidable lady, who had supported many fleeing Jews. Lisa Deyhle, the young woman under whose window the French gardener always sang 'Parlez-moi d'amour', lived next door to the Hammerstein's home in Dahlem. She was looking out of that same window the day two unmistakable Gestapo men came to arrest the old lady. She saw Frau von Hammerstein's Russian maid answer the doorbell, take one look at the men and start screaming. The lady of the house then appeared, but refused to allow the men into her home, making them stand outside while she went back indoors to collect her things. When she reappeared, she put down her small case, rolled up her sleeve and struck the arresting officer a resounding slap across the face for his impertinence. To Lisa Deyhle's amazement, the man made no response. He just waited impassively while the old lady picked up her bag then walked away with them with great dignity, her head held high.

The arrest of the Hammerstein family was part of Hitler's terrible revenge. Against the central conspirators, the Nazis invoked the ancient Teutonic punishment of *Sippenhaft*, 'kith and kin detention'. This meant that the whole of the Stauffenberg family – wife, children, mother, mother-in-law, brothers, sisters, and so on – was liable to imprisonment for Stauffenberg's crime. 'You only need to read the Germanic sagas,' Himmler told a meeting of Gauleiters in August. 'When a man was outlawed, it was said: this man is a traitor, his blood is bad, it contains treason, it will be exterminated.'


THE TRIAL of the first group of conspirators took place on 7 and 8 August, eighteen days after the explosion of Stauffenberg's bomb. There were eight accused: Field Marshal von Witzleben, Generals Hoepner, Stieff and von Hase, Lieutenant-Colonel Bernardis, Captain Klausing, and Lieutenants von Hagen and Count Yorck von Wartenburg (Moltke's friend Peter Yorck). The proceedings were held before the People's Court in the great hall of the Berlin Supreme Court, with Dr Roland Freisler, known as 'the hanging judge', presiding.

Goebbels had ordered that the trial was to be filmed, to be shown to the troops and the general public as an example, and the whole thing was as carefully staged as any Hollywood movie. Freisler wore a magnificent blood-red robe, and the court was hung with great swastika flags, behind which the cameras were concealed. They were started and stopped by signals from Freisler, who conducted the proceedings virtually single-handed. Once the cameras were running, he screamed and shouted at the accused, aiming to show them as little more than common criminals.

The men, however, all behaved with great composure, in spite of the fact that they were kept unshaven and had been dressed in clothes taken from concentration camp victims. Witzleben looked particularly pitiful, since his false teeth had been taken away and his unsupported trousers were far too big, so that he had to keep grabbing hold of them to stop them falling down. As he did so, Freisler screamed at him: 'You dirty old man! Why do you keep fiddling with your trousers?'

Peter Yorck dared to argue at length with Freisler, showing his utter contempt for National Socialism, and insisting on speaking of a man's moral and religious obligations. But the displays of courage counted for little in the end. There was no groundswell of public opinion in the conspirators' favour – they were generally perceived as a small, aristocratic clique, out of touch with ordinary people.

ALL THE defendants in the first trial were condemned to death by hanging – as traitors they were denied the 'honour' of being beheaded. They died that same day, 8 August, at Plötzensee prison in the north-west of Berlin.

The execution chamber was a shabby, red-brick, single-storey building, about the size of a large two-car garage, some twenty-five feet deep and fourteen feet wide. It was divided in half by a black curtain, behind which stood the guillotine that was used for regular executions. The only light in this half of the room filtered through two small windows.

Since hanging was not the normal method used in Germany, the prison had no scaffold. Instead, eight large meat hooks had been fixed at intervals along a roof beam. The nooses used were shaped like a figure eight, with two loops, one for the victim's neck, the other to go over the hook. They were mostly made of hemp rope, but in some later cases piano wire was used. With no drop, the condemned men would not be killed instantaneously by having their necks broken, but more slowly, by strangulation. It could take several minutes for a man to die in agony.

As the half-naked men were led into the room, Dr Kurt Hanssen, the public prosecutor, read out the death sentence to each in turn: 'Accused, the People's Court has sentenced you to death by hanging. Hangman, do your duty.' The executioners then led the man through the curtains, to the far end of the room. There, they placed the noose around his neck, then lifted him bodily, threw the upper noose of the hemp rope on to the hook, and let him fall. After each execution, a smaller black curtain was drawn across to conceal the hanging body. These side curtains, however, ended clear of the floor at about knee height, so although the next victim could not see the man who had gone before, he could see his feet twitching and jerking in the agonies of death.

Unable – or unwilling – to watch the executions in person, Hitler instructed that they should be filmed so that he could watch the men's death agonies at his leisure. He had ordered: 'They must all be hanged like cattle.'

But after recording the first two executions, the two cameramen assigned to the task could not face any more, and refused to continue.

The executioners at Plötzensee were kept busy until the very last days of the war. Even as the Allied armies closed in on Berlin, there was no let-up in the hangings, as the death roll mounted to close on 5,000 souls.

# 9

W HEN HE heard of the failed *putsch*, Dietrich Bonhoeffer knew he was doomed. The case against him was closely linked with that of his brother-in-law, Hans von Dohnanyi, who had been one of the leaders of the conspiracy. So far, they had managed to play complex legal games to keep themselves out of the clutches of the Gestapo, but there could be little chance of continuing that now. Sure enough, Dohnanyi's case was taken over by the Gestapo the day after the coup. He was safe for the moment, since he was in an isolation ward of the prison hospital for contagious diseases at Potsdam, suffering from scarlet fever and diphtherial paralysis, but this could only be a matter of delaying the inevitable.

Being thrown into the hands of the Gestapo was a particularly bitter blow to the two brothers-in-law, for Dohnanyi had learned only a few days before that there was every chance of the case against him being suspended, and of his being safely interned in a sanatorium until the end of the war. Even if this failed, there was still a chance of avoiding the gallows: their fellow member of the Abwehr circle, Josef Müller from Munich, had actually been tried and, to everyone's astonishment, acquitted. He had been arrested again immediately, it was true, but had escaped execution. Now, any such hopes had been removed.

On 22 August, Dohnanyi was moved from Potsdam to the hospital wing of Sachsenhausen, the Berlin concentration camp. There, on 5 October, SS interrogator Walter Huppenkothen walked into his room and threw a sheaf of documents on to the bed. 'There!' he told him triumphantly. 'At last we've got the evidence against you that we've been looking for for two years.'

The documents had been found at the Abwehr offices in Zossen during a raid by the Gestapo on 20 September. They came from a safe in Canaris's office used by Oster and Dohnanyi for their secret files. They included plans for a coup made by Dohnanyi as far back as 1938 and 1939, a call to the German people written for General Beck, and other incriminating papers. Among these were notes concerning Bonhoeffer's foreign visits. Added to his family connections with Dohnanyi, these suddenly made Dietrich Bonhoeffer a prime candidate for execution – unless of course he could escape from Tegel prison, before he was moved to the fastness of the Gestapo dungeons in Prinz–Albrecht–Strasse.

During his time in Tegel, Bonhoeffer had made friends with many of the guards. They all treated him with respect, none more so than Corporal Knobloch, who had passed messages to and from the family and other prisoners. When he was approached by Bonhoeffer's sister Ursula, her husband Rüdiger Schleicher, and their daughter Renate, now married to Bonhoeffer's friend and disciple Eberhard Bethge, he agreed to help. Their plan was bold: armed with a forged pass, Bonhoeffer would don a mechanic's overalls and simply walk out of the prison gates, accompanied by Knobloch in his guard's uniform. They would then disappear together until the war was over.

On Sunday, 24 September, Rüdiger and Ursula Schleicher drove over to Knobloch's home and handed him a parcel containing the overalls and other clothes, together with money and food coupons. These were to be left in a summer-house on a *Schrebergarten*, where the two men could hide until they could be got out of the country. Through their resistance contacts, the family were arranging for false passports and papers, and the chaplain at the Swedish embassy – Maria von Maltzan's friend who had helped so many Jews and other fugitives to escape – was organizing passages to Sweden. Everything was set for the escape attempt to take place in early October.

Then came the bombshell. When Knobloch arrived at the Schleichers' house the next Saturday to discuss details of the plan, he found Dietrich's elder brother Klaus. Klaus, who was also deeply involved in the resistance on his own account, was sheltering from the Gestapo, who were waiting outside his own house in Eichkamp. Knobloch hurried back to tell Bonhoeffer the news. Klaus was arrested next morning.

The arrest of another Bonhoeffer changed everything. The Gestapo had another hostage, and Dietrich knew that if he escaped now they would exact a terrible vengeance on Klaus, as well as his mother and father and probably the rest of the family. He sent Knobloch back to the house on the Monday morning, with a message that the escape was off. Two days later, the Gestapo picked up Rüdiger Schleicher, and shortly after that Eberhard Bethge. They now had five members of the Bonhoeffer family in custody. On 8 October, they moved Dietrich from Tegel prison to the cellars of Prinz–Albrecht–Strasse.

AMONG THOSE whom Bonhoeffer left behind in Tegel prison was Helmuth von Moltke. His connections with the 20 July conspiracy had been established, although having been in the special SS prison at Ravensbrück since January he could have played no part in it. Nevertheless, he had been charged with high treason, and had been moved back to Berlin, to await trial by Judge Freisler. Since there was an enormous backlog of cases, he was likely to have a long wait.

Like the good lawyer he was, Moltke settled down to preparing his defence with meticulous care. Fortunately he was sent to Tegel rather than any other Berlin prison: his good friend Harald Poelchau, himself a member of the so-called Kreisau Circle, was the prison chaplain there. Poelchau was worn down by the strain of his multifarious resistance activities and by the emotional stress of accompanying condemned prisoners – many of them his friends and acquaintances – to the scaffold every day. But he was willing to risk facing the same fate by acting as a messenger between Moltke, his wife and other prisoners, so that they could coordinate their statements and plans. Like Bonhoeffer, Moltke refused to give up hope.

IN PRINZ–Albrecht–Strasse Bonhoeffer found himself in good company: among his old friends and acquaintances were Josef Müller, Canaris, Oster, Goerdeler and Hans Böhm, a fellow pastor and ecumenical officer of the Confessing Church. Later, briefly, Dohnanyi was brought in, too. In the next cell was his fiancée Maria's cousin, Fabian von Schlabrendorff.

Bonhoeffer told Schlabrendorff he had not been tortured, although he had been threatened with it, but he had been questioned with a brutality that he described as 'disgusting'. He said his interrogators had no idea of the extent of his involvement in the Abwehr conspiracy, and that he was doing his best to play down Dohnanyi's role in it. He was determined to resist the Gestapo's efforts to prise information out of him that might endanger the lives of his friends. Somehow, he succeeded in convincing them that he was not guilty of treason, but had opposed the regime simply because he was a Christian.

Schlabrendorff, who had of course been severely tortured himself, was astonished at how Bonhoeffer still managed to be so sweet tempered with everybody. Within a short time he had even won over the SS guards. He would make modest requests of them, said Schlabrendorff, without the least embarrassment, 'or enquire at the right moment about their personal circumstances or worries. He never demanded the impossible from them, since he could see that they too were in a nervous state.'

Within a short time, Bonhoeffer realized that the Gestapo interrogators were more interested in obtaining detailed information about the connections between the various European churches than in getting a quick conviction against him. Knowing this, he believed he could play for time, feeding them slanted facts designed to confuse the issues. Eventually, he might even be able to save the situation. 'The only fight that is lost,' he said, 'is that which we give up.'

# 10

ON 25 JULY, Hitler rewarded Goebbels for his part in foiling the officers'
plot by appointing him Reich commissioner for total mobilization of
resources for war. A few weeks earlier he had bestowed a meaningless honour
on him when he made him city president of Berlin, but there was nothing
meaningless about the new appointment. Goebbels was given unbridled
power over all civilian and party authorities, and was to be answerable
directly and only to the Führer. In an unprecedented move, all complaints
against him were strictly forbidden, even if they were made to Hitler himself.

Goebbels's new task was to squeeze the last drops from Germany's
reserves to stave off the inevitable disaster. Everything the Germans needed to
continue the war was in short supply: raw materials, transport, oil, steel,
munitions, aircraft, food, and, above all, manpower. It had been bad enough
when the war had only been fought on one major front, in the east. Now, with
fresh Allied troops pouring into Normandy, and the American and British
armies poised to break out into the rest of France, the realities of a two-front
war could not be ignored. On 1 July, when Field Marshal Keitel, chief of staff
of the OKW, telephoned Field Marshal von Rundstedt, commander-in-chief
in the west, to ask 'What shall we do?', Rundstedt's answer was short and to
the point: 'Make peace, you idiots. What else can you do?'

That same day, Churchill wrote to Stalin, following the staggering
success of the first week of the main Soviet summer offensive in Belorussia:
'This is the moment for me to tell you how immensely we are all here
impressed with the magnificent advances of the Russian armies, which seem,
as they grow in momentum, to be pulverizing the German armies which stand
between you and Warsaw, and afterwards Berlin.' At last, Berlin had been
named as the ultimate objective that would mark the end of the war in Europe.

THROUGHOUT July and August the invaders charged towards Germany from
east, west and south. In the east, the Red Army scored a series of spectacular
victories on all fronts from the Baltic to the Black Sea – unlike the Germans or
the Western Allies, the Soviets did not organize their major formations into
army groups but into 'fronts'. The four northern fronts drove into the Baltic
States, trapping fifty German divisions in the process. In Belorussia, the
newly promoted Marshal Konstantin K. Rokossovsky's First Belorussian

Front destroyed German Army Group Centre, advancing 400 miles in six weeks before halting only ten miles from Warsaw on 31 July. Next day the underground warriors of the Polish Home Army launched their own offensive, the Warsaw Uprising, against the Germans inside the city.

On Rokossovsky's left flank, Marshal Koniev's First Ukrainian Front, the most powerful in the Red Army, had taken Lvov with a massive two-pronged attack, despite fierce resistance from the German forces, and was rolling on towards the Vistula. To the north of Rokossovky, the Second and Third Belorussian Fronts ground their way through northern Poland and Lithuania.

Shortly before dawn on 17 August, Sergeant Victor Mikhailovich Zakabluk led his section of infantrymen crawling through a clover field to the banks of the River Sheshupe, the border of East Prussia. At 5 am he stood up and shouted 'Charge!' His men scrambled to their feet, raised a ragged cheer and splashed across the river. The first man on the other side, Private Alexander Afanasevich Tretyak, planted the section's red battle flag alongside frontier marker number 56. Soviet soldiers were on German soil at last.

Away to the south, three days later, Soviet forces crossed into Romania and captured the Ploesti oilfields, Germany's last source of natural oil. The Romanians swiftly changed sides, declaring war on Germany on 25 August. The next day, as Hitler ordered the withdrawal of all German troops from Greece, Bulgaria deserted the Nazi fold. On 29 August, there was an armed uprising in Slovakia. A few days later, Finland, too, jumped ship, accepting Soviet armistice terms and turning on the German troops still in the country.

In Italy, meanwhile, the British Eighth Army entered Florence, and the Allies continued to fight their way north, against fierce opposition. In France, the fighting in Normandy had been savage ever since the landing. In mid-July the commander of the German LXXXIVth Corps, General Dietrich von Choltitz, reported: 'The whole battle is one tremendous bloodbath such as I have never seen in eleven years of war.' But on 30 July the tanks of the newly formed US Third Army, under the inspired leadership of General George S. Patton, finally broke out and roared towards Le Mans and Orleans, then turned east towards the Seine. By the time they had reached the river on either side of Paris, there had been a second Allied landing in the south of France, between Cannes and Toulon, and American and Free French forces were advancing fast up the Rhône valley.

On 25 August, General Jacques Leclerc's French 2nd Armoured Division, followed by units of the US 4th Infantry Division, rolled into Paris to be greeted by the men and women of the Resistance, who had risen against the remaining German troops to liberate their city after four years of enemy occupation.

*

HITLER REFUSED to allow his generals to withdraw their battered forces from France, insisting that they fight on. Still deeply distrustful of the officer corps, he prepared a detailed plan himself, though he was 1,000 miles away from the front lines and had little idea of what was really going on. The result was to turn defeat into disaster. Within days the entire German force in France, hopelessly short of fuel and ammunition, was routed, forced to retreat ignominiously into Germany as fast as it could go.

The Allied armies pursued the fleeing Germans at full speed. The Canadian First and British Second Armies under Montgomery covered 200 miles in four days, leaping from the lower Seine right into Belgium. They liberated Brussels on 3 September, the fifth anniversary of Britain's entry into the war, and Antwerp the following day. To their south, the US First Army, under General Courtney H. Hodges, moved equally fast to reach south-eastern Belgium and capture the fortresses of Namur and Liège. Patton's Third Army, meanwhile, was powering its way east to reach the Moselle river and link up with General Alexander Patch's French-American Seventh Army, which had fought its way north from the Riviera.

ONLY WHEN they reached the German frontier were the Western Allies forced to halt their furious progress as they ran out of steam – or rather, out of fuel and ammunition as their lines of supply became overstretched. At 6.05 pm on 11 September, the 85th Reconnaissance Squadron of the US 5th Armored Division, an advance unit of the First Army, crossed the frontier into Germany, near Stalzenburg. But that was as far as anyone went for the time being.

The respite was badly needed and vitally urgent for the Germans: they had to start from scratch, hurriedly preparing the defence of the Fatherland. Since 1940, Hitler had always refused even to consider such a possibility. So there was no master plan, and the fortifications of the Siegfried Line, the West Wall, were unmanned and had largely been stripped of their guns. Now, they had to be re-equipped and reorganized. It seemed an impossible task. Already, the British and Americans were little more than 400 miles from Berlin, and in the east the situation was even worse: the Red Army was barely 300 miles from the German capital, having advanced some 400 miles in six weeks. The Berliners were beginning to wonder anxiously who would get there first.

The Allies were wondering, too. And in the process they were beginning to fall out among themselves. Jealousies and rivalries among Eisenhower's generals, both national and personal, were beginning to affect the conduct of the war in the west. Stalin faced a similar problem with his three leading marshals, Zhukov, Koniev and Rokossovsky, but he put the rivalry to good use. Eisenhower, unlike Stalin, was the most reasonable of men, and in trying to keep all the competing parties happy was prone to compromise.

*

SUCCESSFUL GENERALS must by nature be strong personalities, and there were few stronger than Eisenhower's three leading generals at that time: Montgomery, Patton and Bradley. Each of them believed that he knew best how to win the war, and that he should receive priority over everyone else for supplies and support to enable him to win it. The two Americans, Bradley, and even more so Patton, possessed well-developed egos and were capable of being bloody-minded, but for sheer egotism and opinionated arrogance, Sir Bernard Law Montgomery was in a class of his own. His belief that he always knew better than Eisenhower, that he was the better battlefield commander and planner, meant that he constantly teetered on the brink of insubordination.

Already the darling of the British people as the hero of El Alamein and Tunisia, Montgomery had scored another personal triumph as commander-in-chief of all land forces during the Normandy campaign, which did nothing to reduce his inflated self-esteem. He had been forced to hand over to Eisenhower on 1 September, and to accept relegation to army group command, on an equal footing with Bradley. With the United States now providing the larger share of both men and equipment, it was no longer acceptable in Washington or in France for them to be commanded by an Englishman. Montgomery's pill was sugared to some extent by promotion to the rank of Field Marshal. Nevertheless, he was firmly convinced that he could end the war within weeks if Eisenhower would give him complete control.

Montgomery's eyes were fixed firmly on Berlin. 'I consider we have now reached a stage where one really powerful and full-blooded thrust towards Berlin is likely to get there and thus end the German war,' he wrote to Eisenhower on 4 September. To achieve this, he demanded that he be given all available resources, leaving Bradley's American army group to 'do the best it can with what is left over'. There were, he said, two possible routes: one in the north through the Ruhr, the other through Metz and the Saar. He considered the northern one, involving his army group, would give 'the best and quickest results', and that time was vital. 'If we attempt a compromise solution,' he added, 'and split our maintenance resources so that neither thrust is full-blooded we will prolong the war.'

Eisenhower did not agree. He replied next day, 5 September, but communications between his headquarters at Granville and the front-line commanders 400 miles away were so bad that the second half of his message did not reach Montgomery until 9 am on 7 September, while the first half did not arrive until two days after that. Between receiving the two half-messages, Montgomery continued to press for every scrap of fuel and transport that came ashore in Normandy, arguing that this would be enough for his forty divisions to deliver a single knock-out blow to Berlin. But when he finally saw the opening paragraphs of Eisenhower's reply, his worst fears were confirmed. 'While agreeing with your conception of a powerful and full-blooded thrust to Berlin,' Eisenhower wrote, 'I do not agree that it should be initiated at this moment to the exclusion of all other maneuvers.'

Eisenhower, pressed by political, national and logistic considerations, had chosen to compromise. He had decided to attack on a broad front, splitting available resources between Montgomery's and Bradley's army groups. Plagued by the problems of supplying all his forces through makeshift port facilities in Normandy and Brittany, he believed with good reason that any idea of a thrust to Berlin before the ports of Antwerp and Le Havre were in use was 'fantastic'. He was supported in this belief by virtually all his senior staff officers at Supreme Headquarters, both American and British. Montgomery had already taken the city of Antwerp, but the port approaches along the Scheldt estuary remained in German hands. Now, Eisenhower ordered him to concentrate on freeing those before advancing any further to the east.

Montgomery was furious. He continued to argue, signalling to Eisenhower on 9 September: 'Providing we can have the ports of Dieppe, Boulogne, Dunkirk and Calais, and in addition 3,000 tons per day through Le Havre WE CAN ADVANCE TO BERLIN.' He persuaded Eisenhower to fly to Brussels to confer with him on 10 September; they had not met for fifteen days and communications, as had been proved by the delays to Eisenhower's signal of the 7th, were very bad. They talked in Eisenhower's aeroplane – he had damaged his knee the previous day while helping to push the plane to safety after it had been forced to land on a beach in a high wind, and he found it difficult to climb out.

Insisting that everyone except Air Chief Marshal Sir Arthur Tedder, the deputy supreme commander, should leave the aircraft cabin, Montgomery prepared for a face-to-face confrontation. He pulled Eisenhower's signal from his pocket, then launched into a great tirade, lecturing the supreme commander as though he were an errant staff college pupil. Eisenhower waited until Montgomery paused for breath, then leaned forward and put his hand on the other man's knee. 'Steady Monty,' he said, quietly. 'You cannot talk to me like this. I am your boss.' Montgomery calmed down. 'I'm sorry, Ike,' he muttered, suddenly humble.

The two commanders went on to discuss Montgomery's bold plan for an airborne operation to establish a bridgehead over the Rhine at Arnhem later that month, which Eisenhower supported wholeheartedly. Once that had been accomplished, Montgomery would be able to bypass the Siegfried Line and cut off the Ruhr, ready for an advance into northern Germany. But the idea of a lightning move to land the killer left hook on Berlin was dead. 'The advance to Berlin was not discussed as a serious issue,' Tedder reported.

Five days later, Eisenhower could still write to the field marshal: 'Clearly, Berlin is the main prize, and the prize in defense of which the enemy is likely to concentrate the bulk of his forces. There is no doubt whatsoever, in my mind, that we should concentrate all our energies on a rapid thrust to

Berlin.' The thrust itself, however, would not be concentrated, as Montgomery demanded, but spread across the whole front. 'Simply stated,' Eisenhower continued, 'it is my desire to move on Berlin by the most direct and expeditious route, with combined US–British forces supported by other available forces moving through key centers and occupying strategic areas on the flanks, all in one coordinated, concerted operation.'

Eisenhower was still not prepared to give a date for the start of his broad-based thrust to Berlin. For several more days, while the Arnhem operation, which had been seriously flawed from its conception, turned into a major disaster, Montgomery went on trying to convince Eisenhower that time was vital. But Eisenhower refused to be budged, and it was soon clear that it was too late, as the Germans miraculously managed to rush reconstituted armies into strong defensive positions.

Most German generals later agreed with Montgomery that the opportunity of ending the war that year had been thrown away. Rundstedt's chief of staff, General Günther Blumentritt, admitted after the war that there had been no German forces behind the Rhine at the end of August, and that the front had been 'wide open'. 'Strategically and politically,' he said, 'Berlin was the target. Germany's strength is in the north. He who holds northern Germany holds Germany. Such a breakthrough, coupled with air domination, would have torn the weak German front to pieces and ended the war. Berlin and Prague would have been occupied ahead of the Russians.'

# 11

IN THE three months following the D-Day landings, the German armies lost some 1.2 million men, dead, wounded or missing, on all fronts. Fifty divisions were completely destroyed in the east, and another twenty-eight in the west, where the Wehrmacht lost virtually all its guns, tanks and trucks. All Hitler's European allies deserted him – it was now Germany that stood alone. The losses were by no means confined to one side; the Germans fought hard and inflicted serious casualties on their enemies. But the Allies were able to replace both men and materiel from seemingly limitless resources, and their strength was still growing: the Western Allies already had well over 2 million men ashore by September and were landing more every day, while the Soviets were now fielding no fewer than 555 divisions. Germany, on the other hand, was reduced to scraping every barrel.

This was the reason for the 'total mobilization' measures, and for

Goebbels's new role. The new Reich commissioner promised Hitler he would raise a new army of a million men, and turn the entire resources of German industry over to producing the arms and equipment they needed to drive back their enemies.

Goebbels had first declared the doctrine of total war in his speech to the party faithful at the Berlin Sportpalast in Feburary 1943, but he had been denied the authority then to put his demands into effect. 'If I had received these powers when I wanted them so badly,' he told his assistant during the journey from Rastenburg back to Berlin on 25 July 1944, 'victory would be in our pockets today and the war would probably be over. But it takes a bomb under his arse to make Hitler see reason.'

Like Hitler, Goebbels placed his trust in miracles. Hitler persuaded himself that if Germany could only keep fighting, the Allies would eventually grow tired and fall out among themselves. 'Come what may,' he told his generals on 31 August, 'we will continue this battle until, as Frederick the Great said, one of our damned enemies gets too tired to fight any more. . . . The time will come when the tension between the Allies becomes so great that they break up. All the coalitions in history have disintegrated sooner or later. You just have to wait for the right moment, no matter how hard it is.'

Goebbels took a more positive line, telling the German people in a radio speech: 'We are actually in a position to turn the fortunes of war in our favour in the immediate future. All that is needed to bring this about is there for the taking. Let's take it! Never again will the Almighty reveal his presence to us as clearly as when he worked a miracle on behalf of the Führer, saving his life.'

Goebbels immediately ordered the call-up for full military service of boys aged betweeen sixteen and eighteen, and men between fifty and sixty. He scoured schools, colleges, offices and factories for recruits, conscripting thousands of men who had previously been in reserved jobs. Starting with his own Propaganda Ministry, he demanded a 30 per cent reduction in government staffing levels. This drive produced half a million men, enabling Himmler, as chief of the Reserve Army, to create twenty-five new *Volks-grenadier* divisions. Although many regular army divisions had been reduced to little more than battalion strength, Hitler decided they should not be restored. He believed that troops who had suffered severe defeats no longer had the morale to fight effectively, and such divisions should be left to 'bleed to death', while still existing on paper as full divisions in the German order of battle, creating an illusion of greater strength.

For those already in the armed forces, all leave was cancelled, and men previously considered unfit for active service were routed out of administrative posts and sent to the front. Goebbels had whole battalions formed of men suffering from stomach troubles, ear problems, rheumatism, and gall and kidney stones. He proudly informed his Gauleiters that he had sent 79,874 such men to the front from Military District VIII alone. 'The physician in charge of this military district reckons that in the Reich as a whole one could recruit enough men suffering from these ailments to form one hundred such special battalions,' he told them, 'all in all around two million men fit to be dispatched to the front. We are taking the view that, for instance, a chronic stomach ailment cannot be regarded as a life insurance, and that it could hardly be the aim of this war to send the fit to die while the ailing are preserved.'

To drive home the reality of his total mobilization, Goebbels shut down all theatres, concert halls, acting schools and *conservatoires*. Public transport services were cut drastically, and film production and broadcasting – two activities that he had always maintained as essential morale boosters – were considerably reduced. The nature of the films that were still being made was changed, too – gone were the supposedly realistic war dramas, to be replaced by frothy light comedies designed to raise audiences' spirits.

AT EXACTLY the right psychological moment, Goebbels's campaign to rally the German people was given a great boost from a most unexpected source: the secretary of the United States Treasury, Henry Morgenthau. For some time, politicians and planners in London and Washington had been trying to decide what should be done with a defeated Germany after the war. During the summer of 1944, Morgenthau and the Treasury had drawn up a plan to dismember Germany and destroy all her remaining heavy industry, transferring huge tracts of territory to Poland, the Soviet Union, France and Denmark and turning what remained into a pastoral economy just capable of maintaining its population at subsistence levels.

Roosevelt at first strongly supported Morgenthau's proposals, which were tabled at the Quebec conference between himself and Churchill on 13 September. In fact, wiser counsel soon prevailed – Churchill, for one, was furiously opposed – and the plan died. But Goebbels got wind of it and rushed to broadcast it to the nation as a dire warning of what they could expect if they lost. To a propagandist of his genius, it was a gift of purest gold.

The realization that their backs were truly against the wall stiffened the resistance of ordinary citizens, and their general morale rose as Goebbels's measures brought a new sense of determination. For the Berliners, even the constant air raids by the British and Americans became a matter of routine, with each cellar community creating its own rituals for survival. Faced with a common enemy, the citizens were more united than ever before.

# 12

ALBERT SPEER was furious at losing so many skilled men from his workforce in the armaments industry, but since he was not allowed to complain to Hitler about Goebbels, there was little he could do about it. In fact, the new Reich commissioner went on to deprive him of responsibility for arms production, handing control to the Gauleiters in whose territories the factories were situated. To make up for the shortage, Goebbels ordered the standard working week to be increased to 60 hours. It made little difference, of course, to the foreign workers, who were already working a basic 72-hour week.

Hitler had always resisted the idea of allowing German women to work in factories – under the Nazi ethic their place was in the home. But he had been persuaded to relax his restrictions, and now Goebbels took advantage of the situation to raise the upper age limit for women drafted into war work from forty-five to fifty. He also ordered that school holidays be extended 'indefinitely', so that twelve- to fourteen-year-old children could work in light industry, releasing women and the few remaining men for the heavier work.

To help make up the numbers, thousands of Polish women were brought in from Warsaw, where they had been rounded up from streets and homes. The Polish women were handed over to 'skilled' workers like Irma Diehn to be trained to use their machines. 'They must have thought I was enormously qualified,' Irma recalls. 'But in reality, I had only six days of training myself!'

FOR MOST of the foreign workers who now made up such a large proportion of the city's population, only the prospect of the end of the war made the misery bearable. They were more exposed to the bombing than the Germans, since their shelters were few and inadequate. 'In the Russians' camp we are in danger of being bombed,' fourteen-year-old Eliza Stokowska wrote in her diary on 5 October, 'because it is situated close to the railway station. Living conditions are bad: there are masses of bugs, rooms are damp, there are no stoves, no light, and getting up at four in the morning is terrible. Now we get our food from the Ukrainian kitchen, which means that every second day we get Swedish turnips, dry bread or even less sometimes. Today we had an air alert and even an air raid. In one word: conditions are so bad that I don't want to live any more. Everybody comforts us by saying it will only last another two weeks. And after those two weeks, will we then be in for it?'

SOMEHOW, EVEN with such unskilled and unwilling labour, in spite of all the bombing, and the shortages of raw materials and fuel, arms production actually rose to record levels during the last quarter of 1944: 3,031 fighter planes were built in September, for instance, as against 1,248 the previous January, including about 100 of the new Messerschmitt 262 and Arado 234 twin-jet fighters. Production of guns showed a similar sharp leap. Only tanks were down in number – the Alkett factories in Berlin had been especially targeted by the bombers. It was a remarkable success for Goebbels's total mobilization – but it was also the last gasp of a dying man, drawing on his final reserves of strength and energy.

# 13

THE SUPERHUMAN efforts of the German people and their slaves paid off with what seemed like a miraculous recovery on both fronts. At the end of August, the entire German army in the west had been on the run, disorganized and demoralized. So many men were simply giving up the fight that Himmler had announced on 12 September that the families of deserters would be summarily shot – though there are no recorded cases of this threat being carried out. By the end of September, it had re-formed into a solid front west of the Rhine, which the Allies were unable to break or turn. There had been a notable victory over the British at Arnhem; and the Fifteenth Army was successfully holding on to the Scheldt estuary, blocking access to Antwerp for shipping and denying the Allies the port facilities they needed so badly. As winter approached, the army had won a breathing space for Germany, and was regaining strength at a remarkable rate. As the build-up reached its peak, SHAEF (Supreme Headquarters Allied Expeditionary Force) Intelligence identified 74 divisions or their equivalent, which they reckoned was equal to 39 normal divisions. There was no longer any chance of Montgomery or anyone else from the west reaching Berlin in 1944.

IN THE east, the Soviet advance was also halted. Rokossovsky's First Belorussian Front remained bogged down on the Vistula, ten miles away from

Warsaw. It was both unable and unwilling to move in to help as the underground Polish Home Army led by Tadeusz Komorowski, who used the *nom de guerre* General Bór, fought its hopeless battle against the German occupiers.

Bór-Komorowski had deliberately triggered the rising in advance of the Soviet arrival, fearing the consequences for Poland if the Soviets liberated the capital. The Soviet-controlled Polish radio station, Radio Koscuszko, had encouraged his call to arms. Stalin, however, had no interest in helping Bór-Komorowski and his people, whom he regarded as the army of the anti-communist Polish government-in-exile in London. If the city was to be liberated, then it would be by the Red Army. Ignoring all their pleas for aid, he sat back and waited as the Home Army was annihilated by the Germans.

There were good military reasons to back up Stalin's political inaction. Rokossovsky had already lost 123,000 men in the approach to Warsaw, and rightly feared a German counter-attack from the south on his exhausted troops. He knew that two crack SS divisions, the Viking and the Totenkopf, plus the Hermann Göring Division and the 19th Panzer Division, were being rushed to the defence of the city. Moreover, he was acutely aware of the difficulty of trying to take a large city whose defenders were prepared to contest every street, every building.

Warsaw had held out against the Germans in 1939, forcing Hitler to subject it to a non-stop aerial and artillery bombardment which had killed somewhere between 15,000 and 60,000 civilians before it surrendered. And closer to home there was the memory of Stalingrad, which had swallowed a whole German army as though it were a black hole. With Stalin breathing down his neck, Rokossovsky had no intention of being forced into the position of Field Marshal von Paulus at Stalingrad. The Warsaw Uprising, which had begun with such hope on 1 August, collapsed on 2 October, when Bór-Komorowski finally surrendered to the Germans after two months of slaughter.

Still the Soviet armies were unable to move. The Forty-Seventh Army, which had been in the van of the great drive to the Vistula, had suffered heavy casualties, and the Seventieth Army had also been badly mauled. And to make matters worse, the supply lines, already in the grip of the beginning of the Russian winter, were stretched to breaking point. Stalin sent his deputy supreme commander, Georgi Zhukov, to evaluate the position. He and Rokossovsky conferred and agreed that the First Belorussian Front was exhausted. It needed time to reorganize and regroup, and to bring up fresh reinforcements. Zhukov called Stalin to explain the situation. Ominously, the dictator ordered both marshals to return to Moscow for what he called 'face-to-face discussions'.

In Stalin's second-floor office in the Kremlin, watched by Molotov and General Antonov, who was both chief of operations and first deputy chief of the general staff, Zhukov spread out his maps on the long, green-baize-covered table in front of Stalin's desk. As Zhukov began his explanation, Stalin grew visibly restless. He paced the room, as was his habit, wreathed in the aromatic blue smoke of the shredded Herzegovina Flor cigarettes he burned in his English Dunhill pipe. He moved in to look at the map, then went back to his pacing, from time to time approaching the table again and eyeing Zhukov and Rokossovsky in turn. When he laid aside his pipe, Zhukov recognized it as a sure sign that he was losing his composure, and was displeased.

The atmosphere became tense. Molotov protested that it was idiotic to relax the pressure on the Germans then. Surely, he declared, the enemy was defeated. Zhukov countered by insisting that the Red Army was suffering 'unjustifiably heavy losses'. If they did not regroup, the situation on the Vistula could only get worse.

Stalin turned to Rokossovsky. 'Do you share Zhukov's opinion?' he demanded. Rokossovsky replied that he did. Annoyed, Stalin banished them to the ante-room, 'to think some more'. Obediently, they retired to study their maps. After twenty minutes, they were called back to face him again.

'We have considered it all,' Stalin announced, 'and have decided to agree to our forces passing over to the defensive.'

# 14

FOR THE time being, Germany had been given a reprieve. With winter approaching, Berlin would probably have several weeks, maybe even months, to prepare itself for any assault. But everyone knew that the respite could only be temporary – even Hitler was beginning to acknowledge that Germany's plight was desperate. At the beginning of September he issued orders for a scorched earth policy in the Reich itself. No German, he decreed, should live in territory conquered by the enemy, and anyone who chose to do so would find himself in a desert. Everything was to go: all industrial plants and public utilities were to be destroyed, along with civil records, food supplies, and all buildings. 'Not a stalk of German wheat is to feed the enemy,' the *Völkischer Beobachter* trumpeted on 7 September. 'Not a German mouth to give him information, not a German hand to offer him help. He is to find every footbridge destroyed, every road blocked. Nothing but death, annihilation and hatred will confront him.'

The whole of Germany was now under siege. In early October Goebbels announced that food rations were to be cut again. Youngsters throughout the country were ordered to start digging trenches. And on 18 October, Himmler set up the Volkssturm ('People's Storm'), the equivalent of the British Home Guard. Every remaining male between the ages of sixteen and sixty was to be drafted into service to defend the Fatherland in the final emergency.

The Volkssturm came under the direction not of the army but of the party, and local Gauleiters were responsible for raising, arming and equipping the units in their districts. This meant that Goebbels was in charge of the Berlin Volkssturm. He called its members to take their oath at a parade in the Wilhelmplatz, in front of the Propaganda Ministry, on 12 November. By an ironic coincidence it was the day after the British Home Guard had held its farewell parades as it was disbanded.

There were no uniforms for the Volkssturm – a matter of great regret to many men in a society that traditionally honoured the uniform above almost everything. The only standard issue was an armband. Individual units did what they could to improvise some form of common outfit from what was available, including in some cases captured British battledress. Most men at the oath-taking ceremony had managed to get hold of steel helmets.

Far more serious was the lack of weapons. There were two levies of Volkssturm, the first supposedly armed and the second intended as a replacement. But there were virtually no weapons even for the first echelon. In one battalion, the first company was given only two rifles, the second company several Italian rifles but only a few rounds of ammunition, and the third some machine guns, an old anti-tank gun, and a few Italian rifles. There was a reasonable supply of hand grenades and the new hand-held Panzerfaust anti-tank rocket, a crude but highly effective weapon that actually performed better than the American bazooka on which it was based.

The men were supposed to be trained at weekends and in the evenings, when their regular jobs permitted, but since most of them were working long hours, they did not get much chance to attend. When the crunch finally came, none had been trained to anywhere near the combat level needed to face tough, battle-hardened troops. There was, in any case, precious little enthusiasm for joining the ranks. Ruth Andreas-Friedrich's doctor friend, Walter Seitz, was 'writing his fingers to the bone' providing faked medical evidence for men to obtain exemption. He had been underground since the beginning of December, when he had walked out of his post at the Charité hospital, after refusing to certify sick men fit for duty on the eastern front.

AWAY IN his East Prussian field headquarters, Hitler continued to rant and rave at any suggestion of retreat. But in the garden of the chancellery back in Berlin, the frenzied activity of a construction company called Hochtief betrayed his realization of the true position. Hochtief (literally 'high-deep') specialized in building underground bunkers. They had been responsible, early in the war, for converting the cellar of the new chancellery into a bombproof shelter or bunker. In 1943, as both the raids and the bombs became heavier and more destructive, they were called back to reinforce it. In 1944 they were called back again, this time to build a new, deeper bunker below the existing one, with walls at least six feet thick, and a solid roof of more than sixteen feet of reinforced concrete, further protected by tons of earth piled on top. Throughout the autumn of 1944 they worked furiously, endlessly pouring concrete, sinking an artesian well, racing against the clock to complete the installation of the basic services needed to make it habitable, and to allow it to function as the Führer's last headquarters.

# 15

At the beginning of November 1944 the Soviet general staff completed its outline plan for the greatest campaign in military history, bigger even than Barbarossa: the invasion of Hitler's Reich. They estimated it would take the Red Army up to forty-five days to finish the job. The start date was set for between 15 and 20 January 1945.

Though the offensive as a whole covered the entire eastern front from the Barents to the Black Sea, with Soviet troops fighting in no fewer than eight foreign countries, the principal objective was to penetrate to the 'lair of the Fascist beast', Berlin itself. It was an aim that was shared by all, from the highest marshal of the Soviet Union to the humblest private. 'I am on my way to Berlin,' a Soviet soldier wrote. 'Berlin is precisely the place we *must* reach . . . we deserve the right to enter Berlin.'

No one pretended it would be easy, even though Stalin was committing no fewer than three complete fronts to Operation Berlin: the Germans would obviously concentrate their stiffest resistance in this central sector. The Soviets could draw off some of the remaining German strength by starting with powerful attacks on either flank, into East Prussia and the Baltic States in the north, and against Hungary and Austria in the south, to prevent them reinforcing the centre. But the fiercest and most decisive battles would undoubtedly be fought on the axis between Warsaw and Berlin.

To Stalin, the thrust for Berlin was so important that he refused to entrust its overall direction to anyone but himself. Bypassing both his personal supreme command staff, the Stavka, and the army general staff, he decided to act personally as coordinator of the three fronts directly involved – First and Second Belorussian and First Ukrainian – and a fourth, the Third Belorussian, which would play a vital role on the operation's northern flank. The commander on the ground, in charge of all the troops assigned to capture Berlin, would be his deputy, Marshal Zhukov, who would also take over direct command of the First Belorussian Front, the spearhead of the assault.

GEORGI KONSTANTINOVICH Zhukov was Stalin's favourite general – and also the stuff of which his nightmares were composed. As a military hero, Zhukov became for his countrymen the kind of popular icon that Stalin always feared, carrying with him the menace of Bonapartism. But he was a brilliant and utterly ruthless strategist who never lost a battle, and Stalin knew he could always rely on him to deliver the goods.

Short and stocky, with close-cropped hair, Zhukov had one of those Russian faces that look as if they have been modelled out of dough. He was born on 2 December 1896 – 19 November by the old calendar then in use – in the village of Strelkova, south-west of Moscow, in a cabin covered with moss and grass. His father was a poor shoemaker; his mother worked in the fields. At the age of eleven he was apprenticed to his uncle, a furrier in Moscow, but his training was hardly complete when, in 1915, he was conscripted into the Tsar's army. He proved to be a natural soldier, and rose to the rank of sergeant, seeing action in the Ukraine with the famous 10th Cavalry Division. Badly wounded by a mine which threw him from his horse, he recovered to fight again and be twice decorated with the Cross of St George for bravery.

In 1918, as civil war engulfed Russia following the October Revolution, Zhukov joined the Red Army, where he quickly came to the attention of Stalin, who was then a member of the Revolutionary Council. Stalin appreciated the young furrier's instinctive grasp of military strategy, and took a permanent interest in his career. When two special regiments were formed in the Twenties and Thirties to experiment with the new high-speed tanks, testing the latest German theories about Blitzkrieg and tank warfare, Zhukov was appointed to command one of them.

As a general, Zhukov demanded absolute obedience from his men, particularly his senior officers. They did what they were told, or they were shot. To a large extent, of course, this was only echoing his own relationship with Stalin. Stalin demanded victory at any price, and human lives were the cheapest commodity in the Soviet army: as a military commander during the civil war, Stalin had thought nothing of sacrificing an entire division of 60,000 men, shocking even Lenin. Zhukov now followed a similar course for much of the time, regularly using penal battalions to clear minefields by marching straight through them, for example, and dropping paratroops behind enemy lines to fight to the death with no provision for relief or withdrawal. Sometimes, when parachutes were in short supply, men were dropped into the snow from low-flying planes without them, on the principle that enough would survive to make a fight of it.

In 1939 he had put into practice all his theories of armoured warfare to inflict on the Japanese in Mongolia the worst defeat the Imperial Army had ever suffered; it left them with no appetite for further incursions into the Soviet Far East, and kept them out of the war with the Soviet Union until the final days in 1945. In 1941 he had halted the Germans in front of Moscow; in 1942–3 he had defeated them at Stalingrad. In 1943, alongside Marshal Vasilevsky, chief of the general staff, he had been coordinator responsible for the decisive battle of Kursk.

Since August 1942 he had been deputy supreme commander of all Soviet forces, under Stalin, directing and orchestrating the great revival. Now he had been presented with the ultimate accolade for any Soviet general: the opportunity to conquer the Nazi capital and inflict the final defeat on Hitler, not from behind a desk in the Kremlin, but leading the Soviet armies in the field.

MARSHAL KONSTANTIN K. Rokossovsky, who had led the First Belorussian Front to all its victories until then, was the same age as Zhukov and, like Zhukov, a charismatic leader and a soldier through and through. He was tall, blond and handsome, every inch the dashing half-Polish cavalry officer – his father had been a Polish locomotive driver, his mother Russian. Orphaned at the age of fourteen, he had worked on construction sites until 1914, when he had been conscripted into a cavalry regiment, the 5th Kargopol Dragoons, where he, too, became a sergeant. After the Revolution he had joined first the Red Guard and then the Red Army, commanding a cavalry regiment during the civil war. He had become a Communist Party member in 1919.

Like Zhukov's, his career had blossomed during the Twenties and Thirties. He converted to tanks and by 1936 had risen to command Vth Cavalry Corps. But in 1937, in Stalin's infamous purges of the army, his world fell apart. For some unknown reason, he was arrested, is said to have been tortured, and was condemned to death. However, with the threat of war looming in 1940, he was suddenly released, though he remained under sentence of death, a sentence that Stalin could invoke at any time should he fail, or show signs of faltering loyalty.

During the war he found fame as commander of the Sixteenth Army in the battle for Moscow, of the Don Front at Stalingrad, and the Central Front at Kursk – all serving under Zhukov. The Central Front had become first the Belorussian and then the First Belorussian, always remaining at the forefront of the Soviet drive to the west. More than once, Rokossovsky had defied Stalin, arguing fiercely over plans and decisions – on one occasion, Stalin twice sent him out of the room 'to think things over', before finally giving in to him. In spite of his independent spirit and the suspended sentence of death, Rokossovsky was made a marshal in July 1944.

*

THE THIRD front in Stalin's massive assault plan was the First Ukrainian, until then the most powerful in the Red Army. Operating on Zhukov's left flank, it was commanded by a man whose rivalry with him was far less friendly than Rokossovsky's: Marshal Ivan Stepanovich Koniev. A year younger than the other two marshals, Koniev came from peasant stock near Vologda, 250 miles north of Moscow, where he worked as a lumberjack until he was drafted into the army during the First World War. He served in the artillery and, like the others, ended the war as a non-commissioned officer.

It was in the civil war that his military career took a different path from those of Zhukov and Rokossovsky. While they distinguished themselves as soldiers, he became a political commissar, a role he continued in until 1926, when the Communist Party was eager to increase the number of party members among senior officers. It was safer to train and promote officers who were already trusted communists than to rely on the late conversion of senior officers who had once worn the Tsar's uniform.

Koniev was sent on the advanced course for senior officers at the Frunze Military Academy, emerging with the rank of regimental commander, the equivalent of a colonel. Seven years later, he returned to the academy to graduate from the 'Special Faculty', which trained party members for special intelligence and internal security work. It came under the control of Stalin's personal secretariat, which was then busily recruiting people to carry out what would become the great purges.

In February 1939, as the purges finally died down, Koniev was promoted to the rank of army commander, the equivalent of lieutenant-general, and sent to the Far East, where he took over the task of directing military operations against the Japanese, who were then attempting to expand into Mongolia. He failed, dismally, to dislodge them, and was dismissed, to be replaced by Zhukov, who succeeded brilliantly.

Zhukov's success left Koniev seething with jealous hatred – and the hatred was mutual. While Zhukov was the proverbial 'soldier's soldier', Koniev was the supreme example of the political commissar turned military commander – the only one, in fact, to achieve general rank – the living embodiment of everything Zhukov and most other professional Red Army officers despised.

Stalin was fully aware of the feelings of his two protégés. Indeed, he encouraged them. As early as the end of 1941, he was deliberately grooming Koniev as a rival whom he could play off against his more brilliant contemporary, to counter-balance the political threat of Zhukov's growing popularity. He conferred honours on Zhukov only when he had to, but gave them to Koniev even when there was no particular reason for doing so.

Better educated than Zhukov, Koniev always travelled with a small library of books by classical authors, like some eighteenth-century general. To the surprise of many, he was fond of quoting Livy and Pushkin, rather than Marx. But he could be as brutal as any SS leader. His reputation for ruthlessness was confirmed in February 1944, when he turned his tanks and Cossack cavalry loose on 20,000 Germans trapped in ravines near Korsun, in the Ukraine. 'There was no time to take prisoners,' wrote an officer on his staff. 'It was the kind of slaughter that nothing could stop until it was all over.' Tanks headed straight into the columns of men, crushing them under their tracks as they drove backwards and forwards. The Cossacks cornered and literally cut to pieces those who escaped, slashing with their heavy sabres at men with their hands raised in surrender. The massacre of Korsun earned Koniev promotion to Marshal of the Soviet Union, Zhukov's equal in rank.

DESPITE THEIR personal rivalries, the three marshals would need to work in harness. As Stalin told Rokossovsky when he called him to Moscow in mid-November for a personal briefing, their three fronts were the ones that would end the war in the west. It was vital that their operations should be properly coordinated.

'If you and Koniev don't advance,' he said, 'neither will Zhukov.' To demonstrate what he meant, he took one of the coloured crayons for which he was noted, and drew a large red arrow on the map. 'This is how you will help Zhukov if the First Belorussian Front's advance slows down.' What Stalin did not say, though Rokossovsky and Koniev both realized it very clearly, was that if Zhukov's advance was slowed down or halted, each of them had an outside chance of reaching Berlin first. Although all three were expected to cooperate, they were also expected to compete with each other.

The boundary between Rokossovsky's forces and Zhukov's at the start was to be the confluence of the Vistula and Narew rivers, to the north-east of Warsaw. Rokossovsky foresaw huge problems ahead. His front would approach Berlin from the north, which meant advancing across difficult and varied terrain. On his right, from Lamza to the Alexandrow Canal, there were thick forests and lakes everywhere, making large-scale troop movements hazardous. His left flank, from which would come the thrust towards the River Oder, offered more room for manoeuvre, but the enemy was well dug-in there and would certainly prove hard to smash. If General Chernyak-hovsky's Third Belorussian Front, to the north of him, was held up in heavily defended East Prussia, then his right flank, already stretched thin, might collapse. Stalin assured him there was no need for him and Chernyakhovsky to coordinate their efforts.

Koniev was summoned to Moscow at the end of November to present his plan of operations for his First Ukrainian Front to Stalin and the State Defence Committee. He was to drive towards Berlin from the south, starting with a powerful thrust from the large bridgehead that his forces had established on the Vistula at Sandomierz, a little over 100 miles south of Warsaw. His first objective was to reach the Oder near Breslau, bypassing as far as possible the mining and industrial areas of Silesia – factories and mines tended to consist of sturdy concrete buildings which defenders could all too easily turn into fortresses. Koniev was in a hurry. He had no time to waste on sieges.

Stalin nodded approvingly, and with one stubby finger made a circle on the map around industrial Silesia. 'Gold,' he said. Koniev understood: Stalin was telling him not to damage the area's industrial potential, because he wanted to exploit it himself after the war. Koniev was to liberate, but not to destroy.

Zhukov's own plan was clear. Starting from the First Belorussian Front's bridgeheads over the Vistula at Magnuszczew and Deblin, just below Warsaw, he planned to mount his offensive along the Warsaw–Lodz–Poznan axis, a mighty blow aimed directly at Frankfurt-an-der-Oder, which would bring his troops to within forty-five miles of Berlin.

# 16

ON 16 DECEMBER, mist and fog lay thick in the valleys of the Ardennes, the hilly, wooded region of Belgium, north-eastern France and Luxembourg. The clouds hung low, almost at treetop height. It seemed to rain incessantly – cold, stinging rain, which fell on the high ground as snow. It was the opposite of 'Führer weather', when the sun always shone on Hitler's parades and the rain ceased immediately he stepped out of doors. But Hitler had been praying for weather like this ever since September. Then, confined to bed with jaundice and the after-effects of Stauffenberg's bomb, he had sent for maps marked with the latest military situation in the west. From his study of them, he detected what was undoubtedly the weakest point in the American front line. The Ardennes, through which he and Manstein had staged their lightning strike in May 1940, was manned only by three weak divisions. Hitler saw it as offering him the chance of one last desperate throw of the dice, a gamble for victory or death.

'If all goes well,' he told his staff, 'the offensive will set the stage for the annihilation of twenty to thirty divisions. It will be another Dunkirk.'

Sweeping aside the objections of his generals, Hitler drew up detailed plans himself, with the aid of Colonel-General Alfred Jodl, chief of the OKW operations staff, and transmitted them to Rundstedt with strict orders that they were not to be altered in any way. Convincing himself that the British were at the end of their strength, and that the Americans would cave in under pressure, he believed he could still defeat them in the west. This would leave him free to concentrate all his forces in the east to deal with the Red Army, which in December was still bogged down on the Vistula.

During the last three months of 1944 Hitler had painstakingly re-formed two huge Panzer armies, assembling nearly 600,000 men from the remnants of units shattered by the Anglo-American summer victories, together with the major share of the new troops from Goebbels's comb-out. He had patiently waited for the weather to turn. Planes could not fly in fog and low cloud, and without their eyes in the sky, the Allied forces were temporarily blind. All Hitler needed was a longish period of bad weather and he could strike without warning. Now, at last, the time had come.


THE ATTACK began with a colossal artillery bombardment that numbed the brain. Shells, mortar bombs, everything the Germans could throw, rained down on the American line. And then, out of the mist, came the tanks in a massed attack along a forty-mile front. They caught the US First and Ninth armies totally by surprise, and sent them reeling backwards.

Hitler's plan was to smash the three American divisions facing him in the Ardennes, get his Panzers across the River Meuse and go hell for leather for Antwerp, which had only been finally cleared for use as a port on 28 November. The result would be to drive a wedge between the British and Canadian forces and the Americans, leaving Montgomery's armies in a particularly vulnerable position. In this, at least, it almost succeeded.

It almost succeeded, too, in splitting the Anglo-American alliance. Montgomery was still complaining vociferously that Eisenhower's broad-front policy was not working, and demanding that he be given complete command of the Allied ground forces in the north. When the bulge created by the Germans developed at an alarming rate, cutting off US generals Hodges and Simpson from Bradley, Montgomery was, temporarily, given overall command. He made excellent use of it, but could not resist crowing over the eventual victory, putting American backs up more than ever by claiming it as a personal triumph, when almost all the effort and most of the sacrifices had been made by them.

More bumptious than ever, Montgomery insisted on telling Eisenhower 'I told you so', and renewing his call for a single knock-out blow to Berlin. Relations became so bad that Eisenhower actually drafted a note to the US chief of staff in Washington, General Marshall, saying in effect that either Montgomery or he would have to go. Only at the last moment was Montgomery persuaded to climb down and make an abject apology.

Goebbels stirred the pot vigorously by broadcasting – on a European wavelength normally used by the BBC – a version of Montgomery's tactless press statement, cleverly edited and slanted to cause the most offence to the Americans. In the end, Churchill had to defuse the situation with a statement in Parliament on 18 January 1945, denying any but a minor British involvement in the Battle of the Bulge, and lauding 'the greatest American battle of the war . . . an ever famous American victory'.

On the surface, Montgomery was suitably contrite, agreeing that he had been wrong to hold the press conference and in any case should have been more careful in what he said. But the contrition was tempered by arrogance. 'What I did not say,' he wrote later, 'was that, in the Battle of the Ardennes, the Allies got a real "bloody nose", the Americans had nearly 80,000 casualties, and that it would never have happened if we had fought the campaign properly after the great victory in Normandy. . . . Furthermore, because of this unnecessary battle we lost some six weeks in time – with all that that entailed in political consequences as the end of the war drew nearer.'

# 17

IN THE long run, the Ardennes offensive – labelled 'Operation Watch on the Rhine' by Hitler, and 'the Battle of the Bulge' by the Allies – never had any realistic chance of lasting success. But it was extremely bloody, and the situation was still dangerous by 6 January, when Churchill wrote to Stalin asking for a Soviet attack in the east to prevent troops being switched to strengthen the western front. 'I shall be grateful if you can tell me whether we can count on a major Russian offensive on the Vistula front, or elsewhere, during January,' he said. 'I regard the matter as urgent.'

Stalin replied the next day, saying that in view of the position, 'the supreme command has decided to accelerate the completion of our preparations, and, regardless of the weather, to commence large-scale offensive operations against the Germans along the whole central front not later than the second half of January.' Within twenty-four hours, he had General Antonov phone each of the four marshals involved.

Koniev was first to receive a radio-telephone call. Antonov told him his First Ukrainian Front was to attack on 12 January, not the 20th as had been planned. Although Koniev knew the weather would still be bad enough to deprive him of air cover, forcing him to rely on artillery alone to prepare the way, he agreed at once, without demur. General Chernyakhovsky's Third Belorussian Front, on the operation's northern flank, would start its attack next day. And one day after that, on 14 January, Zhukov and Rokossovsky would begin their attacks. In the race for Berlin, Koniev would have two days' start on his rivals.

\*

As ANTONOV was telephoning the Soviet marshals, Hitler was conferring with his generals in the Adlerhorst, his latest western field headquarters near Bad Nauheim. The great offensive was faltering, and he had reluctantly agreed to allow a limited withdrawal from the Ardennes on 8 January. Now Guderian had the impertinence to wave a recent intelligence report under his nose, saying that a massive Soviet offensive could be expected in the east at any moment. Troops must be pulled out from the west and transferred there immediately. It was not the first time Guderian had tried to make Hitler see reason – he had argued with him at least twice before – nor was it the first time he had been met with the Führer's hysterical rage. The report's information was nonsense, Hitler declared. The man responsible for it must be mad and ought to be locked up in a lunatic asylum. Guderian, never the most diplomatic of men, shouted back that if General Gehlen, his intelligence chief in the east, was crazy, then he, Guderian, had better be certified, too.

When Hitler argued that the eastern front had 'never before possessed such a strong reserve as now', Guderian could scarcely believe his ears: he knew that the reserves for a front of over 750 miles amounted to only twelve divisions. 'The eastern front,' he retorted angrily, 'is like a house of cards. If the front is broken through at one point, all the rest will collapse.'

Hitler, unmoved, turned to Himmler, on whom he relied more and more. What did he think? he asked. Himmler scoffed at Guderian's warning. 'It's all an enormous bluff,' he declared.

# 18

WHILE THE German and American armies were locked in combat in the Ardennes, and in a second counter-attack from the Rhine in Alsace, life in Berlin was becoming grimmer by the day. The air raids continued unabated, but the young *Flakhelfer* who had been manning most of the guns suddenly found they were now needed for other duties in the defence of the city. Fred Laabs and his companions on the anti-aircraft site in Lützowplatz were relieved of their positions in mid-December, replaced by teenage girls drafted in as auxiliaries. Most of the girls were terrified, screaming in fear when their position was attacked by Mustang fighters supporting the Flying Fortresses and Liberators during daylight raids, and by RAF Mosquitoes at night, when their searchlights were obvious targets. But there was nothing they could do to hide – the gunners needed the lights to find their targets. Fred and the other boys had a few days to show the girls what to do, before they were ordered to report to the Hermann Göring barracks at Reinickendorf, in the north of the city.

The barracks at Reinickendorf belonged to the Waffen SS, but the SS uniforms were at first swamped by those of all the other services – army, navy and air force – worn by men who had been rounded up from every possible unit in Himmler's and Goebbels's great comb-out. As they now came under the command of the Waffen SS, Fred and his companions were issued with new uniforms, and with pistols, the first side arms the boys had ever handled.

Formed into new units, the recruits were given a hasty training in anti-tank warfare, being shown how to fire Panzerfaust bazookas, and told the weak points of the Soviet T34 tank. Appalled at the hopeless prospect of facing Soviet troops and tanks with such primitive weapons and so little training, Fred and his closest friend, Karl-Heinz Freund, decided to quit at the first opportunity.

SINCE SEPTEMBER it had been forbidden for anyone to leave Berlin without a special permit: every available person would be needed to help with the final defence of the city. Missie Vassiltchikov's friend Loremarie von Schönburg, under suspicion by the Gestapo since she and Missie had made so many visits to the Lehrterstrasse prison to enquire about friends awaiting trial or execution for their part in the 20 July plot, managed to jump aboard a train as it was leaving, after getting through the station gate with a platform ticket. Missie herself, depressed at the execution of so many close friends, was allowed sick leave in September, and was then diagnosed as suffering from an enlarged thyroid gland. She did not return to Berlin, but went instead to Vienna, where she worked until the end of the war as a nurse in the Luftwaffe hospital.

MARIA VON MALTZAN had no intention of leaving Berlin. She was still harbouring her Jewish lover, Hans Hirschel, in her apartment. The flat was in a sorry state: the windows and front door had long been boarded up after being destroyed by the blast of bombs falling nearby, and the previous autumn the block had suffered a direct hit. Only Maria's flat and the one immediately above it had survived, though Maria's ceiling was in danger of collapsing and had to be propped up by a stout timber beam in the middle of the living room. A Polish family had moved into the wreckage of the flat above, happy to have found somewhere to live, even though it was half-ruined.

Maria's household was bigger now. Besides Hans and her two Scottie dogs, she had also taken in two young Russian girls from Minsk, twelve-year-old Tamara and her seven-year-old sister Lucie, orphans who had been living in a Berlin camp. Tamara spoke some German: she had been a pupil at a

Comintern school in Russia, and she translated for her sister. The girls were not only the filthiest children Maria had ever seen – they were crawling with fleas and head and body lice – but also the most suspicious. They demanded at every turn to know what was going to happen to them, and refused to be parted, even if in the end it meant being gassed together if they could not find a home.

The presence of the children could have been dangerous for Hans, but Maria need not have worried. The girls had been through a great deal, and were experienced far beyond their years. On the first day, when she sent Tamara out to buy bread, the girl asked where Hans's ration card was. When Maria said he didn't have one, Tamara nodded, narrowed her eyes in thought for a moment, then asked, 'Political or Jew?'

'Jew,' Maria replied. 'And if you ever tell anyone that he lives here, you'll kill both him and me.'

'Then you've got nothing to do with the Nazis?' Tamara asked.

'Nothing,' Hans told her.

Tamara regarded him gravely for a moment, then suddenly threw her arms around him and hugged him. Lucie followed suit. Two weeks later, the girls asked Maria and Hans if they could call them 'Mother' and 'Father'.

Hans's illegality was not the only secret the girls had to keep. They also had to learn to keep their mouths shut about the other people who passed through the flat, for Maria was still deeply involved in helping opponents of the regime. In the autumn of 1944 the Jewish problem had become more intense again, as the Nazis started deporting half-Jews and the 'privileged' Jews, those married to Aryans who had been spared after their wives' mass protest outside Gestapo headquarters. More faces started appearing at the door late at night, to stay for a day or two while Maria and her associates in the Swedish church made arrangements to spirit them away. By the end of the war, Maria von Maltzan had personally rescued sixty-two fugitives, and played a part in the survival of many others.

In some ways, the heavy bomb damage made things easier for Maria and the others involved in caring for people who had gone underground. Because of the bombing, the main registries were moved out of Berlin, leaving only small, local record offices, which were frequently hit by bombs. Whenever that happened, Maria and her friends descended on the harassed officials as they tried, like good German bureaucrats, to restore order. Assuming invented names, they obtained 'replacement' cards and papers for those they were supposed to have lost in the raids – with which they could get rations for their illegals.

Towards the end of 1944, Maria was able to help Hans even further. With the help of a fellow conspirator, Werner Keller, and another friend who worked in Goebbels's ministry, she obtained a pass which, complete with photograph, identified him as an official of the authority for the defence of Berlin, part of Goebbels's Total Mobilization Commission. This gave him almost unlimited powers. The wording on the document enjoined members of the SS, SA, the military and police – even the Gestapo – to unquestioning obedience to the orders of the holder. For the first time in nearly three years, it was relatively safe for him to leave the apartment.

Anxious to try out his new papers, Hans took a trip into the countryside of the Mark Brandenburg, to the home of friends of Maria's, with whom she had stored her fur coats – as winter approached, she was starting to feel the cold. Although travel outside Berlin was severely restricted for civilians, Hans could go wherever he chose with his new pass. He would not even need a ticket. He could collect a fur coat for Maria.

Next day, when he boarded a train, Hans was saluted by the controller. He was given a meal in the station restaurant when he stopped to change trains. When he arrived at his destination, the stationmaster insisted on providing a car and driver to take him to Maria's friends' house. It was all magical for a man who had been cooped up for so long – but back in Berlin with the coat wrapped in a parcel under his arm, he decided it was wiser to decline the offer of another car to drive him home. Saying he felt like stretching his legs, he walked back to the flat by the most winding route possible, to make sure he was not being followed.

The fur coat was welcome and useful as winter set in, but Maria had more essential preparations to make for the siege she was certain was coming. All through the autumn she had scrimped and saved to buy extra black market food that would keep – food like hard salamis and smoked bacon. Now, she and Hans dragged their big bathtub away from the wall, fixed hooks under its wide brim, hung the sausages and bacon from them, then pushed the bath firmly back into place. She hid money in pots of that Berlin delicacy *Schmaltz*, a soft lard dripping, confident that Russian soldiers would not want to steal this, unlike jam and sweet conserves. She also preserved dozens of eggs, part of her regular haul from farmers grateful for her veterinary skills, in buckets of water-glass, a solution of potassium silicate. Its dirty appearance not only concealed the eggs, but looked so unappetizing that it could safely be left standing around without fear of theft. Whatever happened, she and her household would be able to eat.

# 19

ON TUESDAY, 19 December, Freya von Moltke arrived in Berlin from Kreisau and made her way to Ruth Andreas-Friedrich's flat in Steglitz. Freya brought news that Moltke's trial was set for 8 am on 8 January, which left little time to organize an appeal. With so many of Moltke's circle already dead or imprisoned, and their mutual friend Hans Peters banished to a Luftwaffe anti-aircraft post in Hamburg, it was up to the women to do everything. Ruth promised to do whatever she could to mobilize her circle of friends. Peters, who had taught Moltke at university and had later been one of the original five members of the Kreisau Circle, could try to see Judge Freisler, but since he had spoken to him before, fruitlessly, about Pastor Wachsmann, this might do more harm than good. They agreed it would be kept as a last resort, if all else failed.

For the next three weeks Ruth and her friends tried to find some string they could pull that just might help. Her lover, Leo Borchard, located a prominent SS informer, and spent time drinking whisky with him, trying to persuade him to make a report saying the Moltke case must be a mistake. Moltke, Borchard argued, was no politician, but a typical German dreamer. Goerdeler had been his opponent, not his friend. There must have been 'some wretched misunderstanding' that had implicated Moltke in the 20 July plot.

Ruth spent days trying to track down a Dr Lenz, who according to Peters had once been Freisler's assistant and was now his personal confidant. Lenz was supposed not to be a Nazi. He might be able to influence Freisler. Day after day, Ruth hunted for him through the chaos of government offices that were constantly being relocated because of the bombing, finally discovering that Dr Lenz had himself been arrested. In desperation, she called Peters three times on 5 January, pleading with him to risk traveling to Berlin to talk to Freisler himself. But the day before, with the fighting in the Ardennes at a critical phase, all official travel had been banned for a week.

Ruth's nineteen-year-old daughter Karin agreed to pay a visit to the People's Court, to see what went on there. She returned white-faced and tearful, shocked by the spectacle of seeing seven defendants receiving seven death sentences.

'It's a farce – a prearranged farce,' she sobbed. 'And the audience sits there as if it were a circus – laughing, shuddering, feeling a pleasant tingle in their stomachs. During the intermission they munch apples and sandwiches!'

One of the accused had been a young girl music student, no older than herself, accused of harbouring communists. Another had been an old greengrocer who didn't seem to understand what was happening or why he was there.

'If anyone speaks the truth, they overlook it,' Karin told her mother. 'If anyone tries to defend himself, they slap his mouth. I swear to you, every sentence is filled out before the session begins. All they do there is give the masses some entertainment.'

FREYA, MEANWHILE, had been busy herself, keeping in touch with her husband and following up countless steps which he suggested to her.

Moltke set great hope on an interview with SS General Heinrich Müller, head of the Gestapo. Freya went to Prinz–Albrecht–Strasse to arrange it. 'He promised to see Helmuth,' she said later, 'but left no doubt in my mind that they were after his life. After the First World War, he said, "their" opponents survived and took over. They would see to it that this was not possible this time.'

Freya also saw Freisler, who talked to her about 'the never-failing justice of the court', but offered her no hope. She was allowed to see her husband four times. Although Moltke was calmly prepared for death, the tension became unbearable for both of them. He had days of depression, but always overcame it, and she noted that as the days and weeks passed he became stronger rather than weaker.

On Saturday, 6 January, Freya arrived at Ruth's flat during the evening with the news that the trial had been postponed for twenty-four hours. It would now begin on the 9th. Ruth still hoped that Peters might make it to Berlin in time, and that as a distinguished lawyer he might even be able to influence Freisler. In fact, Peters staggered into Berlin early on the day of the trial, and went straight to the People's Court. Freisler said he was too busy to talk, and refused to see him.

MOLTKE'S TRIAL was held in camera in a small hall near Potsdamerplatz. Nevertheless, the hall, a former schoolroom, was full to bursting. There were seven other defendants besides Moltke, all connected with the Kreisau Circle. They sat on four rows of chairs in the body of the room, each man flanked by two policemen, facing a long table at which Freisler presided. The trial was not filmed, but was recorded on steel sound tape, the only official record, since taking notes was forbidden. As each man was dealt with, he was brought forward to sit at a smaller table immediately facing Freisler and the microphone.

Even without the movie cameras, Freisler's performance followed its usual course as he bellowed at the accused men.

As though saving the choicest titbit for the end, Freisler left Moltke until last, which meant he was not tried until Wednesday, 10 January. Freisler started at top speed, racing along at a pace that would have confused most men, but not Moltke, whose intellect was more than a match for the Nazi judge. 'Thank God I am quick and found Freisler's speed child's play, which, incidentally, we both enjoyed,' he wrote. At first, everything went smoothly. But then Moltke raised his first objection and, as Moltke told Freya, Freisler had his first paroxysm:

A hurricane was unleashed. He banged on the table, turned as red as his robe, and roared: 'I won't stand for that sort of thing. I won't listen to that sort of thing.' And it continued like that all the time. Since I knew anyhow what the result would be, it all left me quite indifferent: I looked him icily in the eye, which he clearly didn't like, and suddenly I couldn't help smiling.

An SS journalist at the trial was among those who were struck by Moltke's calm dignity. 'A strange sort of fellow, Moltke,' he told Ruth. 'He didn't say a word. He just looked at him. Just looked at Freisler with those huge dark eyes of his. Do you know what it seemed like to me? It was like Christ before Pilate. He only went to work when they charged the others – Gerstenmaier and Reisert. He actually wangled them out of it. He's a queer stick!'

In spite of his impressive display, Moltke and two of his fellow defendants, the Jesuit Father Alfred Delp and Franz Sperr, a retired colonel from Bavaria, were sentenced to death. The others escaped the gallows, largely through Moltke's pleading, but received prison sentences ranging from three to seven years.

Back in his cell at Tegel after the trial, Moltke wrote a long letter to Freya, giving her the details of the secret proceedings. Poelchau carried it back to her that night. The information could be vital in ensuring that other members of the group awaiting trial could coordinate their stories, and must be distributed, but Freya would need to take great care. 'If they find out that you received this letter and passed it on,' her husband wrote, 'you too will be killed.' The information would have to be disguised, so that it did not look as though it had come from him.

Freya did as she was told, typing copies with several carbons. Friends rushed them to the homes of the other prisoners, where their wives and fiancées each baked a little cake, putting the copy in the middle of it. Next day, Poelchau took them to the men in their prison cells.

Even while Moltke was in the condemned cell at Tegel, Freya and her friends continued to petition for clemency, trying to get to Himmler or some other top Nazi. But shortly before 2 pm on Wednesday, 24 January, he was suddenly taken from his cell, 'for proceedings at Plötzensee'. At 4 pm, he was hanged.

# PART FIVE

# *The race*

# 1

THE NIGHT of Thursday, 11 January, was clear on the Vistula. Stars glittered in the sky like jewels as sappers of Koniev's First Ukrainian Front crawled forward to begin the dangerous task of clearing paths through the minefields that both sides had laid in front of their positions. But as the night advanced the weather began to close in, and by morning heavy mist and thick cloud obscured everything. The air was thick with falling snow. Visibility was down to ten yards or even less. So bad was it that when the tanks of General Rybalko's Third Guards Tank Army passed close to Koniev's observation post, he could make them out only because they were moving.

Koniev had taken up position in a small farmhouse on the edge of a wood, close to the front line. At 5 am on the morning of Friday, 12 January, he gave the orders for his guns to open up with a huge rolling barrage – with the Red Air Force grounded because of the weather, there could be no aerial bombardment of German positions, and Koniev had to rely on his artillery to soften up the enemy. With as many as 450 medium and heavy guns deployed in each mile of front, the result was probably the heaviest and most terrifying concentration of firepower ever seen at that time. Behind the barrage, reconnaissance battalions, stiffened by penal units, moved forward to take the first line of German trenches. Once they had accomplished this, the guns began to fire again, in a bombardment so ferocious that the first German prisoners brought in were incoherent and shaking uncontrollably as if suffering from ague.

For one hour and forty-seven minutes a non-stop hail of shells flinging up great spouts of earth transformed the Polish landscape into the kind of desolation that only men who had experienced the western front during the First World War could have recognized. German mobile reserves were caught in position and so badly battered they were forced to disperse. The Fourth Panzer Army's command post was completely destroyed. Great gaps were torn in the German defences, and before they had time even to think of recovery, Koniev hurled in his main force.

By 1.50 pm, General Lelyushenko, commander of the Soviet Fourth Tank Army, was champing at the bit. Ten minutes later, his forces, including two regiments equipped with the new Stalin heavy tanks mounting 122 mm guns as big as medium artillery, were rolling towards the German lines. The sheer weight of their armour was unstoppable. By evening Koniev's troops had broken through on a 25-mile front to a depth of 12 miles, with Lelyushenko's tanks 8 miles ahead of the rest. By the following day, three Soviet armies had broken through the German line west of Kielce into ideal tank country, of which they took full advantage. At the same time, Koniev launched an attack with his left wing in the direction of the ancient city of Krakow.

Five days after the start of the operation, Koniev had blasted a hole in the German defences 75–85 miles deep and more than 150 miles wide. And everywhere his troops were advancing.

THE SPEARHEAD of Zhukov's First Belorussian Front was the Eighth Guards Army, led by General Vassili Chuikov, the hero of Stalingrad. Chuikov, a short, chunky man with the face of an intelligent prize-fighter surmounted by a mop of thick, unruly hair, was probably the finest front-line commander and certainly the most aggressive general of the Second World War. He combined the belligerence of a pit bull terrier with a superb tactical sense. At 7 am on Sunday, 14 January, while it was still dark, Chuikov ordered the field kitchens to be brought up close to the front line. Huge insulated containers filled with hot food were taken out to the men who were about to face German guns. At least they would be able to eat a good breakfast before the attack – who knew when they would get their next meal? By 8 am everything was ready. At 8.25 am, the artillery was ordered to load. At 8.30 came the order to fire.

Instead of a conventional lengthy barrage, Zhukov used the same tactic as Koniev – a short but crushing bombardment lasting only twenty-five minutes, followed by a sudden assault from the Magnuszczew bridgehead by assault battalions supported by artillery, tanks, small arms and machine gun fire. Hard on the heels of the assault battalions came his main force, striking not at Warsaw itself, as the Germans had been led to expect, but south of the city along the rivers Pilica and Radomka. Zhukov had crammed almost half a million men and well over a thousand tanks into the bridgehead, an area only fifteen miles wide by seven miles deep. Chuikov said that when they attacked it was like releasing a compressed spring. By the evening of that first day, Soviet tanks were driving as they pleased as far as twenty miles beyond the breakthrough line. The assault from Zhukov's second bridgehead at Pulawy was even more successful, bringing the XIth Tank Corps to within striking distance of the important industrial town of Radom, well over forty miles from the Vistula.

On the second day, Zhukov pounded German positions with another devastating artillery barrage before flinging more tank armies into the battle.

Moving fast and sweeping all before it, the Second Guards Tank Army smashed through crumbling German defences to the south of Warsaw. By nightfall they had got round behind the city, half cutting it off from the west. When the Forty-Seventh Army managed to establish a new bridgehead across the Vistula just north of Warsaw, where the river bends sharply westwards, the city was in grave danger of being surrounded. Two days later, with the noose on the verge of being pulled tight, the Germans evacuated the city, after razing what was left of it in an orgy of vengeful destruction, shooting, hanging and burning alive thousands of its citizens in their own homes.

To THE north of Zhukov, Rokossovsky faced the rather unnerving prospect of having to fight over ground where the Imperial Russian Army had suffered its most catastrophic defeats in the First World War, at Tannenberg and the Masurian Lakes. His task was to cut off the retreat of German forces from East Prussia and join up with Chernyakhovsky's Third Belorussian Front advancing from the east, though he regarded the Stavka's plan for the whole operation as inept. Among other things, they had ignored the fact that the River Narew, which lay directly across his path, was 300 yards wide and at least 12 feet deep. Even in a freezing Polish January, it was only covered with a thin crust of ice, strong enough in places to bear the weight of a few men but not the passage of tanks or troops in large numbers.

Despite his misgivings, Rokossovsky began his offensive as ordered on Sunday, 14 January, with an intense artillery barrage lasting most of the day. With tank operations severely curtailed, he had to try to break through the German defences with his infantry – which created additional problems, since infantry was the one thing he was short of. He had been given 120,000 men as reinforcements, but they turned out to be a motley collection of no-hopers, largely local conscripts and recently liberated prisoners of war who were in no condition to fight: 39,000 of them were sick and walking wounded dragged from field hospitals, or clerks, orderlies and anyone else who could be squeezed from the system without its actually collapsing. They were hardly the stuff heroes are made of.

Not surprisingly, progress was slow that first day. It was not until Lieutenant-General Gorbatov – another purge victim who had been recalled from the gulags in 1941 – succeeded in holding off attacks on his Third Army by the SS Gross Deutschland Division that Rokossovsky dared to risk his tanks in the battle.

By 17 January, the weather had improved enough for the Red Air Force to provide some much-needed air support for Rokossovsky's advance units. They responded by breaking through on a sixty-mile front. On 19 January they took five towns, and were only seventy miles from the Baltic, developing their advance along the Vistula towards Danzig, and cutting off the German forces in the Baltic region and East Prussia. That same day, the Germans hastily dug up the remains of Field Marshal Hindenburg and his wife, who had been buried at Tannenberg, the scene of his greatest victory, and carried them back to Berlin for safety. They also blew up the national monument at the site, to avoid its falling into Soviet hands.

On 20 January, Rokossovsky received the orders he had feared since the beginning of the Vistula operation. He was to change his entire strategy, turning the majority of his strength north-eastwards towards East Prussia, while at the same time continuing to support Zhukov's First Belorussian Front on his left flank, a truly schizophrenic division of his forces. Both he and Zhukov were furious, but there was little either of them could do. Moscow – that is to say Stalin – had spoken. At one stroke, Rokossovsky found himself disqualified from his place in history as one of the Soviet generals who took Berlin. Unless something totally unforeseen happened, he was relegated to being an also-ran.

THE RATE of advance by Koniev's and Zhukov's fronts was so rapid that the two commanders simply could not keep track of events. Their forces were, as Chuikov put it, 'striking to kill'. In this war of movement, front lines ebbed and flowed like water. Mostly it consisted of a series of confused and confusing engagements, savage and bloody, between fleeing Germans and advancing Russians, scattered across miles of open country. In the midst of it all, however, loyal Nazi units would suddenly stand and fight.

The Stavka had made its plans on the basis of an advance of 10 to 12 miles a day, the rate that had been achieved during the successful summer of 1944. But two days after the start of the offensive, Chuikov's own Eighth Guards Army was covering 15 to 18 miles each day, and on 17 January made a leap of 25 miles. With such progress, even Chuikov, never a general who liked to lead from the rear, found it hard to keep up with his own army.

BY NIGHTFALL on 17 January, Zhukov's central striking force was approaching the main rail line and highway between Warsaw and Berlin, and meeting little resistance. They continued next day, moving so fast that they were already well ahead of schedule. Chuikov was concerned to find himself receiving orders from front HQ to reach a line next day which he had already left far behind. If he was to obey his instructions, he would have to halt his men for at least a day, simply to allow the timetable to right itself. But it was not in the nature of Chuikov and his men to wait while there was still an enemy to be attacked. They raced on, eager to reach the German border.

On the evening of the 18th, Chuikov saw through his binoculars smoke rising from factory chimneys on the edge of a large city. It was Lodz, Poland's second largest city. Out of contact again with Zhukov, Chuikov had to decide for himself whether to attack it, bypass it and leave the city with its large

German garrison behind him, or wait for instructions. He halted his troops, had them fed, and let them rest until midnight. Then, his plan already complete, he started moving them into position ready to attack next day.

The morning of 19 January dawned bright and clear, with the sun glittering on the snow as Chuikov's reconnaissance units scouted the city to get some idea of the strength of the garrison. Twice, Chuikov and his senior officers almost met disaster: once when German artillery fired on his observation post, and once, at the very beginning of the assault, when they were almost strafed by Red Air Force fighter planes. Seeing troops moving on the ground, a large formation of aircraft started moving in to attack, certain that they were Germans – according to the timetable, Chuikov was not due to reach Lodz for another six days! Only at the last moment were they warned off: having no radio contact with the aircraft, Chuikov ordered everyone to spread their greatcoats, groundsheets, tents and everything else they could find on the open ground, while they fired green flares and rockets into the air. The planes banked away at the last moment, realizing what was happening.

The attack on Lodz was so sudden and so successful that the Germans had no time to destroy buildings and services. The conquerors were greeted with flags and flowers by a local population delirious with joy at being released from five long years of Nazi brutality.

That same day, Koniev's forces took Krakow, the ancient seat of Poland's kings and the capital of the Nazi 'General Government'. Then, following instructions, he directed his main armoured thrust north-westward towards Breslau. Bearing in mind Stalin's wish to liberate but not destroy the industrial complexes of Silesia, he encircled and bypassed important centres, enabling his troops to advance even more speedily. Two days later, as Rokossovsky's armies in East Prussia captured Tannenberg, Koniev's men crossed the frontier into German Silesia, only ten miles from the River Oder, the last major natural obstacle on their path to Berlin.

The Oder and its main tributary, the Neisse, formed the ancient frontier of the German empire. Running roughly south for 562 miles from Stettin on the Baltic, through Küstrin, Frankfurt and Breslau, to Czechoslovakia, the rivers acted as a long defensive moat, which for centuries had protected Germany against invasion from the east. By the end of the week, five of Koniev's armies were on or across the Oder, with two major bridgeheads established, one on either side of Breslau, waiting for the ice to thicken on the fast-flowing river so that troops, armour and equipment could cross in greater numbers.

So that there should be no misunderstandings, political officers attached to front-line units nailed up wooden signboards at the frontier. On them, they inscribed in dirty diesel oil: 'You are now in Goddam Germany!' It was a sign to those with scores to settle that revenge could begin.

*

To ALL the scores that remained to be settled with the Third Reich, another was added on Saturday, 27 January. At about 9 am that morning, in the midst of a snowstorm, a lone Soviet scout from the 100th Infantry Division walked into a twentieth-century nightmare. He entered a compound containing a group of wooden buildings, about seventeen miles south-east of Katowice in Upper Silesia. The place was called Monowitz. It was part of the vast Auschwitz-Birkenau complex, which covered an area of fifteen square miles, and was officially known as Auschwitz III, an IG Farben slave-labour factory for the manufacture of Buna artificial rubber. The soldier was entering the grounds of the prison infirmary.

The Germans had started pulling out of Auschwitz eleven days before. The gas chambers and crematoria, in which some 3 million victims had perished, had been closed down nearly three months earlier, on 2 November 1944. Before they left, the Germans had blown up everything, including the factories, and had set fire to the barracks, many with the prisoners still inside. They had shipped the survivors westwards, at least those who could still be of use to the Reich.

The main force of the 100th Division arrived in Monowitz about thirty minutes after the scout. They found nearly 600 sick and dying men and women, out of 850 who had been left behind. The soldiers distributed their bread to the survivors. Later that day, a Red Army doctor and medical staff arrived to tend them.

The rest of Auschwitz-Birkenau fell to the Soviets that afternoon. Two hundred and thirty-one Red Army men died in the fighting. After they had removed the mines from the surrounding area, they were able to enter the death factory, where they found some 5,000 surviving prisoners. They also found mountains of clothes, all neatly baled – 348,820 men's suits and 836,515 women's dresses – grotesque pyramids of dentures and spectacles, and, perhaps most ghastly of all, 7 tons of women's hair.

Koniev did not visit the camp personally. He felt it was more important that he retain his objectivity than rage at the horrors that had been discovered. In military matters, he believed, it was vital to preserve a cool head.

## 2

TERRIFIED OF the advancing Russians, the German civilian population in Silesia began a mass exodus to the west. Most of them headed for Berlin, bringing a new awareness of the situation to the city. Two friends of Ursula von Kardorff, who managed to get the last train out of the beleaguered city of

Breslau, described conditions that Berliners could soon expect to face themselves. For days, they told her, loudspeakers on street corners had been warning all women and children to leave while they could, but the trains were packed and it was impossible to get on board.

'Young girls and women with grown children are urged to leave the city on foot,' the Silesian newspapers announced, 'taking a southerly and westerly direction, in order to save hours of useless waiting at the stations.' The whole city was in a state of panic. Patients in hospitals were being armed with hand grenades, so that, although sick, they could still pull the pin and take a few Russians with them. Fanatical army officers were rounding up anyone in uniform, including the wounded, in an attempt to scrape together enough men to resist the enemy.

There were stories of refugees trampling one another to death, of corpses being thrown out of unheated freight wagons, of convoys stranded on the roads, of demented mothers who refused to believe that the babies they were carrying in their arms were already dead. Ruth Andreas-Friedrich reported the arrival of one train in which an open truck was crammed with frozen children: 'They stood in the cold for ninety-six hours, packed like sardines in a can. The wind blew on them, the snow covered them; they froze and wept; they stood on their feet and died, jammed into a wooden coal car. . . .'

ONE REFUGEE from Breslau who did not have to fight for a seat was Eva Braun's sister, Ilse. She arrived at the Schlesien station on the morning of 21 January, pale and haggard from three nights without sleep and carrying only a small, cloth suitcase. Eva had an official car pick her up at the station and take her to the Adlon Hotel, which was still managing to stay open. 'I'm sorry not to be able to put you up at the chancellery,' she told her, 'but it's full of soldiers and we're rather short of space. But naturally, you're dining with us this evening.'

Ilse found the continuing luxury of the Adlon unnerving after the scenes she had endured, and dining with Eva in the library of the chancellery, with white-gloved stewards serving them from silver dishes, even more so. But when Eva blithely assured her that she had it on good authority that she would be able to go back to her home in Breslau in a fortnight's time, it became too much.

'You wretched creature!' she stormed. 'Wake up. Open your eyes to reality. Breslau is lost. Silesia is lost. Germany is lost. Don't you realize that hundreds of thousands of people are choking the snowy roads, fleeing from the enemy who is ravaging and carrying off everything? Your Führer is a fiend, he's dragging you into the abyss with him, and all of us along with you!'

Eva refused to listen. 'You're mad. Crazy!' she flung back at her sister. 'How can you say such things about the Führer, who's so generous and who told me to invite you to stay at his house at the Obersalzberg until you return to Breslau? You deserve to be stood up against a wall and shot.' Despite her jaundiced view of Hitler, Ilse accepted his offer of hospitality in the south, travelling in the comparative safety of a mail van on a Wehrmacht armoured train. Eva followed on 9 February, sent away for safety by Hitler, who found her presence a distraction; she was forbidden to return to Berlin.

AMONG THOSE fleeing to Berlin from the east the hard way at the end of January was Marianne Gärtner, the little girl who had danced for Hitler at the opening of the Olympic Games in 1936. Now aged nineteen, she had been posted to work in the drawing office of a Todt Organization camp near Posen (Poznan), about 170 miles east of Berlin, tracing maps and marking up trenches and defence positions.

Marianne's father had already managed to scramble back to Berlin early in the new year from Warsaw. He had been posted there in the spring of 1944 to run a steel mill – having been expelled from the Nazi Party for failing to show enough enthusiasm, for not using the raised arm greeting, for describing his local block warden as a pompous ass, and for making jokes about Nazi big-wigs. The posting had been meant as a death sentence, since he would be under threat both from Polish partisans and from the Soviets. But he had won the respect of the workers in the mill, and they had helped him get away.

Now, it was Marianne's turn. For days she had been aware of a deep and constant rumbling carried on the biting east wind, growing steadily louder and more ominous. From her office window she could see westbound trains chugging past, their engines labouring, their coaches covered with antlike figures clinging to buffers, running boards and roofs in spite of the bitter cold. On 26 January, she awoke to the closer sound of artillery. 'The war,' she wrote later, 'was rolling towards the town with the speed of hot lava.'

She dressed quickly, her hands trembling as she buttoned up her dress and searched frantically for her left stocking. As she stepped outside, where a red sun was rising, the frozen snow cracked under her feet like glass. There was pandemonium in the main street. Muffled-up figures hauled heavily laden handcarts, or drove vehicles and horse-drawn carts piled high with pots and pans, mattresses, bedding, suitcases and sacks filled to bursting point. A grandfather clock stuck out incongruously from a load of household chattels.

Suddenly, a German army convoy on its way to the front drove into the fleeing mass, hooting furiously, scattering people and animals, upsetting carts. Aboard the vehicles, Marianne saw what she at first took to be midget soldiers, but were in fact children, boys with smooth, pink 'terrifyingly determined' faces, wearing uniforms two sizes too big.

Marianne scrambled into the cab of a truck already packed with people. They lurched off in the direction of Berlin, crawling slowly along in low gear on roads clogged with refugee columns. The driver, Albert, was a middle-aged Berliner who hadn't slept for forty-eight hours. As a precaution, he gave

Marianne a brief instruction on how to grab the wheel and steer in case he fell asleep – which he did once. At one point, Marianne recalls, a loud hammering on the cab stopped them.

> Suddenly it was very quiet in the back. Then I saw the woman. Holding a tiny, lifeless bundle in her arms, she walked over to the edge of a field, awkwardly, her legs slightly apart, and very slowly as if time were waiting as her executioner. Her frail body was shaken with sobs which seemed to freeze as they reached her lips. Placing the bundle at the foot of a hedge, she hacked with her heel at the ground until it had yielded enough frosted snow to cover the body. As she stooped over it as long as it takes to say a short prayer and make the sign of the cross, standing out sharply against the grim whiteness of the fields, she struck me in the silent torment of her mourning as one of the loneliest figures I had ever seen.

Albert returned and started the engine. 'It was a boy,' he said. 'Poor woman! Didn't have a chance . . . not in an open truck . . . not in this arctic cold!'

Shortly afterwards, the engine spluttered and died as the fuel ran out. Marianne climbed down and joined the lines of figures trudging through the snow, wrapping as many clothes as possible from her suitcase around her body, with woollen socks pulled over her hands as extra mittens. For mile after mile, hour after hour, she limped along in her ill-fitting wooden-soled shoes, through the rest of the day, and into the night, not daring to stop and rest for fear of falling asleep and freezing to death. Towards evening on the second day, they met another convoy of troops, dressed in ill-fitting uniforms, driving eastwards. This time they were 'grey-haired, unsmiling men, some with gold-rimmed spectacles, who looked as if they had been dragged from behind desks, out of classrooms or lecture halls'.

At last, Marianne reached the suburbs of Berlin. There were pretty houses with snowmen in the front gardens, and pavements cleared of snow. The war seemed a million miles away. But as she got further into the city – at first on foot, since the S-Bahn was under repair from the last air raid and all buses had now been taken out of service – she passed through ruined streets where buildings were still collapsing, and where the air was filled with dust and smoke. It was a grim welcome back to her home city. But there was worse to come. When she finally arrived at her destination in Zehlendorf, the house where her mother and grandmother lived was nothing but a hollow shell, black space gaping behind empty window frames.

As she groaned and sank to her knees, an old man shuffled out of the deepening gloom. 'Been looking for family?' he asked. 'Yes, it's been a bad week, what with one raid after another. Amis dropped a lot of firebombs around here.' He told her survivors usually left a note for their relatives on the nearest tree, and pointed to one. Marianne scrambled to her feet, and scanned the scribbled notices pinned to the tree trunk. Among them she saw one in her mother's handwriting – a message, a new address. Thanking the old man, she dragged herself off to the nearest S-Bahn station.

On the train, no one paid much attention to her wild, exhausted appearance – Berliners had grown accustomed to the sight of refugees, and their sympathy was tempered by the knowledge that every new arrival placed an extra strain on the city's limited resources of food and shelter. But her ordeal was not yet over. Less than five minutes into her journey, the sirens started wailing, and at the next station she joined the rush into an underground shelter.

Deaf to the clamour all around her and the reverberations of falling bombs outside, Marianne fell asleep. She woke up when the raid was over, and emerged from the shelter to find the S-Bahn was out of action again. She continued on foot, into a nightmare:

> A row of houses cut in two with the precision of a ruler. I want to retreat, but it is too late. I am trapped between mounds of rubble, smoke and clouds of pulverized masonry. I trip over a body, I flee in horror from a pair of gaping, empty eyes which are fixed on the dusty moon as in a somnambulist's trance. A few staggering steps ahead, close to a bomb crater, where the street has belched up pipes and cables, and the small mosaic of paving-stones forms mole hills, a woman lies twisted around a lamp post which is bent like a stick of plasticine, and not until I am clear of the body do I realize that there are no legs sticking out from under her coat. And as I climb over, or try to bypass obstacles, yet more horrors begin to crowd my yellow-dusted vision: another body; a lump of raw flesh where a face has been; the savage, obscene sight of a laced-up boot sitting on top of a chunk of mortar, still enclosing the bloody stump of a foot . . .

The church clock was striking one when Marianne finally reached her mother's new address – a block of modern flats in a quiet, tree-lined street, with boarded-up windows on all sides. Her mother did not recognize her at first, but then fell on her with enormous relief.

'We were so worried,' her grandmother told her. 'Posen was taken two days ago. . . .'

# 3

IN FACT, Posen had not fallen, though it had been completely surrounded on 27 January. The city was built around a medieval citadel, with fortifications that had recently been strengthened, and here the last 12,000 defenders held out until 23 February against everything the Soviets could throw at them. But although the siege temporarily delayed Zhukov's advance by tying up part of Chuikov's army, it could not halt its momentum – two of Chuikov's rifle corps, the IVth and XXVIIIth, charged round the north of the city, covering nearly forty miles in two days.

The day before, a scouting party of the First Guards Tank Army had captured a large group of Germans at the fortified Meseritz Line. During interrogation, the prisoners revealed that the fortifications were not yet fully manned, but that reinforcements were being rushed in from Germany and the west. At the same time, other intelligence showed that retreating German units were regrouping in strength on the Oder. Clearly, time was crucial. On 27 January, Zhukov issued orders to his army commanders to push on to the Oder as quickly as possible, to establish bridgeheads on the western bank of the river before the Germans could complete their defences. 'If we succeed in capturing the west bank of the Oder,' he concluded, 'the operation to take Berlin will be fully guaranteed.'

It was the first time the city had been specifically mentioned in an operational order. The effect on Chuikov and his fellow generals was electric. 'The word "Berlin" on that memorable order sounded like our next mission,' he wrote. 'One can well imagine how excited we were when we read it. Advancing on a broad front we had covered thousands of kilometres through the flames of battle. Braving the winter cold, crossing water obstacles, and smashing fortifications, we were now approaching the ultimate target.'

ZHUKOV HAD already submitted plans to Stalin for a new, non-stop offensive. Starting at the Berlinchen (Barlinek)–Landsberg–Grätz line on 1 or 2 February, he proposed smashing his way across the Oder and right into Berlin in one massive thrust. A couple of days later, Koniev, not to be outdone, put in his plan. This involved an advance starting on 5 or 6 February which would destroy German forces at Breslau, then press on to the south of Berlin until they reached the River Elbe on about 25 or 26 February. His right-flank armies would then be free to join Zhukov's forces in capturing Berlin.

Stalin approved Zhukov's and Koniev's plans. Both commanders were to be given the chance of writing their names in the history books as conqueror of Hitler's capital. The race for Berlin was now on. No doubt Stalin meant this decision as a goad to his most brilliant general, but it turned out to be a recipe for confusion and delay. He had already designated Zhukov as 'the victor of Berlin': in allowing Koniev to get in on the act, he encouraged both men to take risks they would normally never have contemplated, whipping their commanders into a breakneck gallop.

The result was that the front echelon forces outran not only the directives from Moscow, but also their own vital supplies. Units were having to siphon fuel out of some of their vehicles in order to keep the others running. Tanks were being abandoned across Poland and Silesia like the toys of some impatient child. Supply trucks returning empty from the front areas were joined in pairs, with one towing the other to save fuel. Even more serious was the shortage of ammunition. Chuikov, for example, was having to fall back on using captured German guns and shells. He was also operating beyond the reach of his air support. Plagued by the appalling weather conditions, short of aviation fuel, and still desperately trying to establish airfields closer to the rapidly moving front, the Red Air Force was simply being left behind.

On 31 January, Chuikov's troops finally gained control of the whole of the fortified Meseritz area, routing General Lübbe's newly arrived 15,000-strong reinforcement division. That same day, an advance battle group from the Fifth Shock Army, on Chuikov's right, managed to force the Oder north of the fortress of Küstrin. The Germans, believing the nearest Soviet forces were still some miles away, were caught napping. As the Soviet troops, under Colonel Yesipenko, burst into the town of Kienitz, German soldiers were strolling around the streets, while many of their officers were eating breakfast in the local restaurants. The railway station was open, and trains were running to Berlin, apparently still on schedule.

Recovering from their shock, the Germans counter-attacked fiercely, calling up artillery, mortar fire and air support to try to drive the Soviets back. But at 10 am Colonel Vainrub's 219th Tank Brigade reached the river, and the following day the rest of the Ist Mechanized Corps reached the eastern approaches of Küstrin. Next day, 1 February, Chuikov's IVth Guards Rifle Corps reached the bank of the Oder just south of the town.

Situated on the confluence of the Oder and Warta rivers, Küstrin had been a fortified strategic town even in Frederick the Great's day. The citadel at its centre was a virtually impregnable fortress, built on an island at the meeting point of the two rivers. A major rail and road junction straddling the direct routes to the capital, Küstrin had always been known as the gateway to Berlin. The Big City lay just forty miles away to the west.

*

NEVER A man to await the enemy's convenience – or even his own reinforcements and air cover – Chuikov ordered his troops to cross the river and establish bridgeheads on the west bank. The weather was cold and clear, with a brilliant blue sky. The landscape was white with snow, and the big river in front of them, a formidable obstacle 300 yards wide and 10 feet deep, lined on both sides with steep embankments, was ice bound. But the ice was so thin that it could barely support the weight of a man, let alone tanks and heavy equipment. The army's pontoons, boats and bridging equipment were still far away in the rear. So, too, were their anti-aircraft batteries, struggling through the snow behind the advance guard, while the Red Air Force was still out of touch and out of fuel.

Nevertheless, under cover of artillery fire, Chuikov's guardsmen began to pick their way across the river, laying planks, poles and bundles of brushwood on the ice to make improvised footbridges. They mounted anti-tank guns on makeshift skis and slid them across, in the face of Luftwaffe Focke-Wulf fighters strafing them with machine-gun fire and bombing holes in the ice, flying so low that to Chuikov it seemed their propellers would touch the heads of his men. Without air support or anti-aircraft guns, there was little the Soviet troops could do, apart from using their machine guns and anti-tank guns, which managed to bring down at least two enemy aircraft. By nightfall, they had established two minor bridgeheads on the west bank.

The anti-aircraft division finally arrived on the morning of 3 February. From then on, they were able to provide covering fire against the incoming planes, as Chuikov continued to get troops across the river. During the day, he succeeded in transferring his artillery observation posts to the far bank. There, they could direct fire on to the German formations facing them, while their own troops began to extend their footholds, gradually linking them up until they formed one single bridgehead. Further advance was impossible without the heavy guns and tanks that could still not be moved across from the east bank, but the bridgehead was secure.

That day, Zhukov issued a new directive. It began: 'The troops of the front will consolidate their success by active operations in the next six days, bring up all units that have fallen behind, replenish fuel to two allowances per vehicle and ammunition to two establishments, and in a swift assault take Berlin on 15–16 February.'

# 4

Among the troops facing Chuikov's army across the Oder was Fred Laabs. He and Karl-Heinz Freund had just arrived by truck in the small town of Gorgast, west of Küstrin. They were temporarily billeted in a school, but it was clear to them that despite their pitiful lack of training, they were about to be thrown into the front line, to face Soviet veterans. During their time in the Reinickendorf barracks, the two boys had often discussed plans for escape, but had had no opportunity. Now, with the enemy almost within sight and certainly within sound, they knew there was no time to lose if they were not to become cannon fodder.

The escape itself could not have been easier. Waiting until a truck drove slowly out of the big gates of the school playground, they walked out alongside it, as though escorting it on foot. Wearing full combat gear, complete with gas masks, pistols and steel helmets, they looked the part, and nobody took any notice of them. Once they were clear, they headed for the city of Frankfurt-an-der-Oder, fifteen miles to the south, where Karl-Heinz had a reliable friend. Although they still had all their papers, the biggest danger was from the infamous Feld Gendarmerie, the German military police, who were constantly on the look-out for deserters. The Feld Gendarmerie would shoot anyone they even suspected of desertion, or hang them from the nearest tree without the time-wasting formality of a trial.

Avoiding the main roads and keeping to rural areas, the two friends arrived at their destination without encountering any patrols. Karl-Heinz's friend lived with his mother close to the main bridge over the Oder. He was already in hiding, and his mother was fearful of the idea of putting up Fred and Karl-Heinz. She suggested they burn their uniforms, but they refused, knowing they would need them when the time came to return to Berlin. Without them, they would be far too conspicuous.

The Germans still held both sides of the river at Frankfurt, and the city was not badly damaged. It seemed to be full of people on the move – bedraggled civilian refugees heading west, and reluctant soldiers marching east across the bridge, the last reserves heading for the coming battles with the Soviets. Most of the local inhabitants were joining the trek westwards, so day by day the city became more and more empty. Food and fuel were virtually non-existent. Everyone had to fend for themselves, and Fred and Karl-Heinz joined the rest of the population in forays into the surrounding countryside to find food by grubbing out what little they could find in the frozen fields, or by bartering with farmers. For fuel they used beams and timber from ruined buildings, planks from fences, or the wood from the few remaining trees. Because the situation was utterly chaotic, they were able to live quite openly, still wearing their uniforms, as long as they took care to keep an eye open for Feld Gendarmerie patrols.

# 5

HITLER LEFT the Adlerhorst, his last field headquarters, on 15 January, when it was clear that his Ardennes gamble had failed. He arrived in Berlin early in the morning of the 16th, and was driven straight to the Reich chancellery, the blinds pulled down as usual over the windows of his car to shut out the unwelcome sight of the destruction he had brought upon the city. Hitler never wanted to see the results of air raids, and, in marked contrast to Churchill and the British royal family, never visited the ruins of bombed cities. Goebbels was the only Nazi leader to do so.

The chancellery was even more badly damaged than when Hitler had last seen it. Every window had long since been shattered, but now only the ground floor and cellar were habitable. His large study, where he had always held his daily conferences while in Berlin, was one of the few rooms that remained undamaged, but the west wing of the old chancellery building, which had housed his private apartment, had collapsed. On the advice of SS General Rattenhuber, he moved his office and residence into the barely completed bunker deep under the chancellery garden. For some time, when no daylight air raid was expected, he continued to hold daily conferences in his old study, but more and more he was forced to stay underground, in what the wags among his entourage called his 'cement submarine'.

It would have made more sense had Hitler gone to the OKW bunker in Zossen, which was both more roomy and fully equipped as a military headquarters, and was out of the target zone of the constant air raids. As supreme commander he would have been in direct contact with his general staff, who were all based there. Zossen also possessed the most modern communications systems, while the bunker had only a fairly small telephone switchboard, designed by Siemens for use by one operator in a divisional headquarters or a medium-sized hotel. It did have an army radio transmitter but this worked only on medium and long waves and needed an external aerial which had to be jury-rigged using a length of wire suspended above the bunker by a balloon.

As the situation continued to deteriorate, many people tried to persuade Hitler to move to Zossen or, failing that, to the big Luftwaffe bunker at Wannsee. But he refused, claiming that he was doubtful about the strength of 'army concrete'. The truth was that after the 20 July assassination attempt he no longer felt safe among army officers. In the Führer bunker he was surrounded at all times by his hand-picked SS guards.

THE FÜHRER bunker consisted of eighteen rooms, arranged on either side of a central corridor which was itself divided in two by a partition. One half was used as a conference room, the other as a general sitting room. On one side of the corridor lay Dr Stumpfegger's room and surgery, and the rooms where Hitler's valet and military aides slept; painted battleship grey, these rooms were a uniform eight by ten feet. The telephone switchboard was also located there, as were small offices for Goebbels and Martin Bormann, chief of the party chancellery, who went on right to the end producing what Goebbels called his 'mountain of paper', bureaucracy at its last gasp. On the other side of the corridor was Hitler's private apartment, consisting of bedroom, map room, living room and lobby, each measuring ten feet by fifteen, a private shower and toilet, and Eva Braun's bedroom. A separate small room for Hitler's dogs contained a ladder leading to an unfinished concrete observation tower above the ground. At the end of the corridor was a small room used as a cloakroom, from which four flights of steps led up to an emergency exit in the chancellery garden. Apart from the few rooms that had received a hurried lick of grey paint, all the walls, floors and low ceilings were of bare concrete, much of it still not completely dry.

Almost the only decoration of any sort was Hitler's prized portrait of his hero, Frederick the Great. A life-sized oil painting by Anton Graff, the picture had been bought by Hitler in Munich in 1934. In its specially constructed travelling crate it had to be carried on his private train or Condor aircraft every time he moved his base. Now it was installed in his underground study/living room, where he could sometimes be seen sitting alone in candlelight, staring at the old king as though in deep, silent conversation with him.

The Führer bunker was reached by a wrought-iron spiral staircase, at the foot of which was a bulkhead with a heavy steel door, leading down from the older upper bunker, which consisted of twelve cramped rooms around a wide corridor used as a communal mess area. One of the rooms was the vegetarian kitchen where Hitler's own meals were prepared, the others were storage rooms and servants' quarters, plus accommodation for Hitler's other physician, Dr Theodore Morell, which was taken over by the Goebbels family when Morell was finally banished. A 60-kilowatt diesel generator supplied electricity for lighting, heating, ventilation, radio and telephone, and for the pump to draw water from the artesian well.

Entry to the upper bunker, which was built under the west wing of the old chancellery, was either by a staircase leading down from the butler's pantry, or by a tunnel 120 yards long but only five feet below ground level from the basement of the new chancellery, which served as barracks for the SS troops who guarded the Führer, and for members of his office staff. Work on reinforcing the basement was not finished until February 1945, so the concrete had no time to dry out properly, leaving the walls permanently dripping with water.

At the bunker end of the tunnel was a narrow corridor containing three air- and water-tight double steel doors. One led to the passageway to the old chancellery, known to the denizens of the concrete catacombs as Kannenberg Alley, after Hitler's portly chief steward, Arthur Kannenberg; the second was the entrance to the central corridor in the upper bunker itself; the third closed off a short tunnel and another flight of stairs leading up to the gardens of the Foreign Office, next door in the Wilhelmstrasse. The Foreign Office had its own underground bunker, as did Goebbels's Propaganda Ministry – all told there were at least six large underground bunkers in the Wilhelmstrasse area by the beginning of 1945, most of them connected to the chancellery by a labyrinth of tunnels through which generals, ministers, officials and messengers could scurry beneath the surface, relatively safe from bombs.

BY THE time he returned to Berlin, Hitler was a wreck, both physically and mentally. He had developed a marked tremor in his left hand after the bomb attempt, but this shaking had now spread to the whole of his left side, and his gestures were slow and jerky, like a man in an advanced stage of Parkinson's disease. He had taken to keeping his hand in his pocket, so that the shaking would not be seen, or using his good right hand to hold his left arm against his body. He had become stooped, almost hunch-backed, with a sagging pot belly. He walked with an awkward shuffle, dragging his left leg a little, and had to have his chair pushed under him when he wanted to sit down. With his ashen complexion, he looked like an old man in his seventies rather than a mere fifty-five. But his pale blue eyes, though tired and bloodshot, could be as hypnotic as ever, and he still retained the unmistakable aura of power, and the ability to switch on a commanding presence that could still inspire a certain awe.

Despite his exhaustion, Hitler insisted on running every detail of the war. Indeed, he even increased his involvement: one of the first directives he issued from Berlin, on 21 January, ordered all commanding generals down to divisional level to inform him in advance of every operational movement from their units. 'They must ensure that I have time to intervene in their decisions if I think fit,' he declared, 'and that my counter-orders can reach the front-line troops in time.'

Hitler's interference brought more clashes with the chief of the general staff, Heinz Guderian. He was furious when General Friedrich Hossbach pulled his Fourth Army out of East Prussia, after it had been overrun by Rokossovsky. Hossbach was intent on saving as many of his men as possible and was also trying to keep open an escape corridor for half a million East Prussians fleeing on foot and in horse-drawn wagons. He had cleared the withdrawal with his immediate chief, Colonel-General Hans Reinhardt, commander of Army Group North, but not with Guderian or the Führer. Hitler summoned Guderian – himself an East Prussian, born on the Vistula – and ordered him to dismiss both generals immediately, together with their staffs. 'They deserve to be court-martialled,' he raged, accusing the two men of treason. Guderian protested that he did not consider either man a traitor. Hitler ignored him and replaced Reinhardt with Colonel-General Lothar Rendulic, a committed Nazi noted for his advice to his cornered troops: 'When things look blackest and you don't know what to do, beat your chest and say "I'm a National Socialist – that moves mountains!"'

Hitler had also ignored Guderian's violent objections when he had replaced the commander of Army Group Centre, on Rendulic's right, with another of his favourites, Colonel-General Ferdinand Schörner. In despair, Guderian approached Foreign Minister Ribbentrop, told him the war was already lost, and asked him to try to get an immediate armistice in the west so that troops could be transferred to face the Soviets. Ribbentrop hurried to tell Hitler of Guderian's suggestion, provoking a new row between the two men.

'In the future,' Hitler screamed, 'anyone who tells anyone else that the war is lost will be treated as a traitor, with all the consequences for him and his family. I will take action without regard to rank and reputation!'

Guderian weathered the storm, and once again swallowed his anger at Hitler's irrational meddling. But there was worse to come. On 24 January, as convoys of trucks began moving government documents from Berlin to Bavaria for safe keeping, the Führer approved Guderian's proposal to form a brand-new emergency army group, to be rushed into the gap between Army Groups North and Centre in a last-ditch effort to stem the flood tide of Zhukov's advance. However, he rejected his choice of Field Marshal Maximilian von Weichs, a brilliant and daring field commander then in charge of German forces in Yugoslavia, as its commander. Hitler decreed that the new force, to be known as Army Group Vistula, should be commanded by Heinrich Himmler.

Guderian exploded at the idea of 'such an idiocy being perpetrated on the unfortunate eastern front'. Himmler's only previous military experience was a brief period as an army cadet during his youth. Encouraged by Bormann, who was eager to remove one of his few rivals for their master's affections, Hitler insisted that the SS leader was a great organizer and administrator, and that his very name would inspire the troops to fight to their last breath. Besides, he went on, as commander of the Reserve Army, Himmler was the only man who could instantly form a major new force.

Convinced that his hour of glory had come at last, Himmler accepted enthusiastically, and set off at once for the front, near Danzig. He was armed with one outdated situation map, had only a handful of staff officers, and his new army group barely existed on paper. But as new divisions arrived from the reserves, he began forming them into a defensive line. Incredibly, this ran not from north to south but from east to west, from the northern Vistula to the Oder, offering no protection to Berlin, and only a little to Pomerania in the north. Zhukov ignored it, sweeping around it to the south to reach the Oder.

GUDERIAN LEFT the daily situation conference on 27 January at 6.50 pm, utterly disgusted. For two and a half hours, while the eastern front was disintegrating under the crashing hammer blows of the Soviet assault, Hitler and his toadies had indulged in petty squabbles and wild fantasies of the British and Americans joining the Germans in fighting off the Bolshevik menace from the east. Not one single decision had been taken concerning the critical situation beyond the Oder.

After the conference had broken up, Hitler received a telephone call from Schörner at Army Group Centre. He had consistently forbidden any retreat from the industrial and mining region of Silesia, on pain of death. But now Schörner told him he had ordered its evacuation. Hitler said nothing. Schörner continued: 'These troops have been fighting a heavy battle for two weeks, and now they're finished. If we don't relieve them, we're going to lose the whole Seventeenth Army, and the road to Bavaria will be wide open. We're moving back to the Oder, and there we will stop.'

The silence at the other end of the line continued. Then, after what seemed an eternity, Hitler replied, in a weary voice: 'Yes, Schörner. If you think it's right, I'll have to agree.'

FOR ALBERT SPEER, the loss of Upper Silesia marked the end of all hope. He had already prepared a farewell memorandum to his staff, and ordered his assistants to collect photographs and records of his architectural projects and store them in a safe place – as if such a thing still existed in Berlin. Now he prepared a detailed note for Hitler on the hopeless situation for armaments production. Delivered on 30 January, the twelfth anniversary of Hitler's accession, the report began unequivocally: 'The war is lost.' He went on to detail falling production figures and to forecast what might be possible in the coming three months. Silesia had been providing 60 per cent of Germany's coal supplies. Now there were only two weeks' stocks to fuel factories, railways and power plants. 'From now on,' he concluded, 'the material preponderance of the enemy can no longer be compensated for by the bravery of our soldiers.'

Hitler remained unmoved by Speer's message. He left the chancellery for what was to be his last social engagement outside its walls, afternoon tea with Joseph and Magda Goebbels at their home in Schwanenwerder – his paranoia was so intense that he took his own thermos flask of tea and a bag of cakes.

WHILE HITLER was enjoying his tea and cakes with the Goebbels, others in the city were fighting for their food. At a distribution point in the working-class district of Neukölln, the stoic calm of the Berliners lining up for their handout finally snapped. They charged the trucks, trying to seize the supplies. Several women were killed when they overturned a wagonload of potatoes. In no time the disturbance turned into a full-scale riot, which was only put down when the police opened fire, killing several more women.

If he heard about the riot in Neukölln, Hitler made no mention of it later that day, when he made his last broadcast to the nation. In a speech that was totally blind to reality, he told Berliners that their city was now like a huge porcupine, and would be defended to its last breath. He promised that his new secret weapons would drive the enemy from the Fatherland. 'We are going to force a turn of the tide!' he declared solemnly. 'We are going to show our enemies that our courage and our spirit are made of Krupps steel. Keep up your morale, Berliners! I am with you!

'However grave the crisis may be at the moment,' he assured the long-suffering German people, 'in the end it will be mastered by our unalterable will, by our readiness for sacrifice, and by our abilities. We will overcome this emergency. And in the struggle it will not be the interior of Asia that will win, but Europe, represented by that nation which for fifteen hundred years has defended and will always defend Europe against the east, our Greater German Reich, the German nation!' Germany, he said, would never surrender. Germany would fight on to the last. Hitler expected every man to do his duty, even the sick.

'Now,' said the Berlin wits, 'the Führer has declared war on *us*!'

# 6

THE DAY after Hitler's radio speech to the nation, a sudden panic gripped Berlin. With Silesia cut off, and the Red Army across the Oder, a rumour swept the city that Soviet tanks had reached Strausberg, only eleven miles from the city boundary and less than twenty from the centre. The Volkssturm, 'the last round-up of the old and the lame, the children and the dotards', as it was described, was put on the highest alert. All over the city, men disappeared from their homes. Most reported to their units to receive what few arms were available – at a roll call of 1,000 men a short time before, for example, only eighteen had rifles. Then, fearful but determined, they piled into the trenches they had been digging for weeks, or went to work building makeshift barricades in the streets of the eastern districts.

Other men, far too many to be counted, simply disappeared. Men like Leo Borchardt, who had acquired phoney medical certificates for weak hearts, dangerously high blood pressure or serious kidney disorders, thought it wiser not to be at home when the messengers from their local Volkssturm unit arrived on the doorstep, telling them to be ready to march in one hour. Knowing that resistance was pointless, they were not prepared to face almost certain death simply to prolong Hitler's regime for a few more hours or days. All that mattered to them was that the war should be lost as quickly as possible.

In a vain effort to counter this, Berlin's five surviving daily newspapers carried a prominent warning in bold type on the front of their single page: 'Any person who attempts to avoid fulfilling his obligations towards the community, and in particular any person who so acts from cowardice or for selfish reasons, must be punished at once with appropriate severity, in order to ensure that the state suffers no harm through the failure of the individual citizen.'

Party officials were not drafted into the Volkssturm, but they were now classified into two groups. Those considered too important to be called up for military service until the very last moment were given red identity cards; those who could be spared a little earlier were given white ones.

Police on the beat were ordered to wear steel helmets and carry carbines – but they were clearly meant to keep the population in order rather than fight the Russians. Foreign workers were locked into their camps, with armed guards stationed at the gates in case of trouble. 'But despite all that,' Eliza Stokowska wrote in her diary, 'we were aware of what was going on. We could read everything from the faces of the camp leader and the guards.' The Polish women had started packing several days earlier, getting their belongings together just as they had in Warsaw when they were waiting for the end there. They were cold and hungry, for there was no more fuel and little food. But when they complained, they were told: 'You'll be going home soon – why are you still moaning?'

There were few regular troops anywhere near Berlin now. The remains of the Reserve Army had been shipped to the front, where many fell victim to the Soviet advance before they had even had time to take up positions. To strengthen the Volkssturm, Luftwaffe anti-aircraft units were hurriedly brought into the city from nearby regions. Lieutenant Walter Schmid arrived from Magdeburg in the early hours of the morning, with his troop of about seventy men, most of them youngsters, and two 88 mm anti-aircraft guns. They had been sent to help defend the capital not against aircraft but against tanks – the 88 was one of the most versatile guns of the war, equally effective as a field gun or in an anti-tank role. They found the city in some confusion, as officials scrambled to load as many of their possessions as they could manage into cars hurriedly bought and fuelled on the black market, ready for the anticipated evacuation of the government. Many were already leaving, prepared to risk being hanged as defeatists rather than stay and face the Soviets.

For Schmid the situation was fraught with irony. In 1939, as one of the youngest attachés in the Foreign Office, he had been closely involved in the secret negotiations that led to the Nazi–Soviet Pact. During the first two years of the war, right up to Barbarossa, he had served in the Moscow embassy. He spoke excellent Russian, and like everyone who worked in that embassy, had fallen in love with Russia – with the country, the culture, and above all the people. And now, here he was at the age of twenty-nine, preparing to defend Hitler's Berlin and a regime he detested against the very people he cared for so deeply.

On their arrival in Berlin, Schmid and his men were met by an officer from divisional headquarters at the Zoo flak tower, who guided them to their new location. It was not in the city, but several miles to the east, astride the main road leading to Frankfurt-an-der-Oder. Soviet tanks, he was told, were already on the move; they might attack at any moment. Hastily they dug in their guns and waited for the worst. A week later, they were still waiting.

The panic faded as quickly as it had started, when it was confirmed that the Soviet armies were still only at the Oder. The news was received by Berliners with gallows humour. 'The situation is bad but not serious,' went one joke. 'It will only be serious when you can get to the eastern front by U-Bahn.' Others looked at the half-finished barricades and shook their heads scornfully. 'They'll save Berlin,' they mocked, 'because when the Russians see them they'll die laughing!'

The government was not evacuated. Party officials were not called up. Volkssturm units were stood down. Elderly men and boys clambered out of their trenches and left the uncompleted barricades, to drift thankfully back to their homes. But they hardly had time to enjoy their relief when the city was hit by a fresh catastrophe.

On Saturday, 3 February, at 10.45 am, the first of a giant armada of American bombers appeared over the city. For one and three-quarter hours they filled the sky in a non-stop tidal wave, nearly 1,000 Flying Fortresses and Liberators dropping 2,267 tons of bombs, the heaviest single raid yet.

Once again, the central districts got the worst of the raid. The Reich chancellery was the bull's eye, and suffered accordingly. Bormann described the results in a letter to his wife, his 'beloved girl', who had stayed safely at home on the Obersalzberg, near Berchtesgaden:

The Reich chancellery garden is an amazing sight – deep craters, fallen trees, and the paths obliterated by a mass of rubble and rubbish. The Führer's residence was badly hit several times; all that is left of the winter gardens and the banquet hall are fragments of the walls; and the entrance hall on the Wilhelmstrasse, where the Wehrmacht guard was usually mounted, has been completely destroyed. . . .

In spite of it all, we have to go on working diligently, for the war continues on all fronts! Telephone communications are still very inadequate, and the Führer's residence and the party chancellery still have no connection with the outside world. . . .

And to crown everything, in this so-called government quarter we still have no light, power or water supplies! We have a water cart standing in front of the Reich chancellery, and that is our only supply for cooking and washing up! And worst of all, so Müller tells me, are the water closets. These *Kommando* pigs use them constantly, and not one of them ever thinks of taking a bucket of water with him to flush the place. . . .

Hitler was unharmed in his deep bunker. Others in the city were not so lucky. At the People's Court, Freisler was busy as usual. The day before, he had sentenced Dietrich Bonhoeffer's brother Klaus and his brother-in-law Rüdiger Schleicher to death, along with two other conspirators, Friedrich Perels and Hans John. When the American bombers struck on the Saturday morning, he had been in the middle of trying Fabian von Schlabrendorff. The trial was interrupted as everyone dashed for the shelter.

Schleicher's brother, Rolf, a senior army staff doctor, had been on his way to the court to lodge an appeal for mercy, and was trapped in the Potsdamerplatz U-Bahn station while the raid progressed. When it was over, he emerged and headed for the nearby courthouse, where he was recognized as a doctor because of his uniform, and asked to attend to some important person, the only casualty in the courthouse, who had been hit by shrapnel as he ran across the courtyard to the shelter. All Rolf Schleicher could do was to certify that the man was dead. He did it with pleasure: the man was Roland Freisler.

Seizing his opportunity, Schleicher refused to sign the death certificate until he had spoken personally to the minister of justice, Dr Thierack. Struck by the coincidence, Thierack agreed to a stay of execution for Rüdiger Schleicher until he had reconsidered the verdict in the light of his brother's mercy plea.

Schlabrendorff was taken back to the Prinz–Albrecht–Strasse prison, which had been damaged by bombs. Fortunately, none of the prisoners had been injured. Passing Admiral Canaris as he was being led back to his cell, Schlabrendorff called out 'Freisler is dead!' Within minutes the prison grapevine spread the news throughout the cellars. At last, in the midst of their darkness, the prisoners had something to celebrate.

Hans von Dohnanyi had joined the other conspirators in the Gestapo prison on 1 February, having been carried there on a stretcher when the important prisoners were evacuated from Sachsenhausen concentration camp. As they were returning from the shelter after the raid, Bonhoeffer managed to snatch a brief conversation with him alone in his cell; they were able to update each other on the state of their interrogations, and to go a little further in coordinating their stories.

THE GESTAPO prison and headquarters was so severely damaged in the raid that it could only house those prisoners who were about to stand trial. The others were moved out, to the comparative security of the Flossenbürg and Buchenwald concentration camps. Bonhoeffer was one of the twelve men sent to Buchenwald in an eight-seater prison van. Among his fellow passengers were Gottfried von Bismarck, General Alexander von Falkenhausen, the former governor of northern France and Belgium, and Bonhoeffer's Abwehr colleague from Munich, Josef Müller.

Dohnanyi remained behind in Prinz Albrechtstrasse, where he was handed over for questioning to a particularly brutal commissar called Stawizky. Suspecting that he was malingering, Stawizky refused to allow him any treatment, and for three weeks never even had him taken to the bathroom. 'He thought he could break my spirit by leaving me entirely uncared for,' Dohnanyi wrote to his wife in a letter smuggled out in his laundry parcel after Stawizky was removed from the case. 'That went on for three weeks. I really began to stink. That helped. . . . It was actually very funny, and I often laughed at how I looked. I am using my illness as a weapon. It helps me that people think I'm sicker than I am. . . .'

With the end of the war coming closer all the while, Dohnanyi had to play for time, both for himself and for those who would go down with him if he were broken. 'They want to finish things off by force, and that must be prevented,' he wrote. For all his positive words to his wife, he knew he could not keep up the pretence of illness for much longer. If the illness were real, however, he would not have to fear more interrogation. Making use of the Bonhoeffer family's medical connections, he persuaded his wife to obtain a culture of diphtheria bacilli from the research laboratories of the Koch Institute. She smuggled it in to him inside a thermos flask in a food parcel. Shortly afterwards, seriously ill with diphtheria, he was moved to the prison hospital in Scharnhorststrasse, under the care of a family friend.

# 7

ONCE THE immediate threat to the city had receded, however temporarily, the Berliners picked up the threads of daily routine. A visiting French writer was astonished by what he described as people's indifference to catastrophe. He watched as Berliners 'went about their business, did their shopping amidst mountains of ruins, made their way along pavements obstructed with bricks and mud, as if nothing had happened'.

Shopping had by then become difficult, if not impossible, because those shops that remained open were virtually empty. Their display windows had long since been replaced by heavy wooden boarding, with a small aperture cut at eye level so that customers could see what was inside – though this was usually a pile of empty cartons and a picture of the Führer. The few items still available could usually only be bought by those with a bomb damage certificate stating that their homes and possessions had been destroyed. A few shops on the Unter den Linden were said to be prepared to sell goods in exchange for cigarettes – money had become almost worthless.

Gas and electricity supplies were cut off more and more often, and for longer periods – sometimes for days. The city's reserves of coke were said to be sufficient for only two weeks, and people found it increasingly difficult to find lignite briquettes to burn in the little tubular stoves they had installed in their living rooms for heating and cooking. Water supplies, too, were interrupted more frequently, and the water crocodile became an increasingly common sight on the streets: lines of women queuing at standpipes and hydrants to fill pails, cans and saucepans. The reduced food rations, now down to an average 1,600 calories a day, could no longer be guaranteed. Daily bread had become a weekly loaf, which bakers were not allowed to sell until it was two or three days old, so that it could be sliced more thinly and therefore might last longer.

The basic community unit had become smaller – based no longer on a district, or even a street, but on a cellar. An anonymous woman diarist, who recorded her experiences during the final weeks of the war in a series of exercise books, described cellar life at that time:

> The cellar tribe in this house is convinced that its cave is the safest.
> There's nothing stranger than a strange cellar. I have belonged to this
> one for more than three months and I still feel a stranger in it. Each

cellar has its own taboos, its own fads. In my old cellar they had a rage for extinguishing water; everywhere one bumped into buckets, pitchers, pots and barrels filled with the muddy brew. It didn't stop the house burning like a torch. The whole lot would have been as much use as spitting. Frau Weiers told me that in her cellar they perform the lung ritual. As soon as the first bomb drops, they all bend forward and breathe very carefully, at the same time pressing their hands against their bellies. Someone had told them this would prevent their lungs tearing. Here, they have wall drill. Everyone sits with his back against the wall; the only place where the line is broken is under the air hole. At the first bang, the towel ritual begins: everyone wraps a special towel kept ready for this purpose over his mouth and nose, and knots it at the back of his head.

Travel was becoming increasingly difficult both inside the city and for anyone trying to get in or out by train. All buses had been taken off the streets on 23 January: every gallon of fuel was needed for military vehicles, and in any case it had become almost impossible for them to navigate the rubble-strewn streets. Some trams still operated, running shuttle services along those stretches of track that were still usable, but they stopped at 10 pm. Within the city, a bicycle was more useful than a Mercedes limousine.

Most of the mainline stations were out of action for much of the time, and travellers often had to start or finish their journeys at outlying S-Bahn stations. The S-Bahn trains still ran – their tracks could be repaired between raids. The U-Bahn, however, was more difficult to repair, and was reduced to running shuttle services between the points where its shallow tunnels had been destroyed. As the final weeks passed, more sections of track were put out of service.

Veronika von Below, a young woman fleeing from Pomerania to Bavaria, passed through Berlin at this time. On 5 February, at midday, she was caught on an underground train when the US Air Force arrived. The station they had just left received a direct hit, leaving no survivors. They stopped at the next, which was packed with people sheltering, as bombs exploded nearby. All the lights went out. The earth shook. But to Veronika's surprise, no one moved or made a sound.

When she surfaced after the raid, she was faced with a scene of utter chaos, with tramcars thrown against the walls of buildings like crumpled paper. She picked her way on foot to her destination, where she was astonished to find her relatives sitting behind shattered windows, drinking schnapps and apparently oblivious to the unexploded bomb outside the house. Their sang-froid was typical of most Berliners, who continued to pick themselves up and dust themselves down after each air raid and each setback, true to their centuries-old motto: 'Ich lass mir nicht unterkriegen!' – 'I don't let anything get me down.'

Life just had to go on, regardless. Office workers could be seen riding to work each morning jammed together in the back of open trucks – but they still went every day. Karl-Friedrich Borée worked in a city centre bank that had been bombed several times. The staff conscientiously carried their files, typewriters and calculators down to the cellar every time an alert sounded, and lugged them back up again at the all-clear. But there was an air of surrealism about the place: Borée watched his departmental manager working in the air-raid shelter on the final details of a deal with the state of Estonia – which no longer existed. And the eastern department went on punctiliously writing to clients in Persia which had long since been swallowed by the Soviets.

BEFORE SHE could continue her journey south, Veronika von Below had to make her way on foot to the Alexanderplatz, to collect a refugee certificate. The office was besieged by endless lines of people, for it was also responsible for issuing bomb damage certificates. It took her fourteen hours to obtain the paper allowing her to leave the city. But she had even more frustrations ahead of her: because of the bombing, there was only one train to the south each twenty-four hours from the outlying S-Bahn station that was being used as a mainline terminus. It left at night, to avoid daylight bombers and fighters – but still had to endure the RAF attacks.

The train she managed to squeeze aboard departed on Monday night, but only travelled fifty yards or so through the tunnel before being forced to stop and wait until the next night. It was Thursday night before it was finally clear of Berlin. The journey to Munich took another two days and nights.

FOR THE ordinary Berliner who could not escape, the cinema continued to provide a welcome distraction. 'Morale wouldn't be so high if it weren't for the cinema,' the intellectuals in Marianne Gärtner's communal cellar shelter concluded.

'Two hours of escaping into a perfect world!' someone agreed.
'Of feeling beautifully lachrymose . . .'
'Or splitting your sides laughing . . .'
'And forgetting your empty stomach.'
'Ja, ja – if they can't have bread, give them films!'
'The few remaining city and suburban film-theatres were showing *Heimatfilme*,' Marianne recalls,

German musicals and romantic comedies which, invariably leading to a happy ending, and being mildly erotic, brought all the glitter of show business to the screen, or transported the viewer to peaceful Alpine meadows and stag-and-edelweiss mountains. Ilse Werner whistled through her films, Marikka Röck danced, Johannes Heesters smoothed the brows of female cinema-goers with his songs. Buxom girls with blonde plaits, bejewelled, permed ladies in silk, or demure maidens in white-collared dresses or dirndls were courted by lean, heroic men with the social polish of officers and gentlemen, or by handsome Nordic types with poetry on their lips or marriage proposals in their briefcases. In some films, darkly irresistible Casanovas made women's hearts throb with the ardour of their passion and their dishonourable intentions; in others, hefty, broad-shouldered rustics in *Lederhosen*, experts in lifting a stein and in handling the axe and scythe, went about conquering their women-folk with Bavarian bravura.

Maria Milde, ex-dancer, ex-Hiller girl, product of the Ufa charm school and at one time being groomed as Nazi Germany's answer to Greta Garbo, played in many of the frothy romantic comedies of the period – films with titles like *Spring Melody*. As a film actress, she was cushioned against the worst effects of the war, living a strangely cocooned life. She and her fellow starlets were housed during the last weeks of the war in the draughty splendours of the Jagdschloss Glienicke, a château alongside the famous Glienicke bridge at the southern tip of the Havel bordering Babelsberg and Potsdam. There, outside the target area for most of the air raids and conveniently close to the studios, they were hardly aware of life outside.

Ufa film production continued right up to March 1945, albeit on a reduced scale. When the bombing got so bad that it interfered with the sound equipment in the Babelsberg studios, film units were sent on location, often as far away as Prague. One such unit completed its shooting schedule in territory that was actually being overrun by Soviet tanks during filming. When they had finished they had to cross the front line to return to Berlin. With dedication like that, it is not surprising that, almost to the very end of the war, Ufa producers and directors were still able to get their film processed, and to view their 'dailies' regularly.

For those with more elevated tastes, there were still frequent music concerts in churches, makeshift halls and even in factory workshops, though the musicians were all elderly or sick. Nevertheless, they lifted people's spirits with performances of chamber music, popular overtures and symphonies. Tania Lemnitz sang *Lieder* and operatic arias, Elli Ney played Beethoven, Wilhelm Kempff played Schumann. The Berlin Philharmonic, under Wilhelm Furtwängler, who had rejected a suggestion by Speer that he should escape to the safety of Switzerland, still played in the Philharmonic Hall or the Admiralspalast theatre alongside Friedrichstrasse railway station. Marianne Gärtner went with her grandmother to a performance of Beethoven's Fourth Symphony at the Philharmonic. The experience could not have been in more striking contrast to the harsh world outside, as she sat with eyes closed, transported for a short time to an almost forgotten world of beauty and happiness.

8

Eᴀʀʟʏ ɪɴ the morning of Tuesday, 6 February, Zhukov drove to the command post of General Kolpakchi's Sixty-Ninth Army, for a conference with his five army commanders to discuss the final assault on Berlin. They knew that the Germans were not yet strong enough to mount a serious counter-attack, or even to maintain a solid defence, but believed they were in the process of transferring four Panzer divisions and five or six infantry divisions across from the west, and more troops from East Prussia and the Baltic area. This, according to Zhukov's assessment, would give the enemy enough men to cover the approaches to the city.

If Zhukov was to mount his planned high-speed assault to capture Berlin by 15–16 February, his armies would have to complete all their preparations by the 10th at the latest. By then, they would need to have consolidated their bridgeheads across the Oder and established new ones; they would have to have destroyed all enemy forces still in the rear; the Red Air Force would have to be completely redeployed on new forward airfields, with enough aviation fuel and ammunition at each field to enable every aircraft to fly at least six missions; all tanks and self-propelled guns undergoing repair or refit would have to be ready for action.

It was a tall order, made even more so by seemingly intractable supply problems, and by the depleted state of the forward armies. The great advance had taken a terrible toll – divisions now averaged only 4,000 men, less than one third of their normal size, some of Chuikov's regiments were reduced to two battalions, and companies averaged between twenty-two and forty-five men. At the same time, almost half of his force was still tied up trying to overcome German resistance at Posen, more than 100 miles to his rear. Katukov had lost a fifth of his First Tank Army, and his remaining tanks were short of spares and in need of a refit. And to cap it all, the weather was on the side of the Germans: a combination of heavy snow and rain transformed grass airstrips into quagmires, making take-off and landing extremely hazardous, if not impossible, and bogging down trucks bringing up supplies, heavy artillery and bridging equipment. For once, the Luftwaffe had complete superiority in the air: even the slow and outdated Stuka dive bombers were able to attack tanks and infantry formations almost as they pleased.

Zhukov was also concerned, he claimed later, by a powerful threat to his right flank from the German Second and Eleventh Armies. Heading straight for Berlin would expose his troops to the danger of being cut off by an enemy counter-strike from the north, where Rokossovsky's armies, which were supposed to be protecting his flank, were bogged down, 100 miles adrift.

Nevertheless, Chuikov for one was eager to blast on towards Berlin immediately. He was certain that the German armies, still reeling from the blows they had received, were so shocked and disorganized that they would be incapable of stopping him. Like Montgomery in the west, he was convinced he could end the war with one, powerful, knock-out punch. The generals spread out their maps and began to discuss the operation. They had not got far when the telephone rang. It was Stalin, calling Zhukov from Yalta in the Crimea, where he was in conference with Roosevelt and Churchill – that same day, to highlight the strength of the opposition facing his troops, he jokingly bet the US president that the Americans would be in Manila before the Red Army was in Berlin.

Chuikov was sitting next to Zhukov, and could clearly overhear what Stalin was saying.

'Where are you? What are you doing?' the dictator demanded.

'I am at Kolpakchi's headquarters, and all the army commanders of the front are here, too,' Zhukov replied. 'We are planning the Berlin operation.'

'You are wasting your time. We must consolidate on the Oder and then send all the forces you can to Pomerania, to join with Rokossovsky and smash the enemy's Army Group Vistula. . . .'

Zhukov put down the phone. Saying nothing, he got up from the table, and left, to drive back to his headquarters. The advance on Berlin was postponed, indefinitely.


TWO DAYS later, Koniev's troops broke out from the Steinau bridgehead on the west bank of the Oder. By 11 February, they had smashed a hole in the German defences nearly forty miles deep on a front more than ninety miles wide. They surrounded the fortress of Glogau and then Breslau, trapping 40,000 German troops inside the city. Most of the remaining civilian population fled westwards. Those who chose to stay, still apparently believing the official Nazi line that their city was to become a springboard for a victorious new offensive, faced a bleak future, as Gauleiter Hanke proclaimed 'Every house a fortress!' With this obstinate refusal to submit to the inevitable, Breslau held out until 5 May, at a cost of 29,000 civilian and military casualties.

Koniev was now firmly established on the Neisse, but Stalin was in no hurry to apply the *coup de grâce*. Pointing out that Koniev's left flank was vulnerable to German counter-attack, he ordered him to stay where he was on the Oder and Neisse, and strengthen his position in Lower Silesia.

Although the end was in sight, Stalin had grown cautious – perhaps remembering the near disasters that had almost overtaken the Red Army's assault on Budapest the previous October and November.

Now, with Berlin on the horizon, Stalin knew he did not need to take any more chances. Churchill and Roosevelt had confirmed at Yalta that they would cooperate and not compete with the Soviet Union in the conquest of Germany. They would go on fighting the Germans until they had achieved unconditional surrender, which removed Stalin's recurrent fear of a separate peace allowing the Germans to transfer all their remaining forces to the east. He could afford to take the time to regroup and build up the strength of his armies for the final, irresistible assault.

OF THE three fronts involved in the Berlin operation, only Rokossovsky's Second Belorussian was ordered to keep moving forward. Convinced that with the gap between Rokossovsky and Zhukov still gaping wide the door was open for a counter-attack in the north, Stalin prodded Rokossovsky into action. He was to launch an offensive to destroy German groupings in East Pomerania, capture Danzig, and gain the Baltic Sea coast.

It was easier said than done, however. After weeks of continuous hard fighting, Rokossovsky's infantry divisions had been reduced to one-third of their normal strength, and his supply problem was even worse than the rest of the eastern front. Mud, rain, sleet and snow slowed up everything. The ground turned into a partly frozen morass. Men sank knee-deep into what felt like meringue. Moving supplies by any means was difficult: roads and railways had suffered at the hands of the German demolition squads, and because of the different gauges of Soviet and European rail tracks, everything had to be offloaded and then reloaded from Soviet to European wagons.

Zhukov raged at Rokossovsky, accusing him of lagging behind, and not driving on his troops hard enough. Rokossovsky, who knew Zhukov of old, was philosophic about it all. His old friend's complaints, he wrote later with some irony, were no doubt intended to spur him on. But his problems were not due to inactivity – an attack launched on 10 February foundered, literally, in mud, and in five days of fierce fighting, two of his armies succeeded in advancing only ten miles.

# 9

KONIEV'S ADVANCE to the Neisse brought yet another wave of refugees flooding into Berlin from the east. For them it was catastrophe, but for two people at least it brought salvation. Inge Deutschkron and her mother, Ella, had been living as illegals in a former goat shed at Potsdam for a year, accepted by the locals as bombed-out Berliners. Each day, they travelled into the city to their jobs, Inge in a bookshop and her mother in a textile printing firm, jobs provided by kind friends who were brave enough to take the risk of employing Jews. But the textile firm had been closed down by the Nazis in the autumn of 1944, after the owner had tried to get his adopted child, a half-Jew, into a local secondary school. Soon after, Inge had lost her job in the bookshop when the owner had decided it had become too dangerous to keep her on any longer.

With the help of other friends, Inge managed to find new work – at first ironing shirts for Frau Gumz, the laundry owner who had first sheltered them when they went underground, and then part-time with another stationery and book shop. Since all women under sixty were supposed to be in munitions factories, she said she was only allowed to work part time in the factory, because of an injury, but needed more money to support her widowed mother. To fill the rest of her days, she found another part-time job in a small grocery store, telling them the same story. As well as getting her off the street, the grocery store job had the added advantage of providing food. Ella, meanwhile, found herself work as a tutor for a group of several children whose families had been unable to bear sending them away. The fathers were all SS officers, a neat irony that was not lost on the Deutschkrons.

They had barely settled into their new roles when a fresh disaster struck. Someone denounced the man who was sheltering them in Potsdam, saying he was harbouring Jews. They had to pack up and leave at first light. With them out of the way, the man was able to avoid being charged – the anonymous denouncer turned out to be his wife, seeking revenge for an affair he was having with a girl in Berlin. He was safe, but Inge and Ella Deutschkron, with no papers or permits, were in trouble again.

They solved their problem by becoming refugees. Wearing their shabbiest clothes and carrying one small suitcase tied up with string, they took a train heading south-east out of Berlin towards the battle zone, taking the chance of being stopped for an identity check. Luck was with them – no one thought to question people leaving Berlin in the wrong direction. At Lübbenau, about fifty miles down the track, they got out and squeezed aboard a refugee train heading back to Berlin, crammed to overflowing with women and children, cats and dogs, packages and crates. During the two-hour return journey they listened carefully to what everyone was saying, making mental notes of all their experiences. Most of the others came from Guben, a town astride the Neisse which had just fallen, or from the countryside around it. They all had tales of the horrors of the Red Army – rape, pillage, looting, shooting. There had been hand-to-hand fighting in the streets of Guben, but the women and children had not been allowed to leave until the last minute. By the time the train arrived, the Deutschkrons had a good picture of the town, its streets, and what had gone on there.

Back in the chaos of a Berlin rail terminus in the middle of an air-raid alert, Ella Deutschkron put on a remarkably convincing performance as she described the terrible ordeal they were supposed to have gone through. The NSV helpers were sympathetic, plying them with food, drink and advice. Most of the genuine refugees could hardly eat, but Inge wolfed down the Leberwurst sandwiches with gusto. Tearfully, the two women told the authorities they had come from Guben, giving an imaginary address, confident that no one could check the records in a town now in Soviet hands. They complained bitterly that suitcases containing all their belongings, including papers and ration cards, had been stolen.

The NSV provided Ella Paula Richter and Inge Elisabeth Marie Richter, formerly of Amt Markt 4, Guben, with new papers, cards and clothing coupons – though the coupons proved useless as there was nothing in the shops to buy. They even gave them full, official residence permits, allowing them to live and work in Berlin. Armed with these, Ella and Inge rented a furnished room in the city to give them an address from which they could obtain regular ration cards. At last, they were legal.

# 10

STALIN WAS quite right to fear the possibility of German counter-attacks. Heinz Guderian was fully aware of the parlous state of the Soviet troops, and for days had been demanding approval from Hitler for just such a strike. He had also been badgering him for weeks to agree to the evacuation of German troops trapped in the Courland region of Latvia, beyond Riga, where two armies, the Sixteenth and Eighteenth, totalling twenty-two divisions, were locked up, serving no useful purpose. They could be evacuated comparatively easily by sea through the ports of Libau (Liepaja) and Windau (Ventspiels), to strengthen the eastern front before Berlin.

Guderian also wanted to pull back German troops from Italy, the Balkans, Norway, and finally East Prussia, to build up effective forces to mount counter-attacks and drive the Soviets back from Berlin and the body of northern Germany. He had had at least two blazing rows with Hitler – once, his aides grabbed him by the coat tails and yanked him backwards as Hitler prepared to hit him with his fists. But it had been no use. Hitler had reluctantly agreed to allow one single division to be evacuated from Courland, but instead of pulling troops back from the south, had actually continued to send reinforcements, including the Sixth SS Panzer Army, Germany's most powerful fighting force, from the north and west to fight in Hungary.

On the afternoon of 13 February, the day after the communiqué at the end of the Yalta conference had confirmed Allied insistence on unconditional surrender, punitive reparations and the division of Germany into occupation zones, Guderian arrived at the chancellery prepared for a showdown with Hitler. On the way in from Zossen for the daily Führer conference, he told his chief of staff, General Walther Wenck, 'Today, Wenck, we're going to put everything at stake, risking your head and mine.'

As the American bombers had already raided Berlin that morning, and there were unlikely to be any British attacks until night time, the conference was held in Hitler's study in the remains of the chancellery itself. Forced to take a roundabout route because so much of the building had been damaged, Guderian and Wenck, accompanied by Guderian's adjutant, Major Bernd Baron Freytag von Loringhoven, and his ADC, Captain Gerhard Boldt, marched grimly through corridors and ante-rooms, with their boarded-up windows and bare, cracked walls and ceilings. At each turning their passes were inspected by SS sentries armed with machine pistols, and when they arrived outside the ante-room to the study they were given another, even more rigorous check by SS officers and guards. They surrendered their weapons. Their briefcases were taken from them and minutely examined – not even the chief of the general staff was above suspicion.

This part of the chancellery had so far escaped serious damage. Unlike the rooms and corridors through which the four men had just passed, which had been stripped of all pictures, tapestries, curtains and carpets, these two rooms had been kept fully furnished and repaired. Here, the shattered city outside seemed as remote as another world. In the ante-room, where the generals and admirals gathered, long tables were set with refreshments – sandwiches, coffee, schnapps. While Guderian and Wenck helped themselves to coffee and talked to the other chiefs, Boldt and Freytag carried their maps through into Hitler's room to lay them out, in sequence, on the enormous red marble table halfway along one wall, on which stood a telephone, a bell push, two heavy paperweights, a desk set and a few coloured pencils.

The study was a vast room, with a high, heavily gilded ceiling, from which hung ornate crystal chandeliers, its floor covered with a rich, pastel-coloured carpet. Apart from the map table and a black upholstered chair standing behind it, positioned so that Hitler had a view of the garden when seated in it, there was little furniture. Hitler's elaborate desk stood at the far end, its front decorated with inlays depicting a half-drawn sword and three heads, one of them of Medusa, complete with writhing snakes. At the other end of the room was a heavy, round table. Big leather armchairs and a couch stood along the walls to left and right, one of which was broken by four full-length windows, hung with heavy grey curtains, and a glass door opening on to the devastated garden.

Back in the ante-room, the gathering was complete: Martin Bormann; Field Marshal Keitel, chief of the High Command; General Jodl, his chief of staff; Grand Admiral Dönitz, commander-in-chief of the navy; SS Reichs-führer Heinrich Himmler; General Fegelein, chief of the Waffen SS and Himmler's personal representative to Hitler, who was married to Eva Braun's sister, Gretl; Ernst Kaltenbrunner, head of the RSHA; Hermann Göring; General Burgdorf, Hitler's chief adjutant; and so on.

Burgdorf disappeared into the study for a moment, then returned and announced: 'The Führer would like you to come in.' In strict order of rank, with Göring leading the way, everyone filed in. Hitler stood alone in the middle of the huge room, his head shaking slightly, his left arm hanging limply by his side, the hand trembling perceptibly. He greeted each man individually with a silent handshake. Boldt noted that it was 'loose and flabby, quite devoid of strength or feeling'.

The conference began normally, with reports from the obsequious Jodl, covering the general situation on all fronts. Then it was Guderian's turn. Wasting no time on preliminaries, he quickly described the situation in the east, and demanded that the counter-attack begin in two days. Himmler, as commander of Army Group Vistula, stammered a protest. It could not be done, he said. The front-line units needed more ammunition and more fuel. Agitated, he took off his pince-nez and started polishing them.

'We can't wait until the last can of petrol and the last shell have been issued!' Guderian shouted. 'By that time the Russians will be too strong!'

'I will not allow you to accuse me of procrastination,' Hitler snapped back, clearly stung.

'I'm not accusing you of anything,' Guderian replied. 'I'm simply saying that there's no sense in waiting until the last lot of supplies has been issued – and the favourable moment to attack has been lost.'

'I've just told you that I won't allow you to accuse me of procrastinating!'

Guderian brushed the attempted rebuke aside, and went on. 'I want General Wenck at Army Group Vistula as chief of staff. Otherwise there can be no guarantee that the attack will be successful.' He glared at the hapless figure of Himmler. 'The man can't do it. How could he do it?'

Hitler rose to his feet. 'The Reichsführer is man enough to lead the attack on his own,' he declared.

'The Reichsführer doesn't have the experience or the right staff to lead the attack without help. The presence of General Wenck is absolutely necessary.'

'How dare you criticize the Reichsführer! I won't have you criticize him!'

Guderian remained unbowed, repeating his demand: 'I must insist that General Wenck be transferred to the staff of Army Group Vistula to lead the operation properly.'

With neither man prepared to give ground, the argument became more and more heated. One by one, the other men around the table slipped unobtrusively away to the ante-room, until only Hitler, Himmler, Guderian, Wenck and their adjutants remained.

Guderian himself described what happened next, as he continued to argue for a counter-attack, to be masterminded by Wenck:

His fists raised, his cheeks flushed with rage, his whole body trembling, the man stood there in front of me, beside himself with fury and having lost all self-control. After each outburst of rage, Hitler would stride up and down the edge of the carpet, then suddenly stop immediately before me and hurl his next accusation in my face. He was almost screaming, his eyes seemed to pop out of his head and the veins stood out on his temples.

After two hours of this, with Guderian still refusing to budge, Hitler suddenly gave way. 'Well, Himmler,' he said, stopping in front of the Reichsführer's chair, 'General Wenck is going to Army Group Vistula tonight, to take over as chief of staff.' Turning to Guderian with his most charming smile, he told him: 'Now let us please continue with the conference. Today, Colonel-General, the general staff has won a battle.'

The remainder of the conference was soon over. Guderian walked through to the ante-room and sat, exhausted, at a small table. Keitel and the other generals rebuked him for daring to upset the Führer. He regarded them with cool contempt, then turned to Wenck and told him to issue the orders for a counter-attack, to start in two days' time, on 15 February.

# 11

WHILE HITLER and Guderian were quarrelling, Marianne Gärtner was anxiously trying to escape from Berlin. Two days before, she had returned home to discover that the entire façade of her block of flats had been blown off during that morning's raid by a bomb that had fallen in the street outside. She had been to register as a student at the university, where a few classes were still being held, in the hope that she might avoid being drafted into factory work – only the day before, it had been announced that all women between the ages of sixteen and sixty were expected to serve in the Volkssturm. Although half the flat had gone, with the front rooms exposed to the street like a stage set, her mother and grandmother were unhurt. Amazingly, the engineers of the emergency services pronounced the remaining half of the flat to be safe. The three women spent the evening rescuing anything they could reach from the damaged rooms before locking doors that led into space. Then they settled down to sleep together in Marianne's mother's room at the back – until they were roused by the sirens announcing the arrival of the RAF.

Next morning, to her dismay, Marianne received an official letter; somehow, the postal service was still working. So was the bureaucracy – the letter was from the local party headquarters, following her registration only the previous day as a student, ordering her to report for work as a machine operator at Borsig at 7 am next Monday. Alarmed, she called her father.

He told her not to worry. 'There is an excellent college of languages in Dresden,' he said. 'I know the director. I'll try and get you in there. Just pretend you didn't get the letter. Enemy bombers won't touch Dresden . . . all that baroque and rococo . . . they wouldn't dare harm it! You'll be safer there . . .'

That night, the RAF bombed the rail lines to the south-east of Berlin. There would be no trains to Dresden for at least twenty-four hours; Marianne would have to delay her departure. The next night, 13 February, Berliners enjoyed the rare pleasure of an uninterrupted night's sleep. For once, the bombers left the city alone: they were too busy destroying Dresden. The fire storm caused by the raid, and by follow-up attacks next day by the USAAF, not only razed the historic city to the ground, but also killed between 35,000 and 135,000 people – the blaze was so intense that there were no bodies left to be counted, in a city whose population of 600,000 had been swollen to at least a million by unnumbered refugees from the east.

On the morning of Wednesday, 14 February, Marianne's father called, in a state of shock. He had just received his call-up papers, drafting him into the Luftwaffe, despite his age and poor eyesight. But he had twenty-four hours in which to settle his business affairs – and to wangle travel permits for Marianne, her mother and grandmother to leave Berlin. They left next day, to stay with relatives in Tangermünde on the Elbe, fifty miles west of the city, hopefully well away from the bombers and the Soviet troops.

As MARIANNE was leaving, Hans-Georg von Studnitz was returning to the city from Eberswalde, where he had been helping a friend move belongings from his house there to the capital. In Eberswalde station, Studnitz saw a freight train loaded with troops. They were, he said, 'child-soldiers, kids of twelve to sixteen years of age in baggy air force uniforms, who glared at us with animal-like eyes set in emaciated, prematurely knowing faces'. While their train was waiting in the station, another drew up on the next track. This one was filled with members of the Women's Auxiliary Anti-Aircraft Force, pretty girls with open faces, broad smiles and beautiful long hair.

The freight trains had no toilet facilities, and when they moved out, Studnitz saw to his horror that the space between the lines where they had stood was 'a mass of excreta, old tins, paper and rubbish of every kind'. The idea of boys and girls squatting together to defecate offended Studnitz's sensibilities; the insanitary results and the girls' shrieked obscenities somehow typified for him the final breakdown of decency and order.

The boys on the train, however, were facing a much greater and more serious breakdown of decency. They were on their way to the front, where Wenck had that day launched the Third Panzer Army against Zhukov's exposed right flank to start the planned counter-attack with a powerful thrust that sent the Soviets reeling. Wenck's troops succeeded in recapturing the town of Pyritz, south-east of Stettin, and the Soviet situation rapidly deteriorated under constant German pressure. But Zhukov's luck held. Two days later, driving back to the front at dawn after spending all night briefing Hitler in Berlin, Wenck took over the wheel of his staff car from his exhausted driver. Before long, he too fell asleep, and the car smashed into the side of a railway bridge. Wenck was trapped inside as it burst into flames, and was only just pulled out in time. His injuries included a fractured skull and five broken ribs. Deprived of his leadership, the counter-attack fizzled out.

Within a week, the Soviets hit back. Rokossovsky ripped a great hole thirty-five miles wide and thirty miles deep in the German defences, as he launched a new offensive towards the Baltic coast at Stettin. In the next four days, he advanced another forty-five miles. Aimed at cutting off German forces in Danzig and Gdynia, this operation would bring his armies to the mouth of the Oder, only seventy-five miles north-east of Berlin, a position from which he could sweep around the city, and possibly descend on it from the north.

Prodded by Stalin, Zhukov joined in on 1 March. After an artillery barrage that convinced the Germans that this was the final bombardment before his tanks struck directly at Berlin, he astonished them by turning his armies northwards, taking Stargard and breaching the defences on the approach to Stettin, to link up with Rokossovsky. Stalin was still taking no chances in his massive build-up for the final assault. Before it started, he wanted to have his entire force lined up on the Oder.

# 12

IN THE west, with the Ardennes battles safely behind them, the Allied armies were moving forward again. On 8 February, Montgomery's Twenty-First Army Group started its assault on the Rhine. In an operation codenamed 'Veritable', the First Canadian Army and the British Second Army drove forward from the River Meuse (known as the Maas in Holland) between Nijmegen in the north and Venlo in the south. At the same time, in a linked operation codenamed 'Grenade', Lieutenant-General William H. Simpson's US Ninth Army, under Montgomery's control for this operation, was due to advance between Venlo and Julich on the River Roer, to join up with the British and Canadians on the west bank of the Rhine.

Both operations met with surprisingly fierce opposition. Veritable, also known as the battle of the Reichswald Forest, was described as 'unmitigated hell', with conditions more like those of 1914–18 than any other operation of the Second World War: the First Canadian Army sustained 15,000 casualties before it was over. Both Veritable and Grenade also had to contend with problems of terrain. In the northern sector, both the Rhine and the Meuse had overflowed their banks, and the ground everywhere was sodden and treacly, confining tanks to the paved roads. In the south, Simpson's main attack was delayed for two weeks when the Germans opened the dams further upstream on the Roer, making the river uncrossable. But eventually Montgomery's armies prevailed. By the beginning of March they had shattered nineteen German divisions, which had lost 90,000 irreplaceable men, to occupy the entire west bank of the Rhine from Nijmegen to Düsseldorf.

To their south, General Omar Bradley's Twelfth Army Group was busy clearing the eighty miles of the west bank from Düsseldorf down to Koblenz.

Lieutenant-General Courtney H. Hodges's US First Army, fighting alongside the Ninth, captured Cologne on 7 March. That same day, by a great stroke of good fortune, part of Hodges's army, the 9th Armoured Division, found the railway bridge across the Rhine at Remagen undestroyed. The advance guard charged over it, others followed swiftly and before long there were four divisions across the Rhine, establishing a bridgehead several miles deep. The following day, Lieutenant-General George S. Patton's Third Army also reached the Rhine, only three days after launching its attack from the Moselle. Another 49,000 German soldiers had been removed from the war during Hodges's advance, captured when they were immobilized by lack of fuel.

Eisenhower's broad front was lined up and ready to advance from the Rhineland into the heart of Germany – but for the moment any thought of beating the Red Army to Berlin could be dismissed as wishful thinking, for the Western Allies were still at least 285 miles away from the ultimate target.

# 13

UNKNOWN TO the Americans as they rained down their bombs on Berlin in the spring of 1945, one of the most senior USAAF officers was in the city beneath them. Brigadier-General Arthur W. Vanaman was the highest-ranking American officer to be captured by the Germans. Until 27 January, he had been in Stalag Luft III in eastern Poland, along with 9,500 other American airmen. But that day – the same day that the Red Army took Auschwitz – the Germans had moved them all out, partly to keep them away from the Soviets, partly in the belief that they might be a valuable bargaining counter with the Western Allies. Without adequate food or shelter from the bitter cold, they were force-marched to Spremberg in Germany, where all but Vanaman and four other officers were loaded like some valuable herd into cattle trucks bound for Nuremberg and Munich.

Vanaman and his group – Colonels Bill Kennedy and Delmar T. Spivey, Captain 'Pop' George, and Lieutenant Willard Brown – were taken to Berlin. They were told they were due for early repatriation as a reward for their leadership during the march from Poland, but none of them believed that. After a hideous trek across the city at night, from one railway station crowded with terror-stricken people to another, they were put aboard a train to Luckenwalde, about twenty-five miles to the south, where there was a camp housing 40,000 Allied prisoners of war. The camp commandant was not pleased to see them, having been given no warning that they were coming.

Vanaman had long suspected that the enemy would try to make use of him for propaganda or some other purpose: as well as being a senior officer he also had a diplomatic background, having served as assistant military attaché for air in the US Embassy in Berlin from 1937 until 1941. In mid-February, after he had been in Luckenwalde for two weeks, his suspicions were strengthened when he had a surprise visitor. SS Hauptsturmführer (Captain) Dr Helmut Bauer was a doctor on the headquarters staff of SS Obergruppen- führer (Lieutenant-General) Gottlob Berger. Speaking perfect American English with a Midwestern accent – he had lived in the United States from the age of three until he returned to Germany to begin his medical studies – he asked as a matter of courtesy if there was any way he could help General Vanaman.

Vanaman told him there was. For some time, Red Cross food parcels had not been getting through to the PoW camps, with the result that many men were suffering from malnutrition, and sickness was rife. He asked to be allowed to go to Switzerland, to sort out the problem. He gave his parole, as an officer and a gentleman, that he would return to Germany as soon as the job was finished. Bauer returned after a few days and told him that Berger had agreed to the request. However, he warned that there might be delays before Vanaman could leave for Switzerland, because of problems Berger was having with Goebbels and Bormann. This was certainly true – but it was only part of the truth. The situation was far more complex. Without knowing it, Vanaman had become involved in the efforts of top SS chiefs to save their skins by negotiating a separate peace with the Western Allies.

Leading the peace negotiations was one of the sleekest and slickest of the 'golden pheasants', as the Nazi big-wigs were known to the Berliners, Obergruppenführer Walter Schellenberg. Schellenberg, supreme head of the combined SD and Abwehr intelligence service since the downfall of Admiral Canaris, had had a meteoric career in the SS, most of it spent lurking in the shadows. Fascinated ever since his university days by Renaissance politics, particularly the philosophy of Machiavelli, he was addicted to intrigue in the way some men are to sex or speed. He had been involved in a whole string of cloak and dagger operations, including the snatching of the top two British intelligence officers in Holland at Venlo in 1939, and the attempted kidnapping of the Duke of Windsor in Portugal a year later.

Convinced that the invasion of the Soviet Union had been totally mistaken, he had tried to persuade Himmler to investigate the possibility of a negotiated peace with the Allies as far back as August 1942. Now he was about to launch another peace feeler with the aid of the captured American general and the nephew of the king of Sweden.

*

COUNT FOLKE Bernadotte, nephew of King Gustav V and vice-chairman of the Swedish Red Cross, visited Berlin on 17 February. His stated purpose was to negotiate the repatriation of Swedish-born women who had married Germans but were now either widowed or deserted. In fact, he hoped to achieve the release of all Scandinavian prisoners, and others if possible, from the concentration camps. In return, he was prepared to cooperate with the regime in any way that he could.

From Schellenberg's point of view, the situation looked promising. Surely, with both Bernadotte and Vanaman as go-betweens, some kind of deal could be done with the Americans and British? But he needed Himmler's authority, and as always, Himmler hesitated. He had already tried to open his own peace negotiations using the International Red Cross in Switzerland as intermediary, but these had foundered when Ernst Kaltenbrunner, head of the RSHA, informed Hitler what was going on. In the end, Himmler decided that he was not prepared to release Scandinavian concentration camp prisoners unless Bernadotte could guarantee that Danish and Norwegian resistance fighters would cease harrying the Germans. Since Bernadotte could not make deals on behalf of the resistance movements in other countries, the whole negotiations were on the verge of collapse, until Schellenberg persuaded his chief to agree that all Scandinavian prisoners would be gathered into one camp, where they could be looked after by the Red Cross.

Bernadotte was now willing to cooperate, since he had achieved at least part of what he had come to Berlin for, and Schellenberg worked on Himmler to persuade him to sanction the opening of negotiations with the West. According to Schellenberg, Himmler finally agreed, but changed his mind again the very next day. He had realized, as surely as Schellenberg had done, that if they proceeded it would mean organizing an SS *putsch* against Hitler and the crew of the 'cement submarine'. In the end, he could not bring himself to betray his Führer – not, that is, on his own doorstep. For at that same time, his chief of staff, Obergruppenführer Karl Wolff, was in Berne, the capital of Switzerland, negotiating with the OSS chief in Europe, Allen Dulles, for an armistice in Italy that would allow troops to be withdrawn to fight in Germany.

Vanaman was not yet fully aware of the dangers, but he was by now in an embarrassing and potentially lethal position. The embarrassment arose from his fear that he might be accused by his own government of collaborating with the enemy. But in all conscience, he could not ignore any opportunity for improving the lot of his fellow PoWs. The danger lay in the fact that his survival in Berlin depended on the goodwill of men like Schellenberg and Berger, men who were not noted for their general benevolence. As long as Schellenberg regarded him as a valuable negotiating tool, his life was safe. But if for any reason he should become a threat, he could easily disappear in the rubble of Berlin, simply another casualty of US bombs.

For the moment, Vanaman was useful to Schellenberg. While they were awaiting the outcome of their machinations, Schellenberg and Berger sought to demonstrate their concern for Allied prisoners by holding a conference on their welfare. Along with a number of Allied doctors temporarily released from prison camps, Vanaman and Colonel Spivey attended this conference, held in a house that had belonged to the Danish Embassy near Goebbels's home on Schwanenwerder. It turned out to be an ill-tempered affair, with everyone convinced that the whole thing was a propaganda exercise. On one level it certainly was just that, but it also served to explain Vanaman's forthcoming trip to Switzerland, should the two SS generals ever be called upon to justify it.

After the conference, while the others were returned to their PoW camps, Vanaman and Spivey remained in Berlin. They met and were entertained by Max Schmelling, the former boxing champion. He also had an axe to grind – he asked Spivey to sign a paper certifying that he had visited Allied PoW camps and had even sparred with US prisoners. Spivey assured him that because of his two fights with Joe Louis, he was still extremely popular in the States.

# 14

O N 5 MARCH, the telephone rang in Lieutenant-General Helmuth Reymann's home on the outskirts of Dresden. It was Hitler's adjutant, General Wilhelm Burgdorf, who told him: 'The Führer has appointed you military commander of Dresden.' The fifty-three-year-old Reymann, still heartbroken by the total destruction of his beautiful old city in the Allied firebomb raids, reacted furiously. 'Tell him,' he shouted, 'there's nothing here to defend except rubble!' And he slammed down the receiver. An hour later, Burgdorf called again. 'The Führer has appointed you military commander of Berlin instead,' he told an incredulous Reymann.

It was only when Reymann took up his post next day that he discovered, to his horror, the true state of affairs in Berlin. Reymann was replacing Lieutenant-General Bruno Ritter von Hauenschild, who was sick – but he could find no sign that his predecessor had actually done anything to prepare the city against attack. This was perhaps understandable, for Hitler and Goebbels were still insisting that any suggestion of the Soviets being able to reach the city was defeatist talk, and punishable by death.

Nothing had been done to protect the civilian population from ground attack, or to evacuate the remaining children, or the sick and elderly. There were not even any plans, let alone stocks of food, for feeding them under siege conditions. The barricades, road blocks and improvised tank traps that Berliners had begun to erect in their near panic at the end of January remained unfinished – though they had caused considerable problems for people trying to escape the enormous fires started by an RAF raid on 26 February, which had destroyed the area around Alexanderplatz and the Frankfurterallee.

Hitler, it seemed, preferred to rely on the coming of a miracle, rather than any carefully prepared strategy. 'No game is lost until the final whistle,' he declared on 6 February to Bormann, to whom he was dictating his memoirs:

> A desperate fight remains a shining example for all time. Remember Leonidas and his 300 Spartans! No! There is no such thing as a desperate situation! Think how many examples of a turn of fortune the history of the German people affords. During the Seven Years War, Frederick found himself reduced to desperate straits, then behold – the Czarina died unexpectedly and the whole situation was miraculously reversed . . . if Churchill were suddenly to disappear, everything could change in a flash. We can still snatch victory in the final sprint!

On 9 March, three days after Reymann had taken up his post, a 'fundamental order for the defence of the Reich capital' was issued at last. Reymann later denied that he had had anything to do with it, though it was issued in his name and over his signature. In fact, the 33-page document bore the unmistakable stamp of Goebbels's hysterical prose, though it also contained a fair amount of practical detail as well as a great deal of wishful thinking. Much of it is typically grandiose, imprecise and emotional, a scenario for *Götterdämmerung*:

> The capital will be defended to the last man and the last bullet . . . the forces available for the defence of the capital will not engage the enemy in open battle but in *street and house fighting*. The struggle must be conducted with
>
> > *Fanatical resolution*
> > *Imagination*
> > Every means of *deception, artifice and cunning*:
> > *Stratagems of all kinds*, devised in advance or on the spur of the moment
> > *on*
> > *above* and
> > *beneath the ground.*
>
> In the battle, every advantage arising from our familiarity with

the terrain and from Russian nervousness in facing a sea of strange houses must be exploited to the full.

Exact local knowledge, utilization of the underground railways and sewers and of existing means of communication, of the excellent cover and camouflage provided by houses and blocks of flats, particularly those built of reinforced concrete – all these make a defender *immune to any enemy*, no matter how superior in numbers or supplies he may be.

The enemy, who shall not be given a minute's respite, must be bled to death in the meshwork of our resistance strong points, defence bases and fortified buildings. Every house or base captured by the enemy must be *recaptured at once*. Shock troops will penetrate behind the enemy lines through the underground, to take him by surprise in the rear.

It is a condition for the successful defence of Berlin that

> *Every building*
> *Every house*
> *Every floor*
> *Every hedge*
> *Every shell crater*
> *be defended to the utmost!*

It is not nearly so important that those defending the capital have a detailed knowledge of the mechanics of their weapons; *what matters is that*

> *every man*
> be inspired and suffused with a
> *fanatical resolve*
> *with a WILL TO FIGHT*
> *realizing that the world is watching us with bated breath and*
> *that the struggle for Berlin may decide the war.*

The document stated that the defenders would be alerted by the codeword 'Clausewitz'; the signal for the start of the battle proper was 'Kolberg'. Greater Berlin and its surroundings were divided into a series of concentric rings: an outer restricted zone, an outer defence zone, an inner defence zone, and finally 'Sector Z', for *Zitadelle* (Citadel), around the government quarter.

'The mass of our forces' – these were not defined in any way – was to be deployed in the outer defence zone, which coincided roughly with the city borders. Here there was to be a 'green battle line' behind which the troops would form 'an impregnable wall by taking up strong positions in depth'. Deploying 'heavy weapons and artillery' in this 'main battlefield' would involve blowing up whole districts.

The perimeter of the inner defence zone followed the S-Bahn. Again, the order gave no details, simply the exhortation: 'The elevated railway battle line will be held!'

The entire defence area, with a diameter varying between twenty-four and thirty-six miles, was divided like a cake into eight sub-sectors radiating from the Citadel, plus Potsdam, which lay outside the city boundary. The central command post was in the Wehrmacht headquarters on the Hohenzollerndamm in Wilmersdorf, but was to move into the Zoo flak tower six hours after the alert.

All 'provocateurs and rebellious foreigners' were to be 'seized and ruthlessly put down'. There would be 'flying court martials' empowered to reach only two decisions: execution or acquittal.

To THE east and north-east, the Berlin defence area ran as far as the west banks of the Oder and Neisse, joining up with the defence system of the Oder front itself. This, too, consisted of three lines. The first, stretching back between two and six miles, was fortified by trenches, buildings hurriedly converted into blockhouses with bricked-up windows, barbed-wire entanglements and minefields, though there were hardly any mines available and barbed wire was in desperately short supply. The second line, in wooded countryside some twelve miles to the rear, was a pitiful affair, with no continuous trenches and few bunkers, while the third line, a further six to twelve miles back, consisted only of occasional strong points, road barriers and tank traps, and was manned by civilians who were too old even for the Volkssturm.

According to the official maps supplied by the Reich chancellery, the defence zones were a mass of major strong points. In fact, they were nothing more than a feeble pretence, lacking both troops and weapons. The city's own inner defence lines were little better. The outer ring, some sixty miles in circumference, contained no proper fortifications, but included lines of trenches and uncompleted barricades made from old railway coaches and wagons, tramcars filled with stones, and building rubble, with occasional concrete-block walls and converted air-raid bunkers. It was interspersed with the natural barriers of Berlin's many lakes and waterways.

The second ring, following the line of the S-Bahn, was more promising, for the railway alternated between deep cuttings that made perfect tank traps overlooked by buildings from which gunners could pick off tanks or infantry trying to cross the line, and steep embankments which would become high ramparts for the defenders. Given seasoned troops, good weapons and plentiful ammunition, the twenty-five miles of S-Bahn could present a formidable obstacle to any invader. Reymann's only problem was that he had neither the troops nor the weapons to man it effectively.

The final defensive ring, around the Citadel itself, was defined by the River Spree, the Landwehr Canal, and the Tiergarten. Most of the great buildings in the heart of the government quarter had been destroyed or seriously damaged by bombing, but enough remained to give ample cover to defenders. They were to be linked by barricades and concrete block walls.

REYMANN'S TASK of defending Berlin was complicated, like so many things in Nazi Germany, by a confused tangle of responsibilities. Although Reymann was now fortress commandant, General Hauenschild remained commanding general, and yet another general, Major-General Georg Hofmeister, had the title of city commandant. Since both Hauenschild and Hofmeister were supposed to be seriously ill – there is no way of telling if their ailments were genuine or simply convenient – Reymann did not have to worry about them. But their overlapping roles give a clear picture of the bureaucratic convolutions that clogged up the German system even at that late hour.

Reymann had been appointed by Hitler and was directly answerable to him – though he never got to see him again after he had first reported to him on 6 March – so the general staff of the army did not regard him as its responsibility. This made it almost impossible for him to obtain the senior officers needed to set up a proper chain of command, or to establish a workable liaison with the Oder front. To make matters worse, Berlin had not been officially declared a battle zone, so it was still under the civil control of the party, which meant Goebbels as Gauleiter. It was Goebbels who refused even to consider evacuating any of the 3 million civilians remaining in the city, even the 120,000 children under the age of ten. And when Reymann asked what provision had been made to provide infants with milk if the city were cut off, it was Goebbels who told him, quite wrongly, that he had enough canned milk in store to last three months.

As defence commissar, Goebbels was also in charge of the military situation, holding meetings of the Defence Council at a house near the Brandenburg Gate which Reymann had to attend as his subordinate. He demanded a weekly report on the army's stocks of food, fuel, weapons and ammunition, and on how many fit men were available. When the first report was submitted on 10 March, Goebbels noted in his diary: 'Taken as a whole, the situation is extraordinarily satisfactory.' He interpreted the figures as suggesting that the city had enough men, weapons, food and coal to hold out for eight weeks under siege. 'Eight weeks is a long time, during which a lot can happen,' he noted with astonishing complacency. 'In any case, we have made excellent preparations and above all it must be remembered that, if the worst should happen, an enormous number of men with their weapons would flow into the city and we should be in a position to use them to put up a powerful defence.'

Such vague hopes had no place in the thinking of a trained soldier like Reymann, who had been working night and day since he arrived in Berlin, trying to create some sort of order out of the chaos he had inherited. He had to do almost everything himself, and did not even have a chief of staff until 20 March, when he finally succeeded in getting Colonel Hans 'Teddy' Refior, a highly professional officer who had played the same role for him in a war game at a staff lecture at Hirschberg a few weeks before.

Goebbels was not impressed by Reymann: 'He is the typical sort of bourgeois general who will do his duty faithfully and honestly but from whom no extraordinary output is to be expected.' His opinion may have been affected by the fact that Reymann disagreed with his view on the state of the city's defences. He interpreted the weekly figures differently, pointing out 'a number of gaps', in particular a serious shortage of ammunition. He also spotted other disturbing discrepancies that Goebbels seemed to have overlooked: according to the records of Berlin railway stations, there should have been 'an enormous quantity of military equipment – including ammunition – stored away somewhere in sidings'. No one seemed to know where it all was, if indeed it existed at all.

Goebbels in turn did not agree with parts of Reymann's plan, and had no hesitation in interfering. He commented indignantly that preparations for demolition were far more extensive than was necessary, adding acidly that the pioneers were working as though they were in enemy territory. In the last resort, they intended to blow all the bridges leading into Berlin. 'If this were done,' he wrote in his diary, 'the Reich capital would inevitably starve. I am putting things to rights here and ensuring that the pioneers do not look upon their job purely from the pioneer point of view.'

Reymann was no Guderian, prepared to rant and rave at the idiocies of his master. In any case, he was in a very tricky situation. Flying court martials under Lieutenant-General Dr Rudolf Hübner had been set up a few days before to deal with generals who tried to make their own military decisions. They were not operating in Berlin – Goebbels felt that the People's Court, even without Freisler, was capable of handling anyone in the city – but Reymann must have been aware that Hübner had just executed the commanding general who had failed to blow up the Remagen bridge, along with seven other senior officers. The unfortunate men had been tried, condemned and shot, all within two hours. In addition, General Fromm, the executioner of Stauffenberg, had been shot on 9 March. Although the Gestapo had not been able to nail him as a supporter of the 20 July plot, he had been charged with 'cowardice in the face of the enemy', for not doing enough to stop it. Now, another general was about to be tried, for refusing to allow a Nazi leadership officer – the equivalent of a political commissar – time to indoctrinate his troops. It would be suicide for Reymann to oppose Goebbels too strongly, however much he may have despised his criminal negligence.

Reymann needed Goebbels to provide him with men and materials to build what physical defences were possible in the short time remaining before the Soviet attack. He asked for a minimum of 100,000 men a day. He got fewer than 30,000, and many of those were wasted as the chaotic bureaucracy ordered men from Spandau on the city's western edge to work at Karlshorst, way over to the east, while sending men from Tempelhof to work in Spandau. With most transport services at a standstill, and those trains that were running disrupted by air raids, much of the labour force spent all day struggling to and fro across the ruined city.

The men who did arrive found little in the way of equipment – most of the heavy earth-moving machines had long ago been sent to the Oder front, and there was no fuel for those that were left. Often they did not even have hand tools. The authorities were reduced to making appeals through the newspapers for picks and shovels, but few Berliners were prepared to part with tools that might be essential to their own survival in the months ahead. A disappointed Colonel Refior noted: 'Berlin gardeners apparently consider the digging of their potato plots more important than the digging of tank traps.'

But even if Reymann could achieve the impossible and get the defence lines into a reasonable state before the Soviet assault started, he was faced with the still bigger problem of who was to man them. He believed that in ideal circumstances, he would need at least 200,000 well-trained and well-armed men to defend the city. After doing his first sums, he estimated that he would have no more than 125,000 troops. In fact, including the last-ditch levies he had as few as 94,000, 60,000 of whom were untrained Volkssturm members, who came under the jurisdiction of the party, not the army. Most of these had no weapons, but when Reymann raised the matter with Goebbels, he was told that the factories were working flat out to supply the Oder front armies, but if the city was encircled then they would be able to provide adequate quantities to the defenders. Knowing that when the city was surrounded there would be no factories still working, Reymann was not reassured.

TWO DAYS after issuing the order for the basic defence of Berlin, Reymann had to attend the annual ceremony for Heroes' Remembrance Day at the Tomb of the Unknown Warrior in Schinkel's Neue Wache. Keitel, Göring and Dönitz represented the three arms of the Wehrmacht, but Hitler did not make his customary appearance. He was paying a fleeting visit to the eastern front: it was to be the last time he ever left the chancellery. Göring – who appeared in a plain uniform with no medals – laid a wreath on his behalf. There were representatives from all the front-line regiments on parade, about 120 men of all ranks, nearly all of them wearing the Knight's Cross, as well as official representatives of the party and the city; but there were no spectators. 'It would have been wrong to expose masses of people to a possible enemy air raid,' Reymann noted.

The absence of crowds gave the occasion a ghostly feeling, and the state of the surrounding buildings, Reymann wrote, added to the effect:

On the one side was the palace, completely gutted and severely bombed; on the other was the ruined cathedral. Opposite the war memorial stood the craggy shell of the Berlin Opera; it had been hit again the night before. Shortly before the beginning of the ceremony, Göring appeared in his big car, got out and looked at this picture of desolation, shaking his head. Then he and several other officers, including me, went up to the memorial which, strangely enough, was almost completely undamaged. Göring laid a wreath, saluted, and then left the memorial without saying a word. The strangeness of the situation probably struck all of us who took part. We remembered the dead who had laid down their lives for a cause that was now on the point of collapse. I was shaken when I returned to my command post.

# 15

THE 13TH OF March, the day he first met Reymann, was Goebbels's twelfth anniversary as minister of propaganda. That evening, he received what he described as 'the worst conceivable omen for the next twelve years': in the nightly Mosquito raid, his ministry building was totally destroyed by a bomb. Goebbels was at home when it happened, but drove to the Wilhelm-strasse immediately to survey the damage. He had taken great pride over the years in restoring the old palace, and for once was genuinely upset. 'One's heart aches to see so unique a product of the architect's art, such as this building was, totally flattened in a second,' he wrote in his diary. The building was still blazing when he got there, and he was terrified that 500 Panzerfaust missiles stored in the basement would explode.

At home, later, he passed what he described as 'a somewhat melancholy evening' with his family. 'Slowly one is beginning to realize what this war means for us all,' he wrote – an astonishing admission after nearly six years of slaughter. But even then, on paper at least, he refused to face the possibility of defeat: 'We had all taken the Ministry so much to our hearts. Now it belongs to the past. I am firmly convinced, however, that when this war is over, not only shall I reconstruct a new monumental ministry – as the Führer says – but restore the old Ministry in all its glory.'

IN SPITE of all Goebbels's bluster, his wife, Magda, knew the end could not be far away. She feared not only for her husband but also for herself and their six children when Berlin fell. Goebbels suggested she take the children and move out westwards, where she might find shelter with the British, but she refused to leave him. Sometimes, in the evenings, she went into the room where Rudolf Semmler, one of Goebbels's more reasonable assistants, was working. Semmler felt sorry for her. 'She sees her future quite clearly,' he noted. 'She admits she is afraid of death and she knows it is drawing closer every day. She does not like talking to her husband about such matters.'

Without telling him, she went to Dr Morell and asked him to provide her with enough poison to kill herself and the children when the time came. She had gone to the right man – for nine years, Morell had fed the Führer mysterious cocktails of pills and potions, including vast doses of amphetamines which were contributing significantly to the tremors that affected him so badly. He had grown rich on the proceeds of treating Hitler and his top associates and their families, and had his own pharmaceutical company. He was happy to provide her with what she needed to end her children's lives.

'When I think that in a few weeks' time I may have to kill these innocent creatures,' she told Semmler, 'I go nearly crazy with grief and pain. I am always wondering how I will do it when the time comes. I cannot talk about it with my husband any more. He would never forgive me for weakening his resistance. As long as he can go on fighting, he thinks that all is not lost.'

That may have been what Goebbels told his wife, but with his staff he kept discussing different scenarios for the end, always looking for the most dramatic and Wagnerian last act. One of his ideas was to lead his long-suffering staff in a fight to the finish in the Zoo flak tower bunker, blowing it up in the final stages of the battle with himself and everyone else inside it. In another vision, he saw himself dying a hero's death on the barricades, swastika in hand. His staff were less inclined to indulge in such theatrics. Few of them had any appetite for suicide: they saw themselves as civil servants, not samurai warriors. They decided to take no part in what they regarded as their boss's ridiculous schemes, but to keep in close touch with each other to plan their escape from Valhalla.

ESCAPE WAS uppermost in everyone's mind. The problem was, how? Hans-Georg von Studnitz recorded in his diary that the most cherished possession in Berlin was a car with petrol, and that unlimited supplies of coffee, spirits and cigarettes were being offered in exchange for one. Black market petrol prices soared with each passing day: in early March, a litre of petrol was fetching 40 marks, or 20 cigarettes; a pound of coffee or a kilo of butter would buy 20 litres, about 5½ gallons. Tyres cost 2–3,000 marks, small trailers 20,000 marks. Even an old car could not be had for less than 15–20,000.

Even those who had both a car and fuel faced the problem of papers. Forgery flourished, at a price. A complete set of false papers, consisting of a travel permit allowing the holder to leave Berlin without being arrested and shot, a military pass, and a 'Z' card giving exemption from Volkssturm duty, cost 80,000 marks. Some of the forgeries were better printed than the genuine articles. In one instance, a soldier was stopped in the street carrying a suitcase filled with bogus rubber stamps, which were so much better cut than the official originals that the SS unit that made the arrest immediately confiscated them for its own use.

The most ironic, and sickest, demand in the final weeks was for authentic Jewish stars, which changed hands for large sums in the belief that a yellow star was a passport to sympathy for anyone who surrendered to the Allies.

SOME PEOPLE decided to ignore everything and go down in Neronian style. The most prominent of these was Dr Vladimir Kosak, the Croatian minister in Berlin, who held a nightly series of farewell parties from November 1944 onwards, sometimes at the legation, but more often in his villa in Dahlem. The parties, consisting of a banquet followed by a gargantuan drinking bout, swiftly became a highlight of the dwindling social scene, attended by everyone who was anyone – foreign diplomats, Nazi officials, stars of stage and screen. At about midnight, a Croatian choir would appear to sing folk songs, and when the all-clear had sounded after the nightly Mosquito raid, the gunners of a Croatian anti-aircraft battery stationed nearby would join the party and spend the rest of the night playing jazz. With the music and the alcohol, the situation often got out of hand. Studnitz, a frequent party-goer, noted that the revellers often fired their revolvers off into the air, and that the legation porter lost three fingers 'as a result of such horseplay'.

Ribbentrop attempted his own version of a last party aboard the *Titanic*, with a diplomatic reception on Wednesday, 7 March. But, like almost everything he touched, it did not quite come off. Not only was it on a less heroic scale than the Croat jamborees, but in spite of his wine trade connections, it was non-alcoholic. Nevertheless, the gesture was much appreciated by foreign journalists and junior diplomatic staff of the various foreign embassies – most of the ambassadors had already contrived to escape from the city. There were three tea tables, each with fifteen guests, served by waiters in ill-fitting liveries. Ribbentrop moved from table to table, devoting thirty minutes to each, while he unburdened himself of long, rambling monologues on the menace of Bolshevism. After Germany, he told everyone, the Russians would overrun France and Britain and bolshevize the whole earth. By 6.15 pm, when the reception ended before the RAF arrived, the guests were glad to leave.

## 16

ON 9 MARCH, the main force of the US Third Army reached the Rhine and began linking up with the First Army. Hitler reacted by issuing another decree against cowardice: 'Anyone captured without being wounded or without having fought to the limit of his powers has forfeited his honour. He is expelled from the fellowship of decent and brave soldiers. His dependents will be held responsible.' Seeking someone to blame for the disasters, he fired the commander-in-chief of the western front, Field Marshal von Rundstedt, and replaced him with Kesselring – who, ironically, was at that moment trying to negotiate surrender terms for German forces in Italy.

But there was little any German commander could now do against the overwhelming might of the Allies. The last German force west of the Rhine – what was left of the German First and Seventh Armies – was contained in a large salient between the River Moselle from Koblenz to Trier, and the Siegfried Line, running back to the Rhine itself. On 15 March, the US Third and Seventh Armies, with elements of the First French Army, attacked from both sides. The Germans fought well, but having reached the Rhine north of Koblenz, Patton achieved total surprise by turning five divisions south to cut through the German rear and link up with his XXth Corps, which had burst through the bulge south of Trier. By 21 March the much-feared Siegfried Line, or West Wall, was completely cut off, bringing the tally of German prisoners taken since the beginning of the Allied offensives in February to more than 280,000, and overall German losses to 350,000 men.

## 17

ON 18 MARCH, a beautiful, sunny Sunday, 1,250 American bombers supported by 700 fighters pounded Berlin in yet another destructive daylight raid. They were opposed by twin-jet Messerschmitt 262s, flying in significant numbers for the first time: 28 jets shot down 15 US planes, but neither they nor the flak, which accounted for another 7, could prevent the bombers bringing the city to a standstill. The Luftwaffe was so short of fuel, aircraft and pilots that to all intents and purposes Berlin had become an open city to attack from the air. The raid, concentrated mainly on the city centre and northern and north-eastern districts, killed at least 1,000 people and made some 65,000 homeless. When the RAF Mosquitoes arrived as usual that night, their way was lit by the fires that were still raging.

Hitler was concerned about the state of the city, and telephoned Goebbels for a situation report as soon as he rose at midday. But he was also prepared to destroy Berlin to deny it to the Soviets. His scorched earth policy was to apply to the whole country, including the capital. Albert Speer tried to dissuade him, taking the risk of presenting him with a report on 18 March giving a truthful assessment of the country's position: the final collapse of the economy was certain within four to eight weeks, after which the war could not be continued. Appealing to Hitler's humanity, Speer said that they had to do what they could to maintain at least the basics for the survival of the people. 'At this stage of the war,' he wrote, 'it makes no sense for us to undertake demolitions which might strike at the very life of the nation . . . it cannot possibly be the purpose of warfare at home to destroy so many bridges that, given the straitened means of the postwar period, it will take years to rebuild the transportation network. . . . Their destruction means eliminating all further possibility for the German people to survive.'

Turning specifically to Berlin, Speer wrote: 'The planned demolition of the bridges in Berlin would cut off the city's food supply, and industrial production and human life in the city would be rendered impossible for years to come. Such demolitions would mean the death of Berlin.'

Hitler rejected Speer's pleas with contempt. 'If the war is lost, the nation will also perish,' he told him. 'Besides,' he concluded, 'those who remain after the battle are only the inferior ones, for the good ones will have been killed.' Next day, he issued his 'Nero Order', for the destruction of all industrial plants about to fall into enemy hands, all important electrical facilities, water works, gas works, food and clothing stores, all bridges, all railway and communications installations, all waterways, all ships, freight cars and locomotives.

The Nero Order was supplemented by another, calling for the entire population of areas threatened by the enemy in the west to be evacuated, on foot if necessary. Sick to death of the war, the civilian populations of small towns and villages were doing their best to prevent Kesselring's men defending them. All they wanted was to get it over with as quickly and as painlessly as possible.

IN BERLIN, it seemed there would be no need for the Nero Order – the Allied air raids would soon have completed the destruction of everything that mattered. Eliza Stokowska, the young Polish forced labourer, was mourning her friends killed in the Borsig works that Sunday morning. Three Polish women had been dug out of the rubble: they were found standing with their backs to a wall, the only survivors after the entire shelter had collapsed. No one knew how many foreign workers had been in it.

The survivors were put to work clearing up among the rubble. It was not pleasant or easy. 'Black clouds of smoke surround us,' Eliza wrote in her diary. 'There is no sun any more. The wind blows. The sirens wail. The bombs have destroyed Borsig over the entire area. They tore off several storeys from buildings. The steel cranes and the steel structures of the halls are bent.' She noted that the Germans worked frenziedly, with 'raving energy' to repair and rebuild the damaged factory. But the main burden fell on the 15,000 foreign workers, slaving from 7 am until dark, clearing the rubble with their bare hands. They had to march to and from the works, as the S-Bahn had been destroyed. 'Tomorrow I will go to work in the Western Hall. Half of it has collapsed and all the shelters are destroyed. We will dig there and get everything on its feet again.'

Two days later she was still digging, by now in her own department in the Western Hall. Her workplace had been reduced to a heap of twisted rails, with bomb craters between them. The Dutch boys, Jo, Jaap and Karel, had been moved out of their hostel yet again, and had lost everything but what they were wearing. 'I clear a corner of the shelter, where the doctor used to work,' Eliza continued. 'Two corridors and some rooms are full of rubble. Dead bodies and a stench that could suffocate you. We had to clean two rooms and the kitchen there. We fetched the water from the nearby lake; there is none on the premises any more.

'All our interest is concentrated on surviving somehow . . . two kilograms of bread and a little soup per week, nothing else. Three to four air raids every night, each about one hour, and nine hours of heavy work in each shift. It is very cold and we have not the slightest hope.'

# 18

HITLER AT this time was totally preoccupied with the military situation in the west. Guderian, on the other hand, was far more anxious about the eastern front – after all, apart from the one bridgehead around Remagen, the Allied armies were still behind the Rhine and had 285 miles and two more major rivers, the Weser and the Elbe, between them and Berlin. The Soviets were almost within heavy artillery range of the city. Although Rundstedt had been dismissed, in Kesselring the western front had an experienced, professional soldier in command. The eastern front had Himmler supposedly commanding its most vital sector, Army Group Vistula.

Since Wenck's accident, the general staff had not received a single situation report from Himmler. With every day bringing fresh evidence of a gigantic build-up of Soviet strength and mounting enemy activity around the remaining German bridgeheads at Küstrin and Frankfurt, Guderian could not afford to wait any longer. On 19 March, he set out for Himmler's headquarters, a monstrous, pillared mansion set deep in woodland at Birkenhain, near Prenzlau, which the Reichsführer had built as his personal retreat some years earlier. Himmler was not there, but Guderian was greeted by his chief of staff, SS Brigadeführer (Brigadier-General) Heinz Lammerding, who asked him: 'Can't you rid us of our commander?' Guderian dryly told him that that was a matter for the SS, and asked where Himmler was.

Himmler, it transpired, had retired to a clinic at Hohenlychen, twenty miles away, where he was being treated by Professor Gebhardt. Exactly what he was being treated for was a mystery – Goebbels, who had visited him a week before, believed he had suffered a severe attack of angina, others thought it was tonsillitis, Lammerding told Guderian he was down with the flu. Guderian, when he found him, thought he looked perfectly well apart from a slight head cold – but had already realized that Himmler's health could provide the answer to his problem. He expressed sympathy, and suggested that perhaps he had been overworking, reminding him that as well as being commander of Army Group Vistula he was also national leader of the SS, chief of all German police, including the Gestapo, minister of the interior, and commander of the Reserve Army. Such a portfolio, he said, would surely 'tax the strength of any man'. Why not give up one of them – such as the Army Group?

Himmler seized on the possibility. Yes, he told Guderian, it was only too true that his many positions really taxed his endurance. 'But how can I go and say that to the Führer?' he asked. 'He wouldn't like it if I came up with such a suggestion.'

'Would you authorize me to say it for you?' Guderian asked quickly. Himmler nodded his agreement. Guderian then began sounding him out on the vital need for an immediate armistice, but although he listened sympathetically, Himmler refused to be drawn.

Guderian sped back to Berlin, where Hitler agreed – 'but only after a lot of grumbling and with obvious reluctance' – to relieve the overworked Reichsführer. As a replacement, Guderian suggested Colonel-General Gotthard Heinrici, who was then commanding the First Panzer Army in the Carpathians, in eastern Czechoslovakia.

Hitler, inevitably, opposed the idea of Heinrici, a cousin of Rundstedt, but Guderian persevered. Heinrici, he insisted, was the one man for the job.

'He's especially experienced with the Russians,' he said. 'They haven't broken through him yet.' Finally, Hitler was convinced, and a telegram was sent to Heinrici on 20 March, informing him of his new appointment.

GUDERIAN MET Himmler at the chancellery next day, walking with Hitler. He asked to speak to him in private, and Hitler, no doubt believing it was to do with the handover of command, left them to it. But the chief of the general staff had other things on his mind, and plunged into the heart of the matter immediately, picking up the question of peace where he had left off the previous day.

'The war can no longer be won,' he told Himmler. 'The only problem now is finding the quickest way of putting an end to the senseless slaughter and bombing. Apart from Ribbentrop, you are the only man with contacts in neutral countries. Since the foreign minister is reluctant to ask Hitler to open negotiations, you must go with me to Hitler and urge him to arrange an armistice.'

Again, Himmler appeared receptive and interested, but again refused to commit himself, or to offer support. Hitler, he said, would have him shot if he were even to approach him with such a proposal. Despite his apparent sympathy – and the fact that he was, of course, busily trying to arrange peace negotiations on his own account – he seems to have faithfully reported the conversation to Hitler. That evening, after the daily conference, the Führer asked Guderian to stay behind.

'I understand that your heart condition has taken a turn for the worse,' he said, ominously. He urged Guderian to take a cure at a spa, at once.

Guderian, fully aware of what lay behind Hitler's words, played for time. 'I cannot leave my post at the moment,' he replied, 'because I have no deputy.' This was true – his deputy, General Hans Krebs, had been wounded in an air raid on the OKH headquarters at Zossen. 'I'll try to find a replacement as soon as possible, and then I'll go on leave.'

HEINRICI ARRIVED at Zossen early next morning, 22 March, having been travelling since dawn, first by plane to the Czech–German frontier, then by car. A short, chunky man, with steady blue eyes, greying fair hair and a clipped moustache, he cared little for appearances, wearing his uniforms until they were threadbare, and keeping out the cold with a shabby old sheepskin coat. He was the son of a Lutheran pastor, and was a devout Christian, reading his bible every day and attending church every Sunday without fail, even though he was warned by high-ranking party officials that Hitler strongly disapproved. On his mother's side, he was descended from a line of aristocratic soldiers stretching back to the twelfth century – another reason why he never found favour with the Führer.

By nature, Heinrici was no dashing warrior but an efficient, utterly reliable professional soldier, unequalled as a defender of seemingly hopeless positions. 'Heinrici retreats only when the air is turned to lead,' one of his staff officers said, 'and then only after considerable deliberation.' His reputation had been made at the beginning of 1942, when his tattered and frozen Fourth Army held out in front of Moscow for almost ten weeks, against everything the elements and the Soviets could throw at him, stabilizing the line when it seemed the entire German army was about to collapse. Since then, he had fought a number of stubborn rearguard actions, always making the Red Army pay dearly for any advance. If anyone could stop them at the Oder, it was Heinrici.

Heinrici knew little of the situation on the Oder, and was shocked to discover from Guderian just how weak his forces were. He was even more shocked to find how little detailed information Guderian had about them, as a result of Himmler's failure to report. To hold back the Soviet might, he had just two armies: Colonel-General Hasso von Manteuffel's Third Panzer Army facing Rokossovsky's Second Belorussian Front along the northern reaches of the Oder from Stettin to about twenty-eight miles north-east of Berlin, and further south, facing Zhukov's front, the Ninth Army, commanded by the forty-seven-year-old General Theodore Busse. Both generals were good professionals, known and trusted, but Guderian could not tell Heinrici much about the strengths or weaknesses of the divisions that made up their armies. He would have to find this out for himself. Their names gave little away, for they were all strange to him, units that had been cobbled together from the remnants of better days and given grandiose titles.

What Guderian was able to tell Heinrici was that Busse was scheduled to launch an attack within the next forty-eight hours against the Soviet forces around the fortress of Küstrin, which was still in German hands. The citadel, on its island at the junction of the Oder and Warta rivers, controlled the only existing bridges across the Oder in that area.

Since early February, Küstrin had been a thorn in the side of Chuikov's Eighth Guards Army and Berzarin's Fifth Shock Army, preventing their linking up their bridgeheads on the west bank. Over the weeks, they had slowly managed to reduce the gap between the two armies to a narrow corridor some two miles wide, but German supplies were still getting through across the Oderbruch, the flat, marshy valley bottom stretching back from the raised west bank of the river for about ten miles. Neither Chuikov nor Berzarin had the artillery or the ammunition to storm the fortress. They were still having to use captured German guns and shells while they stockpiled Soviet-made ammunition for the final assault on Berlin, and many of Chuikov's best troops had been temporarily withdrawn for special training in street fighting. The situation was made doubly difficult by the weather. As the snow thawed, early spring floods covered the approaches to Küstrin and its fortified suburb of Kiertz.

If the Germans could destroy the Soviet bridgeheads around Küstrin, and reinforce their own defences there, it would be a significant help in holding back the assault on Berlin. But even though Chuikov had problems in both supply and manpower, his forces were still immeasurably stronger than Busse's. The German attack had been ordered and planned by Hitler himself, and Heinrici could see from his first glance at the maps that it was suicidal. 'It's quite impossible,' he told Guderian, who agreed wholeheartedly.

Hitler had ordered Busse to send five Panzer grenadier divisions across the river at Frankfurt into the German bridgehead on the east bank. From there they were to drive up the east bank to cut off the Soviet forces around Küstrin from the rear. The plan was madness, calling for five divisions to cross the river by the single bridge at Frankfurt, within easy range of Soviet artillery. If they ever managed to get across, the area on the other side was too small for them to assemble, and the sheer number of Soviet forces between there and Küstrin was so great that they would never stand a chance of breaking out. 'Our troops will be pinned with their backs to the Oder,' Heinrici stated. 'It will be a disaster.'

Before the discussion could go any further, Guderian suddenly looked at his watch, and groaned. He had to leave for the daily Führer conference. Flying into a fine rage, so violent that his face turned crimson and Heinrici feared he was about to have a heart attack, he fulminated against the idiocies of Hitler and the group surrounding him in the chancellery. When he calmed down again, he told Heinrici: 'Hitler is going to discuss the Küstrin attack. Perhaps you'd better come with me.'

Heinrici refused. His place, he said, was at his Army Group. He was completely uninformed, and needed to be briefed before he could do anything. He could not afford to waste half a day. 'Hitler can wait a few days to see me,' he concluded.

MEETING HIMMLER for the first time, for the hand-over of command, Heinrici found all his worst fears confirmed. The Reichsführer was more concerned with treating him to an interminable speech of self-justification than with giving him details of the forces under his command or a proper assessment of the situation. The monologue had gone on for forty-five minutes and showed no sign of abating when the telephone rang. Himmler paused to answer it, listened for a moment in silence, then handed it to Heinrici.

'You're the new commander,' he said. 'You'd better take this.'

Heinrici took the telephone, and introduced himself. On the other end was Busse. 'The Russians have broken through,' he said, 'and have enlarged their bridgehead near Küstrin.'

Heinrici relayed the information to Himmler, who shrugged nervously. 'Well,' he said, 'you're the new commander of Army Group Vistula. Issue the proper orders.'

Heinrici glared at him. 'I don't know a damn thing about the army group. I don't even know what troops I have or who's supposed to be where.'

Himmler said nothing. Clearly, Heinrici could expect nothing from him. Turning back to the telephone, he asked Busse what he proposed.

'As soon as possible I'd like to counter-attack to restabilize my forces around Küstrin,' was the reply.

'Fine. As soon as I can I'll come to see you and we'll both look over the front lines.'

As Heinrici replaced the receiver, Himmler started talking again as though nothing had happened. The general cut him short. It was vital, he told him, that he should have the Reichsführer's considered opinion of the overall situation, and of Germany's current war aims. Himmler pulled a disagreeable face, then said, conspiratorially, 'I want to tell you something personal.' Leading Heinrici to a couch on the other side of the room, where the stenographer who had been recording the conversation could not hear, he told him, 'I have taken the necessary steps to negotiate a peace with the West.'

'Fine,' Heinrici responded, 'but how do we get to them?'

'Through a neutral country,' Himmler told him. 'I'm telling you this in absolute confidence, you understand?'

Himmler did not enlarge upon his statement any further. All he wanted to do now, it seemed, was to get away as quickly as possible. 'He was only too happy to leave,' Heinrici told his former chief of staff in the Carpathians in a telephone call that night. 'He couldn't get out of here fast enough. He didn't want to be in charge when the collapse comes. No – he wanted just a simple general for that, and I'm the scapegoat.'

EARLY NEXT morning, Heinrici began visiting his front to meet his generals and see things for himself. All day, he drove along behind the front line, scouting out the terrain. By evening, he was convinced that there was only one place where the Soviets would strike: the twenty-five-mile sector between Frankfurt and Küstrin. He had also decided where he would establish his main defence line: on the ridge known as the Seelow Heights which marked the edge of the Oderbruch, the flood plain alongside the river. Heinrici had little choice – the escarpment, rising between 100 and 200 feet from the swampy valley bottom, itself studded with ponds and criss-crossed with canals and ditches, was the only natural defence position between the river and Berlin.

Heinrici set about reinforcing his troops in the region, ordering all the divisions that had escaped from Pomerania ahead of Rokossovsky's advance to transfer at once to the critical area. Then, echoing the move that had caused such difficulty to the US Ninth Army in its drive to the Rhine, he ordered the sluice gates holding back the Ottmachau, a large artificial lake emptying into the Oder some 200 miles upstream, to be opened. As the raised water level in the river reached the low-lying Oderbruch, it would flood it to a depth of two feet, creating an added obstacle for Chuikov. In the meantime, he ordered Busse to launch another attack on Küstrin, since the first had failed. This second attack, too, was doomed before it even started, but by this time things were so desperate that every remote chance had to be tried.

# 19

GEORGE PATTON had scored a major success in eliminating the Trier pocket, but he was still not satisfied. He knew that Montgomery in the north was about to launch his much-planned and meticulously prepared crossing of the Rhine on 23 March, and saw a chance of scoring a few personal points by beating him to the punch. He also believed a quick, surprise crossing would save American lives and at the same time put him in position for the start of a spectacular advance into the centre of Germany.

Bradley had forbidden Patton from attempting a crossing in the region of Koblenz, since this might interfere with Montgomery's operation. But he had given permission for a crossing further south, near Mainz – and Major-General Manton S. Eddy's XIIth Corps was within striking distance of the Rhine at Oppenheim, just south of Mainz. Patton flew to Eddy's head-quarters at Simmern, and, in Eddy's words, 'tramped up and down and yelled' at him. At 10 pm on 22 March, men of the 5th Division pushed off silently from the west bank in assault boats. There had been no aerial bombing, no preliminary artillery barrage, no paratroop drops, no smoke screens, not even a signal flare.

Bradley was just finishing his second cup of coffee at breakfast next morning in the sunlit dining room of his headquarters, the Château de Namur, when Patton telephoned.

'Brad, don't tell anyone, but I'm across,' he said.

'Well, I'll be damned,' Bradley replied. 'You mean across the Rhine?'

'Sure am. I sneaked a division over last night. But there are so few Krauts around they don't know it yet. So don't make any announcement – we'll keep it a secret until we see how it goes.'

The Americans were understandably cock-a-hoop. 'While Monty flexed his muscles ostentatiously farther north,' as Bradley himself put it, they had achieved the first military crossing of the Rhine by boat since Napoleon, at a cost of thirty-four American casualties. That night, Patton called Bradley again, his high voice trembling with excitement.

'Brad,' he shouted, 'for God's sake tell the world we're across. We knocked down thirty-three Krauts today when they came after our pontoon bridges. I want the world to know Third Army made it before Monty starts across.'

Bradley was delighted. He told Patton he could put ten divisions into the new bridgehead. He then said he was also giving Hodges ten divisions to break out of the Remagen bridgehead. The US Twelfth Army Group would be well placed to challenge Montgomery's Twenty-First Army Group in any race for the heart of the Reich.

MONTGOMERY'S MASSIVE operation began on schedule on Friday, 23 March, at 10 pm, against German forces who had had plenty of time to prepare. Throughout that night and the next day, 80,000 men, British, Canadian and American, forced their way across the river at ten points along a twenty-mile front, with two airborne divisions dropped behind enemy lines.

It was the moment Winston Churchill had been waiting for since 3 September 1939, and he made sure he was there to see it for himself. Wearing the uniform of his old cavalry regiment, the 4th Hussars, he flew in from London by Dakota during the afternoon of the 23rd, had dinner with Montgomery in his caravan, then spent two hours going over the plans on the maps. In the distance, they could hear the roar of the opening artillery barrage. At 10 pm, as the first green-bereted Commandos were making their way across the river, Montgomery retired to bed – he had never allowed anything, not even a visit by the king, to interfere with his routine. Churchill, a habitual night-owl, was far too exhilarated for sleep, and spent a couple of hours pacing up and down in the moonlight outside, talking to the chief of the imperial general staff, Field Marshal Alan Brooke, before returning to his caravan to deal with the papers that had arrived for him in his boxes.

In the morning, from a selected vantage point on a nearby hilltop, Churchill watched enthralled as over 2,000 aircraft flew over his head carrying the paratroops, while assault craft continued to ferry men, guns and machines across the wide river below. Later, he and Brooke were taken ten miles north to another hilltop overlooking the river, from which they could watch the 51st Highland Division crossing the water. The prime minister was as excited as a small boy, and Brooke had great difficulty dissuading him from joining them.

Churchill's private secretary, Jock Colville, who had been sent off on other business for the PM, actually crossed the river at 11 am, and had a narrow escape when German shells began landing almost on top of his party. He returned to headquarters covered in blood from a driver who was wounded by shrapnel while standing next to him. Churchill secretly thought it rather a lark, but Montgomery was furious that Colville had exposed himself to such danger without his permission.

On Sunday, 25 March, after attending the Palm Sunday church service, Churchill and Montgomery joined Eisenhower, Bradley and Simpson for lunch at a castle overlooking the river at Rheinberg. Afterwards, at a house on the riverbank, Churchill again looked longingly at the landing craft ferrying to and fro. 'I'd like to get in that boat and cross,' he said.

Eisenhower responded firmly. 'No, Mr Prime Minister,' he said. 'I'm the supreme commander and I refuse to let you go across. You might be killed.'

Churchill submitted, but as soon as Eisenhower had left for another appointment, he turned to Montgomery. 'Why don't we go across and have a look at the other side,' he pleaded, pointing to a small US Navy launch nearby.

To his surprise, Montgomery agreed, and they climbed aboard the landing craft, along with a worried Simpson and several other officers. On the other bank, a jubilant Churchill, cigar in his mouth, started marching straight towards the front, and had to be restrained. His enthusiasm was still undimmed on the return journey, when he tried to persuade the skipper of the launch to take them down the river to Wesel, where fighting was still going on. A chain across the river prevented this, but when they landed, Montgomery took the PM in his car to the railway bridge at Wesel, which was under enemy fire. Even with shells and mortar bombs landing all around, and the constant danger of sniper fire, Churchill could only be prised away from the scene with the greatest difficulty, leaving a highly relieved Simpson behind as he was driven happily back to Montgomery's headquarters.

# 20

THE ONLY thing to spoil Churchill's delight during the glorious weekend on the Rhine were the signals concerning the Soviet Union delivered to him in his red-leather-covered ministerial boxes. The accord that had been reached between the three powers at Yalta only the previous month was rapidly falling apart as the end of the war came into sight.

On the first night on the Rhine, Churchill received what Jock Colville described as a venomous telegram from Molotov, bitterly denouncing the negotiations taking place in Switzerland, accusing Britain and America of lying, and of secretly opening negotiations for a separate peace, 'going behind the back of the Soviet Union', the county that was bearing the brunt of the entire war. This brutally insulting note was the latest shot in a row that had been building ever since Himmler's envoy, Karl Wolff, had made contact with Allen Dulles.

Stalin had been kept fully informed of what was happening, but his paranoia could not be assuaged. He judged other leaders by his own standards, and his suspicions were undoubtedly fuelled by intelligence reports of all the other German peace manoeuvres being secretly set up by Ribbentrop, Schellenberg, Berger and others – even Goebbels was openly talking about the possibility of a deal with the West to join Germany in driving the Bolsheviks back, the thing that Stalin had always feared most. The fact that Ribbentrop was also trying to persuade the Japanese ambassador in Berlin, General Hiroshi Oshima, to act as an intermediary in seeking a separate peace with the Soviet Union, could be ignored.

For his part, Churchill was increasingly disturbed as Stalin broke his word by imposing communist regimes on the countries in Eastern Europe liberated by the Red Army. Poland was the most contentious issue, causing great upset, particularly to Britain, which had hosted and supported the Polish government-in-exile throughout the war. Stalin was refusing to have anything to do with what he contemptuously described as 'the London Poles' and was ignoring all Allied protests as he installed his own government composed of Polish communists who had spent the war in the Soviet Union. It was the same story in Romania, Bulgaria, Hungary and Yugoslavia.

Churchill had never trusted Stalin, but had been overridden by Roosevelt and his advisers at Yalta. Now he refrained from saying 'I told you so', and tried to persuade Roosevelt to join him in taking a tougher line with Uncle Joe. Every Soviet action, every hostile word from the Soviet dictator and his henchman, Molotov, increased Churchill's lurking fear that if Stalin could tear up the Yalta agreements over Poland and Eastern Europe, he could do the same over Germany, and Berlin. If they swept far across Germany, could the Soviets be trusted to pull back to the agreed demarcation line? If the Red Army got to Berlin first, could they be trusted to hand over two-thirds of it to the Allies – especially since they clearly believed they had done all the fighting for it? 'I hardly like to consider dismembering Germany,' he told Colville that night, 'until my doubts about Russia's intentions have been cleared away.'

After his initial anger had died down, Churchill decided not to reply to Molotov's insulting letter. But he showed it to both Montgomery and Eisenhower. Eisenhower, he wrote later, 'was much upset and seemed deeply stirred with anger at what he considered most unjust and unfounded charges about our good faith.' But it was Montgomery who took its message to heart, and who started pressing again for a drive to Berlin. 'I had always put Berlin as a priority objective,' he wrote in his memoirs. 'It was a political centre and if we could beat the Russians to it things would be much easier for us in the post-war years.'

Eisenhower was not so sure. He consulted his American generals, including Omar Bradley, who had no doubts about what course they should take. Even when they reached the Elbe, he argued, the Allies would still be fifty miles from Berlin, while the Soviets were already within thirty-five miles. 'I could see no political advantage accruing from the capture of Berlin that would offset the need for quick destruction of the German army on our front,' Bradley recalled later. 'As soldiers we looked naïvely on this British inclination to complicate the war with political foresight and nonmilitary objectives.'

A second element in Bradley's and Eisenhower's thinking was the fear that if they went for Berlin, Hitler and his government would abandon the capital and make for the Alps on the borders of Bavaria and Austria, where they could hold out for months in a fabled 'National Redoubt'. In fact, the redoubt was nothing but a hollow legend, created in the imaginations of a few Nazis as the site for a Wagnerian last stand. But during the final months of the war it became something of an obsession, particularly with Bradley, shaping much of his thinking. Determined to avoid a lingering end to the war in the mountains, he was most concerned with cutting off any possible retreat from Berlin to the south, by turning two of his armies south-east to link up with the Soviets on the Danube.

EISENHOWER SAID nothing about his doubts to Montgomery, Churchill and Brooke when they met on 25 March. Nor did he say that he was already considering shifting the main attack from the north to the centre, removing the US Ninth Army from Twenty-First Army Group and giving it back to Bradley. This would divert Montgomery entirely from the road to Berlin, leaving him only to complete the capture of north-western Germany and to seal off Denmark before the Soviets could 'liberate' it. Eisenhower did, however, order that the Ruhr was to be surrounded and mopped up before any advance to the east began.

Blithely ignoring the Supreme Commander's specific orders, Montgomery went ahead with his plans for the great drive across the plains of northern Germany with his armour speeding towards both the Baltic and Berlin. By 27 March, his armies were rolling forward so fast, and meeting so little serious opposition, that he felt confident enough to issue orders to his army commanders to go for the River Elbe 'with all possible speed and drive'. He reported this to Eisenhower, ending his signal: 'My Tac HQ moves to the north west of Bonninghardt on Thursday, 29 March. Thereafter my HQ will move to Wesel, Munster, Widenbruck, Herford, Hanover – and thence by autobahn to Berlin I hope.'

Eisenhower was already close to breaking point with the strain of trying to reconcile the political demands and national jealousies of Britain and America. When he received Montgomery's imperious and typically tactless signal, usurping his authority over the master plan for the advance into Germany, he finally blew up. His anger made his reply for once clear and uncompromising. There was to be no drive for Berlin. Ninth Army was to revert to Bradley's Twelfth Army Group as soon as it had joined hands with the US First Army to complete the encirclement of the Ruhr. Bradley would be responsible for mopping up and occupying the Ruhr and then would 'deliver his main thrust on the axis Erfurt–Leipzig–Dresden to join up hands with the Russians. . . . The mission of your army will be to protect Bradley's northern flank.'

Eisenhower told Montgomery that he was coordinating his plans with Stalin. And indeed he had pre-empted any decision but his own by sending a telegram to the Soviet leader that very day, telling him of his intentions. He asked for details of Soviet plans, so that the operations of the two armies advancing from east and west could be harmonized. It was most unusual, though not unprecedented, for a general to communicate directly with an allied head of state, and quite a few hackles were raised in the British camp, not least Churchill's. Eisenhower had not even consulted his deputy supreme commander, Air Chief Marshal Tedder, over his change of plan, and he had failed to mention it to the combined chiefs of staff. For the next few days the resulting row raged between politicians and statesmen as well as soldiers, threatening to split the Allies.

Churchill backed Montgomery, and sent a strong message to Roosevelt: '. . . I say quite frankly that Berlin remains of high strategic importance. Nothing will exert a psychological effect of despair upon all German forces of resistance equal to that of the fall of Berlin. It will be the supreme signal of defeat to the German people. On the other hand, if left to itself to maintain a siege by the Russians among its ruins, and as long as the German flag flies there, it will animate the resistance of all Germans under arms.'

To Eisenhower himself he wrote:

> If we deliberately leave Berlin to them, even if it should be within our grasp, [it] may strengthen their conviction, already apparent, that they have done everything. Further, I do not consider myself that Berlin has yet lost its military and certainly not its political significance. The fall of Berlin would have a profound psychological effect on German resistance in every part of the Reich. While Berlin holds out great masses of Germans will feel it their duty to go down fighting. . . . While Berlin remains under the German flag, it cannot, in my opinion, fail to be the most decisive point in Germany.

Eisenhower rode out the storm. With his usual diplomatic skill, he pacified Churchill, promising that if there were a collapse anywhere along the front 'we would rush forward', and that 'Berlin would be included in our important targets'.

Stalin was both delighted with Eisenhower's signal and highly suspicious of it. Before replying, he sent a signal to the US chief of staff in Washington,

General Marshall, complaining that information passed to Moscow by the Americans about the movements of the German Sixth Panzer Army had been false. He more or less accused the Americans of deliberately trying to mislead the Soviet Union. He did not mention Eisenhower's telegram, but clearly he suspected that the Americans were trying to lull him into a false sense of security to allow them to snatch the final prize – and once it was in their possession, who was to say that they would be prepared to give it up again?

At that moment, Stalin was actually in the process of presenting the Soviet general staff with two alternative plans from Zhukov for the assault on Berlin. When he received Eisenhower's message he telephoned Zhukov and ordered him to come to Moscow immediately, to discuss the details of the operation.

# 21

UNTIL KÜSTRIN was taken, there could be no attack on Berlin by the First Belorussian Front. Unfortunately, however, Stalin was making his plans in the belief that Küstrin had already fallen. Front headquarters had reported its seizure early in February, when Berzarin's forces had reached the town, and had failed to correct the misapprehension. This promised to be a source of considerable embarrassment to Zhukov, to say the least – the great victory had been celebrated in Moscow with a salute of guns.

On 24 March, knowing he would shortly be called to Moscow to discuss his plans with Stalin, Zhukov decided it was time to put things right. His chief of staff, General Malinin, telephoned Chuikov.

'When is the Eighth Guards Army going to take Küstrin?' he demanded.

Mischievously, Chuikov professed astonishment at the question. After all, Küstrin had been reported as having fallen to the Fifth Shock Army over a month ago. Surely, he said, it was unnecessary to take a place a second time?

Malinin was not amused. Mistakes occur in war, he said, and Küstrin was one of them. In the middle of the conversation, Zhukov himself grabbed the phone. Gruffly, he told Chuikov, 'Mistakes happen and they have to be put right.' Chuikov was to get on and take the damned place as quickly as possible.

Chuikov replied that provided he was given adequate air support, including dive bombers, he guaranteed not only to take the fortress but to do so before Zhukov was due to see Stalin. Zhukov agreed to provide all the air cover needed.

Before Chuikov could move, Busse launched another German attack, with two additional divisions, on Tuesday, 27 March. It had been ordered by Hitler and Guderian, very much against the wishes of Heinrici, who had described it as crazy. He believed the only sensible thing to do was to order the Panzer units inside Küstrin to break out, abandoning the fortress, but he was overruled. The new attack caught the Soviets by surprise, and achieved an initial advance of about two miles. But once again the overwhelming superiority of the Soviet armies soon crushed the attack, inflicting heavy losses. Bitterly, Heinrici reported the result: 'The attack is a massacre. The Ninth Army has suffered incredible losses for absolutely nothing.'

Next day, the Red Air Force began the Soviet attack on the Küstrin citadel. Early the following morning, the air strikes were renewed until 10 am, when the planes returned to base. As they departed, a forty-minute artillery barrage opened up from guns of all calibres, including heavy artillery firing over open sights. The first boatloads of assault troops landed soon after. There was savage fighting until noon. Officers of the operations section of Chuikov's staff entered the fortress at about 2 pm. As soon as they were in, he put through a phone call to Zhukov, who had just arrived in Moscow.

'Did you give it to them hot?' Zhukov asked.

'As hot as we could,' Chuikov replied.

'Good. Thanks,' said Zhukov, as laconic as ever.


ZHUKOV WAS called to Stalin's office in the Kremlin late that night. Stalin had just finished a conference with the GKO, the State Defence Committee, the central decision-making body which ran the whole Soviet war effort, but he was settling down to work through the night, as usual. Puffing on his pipe, he thrust out his hand to Zhukov, then launched straight into business, as though they were continuing an interrupted conversation. 'The German front in the west has collapsed for good,' he told the marshal, 'and probably the Hitlerites don't want to do anything to halt the advance of the Allied forces. In the meantime, they are reinforcing all their army groups facing us.' To back this up, he produced a letter, supposedly from 'a foreign well-wisher', which told of secret meetings between Nazi and Allied representatives. The writer said that although the Allies had rejected German peace overtures, Stalin should be aware of the possibility that the Germans might be doing a deal that would give the Allies a free run to Berlin.

Stalin asked to see Zhukov's detailed plans for the last great battle of the war in Europe, the battle for Berlin. When would he be ready to begin the offensive?

'Not later than two weeks' time,' Zhukov replied. He added that he thought Koniev could be ready by then, too, but Rokossovsky would probably not be in position on the lower Oder until mid-April.

'Well, then,' Stalin told him, 'we shall have to begin the operations

*Right:* Marshal Koniev, commander of the 1st Ukrainian front, at a forward observation post. An ex-political commissar, Stalin exploited his rivalry with Zhukov to spur the latter on to greater efforts. (Novosti) *Left:* Marshal Zhukov, commander of the 1st Belorussian front and Stalin's most successful general, just before the start of the final assault on Berlin. (Novosti)

*Left:* Marshal Rokossovski, initially commander of the 1st Belorussian front, who was transferred on Stalin's orders to the 2nd Belorussian front, before the Red Army crossed the Vistula. (Novosti) *Right:* On 16 April a cheerful Gen. Chuikov, commander of the 8th Guards Army, one of the most aggressive front line commanders of the Second World War, at his forward observation post on the west bank of the Oder. Gen. Telegin is on his right, Gen. Kazakov on his left. (Novosti)

One of the victims of Allied bombing. The French cathedral in Berlin goes up in flames. (HULTON-DEUTSCH COLLECTION)

Soviet combat engineers working waist-deep in the freezing water of the Oder to complete a make-shift bridge suitable for tanks and self-propelled guns. (Novosti)

At 5 a.m. Moscow time on 16 April thousands of Soviet guns and mortars – 'guns lined up virtually wheel to wheel, one every four yards: 400 guns for every mile of front' – began a huge bombardment of the approaches to Berlin. (Novosti)

An itemised bill sent to the victim's widow by the People's Court for the cost of trying and executing her husband, Erich Knauf (POPPERFOTO):

| | |
|---|---:|
| Fees, accrdg. to Para 49, 52 SGKG for the death penalty | 300,00 M |
| Postage, accrdg. to Para 71, 1 SGKG | 1,84 M |
| Fees for obligatory defender Lawyer Ahsdorff, 10a Gartnerstrasse, Berlin-Lichterfelde-Ost | 81,60 M |
| Time served in prison from 6.4.44 to 2.5.44 | 44.0 M |
| Cost of execution | 158,10 M |
| Total | 585,74 M |

On 23 April Hitler issued an order setting up tribunals for the execution of 'traitors and deserters'. Here, after one such drumhead court martial two men are executed by firing squad. (POPPERFOTO)

Katyusha multiple rocket launchers firing in the streets of Berlin: these so-called 'Stalin Organs' were mounted on trucks and could be moved from place to place. (NOVOSTI)

Soviet guns inside Berlin firing on German positions only a few blocks away. (NOVOSTI)

Fresh Soviet tank reinforcements enter what is left of Berlin as the fighting in the centre draws to a close. (Novosti)

Thousands of Hitler Youth, thirteen and fourteen-year-olds, fought and died for the Führer during the last days of Berlin. (Novosti)

Amid the litter of war – damaged half tracks and dead soldiers – German civilians flee their cellars during a lull in the fighting in Berlin. (Novosti)

Berlin surrenders. On 2 May Berliners hung white flags – sheets, towels, table cloths: anything white – from their windows. For them the war was over. (Novosti)

Probably the most celebrated photograph of the Second World War – Soviet troops raising the victory banner over the Reichstag. In fact, this photograph was specially posed, when the first photograph taken the preceding evening was deemed inadequate. Both photographs were premature. Fighting still continued in the basement of the Reichstag for another twenty-four hours. (NOVOSTI)

without waiting for Rokossovsky. And even if he's a few days late, that's no problem.'

Leaving Zhukov to work on his maps with Antonov, Stalin ordered Koniev, too, to come to Moscow to present his plans for the First Ukrainian Front's part in the Berlin operation. But when he replied to Eisenhower on 1 April, the Soviet dictator told him his forces would launch the main thrust of their attack towards Leipzig and Dresden, to link up with the Western Allies. 'Berlin has lost its former strategic importance,' he said. He would commit only secondary forces in that direction. He told Eisenhower that he planned to launch his offensive in the second half of May.

# 22

HITLER WAS frantic with rage when he heard of the failure of the final German counter-attack on Küstrin. He railed wildly against Busse at the daily conference in the cramped space of the Führer bunker on 27 March, and ordered Guderian to bring him to the next day's conference to give an account of himself. The meeting on 28 March began badly. Busse was given a frosty reception and had hardly begun speaking when Hitler interrupted him with a torrent of personal invective.

'Why did the attack fail?' he yelled. 'Because of incompetence! Because of negligence!'

Busse, a large, steady man, regarded Hitler calmly through his glasses. He tried patiently to explain why the three attacks had all been doomed to fail. But Hitler interrupted again. 'I am the commander!' he cried. 'I am responsible for the orders!' He proceeded to savage Busse, Guderian, Heinrici, the whole military command.

'The Küstrin attack was launched without sufficient artillery preparation,' he declared.

Guderian butted in to say that Busse had not had enough ammunition for a full-scale artillery barrage. Hitler demanded to know why, if that was so, Guderian had not provided him with more. At this, Guderian finally lost control. At the top of his voice he started hurling at Hitler all the arguments he had used the night before. 'Yesterday, I explained to you in detail, both vocally and in writing, that General Busse was not to blame for the failure of the Küstrin attack,' he shouted. 'He followed orders. Ninth Army used the ammunition that had been allotted to it. All of it. Look at the casualty figures! Look at the losses! The troops did their duty – their self-sacrifice proves that!'

'They failed! They failed!' Hitler yelled back.

His face growing purple with rage, Guderian began pouring out his scorn at Hitler's amateur meddling in military matters. The rows the two men had had previously paled into insignificance as he got into his stride. Hitler, unable to get a word in, slumped lower and lower in his chair, the colour draining from his face. The generals and aides in the narrow room stood silent, stunned.

Suddenly, with an agility that surprised everyone, Hitler leapt from his chair. His face was covered with vivid red blotches, his arm and the whole left side of his body trembled more violently than ever. It looked as though he was about to hurl himself bodily at Guderian. For several seconds there was no movement, not a sound apart from the heavy breathing of the two men as they stood glaring into each other's eyes. Then Hitler began screaming again. He unleashed a torrent of hatred against the whole of the general staff, the whole of the officer corps. He blamed them for every disaster, every failure of the last few months. He called them 'spineless', 'fools' and 'fatheads'. He claimed that they had constantly misled and misinformed him, deliberately tricking him. All his accumulated hostility to the aristocratic military establishment exploded like pus from a burst abscess.

Guderian roared back at him, blaming his misjudgement and military incompetence for the débâcles in the Ardennes, in the east, in Hungary, in the Baltic. He attacked the most recent piece of ineptitude: when was Hitler going to bring back the eighteen desperately needed divisions from Latvia?

'Never!' Hitler shouted.

At last, the paralysed bystanders came to their senses. Freytag von Loringhoven, terrified that his chief was about to be arrested and shot, hurried out to the ante-room, to telephone Guderian's chief of staff at Zossen, General Hans Krebs. Swiftly, he told him what was happening, then dashed back to take Guderian by the arm and tell him Krebs had urgent news for him from the front. Generals Jodl and Thomale, meanwhile, were trying to pull Guderian away from Hitler, and Hitler's adjutant, SS General Burgdorf, was easing his master back into his chair.

Krebs was a skilled diplomat – he had never commanded troops in battle, but had been military attaché in Moscow in 1940–41 – and managed to calm Guderian down. For fifteen minutes he talked to him, until Guderian had regained control and was fit to face Hitler again.

By the time he returned, Hitler was also calm. He asked everyone but Keitel and Guderian to leave the room for a few minutes.

'Colonel-General Guderian,' he said coldly as soon as they were alone, 'the state of your health requires that you take six weeks' sick leave immediately.'

'I'll go,' Guderian replied, equally coolly, and extended his arm in a stiff salute.

'Please wait until the conference is over,' Hitler told him.

The conference finished early that day – everyone was eager to get away. At the end, Hitler asked Guderian to stay for a moment. 'Please take good care of yourself,' he told him, suddenly quite solicitous. 'In six weeks the situation will be very critical. Then I shall need you urgently. Where do you think you will go?'

Keitel, too, was eager to know where Guderian would go, and suggested Bad Liebenstein, a spa in southern Germany. Acidly, Guderian told him it was already in American hands. He said he would pick somewhere that wouldn't be overrun during the next forty-eight hours. Suspicious of their sudden concern, he decided it would be wiser not to tell them where he planned to go.

# 23

WHILE GUDERIAN was having his final row with Hitler, Reymann and his chief of staff, Colonel Hans Refior, were involved in a less dramatic but equally hopeless battle with Goebbels. They had learned that day that fourteen more heavy anti-aircraft batteries were being removed from Berlin and sent to the eastern front. During the previous few days the last units of the Reserve Army had left the city, followed by the entire complement of the military training establishments. Most of the 88 mm anti-aircraft guns and their crews had already moved east. Soon, there would be nobody left to defend the city but the Volkssturm. While the army command still had no responsibility for the city's defences, there could be no hope of reinforcements. But Goebbels continued to insist on retaining control, despite all Reymann's efforts.

Once again, one of Reymann's main concerns was the evacuation of the civilian population of Berlin, particularly the children. He had even tried raising the question with Hitler, but the Führer had refused to listen – 'There are no children of that age group left in Berlin!' he had declared. During their earlier meetings, Goebbels had rejected all idea of an evacuation as 'out of the question'. But Reymann had persevered, and eventually Goebbels had admitted that there was already a plan, prepared by the SS and the police.

When Refior had investigated, he had discovered that the so-called plan consisted of one small-scale map, on which possible evacuation routes through the city to the south and west had been inked in. The idea, it seemed, was for evacuees carrying only hand luggage to make their way on foot for up to twenty miles along the chosen roads to suburban rail stations. There was no provision for sanitation stations, food distribution points, or transport for the old and sick. Nor was there any indication of where the trains to carry them to safety would come from.

Accepting that there was little chance now of organizing an orderly evacuation, and that he would be stuck with millions of civilians when the Soviets attacked, Reymann turned to the problem of feeding them in the event of a siege. Where was the food to come from? How were babies to be provided with milk? Goebbels referred him to the mythical three months' supply of canned milk, but then produced a more imaginative solution.

'How will we feed them?' he asked, rhetorically. 'We'll bring in livestock from the surrounding countryside – that's how we'll feed them!'

The thought of bringing cattle into the middle of a battle zone, where they could not be fed, herded, milked or protected, struck Reymann as ludicrous. He returned to the attack on evacuation. 'Surely, we must consider an immediate evacuation programme,' he pleaded. 'We cannot wait any longer. Each day that passes will multiply the difficulties later on. We must at least move the women and children out, before it's too late.'

Goebbels did not answer for a moment. Then he said, mildly, 'My dear General, when and if an evacuation becomes necessary, *I* will be the one to make the decision.' His voice hardened as he concluded: 'But I don't intend to throw Berlin into a panic by ordering it now! There's plenty of time! Plenty of time! Good evening, gentlemen.'

Reymann knew that there was not plenty of time. By now, surely, not even Goebbels could doubt that the Soviet attack was imminent. At 11 am that morning, shortly before 600 US bombers hit industrial installations at Siemensstadt and Marienfelde, knocking out the Daimler-Benz factory among others, the city had been taken completely by surprise by an unusual low-level aerial attack. The aircraft, mostly fighters, strafed the streets with cannon and machine-gun fire for about twenty minutes. They came not from the west but from the east, bearing the red star of the Soviet Air Force.

There was one ray of hope for Reymann that day. When he returned to his headquarters he received a call from OKH, the army high command, to say that arrangements were being made for the Berlin defence area to be put under the control of Army Group Vistula. Reymann was heartened at the prospect of serving under Heinrici, whom he knew well. But Heinrici had quite enough problems simply trying to hold the Oder front, and had no intention of being burdened with the even more hopeless task of defending Berlin. He refused to accept it, leaving Reymann and the city exactly where they were.

# 24

WHILE BERLIN was full of people trying to find a way out of the doomed city, some Berliners were anxious to get back in. Gerald Rahusen, the youth who had cycled curiously past the decoy factories on the heath near his home in 1941, had spent the rest of the war working on a big farm estate near Magdeburg, south-west of Berlin. Since he had kept his Dutch citizenship and was classed as an enemy alien, he had not been liable to conscription. For a while after the invasion of Holland, he had had to report regularly to the police, but this had soon been forgotten. SS recruiting officers tried to persuade him to join the SS Flanders Division, but when he jokingly told them he would join when the war was over, they left him alone. By the time things became more difficult, he was able to argue that he was doing his bit by growing food to feed the army and the munitions workers – the estate grew mainly potatoes, with some rye and poppies, the seeds of which were used to produce badly needed oil.

Gerald had always dreamed of becoming a planter in the Dutch East Indies, but when he finished school the German authorities would not allow him to go on to university to study agriculture unless he took an oath of allegiance to Hitler. This he was not prepared to do, so he decided to gain practical experience instead, and found work as a volunteer on the land.

The owner of the estate, Baron Günter von Wolfen, took a liking to the young man, and before long appointed him as his overseer, responsible for about 120 Eastern workers from Poland, the Ukraine and Russia. The baron was involved in the conspiracy against Hitler, acting as the link between a group of Prussian noblemen and Goerdeler, whom he knew well. During 1944 Gerald did his bit by sending and receiving letters between Wolfen and Goerdeler. Fortunately, the Gestapo never discovered the connection.

Gerald was popular with the Eastern workers – his mother, who had grown up in Odessa and spoke nine languages including Polish, Ukrainian and Russian, was worshipped by them when she visited him. As the Soviets strengthened their position on the Oder, one of the workers came to him and told him: 'Look, your mother is alone in Berlin. The Russians are on their way. You must go back there to your mother.'

Gerald tried to explain that leaving his job was a serious offence, for which he could be shot, and that in any case he had to stay where he was to protect the workers from possible reprisals by the Germans. But they persuaded him that they were well able to look after themselves, and that his mother needed him more. Shortly afterwards, in the middle of the night, they escorted him through the woods to the railway station. He did not have a travel pass, but overcame this by wearing his fire service officer's uniform. As always, an official uniform worked wonders. He was not questioned – the military police on the train simply saluted and passed on. On arrival at the Anhalter station, already little more than a heap of ruins, he was not even ordered to go into the shelter when an air raid began – the fire service uniform allowed him to stay and watch, unchallenged.

At home in Frohnau, on the northern edge of Berlin, Gerald and his mother set about preparing the basement of their house for a siege. Frau Rahusen had lived through the first Russian revolution in Odesssa in 1905, and had a good idea what to expect when the Red Army arrived, as it surely would in a very short time.

# 25

ON EASTER Sunday, 1 April, Zhukov and Koniev reported to Stalin's study to present their plans to the State Defence Committee. Rokossovsky was not called to Moscow, as his front was still involved in heavy fighting around Danzig and he could not leave his headquarters. As the two marshals prepared their maps and papers, the committee filed in – unlike Hitler's conferences, there was no formality, no order of precedence. But these were the seven most important men in the Soviet Union after Stalin himself: Vyacheslav M. Molotov, foreign minister and former prime minister, the committee's deputy chairman; Lavrenti P. Beria, head of the NKVD, the state security organization; Georgi M. Malenkov, secretary of the central committee of the party; Anastas I. Mikoyan, trade and industry minister; Marshal Nikolai A. Bulganin, the representative of the Supreme Command to the Soviet fronts; Lazar M. Kaganovich, transport minister; and economic supremo Nikolai A. Voznesensky. The chief of the general staff, General A. A. Antonov, and the operations chief, General S. M. Shtemenko, were in attendance.

As soon as everyone was seated, Stalin got down to business. He did not mention Eisenhower's telegram, nor the fact that he had replied to it earlier that day saying Berlin was of no importance. He said he had received information about the Allies' plans, which he considered to be 'less than allied'. 'The little allies,' he said, 'intend to get to Berlin ahead of the Red Army.' Nodding to Shtemenko, he ordered: 'Read the telegram.'

The telegram turned out to be a report from the Soviet mission to Eisenhower's headquarters, detailing his plan to surround the Ruhr and then, having destroyed the enemy forces there, advance to Leipzig and Dresden. But it went on to say that British and American forces under the command of Montgomery would attack north of the Ruhr, driving by the shortest route directly to Berlin. The telegram concluded that 'according to all the data and information, this plan – to take Berlin before the Soviet Army – is regarded at the Anglo-American headquarters as fully realistic and that preparation for its fulfilment is well advanced.' Clearly, the Soviet mission had got hold of Montgomery's telegram to Eisenhower, and were taking it seriously.

Stalin turned to his two marshals. 'Well, now,' he demanded softly. 'Who is going to take Berlin? We or the Allies?'

Koniev got in first. 'It is we who will be taking Berlin,' he said, 'and we shall take it before the Allies.'

'So that's the sort of fellow you are,' Stalin said, with a faint smile. His tactic of playing one rival off against the other was working well. Koniev had spoken too quickly: he had not had time to think about the proposition. Stalin probed further.

'How will you be able to organize a proper strike group for it? Your main forces are on your southern flank. Wouldn't you have to do a lot of redeployment?'

'You needn't worry, Comrade Stalin,' Koniev replied. 'The front will carry out all the necessary measures, and we shall organize the forces for the Berlin offensive in good time.'

Stalin nodded, and turned to Zhukov, who spoke with quiet confidence. 'With respect,' he began, nodding to Koniev, 'the men of the First Belorussian Front do not need any regrouping. They are ready now. We are aimed directly at Berlin. We are the nearest to Berlin. We shall take Berlin.'

Stalin smiled again. 'Very well,' he told them. 'You will both stay in Moscow and prepare your plans with the general staff. You will report them to the Stavka within forty-eight hours. Then you can go back to your fronts with fully approved plans in your hands.'

Both marshals were staggered by the short time they were being allowed, for both knew they still faced enormous problems of supply and logistics. But Stalin was not done with them yet. As the meeting broke up, he gave a final turn of the screw. 'I must tell you,' he emphasized, 'that we shall pay special attention to the starting dates for your operations.'

THE TWO men reported to the Kremlin again on the morning of 3 April, their briefcases and map cases bulging with the detailed plans they had been working on night and day. Stalin heard Zhukov first, then Koniev. There was some discussion, but in essence both plans were agreed with remarkably little argument. The only thing that remained to be decided was the boundary between the operational areas of each front. Zhukov's eight armies were poised along the Oder and part of the Neisse, from just above Guben in the south to just above Schwedt, about twenty-eight miles from Stettin, in the north. To the south of Zhukov, the five armies of Koniev's First Ukrainian Front lay stretched along the Neisse. The two fronts were to launch their attacks simultaneously. With massive superiority in men and equipment, Stalin expected Berlin to fall within twelve to fifteen days.

Koniev argued passionately for greater freedom of action. Once across the Neisse, his armies were in a position to strike towards the Spree and then on to the Elbe, where they expected to link up with the Americans by the time Berlin fell. The question that haunted Koniev was how far his front boundary would extend. If Stalin drew a long line right across the map of Germany, then the nearest Koniev could expect to get to Berlin would be Potsdam, as his armies swept round the city from the south-west to encircle it. But if Stalin drew a short enough boundary between the First Belorussian and the First Ukrainian fronts, then – just possibly, if luck was on his side and Zhukov was held up by the Germans in the east – Koniev's tanks would be able to roll northwards and into the southern suburbs of the capital. The prize would be his. He and not his hated rival would be the conqueror of Berlin.

Everything depended on Stalin – who was, of course, fully aware of his protégé's thirst for glory. He thought about the problem for a moment, then stepped up to the map table and, with one of his coloured crayons, drew the boundary between the two fronts. The line extended only as far as Lübben, a town on the Spree about thirty-five miles south-east of the city boundary. 'In the event of stiff enemy resistance on the eastern approaches to Berlin,' he ruled, 'and the possible delay of the First Belorussian Front's offensive, the First Ukrainian Front will be ready to deliver a strike on Berlin from the south.'

Later, he put it more succinctly: 'Whoever breaks in first, let him take Berlin.'


ALTHOUGH ROKOSSOVSKY was not present at the Kremlin meetings, he was not forgotten. The Stavka ordered him to regroup his forces and take over Zhukov's right flank on the Oder by 15–18 April, in order to reduce Zhukov's front by about 100 miles and allow him to concentrate all his power on Berlin. This meant a huge redeployment of much of the Second Belorussian Front, a complete about-turn followed by a 185-mile trek across devastated country-side. The only practical way of transporting the tanks was by rail, but there was not much left of the rail network, and even less rolling stock, and they could only travel at snail's pace. The rest of Rokossovsky's men travelled on trucks and horses, or, like the rifle units, on their own feet. They were an extraordinary sight as they marched along recently captured roads, every man a walking arsenal festooned with machine pistols, ammunition, grenades, fighting knives, dry rations and so on, covering some twenty miles a day. The loot they had acquired accompanied them on trucks.

FOR SECURITY, the starting date was not included in the written directives. But Stalin, Zhukov and Koniev were all agreed: it was to be 16 April, one full month earlier than Stalin had told Eisenhower. Early on the morning of 4 April, with the plans now included in formal written directives, the two marshals sped to the airfield, boarded their planes, and took off in swirling fog within minutes of each other. From now on, every moment counted: the race was on.

# 26

AT ABOUT the same time as the two Soviet marshals got back to their headquarters, Hitler was convincing himself that the Soviet preparations for an attack on Berlin were all a huge deception. Operation Berlin, he declared, was only to be a minor, secondary thrust. The real offensive would be directed further south, at Prague, and this was where the main German defence effort should be concentrated.

Hitler was encouraged in this belief by Colonel-General Ferdinand Schörner, now commanding Army Group Centre, which faced Koniev in the northern part of its sector and the Fourth Ukrainian Front further south in Czechoslovakia. Schörner was already one of Hitler's favourites. A dyed-in-the-wool Nazi, he had been held up to the Führer as a shining example by Goebbels only a few days before, for the way he dealt with deserters and 'professional stragglers' by hanging them from the nearest tree with placards round their necks saying: 'I am a deserter. I have refused to defend German women and children and therefore I have been hanged.' Now this same Schörner had written to Hitler: 'My Führer, it is written in history. Remember Bismarck's words. "Whoever holds Prague holds Europe."'

Hitler rewarded Schörner for his zeal by promoting him to Field Marshal. He then issued a directive transferring four of Heinrici's Panzer divisions from the Oder front to Czechoslovakia. To Heinrici this was a major catastrophe – at one stroke Hitler had deprived him of half his armour. Army Group Vistula was reduced to only twenty-five scratch divisions to cover the whole 100 miles of the Oder front. Schörner's northern flank, facing

Koniev, had another ten. The three Soviet fronts in Operation Berlin, each a massive army group in its own right, between them totalled 192 full divisions.

HEINRICI MET Hitler for the first time the following afternoon in the Führer bunker, for a detailed review of the situation on the Oder front. Like everyone who saw him at that time, he was shocked: he thought Hitler 'looked like a man who had not more than twenty-four hours to live. He was a walking corpse.' The handshake he received was so feeble he could feel no returning pressure. Hitler, wearing green-tinted dark glasses, shuffled painfully into the conference room and collapsed into his chair without a word. Bormann and Krebs, who had replaced Guderian, took their places on the bench against the wall behind him. Heinrici was ushered to stand on Hitler's left, and his operations chief, Colonel Hans Georg Eismann, on Hitler's right. Keitel, Himmler and Dönitz sat facing them across the table. Krebs introduced Heinrici and Eismann, and suggested they give their report immediately, so that they could get back to their headquarters.

Heinrici began to give a precise account of the position as he saw it. He explained how and where the Soviet armies were building up for 'an attack of unusual strength and unusual force'. The main blow would be against Busse's Ninth Army in the central area, he said, and he was doing everything he could to provide strength there. But this was weakening Manteuffel's Third Panzer Army – 'Panzer' in name only these days, since it had so few tanks – on the left flank. Manteuffel's troops were of extremely doubtful quality, including ageing Volkssturm battalions from Stettin and Potsdam, foreign volunteers, Hungarian units, renegade Russian ex-prisoners under former Soviet General Andrei Vlasov, Hitler Youth, and even youngsters of the Reich Labour Service. In the middle and northern sectors they had no artillery whatsoever. 'Anti-aircraft guns cannot replace artillery,' Heinrici said, 'and in any case there is not enough ammunition even for those.'

Krebs promised they would be getting artillery soon. But Heinrici needed more than promises. He went on without pausing, to warn that as soon as the spring floods on the Oder began to subside, Rokossovsky would attack the Third Panzer Army. But more immediately urgent was the need to continue strengthening the Ninth Army in the centre, particularly around Frankfurt. Heinrici proposed that the fortress of Frankfurt should be abandoned. This would release eighteen battalions, 30,000 men, for service in the main defence lines.

This was dangerous ground. Hitler was firmly wedded to the idea of fortresses, and had consistently refused to allow any fortified town to be abandoned – as Guderian had found to his cost with Küstrin. Heinrici's proposal at last brought Hitler to life. For the first time that afternoon he spoke: 'I refuse to accept this,' he said harshly.

Unlike Guderian, Heinrici did not fly into a passion, but continued to explain his reasons calmly and quietly, producing answers to every argument put up by Hitler, backing them up with facts and figures supplied by Eismann. Hitler listened with respect, and examined each paper carefully as it was laid before him. He seemed impressed.

'My Führer,' Heinrici told him firmly, 'I honestly feel that giving up the defence of Frankfurt would be a wise and sound move.'

Astonishing everyone, Hitler nodded thoughtfully, then turned to Krebs. 'Krebs,' he said, 'I believe the general is right. Prepare the orders.'

Heinrici's face did not betray the relief or the triumph he must have felt at such an easy victory. Eismann noted that he seemed completely unmoved, 'But he gave me a look which I interpreted as "Well, we've won!"'

Suddenly, however, there was a commotion in the corridor outside the room. The door was flung open and Göring marched in, noisily excusing himself for being late, and explaining that he had just visited his division of Luftwaffe airborne troops on Heinrici's front. He pumped Hitler's hand in greeting, forced himself into a seat between Dönitz and Keitel, and launched into an anecdote about his trip to the front.

He got no further than the opening words when Hitler shot up from his seat and started screaming in rage. 'Nobody understands me!' he yelled. 'Nobody's doing what I want! Again and again, fortresses have proved their value. Look at Posen. Look at Breslau, and Schneidemühl. Look at how many Russians we've kept pinned down there. Every one of those fortresses was held until the very last man! History has proved me right in my decision to order that every fortress should be held to the last man! That's why Frankfurt is to retain its position as a fortress.'

As suddenly as he had begun, he stopped, falling back into his chair as though exhausted, his entire body shaking violently. Heinrici waited for a moment, then began his patient arguments again, unsupported by Krebs or Keitel. This time, however, Hitler refused to give in. The best Heinrici could manage to get from him was permission to withdraw six battalions from Frankfurt. It was better than nothing, but it gave him little more hope – and he had the nerve to say so.

'My Führer,' he said gravely, 'I do not believe that the forces on the Oder front will be able to resist the extremely heavy Russian attacks that will be made on them.' He complained about the transfer of the Panzer divisions to the south. There was not much left of his Ninth Army, he said, and the troops that remained had no combat experience and precious little training. Even their officers were mostly men from administrative positions who had never seen a battle. As an example, he quoted the 9th Parachute Division – the very unit Göring had been visiting that morning. 'They are young men, well armed,' he said. 'In fact, overarmed, while the infantry on their flank is only half armed. But these people are not experienced. Most of them are recruits with only two weeks' training, and they are led by pilots.'

'My paratroops!' Göring protested. 'You are talking about my paratroops!

They're the best there are. I won't listen to such scurrilous talk. I personally guarantee their fighting ability!'

'I'm not saying anything against your men,' Heinrici responded. 'But they've had no battle experience. And my experience has taught me that untrained units – especially those led by green officers – can be so shocked by their first exposure to artillery bombardment that they're not much good for anything afterwards.'

Hitler, who had now calmed down, joined in. 'Everything must be done to train these formations,' he said. 'There is time to do this before the battle.'

Heinrici assured him that everything that could be done would be done. But it would not be enough. He explained that losing the Panzer divisions to Schörner meant that all his troops had to be used in the front line immediately. He had no reserves. And each division could expect to lose at least a battalion every day once the Soviet onslaught began, which would add up to a complete division each week. 'We cannot sustain such losses,' he said gravely. 'We have nothing to replace them with – and I need at least 100,000 men. My Führer, the fact is that we can only hold out for a few days at the most. Then, it will all come to an end.'

There was a deathly silence. Then Göring rose to his feet. 'My Führer,' he declared, 'I will give you 100,000 men from the Luftwaffe!'

Dönitz was next on his feet: 'I can give you 12,000 men from the navy!'

Himmler followed suit. 'My Führer,' he piped shrilly, 'the SS has the honour to supply 25,000 fighters for the Oder front!'

Heinrici could not believe his eyes or ears. Göring, Dönitz and Himmler were bidding for Hitler's favour with human lives. But the ghastly auction was not yet over. Hitler sent for Major-General Walter Buhle, who was responsible for the Reserve Army's organization. Buhle was at the refreshment table in the ante-room, where he had progressed from coffee to brandy. He reeled into the room, to Heinrici's great disgust, but no one else, not even Hitler, seemed to notice. Hitler questioned him about the Reserve Army's remaining manpower and arms supplies, and concluded that another 13,000 troops could be found for Heinrici.

'There,' he told him triumphantly. 'You have 150,000 men. About twelve divisions. You have your reserves.'

In vain, Heinrici sought to make Hitler and the others understand that it was simply not possible to throw unprepared men – clerks, storemen, airmen, sailors – into battle against the toughest and most experienced troops in the world. 'These men will all be slaughtered at the front!' he stormed. 'Slaughtered!'

Hitler was unperturbed. 'Very well,' he said. 'We will place these reserve troops in the second line about eight kilometres behind the first. The front line will absorb the shock of the Russian artillery barrage. Meanwhile, the reserves will get used to battle and if the Russians break through, then they'll fight them. If the Russians do break through you will have to use the Panzer divisions to throw them back.'

Heinrici still persisted with his demand that the battle-hardened armoured divisions be returned to him. 'I must have them back,' he said very slowly and clearly.

General Burgdorf hissed angrily into Heinrici's ear from behind him: 'Finish! You must finish!'

Heinrici ignored him. 'My Führer,' he reiterated, 'I must have those armoured units back.'

Hitler waved him away. 'I am very sorry,' he said. 'But I had to take them from you.' He explained that Schörner's need for them was far greater than Heinrici's. 'The main Russian attack,' he told him, 'will not be directed against Berlin, but against Prague. So, Army Group Vistula should be well able to withstand the secondary attacks.'

Heinrici stared in disbelief. Now he knew that Hitler and his associates in the bunker 'were all living in Cloud-cuckoo-land'. But, like the ruthlessly honest man he was, he had to tell Hitler that he could not guarantee to repel the Soviet attack towards Berlin.

Hitler hauled himself to his feet again and started shouting at Heinrici: 'Faith and strong belief in success will make up for all these deficiencies! Every commander must be filled with confidence! *You* must radiate this faith! *You* must instil this belief in your troops!'

'My Führer,' Heinrici replied, ignoring the urgent whispers at his back for him to finish, 'I must repeat – it is my duty to repeat – that hope and faith alone will not win this battle.'

'I tell you, Colonel-General,' Hitler continued, 'if you are conscious of the fact that this battle should be won, it will be won! If your troops are given the same belief – then you will achieve victory, and the greatest success of the war!'

Heinrici left the meeting, exhausted. The result of the grandiose offerings eventually amounted to some 30,000 men, all unarmed and totally unprepared for combat. Army Group Vistula was able to find only 1,000 rifles between them.


HEINRICI KNEW that it would take a miracle to save Germany now, and he did not believe in miracles. Hitler, however, did – it was all he had left to cling to. So, too, did Goebbels, who visited him that night after the generals had all been dismissed, bringing with him one of his favourite books, Carlyle's *History of Frederick the Great*. To comfort the Führer, Goebbels read aloud to him from the book, which he considered 'extraordinarily instructive and uplifting'. The chapter he chose told of the turning point in the Seven Years War in 1762, when Prussia faced overwhelming odds against an alliance of Russia, Austria and France. Like Hitler, Frederick, too, 'sometimes felt that he must doubt his lucky star', Goebbels wrote in his diary, 'but, as generally happens in history, at the darkest hour a bright star arose and Prussia was saved when he had almost given up hope.'

Frederick had said he would give up the fight and commit suicide if things had not improved by 15 February. Goebbels read Carlyle's apt and dramatic words with relish: 'Brave King! Wait yet a little while, and the days of your suffering will be over. Already the sun of your good fortune stands behind the clouds, and soon it will rise upon you.' Shortly afterwards, the 'miracle of the House of Brandenburg' had come to pass: Czarina Elizabeth of Russia, Frederick's most deadly enemy, died; her successor made a separate peace, to become an ally; and Prussia went on to victory. Hitler saw the parallel at once, and his eyes, Goebbels said, 'were filled with tears'.

It seemed particularly portentous that such a prophecy came from a British writer. Filled with excitement, they sent for two horoscopes. One was for Hitler, cast on 30 January 1933, the day he took office as chancellor. The other was for the German republic, drawn up on 9 November 1918, the date of the Kaiser's abdication. To their amazement, they found that both could be interpreted as predicting the outbreak of war in 1939, the victories until 1941, followed by a run of defeats and difficulties reaching a peak in mid-April 1945. In the second half of April Germany was to have a temporary success, leading to a period of stagnation until August, when there would be peace. This would be followed by three years of hard times, after which the nation would rise again.

Hitler was convinced. The next day, Goebbels issued a proclamation to rally the hard-pressed troops:

> The Führer has declared that there will be a change of fortune in this very year. . . . The true quality of genius is its awareness and its certain knowledge of approaching change. The Führer knows the exact hour of its arrival. This man has been sent to us by destiny, so that we, in this time of great external and internal strain, shall testify to the miracle . . .

Goebbels's ringing words may have comforted Hitler, and those rabid Nazi supporters who still believed he was their saviour, but they were small consolation to soldiers without weapons, or to people without food. Two days before there had been a riot in the Rahnsdorf district of Berlin, when a crowd of about 200 ransacked two bakeries. Goebbels had reacted immediately: 'I decided to take brutal action,' he wrote. The same afternoon the People's Court sentenced to death a man and two women judged to have been the ringleaders. Goebbels pardoned one of the women, but the other two were beheaded that night. He had placards posted to announce this, and broadcast the news of the sentences over the radio. 'I think this will have a most sobering effect,' he complimented himself. 'I am of the opinion that no more bakeries in Berlin will be looted in the immediate future.'

# 27

THE LUNATIC ravings emanating from the Führer bunker might have convinced the brainwashed children of the Hitler Youth and other Nazi fanatics that there was still hope, but for an increasing number of party notables they were a signal that the time had come to look to their own futures. Obergruppenführer Gottlob Berger, the SS general in charge of all prisoners of war, sent for his two prize American captives, Brigadier-General Vanaman and Colonel Spivey, on 3 April. He talked to them in his office until 4 am next morning, explaining his plan for an anti-Bolshevik crusade. The only way the red tide could be prevented from engulfing Europe, he believed, was for the West to join Germany in fighting the Soviet Union.

Berger knew the Allies would never agree to join hands with Germany while Hitler was still in power. However, he told Vanaman and Spivey, he might not remain in power much longer: there was a plot to remove him, along with Göring, Himmler and Bormann. All the conspirators needed was a little encouragement, some sign, from the West. This was the reason for the American officers' proposed trip to Switzerland – from there they could make direct contact with President Roosevelt and the US government. So that they could keep in touch with the anti-Hitler conspiracy, Berger gave them a system of radio codes and frequencies.

Vanaman demanded Berger's assurance that he would continue to protect Allied PoWs – Goebbels was advocating their wholesale murder, believing that the fear of Allied retaliation would stop any more German soldiers surrendering or deserting, and Hitler was seriously considering the idea. Berger readily assured Vanaman that he would look after the prisoners. The following day, the two Americans were introduced to the leader of the conspiracy, Walter Schellenberg, who briefed them and assigned SS Sturmbannführer (Major) Heinz Lange to be their escort. They were given a pass, signed with Himmler's forged signature, guaranteeing them safe conduct out of Germany. At 3 am on 5 April, between RAF Mosquito raids, they left Berlin.

After an eventful trip to the south, which included a car crash and being machine-gunned by US Lightning fighters, they arrived at Meersburg on Bodensee (Lake Constance). From there, they took a ferry to Konstanz, on the Swiss border, where they awaited further orders from Berlin. When these arrived, Lange informed them that there had been a change of plan: they must return to the capital. But Vanaman, who spoke excellent German, saw the message for himself: it ordered Lange to liquidate them. Fortunately, Lange very sensibly decided that it was too late in the war to risk murdering two senior US officers, and delivered them safely to the Swiss authorities. Their part in Schellenberg's peace machinations was over.

# 28

ON 5 APRIL, Zhukov's senior commanders converged on his head-quarters, a grey stucco, three-storey house on the outskirts of Landsberg. There, he gathered them around a large table, covered with a dust sheet. When he pulled off the sheet, he exposed a huge scale model of Berlin and its surrounding suburbs, complete with miniature buildings, bridges, railway stations, airfields and defensive positions. The principle streets and canals were shown in relief, with anticipated German defensive positions, flak towers and bunkers specially marked. The main objectives were picked out with green flags bearing numbers: 105 was the Reichstag, 106 the chancellery, 107 the Interior Ministry, 108 the Foreign Office, and so on.

'I ask you to turn your attention to objective 105,' Zhukov said, after giving his generals time to take in some of the details. 'That is the Reichstag. Who is going to be the first to reach it? Chuikov and his Eighth Guards? Katukov and his First Guards Tanks? Berzarin and his Fifth Shock Army? Bogdanov with his Second Guards Tanks? Who is it going to be?' Like Stalin, Zhukov was encouraging competition between his generals. For some strange reason, he saw the Reichstag – burnt out and unused since 1933 – as the final target, the final prize that would go to the winner of the race. No one took up his challenge, however, and he turned his attention to objective 106.

Having had his moment of fun, Zhukov got down to the serious business for which he had had the model constructed. For two solid days, he conducted detailed briefings followed by intensive war games, working through every conceivable scenario for the attack on Berlin. War games had always played an important part in Red Army planning, but Zhukov was particularly keen on them. He believed in leaving nothing to chance, nor in allowing any uncertainty. When Bogdanov complained that he needed more room to manoeuvre for his outflanking movement to the north of the city, Zhukov asked him sardonically if he intended to take part in the assault on Berlin, or to go off northwards on his own. Several commanders suggested that the main German defences would be concentrated in the second line of fortifications, and that the Soviet artillery barrage should be directed against this and not against the immediate front line, but Zhukov refused to accept the idea.

Once the generals had finished, they went back to their own headquarters to conduct exercises and war games of their own, first with corps and divisional commanders, then moving down the line of command to battalion and company level.

AWAY TO the south, Koniev was also involved in feverish preparations and war games of his own, complicated by the fact that he had not yet crossed the Neisse, and had no bridgeheads established. His attack would have to begin with a river crossing under fire – but he warned his two tank army commanders not to use up their bridging equipment on the Neisse, but to save it for the Spree, which they would have to cross if he had the chance to turn them north towards Berlin.

To Zhukov's north, meanwhile, Rokossovsky's armies were still trekking across country to their start line on the east bank of the lower Oder. The first units reached it on 10 April. Before them stretched a most unpromising scene – conditions for a crossing looked almost impossible. The river forked into two wide channels, and the land between them was flooded by water too shallow for boats or pontoons. In all, they faced a water barrier over three miles wide. There were marshes nearly a mile wide all along the eastern bank, while on the German side the land rose much higher, providing the enemy with a formidable defence line.

Intelligence reports indicated that Manteuffel's Third Panzer Army was well prepared on the west bank. There was an elaborate system of trenches and strong points stretching back for a depth of between six and seven miles from the river, with a second line about twelve miles from the Oder, and a third defence line behind that. It would be no picnic, but Rokossovsky would be ready to launch his attack four days after Zhukov's, to protect the First Belorussian Front's right flank as it powered its way into Berlin.

# 29

WHILE ZHUKOV was occupied with finalizing his plans and completing the immense build-up for the great attack, there was still plenty of activity on the Oder front. Patrols were constantly probing the German defences, scouting out the land and seizing prisoners for interrogation. The

Soviet generals went on trying to expand their bridgeheads, pushing back their boundaries with continuous small-scale skirmishes.

In Frankfurt, Fred Laabs and Karl-Heinz Freund heard the sounds of Soviet artillery and tanks getting closer every day. From their friend's house near the western end of the bridge they kept watch on the other bank. One day in early April, they saw the first silhouettes of Soviet tanks on the hills behind the eastern bank, and shortly afterwards they could make out Soviet infantrymen through their binoculars. That was enough for them – it was time to go. Both lads had been thoroughly indoctrinated with Nazi propaganda telling them that the Bolsheviks would cut their throats, or at the very least cut off their ears and tongues, deport men to Siberia, and rape all the women.

Still wearing full uniform, carrying all their equipment and their military identity cards, they set out for Berlin. They did not follow the direct westerly route to the city, but struck out north, along the river towards Küstrin. From there they turned west to make the fifty-mile trek on foot. They avoided towns and villages where possible, and from time to time joined one of the many refugee columns, occasionally being given a lift on a peasant's horse-drawn cart. They slept in barns or in the cellars of ruined buildings. Carefully skirting the garrison town of Strausberg, they approached Berlin through the north-western borough of Weissensee, timing their arrival at Fred's home for late afternoon when dusk was falling.

The city was busy everywhere with preparations for the last battle. A barricade was being built near Fred's home, so they had to make a detour to avoid being caught. Fred knew that many of the other tenants of his block were still one hundred per cent Nazi, and would have no hesitation in denouncing them as deserters, so he kept clear of the front door and got into his family's flat via an iron fire escape from the next building. Apart from broken windows and minor damage to some furniture, the Laabs' flat was intact, though the rear of the building had been virtually destroyed.

After the first, joyful reunion, Fred's mother agreed to offer Karl-Heinz refuge for the night. Next morning, he set out to join his own family, promising to make contact again 'as soon as everything is over'. Fred never knew if he made it home, or what happened to him. He never heard of him again.

Frau Laabs kept Fred safely inside the flat, burning his uniform and telling him to get rid of his pistol, which she did not want to touch. He wrapped it in an oil-soaked rag and hid it in a bucket of sand, kept by the door for firefighting. But hiding in the flat had its problems. Fred could not accompany his mother, elder sister and grandmother to the shelter during air raids; there was too much risk of being denounced by some eager Nazi. After a few days, his mother told the neighbours that she had heard from her son that he was about to be discharged from military service for medical reasons. Surprisingly, considering that so many invalids were being called up, the story was believed by everyone, including the senior Nazi official who lived in the next flat, and who had a bunch of deserters hanged from a tree at the corner of the nearby Friedrichshain park in front of Fred's horrified eyes.

# 30

WITH THE Red Army threatening to attack Berlin any day, the Nazi hierarchy decided it was time to settle scores with those conspirators who were still in custody. Canaris's remaining diaries and notes had been found at Zossen early in the year, so there was little need to go on interrogating his associates.

Late in the evening of Easter Tuesday, 3 April, Dietrich Bonhoeffer and the others in the group who were being held at Buchenwald were loaded into a heavy lorry, which had been adapted to run on gas generated in a wood burner. It set out into the night, making slow progress since its top speed was only 20 miles an hour and it had to stop every hour for the air filters to be cleaned and the generator stoked for fifteen minutes.

The prisoners feared they were being taken to the annihilation camp at Flossenbürg for immediate execution. They were vastly relieved when they reached Weiden, at the start of the valley in which the death camp lay, at noon on Wednesday, to hear someone outside saying: 'Drive on. We can't take you . . . too full!' The lorry rolled on, heading south-east, but after a few miles it was stopped by two police motorcyclists. The policemen had a list of names. They called Dr Josef Müller, then Korvettenkapitan Franz Liedeg, out of the truck. Suspecting that he would be the next to be called, Bonhoeffer kept his head down. Captain Ludwig Gehre, however, a close friend of Müller's, jumped out to see what was happening, and the police took him.

Bonhoeffer stayed in the truck, which rolled on to Regensburg, on the Danube. There the remaining prisoners were locked up overnight in the local courthouse jail. Next day, air raids kept them in their cells until dark, when they could start their journey again. Driving along beside the river, in darkness and rain, the truck went into a skid, breaking its steering. It was noon next day before a replacement vehicle arrived – a comfortable bus, in which the men were driven to Schönberg, north of Passau. There they spent the night in a local schoolhouse, where they enjoyed the delight of sleeping in proper beds with coloured blankets. The door was locked, of course, but there was a holiday atmosphere among the prisoners.

Saturday was a beautiful day, and they took advantage of the spring weather to sit in the first-floor windows of the school, soaking up the sun.

Bonhoeffer passed the time learning Russian from one of his companions, Vassiliev Kokorin, a Russian air force officer who was a nephew of the Soviet foreign minister, Molotov. The following day they celebrated Low Sunday with a service conducted by Bonhoeffer. For the first time, they felt they could really start to believe that with the war almost over there would be no more trials, and that they might all be saved.

For the others, the hope was justified. For Bonhoeffer, however, fate was to prove more cruel. On Friday, 6 April, Dohnanyi had suddenly been moved back to Sachsenhausen, where SS interrogator Walter Huppenkothen, together with the camp commandant, had conducted a hasty court martial. Dohnanyi, still genuinely ill, had been condemned to death while lying on a stretcher, heavily drugged into semi-consciousness. He was executed shortly afterwards.

Huppenkothen had then travelled to Flossenbürg, arriving on the Saturday, to set up a summary court martial for the other conspirators. It was not until he surveyed the prisoners, who included Canaris and Oster, that anyone realized Dietrich Bonhoeffer was missing. Huppenkothen ordered an immediate search, and after an initial panic Bonhoeffer was located at Schönberg. He had just finished the Sunday morning service when two men arrived in a car to collect him. His brief holiday was over. By the time he arrived at Flossenbürg, the court had already tried and convicted Canaris, Oster, Count Sack, Dr Theodor Strünck, and the unfortunate Captain Gehre. In each case, the sentence was the same: death by hanging. Bonhoeffer's fate was a foregone conclusion.

About 5.30 am on 9 April, the condemned men were forced to strip. Then they were led out to be hanged. The camp physician, Dr Fischer-Hüllstrung, described how Bonhoeffer faced his end:

> Through the half-open door of one of the huts I saw Pastor Bonhoeffer, before taking off his prison garb, kneeling on the floor praying fervently to his God. I was most deeply moved by the way this lovable man prayed, so devout and so certain that God heard his prayer. At the place of execution, he again said a short prayer, then climbed the steps to the gallows, brave and composed. His death ensued after a few seconds. In the almost fifty years that I have worked as a doctor, I have hardly ever seen a man die so entirely submissive to the will of God.

Immediately after the hanging, Bonhoeffer's body and all his possessions, like those of his fellow victims, were burned. Two days after his execution, the companions he had left behind in Buchenwald were free: the camp was abandoned by its SS guards shortly before an armoured spearhead from Patton's US Third Army rolled through the gates.

# 31

WHILE HITLER and his generals were disagreeing about the immediate danger from the east, Berlin suddenly found itself threatened from the west, too. The great American trap had snapped shut around the Ruhr on 1 April, as the US First and Ninth Armies linked up near Paderborn. Surrounded inside the ruins of the great industrial area was an entire German army group, Field Marshal Model's Army Group B, with two Panzer armies, some twenty-one divisions, amounting to almost 325,000 men. This was a staggering loss to Germany, leaving a gap 200 miles wide in the western front, with only a few disorganized divisions standing between the Ruhr and Berlin. Montgomery had been diverted to the north, but the road was now open for the fast, highly mobile US armoured formations to strike for Berlin.

Bradley chose not to seize the opportunity. He was, as he later admitted, obsessed with the idea of the Alpine Redoubt. Intelligence assessments indicated that Hitler intended to dash south for a last stand in the mountains – what other sensible explanation could there be for his moving Panzer divisions south at this time, away from Berlin and the Oder? So instead of unleashing the Ninth Army to charge north-east across Germany, Bradley committed eighteen American divisions to reducing and dividing the Ruhr pocket – it was to take until 18 April before the Germans there surrendered – after which he planned to move south-east to link up with the Soviets and cut Germany in two. Only eight divisions were left free to continue the advance to the north-east, while no fewer than thirty-one were headed south.

Lieutenant-General William H. Simpson, however, as commander of the Ninth Army, still had his eyes fixed on Berlin, and for a while it seemed Bradley and Eisenhower might give him his head. On 4 April, the day Ninth Army was removed from Montgomery's control and returned to Twelfth Army Group, Simpson's advance units were already crossing the Weser. Bradley ordered him to attack eastward towards Magdeburg, and from there 'to exploit any opportunity for seizing a bridgehead over the Elbe and be prepared to continue to advance on Berlin or to the north east'.

Simpson needed no further bidding. 'We'd been the first to the Rhine,' he recalled later, 'and now we were going to be the first to Berlin. All along we thought of just one thing – capturing Berlin, going through and meeting the Russians on the other side.' He issued his own instructions at once, telling his staff that as soon as he had reached the phase line along the Leine River, which he expected to do within a matter of days, he planned 'to get an armoured and an infantry division set up on the autobahn running just above Magdeburg on the Elbe to Potsdam, where we'll be ready to close in on Berlin'.

The word spread quickly throughout Ninth Army, to the dismay of those divisions committed to the reduction of the Ruhr and the delight of those apparently chosen to go for the big prize. Major-General Isaac D. White, commanding the 2nd 'Hell on Wheels' Armored Division, was way ahead of his army chief. He had already completed his detailed plan to drive for Berlin, 'generally along the autobahn' – in fact, his maps had been ready since 25 March. Now, covering an average of thirty-five miles a day and only eighty miles from Magdeburg, he was confident that once he had established a bridgehead there, he could be in Berlin within forty-eight hours. On White's right, Major-General Robert C. Macon's 83rd 'Thunderbolt' Infantry Division, now also known as 'the Rag-Tag Circus' because of its motley collection of captured German vehicles, was pressing forward just as fast. Further along the line, 5th Armored and 30th, 84th and 102nd Infantry Divisions all had the bit firmly between their teeth.

At times, they all met stiff resistance from individual German units, but this was spotty and uncoordinated, and the momentum of the advance continued to grow. By 7 April, even Eisenhower was hedging his bets, writing to General Marshall and the Combined Chiefs of Staff to say that he regarded 'the capture of Berlin . . . as something that we should do if feasible and practicable as we proceed on the general plan'. He went on to say that he thought it was 'militarily unsound . . . to make Berlin a major objective, particularly in view of the fact that it is only 35 miles from the Russian lines'. However, if the Combined Chiefs decided that it was politically desirable to go for Berlin, 'I would cheerfully readjust my plans and my thinking so as to carry out such an operation'. Marshall did not reply, or even discuss the question of Berlin with the chiefs. He was happy to leave the decision to Eisenhower.

Next day, Eisenhower joined Bradley for a visit to Major-General Alexander R. Bolling's 84th Division on the outskirts of Hanover. Bolling was worried that an order to capture this city of 400,000 inhabitants, rather than skirting it, would slow down his advance. The order stood, but Eisenhower parted from Bolling by asking him, 'Alex, where are you going next?'

Bolling replied, 'General, we're going to push on ahead. We have a clear go to Berlin and nothing can stop us.'

Eisenhower put his hand on Bolling's arm and told him: 'Alex, keep going. I wish you all the luck in the world and don't let anybody stop you.'

Bolling captured Hanover on 10 April – it took him only one day, thanks to finding a map of the city's defences on a captured German soldier. That day, as so often during the later stages of the war, the US Air Force staged a particular heavy raid on Berlin with 1,232 B-17s and B-24s, to draw German fighter defences away from ground operations in the west. The Luftwaffe sent up fifty Me-262s against them, the largest concentration of jet aircraft it had ever mustered. The bombers and their P-51 Mustang escorts shot down thirty of them. Hitler's last 'wonder weapon' had failed him.

Though Bolling's charge was slightly delayed, other American units were racing onward. On 11 April, forward units of 2nd Armored Division covered almost sixty miles in thirteen hours, in spite of being held up by civilian traffic jams in some of the towns they passed through. Shortly after 8 pm, Colonel Paul A. Disley of the 67th Armored Regiment called General White at Divisional HQ. 'We're on the Elbe,' he announced. Inside twenty-four hours, other units of both 2nd and 5th Armored Divisions had reached the Elbe at Wittenberge, Werben and Sandau. US troops were within fifty miles of Berlin.

BRADLEY HAD ordered Simpson 'to snatch a small bridgehead across the Elbe as soon as he reached its bank', and Simpson had managed to do so, with men of the 83rd Infantry Division getting two battalions across the river at Barby, fifty miles upstream from Magdeburg. With little opposition to be seen from the Germans, Colonel Edwin 'Buckshot' Crabill strode up and down the west bank, urging men into assault boats and amphibious DUKWs. 'Get across! Get across!' he yelled. 'And keep moving – you're on your way to Berlin!'

But Bradley, as cautious as ever, had not told anyone the real reason why he wanted the bridgehead. 'This was not in preparation for an advance on Berlin,' he wrote later, 'but only to establish a threat that might draw off German resistance from east of Berlin in front of the Russians.' Having got his 'diversion', he was not keen to go further. He was visiting Simpson at his command post a few days later when the phone rang. Simpson answered, listened, then told Bradley, with his hand held over the mouthpiece: 'It looks as though we might get the bridge in Magdeburg. What'll we do if we get it, Brad?'

'Hell's bells,' Bradley answered. 'We don't want any more bridgeheads on the Elbe. If you get it, you'll *have* to throw a battalion across it, I guess. But let's hope the other fellow blows it up before you find you're stuck with it.' The Germans blew the Magdeburg bridge a few minutes later, so the decision never had to be taken.

THE BRIDGEHEAD at Barby did not draw German forces from the eastern approaches to Berlin, as Bradley had hoped. But his troops found themselves facing unexpectedly fierce resistance. For the first time in thirty months of combat, 2nd Armored was thrown back when it tried to establish another bridgehead just south of Magdeburg. The main opposition came from new mobile combat units of the Potsdam, Scharnhorst and Ulrich von Huten divisions of the German Twelfth Army, which was commanded by the former chief of staff to Guderian and Army Group Vistula, General Walter Wenck.

After six weeks in hospital following his serious car accident in February, Wenck had been recuperating on the beautiful Chiemsee lake between Munich and Berchtesgaden when he had received a telephone call from Hitler's adjutant, General Burgdorf. It was 6 April, the day Heinrici was promised his 'reinforcements' by Göring, Himmler and Dönitz. Wenck was still far from fit – he had to wear a surgical corset from chest to thighs to support his damaged ribs – but he was ordered to report to Berlin the following day.

'The Führer has appointed you commander of the Twelfth Army,' Burgdorf told him.

'The Twelfth Army?' Wenck asked. 'Which is that?'

'You'll learn all about that when you get here,' he was told.

'I've never heard of a Twelfth Army,' Wenck persisted.

'The Twelfth Army is being organized now,' Burgdorf replied.


THE TWELFTH Army existed mostly on paper, another straw for Hitler to clutch while awaiting his miracle. It was intended to relieve Army Group B, trapped in the Ruhr, and to defend the centre of the western front, from the junction of the Havel and the Elbe in the north, down to just below Leipzig. But it had precious little with which to do either. It did have four experienced corps headquarters, but two of these had insufficient signals equipment to operate. Its troops, still being hurriedly assembled while Wenck flew north from Bavaria to take command, consisted of the last scrapings from military depots, the remnants of units that had been shattered in the Rhine battles, and youngsters from the Reich Labour Service and the Hitler Youth. The officers and non-commissioned officers from training establishments were excellent, but 90 per cent of the troops under their command were green youths between seventeen and eighteen.

When Wenck took command, he found he had little artillery apart from fixed anti-aircraft guns set around key sites along the Elbe, such as Magdeburg and other bridge crossing points. He had a few self-propelled guns and armoured cars, but only about a dozen tanks – he would have to wait for more until they came off the damaged production lines. He was promised ten divisions, about 100,000 men, but the promise was unlikely ever to be fulfilled. The best he could expect was five divisions, giving him a total of about 55,000 troops.

This was the force that was opposing Bradley's men, and even driving back the veterans of units like the 2nd Armored Division. They did it through brilliant anticipation by Wenck, concentrating the men he had into mobile shock troops and rushing them to the points where he expected trouble – and by the sheer energy and dedication of young men who had been thoroughly indoctrinated with Nazi fanaticism. In the long run, they could not hope to defeat the vastly superior American forces. But for now they could hold them on the Elbe, breaking down the momentum of the great rolling advance and bringing it to a halt.

# 32

EVEN RIBBENTROP was now feeling the jaws of the vice tightening on Berlin, and on 12 April he asked the remaining diplomats to leave the city. But Goebbels still kept up his show of confidence. He visited General Busse that day at the front near Küstrin, and took the opportunity of making a speech to the officers, reminding them of the miracle that had saved Frederick the Great. One of the officers asked pointedly which Czarina was going to die this time. 'I don't know,' Goebbels replied in all seriousness, 'but fate holds all kinds of possibilities.'

As he arrived back at his office in Berlin just after midnight, its exterior lit by fires from the Adlon Hotel and the chancellery, both of which had been hit during the evening raids, a group of his staff were waiting for him on the steps.

'Herr Reichsminister!' one of them shouted. 'Roosevelt is dead!'

Goebbels stood still for a moment, unable to believe what he had heard. Then, trembling with emotion, he cried: 'Bring out our best champagne! I must telephone the Führer!'

He hurried inside, to his office, where his press officer, Rudolf Semmler, confirmed the news. Goebbels's face went pale.

'This is the turning point!' he exclaimed, then incredulously: 'Is it really true?'

Semmler assured him it was. Harry S. Truman was the new president of the United States of America. Goebbels immediately picked up the phone and called Hitler. 'My Führer,' he said in a fever of excitement, 'I congratulate you. Roosevelt is dead. It is written in the stars that the second half of April will be the turning point for us. This is Friday the thirteenth! Providence has struck down your greatest enemy. God has not forsaken us. Twice he has saved you from savage assassins. Death, which the enemy aimed at you in 1939 and 1944, has now smitten your most dangerous enemy. It is a miracle! It is like the death of Czarina Elizabeth.'

Hitler was overjoyed. When Ribbentrop visited him next day, he found him, he said, 'in seventh heaven'. At the daily conference, his mood was still ecstatic. Not even the news that Vienna had fallen to the Red Army could lower his spirits. He announced that the war would be won in Berlin: units falling back from the Oder front would form a hard nucleus that would draw the Soviet troops towards it. German armies would then be able to attack from the outside, to destroy the enemy in a decisive battle. He would remain in Berlin, to inspire his forces to victory.

His generals were less than convinced by this strategy, and several tried to persuade him to leave the city and go south, to the comparative safety of Berchtesgaden. But he refused even to consider it, and when they had gone he began drafting a new proclamation to the troops, so bombastic that even Goebbels thought it too far-fetched, and held off distributing it until the Soviet attack began.


NEXT DAY, Saturday, 14 April, Zhukov's artillery opened up all along the front. After only ten minutes Soviet troops began attacking in battalion-strength groups, catching the Germans by surprise and making inroads of up to three miles. Heinrici was not fooled by the attack. He recognized it for what it was – the standard Soviet tactic of reconnaissance in force, with each division using about one battalion with armour and artillery support to check out the enemy's first line of defence. The troops on the ground were not fooled, either. A German corporal taken prisoner by Chuikov's men was quite open during his interrogation. 'Germany will be finished in a fortnight,' he told his captors. When asked why he said this, he replied: 'Your offensive isn't the main one. It's only a reconnaissance. You'll start the real thing in two or three days. It'll take you about a week to reach Berlin and another week to capture it. So, Hitler will be kaput in fifteen to twenty days.'

Heinrici already knew the attack was imminent, for he had been watching Zhukov's awesome preparations. Every day, he had flown over the Soviet lines in a scout plane, to see for himself as more and more guns and tanks, ammunition and men, piled into position. Every night, he had studied the intelligence reports and prisoner interrogations. From the Seelow Heights the Germans could watch every move made in the all-important Küstrin bridgehead and even over the river on the eastern bank. There were few trees to hide tanks, guns or equipment, and those that remained were not yet in leaf. Digging in was impossible in the marshy, waterlogged ground, where every hole immediately filled with water. When darkness fell, the Germans used searchlights from Seelow to sweep across the Soviet positions, augmented by flares dropped from light aircraft. The only secret the Soviets were able to keep was the exact timing of the assault.

# 33

THE US 83RD Infantry Division's bridge over the Elbe at Barby was doing good business. Units of the 2nd Armored Division, driven back from their own bridgehead by Wenck's youngsters, had recovered their breath and headed south at full speed to join the men of the Rag-Tag Circus pouring across the river. A second bridge was constructed alongside the first, to speed up the flow, but traffic was so heavy that there was considerable congestion, slowing everyone down. Nevertheless, General White planned to set his armoured columns moving again just as soon as they had reassembled on the eastern bank, and advance patrols from the 83rd were already in the town of Zerbst, less than forty-eight miles from Berlin.

When Bradley called Eisenhower at his headquarters in Rheims, he found the supreme commander in a sombre mood. Eisenhower had spent part of the day inspecting his first concentration camp, near Gotha, and had been appalled by the experience. 'I have never at any other time experienced an equal sense of shock,' he recalled later. Bradley told him of the continuing success of the bridging operation. Eisenhower listened carefully, then asked, 'Brad, what do you think it might cost us to break out from the Elbe and take Berlin?'

Bradley had his answer ready; it was something he had thought about a great deal during the previous few days. He believed his troops could get to Berlin fairly easily, but that once there they would suffer heavy losses as the Germans fought hard for their capital. 'I estimate that it might cost us 100,000 casualties,' he said. Eisenhower did not reply, and Bradley went on: 'A pretty stiff price to pay for a prestige objective, especially when we've got to fall back and let the other fellow take over.'

Eisenhower said nothing. Two weeks earlier, at the end of March, he had stipulated that Twelfth Army Group was not to push on from the Elbe without further orders. Now, with his generals champing impatiently in the starting gate, he had to decide whether or not to give them those orders. Simpson was eager for his Ninth Army to drive on to Berlin, convinced that he could get there before the Red Army. He had completed his plan, and presented it to Bradley early on 15 April.

But Eisenhower knew that any American drive for Berlin could not start with more than about 50,000 men, the spearhead of a force that had just covered 250 miles in two weeks and was nearing the limits of its lines of communication. The three Soviet fronts in Operation Berlin were not only fifteen miles closer to the city already, but they numbered 2.5 million men and had had the best part of two months to prepare themselves and build up their strength. In his view, it was no contest.

By the time Bradley received Simpson's plan, Eisenhower had made his decision, and telegraphed it to the Combined Chiefs of Staff. His intentions were, he said: 'A. In the central area to hold a firm front on the Elbe. B. To undertake operations to the Baltic at Lübeck and to Denmark. C. To make a powerful thrust in the Danube valley to join with the Russians and break up the southern redoubt. D. As the thrust on Berlin must await the success of these three operations I do not include it as part of my present plan. The essence of my plan is to stop on the Elbe and clean up my flanks.'


On Sunday, 15 April, shortly after he had received Simpson's plan, Bradley called him to fly at once to his headquarters at Wiesbaden. 'I've something very important to tell you,' he said, 'and I don't want to say it on the phone.'

Simpson, naturally, assumed Bradley wanted to know exactly when he could jump off for Berlin, and spent the flight going over his plan in his mind. When he stepped out of the plane, Bradley was waiting to greet him. They shook hands, and without wasting a moment more, Bradley said: 'I want to tell you right now. You have to stop right where you are on the Elbe. You are not to advance any further in the direction of Berlin. I'm sorry, Simp, but there it is.'

'Where in hell did this come from?' Simpson demanded. 'I could be in Berlin in twenty-four hours.'

'From Ike,' Bradley told him. He went on to outline his own orders, which were that Simpson was to defend the line of the Elbe. There were still many pockets of fierce resistance, including the city of Magdeburg, and his supply columns and communications as far back as Hanover, Brunswick and the Harz mountains were constantly being attacked, often with tanks and assault guns, by German groups holed up in the heavy woodlands that covered the area. He was to hold the bridgehead at Barby 'as a threat to Berlin'.

A disconsolate Simpson flew back to his own headquarters, and then on to the Elbe, where he met up with Brigadier-General Sidney R. Hinds, commander of 2nd Armored Division's combat command B, who had been driven back across the river at the other bridgehead. He asked how things were going.

'I guess we're all right now, General,' Hinds replied. 'We had two good withdrawals. There was no excitement and no panic and our Barby crossings are going good.'

'Fine,' said Simpson. 'Keep some of your men on the east bank, if you want to. But they're not to go any further. Sid, this is as far as we're going.'

Hinds stared at him in disbelief. 'No, sir!' he protested. 'That's not right. We're going to Berlin.'

'We're not going to Berlin, Sid,' Simpson told him flatly. 'This is the end of the war for us.'

## 34

By 15 April, the tension on the Oder front was becoming almost unbearable. Heinrici had prepared his defensive plan meticulously, deploying his meagre resources to the best possible advantage. With his forces outnumbered by a ratio of 10:1, he depended on good intelligence and bold anticipation, so that he could concentrate what strength he had in the right places at the right time. But what he had was pitifully weak by comparison with the Soviet forces facing him. The three Soviet fronts of about 2.5 million had 41,600 guns and mortars, 6,250 tanks and self-propelled guns, more than 1,000 multiple rocket launchers and 7,500 aircraft. The First Belorussian Front alone had accumulated a stockpile of 7.147 million shells. Army Group Vistula had at the very most 250,000 poorly armed men, with about 850 tanks, 500 anti-aircraft batteries serving as artillery, and 300 aircraft, which had virtually no fuel.

To ride the first, smashing blow, Heinrici had developed a technique that was highly effective, but which depended entirely on his being able to forecast exactly when the blow would be struck. Knowing that the Soviets always preceded their attacks with a massive artillery bombardment to shatter the troops in the first defensive line, he would pull all his men out of the forward positions shortly before the barrage began. The shells would fall on largely empty trenches, with the troops safely installed in the main defence line, ready to resist the main attacking force. It was exactly what Chuikov and some of the other generals had tried to warn Zhukov about during their war games. Zhukov had refused to listen, and now believed his judgement had been vindicated – the Soviet reconnaissance in force on the Saturday had found the German front lines fully manned. So far, Heinrici's ploy was working. Now it was up to him to judge the right moment to make the switch – and everything pointed to that Sunday night.

At such a time, Heinrici needed no distractions, no visitors at his command post near Prenzlau. He was not pleased when Albert Speer arrived, in a highly nervous state, accompanied by the Berlin city superintendent of roads and the Berlin chief of the state railways. Speer wanted Heinrici's support in resisting Hitler's scorched earth orders to destroy all industrial plants, power stations, bridges and so on.

'Why should everything be destroyed,' he asked, 'with Germany already defeated? The German people must have the means to survive.'

Heinrici assured him that he would do all he could to avoid blowing anything up, but that for the moment he had to fight the coming battle as well as he could. 'The rest,' he said, 'is in the hands of God. But I will promise you this: Berlin will not become another Stalingrad. I will not let that happen.'

While they were still talking, Reymann arrived from Berlin, with his chief of operations, Colonel Eismann. Heinrici had asked Reymann to come, to discuss the defence of the city. He wanted to explain to him in person why he was unable to make the Berlin garrison part of his command. Reymann explained his hopeless situation, but Heinrici had to tell him 'not to rely on Army Group Vistula for support'.

'Then I don't know how I can defend Berlin,' Reymann replied, his last hope gone.

Heinrici told him that as far as he was concerned, there would be no battle for Berlin. If the Russians broke through, he said, he would try to withdraw to the north and south of the city, not into it. 'Of course,' he concluded, 'I may be ordered to send units into Berlin, but you should not depend on it.'

Speer was particularly anxious about Berlin's bridges, which Reymann had been ordered by Hitler to destroy. With so many waterways, the city had hundreds of bridges – Speer put the number at 950. Besides being vital arteries in the road and rail network, many of them carried essential services – water pipes, gas mains, electricity cables.

'If you destroy these supply lines,' Speer declared, 'the city will be paralysed for at least a year. It will lead to epidemic and hunger for millions. It's your duty to prevent this catastrophe! It's your responsibility not to carry out these orders!'

Reymann was shocked at the suggestion that he might disobey direct orders from the Führer, to whom he had sworn an oath of obedience. He also remembered what had happened to the officers who had failed to blow up the bridge at Remagen. Eventually, Heinrici consulted a map and marked bridges that carried no water, gas or electricity. Those, he said, could be blown up if need be. Any others would have to be cleared with him.


AT LAST, the visitors left. Heinrici could return to the task of forecasting the timing of the Soviet attack. For the rest of the afternoon and early evening he studied every detail of the latest intelligence reports, analysed the possibilities with his staff, and talked to his field commanders by telephone. He paced the floor of his office, hands behind his back, his head bowed in concentration, trying to put himself inside Zhukov's mind. Shortly after 8 pm he stopped, and raised his head. One of his aides thought 'it was as though he had suddenly sniffed the very air'.

'I believe,' he said, 'the attack will take place in the early hours tomorrow.'

He turned to his chief of staff, and dictated an order to be sent at once to Busse at Ninth Army: 'Move back and take up positions on the second line of defence.'

# PART SIX

# *Encirclement*

# 1

To the men of the First Belorussian Front, the night of 15–16 April seemed to last for ever. Normally, Soviet troops were not told exactly when they were about to launch an offensive. They usually found out for themselves: tanks and guns would be brought forward to the front line during the hours of darkness, companies reinforced with extra men, the sergeant-majors would suddenly be more generous with the issue of ammunition, the soup would be thicker and have more fat in it. But this time, everyone was informed by small leaflets handed out to each man, even those crouching in the most forward foxholes, right under the noses of the Germans. Zhukov's order of the day for 16 April was short and very much to the point: 'The enemy will be crushed along the shortest route to Berlin. The capital of Fascist Germany will be taken and the banner of victory planted over it.'

There had been stirring speeches from political officers: over 2,000 men of Zhukov's front applied for party membership on 15 April. Some joined from enthusiasm, others were more interested in safeguarding their futures, or making sure that if they fell in the coming battle their families would be told – the army did not as a rule inform families of casualties, but the party did so for its members.

As night fell, every unit had been ordered to take its Guards colours to the front-line trenches, 'so that every soldier will see that he and his companions, men and officers, are going into battle with the unit's most precious symbol – the Red Banner symbolizing the revolutionary ideals and cherished aspirations of all honest men on earth to freedom and happiness for mankind'. Facing the banners, they renewed their pledges of allegiance.


PRIVATE VLADIMIR ABYZOV, a former aeronautical engineering student, now an infantryman with the 236th 'Bogun' Regiment in the centre of Chuikov's Eighth Guards Army, spent the night crammed with the rest of his platoon in the dugout they had built in the foundations of a demolished manor house. The cellar was dank and musty, smelling of unwashed bodies and the damp hay of their bedding. Mist and drizzle seeped in from outside. Some men slept, snoring loudly. Others, like Abyzov himself, stayed awake, sitting on their groundsheets, leaning against the walls. Some tried to write letters home in the dim light of the single kerosene lamp, borrowing stumps of pencil from each other. The stillness was heightened by the sound of occasional shell bursts and the sporadic rattle of machine-gun fire from the German lines.

About an hour before the artillery barrage was due to begin, the sergeant-major called two men to fetch food and drink – two pails of steaming, thick pea soup with canned pork, and thermos flasks of tea. The sleepers awoke. Spirits began to rise. Yurka, the platoon's musician, started playing his mouth organ, and for a while the men joined in the songs. But as the start time approached, their voices gradually died away, and Yurka tapped the spittle out of his harmonica and tucked it into the top of his boot.

The platoon commander, Lieutenant Kiselyov, a fat, middle-aged former schoolteacher, entered the dugout to give his final instructions. When he asked if the men were nervous, Yurka replied with some bravado: 'Why should we be, Comrade Lieutenant? Let the Fritzes do the worrying – let them be nervous!'

'Shut up, musician!' one of the others chipped in. 'You can start celebrating when we get to Berlin.' He paused, then added, 'It would be a pity to get killed here at the very end of the war.'

Kiselyov began to answer, but was cut short by a violent blast and a blinding flash. The door blew off. Half the roof fell in. Everything went black. A German shell had landed right alongside. As the dust settled men called for help. Two were seriously wounded, two others killed. The survivors scrambled out of the cellar into the trench outside, to stand on flimsy, squelching planks in the blackness, waiting to climb out and begin their advance. It was five minutes before zero hour.


AT THE foot of the eastern end of the Seelow ridge, eighteen-year-old Gerhard Cordes crouched in a trench, also waiting nervously. He and the rest of his squad of Luftwaffe paratroops were armed with hand grenades, machine pistols, rifles and Panzerfausts. Dug in alongside them were a handful of 105 mm anti-aircraft guns and anti-tank guns. No one had told them that most of the German troops around them were being surreptitiously withdrawn during the night, leaving them and a few others to hold up the Soviet attack for as long as they could. The day before, when the Soviets had shelled the line, they had been ordered to dig in deeper. Now, the only shells being fired were from German guns on the Heights behind them. From the Soviet side, there was nothing but an ominous silence.


CHUIKOV'S COMMAND post was on a sandy hill overlooking the village of Reitwein on the west bank of the Oder. Zhukov and his staff arrived well before dawn. A Russian woman soldier named Margot made them hot, strong tea to drink while the last few minutes passed. Zhukov had decided to go for extra surprise by starting his attack in the middle of the night, at 3 am local time, 5 am Moscow time. In the forward trenches men stood or leaned against the sides of the trenches, helmets glistening with moisture, quilted jackets sodden. They smoked their last cigarettes, front-line fashion, cupping the lighted ends in their hands, close to their sleeves, to shield them from the weather and hide the glow from the enemy. Further down the line, tank crews stood in the lee of their vehicles, ready to mount. Artillerymen gripped their firing lanyards. The command was given to bring forward the colours.

With three minutes to go, Zhukov and his officers emerged from the dugout and took their places in a specially constructed observation post. At exactly 3 am, three red flares shot into the sky. 'Now, Comrades,' Zhukov muttered. 'Now!'

The blackness was shattered by the flash and roar of guns and mortars, the unearthly screech of the 'Stalin organs', Katyusha multiple rocket launchers. Guns lined up virtually wheel to wheel, one every four yards, 400 guns for every mile of front, produced a deafening, stupefying concentration of firepower. The whole Oder valley seemed to rock as the barrage crept forward over the Germans' first line. A sudden hot wind scorched across the battlefield, whipping up dust and debris, bending trees and bushes. To the terrified Gerhard Cordes, it seemed that every square yard of earth around him was erupting.

For thirty minutes the bombardment continued, pouring half a million shells on the German lines to a depth of five miles. There was no answer from the German guns. Then a single searchlight beam shining vertically upwards pierced the sky, followed by thousands of multi-coloured flares. It was a signal for 143 other Soviet searchlights to burst into life. Operated by women soldiers, who had arrived at the front a few days earlier to the cheerful cat-calls of appreciative men, the lights were positioned at 200-yard intervals along the front.

They were intended to be Zhukov's secret weapon, turning night into day so that his troops could attack in the small hours. The British army had used lights in this way in the west, bouncing the beams from the clouds to create 'artificial moonlight'. Zhukov, however, had decided to direct them horizontally, to blind the Germans while lighting up the ground ahead for the Soviet troops.

At the signal, the men of Chuikov's army scrambled from their trenches and began surging forward from the Küstrin bridgehead. Behind them, to the north and south, Soviet units on the other side of the Oder literally hurled themselves at the river, cheering and shouting wildly. While the engineers were launching pontoons and bringing up prefabricated bridge sections, men were already making their own way across in all sorts of assault boats. Hundreds, too impatient to wait, plunged into the water and began swimming, despite being weighed down by all their equipment. Many paddled across, supported by tree trunks, branches, empty fuel cans or planks.

In the centre, Chuikov's infantrymen were running into problems. The waterlogged ground criss-crossed with drainage ditches made progress slow and difficult. But what was worse, they felt like easy targets silhouetted for the enemy by the searchlights behind them, and the contrast between the harsh white light and the intense black shadows gave them night blindness. The lights failed to pierce the enormous clouds of dust and smoke, cast unnerving shadows and made the screen look impenetrably solid – like driving a car into thick fog on full headlights. Frantic troop commanders passed back orders for the lights to be switched off – only to find themselves completely blind in the sudden darkness, then dazzled as fresh orders were issued to switch them on again. Many units simply stopped and took what cover they could find, waiting for the natural light of dawn. Confusion increased as the first troops reached the German lines. They were unnerved to find most of them deserted, while there was sudden, unexpected fire from occasional strong points. They faltered, unsure of themselves.

In the command post, Chuikov and Zhukov could not see what was going on, and as wind blew the dust clouds towards them their visibility was reduced to zero. They had to rely on radio telephones and messengers to direct the troops. Zhukov's temper began to flare as reports poured in that the tank detachments and self-propelled guns supporting the infantry were falling behind, and that coordination was rapidly breaking down. The bridges across the Old Oder, a small river running through the valley, and the Haupt-Graben canal had been blown, creating troublesome obstacles, and the engineers could not get through with their bridging equipment, as armoured vehicles piled up along jammed roads. The tanks and guns could not leave the few roads and causeways – if they did, they risked becoming instantly bogged down in a quagmire of mud, or being blown up by mines. Air support from the Red Air Force was also hampered by poor visibility – even with the help of the searchlights, pilots found great difficulty in penetrating the dust clouds, which by now had risen to a height of 3,000 feet.

HEINRICI'S PLAN had worked perfectly. He had kept his guns and armour and most of his manpower intact, and now had drawn the enemy into his trap. The Heights were held by the LVIth Panzer Corps – a renowned formation, but one that bore little resemblance to its former self. It now consisted of Göring's 9th Parachute Division and the scratch 20th Panzergrenadier Division, with the understrength Müncheberg Panzer Division in reserve. But its commander was a tough and experienced soldier, the highly decorated Lieutenant-General Helmuth Weidling, a grim-faced man of sixty with a rimless monocle screwed in his right eye. Known to his friends as 'Smasher Karl',

Weidling had been flown out of East Prussia only a few days earlier to take charge of the reconstituted corps.

As dawn broke, the weather cleared, promising a bright spring day. Through the rapidly settling dust Weidling's gunners, safely installed on the Seelow Heights, could see the Soviet forces crowding the roads below. They opened fire with everything they had on the tightly bunched troop-carriers, tanks and guns. Heinrici had designated the last mile between the Haupt-Graben canal and the foot of the escarpment as the main killing ground, and Weidling had dug in his artillery observers, infantry units, tanks and guns all along the line of the Heights. His main artillery was concealed in gullies, with anti-tank weapons, including 88 mm guns, covering all the possible routes up the slope.

The canal brought the flagging Soviet assault to a stop. 'The spring floods had turned it into an impassable barrier for our tanks and self-propelled guns,' Chuikov wrote later. 'The few bridges in the area were kept under enemy artillery and mortar fire from beyond the Seelow Heights and from dug-in tanks and self-propelled guns, all well camouflaged.'

Vladimir Abyzov was one of the first infantrymen to reach the canal. 'We hugged the ground,' he said, 'waiting for the combat engineers to arrive. Shells continued to burst around us. Flares shot up into the grey sky.' Eventually, someone shouted, 'We have a bridge!' and the platoon jumped up and started to run again.

'We felt no fatigue,' Abyzov recalled, 'and we didn't realize that we were soaked to the skin. We did not even notice night change into day. Beyond the canal there was no mud, though there were many shell craters in the ground. The field was green with silky winter wheat. We ran across this field till the enemy met us with a wall of fire. We fell to the ground and quickly began to dig in. For the first time, the sky was clear of clouds. We saw hills before us. They were not high, but rather steep, some of them crowned by church spires. . . . The Germans could see us as clearly as if we were in the palm of their hand. They spared neither shells nor bullets, but we held our ground. We did not fire back – it would have been useless, because they were well out of range of our sub-machine guns.'

BY THE time the initial assault had been halted, it had already brought the end of the war for Jaap Knegtmans, one of the Dutch students who had been working in the Borsig plant at Tegel. Jaap had been arrested at the factory a couple of weeks earlier for some unspecified crime and transported to a barbed-wire enclosure on a farm near Küstrin, directly in the line of Chuikov's advance. Most of the other prisoners came from Sachsenhausen. They had been put to work digging trenches, ready for the Soviet attack. But when the artillery barrage began, over their heads, their guards simply disappeared. Chuikov's men soon swept through the compound. Jaap and his companions were free.


In his advance command post in the Schönewald forest to the north of Berlin, Heinrici stared at the map table in the middle of the operations room. He watched his staff officers busily marking and moving red arrows on the map, showing Soviet movements. He knew that eventually the Soviet offensive must succeed, for the Ninth Army only had enough ammunition reserves for two and a half days. All he could hope to do with his limited forces was to delay the inevitable. If he had had the four Panzer divisions that Hitler had sent to Czechoslovakia, there might have been a chance. 'If I had *them*,' he told Colonel Eismann, Ninth Army's chief of operations, 'the Russians wouldn't be having much fun now.'


Chuikov's forces were not having much fun – they were taking heavy losses as German fire poured down on them, wiping out men by the thousand and turning tank after tank into blazing wrecks. Chuikov screamed for air support, while he tried to redeploy his artillery for a fresh barrage. Zhukov, never the most serene of commanders, was practically apoplectic with rage.

'What the hell do you mean – your troops are pinned down?' he yelled at Chuikov.

Chuikov did not cringe – he had had experience of Zhukov's rages before. 'Comrade Marshal,' he replied, reasonably enough, 'whether we are pinned down or not, the offensive will almost certainly succeed. But resistance has stiffened for the moment and is holding us up.'

Zhukov was not placated. He stood and swore, loud and long. Berlin was rightfully his. But with every hour's delay, he could see his place in history being snatched away from him by Koniev.


Fifty-five miles south of Seelow, Koniev's operation was going well. The operation as a whole was spread across a front of 250 miles, but the main thrust was in the eighteen-mile reach of the Neisse between the little towns of Forst and Muskau, with three armies. He had good reasons for choosing this sector, although the German defences on the west bank of the river were particularly strong. It gave his troops a run of fifteen miles before they had to face another river crossing, over the Spree; from just south of Forst, there was an autobahn sweeping past Cottbus right into south-eastern Berlin; but above all, it was the shortest possible approach to Lübben, where Stalin's demarcation line between his front and Zhukov's ended. If he reached Lübben before Zhukov was clear of the Seelow Heights, he could swing north and go for Berlin. With this in mind, he had placed two tank armies, the Third and Fourth Guards, towards the right of his line.

Koniev's plan for this vital sector demanded a river assault over no fewer than 150 crossing places between Forst and Muskau – unlike Zhukov, he had no existing bridgeheads on the west bank. Once bridgeheads had been established, his armoured divisions could be thrown into the attack, and the drive for Lübben could begin. Everything depended on his engineers getting bridges into place as soon as possible – not an easy task, because the Neisse was fast-flowing, as much as 150 yards wide.

Koniev viewed the start of his offensive from the observation post of General Nikolai Pukhov's Thirteenth Army, a small dugout and a slit trench on the edge of a pine forest. Directly in front of them the ground sloped steeply down to the river. Koniev studied the opposite bank through powerful binoculars mounted on a tripod – and nearly fell victim to a German sniper's bullet, which buried itself in the mounting.

At 4.15 am the artillery barrage opened up along the whole 250 miles of the front. At the same time, aircraft of the Second Air Army's VIth Guards Air Corps began bombing the German rear areas and communications centres. After forty minutes of saturation bombardment, Soviet fighter planes screamed along the river dropping smoke bombs, again along the entire front, filling the valley with a dense screen. Under its cover, the first battalions started crossing at 4.55 am.

While a hail of fire from heavy machine guns and field artillery on a flat trajectory screamed over them to keep German heads down, the first wave of troops got across in boats, on rafts, on anything that floated, to secure a foothold on the far bank. The second wave went across dragging sections of pontoon bridges with them. At the same time, hundreds of engineers, neck deep in the near freezing water which constantly threatened to sweep them away, held wooden beams above their heads while their comrades drove piles into the riverbed to support them. Boats hauled cables across, which were then attached to winches to haul more sections of pontoons carrying light field guns and tanks. Some heavier artillery pieces were simply dragged across under water, using the stony riverbed as a roadway.

Within twenty minutes of the start of the crossings, Koniev learned that his first bridgehead had been secured. An hour later, the tanks and self-propelled guns that had been ferried across were already in action. At 6.55 am, two hours and forty minutes after it had begun, the preliminary artillery barrage was lifted. The guns were switched to blasting broad avenues through the enemy lines further back, for the tanks and troops to advance along. The shells and bombs combined to start fires blazing in the thick pine forests, bringing additional danger to both sides.

By this time, Koniev knew that 133 of his 150 planned crossing places had been secured. Men of the Thirteenth Army, supported by detachments of Marshal Rybalko's Third Tank Army, were already fighting their way out of the bridgehead, and the German defences were cracking before them. At 11 am the first two brigades of General Lelyushenko's Fourth Tank Army went into action on the west bank. Their commanders had orders to cut loose from the infantry, leaving them to their own resources, then to smash through enemy defences and race as hard as they could go for the Spree – the river that flowed through the heart of Berlin. At the Spree, they were not to wait for the engineers and bridging equipment, but take the river in their stride, fording it themselves. They were to keep going, not to stop anywhere under any circumstances.

By 10 AM, the Red Air Force had silenced most of the German guns on the top of the Seelow Heights. Elements of Chukov's Eighth Guards Army had overrun the first two defence lines at the foot of the Heights, but the third, on the slope itself, was proving difficult. Chuikov could not get tanks or self-propelled guns up because the gradient was too steep. The only way up for them was along the roads to Seelow itself and to the neighbouring villages of Freidersdorf and Dolgelin, but these were controlled by fortified German strong points which could only be overcome by heavy artillery fire. Chuikov ordered his guns to move forward. They were to redeploy, then hit the slopes with a twenty-minute barrage, to prepare the way for a fresh infantry assault.

At this point, Zhukov's patience finally ran out. Sweeping aside Chuikov's plan, and ignoring the protests of all his infantry commanders, he ordered his two tank armies into the attack. This was directly contrary to the battle plan agreed with the Stavka in Moscow, which stated categorically that the tanks were to be held back until the Seelow Heights had been taken; they were then to be deployed on the plateau leading to Berlin. But by then Zhukov was past reasoning. As he stormed out of the bunker, he turned on General Katukov, commander of the First Guards Tank Army. 'Well?' he roared, like the sergeant-major he had once been. 'Get moving!'

Zhukov's change of tactics was a desperate attempt to achieve an immediate breakthrough, hurling 1,377 tanks and self-propelled guns across totally unsuitable terrain. Far from achieving the result he intended, it succeeded only in snarling everything up. It hampered the movement of the artillery and made life even more nightmarish for the infantry, forcing guns and troop carriers off the roads. Tank crews and truck drivers, gunners and foot soldiers, struggled through the soggy, mine-strewn morass, screaming and cursing each other in the increasing chaos and gloom.

At 1 pm, Zhukov reported to Stalin in Moscow, telling him he had sent in both tank armies and expected to take the Seelow Heights by the evening of the next day, 17 April. Stalin advised him to use bombers as well as tanks, and told him to report again later. As for Koniev, Stalin informed him silkily, things were going well. The enemy forces had proved weaker than expected: 'We have forced the River Neisse without difficulty and are pressing forward without too much resistance.'

# 2

I N BERLIN, while the battles were raging only a few miles away, life went on as normal. People struggled to work in offices, shops and factories. Housewives queued for what provisions were available, gossiping and grumbling as on any other day. They waited patiently in line for as much as three hours in the hope of being able to stock up with extra supplies for the difficult times ahead. The law courts were in session – a man who had been caught drawing rations for an imaginary couple was sentenced to three years in jail. The Ministry of Food announced with due seriousness that new issues of ration coupons would no longer be perforated. Ordinary mail was still delivered, but the Post Office announced that it could no longer handle parcels, even to 'accessible' areas of the Reich. Newspapers published hints 'for the new allotment-holders among us', under the title 'As you sow, so shall you reap.' A woman dragged the body of her dead fiancé, who had been killed in an air raid, to the register office and was married to him. In the afternoon, those cinemas that were still standing opened on time. A cinema near Potsdamerplatz that was reserved for soldiers was packed with troops from the Berlin garrison watching an historical epic in full colour called simply *Kolberg*, telling the story of Gneisenau's famous defence of that city against all odds during the Napoleonic Wars.

Everyone knew that the Soviet offensive had begun – indeed, in the most easterly districts they had been woken by the sounds of battle, and in the morning darkness the flashes of light had lit up the sky like a sinister aurora borealis. But there was no panic, only a helpless fatalism. The general greeting between Berliners had become '*Bleib übrig*' – 'Survive'. They mocked Goebbels's proclamations that the turning point was coming, and that Hitler knew exactly when the miracle would take place. 'Don't worry,' they assured each other ironically, 'Gröfaz will save us.' 'Gröfaz' was their abbreviation for '*Grösster Feldherr aller Zeiten*' – 'the greatest general of all time'.

Goebbels held his weekly meeting of the defence council that morning, as though nothing unusual was happening. He gave no orders for a general alert. He did not consider it was time for the 'Clausewitz' order, calling up the main levy of the Volkssturm. When Reymann asked once again for arms, he gave the routine reply: Reymann would get everything he wanted, if and when Berlin was surrounded. 'If the battle for Berlin was on right now,' he repeated, 'you would have at your disposal all sorts of tanks and different calibre field guns, several thousand light and heavy machine guns, and several hundred mortars, plus large quantities of ammunition.'

But not even Goebbels could ignore the fact that the Red Army was coming. 'When the battle for Berlin begins,' he asked Reymann, 'where do you intend to set up your headquarters?' The order for the defence of the city issued under Reymann's name on 9 March had specified that once the battle began the commander was to leave his office on the Hohenzollerndamm and move into the Zoo bunker. That was where Goebbels himself intended to go, and he tried to persuade the general to agree to move in with him. But being shut in with Goebbels was the last thing Reymann wanted. He excused himself, saying they should not run the risk of both being eliminated at the same time by a direct hit from a bomb.

Reymann had succeeded in extracting one concession from Hitler himself. Once the city was surrounded and the defenders were falling back into the inner defence zones, there would be no way in or out except by air. If the airfields on the outskirts were captured, the Citadel would be entirely cut off, unless some alternative could be found. With this in mind, Reymann had suggested that the East–West Axis between the Brandenburg Gate and the Victory Column in the Tiergarten would make a good emergency airstrip. Hitler had agreed. He had even agreed that Reymann could remove the ornate bronze lamp standards along the road. But when Reymann went on to say he needed to cut down the trees for about 100 feet on either side, Hitler refused point blank – perhaps he was belatedly remembering the old legend about the trees on Unter den Linden, which had caused such a furore among Berliners at the time of the Olympic Games.

The trees would prevent large aircraft landing, but at least without the lamps light planes would be able to use the improvised strip. Reymann had given the order, and his men had started carefully dismantling the lamps that morning. As he left the meeting with Goebbels, he was told Albert Speer wanted to see him in his office in the house next door, the former French embassy.

Speer was hopping mad. Pointing out at the scene beyond the gate, he demanded to know what was happening. Reymann tried to explain, but Speer refused to listen. 'You cannot take down my lamp posts!' he exclaimed. 'You don't seem to realize that I am responsible for the reconstruction of Berlin.' To Reymann it was incredible that anyone should question his actions at such a time, but no matter how hard he argued, Speer refused to give in. He declared that he would take the matter up with the Führer himself. Until then, the lamp posts stayed.

This seemed even more lunatic than the question of blowing up Berlin's bridges, over which they had quarrelled the night before. In fact, Speer started arguing about the bridges all over again, insisting that no bridge should be destroyed. But this time it was Reymann who refused to listen – the order had come directly from Hitler, and his oath bound him to obey.

Reymann left Speer's office to visit the outer defence sectors in the east of the city – always a depressing experience. He had given instructions that barricades should start to be closed, blocking off roads and streets apart from narrow openings. From the beginning of the Soviet artillery barrage early that morning, the sound could be heard in districts like Mahlsdorf, Köpenick, Hellersdorf and Marzahn like distant thunder, rattling and even breaking windows, mirrors and pictures. But still the defence preparations were far from complete. General Max Pemsel, who had been chief of staff for the Seventh Army in Normandy on D-Day, described them as 'utterly futile, ridiculous!' He was thankful to be leaving Berlin that day, having been posted to the Italian front. Back in his headquarters, Reymann stood staring at the wall map in his office, wondering 'what in God's name I was supposed to do'.

REYMANN, HEINRICI and the other soldiers could expect little help or understanding from a Führer who was growing increasingly detached from reality. Hitler still seemed to believe that the war could be won with brave words. At about noon, Goebbels issued Hitler's last order of the day to the troops of the eastern front, the proclamation he had been holding on to for the past three days, drafted immediately after the news of Roosevelt's death. Its hollow rhetoric made it a suitable epitaph for the Führer's relationship with the Wehrmacht that he had created and had now destroyed:

Soldiers of the eastern front!
For the last time our deadly enemies, the Jewish Bolsheviks, have rallied their massive forces for an attack. They intend to destroy Germany and to exterminate our people. Many of you eastern soldiers already know well the fate that awaits German women and children especially: old people, men and children will be murdered, the women and girls turned into barrack room whores. The rest will be marched off to Siberia.
We have been expecting this attack, and since January of this year have done everything to build up a strong front. A colossal amount of artillery will confront the enemy. Gaps in our infantry have been filled by countless new units. Emergency units, newly raised units and Volkssturm are reinforcing our front.
This time, the Bolsheviks will meet the ancient fate of Asia, which means they shall and must bleed to death before the capital of the German Reich.
Whoever does not fulfil his duty at this moment is behaving as a traitor to our people. Any regiment or division that abandons its position will be acting so disgracefully that it will be shamed before the women and children braving the bombing in our cities.
Above all, be on your guard against those few treacherous officers and men who, in order to save their pitiful lives, will fight

against us for Russian pay, perhaps even wearing German uniform. Anyone ordering you to retreat, unless you know him well, is to be arrested immediately and if necessary killed on the spot, no matter what rank he may hold.

If every soldier on the eastern front does his duty in these coming days and weeks, the last onslaught of Asia will be smashed, just as the invasion by our enemy in the west will fail in the end, in spite of everything.

Berlin will remain German, Vienna will be German again, and Europe will never be Russian.

Form sworn brotherhoods to defend not just the empty concept of a Fatherland, but your homes, your wives, your children and therefore our future.

In these hours, the whole German nation looks to you, my eastern warriors, and hopes only that by your resolution, your fanaticism, your weapons, and under your leadership, the Bolshevik assault will be drowned in a bloodbath.

In this moment, when fate has removed the greatest war criminal of all time [Roosevelt] from the earth, the turning point of this war will be decided.

*signed*: Adolf Hitler

ALBERT SPEER had plenty of time on his hands to worry about bridges and lamp posts and the reconstruction of Berlin, for he had nothing else to do. He had been replaced as armaments minister by his deputy, Karl Saur, on 27 March, after trying to persuade Hitler that the war was lost. In any case, there was virtually no armaments industry left, though a few factories in Berlin were still producing guns and ammunition, and building and repairing tanks. As each tank or self-propelled gun was ready it was fuelled up and driven straight from the production line to the front, to join in the fighting. Now, Speer spent most of his time flitting about the remains of the Reich, attempting to block Hitler's scorched earth orders and prevent the demolition of factories, power stations, bridges and other essential installations.

When he had finished arguing with Reymann, Speer turned to another of his tasks in his self-appointed role as preserver of Berlin's heritage: saving the Berlin Philharmonic Orchestra. Music had always played an important part in his life. Throughout the war he hardly ever missed a Philharmonic concert – Goebbels considered the orchestra such a vital propaganda tool and morale booster for Berlin that he had exempted all its 105 musicians from military service. In mid-March, however, the orchestra's leader, the brilliant twenty-three-year-old violinist Gerhard Taschner, had gone to Speer to tell him Goebbels had decreed that the entire orchestra was to be included in the final draft for the Volkssturm. Speer had telephoned Goebbels, to protest. Not surprisingly, Goebbels was unsympathetic.

'I alone raised this orchestra to its special level,' he told Speer. 'My initiative and my money have made it what it has become, what it represents to the world today. Those who follow have no right to it. It can go under along with us.'

It was unthinkable to Speer that this unique ensemble should perish on the barricades. He told Taschner not to worry, and sent Colonel Manfred von Poser, his liaison officer with the general staff, to the draft board to extract and destroy the musicians' papers – a trick Hitler himself had used at the beginning of the war to save his favourite artists from call-up. Then he formulated a plan to spirit the entire orchestra away from the city at the last minute before the Soviets attacked it. The first part of the plan had gone into effect on 28 March, when he had had most of the orchestra's library of scores, together with its pianos, harps and Wagner tubas, and the musicians' dress suits, loaded into trucks and driven away for safe storage at Plassenburg, a small town near Bayreuth. Now, with the Soviet forces advancing from the Oder, Speer decided it was time to evacuate the musicians themselves.

That day, the orchestra was due to give a concert at 5 pm in the Beethoven Hall, conducted by Robert Heger. The advertised programme consisted of Beethoven's Egmont Overture, the Brahms Double Concerto, and Strauss's *Tod und Verklärung*. But Speer sent word to the orchestra's manager, Dr Gerhart von Westermann, that there should be a change of programme. The concert should open with the finale from Wagner's *Die Götterdämmerung*, the Twilight of the Gods, which depicted the destruction of Valhalla, the death of the gods, and the end of the world. This would be followed by Beethoven's Violin Concerto, played by Taschner, and then Bruckner's Romantic Symphony. The music was the signal agreed with the orchestra that they were giving their last performance, and that after the concert there would be a bus waiting to take all those who wished to leave the city to safety in the Kulmbach-Bayreuth area, which was about to be taken by the Americans. During the afternoon, Westermann put out the new scores. The musicians needed no rehearsal; the works were all familiar to them.

At 5 pm the concert began. The ornate red and gold auditorium was unheated, and the audience, unaware of the significance of what they were hearing, huddled in their overcoats to keep warm. Normally, the electric power was cut at that time of day, but Speer had managed to keep it switched on for the duration of the concert, so although the hall itself was in darkness, lights glimmered on the music stands. Speer sat alone, savouring the tragic emotion of the occasion, in his usual seat in the centre of the front row. But there was no bus waiting outside – the musicians had voted to stay in Berlin. Only Taschner had agreed to leave, with his wife and two children and the daughter of another musician, Georg Diburtz. They were driven south in Speer's own car, escorted by his adjutant.

*

As DARKNESS fell, Heinrici returned to his command post. He had spent most of the day driving from one headquarters to another along the entire front, his progress impeded by swarms of refugees crowding the roads and interfering with the movement of troops and armoured vehicles. It had been a day of savage fighting, with terrible casualties on both sides, but the men of the Ninth Army could be proud of their achievement in holding back the gigantic red tide. Weidling's LVIth Corps had knocked out 150 Soviet tanks and 132 aircraft, turning Chuikov's attack and Katukov's drive with the First Guards Tank Army into a confused and bloody mess. The Soviet armies on either side of Chuikov had fared little better, and in fact the Germans had retaken some positions on the southern edge of the Heights, and around Frankfurt.

It had been a disastrous day for Zhukov, but Heinrici was under no illusions about the prospects for his forces. 'They can't last much longer,' he told his staff. 'The men are so exhausted that their tongues are hanging out. Still, we are holding. That's something Schörner couldn't do – that great soldier hasn't been able to hold Koniev even for one day.'

# 3

IT WAS late that night when Zhukov reported to Stalin again. No doubt he delayed making the call for as long as possible, in the hope of having better news – and indeed he did have some. He had ordered Chuikov and Katukov to go on fighting in the dark, and they had at last made some headway. They had taken fearful losses as tanks and infantry were blasted by heavy German fire at point blank range from 88 mm and 155 mm guns, which knocked out tank after tank, their blazing hulks lighting up the foot soldiers toiling up the slope, exposing them to machine-gun and small-arms fire. But they had been driven on relentlessly, and around midnight, Chuikov's infantry captured three houses on the edge of Seelow. It was a foothold, but it was far from a breakthrough.

Stalin was unimpressed, and became increasingly unsympathetic as Zhukov's tale of the day's calamities unfolded. He lashed him for departing from the agreed plan. 'You should not have sent in the First Tank Army on the Eighth Guards Army's sector, instead of where GHQ had ordered,' he told him severely. 'Are you sure you will take the Seelow Heights tomorrow?'

Struggling hard to keep his composure, Zhukov reiterated his earlier claim, and pointed out that the delay might not be entirely a bad thing. 'I feel that the more troops the enemy throws in to counter our forces here,' he said, 'the quicker we shall then capture Berlin, as it will be easier to smash the enemy troops on an open battlefield than in a fortified city.'

Still unconvinced, Stalin rubbed salt into Zhukov's wounded pride. 'We have been thinking,' he told him acerbically, 'of ordering Koniev to swing Rybalko's and Lelyushenko's tank armies towards Berlin from the south, and ordering Rokossovsky to speed up forcing the river and then also to strike at Berlin from the north.'

Zhukov was forced to agree that the proposed change in plan for Koniev made perfect military sense. However, he said, he doubted whether Rokossovsky would be able to get across the Oder and into position to attack Berlin before 23 April. But Stalin was in no mood to continue the conversation. He had made his point, now Zhukov could sweat on it. '*Do svidaniya* [goodbye],' he said, and abruptly hung up.


DURING THE night, Zhukov managed to regroup and reorganize his artillery and scattered armour, while 800 bombers attacked German positions from the air, denying the already exhausted defenders any rest or respite. By 8 am the weather had changed, with a cold drizzle drifting down from low clouds as he started his assault on the Heights all over again with a thirty-minute artillery bombardment, while wave after wave of aircraft pounded the enemy defences.

At 8.15, while the barrage was still at its height, the first tanks jumped off, with hundreds of Chuikov's riflemen clinging to their sides and thousands more loping along behind, heading for the smoke-shrouded ridge. Again they were met by devastating fire from 88s over open sights and showers of Panzerfaust projectiles, while heavy machine guns sliced through the infantry. Tank after tank burst into flames or slewed to a halt with broken tracks. The Panzerfaust was a formidable weapon, even in the hands of untrained children, but Soviet tank crews had learned from their experiences of the previous day, and had devised a crude but effective protection against it: they tied wire mattresses snatched from the beds of wrecked German homes around the front of their tanks, to deflect or reduce the impact of the Panzerfaust rockets.

As the day wore on, the sheer volume of Soviet high explosive had its effect. German resistance on the Heights began to slacken. Heinrici, Busse and Weidling had no reserves left from which to find replacements for their dead and wounded, yet somehow they managed to hang on, and to extract a high price from the Soviets. The carnage was appalling as Chuikov threw more and more men forward in mass attacks. By the end of the day he was having to dredge up men from the rear services to send into the line as infantry. Just before nightfall he succeeded in capturing the small town of Seelow, but the Heights remained in German hands. It was little enough to show for a hard day's fighting, when according to the master plan the Eighth Guards Army should have been two-thirds of the way to Berlin.

WHILE ZHUKOV fumed and raged at his front's lack of progress, Koniev had every reason to feel delighted with his day's work. He had started by briefing his two tank generals, Rybalko and Lelyushenko, in person. His orders had been simple and direct, amounting in essence to: 'Don't let anything hold you back. Don't attack enemy strong points, and avoid frontal assault. Outflank the enemy wherever possible. Concentrate on speed and manoeuvrability. Conserve your equipment. And above all, try to keep enough strength in reserve for that final, vital charge on Berlin itself.'

After a short artillery bombardment, he had unleashed his main assault at 7 am. His tanks raced through blazing woods towards the River Spree, leaving dozens of small but fierce skirmishes behind them. Koniev himself followed close behind, eager to see Rybalko's Third Guards Tank Army cross the river. But fast as they travelled, the Germans were quicker. They had outrun the Soviet armour and had begun to establish a defence line on the Spree. When the first tanks arrived they were met with spasmodic and uncoordinated fire, mostly from machine guns and sub-machine guns, from the western bank.

Koniev could not afford to allow the Germans to hold him up: he had to get his tanks across the river before they could bring up heavier weapons. The Spree was fifty to sixty yards wide at this point. The question was – was it fordable? Could tanks get across without the aid of the engineers and their bridging gear? There were rumours about a ford, but there was only one way to find out if they were true. Koniev talked briefly to Rybalko, and he ordered a single tank with a hand-picked crew to try to rush across in the face of small-arms fire. With bullets pinging harmlessly off its sides, the chosen tank ploughed into the water – and found it was only about three feet deep. Other tanks roared into life again and followed. In no time, the leading brigades were all across, and the German line was shattered.

KONIEV SET up his headquarters in an old castle above the river just outside Cottbus, halfway between the Neisse and the end of the demarcation line between the fronts at Lübben, now barely twenty miles ahead. From its ancient baronial splendour, disturbed only by persistent but inaccurate long-range German artillery fire, he talked to Rybalko and Lelyushenko. Then he called Stalin, to report that his tanks were rolling forward west of the Spree.

Stalin suddenly interrupted him. Things were not going too well for Zhukov, he said – he was still trying to break through the German defences. Then, abruptly, he fell silent. Koniev waited, hardly daring to breathe. Was he at last to be given his chance to be first into Berlin? Stalin came back on the line. Was there any way, he asked, that Zhukov's mobile forces could somehow be funnelled through the gap torn in the German lines by Koniev?

This gave Koniev his opportunity. 'Comrade Stalin,' he replied, 'that would take too much time and would only add to the confusion. There is no need to send the First Belorussian Front's armoured troops into the gap we have made. The situation on our front is developing favourably. We have enough forces and we can turn both our tank armies towards Berlin.'

He suggested using the little town of Zossen, fifteen miles south of the capital, as the hinge on which his armies would turn, to wheel northwards.

'What map are you using for your report?' Stalin asked.

'The 1:200,000.'

There followed a pause while Stalin searched for Zossen on his own map. At last, he said: 'Very good.' Then he continued, 'Do you know that the German general staff HQ is in Zossen?'

'Yes, I do,' Koniev replied.

'Very good.' There was another slight pause, then the words Koniev had been waiting to hear: 'I agree. Turn your tank armies towards Berlin.'

AT 12.47 AM on 18 April, Koniev issued Directive Number 00215 to his commanders. Rybalko was ordered 'to force the Spree and advance rapidly in the general direction of Fetschau, Golsen, Barut, Teltow and the southern outskirts of Berlin'. He was also given a precise timetable in which to achieve this: the Third Guards Tank Army was to break into Berlin from the south on the night of 20 April. Lelyushenko's orders were equally precise. The Fourth Guards Tank Army, which was upriver and to the south of Rybalko's, was ordered 'to force the Spree near Spremberg and advance rapidly in the general direction of Drepkau, Kalau, Dane and Luckenwalde'. It, too, had a timetable: by the end of 20 April it was to capture the area of Beelitz, Treuenbritzen and Luckenwalde, and to take Potsdam and the south-western part of Berlin that night.

'The tanks will advance daringly and resolutely in the main direction,' the directive stated. 'They will bypass towns and large communities and will not engage in protracted frontal fighting.' It was to be impressed on the minds of corps and brigade commanders that 'the success of the tank armies depends on boldness of manoeuvre and swiftness of operations'. Koniev intended to make quite sure no one was in any doubt about what he wanted.

IT WAS Stalin himself who told Zhukov that Koniev was now on course for Berlin. Zhukov's reaction was predictable: his senior commanders experienced the full, blast-furnace heat of his invective. As Lieutenant-General N. K. Popiel, chief of staff of the First Guards Tank Army, remarked to his fellow officers: 'We have a lion on our hands!' Zhukov was a lion with sharp teeth and a reputation for eating senior commanders for breakfast. 'Now take Berlin!!!' he roared at them.

On the morning of Wednesday, 18 April, Zhukov issued fresh orders to his commanders. They were to go up to the front line themselves, to make full assessments of the situations both of their own units and of the enemy, and they were to speed up everything ready to resume the main advance by noon next day. Everything was to be moved forward, nothing held back in the rear. This battle was consuming their strength and their reserves: it must be ended quickly. Commanders who showed any lack of resolution, or who proved incapable of carrying out these orders, were under threat of immediate dismissal, which meant instant demotion to the rank of private in a punishment battalion, with a life expectancy only marginally greater than facing a firing squad.

At 5 am, after yet another artillery barrage, Chuikov's troops attacked again, and shortly afterwards all the other Soviet armies in the sector hurled themselves forward into another furious battle. All day, the German troops clung on desperately – at one point, Busse even shook the Soviets by staging a fierce counter-attack – but gradually their lines crumbled. Weidling's LVIth Panzer Corps, still bearing the brunt of the assault, was in desperate need of reinforcements. Weidling had been promised two more Panzer divisions, the SS Nordland and the fully operational 18th Panzergrenadier, but there was no sign of either. One man from the SS division did appear during the day – the commander, Gruppenführer (Major-General) Jürgen Ziegler, who arrived at Weidling's headquarters by car to say almost casually that his division had run out of fuel, miles away. The 18th Panzergrenadier, which should have been there the day before, when its strength might have been decisive, eventually arrived that night. But by then it was too late. Chuikov had achieved his breakthrough on to the Heights, and the entire corps was withdrawing.

The new division could only join them in a retreat led by the paratroops of the 9th Parachute Division, who had finally collapsed after bearing the full force of the maelstrom for forty-eight hours. Göring's much-vaunted young men were taking to their heels and, according to Weidling's corps artillery commander, Colonel Hans Oscar Wöhlermann, were 'running away like madmen'. The remainder of the corps withdrew in reasonably good order to regroup back on the next line of defence, but the Heights were lost.

Weidling had had to move his headquarters back twice during the day. By that night he was installed in a cellar in Waldsieversdorf, a village just outside Müncheberg, ten miles back from Seelow. There he received a surprise visit from Ribbentrop. Both Weidling and Wöhlermann, who joined them in the cellar, expected him to tell them something vitally important, for they had received a mysterious signal earlier in the day from Busse, telling them: 'Hold out for another two days and our objective will have been achieved.' Busse, it seemed, had swallowed Goebbels's propaganda line that the Americans would reach Berlin within two days, and would then join forces with

Germany against the Soviet Union. But Ribbentrop was only trying to find out for himself just how hopeless the situation really was. What they told him, says Wöhlermann, 'had a shattering effect on the foreign minister'. He asked a few questions in a hoarse, quiet voice, then left.

Shortly after the foreign minister had left, another top Nazi arrived – the thirty-two-year-old, one-armed head of the Hitler Youth, Artur Axmann. To Weidling's anger and disgust, Axmann offered the services of the twelve- to fifteen-year-old boys of the Hitler Youth, who were ready to fight to the death. At that moment, he announced, they were already manning the roads to the rear of the corps. Weidling was at first speechless with fury, then 'using extremely coarse language', he told Axmann what he thought of his offer. 'You cannot sacrifice these children for a cause that is already lost,' he raged. 'I will not use them and I demand that the order sending these children into battle is rescinded.' Axmann left in some confusion, promising to withdraw the order – but hurried back to Berlin to find other ways of sacrificing the boys under his command.

CHUIKOV HAD achieved his first objective. He had won control of the Seelow Heights and broken the Germans' first main line of defence. Now, his troops sat astride the main road leading straight as an arrow into the centre of Berlin, thirty-seven miles away. But the price had been terrible: the battle for the Seelow Heights had cost the First Belorussian Front the lives of 30,000 men.

---

4

---

BERLIN AWOKE on the morning of Thursday, 19 April, to the sounds of scrubbing. Overnight, anti-Nazi resisters had been at work throughout the city with paint, charcoal and chalk, daubing the one word 'Nein!' ('No!') on every shop window and available surface. It was the biggest resistance action since 1933, a belated answer to the Nazis' last referendum question: 'Do you approve the policies of Adolf Hitler?' 'No' was also a public rejection of Hitler's policy of defending the city to its death. Ruth Andreas-Friedrich and her friends had been at the heart of the campaign. They had spent the entire night since the last RAF plane left at 2 am scurrying through the streets with paint pots and brushes, dodging police patrols – in spite of the manpower shortage there were still 12,000 policemen in Berlin. Now, in the morning light, the painters were out and about admiring their handiwork.

The resisters had been busy in other ways, too, over the past week. In addition to providing thousands of fake passes and documents, they had also been involved in sabotage. Electrician Kurt Eckhard had cut eight important cables between Berlin and Nauen that were supposed to carry orders for the defence of the capital, and had removed the cable shoes. 'No matter how hard they hunt,' he said, 'they'll be a long time getting those together again.' He had also managed to get himself locked inside a government garage two nights earlier, and had located the secret store of fuel being saved for Nazi officials to escape from Berlin; he poured all 500 litres down the drain. A few days earlier he had ruined his factory's entire supply of high-grade lubricating oil by salting it with emery.

Walter Seitz had been particularly busy providing prescriptions for Atabrine, Pervitin and other pills and potions, to create false symptoms of infectious jaundice, heart murmurs and kidney complaints, which would keep men out of the Volkssturm. Quite separately, in Wilmersdorf, Maria von Maltzan played her part by infecting the wounds of injured soldiers with cultures from diseased animals, and injecting men due for Volkssturm service with a serum that she used to produce a high fever in animals as part of an unorthodox treatment for restoring paralysed limbs. Few people had any interest or enthusiasm for a fight to the death.

THE CITY was experiencing yet another influx of refugees from the towns and villages to the east and south. To Reymann, still trying to organize his last-ditch defences, the newcomers added to his burden without given him any extra manpower. That day, 19 April, his forces in Berlin were officially numbered at 41,253 men, of whom fewer than 15,000 were trained soldiers from the army, Luftwaffe or navy. The rest included 1,713 policemen, 1,252 Hitler Youth and Labour Service, and 24,000 Volkssturm. The 'Clausewitz Muster' – the second levy, which was supposed to be ready at six hours' notice when the final alarm was given – would, on paper at least, produce another 52,841 men. Arming them was another problem. There were 42,095 rifles available, 773 sub-machine guns, 1,953 light machine guns, 263 heavy machine guns, and a smattering of mortars, field guns, anti-tank guns and anti-aircraft guns.

It was, Reymann knew, a pitifully weak force to pit against the might of the Soviet armies already closing in from the east and the south. Attempting to defend the city with such forces was so hopeless it was criminal, but there was worse to come. Busse's Ninth Army was still hanging on around Frankfurt – Hitler had specifically forbidden Heinrici to withdraw it, even from the fortress on the eastern bank, which was still holding out. Overriding Heinrici, Goebbels kept in touch with Busse, telephoning him constantly, and offering whatever help he could. On the night of 17–18 April, Busse had asked for a battalion of trained troops from the Berlin garrison, and Goebbels sent him one, in a fleet of Berlin buses. Now Busse's chief of staff, Colonel Hölz, asked for at least another four battalions, to help in the defence of Buckow, less than twenty miles from the city boundary.

Only now did Goebbels address the basic question of whether Berlin should be defended from outside or inside the city. 'He is not for half-measures,' his devoted press officer, Wilfred von Oven wrote in his diary. 'If the view is that the Russians should be hit on the approaches to Berlin with the assistance of the forces that have been prepared for the defence of the capital, then he is prepared to strip Berlin of troops completely. However, he is against sending only four battalions if Busse does not use them and this imperils the defence of Berlin.'

Reymann was aghast at the idea of being deprived of four precious battalions of troops. He remonstrated frantically with Goebbels, who was not pleased at being reminded so forcefully of the true state of affairs. Reymann's attitude, wrote Ovens, clearly echoing Goebbels, 'shows him to be defeatist and lacking in courage and he should be replaced by a younger, more aggressive officer'. But the leader of the Berlin SA, Obergruppenführer Graentz, who was responsible under Goebbels for the Volkssturm, supported Reymann. 'All we have available in Berlin,' he pointed out, 'is the Guard Regiment, thirty Volkssturm battalions (only partly armed) and some police, flak, and Hitler Youth units of little account.'

Reymann and Graentz insisted that if the four battalions were sent, then the question of the defence of Berlin would be settled. This was a responsibility Goebbels was not prepared to take on his own. He called General Burgdorf in the Führer bunker, and asked him to get Hitler's personal decision. The question was raised at that day's conference, and Hitler gave his answer: the troops were to be sent to the front.


THAT EVENING, Goebbels broadcast to the nation on the eve of Hitler's fifty-sixth birthday. It was a remarkable speech, a rambling and emotional panegyric to Hitler as the saviour of his people, whom they should follow 'faithfully, without reservation, without excuse or limitation . . . to trust in the lucky star that looks down on him and all of us now as before'.

Goebbels called on the German people 'on no account to give a gleefully watching world the satisfaction of witnessing the spectacle of belly-crawling submission, but proudly to unfurl the swastika in the face of the enemy instead of the white flag of surrender he is expecting to see. . . . Once more, the armies of the enemy powers storm our defences; in their wake, foaming at the mouth, international Jewry, which does not want peace because their diabolical aim is to see the world destroyed. But in vain. God will throw back Lucifer, as he has done before when the dark angel stood before the gates of power, back into the abyss from whence he came. . . . Germany is still the land of loyalty; in the hour of danger she will celebrate her greatest triumph.

Never shall history say that the people have abandoned their Führer, or that the Führer has abandoned his people. And this means victory.'

While Goebbels was pouring out his hollow bombast, the resisters were out again with a different message, this time printed on leaflets which they pasted on walls, doors and windows:

> Berliners! Soldiers, men and women! You have heard the order of the lunatic Hitler and his bloodhound Himmler to defend every city to the utmost. Anyone who still carries out the orders of the Nazis today is either an idiot or a scoundrel. Berliners! Do as the Viennese did! By overt and covert resistance the workers and soldiers of Vienna prevented a bloodbath in their city. Is Berlin to share the fate of Aachen, Cologne and Königsberg?
>      'NO!'
> Write your No everywhere! Form resistance cells in barracks, shops, shelters! Throw all the pictures of Hitler and his accomplices out into the gutter! Organize armed resistance!

# 5

ZHUKOV HAD hoped to have taken Berlin, or at least to have reached the eastern suburbs, by 19 April, the fourth day of his attack. But he was still almost twenty miles from the city boundary, and still being held up by determined German resistance. Vladimir Abyzov and his comrades, for instance, had pressed on after taking the Seelow Heights, pausing only for 'a rushed snack and replenishing our supplies of ammunition'. They rode on tanks, at first meeting practically no resistance. 'Then we rushed into an inhabited locality,' Abyzov wrote, 'call it a big village or a small town. Already on its outskirts there was a terrific exchange of fire. The Germans put up such a frenzied resistance that we could not advance even a metre forward in half a day. But what can you do, if you are faced with enemy tanks dug into the ground? Not one or two, but fifteen or more. We decided to wait until darkness set in to close on them under the cover of night.'

WHILE ZHUKOV was fuming at the delays to his front, Koniev's tank army commanders were concerned by the headlong speed of their advance. They were worried that they had no support on their flanks, and that the Germans might cut their communications and attack them from the rear. But when Rybalko called him to express his fears, Koniev reassured him: 'Don't worry, Pavel Semonovich. Don't worry about being detached from the infantry. Keep going.'

Rybalko and Lelyushenko kept going. That day Rybalko's Third Guards Tank Army advanced between 21 and 25 miles, fighting all the way. Lelyushenko did even better – his Fourth Guards Tank Army covered over 30 miles.

BY THE evening of 19 April, Rokossovsky reported to Stalin by phone that his troops were in position and ready to go on the morrow, as planned. Even as he spoke, German positions on the west bank of the Oder were being blasted by squadrons of Soviet bombers, among them aircraft from the Women's Night Bomber Regiment. Many of the pilots in this all-female unit, commanded by the formidable Yevdokia Bershanskaya, had seen continuous action with it since the battles in the northern Caucasus in 1942. At the same time, Soviet special forces were paddling their inflatable boats across the river under cover of darkness. Their mission was to gain control of the floodlands between the two wings of the Oder and, if possible, establish a few toeholds on the German side.

At 4 am on the morning of 20 April, the Sixty-Fifth Army began crossing near Stettin, while further north the Nineteenth and Second Shock armies prepared to go. An hour later, the Seventieth and Forty-Ninth armies, each supported by one tank corps, one mechanized and one cavalry corps, began their assaults on the southern part of the front.

Manteuffel had been expecting the assault, and had done everything he could to prepare for it. His defences stretched back for up to seven miles from the river, and proved remarkably effective. His Third Panzer Army put up a magnificent fight against overwhelming odds, frustrating attack after attack throughout the day.

While Manteuffel held out, the chances of Rokossovsky's being able to strike at Berlin from the north grew steadily more remote. But with the Third Panzer Army fully occupied where it was, it could play no direct part in the defence of the city. Heinrici was left with nothing but the remnants of the Ninth Army, most of which were still held on the Oder at Hitler's insistence, in imminent danger of being surrounded.

VLADIMIR ABYZOV's unit was now safely in Müncheberg, halfway between the Oder and Berlin, astride the main road to the city. Hoping for a night's rest, his platoon – or what was left of it, for it had suffered heavy casualties – chose a deserted, two-storey mansion in the western part of the town. They took their meal together in the spacious dining room on the ground floor, delightedly emptying the contents of their mess tins on to porcelain plates, Kiselyov, the former schoolteacher, sat at the head of the table as platoon commander and father figure, silent and weary. Relaxing for the first time in days, the men chatted easily. Yurka the musician pulled his mouth organ from the top of his boot, to play a tune.

The calm was broken by the battalion clerk, Sasha Dymshyts, who appeared in the doorway, looking excited. 'Comrades!' he announced. 'Anybody who would like to see our artillery firing on Berlin, follow me!'

'But it's still twenty if not thirty kilometres to Berlin,' the men shouted.

'So what?' Sasha replied. 'The artillerymen say that the city is in range.'

Suddenly, everybody was laughing. Chairs were pushed back hurriedly. A plate was knocked off the table; it spun around on the floor as the room emptied.

A gun had been positioned five or six houses away, with an artillery lieutenant-colonel, several sergeants and privates gathered around it. Abyzov and his companions rushed forward, but stopped as they became aware of a group of senior officers.

'What are you afraid of, lads?' one of them called out. 'Come on! This is something you haven't seen before – artillery firing on Berlin.'

More and more officers and men arrived, forming a tight ring around the gun. A row of shells was neatly laid out on the carriage, each with a chalked inscription: 'Regards from Stalingrad!' 'Hitler, this one is for you!'

After a few minutes, two jeeps pulled up, and several more officers got out, led by Major-General D. E. Bakanov, commander of 74th Rifle Division. Lieutenant-Colonel Kolmogorov greeted him, and asked permission to proceed. Bakanov waved a gloved hand. 'Go ahead,' he told him.

His quivering voice betraying his excitement, Kolmogorov gave the order: 'On the den of the enemy, Berlin – fire!'

The gun roared. Troops cheered and loosed spontaneous bursts of sub-machine gun fire into the sky. As shell after shell sped on its way to explode somewhere in Berlin, the whole crowd, generals included, burst into delighted laughter.

# 6

HITLER'S BIRTHDAY had been a national holiday since 1933, and even with the Red Army hammering on the door, the party faithful still felt they had to celebrate it. But public displays of loyalty were few and far between. Max Buch, a Jew who had been living as an illegal since 1943, was delighted when he ventured on to the balcony of the apartment he was occupying in Meinekestrasse, just off the Kurfürstendamm. 'Today,' he wrote in his diary, 'a day on which normally flags with their ugly symbol of evil fly all over the land – more or less by order – not a single flag in sight, not even on official buildings!' Normally, he noted, there would be flags and fanfares, but now the only fanfares were of a different kind: the sound of muffled gunfire from the east.

There were banners, too, but their messages were decidedly ambivalent. A vast notice on a ruined building in Lützowplatz declared: 'We thank our Führer for everything. Dr Goebbels.' In the central workers' district of Moabit, near the jail, a banner was strung across the street: 'We all pull on the same rope. Up the Führer!'

Three men who were not celebrating that morning were Generals Weidling, Heinrici and Busse. Overnight, the Ninth Army's situation had deteriorated still further, and the four battalions of troops that Busse had been promised were simply not enough to man the city's forward defences, which now formed the second defence line for his collapsing front. Goebbels called Burgdorf in the chancellery again, and told him to ask Hitler to authorize the immediate dispatch of all the troops in Berlin. Hitler agreed, and Reymann was ordered to send ten Volkssturm battalions and a flak battalion of the Grossdeutschland Guard Regiment, in the fleet of city buses and taxis which Goebbels already had waiting. Reymann watched them go, then turned angrily to Goebbels's representative. 'Tell Goebbels,' he said, 'that it is no longer possible to defend the Reich capital. The inhabitants are defenceless.'

HITLER ROSE at 11 am. From midday the members of his inner circle arrived at the bunker in a continuing stream, to offer their congratulations and best wishes. Bormann, of course, was first on the scene, swiftly followed by Goebbels, and then Ribbentrop, Speer, Himmler and Göring – who was now dressed in a plain olive drab uniform like a US general's, shorn of all his

333

extravagant decorations. All except Goebbels did their best to persuade Hitler to leave Berlin and fly south, while there was still some chance of escape.

Göring had left Karinhall, his estate near Eberswalde, north-east of the city, early that morning, shortly after learning that Rokossovsky had started crossing the Oder, barely twelve miles away. The most valuable contents of the castle, including much of the loot he had plundered from countries occupied earlier in the war, had been packed into twenty-four heavy lorries, ready to be transported south to his house on the Obersalzberg – clearly, there was no fuel shortage for the Reichsmarschall. His last act before driving out through the gates was to press the plunger of the detonator to blow up the building. He would not be returning. Whatever Hitler chose to do, Göring had no intention of being trapped in or near Berlin. He parked his convoy of lorries under guard at Luftwaffe headquarters in the game park at Werder, just south-west of Potsdam, while he drove into the city to give Hitler his birthday greetings and to attend his last Führer conference.

Göring was far from alone in wanting to get out while there was still time. All the government officials who had not already left joined the stampede to the south – petrol and vehicles appeared miraculously from secret hoards. Reymann's office issued over 2,000 exit permits that day, even though Goebbels had ordered that 'No man capable of bearing arms is to leave Berlin.' And so the 'golden pheasants' flew the coop, scooting out of the city past lamp post after lamp post from which dangled the bodies of those hanged by Nazi fanatics for supposed desertion, cowardice or defeatism.

While the majority of the civil population could not leave the city, many could get out of the central districts and into the suburbs, and they did so in droves, leaving the centre almost empty. Among those who got out were Inge and Ella Deutschkron. When they heard the announcement that only the holders of red passes would be allowed to use public transport of any sort they realized this was their last chance to get out to their goat shed in Potsdam. Packing up their meagre possessions – cereals, a little flour, some potatoes, coal – into bags and haversacks, they left their furnished room in central Berlin and trudged on foot to the Potsdam station.

The trains were packed with people, all carrying similar baggage, all silent and on edge. At Potsdam, which had been heavily bombed for the first time a few nights before, the Deutschkrons found a Ukrainian forced labourer to help them carry their stuff. There were many foreign workers hanging around the station – they had been bombed out of their camps, their guards had been drafted into the Volkssturm, and there was no one to provide for them, but while the fighting continued they had no way of getting home.

BEFORE THE daily conference, Hitler climbed painfully up the stairs from the bunker to the rubble-strewn wreckage of the chancellery garden, to inspect his last birthday parade. It was a far cry from the glory days when

40,000 men with 600 tanks had taken nearly three hours to march past him in salute. Today there was only a handful of men and boys from two formations: the SS Frundsberg Division, which had finally been evacuated from Courland in Latvia, and Artur Axmann's Hitler Youth. While a movie cameraman recorded the occasion on colour film, Hitler tottered along the line of pale-faced lads, pressing their hands, patting their cheeks, and with trembling fingers pinning Iron Crosses on the chests of those who Axmann told him had 'recently distinguished themselves at the front'. He shuffled past the SS men, shaking hands with each of them and assuring them that the enemy would be destroyed in front of Berlin. Then he staggered back into his hole in the earth, away from the oppressive sounds of bombs and guns. He was never again to leave the bunker alive.

THE ALLIES, from both east and west, made their own contributions to the birthday celebrations. Shortly before 10 am the last 1,000-bomber American raid began. The silver planes were clearly visible in the open blue sky, flying straight and level in perfect formation. Too high for the flak and with no German fighters to trouble them, they rained their bombs unhindered on a defenceless city. The raid went on for two hours, and was followed by sporadic attacks by RAF Mosquitoes throughout the rest of the day. That night, the RAF returned for its final raid, and next morning the Americans paid their farewell visit. From then on the Red Air Force took over the job completely. Its bombs were smaller than the RAF blockbusters, but just as unwelcome to the Berliners.

The Soviets, meanwhile, had given the city notice of a new terror. At 11.50 am, long-range guns of Zhukov's LXXIXth Corps fired a salvo on the city centre as a birthday salute to Hitler. The shells fired by Vladimir Abyzov's unit the night before had landed in the suburbs. Another salvo fired at 9 am that morning to celebrate the taking of Bernau, a town only seven and a half miles from the city's north-eastern boundary, had landed nearer to the centre, almost by accident. But now, the heart of the city was within range of the heavier guns. That first 'birthday' salvo was little more than a symbolic gesture, but it was a warning of what was to come. Soviet engineers were busily repairing the main railway line from Küstrin to carry German heavy siege artillery captured in Silesia that could easily reach the city centre with shells weighing half a ton each.

The Allied raids finally put paid to the city's water and gas supplies, sewage services, and most of its electricity. From 10.50 am on 20 April, there was no power apart from brief spells of a few minutes at a time. The last factories were forced to close down, and throughout the entire city, using electricity for cooking became an offence punishable by death. Water could only be obtained from wells, via ancient hand pumps in the streets, left over from the days before the first water mains were installed 100 years earlier.

There were no more trams, no more U-Bahn trains, no more long-distance trains in or out of the city.

The last barricades were being closed to create Fortress Berlin, but it was a fortress with paper walls. The 42nd Battalion was typical of many Volkssturm units. It had a nominal roll of 400 men, but their commanding officer told his local party leader that he could not accept the responsibility of taking men into battle in civilian clothes – the ingrained respect for a uniform, any uniform, still survived. There was also the small matter of weapons. The commanding officer recalled later: 'We were given 180 Danish rifles, but no ammunition. We also had four machine guns and 100 Panzerfausts. None of the men had received any training in firing a machine gun, and they were all afraid of the anti-tank weapons. Although my men were quite ready to help their country, they refused to go into battle without uniforms and without training. . . . The men went home; that was the only thing we could do.'

Another man, drafted into the second Volkssturm levy and appointed a company commander on the strength of having been an NCO in the Kaiser's army in 1917, tried to avoid action by reporting sick. He still received an order to muster his company and join in the fighting, but saved his men from certain death by simply ignoring it.


ALTHOUGH THE vast majority of Berliners wanted the war ended as quickly and as painlessly as possible, there were many who were prepared to fight to the death for Hitler. Some 2,000 volunteers actually made their way into Berlin at this time to join in the defence as the 'Freikorps Adolf Hitler'. There were also several dedicated SS units in the city, including the 1,200 combat-experienced men of Hitler's personal bodyguard. Their commander, SS Brigadeführer Wilhelm Mohnke, was the designated head of the central Citadel sector in the Berlin defence plan.

Thousands of convinced Nazis still believed in the Führer's promised miracle. These were the men, mostly from the SS and SA, who combed the streets and searched houses and apartments for deserters and shirkers, carrying guns and ropes to dispose of anyone they caught. These were the men who were prepared to become 'werewolves', who would go underground to continue fighting and killing after everyone else had surrendered. As the Red Army moved closer, they stashed away weapons and ammunition to be used later.

And finally, there were the brainwashed youngsters of the Hitler Youth. Denied the opportunity of sacrificing them on the battlefield with Weidling, Axmann was now organizing them to play their part in the defence of the city. 'There is only victory or annihilation,' he had told them a few weeks earlier. 'Know no bounds in your love of your people; equally, know no bounds in your hatred of the enemy. It is your duty to watch when others tire, to stand when others weaken. Your greatest honour is your unshakeable fidelity to Adolf Hitler!'

Axmann and his aides issued the boys with rifles, grenades and Panzerfausts, and gave them basic training in how to use them. Then they dispatched them to join the Volkssturm in the trenches and on the barricades. Many of them were assigned to a special Hitler Youth regiment deployed to guard bridges. Others became part of the Axmann Brigade, which began operating in the Strausberg area on 21 April. Mounted on bicycles and armed with Panzerfausts, they rode off to hunt and destroy Soviet tanks, or die in the attempt. Thousands did both.

# 7

ON 20 APRIL, things were going well for Zhukov at last. His forces had already battered their way through three German defence lines and were closing on Berlin rapidly, leaving a trail of desolation in their wake. Koniev's two tank armies were also streaking for the south of Berlin, driven on by threats, while the rest of his First Ukrainian Front followed on their heels heading west to cut Germany in half. But Koniev's eyes were still fixed on Berlin. At 5.40 pm he sent another succinct radio message to his tank generals: 'Personal to Comrades Rybalko and Lelyushenko. Order you categorically to break into Berlin tonight. Report execution.'

Well aware of his rival's progress, Zhukov decided that a touch of the knout was needed to spur on his First Guards Tank Army. He sent a radio signal of his own to its commander and chief of staff: 'Katukov, Popiel. First Guards Tank has been assigned an historic mission: to be the first to break into Berlin and raise the Victory Banner. Personally charge you with organizing and execution. Send up one of the best brigades from each corps into Berlin and issue following orders: no later than 0400 hours [0200 Berlin time] 21 April at any cost to break into outskirts of Berlin and report at once for transmission to Stalin and press announcement.' Zhukov wanted not only Stalin but the whole world to know when he broke into the capital of the Reich. The only thing missing from the signal were the words 'or else' – but there can be no doubt that Generals Katukov and Popiel were fully aware of the consequences of failure.

# 8

THE FÜHRER conference that followed the birthday reception was another weird affair, more concerned with fantasy than reality. Hitler refused to listen when the true seriousness of the situation was explained. In the north, Rokossovsky had succeeded in establishing two firm bridgeheads and was advancing on Prenzlau; he had now cut off most of Manteuffel's Third Panzer Army from the rest of Army Group Vistula. In the centre of the front, Zhukov's forces were in the process of taking Strausberg; they had already taken Bernau and it could only be a matter of hours before they captured Ladenburg and Zepernick, a north-eastern suburb within the boundary of the city itself; other units of the First Belorussian Front were sweeping on around the north of Berlin towards Oranienburg, to the north-west. Back on the Oder, the whole of Busse's Ninth Army apart from Weidling's LVIth Panzer Corps was about to be encircled and destroyed: Koniev had smashed a great gap between it and Fourth Panzer Army, to its south. While his right wing was striking north behind the German Ninth Army, his tanks were rapidly approaching Zossen, due south of the city. During the day, at least 400 German aircraft had been destroyed, and the Luftwaffe was no longer capable of offering any worthwhile air cover.

There was no comfort to be found in the news from other parts of Germany that day. The noose was being drawn tighter and tighter around Model's 325,000 troops trapped in the Ruhr pocket as the Americans closed in from all sides. Montgomery's troops were beginning their assault on Bremen, and the British 11th Armoured Division reached the Elbe. The US 2nd and 69th Divisions completed the capture of Leipzig. French troops entered Stuttgart. The Second Polish Army took Rothenburg. And worst of all for Hitler, the Nazis' holy city, Nuremberg, fell to three US divisions.

Berlin itself was already half encircled, from the north, east and south. Its only vague hope of survival was for the Ninth Army to be pulled back from certain annihilation on the Oder, but Hitler stubbornly refused to allow any withdrawal. Heinrici, when Krebs told him for the third time that day that he was not allowed to pull the Ninth Army back, knew it was doomed. He also knew that the question of retreat was becoming academic. All day he had been driving around his front, and everywhere he had encountered men heading away from the front as fast as their legs or their remaining vehicles could carry them. He had managed to instil a little order, but it could only be temporary.

With Zhukov and Koniev threatening to complete their vast pincer movement to encircle the city, Heinrici appealed repeatedly to Krebs and the OKH to give him more troops to hold the line of the Havel river between Oranienburg and Spandau, to the north-west of Berlin. He was promised the so-called 'Müller Brigade', another mystery formation consisting of a few understrength battalions cobbled together from what was left of the Assault Artillery School. The brigade was part of Wenck's Twelfth Army on the east bank of the Elbe, but since it had little transport, there was no chance of its being able to reach the Havel in time to be of any use whatever.

In an effort to stop Rokossovsky cutting off the Third Panzer Army completely, Heinrici ordered SS Obergruppenführer (Lieutenant-General) Felix Steiner, commander of the army's reserve, the SS Germanic Panzer Corps, to move his headquarters to Eberswald and take over the scattered remnants of the forces he had found milling helplessly around in the forest there. To make up the numbers, Heinrici threw in the still-forming 4th SS Police Grenadier Division, and ordered the 3rd Naval Division – the sailors promised by Dönitz – to be hurried by rail from Swinemünde on the Baltic coast. He also planned to scrape together a few odd units from Luftwaffe personnel, clerks and storemen, and local Volkssturm. But all this would take time to organize, and until then, Steiner was a general with a headquarters but no troops.

As IF the chaos and confusion on the front was not enough, Heinrici's troubles were now increased still further – Hitler decreed that he was to take Reymann and the Berlin Defence Zone under his command. Heinrici called Reymann. He had two immediate orders for him. The first was not to blow up any of Berlin's bridges. The second was to send all his remaining Volkssturm forces to the front. He was determined that the battle for Berlin should take place outside the city, and that no troops under his command should be involved in house-to-house fighting. Berlin would not become another Stalingrad if he could help it.

Now that he was at last part of a military command, Reymann was given reinforcements, in the shape of the newly created Wünsdorf Tank Formation, and the Friedrich Ludwig Jahn Division of Wenck's Twelfth Army. The tank formation turned out to be half a dozen tanks from the Wünsdorf Tank School, all of which either broke down or were quickly put out of action by enemy fire. The infantry division was something of a mystery: no one seemed to know anything about it, what it consisted of, or where it was. Reymann had to send out motorcycle dispatch riders to hunt for it. Its command post was eventually located in a village near Trebbin, about ten miles west of Zossen. Reymann set out to visit them, but arrived just in time to learn that there had been a disaster.

The division, such as it had been, no longer existed. It had been forming up on the parade ground at the Wehrmacht's main ammunition depot at Jüterbog, about fifteen miles further south, apparently unaware that it was in the direct path of Lelyushenko's rampaging Fourth Guards Tank Army. The Soviet tanks had caught it completely by surprise. All its guns had been lost, and most of its men killed or wounded. One of its three regiments had managed to scatter, but no one knew where it was, and the divisional commander had been captured while searching for it.

Reymann just got back to his headquarters that night in time to receive a telephone call from Krebs, with a new order: 'Together with the Friedrich Ludwig Jahn Division, you will attack the enemy spearhead and drive it back to the south.' Reymann's chief of staff, Colonel Hans Refior, could hardly believe what he was hearing. 'Our report that the division was in no state to enter into active military operations was rejected out of hand,' he noted, 'and so were all further objections. The "enemy spearhead" turned out to consist of "only" two Russian tank armies. . . .' Reymann dealt with the ludicrous order by ignoring it.

ONCE AGAIN, everyone at the Führer conference tried to persuade Hitler to leave Berlin and set up his government in the south, on the Obersalzberg. Over the previous ten days, everyone who was not absolutely vital to the Führer headquarters had been sent off there in special trains and convoys of lorries, together with advance contingents from the staffs of the OKW and OKH. Planes were standing by at Tempelhof to fly out the final top brass, including Hitler, Keitel and Jodl, at a moment's notice. But once again, Hitler refused to commit himself. He would go no further than confirming the instructions he had given on 14 April that if the Soviets and Americans cut the country in two, the fight would be continued under separate commands for the north and south. For the northern half, he now formally transferred command of the armed forces to Grand Admiral Dönitz. Kesselring had been named as supreme commander in the south, but Hitler refrained from handing over to him, keeping open the option of taking command himself for the last stand in the so-called Alpine Redoubt.

As the meeting broke up, however, Hitler spoke quietly to General Alfred Jodl, the OKW operations chief. It was only the second time he had ever talked to him about anything other than military affairs – the other had been when Jodl's first wife died. 'Jodl,' he said, 'I shall fight as long as the faithful fight next to me, and then I shall shoot myself.'

Göring hurried out of the bunker after an icy farewell from Hitler, and headed back to his convoy at Werder. On the way, he was caught in an RAF raid, and had to duck into a series of public shelters, where he entertained the people with jokes against himself, playing up his jovial image to the very last. When the raiders had passed he continued to Werder, where he collected his treasures and hit the one remaining road to Bavaria at top speed, not even pausing to acknowledge the farewell salute of his chief of staff, Colonel-General Koller.

Himmler sped away from the city to his castle at Ziethen, where Schellenberg waited to bring him up to date on the latest state of their treasonous peace negotiations. Speer headed for Hamburg, where he recorded a radio speech calling on the people to give up the fight now, to resist all efforts to put Hitler's scorched earth orders into operation, and forbidding all Werewolf activities.

AFTER ALL the senior Nazis had left, Hitler's secretaries Traudl Junge, Gerda Christian, Christa Schröder and Johanna Wolf, sat with him and other members of his personal entourage in the small study beside his living room in the bunker, toasting him in schnapps. In the close atmosphere, with so many people jammed into such a small space, Traudl Junge realized that she could smell herself. She became acutely conscious of the fact that she was filthy but there was nothing she could do about it. Her clothes were dirty, yet there was nowhere she could wash them. Everyone in that cramped, oppressive room stank.

For months now, Hitler had preferred the company of the female members of his staff, perhaps feeling that they were more devoted and more loyal – as indeed events were to prove. But the most devoted of all his women was Eva Braun, who sat alongside him. She had defied his orders and returned to Berlin on 15 April, to stay with him to the end, getting soldiers to carry her bed and dressing table down from the chancellery to the room next to Hitler's bedroom. He had pretended to be angry, but it was clear to everyone that really he was delighted. 'Who else would have come back to Berlin,' he kept saying, 'when they had the opportunity to go to the Berghof?'

Gerda Christian recalled that Eva's arrival was greeted in silence. 'We all knew what it meant,' she said. 'I was now convinced that he would never fly off to the Obersalzberg. Berchtesgaden, in the person of Eva Braun, had come to Berlin.' The question was in everybody's mind, but none of his staff had dared to ask him. Now, on his birthday, the secretaries plucked up the courage to do so. Was he going to leave Berlin?

Hitler shook his head. 'No, I can't,' he told them. 'If I did, I would feel like a lama turning an empty prayer wheel. I *must* bring about the resolution here in Berlin – or else go under.'

For the first time, all those in that room realized that Hitler no longer believed victory was possible. Shortly afterwards, he retired to his room, accompanied by Eva, but she returned after a few minutes and led everyone upstairs to the living room of Hitler's private apartment in the old chancellery. She was determined to celebrate his birthday, come what may. The room was empty apart from a large circular table – all the other furniture had been moved down to the bunker. Someone brought a wind-up gramophone, but there was only one record, a pre-war hit called 'Red Roses Bring You Happiness'. They played it over and over again, while they drank champagne and danced – even Bormann and fat Dr Morell. Outside, there was the constant rumble of Soviet guns. Suddenly a shell landed close by. A telephone rang and someone hurried to answer. The party atmosphere evaporated, and people began to return to the bunker.

Next day, the exodus of some of the personal staff began. Johanna Wolf, Hitler's senior secretary, was in tears. She had worked for him for twenty-five years. Now she knew she would never see him again.

# 9

COLONEL HANS-OSCAR Wöhlermann, Weidling's chief of artillery, and his reduced staff of twenty were so exhausted after five solid days of battle that they all fell asleep in their command vehicle, parked in a clearing near Elisenhof. So, too, did the sentries they had posted. They were woken at 4 am on Saturday, 21 April, by the arrival of a courier, to discover that they were on their own. The rest of the corps HQ had fled during the night, when Soviet tanks had started getting close. While Wöhlermann was trying unsuccessfully to raise them on the radio the tanks suddenly closed in, pumping shells and machine-gun fire into the area. They got out fast.

Weidling, in fact, was pulling the whole LVIth Corps back to the Köpenick-Biesdorf road, well inside the city limits, to avoid being encircled as Chuikov's forces drove forward south of them, cutting them off from the remainder of the Ninth Army. He had completely lost contact with Busse and everyone else, including the Führer bunker. This total breakdown in communications may not have been entirely accidental: under the Führer order issued in January, any commander of a division or larger formation had to seek Hitler's personal permission before withdrawing his troops, and Hitler never gave that permission. Heinrici had discovered that to his cost. That was why the Ninth Army was about to be lost. Weidling had no intention of seeing his corps go the same way.

AT ZOSSEN, to the south of Berlin, Captain Gerhard Boldt was woken at 6 am by a telephone call to his underground room. Boldt, highly decorated and many times wounded, had been ADC to the chief of the general staff since 20 January, and had stayed in the post when Guderian was fired. His closest associate, Major Bernd Freytag von Loringhoven, Guderian's tall, immaculate adjutant, had also been persuaded to stay on, if somewhat reluctantly. They now lived almost permanently in the bunkers of the command headquarters, emerging only to attend Hitler's conferences in the Führer bunker. The drive to and from central Berlin, however, gave them a good idea of the state of the city and its inhabitants. A few days previously, Freytag had returned shaken after one such journey with Krebs: Berliners on the street had shaken their fists at them and cursed them with shouts of 'Vampires!'

Boldt's phone call was from Lieutenant Kränkel, commander of the OKH's 250-man armoured guard squadron. Krebs had sent the squadron out on a reconnaissance mission the previous afternoon, after learning of the approach of Koniev's tanks. Kränkel's news was not encouraging. 'About forty Russian tanks have passed us, as well as mounted infantry,' he reported. 'I shall go in to the attack at 0700 hours.'

Boldt dressed hurriedly, then reported Kränkel's information to Krebs and the rest of the general staff. There was an air of gloom in the massive bunker complex. Everyone knew that Zossen was doomed, and that it could only be hours before the Soviet troops got there. The outlook for Berlin as a whole was equally grim; even the most optimistic officers knew the German army now had no reserves whatever, and those who still clung to the notion that Wenck's Twelfth Army might be strong enough to hold off the Soviets realized that there simply was not enough time to bring it back from the Elbe.

At 9 am, Kränkel called again. 'My attack has failed, with heavy losses,' he reported. 'My reconnoitring tanks report further enemy tanks advancing north.' This meant they were heading for Berlin, and that Zossen was directly in their path. Krebs immediately phoned the Führer bunker, asking permission to evacuate the headquarters. He pointed out that if he and his staff were captured or killed, there would be no one to direct the army. Burgdorf promised to ask Hitler for a decision. The answer, when it came, was no.

By that time, bad news was pouring in from north and south. 'It spread like wildfire through headquarters,' Boldt recalled, 'and I hardly had a chance to put the telephone down. Everyone wanted to know whether, in view of the grave news, there would still be a conference that day. My reply was always the same: "At 11 am as usual." However, contrary to my chief's orders, I issued instructions for everything to be prepared for a hasty evacuation.'

As the time for Krebs's daily briefing approached, Boldt's room was buzzing as clerks, orderlies and adjutants hurried in and out. Colonels and generals were talking so loudly that several times Boldt had to ask them to be quiet so that he could hear what was being said on the phone. Then suddenly, just before 11, everything went deathly silent. From outside, an ominous sound penetrated the earth and concrete around the underground bunker.

'There it was again,' Boldt wrote, 'that hoarse, barking report that anyone who has ever been out there at the front knows only too well. We all looked at each other more in dismay than astonishment, until someone broke the silence. "That must be the Russian tanks at Baruth, that's ten or perhaps even fifteen kilometres from here, I think. They could well be here in half an hour."'

At that moment, Krebs emerged from his room. 'If you're ready, gentlemen,' he said calmly, beginning the briefing as though nothing unusual was happening.

The conference had hardly begun when Boldt was called out. Kränkel had arrived, exhausted and covered in mud. Only about thirty or forty men were left from his squadron, he said, plus a handful of vehicles. The Soviets had taken Baruth, but then, unaccountably, they had stopped. Did Boldt have any further orders for him?

'Yes,' Boldt replied. 'Keep your men and your vehicles ready for action.' He hurried back into the conference room and reported what Kränkel had just told him. Krebs phoned the Führer again for permission to move out. Again, Hitler refused. 'There was only one thought written on the faces of all the officers as they took their leave,' Boldt noted. 'A Russian prisoner-of-war camp.'

For the staff at Zossen, the next hour was one of almost unbearable tension, knowing that the Soviet tanks were lined up, virtually unopposed, only ten or eleven miles away. Then, at 1 pm, Burgdorf called again. The Führer had finally relented: OKH headquarters was to be moved at once. The main body was to drive south to the Obersalzberg; Krebs and his immediate staff were to establish a new headquarters at the Luftwaffe barracks in Potsdam-Eiche. The OKW operations staff, meanwhile, would move into nearby army barracks at Krampnitz. Meanwhile, Burgdorf informed Krebs, the daily Führer conference would go ahead, but half an hour earlier than usual, at 2.30. To get there in time, Krebs and Freytag would have to leave immediately.

After an hour of frenzied packing, Boldt started the main convoy of trucks packed with men, office equipment and documents, on its way south. Then he drove out of the gates of the Zossen complex with the smaller column of trucks and cars headed for Potsdam. They made slow progress, under frequent aerial attack by Soviet fighters. The roads were clogged with hundreds of thousands of refugees, most of them on foot, with the now familiar collection of horse-drawn carts, bicycles, hand carts, wheelbarrows and baby carriages, all heading west. Anti-tank barricades outside each village or small town slowed everything down still further, allowing only a trickle of people through at a time. The huge barricades were a bizarre playground for local children whose families had not yet fled. 'They waved to us,' Boldt noted, 'wearing paper helmets and brandishing wooden swords.'

# 10

D R WALTER SEITZ was pedalling down the Linden on his bicycle at
11.30 am when something went whizzing past his ears and exploded on
the pavement behind him. The blast threw him over the handlebars, flattening
him on the ground outside the Adlon Hotel, winded but unhurt. It took
several seconds for him to realize what was going on, as more explosions
followed, accompanied by a strange whistling and screaming sound: the
centre of Berlin was under artillery attack, with shells pouring in from the
east.

Max Buch, the Jewish illegal, was also in the neighbourhood when the
shelling started, on his way to Oranienstrasse to return the keys to his best
friend's house outside the city, where he had stored some of his belongings.
He had just reached Dorotheenstrasse when a shell scored a direct hit on the
eastern side of Friedrichstrasse railway station. He decided it was time to take
cover in the U-Bahn.

As he hurried home again afterwards, he was intrigued to see soldiers
driving a herd of cows through the Tiergarten. The big guns on the Zoo flak
tower were firing eastwards. On the sides of the tower beneath them, new
propaganda slogans had been painted in huge white letters: 'BETTER DEAD
THAN SLAVES' and 'OUR HONOUR IS CALLED FAITHFULNESS'. There was a great
deal of military activity around the towers, with supplies of food and
ammunition being carried in, in preparation for a siege. It had started to rain,
hard.

BY A terrible irony, the streets were more crowded when the Soviet shelling
started than they had been for some time, as people believed it was safe for the
moment to come out of the shelters. Fred Laabs and his family heard on the
radio in their cellar that the RAF raid during the night and the US Eighth Air
Force raid at 9.25 that morning were the last Allied bombing raids – there
would be no more. As everyone in the cellar started to celebrate the end of
what had been their greatest fear for the past three years, the announcer went
on to say that from now on the Soviet Air Force would take over. But they all
knew that Soviet air raids were far less severe than the British or American, so
when the last Flying Fortress left, they came out of hiding. So, too, did
thousands of others throughout the city. Their numbers were increased by

columns of refugees trudging through from the east and north, including many peasants herding cows and horses before them. The police kept them moving on to the south and west, trying to clear them out of the city centre.

That morning, the newspapers had announced an extra issue of rations in honour of Hitler's birthday – a pound of meat, half a pound of rice, half a pound of beans, peas or lentils, a pound of sugar, three and a half ounces of malt coffee, a tin of fruit and one ounce of real coffee. They also announced that standard rations for the next two weeks would be available in advance – and that up to 1,000 marks could be withdrawn from Post Office savings accounts without the usual advance notice. Knowing that this might be their last chance of obtaining food supplies before the final siege, thousands of Berliners left their shelters and formed long lines outside food shops, to use up all their remaining coupons. There were long queues, too, beside every water pump or standpipe, as people took the opportunity to fill buckets and bowls.

The artillery fire took them completely by surprise. In Hermannplatz, the queues were particularly thick outside the boarded-up windows of the famous Karstadt's department store as shells started exploding in their midst. Within seconds, blood and guts and dismembered body parts were splattered everywhere. Shocked and injured people screamed in pain. This was no isolated incident, no ironic 'salute' to Hitler, this was a grimly systematic barrage, laid down with all the awesome power of the Red Army's speciality, massed heavy artillery.


THE EXPLOSIONS even rocked the deep Führer bunker, which was normally cushioned by the soft alluvial soil around it. Hitler, no doubt reminded of his days in the trenches during the First World War, telephoned General Karl Koller, the Luftwaffe chief of staff, to get something done to silence the Soviet guns.

'Do you know that Berlin is under artillery fire?' he asked. 'The centre of the city?'

'No,' Koller replied.

'Can't you hear it?'

'No, I am in the Werder Game Park.'

'There is great agitation in the city over this long-range artillery fire. They tell me the Russians have brought up heavy guns on railway trucks. They are supposed to have built a railway bridge over the Oder. The Luftwaffe must attack and eliminate these bridges at once.'

'The enemy has no railway bridges over the Oder,' Koller assured him. 'He may have captured a German heavy battery and turned it round. But he is probably using his own medium guns – he is close enough to hit the city with them.'

Hitler did not want to believe this. He ordered Koller to locate and destroy the Soviet guns. He was still not convinced when Koller told him he was already using the guns on the Berlin flak towers to engage enemy batteries near Marzahn, which were probably using 152 mm guns with a range of nine miles.

Salvo after salvo poured into the heart of Berlin. Sometimes there would be a pause of thirty seconds, perhaps even a minute, as the unseen gunners, miles away on the city's eastern boundary, recharged and relaid their guns, before the storm broke again with renewed vigour. Around the Wilhelm- strasse, shells were landing at the rate of one every five seconds. The Brandenburg Gate was hit, and one of its wings collapsed. The ruined Reichstag burst into flames once more. Unter den Linden erupted all along its length. At the far end, the old Royal Palace, already little more than a battered hulk, blazed again. In the west end, the Kurfürstendamm was a scene of wild panic, as shoppers fled and a herd of horses stampeded from a burning riding stable on the edge of the Tiergarten, their manes and tails aflame.

This was a new horror for the Berliners. Those still living in the central districts dived back into their cellars and shelters and stayed there. Most emerged only to make quick forays for food and water. There was nothing else they could do, for there was no regular pattern to the shelling, as there had been for most of the time with the air raids. There was no warning, no alert: shells simply screamed in at any time of day or night. The shelters were permanently overcrowded, and the already poor conditions became appal- ling. There was no heat and no light, apart from candles and the occasional smoky oil lamp. With no water, there was no sanitation and people were forced to relieve themselves where and when they could. The noisome stench was overpowering. Most Berliners lost all sense of time. Days and nights merged into one dark, stinking nightmare as they waited helplessly for the end.

# 11

KONIEV'S TANKS had stalled outside Baruth for a very simple reason: the leading brigade of the VIth Tank Corps had been pushed so hard it had run out of fuel. The tanks sat helplessly waiting for supplies, but the Volkssturm and Hitler Youth got there first. With their crude but deadly Panzerfausts, they proceeded to destroy the brigade, tank by tank. The few operational German aircraft, seeking Koniev's tanks, found and attacked what looked like a large supply column – it turned out to be the main convoy of the OKH, driving away from Zossen.

Koniev was already furious at the delays, which were aggravated by the fact that the nature of the terrain made it difficult for a tank army to operate in open battle formation. 'Comrade Rybalko,' he signalled the Third Guards Tank Army commander, 'you are moving like a snail. One brigade is fighting, the rest of the army is standing still. I order you to cross the Baruth–Luckenwalde line through the swamp along several routes deployed in battle order. Report fulfilment.'

By afternoon, the rest of Rybalko's army had caught up, and the local Volkssturm had run out of Panzerfausts. The advance resumed, tanks pressing on across the swampy land as ordered. Even advancing cautiously, it was not long before they were entering the gates of the Zossen complex. The large, sprawling compound was a masterpiece of camouflage. No casual observer would ever have guessed it was a military headquarters at all, let alone the most important in the Reich. To the casual eye, and particularly from the air, the place looked like just another rural village. Groups of picturesque red-brick cottages and a red-brick church stood on the edge of a dense pine wood. Pigeons – those that had not been shot and eaten – still nested in the eaves. It was like a German Grantchester. But there was a curious absence of human clutter. There were no bits and pieces of decaying farm machinery outside the sheds and barns. Everything was too neat and tidy – even the ground under the trees looked as though someone had been over it with a vacuum cleaner.

Grouped in clearings in the wood, linked by sandy tracks, were twenty-four concrete buildings, all heavily camouflaged, with netting hung across the concrete footpaths around them so that they would not be visible from the air. These comprised two main centres, codenamed Maybach I and II, sealed off from each other by barbed-wire fences, which housed the OKH and the OKW respectively. But the most important parts of both, including the operations rooms, were buried deep underground. Between them, buried even deeper at about seventy feet below the surface, was Exchange 500, the all-important communications centre for the OKW, OKH and the Reich government, the hub of a vast telephone, teleprinter and radio network that had once stretched from the Arctic to the Black Sea, and from the Atlantic coast of France in the west to the Caucasus mountains deep in the Soviet Union. It was completely self-contained, with its own power generators, water supplies and air conditioning filtered against poison gas.

The first Soviet troops on the scene were amazed at the extent and complexity of the underground installations. Hans Beltow, the engineer in charge, had stayed behind when the others fled. Like some obliging janitor, he took his captors on a conducted tour. The lifts were not working, so they had to descend by a spiral staircase, winding downwards to seemingly endless corridors lined with numbered doors. Behind them were offices, store rooms, bedrooms, their floors strewn with documents, maps and reference books, all the discarded paraphernalia of a military headquarters. In Krebs's bedroom a dressing gown lay flung over a writing desk, a pair of carpet slippers lay on the floor. The bed in the adjoining room was unmade. On a small table stood a bottle of wine, a couple of half-full glasses, and a dish of apples. Underwear and family photographs spilled out of an open suitcase.

In Exchange 500, telephones and teleprinters were still working, the printers spewing out messages from Berlin. Cheekily, some German clerk had left large printed notices in schoolboy Russian on the teleprinter consoles, warning: 'Do not damage this equipment. It will be valuable to the Red Army.' A Soviet soldier answered one of the phones. A voice demanded some general or other. With great delight, the soldier replied: 'Ivan is here. You can go —!'

The sole defenders of Zossen were four fat, drunken German soldiers, three of whom immediately surrendered; the fourth was too intoxicated to do anything, and had to be carried away on a stretcher. The nerve centre of Hitler's mighty war machine ended not with a bang but a drunken burp.

KONIEV DID not allow Rybalko's men to waste time gawping at the wonders of Zossen. Even while political commissar Major Boris Polevoi was inspecting Krebs's room and listening to wire recordings of the last telephone messages received in the main communications room, the rest of the army was racing on towards Berlin.

Lelyushenko's Fourth Guards Tank Army, on Rybalko's left, was also closing on the city without pausing, though separated from Rybalko by a widening and potentially dangerous gap of nearly twenty miles. During the afternoon, he swept right round to the south-west of Berlin, taking Babelsberg, the home of the Ufa film studios, on the Havel between Potsdam and Wannsee. There, one of his brigades liberated a concentration camp holding many important foreigners, including the former French prime minister Edouard Herriot and his wife. By Saturday evening both armies had crossed the outer Berlin ring road, and were ready to press on towards the centre.

TO THE east of the city, Zhukov's tanks and infantry were already in control of the whole of the Berlin ring road from Bernau to Wusterhausen. Some of his units had broken into the outer suburbs. The advance formations of the 1st Mechanized Corps crossed the city boundary from the north-east on the Lindenberg–Malchow road. Meeting fierce resistance at Malchow, they swung round the town and pressed on towards Weissensee, which was little more than four miles as the crow flies from the Führer bunker.

Chuikov's Eighth Guards Army, meanwhile, was ordered to swing towards the south, to storm the city from the south and south-east.

# 12

LIEUTENANT WALTER SCHMID, the former diplomat who had served in the Moscow embassy until 1941, was still waiting to face the Soviets with his two 88 mm flak guns at Mahlsdorf, on the boundary ten miles due east of the city centre. He and his troop of seventeen- and eighteen-year-old Luftwaffe anti-aircraft gunners had been stationed near the main road from Frankfurt since mid-February, their guns dug in with barrels depressed, ready to fire at any Soviet tank that hove into view.

Schmid had been ordered to dig extensive trenches alongside the gun pits, though he had no men to put in them. He was told that when the battle started, infantry units falling back from the front would occupy them. On 20 April, retreating troops – regular soldiers, not Volkssturm – had indeed arrived to fill the trenches. But within half an hour they had all disappeared: they had deserted, to a man.

Schmid's youngsters, however, were keen to show how brave they were. They wanted action after sitting waiting for so long. When they heard tanks approaching in the distance, they begged him to give them Panzerfausts and allow them to go hunting. He put them under the command of a subaltern, and they set off eagerly. But after half an hour they were back, disappointed that they had been unable to do anything, though they had seen boys from other anti-tank positions engaging the enemy.

Schmid could hear the sounds of firing in the distance, while Red Air Force planes zoomed overhead, machine guns blazing. They were not shooting at his unit, but at others a little further forward. Communications were virtually non-existent, but during the morning Schmid heard that the commander of a nearby flak troop had been killed in an engagement with Soviet tanks. As the day dragged by, the Soviet strafing, bombing and shelling grew more intense, but still he could get no clear information. There were no connections with the regimental staff, or battalion, or divisional HQ. Nor was there any link with the infantry units in the area. The entire military organization was in a state of total chaos. All Schmid could discover were rumours that the Soviets were already behind them, and that they were in danger of being encircled.

In the evening, the major commanding a nearby infantry battalion arrived. 'I've got to withdraw my people,' he told Schmid, 'and within a very short time there will be nobody in front of you. It's up to you to decide what to do.'

Faced with the prospect of trying to fight the Red Army alone, with only two 88 mm guns, a few rounds of ammunition and a handful of aged French machine guns and rifles, Schmid had little choice. He ordered his men to pull out. His battalion commander had told him previously that if they had to withdraw, they should reassemble at the Ostkreuz S-Bahn station, near the east bank of the Spree at Rummelsburg, about six miles west of their present position.

Schmid sent his men off to find the assembly point, while he stayed behind with some of his sergeants to blow up the guns – with no trucks to tow them he could not take them with him. Just as they were finishing the job, a German armoured car pulled up alongside and offered them a lift. It was, its commander said, the last vehicle withdrawing from the front in that sector. To their surprise, they met no Soviet troops on their way back to Rummelsburg – the rumours had been wrong.

Amid the confusion outside the Ostkreuz S-Bahn station, Schmid found his battalion commander, a much-decorated major with a distinguished record of bravery on the eastern front. When Schmid reported to him, and told him he had had to pull out, the major was furious. 'How dare you give up your position!' he shouted. 'I shall have you court-martialled!'

A charge of deserting his position would mean an automatic and immediate death sentence at the hands of the flying court martials that were now in permanent session throughout Berlin. Schmid acknowledged the threat wearily, then turned his attention to bedding his men down for the night. There would be time enough to think about execution squads in the morning.

ON SCHMID's way back to Ostkreuz, the first district he passed through was Kaulsdorf, a pleasant suburb with an important waterworks. As part of the front, it was swarming with police and SS squads, there to keep the foreign workers and the Danish and Dutch Waffen SS troops in line, busily shooting and hanging any who showed signs of reluctance to die any other way. The walls of the town were covered with slogans: 'Berlin a fortress! Every house a fortress!' The town's Lutheran pastor, Dr Heinrich Grüber, remonstrated with the die-hard Nazis who were chalking them up: 'If Berlin is a fortress there shouldn't be any children or sick in it. If they are left inside, it's criminal to fight on.' Their only reply was that the Führer was sure to find a way out.

That night, an elderly woman parishioner sought out Dr Grüber, to tell him she had overheard a group of young Werewolves in her apartment house planning to hang him and then blow up the waterworks. But Grüber was no pushover. He had survived the Nazi years unscathed, and was not going to be beaten now. When the youths arrived to string him up they were confronted by a bunch of tough trade unionists armed with heavy clubs, who soon put them to flight. Both the pastor and the waterworks survived.

# 13

IN THE FÜHRER bunker Hitler's mood had swung during the day, after his initial shock at learning how close the Soviet guns were. His optimism was rekindled first by the arrival of General Schörner, commander of Army Group Centre, which was operating from just south of Frankfurt-an-der-Oder right down to the Carpathians. Schörner told him he had mounted a strong counter-attack against Koniev's southern armies, successfully holding up their advance on Dresden. Hitler rewarded him by promoting him on the spot to Field Marshal.

Hitler's mood change was also affected by the drugs that had brought about much of his mental and physical deterioration. Dr Morell was still in the bunker with him, and almost certainly gave him one of his massive amphetamine injections that day. His valet, Heinz Linge, certainly administered a large dose of the drops that had been prescribed the previous year for a mystery eye complaint: that day, at Hitler's request, Linge increased the dose from one drop to five. Their main constituent was cocaine.

At the daily conference that afternoon, Hitler's renewed confidence was boosted still further by the unexpected arrival of Wenck, who reported that his Twelfth Army's XXXIXth Panzer Corps was about to launch an ambitious counter-attack on American forces in the Harz Mountains and on the Elbe. Keitel was staggered at the impression Wenck's plans made on Hitler. 'In view of the improvised nature of his formation, the complexity of the situation, which was tying down our forces on every hand, and the numerical weakness of the army in question,' he wrote later, 'I was unable to understand either the Führer's optimism or that of General Wenck.' Keitel's doubts were well justified – unknown to Wenck, the XXXIXth Panzer Corps was being wiped out as he spoke.

In his new enthusiasm, Hitler leaned over his maps and looked for new ways of halting the Soviet advance on Berlin. He called the Luftwaffe chief of staff, General Koller, at Werder and ordered him to send jet fighters from Prague to attack Soviet forces south of Berlin, and to air-drop supplies to German troops in Spremberg. In fact, there were no German troops left in Spremberg: the Soviet Fifth Guards Army had already finished mopping up in that area. Koller had to tell Hitler that there was no possibility of involving the jets: communications with Prague were almost non-existent, and in any case they would never be able to take off, as the Soviets had total air superiority over the fields.

Undeterred, Hitler decided to pull back the LVIth Panzer Corps to the city boundary, not realizing they were there already. The map showed that they could then link up with another formation on their left, Steiner's SS Germanic Panzer Corps.

The name Steiner had an electric effect on Hitler. It had been Steiner, then commanding the Eleventh Army, who had led Army Group Vistula's counter-attack against Zhukov in February, at the time of Wenck's car accident. Steiner was indeed one of the best SS generals, one of the few who was respected by regular army commanders. Hitler believed he had found his saviour for Berlin. Steiner, he ordered, must be given every available man to enable him to form a special group, 'Army Detachment Steiner', to strike southwards from his position in Eberswalde and cut off the line of Zhukov's advance. At the same time, he decided, Busse's Ninth Army would strike northwards, and the two would meet up to re-establish a continuous German line.

On paper, Hitler's new plan looked like a bold and imaginative move that was bound to succeed. But unfortunately it was imaginative in the wrong way: Steiner's detachment only existed on paper. It was still basically nothing more than a headquarters. The rag-bag of troops, sailors, airmen, police and Volkssturm under his command was still being assembled, and had little in the way of arms or equipment. Hitler, however, was oblivious to this, and it seemed there was no one in the bunker prepared to disillusion him. The switchboard operator managed to make contact with Steiner, and Hitler spoke to him excitedly.

'Steiner,' he told him, 'are you aware that the Reichsmarschal has a private army at Karinhall? This is to be disbanded at once and sent into battle. Every available man between Berlin and the Baltic Sea up to Stettin and Hamburg is to be drawn into this attack I have ordered.'

Steiner had no idea what Hitler was talking about. But when he tried to explain his situation, Hitler simply put down the phone. Puzzled and alarmed, Steiner rang Krebs and tried to find out from him what was going on. He was halfway through telling him he had no troops or heavy weapons when Hitler picked up the phone again and cut in. He gave Steiner a long lecture, which he ended by saying: 'You will see, Steiner. You will see. The Russians will suffer their greatest defeat before the gates of Berlin!'

Later that night, Steiner received the official order for the great attack. It concluded: 'Any withdrawal to the west by any section is expressly forbidden. Officers who do not comply unconditionally with this order are to be arrested and shot immediately. You, personally, are answerable with your head for the execution of this order. The fate of the Reich capital depends on the success of your mission. Adolf Hitler.'

Still full of enthusiasm, Hitler then called Koller again, and told him to send all available Luftwaffe personnel, including Göring's bodyguard from Karinhall – a whole division of paratroops equipped with a double comple-ment of modern weapons – to join Army Detachment Steiner at once. This was the first Koller had heard of any Army Detachment Steiner, but when he tried to ask about it he was cut off. He did his best to comply with Hitler's order, but no one seemed to know where Steiner was, and Göring's much-vaunted private army seemed to have shrunk to less than a battalion. When he called Hitler again to report this, he was abruptly ordered to send it to Steiner immediately. Then the phone was put down. Frantic enquiries in all directions discovered that Steiner had last been seen near Oranienburg that afternoon, accompanied by one single staff officer.

In some desperation, Koller called the Führer bunker again, and eventually got hold of Krebs. Where was he supposed to send the men he was raising? he asked. Before Krebs could answer, Hitler picked up the phone and cut in. 'Do you still doubt my orders?' he demanded. 'I thought I had made myself quite clear. All available Luftwaffe personnel north of the city are to join Steiner and take part in a ground attack. Any commanding officer who keeps back men will forfeit his life within five hours. They must be told of this. You, yourself, will guarantee with your own head that every last man gets into battle.'

During the night, Koller managed to scrape together 12–15,000 ground staff, the equivalent of about a division, but untrained, of course, and mostly unarmed. When he reported this to Hitler, somewhat fearfully, he was surprised that there was no outburst of rage at the other end of the line. Instead, the Führer spoke encouragingly, repeating what he had earlier told Steiner: 'You will see – the Russians are about to suffer the bloodiest defeat of their history at the gates of Berlin!'

There was still total confusion about where the men were to go. The OKW insisted that Steiner was based near Oranienburg, north-west of Berlin. Krebs insisted that the attack was to be launched from Eberswalde, in the north-east. Playing safe, Koller had his new force split in two, and sent half to each location.


HEINRICI WAS one of the last to know what Hitler had ordered for his front. He found out from Steiner, who was appalled at what was expected of him. Heinrici called Krebs, to protest angrily that Steiner did not have the strength to mount an attack. 'I reject the order,' he barked down the phone. 'I insist on the withdrawal of the Ninth Army. Otherwise, the only troops still capable of defending Hitler and Berlin will be lost.' He went on to say that if this request was refused yet again, he would demand to be relieved of his command. He would rather serve as a simple Volkssturm man than continue to take the responsibility for his troops in such circumstances. Krebs rejected his appeal. 'That responsibility is held by the Führer alone,' he reminded him, sharply.

The Ninth Army was indeed in serious trouble. Chuikov's Eighth Guards Army, driving south to the Dahme, the broad waterway that flows north to join the Spree at Köpenick, had already cut off Busse's northern flank from Berlin. Now, advance units of Rybalko's Third Guards Tank Army, driving north, reached Königs Wusterhausen on the other side of the Dahme. The Ninth Army was effectively encircled in the woods of the Spreewald. Tens of thousands of refugees camped among the trees were hopelessly entangled with the troops, while Soviet aircraft from three air armies constantly attacked the area. Fuel and ammunition stocks were dangerously low. That evening, the artillery finally ran out of shells.

Heinrici told Busse to pull back from the Oder, and start trying to break out before it was too late. But Busse refused to withdraw without a direct order from Hitler himself. He was not prepared to break his oath of obedience, even at this late stage. He was also loath to abandon the garrison in Frankfurt, which was still holding out against everything the Soviets could throw at it.


As NIGHT came, Hitler was still riding his wave of optimism, convinced that victory could be achieved, given the right leadership. All the defeats his armies had suffered so far, he argued, were the result of treachery or weak commanders. Heinrici was a good general, but clearly he was in danger of succumbing to the virus of defeatism. His resolve needed stiffening, and Hitler felt he knew how to do it. He gave him a new chief of staff, Major-General Thilo von Trotha, an ardent Nazi who could be relied on to see that Heinrici toed the Führer's line. To Heinrici, the very idea of such a change at a critical point in the battle was ridiculous. He decided to ignore Trotha, and deal only with his trusted chief of operations, Colonel Eismann.

But Hitler's changes did not stop there. Turning to the defence of Berlin itself, he recalled that Reymann had done nothing to implement the order he had been given the day before to attack the enemy with the non-existent Friedrich Ludwig Jahn Division. Reymann was another general who was showing signs of defeatism. He would have to be replaced with someone bolder and more trustworthy. The new commander was named during the night as SS Standartenführer (Colonel) Ernst Kaether, who had served on the eastern front as a regimental commander in the Waffen SS, but who was now chief of staff to the Wehrmacht's chief political commissar. Kaether was promoted immediately to Major-General. Reymann was ordered to quit Berlin and take over the defence of Potsdam.

# 14

I N THE small hours of the morning, Walter Schmid was woken by one of his sergeants. 'Will you come with me, please?' the man asked. 'I've been looking around and I see that most of the other units are leaving.'

Schmid followed him outside the building where he had been sleeping, to the square in front of Ostkreuz S-Bahn station. 'Look,' the sergeant said. 'They've gone.'

Schmid looked around. The place was almost empty. His commanding officer had gone, too, abandoning his threat of a court martial along with his troops. Schmid asked around among the people still left, and discovered where the next assembly point was. Then he formed up his men, and marched them away, in good order, as daylight broke. The rain of the day before had cleared, and they marched calmly along through the bright, sunny, Sunday morning streets, disturbed only occasionally by random shelling.

At the assembly point there was no sign of the regimental commander, or any form of higher authority. The place was a mass of guns, vehicles, equipment and men, all milling about aimlessly. Schmidt didn't like the look of it: with Soviet aircraft filling the sky, the square made too good a target. A couple of bombs in the middle would finish everything. He decided he had to get his men away as quickly as possible. They had just left when the place was hit by shell fire.

Schmid had acquired an elegant Maybach car – made by the firm that had built the engines for the Zeppelin airships – intended to tow a small, 20 mm anti-aircraft gun. He put two or three men in it, loaded it up with all the unit's provisions, including a huge bottle of cognac that they had 'found' somewhere along the way, and sent it on ahead to wait for the troops at prearranged meeting points along their route. And so they made their way towards the city centre.

Schmid knew it was his duty to find someone who could allocate them to a defence line, but there was no one to ask. They encountered several other flak troops in the same situation. At a time when the defences were screaming for men, the city was full of troops marching in all directions, looking for something to do. Mostly, however, they were marching west, hoping that somehow they just might be able to find the Americans, though they all knew this was nonsense – it was rumoured everywhere that the Russians had already encircled the city. Even when they arrived at the Air Ministry in Leipzigerstrasse, Schmid could find no one to tell him where he could go, or what he could do.

After a short rest for food in the Tiergarten, interrupted by Soviet shells landing around them, Schmid decided to move on. He knew that Spandau had been designated as an assembly point for units that had lost contact, and prepared to march there, though it was another seven or eight miles west. But they got no further than the Zoo station, where they encountered closed barricades and were turned back. As they did so, a column of German tanks appeared from the west. The commander of one, a young SS lieutenant, told Schmid they had found their way through American lines to return to the capital, on the personal orders of the Führer. To Schmid it was quite Kafkaesque to see these enthusiastic, brave young men, preparing to commit suicide for Hitler.

Schmid stood his own men down, then made contact with his divisional headquarters in the flak tower. They told him to stay there overnight. In the morning, someone would decide what to do with them.

## 15

BERLIN WAS nearly lost within the embrace of the Russian bear. By the end of the day, the squeeze would begin. There were now no fewer than nine complete Soviet armies engaged in the giant encirclement operation, with Zhukov's forces moving in from the north, east and south-east, and Koniev's poised to advance from the south and south-west.

During the day, Zhukov rapidly extended his grip on the northern outskirts of the city, sending the Forty-Seventh Army, backed up by the IXth Guards Tank Corps, in a great lunge to seal off Berlin from the north. His tanks fought across the Havel near Hennigsdorf, then prepared to strike south to link up with Lelyushenko's Fourth Guards Tank Army, which was driving north from Potsdam. Only twenty miles now separated the two fronts. When they linked up, the capital would be locked in tight, with no hope of relief.

To the south-east of the city, the two fronts were also close to joining up. Chuikov's men were in the suburbs, and his left wing reached the Dahme during the afternoon. From Koniev's front, Rybalko's Third Guards Tank Army, smashing its way northwards, was barely seven miles away.

Those armies that were not still racing round the perimeter were busily reorganizing for their plunge into the heart of the city. With each corps holding at least one full division in reserve, they divided into battle groups and assault detachments, specially designed for street fighting. Most groups were composed of an infantry company plus two or three 76 mm guns, a couple of 45 mm guns, a few tanks or self-propelled guns, two or three platoons of sappers and a flame-thrower platoon. The flame throwers were widely used against bunkers and strong points, turning the occupants into screaming, flaming torches. Alongside and behind them, they were supported by massed artillery and Katyusha rocket launchers, while the air force flew continually overhead, striking when and where they chose.

AT 9 AM the Berlin fire chief, Police Major-General Walter Goldbach, received orders to send 1,400 fire engines out of the city to preserve them from destruction. In fact, there were only about 700 operational engines left in the city. They could do little about the numerous fires started by the non-stop bombardment, but they could and did rescue people from the ruins. At noon the order was rescinded, but by that time most of the crews from the eastern part of the city were already well on their way, mostly on the roads to Hamburg or Brunswick. Those in the central and western districts had been too busy to stop work, and were still hard at it.

Later that morning the city's telegraph office closed for the first time since 1832, when it was started by an Englishman called Watson with a mechanical semaphore system. And the last commercial flight left Tempelhof airport, carrying nine passengers to Stockholm.

THE EASTERN suburb of Kaulsdorf, from which Weidling had just moved his headquarters, was coming under heavy artillery attack. Pastor Grüber got on his bicycle and rode through the shells to visit his parishioners in their bunkers and cellars, offering comfort and prayer. In most places he conducted a short service, consisting of a lesson, a hymn and the Lord's Prayer. 'I believe,' he wrote later, 'that these services meant more to the congregation than all the pastoral care I had given them for a whole year.' As the intensity of the attack grew, more and more of Grüber's flock were killed or wounded.

By afternoon, the Soviets were fighting the remaining SS men in the streets, but Grüber refused to take cover: he could not bear listening to the screams and moans of wounded civilians. He pleaded with a Soviet officer to allow him and a deaconess from his church to move around from cellar to cellar, dressing the wounds of injured civilians. They were given permission – but warned that if they were caught spying they would be shot. Grüber and his woman helper dodged shells and bullets for the rest of the day, tending to the injured until their bandages and first-aid supplies ran out.

When the fighting stopped, Soviet troops began entering cellars and shelters. Once they had confirmed that there were no soldiers, they turned to demanding watches from all those present. To everyone's surprise, they did not touch a single woman. There was none of the wholesale rape that was so dreaded – but these were front-line troops, disciplined and well turned out, even for the most part neatly shaved. The brutalized second-echelon men were still to come.

WEIDLING HAD set up his new corps headquarters in the basement of an old people's home at Wuhlheide, on the right bank of the Spree in east Berlin. The area was under constant shelling, but Colonel Wöhlermann was horrified to see many children still playing in the street. He tried to convince one of the mothers of the danger, but got short shrift. 'This good woman,' he wrote, 'a dyed-in-the-wool Berliner, placed her brawny arms akimbo and said: "Come off it, them little bangs don't mean a thing. We've got used to much bigger than that."'

Weidling called all his senior officers, from regimental commander upwards, to a special council of war during the day. He had something important to discuss with them. Although he had still not managed to re-establish two-way communications with the higher commands, he had received signals from Busse and Hitler, neither of whom knew where LVIth Corps actually was. Both were threatening to have him shot – Hitler if he did not instantly move the corps further into the city, Busse if he did not immediately move south-east to link up with the Ninth Army. As far as the officers were concerned, the choice was easy. 'All of us agreed,' said Wöhlermann, 'that bringing the Panzer corps into that inhabited heap of ruins with all its tank traps would lead to the certain and pointless destruction of the entire corps.'

Having decided not to obey Hitler's orders, however, there was little Weidling could do to comply with Busse's, either. The Soviet forces had completely surrounded the main body of the Ninth Army, and were steadily pushing LVIth Corps back towards the city. Shortly after his council of war finished, Weidling was forced to abandon his headquarters again. Rather than move back into the city, he relocated about four miles south-west, at Rudow.

# 16

HITLER HAD come down from his high of the previous day, and was now suffering the reaction to his euphoria. He may also have been suffering drug withdrawal symptoms, without his daily dose of amphetamine: he had dismissed Morell from the bunker that morning, after the doctor had offered him an injection of morphine to calm him. Hitler had suspected Morell of wantıng to knock him out so that he could be removed from Berlin and flown to Berchtesgaden. When Keitel arrived for the daily conference at 3 pm, he sensed at once that 'leaden clouds lay heavily over the atmosphere'. Hitler's face was a yellowish-grey and his expression was stony. He was nervy, and unable to concentrate. Twice during the conference he got up and wandered into his private room next door.

Communications were so bad that Keitel and Jodl knew virtually nothing of the military position. It was left to Krebs to make the situation report, which could hardly have been grimmer, particularly around Berlin. With the noose tightening every minute, Koniev's forces had now taken the German army's biggest and most important munitions depot at Jüterbog, containing most of its dwindling reserves of arms and ammunition. And although Heinrici had at last been given permission at 12.30 pm for the Ninth Army to make a partial withdrawal, it had come too late: Busse's army was now trapped, with the exception of his strongest remaining force, the LVIth Panzer Corps – which was missing. There was a rumour that Weidling had pulled out his corps and retreated with it to the Olympic village at Döberitz, on the western side of Berlin. A general was dispatched to Döberitz to find and arrest him.

Hitler seemed barely to listen to all this. But when Krebs began describing the situation north of Berlin, he suddenly took an interest. Where, he asked, was Steiner's army detachment? What progress was his attack making? Hesitantly, Krebs told him Steiner had not even given the orders for an attack to begin. For a moment, there was an ominous silence. Icily, Hitler ordered everyone except Keitel, Krebs, Jodl, Burgdorf and Bormann to leave the room. Then he went berserk. He leapt to his feet and began to rant and rave. His face turned first white and then purple. His limbs shook uncontrollably. The men with him had seen him angry before, but they had never seen him like this. His voice cracked as he screamed and cursed them all for cowardice, treachery, incompetence, insubordination, disloyalty. Even the SS now told him lies. At the climax of his wild outburst, he yelled: 'The war is lost! Everything is falling apart.'

Regaining some control, he cried that he would stay in Berlin, with the Berliners. He would lead the final battle himself, in person – and when the last moments came, he would shoot himself. 'Alive or dead, I shall not fall into the hands of the enemy,' he declared. 'I can no longer fight on the battlefield; I'm not strong enough. I shall kill myself.'

Then, quite suddenly, his rage evaporated and he began to crumple. Slowly, he sank back into his chair, collapsing into himself. Shrunken, deflated, he began to cry like a small child. 'It's all over,' he sobbed. 'The war is lost. I shall shoot myself.'

For almost five minutes the others stood watching him, silent and embarrassed. Then, incredibly, they tried to persuade him that there was still hope, that he must remain in charge of the nation, that he must move out of

Berlin to Berchtesgaden, and continue directing the war from there. He rejected their appeals. They could leave him, he said bitterly, they could all leave Berlin, but he would stay. 'I order an immediate radio proclamation to the people of Berlin,' he continued, 'of my resolve to remain with them to the end, whatever may happen.'

Dismayed by Hitler's collapse, Keitel asked to speak to him with only Jodl present. But Jodl was called away to the phone, so the two men were left alone together. Keitel began trying to reason with Hitler, telling him there were two options open before Berlin became 'a battleground of house-to-house street fighting': 'We either have to offer to surrender, or escape by flying out to Berchtesgaden by night to commence surrender negotiations from there.' Hitler interrupted before he could get any further.

'I know what you're going to tell me,' he said. 'The decision has got to be taken now. I have already taken my decision. I will never leave Berlin again; I will defend the capital with my dying breath. Either I direct the battle for the Reich capital – if Wenck can keep the Americans off my back and throw them back across the Elbe – or I shall go down with my troops in Berlin, fighting for the symbol of the Reich.'

Keitel told him this was madness. 'I am obliged to demand that you fly to Berchtesgaden this very night, to ensure the continuity of command over the Reich and the armed forces, which cannot be guaranteed in Berlin, where communications might be severed any minute.'

'There is nothing to stop you flying to Berchtesgaden at once,' Hitler replied. 'In fact, I order you to do so. But I myself am going to remain in Berlin.'

Jodl returned, and joined Keitel in refusing to fly out without Hitler. The main cable to the south had already been cut in the Thüringian forest, he explained, and if communications with Berlin were to break down altogether there would be no possibility of directing the operations of the army groups still fighting in the centre, west and south of Germany, and in Croatia and Italy. The split command arrangement for north and south would have to come into effect at once, with Dönitz in the north and Hitler in the south.

In response, Hitler called Bormann back into the room, and ordered the three men to fly out that night. Keitel was to take command of the armed forces in the south, with Göring acting as Hitler's personal deputy. All three refused to go.

'In seven years, I have never refused to obey an order from you,' Keitel said, 'but this is one order I shall never carry out. You cannot and should not leave the Wehrmacht in the lurch at a time like this.'

'I am staying here,' Hitler replied obdurately. 'And that is that. If there has to be any negotiating with the enemy, as there has to be now, then Göring is better at that than I am. Either I fight and win the battle of Berlin – or I am killed in Berlin. That is my final and irrevocable decision.'

There was clearly no point in continuing the argument. Keitel announced that he would drive to see Wenck at his headquarters immediately, cancel all previous orders, and direct him to march on Berlin at once, to link up with the Ninth Army. He would report back to Hitler at noon next day, and they would plan ahead then. Hitler agreed on the spot. 'Obviously,' wrote Keitel afterwards, 'it brought him a degree of deliverance from the frankly horrifying position in which he had put both himself and us.'

After fortifying himself for the journey with a bowl of thick pea soup, and collecting a hamper of sandwiches and cognac ordered from the kitchen for him by Hitler, Keitel set out to find Wenck. Jodl stayed behind to put in hand the arrangements for the transfer of the remaining OKW and OKH staff to Berchtesgaden. He also visited Steiner, to help organize his planned counter-attack from Oranienburg.

WORD OF Hitler's outburst and collapse had been passed swiftly to all the Nazi chieftains not in the bunker. In telephone call after telephone call during the afternoon and evening they all spoke to Hitler, entreating him to fly out to the south, to save both himself and Berlin. Dönitz phoned from his new headquarters at Plön, some fourteen miles south-east of Kiel, promising to send more naval troops to help defend Berlin. Ribbentrop called to offer hope of a great diplomatic coup that would solve everything even then. Himmler made an impassioned speech over the phone, and then sent two of his subordinates to assure Hitler of his support and to offer him his personal SS escort squad of 600 men. But Himmler did not go himself – 'They're all mad in Berlin,' he declared. 'What am I to do?'

Despite all his later protestations, Albert Speer was still under Hitler's spell. When he heard about the collapse he didn't telephone, but set off at once from his estate at Bad Wilsnack, north-west of Berlin, to see his idol for one last time. It took him ten hours. He started by car, on roads jammed solid with refugees, trucks and Berlin fire engines heading for Hamburg, but had to abandon that as hopeless. Then, in spite of the desperate shortage of aircraft and fuel, he persuaded Luftwaffe contacts to provide him with a plane and a fighter escort to Gatow, from where he flew on in a Fiesler Storch to the East–West Axis, putting down before the Brandenburg Gate on the landing strip he had tried to prevent. There was no useful purpose to the trip. It was purely personal: Speer could not bear the thought that Hitler would die without his having said a proper farewell. He also felt the need to confess his sins in sabotaging the Führer's scorched earth orders, and in publicly stating that the war was lost. He felt the trip had been worthwhile when Hitler apparently forgave him, and he flew out again, gratified by his absolution.

THE ONE paladin who did not seek to persuade Hitler to leave was Goebbels. Consumed as always by his thirst for the grand dramatic gesture, he was resolved that the Führer should go out, literally, in a blaze of glory like a mythical Nordic warrior. He would go with him, for he was determined to die in Berlin, the city he believed he had made his own. He planned the same fate for Magda and the children. 'My wife and family are not to survive me,' he had told Albert Speer earlier. 'The Americans would only coach them to make propaganda against me.' Knowing this, Hitler now invited Goebbels and his family to move into the bunker with him. They arrived in two cars, each of the six children clutching the one toy they had been allowed to take.

Magda and the children were given Dr Morell's old suite of four small rooms in the upper bunker. Goebbels had a room in the deep bunker, alongside the Führer. The children regarded the whole thing as a huge adventure. They liked 'Uncle Adolf' and were delighted when Traudl Junge took them upstairs into the ruined chancellery building, to find the boxes of presents that had been sent to Hitler on his birthday. They were allowed to pick out what they wanted, and take the things back downstairs. They had been told by their parents that they would soon be given injections so that they would not get sick.

HITLER, MEANWHILE, devoted himself to sorting out his papers and documents. Those he no longer wanted were burned in the chancellery garden. Those to be kept for posterity were packed into metal boxes and taken to airfields around Berlin, along with the forty or so members of staff who had opted to leave. They were flown out that night in ten aircraft, nine of which reached Munich safely, though ground staff at Gatow delayed some departures by scattering baggage on the runway as a protest against this privileged departure. The aircraft carrying Hitler's documents crashed *en route*, killing all the crew except for the rear gunner. The chests of documents disappeared, to become one of the abiding legends of the Third Reich.

# 17

FEARFUL THAT he might lose the race for Berlin at the last hurdle, Zhukov was anxiously watching Koniev's progress. Chuikov and Katukov were to be his standard bearers. On 22 April, Lenin's birthday, he gave them categorical orders to force the Spree and be in the southern districts of Tempelhof, Steglitz and Marienfelde not later than Tuesday, 24 April. Bogdanov and his Second Guards Tank Army were to drive for

Charlottenburg and the western districts. Zhukov ordered them all to mount round-the-clock operations, with assault squads fighting by night as well as day.

Chuikov responded quickly. As night fell, some of his units made an unexpected breakthrough near Köpenick, where the River Spree is joined by the wider Dahme. Advancing through woodland from the direction of the Berlin ring road, Captain Afanasy Semakin and his 2nd Rifle Battalion suddenly came upon an enemy company dug in to prevent any crossing of the Spree. Without waiting for artillery or tank support – in fact, without waiting for anything – Semakin and his men charged the enemy defences. The Soviet troops poured out of the woods on three sides of the Germans, overwhelming them in savage hand-to-hand fighting, taking 100 prisoners and destroying three armoured personnel carriers.

A few hundred yards further on, they came to the banks of the river. Again without waiting, they slipped into the water and swam across in the darkness, poor swimmers using improvised rafts, to fall upon the unsuspecting Germans on the far bank. 'They rose up before us like ghosts!' said one captured German officer. Pressing on again, virtually unopposed, Semakin crossed the peninsula between the two rivers, and was soon on the banks of the Dahme. Again, the battalion swam across, to establish a foothold on the western bank, paving the way for the rest of the division to pour over the river and consolidate the success.

Other units were luckier in that they did not have to swim at all. The XXVIIIth and XXIXth Guards Rifle Corps came across a fleet of pleasure craft – skiffs, rowing boats, motor boats, dinghies – and several large barges tied up on the bank of the Spree. Without waiting for further orders they piled into them and used them to cross first the Spree and then the Dahme. By dawn, they had taken the suburb of Falkenberg.

The commander of the 82nd Division, Major-General Mikhail Duka, a tough ex-partisan fighter, took matters into his own hands when he reached the river bank with his forward units. Seeing his scouts hesitate, he promptly took off his own tunic and boots and made a perfect swallow dive into the icy water. He swam quickly across, then returned with two rowing boats he had found on the other side. His men swiftly followed his example, and the division was soon across, without casualties.

Further to the right, in Köpenick itself, the 39th Rifle Division did even better. After a short fight they captured the town's two bridges intact, and crossed both rivers complete with all their artillery and armour. During the rest of the night, engineers constructed pontoon bridges to speed up the flow of men and equipment. The last major natural obstacle between Zhukov's left wing and the city centre had been cleared.

Zhukov's right wing, meanwhile, was making rapid progress. The Forty-Seventh, Sixty-First, and First Polish Armies were driving hard across the north of Berlin. The Sixty-First, on the extreme northern flank, crossed the Oder-Havel canal below Manteuffel's Third Panzer Army, to cut it off completely from Steiner's army detachment and the other scattered elements of Army Group Vistula.

During the night of 22–23 April the First Polish Army, supported by artillery, rocket launchers and aircraft, attacked Oranienburg, and the centre of Steiner's beleaguered force. Steiner was desperately short of troops – most of the reinforcements he had been promised had failed to arrive – and was unable to man the line of the Havel south of the town. All he had to throw into the battle were two newly arrived battalions of the 3rd Naval Division, the only ones who had managed to get through from the coast, and local Volkssturm and Hitler Youth.

One of those boys of the Hitler Youth, Helmut Altner, described afterwards how he and his friends had been fetched from their homes and attached to SS and Volkssturm units. 'We first saw action to the north-east of the town,' he wrote in his diary.

> Most of us were killed by infantry fire, because we had to attack across open fields. Then the fighting in the town – two days of it. In two days and nights, Oranienburg changed hands four times. That finished another part of us. Then the Russians started bombarding the town with Stalin Organs, and when we wanted to finish and go home, we were stopped and made to join the escape across the canal. My platoon leader, who refused, was strung up on the nearest tree by a few SS and an SA man – but then, he was already fifteen years old.

The Forty-Seventh Army crossed the Havel at Hennigsdorf, meeting only light resistance and finding the main bridge intact. They could now wheel left and strike south around the west of the city. By evening they had advanced another fifteen miles, bringing their right flank to the outskirts of Nauen, about nine miles due west of the city, while the left flank units closed up to the defences of Spandau and Gatow airfield. They were now less than fifteen miles away from meeting the forward units of Koniev's front, advancing north-west from Potsdam, to complete the encirclement of the city.

KONIEV'S OTHER spearheads, hammering their way into the city from the south and south-west, were now meeting stiffer opposition. Rybalko's Third Guards Tank Army had been halted at the Teltow Canal. This arterial waterway, forty to fifty yards wide and ten feet deep, runs right across the southern half of the city to join the Havel at Babelsberg. For much of its length its steep concrete banks turn it into a broad moat lined with warehouses and factories, some with walls three feet thick, like medieval ramparts. The bridges had all been blown, and the attackers could clearly see lines of trenches, pill-boxes and tanks buried in the ground up to their turrets. Koniev decided to take no chances. He ordered up his heavy guns to join the rest of the artillery along the southern bank of the canal to form an unimaginable concentration of firepower to blast away the obstacles. During the next day, he lined up 1,050 guns for every mile of front.

Koniev believed that he was faced by 15,000 well-armed troops. In fact, at that time there were only a few scattered Volkssturm companies, with minimal weapons. Volkssturm Lieutenant von Reuss, in charge of a platoon of one such company, the only complete unit in the sector, described the defences as a few trenches, with machine-gun emplacements at 600-yard intervals hastily thrown together from concrete slabs. The sector's artillery consisted of two anti-aircraft guns and one rocket launcher. Reuss's own platoon was armed with one Czech-made machine gun, which seized up the first time it was fired, and an assortment of foreign rifles. The neighbouring Volkssturm platoon packed up and went home for the night after its first engagement with the enemy, returning in the morning to continue the fight.

WHILE KONIEV fumed at the delay, Stalin issued new orders to the three fronts involved in Operation Berlin. Now that Zhukov had outflanked it on the north, Rokossovsky was no longer needed for the final assault on the city. He was to revert to his subsidiary role of protecting Zhukov's flank, while pushing on westwards to destroy German forces in and around Stettin and drive Manteuffel's Third Panzer Army and Steiner's two divisions into the arms of the British.

Stalin now defined the new boundary between Koniev's and Zhukov's fronts – a vital precaution if they were not to find themselves fighting each other by accident now that they were close. Stavka directive number 11074 was decisive. It carried the line on from Lübben, where it had previously ended, into the city through Mariendorf, due south of Tempelhof, right through to the Anhalter station. Its end left Koniev's front just 150 yards to the west of the Reichstag, the ultimate Soviet target. The final prize was to go to Zhukov, after all, though for some reason Stalin chose not to tell him for the moment – no doubt he wanted to squeeze the last drops of advantage from the competition between the rival marshals.

# 18

As THE Soviet forces moved in on Berlin, they released thousands of prisoners from camps in the outer parts of the city. Some were slave labourers, others were foreign workers or prisoners of war. When Soviet troops approached, the guards fled. The Soviets swept past the camps, pausing only to drop off food and drink, and to collect and arm any Russian prisoners, who found themselves instantly drafted back into active service as second-echelon troops.

In the jails in central Berlin, political prisoners were still being held, still being tried, and still being executed. At last, however, there seemed to be a ray of hope: twenty-one prisoners, mostly from religious groups like the Jehovah's Witnesses, were released from the Lehrterstrasse Prison during the day of 22 April. At night, another sixteen men were called from their cells and handed back their personal possessions. Among them were Klaus Bonhoeffer, Rüdiger Schleicher and Albrecht Haushofer. They were told they were being transferred to another prison, ready for release. After being kept standing in line for an hour and a half, they were marched up the steps and out of the door. Outside, it was raining. The darkness was broken by the glow of burning buildings all around, and artillery fire echoed through the ruins. An SS officer with a flashlight attached to his belt warned them that anyone who attempted to escape would be shot, then he gave the order to march. The column set off along the rubble-strewn street, an SS man holding a gun on each prisoner.

In the Invalidenstrasse they were led from the street into the remains of the Ulap exhibition hall, supposedly to take a short cut through it. Once inside, the SS guards suddenly grabbed the men by the collar, shoving them forward to stand with their faces against a wall, the cold barrel of a gun pressing into the back of each neck. There was a volley of shots. Sixteen bodies fell to the ground. The SS men left them lying there. Amazingly, one man, Herbert Kosney, a former member of a communist resistance group, survived to drag himself away and tell the tale. He had moved his head at the fateful moment, and the bullet had passed right through his neck.

When the bodies of the others were found three weeks later, Haushofer's fingers were still clutching a tattered sheaf of papers, on which were some of the sonnets he had written during his years of imprisonment. One fragment read: 'There are times when only madness reigns / And then it is the best that hang . . .'

# 19

KEITEL ARRIVED back at Krampnitz at 11 am on Monday, 23 April, exhausted after his journey to and from Wenck's headquarters. He had had a hard time finding Wenck, who was installed in a gamekeeper's cottage deep in the Wiesenburg forest east of Magdeburg. He had ordered him to turn his army about and drive east to save Berlin and the Führer. Wenck had not argued, and even dictated an order to his army on the spot, so that Keitel could take a copy back with him for Hitler. Keitel then departed as quickly as possible – Wenck thought this was the closest he had ever been to a front line in his life, but of course central Berlin was then even closer. On his way back, Keitel called on as many divisional commanders as possible, to pep them up for the tasks ahead, strutting around mouthing empty exhortations and demanding impossible actions.

As soon as Keitel had gone, Wenck called his staff together and told them he had no intention of leading them into Berlin. He would hold on to his positions on the Elbe as an escape route to the west, drive as close to the capital as possible, and try for a link-up with the Ninth Army, in order to get out every soldier and civilian who could make it. If they were to be taken prisoner, as they undoubtedly were, he knew which side he wanted as his captors.

KEITEL HAD no inkling of Wenck's real intentions. Back in Berlin, he snatched an hour's sleep before the afternoon conference, where he proudly presented Wenck's order to the Twelfth Army to Hitler. Hitler had regained his composure. He was ready to hear good news – and the news that Wenck was about to ride to the rescue was as good as it could be. Had contact been established yet between the Ninth and Twelfth Armies? he asked. No one could tell him. Communications with Busse were still in confusion. Hitler ordered Krebs to tell Busse to make contact with the Twelfth Army at once, and to 'mop up the enemy forces between them'. Then, exuberantly, he dictated a message to the troops of the Twelfth Army:

*Führer's Order, 23 April 1945*

Soldiers of Wenck's Army!
At this crucial hour, you are being called away from battle against our

368

western enemies and set marching eastwards. Your task is clear: Berlin must remain German. The objectives you have been given must be achieved at all costs. Other units are advancing from the opposite direction, with the common object of saving the capital and inflicting a decisive defeat on the Bolsheviks. Berlin will never surrender to Bolshevism. The defenders of the capital have found renewed courage at the news of your swift approach and are fighting on bravely in the knowledge that they will soon hear the roar of your guns. Your Führer has summoned you, and you have gone into the attack as in the days of conquest. Berlin is waiting for you! Berlin longs for you with all its heart!

Goebbels seized on the order eagerly. He had copies of it circulated throughout the city as leaflets, and printed it prominently in the newspapers that were still appearing, alongside announcements confirming that Hitler was still in Berlin, and was directing the battle in person. He also had similar messages broadcast on the radio:

Hitler is with you! Hitler is with you! Hold out, Berliners! The reserves of the Reich are on the way. Not just the reserves of a fortress, but the reserves of our great Reich are rolling towards Berlin. The first reinforcements arrived in the early hours of today: anti-tank gun after anti-tank gun, tank after tank, rumbled through the streets in long columns. The troops that man them understand the gravity of the hour.

Supposed eye-witness reports were thrown in for good measure:

'Approaching Berlin I can see the huge fires in the centre, and hear the boom of the Russian artillery. Grenades and shells whistle through the air. Flames light up the night. The guns are rumbling in this hellish battle. Our Führer is under shell fire!'

'Up, Berliners, and rally round the Führer! As a tower of strength he is amongst us at this critical hour in the history of the Reich capital. Those who desert him are swinish cowards.'

'Berlin trusts the Führer! Berlin fights on, though the hour is grave!'

Goebbels's rallying cries may have fooled a few thousand gullible citizens, though with no electric power only those with battery-operated sets could hear the radio messages. But the word spread quickly enough, and for most Berliners it was a clear signal that the crisis was now out of control. If Hitler went on refusing to leave or surrender, the city would be under siege, and no one could tell how long it would last.

For the general population, there was no way out. Goebbels had teams of Feld Gendarmerie, police and SS setting up roadblocks in the western suburbs to stop people fleeing, while others worked their way through cellars and shelters, combing out men who could still stand, no matter how old or young, and searching for deserters. One of the most fearsome of these twentieth-century witch-finders was a one-legged SS Hauptscharführer (sergeant-major), who stumped through the streets, machine pistol at the ready, a gang of thugs at his heels. When they found any man who looked fit enough to fight, or whom they didn't like the look of, they would drag him out of the shelter, shove a rifle into his hands, and order him straight to the front. Anyone who hesitated was shot.

Women, small children, the old and infirm, could stay huddled in their squalid shelters, but they began to fear starvation almost as much as they feared bombs, shells, the Russians and the SS. Everyone knew there were great supplies of food stored in warehouses, and locked in freight wagons in the rail marshalling yards. On 23 April, they decided to do something about it.

Ludwig von Hammerstein, the officer who had escaped the Gestapo after the 20 July plot, was still living in the back room of the Kerp family pharmacy at 36 Oranienstrasse in Kreuzberg. As long as there was electricity he and the Kerps had kept in touch with reality through radio news from London, Beromünster and Moscow. Now, like everyone else, they had only rumours to go by. Today, the rumour was that there was food for the taking – the warehouses in the east harbour, only a few hundred yards from the Kerps' shop, had been thrown open for plundering. Crowds surged from the shelters, braving shells and bombs to storm the docks. There were wild scenes as normally respectable folk battled over the loot. People staggered back along Oranienstrasse hauling churns of butter and sides of beef. Mother Kerp dug into her savings to buy butter and lard from looters.

Hammerstein braved the streets to go in search of more. But he was too late. The Warschauer bridge over the Spree, leading to the warehouses on the east bank, had been closed off and was about to be blown up. The charges were already in position. The only people now coming across from the other side were fleeing soldiers and exhausted youths of the 'Kinderflak' – Soviet troops were approaching fast. Hammerstein was horrified to see several dead bodies sprawled on the road, with cardboard signs from the SS on their chests reading 'We still have the power!' Some looters had been unlucky.

Elsewhere in the city there were similar scenes that morning, as crowds ransacked warehouses, freight trains and shops. Shopkeepers who had been hoarding food for sale on the black market were forced to hand it over without payment. The Karstadt department store was packed with people fighting and struggling to grab anything they could. Rumour had it that the SS had stored 29 million marks' worth of supplies in the basement, and were about to blow the place up to stop the Russians getting their hands on it. There were no sales assistants any more, but supervisors guarded the exits, stopping people taking out anything but food. Amazingly, even at such a time, the Berliners meekly accepted their authority and dropped furs, dresses, blankets and other goods on to the growing piles at each door. That afternoon, the SS fulfilled their threat and blew the store up with huge explosives charges, killing women and children in the process.

AT THE end of the brief conference, Keitel tried again to persuade Hitler to move out of Berlin. Once again he received a blank refusal. This time, however, Hitler was perfectly calm and lucid. It was vital, he said, for him to remain, for the very knowledge that he was there would inspire his troops with a determination to stand fast, and would stop the people panicking. The success of the operations now in hand for the relief of Berlin, and in the battle that would follow for the city itself, depended entirely on his presence. There was only one factor that would determine the outcome: the people's faith in him. East Prussia had held out as long as he had his headquarters in Rastenburg, but had collapsed as soon as he had 'failed to support it with his presence'. The same would happen in Berlin, therefore he would not leave. He would not break his pledge to the army and to the city's population.

Hitler announced that he would personally direct the battle for Berlin in a fight to the finish. After one day as commandant of Fortress Berlin, Major-General Kaether was a colonel again, and out of a job.

BEFORE HE left, Keitel managed to get Hitler to himself. With the danger of finding himself cut off from the Führer bunker at any moment, he needed to know if any peace negotiations had been started. Hitler tried to evade the issue by saying it was still too early to talk of surrender. Keitel, who had a pretty good idea of what was really going on, pressed him again. Hitler insisted that it was always better to negotiate after one had achieved some local victory: in this instance, the 'local victory' would be the battle for Berlin. When Keitel said he was not satisfied with this answer, Hitler finally said he had been putting out peace feelers to Britain via Italy for some time, and had summoned Ribbentrop that very day to discuss the next steps. He would say no more, except that he would certainly not be the one to lose his nerve.

Keitel drove back to Krampnitz with Jodl, thoroughly depressed. Hitler had clearly decided Berlin was to be his funeral pyre, and there was nothing they could do about it. The bunker sycophants like Bormann, Burgdorf, Goebbels and the SS adjutants, backed by the SS guards, would never allow them to move him out by force. Jodl felt their only hope was Göring – he had sent General Koller to Berchtesgaden the previous night, to tell Göring about Hitler's collapse and to ask him to intervene. They would have to wait for his response.

When they arrived at Krampnitz, the two chiefs were in for another shock. The whole OKW was moving out again. There had been reports of Soviet cavalry patrols scouting nearby, and the staff had panicked. The camp commandant – 'this hysterical gentleman', as Keitel described him – had already blown up the vast ammunition dump nearby, which had contained most of Berlin's remaining reserves.

Jodl discovered a camp that had been built for Himmler at Neu Roofen, a small village in the woods not far from Ravensbrück concentration camp, about forty miles north of Berlin, which would suit the OKW admirably. It was empty and unused, and came complete with signals and communications equipment. What was more, it was well on the way to Lübeck, which was in the path of the British advance. Leaving Jodl to supervise the evacuation, Keitel hurried off to seek Wenck again, to urge him to speed up his rescue operation.

# 20

WEIDLING HAD been forced to move his headquarters yet again during the night of 22–23 April. He was now in Rudow, barely two miles from Chuikov, and well inside the city limits. At long last he had managed to re-establish communications with OKH and with Busse by using the public telephone system, which was still working. Busse's chief of staff, Major-General Hölz, ordered him to move his corps south, cutting through the Soviet ring to link up with the northern flank of the Ninth Army near Königs Wusterhausen.

Weidling was greatly relieved to be ordered back, away from the city, and wasted no time issuing the orders. But while his troops were preparing to pull out, he set off for the centre, accompanied by his intelligence officer, Captain Kafurke. He had urgent personal business in the Führer bunker. He had been enraged to learn from Hölz that Hitler had ordered him to be shot for supposedly deserting his position and moving his corps to the old Olympic village at Döberitz, on the west of the city, and wanted to clear the matter up at once. The two men arrived at the chancellery at about 6 pm and were ushered through the underground warren, being passed from checkpoint to checkpoint and growing steadily more depressed at everything they saw, until they were finally ushered into the adjutants' bunker. Krebs and Burgdorf received them coolly.

Weidling pitched into them at once, demanding to know what the hell was going on. Why was there an execution order out for him? He could prove unequivocally that he had rarely been more than a mile from the front line for days, and as for moving his corps to Döberitz, it had never crossed his mind to do anything so damned stupid. The only people from his corps who could be in that part of Berlin were non-combat troops whom he had had to get out of the way to stop them being killed or captured – Turkish and Russian volunteers from a work battalion, sick and wounded, cooks, and so on, men whose presence at the front was interfering with the fighting. Under his blistering attack, Krebs and Burgdorf backed down. There had obviously been a misunderstanding, they said, trying to pacify him. They would clear things up with the Führer right away.

Before they went to see Hitler, however, they wanted to know the present position of the LVIth Corps. Weidling told them he had received orders from Busse to make a fighting withdrawal to Königs Wusterhausen, and that this would begin in about four hours. There was no time to lose, he added, for as he left his headquarters at Rudow, he had received a report that Soviet tank spearheads had been seen in the area. Krebs seized on this information. In that case, he said, Busse's order was cancelled. The LVIth Panzer Corps would have to concentrate on the defence of Berlin.

While Krebs and Burgdorf hurried away to speak to Hitler, Weidling sent his intelligence officer out to phone his chief of staff, Colonel Theodor von Dufving, to tell him their orders had been changed. Kafurke came back looking agitated. Dufving had been informed by teletype that Weidling was no longer in command of the corps. He had been replaced by General Burmeister.

Weidling was beside himself with fury. When Krebs and Burgdorf came back from Hitler he told them, with icy self-control, just what he thought of the irresponsible way he had been relieved of his command. They placated him again, promising that the offending order would be revoked. More immediately, however, Hitler wanted to speak to him.

Off they went again, through more corridors and more checkpoints, at the last of which Weidling's revolver and holster were taken away. They moved on, through a kitchen and the corridor that served as the SS officers' mess, then down into the lower bunker and Hitler's ante-room, where a number of men sat waiting. Among them was Ribbentrop.

They squeezed through into the private study. There, Weidling re-counted later,

Behind a table covered with maps sat the Führer of the German Reich. He turned his head as I entered. I saw a bloated face and delirious eyes. When he tried to stand up, I noticed to my horror that his hands and one of his legs were trembling. He managed to stand up with great difficulty. He offered me his hand. With a distorted smile and in a barely audible voice he asked whether we had met before.

When I replied that he had decorated me with the oak leaves to my Knight's Cross on 13 April 1944, he said: 'I recall the name, but I can't remember the face.' His own was like a grinning mask. He then laboriously got back into his armchair. Even while he was sitting down, his left leg kept twitching. His knee moved like the pendulum of a clock, only faster.

Hitler asked for a briefing on the LVIth Corps' position, and when Weidling had given it, he confirmed that the corps was to stay in Berlin and take over the southern and eastern defence sectors. He then expounded his plan for the relief of the city: he would pull in Wenck's army from the west, Busse's from the south-east, and Steiner's army detachment from the north. Somehow, these forces were to drive the Soviets back and cut them off. Weidling listened to the Führer's 'big talk' with growing astonishment. He knew the truth: 'Short of a miracle, the days until final defeat were numbered.'

Weidling returned to his headquarters with a heavy heart. That night, with severe losses, he managed to disengage his corps from the Soviet forces in the south, turned it and led it back into the graveyard that was Berlin.

BACK IN the bunker, there was fresh excitement. Hitler had received a cable from Göring:

> My Führer!
> In view of your decision to remain in the fortress of Berlin, do you agree that I take over at once the total leadership of the Reich, with full freedom of action at home and abroad, as your deputy, in accordance with your decree of 29 June 1941? If no reply is received by 2200 hours, I shall take it for granted that you have lost your freedom of action, and shall consider the conditions of your decree as fulfilled, and shall act in the best interests of our country and our people. You know what I feel for you in this gravest hour of my life. Words fail me to express myself. May God protect you, and speed you quickly here in spite of everything.
>
> Your loyal
> Hermann Göring

Göring's cable was perfectly sound and reasonable – given the entirely unreasonable circumstances. He had thought about the matter very carefully. He had discussed it with Hans Lammers, Hitler's closest legal adviser and head of the Reich chancellery, who had already flown to Munich. He had consulted his staff, and Koller, who had brought the news of Hitler's collapse together with Jodl's request for Göring to assume the responsibility which

Hitler was no longer capable of exercising. Jodl had told Koller of Hitler's remark that Göring would be better than him at negotiating with the Allies.

In fact, Göring's response was cautious, for he suspected it might all be a plot instigated by Bormann, to trick him into a premature takeover, in order to destroy him in Hitler's eyes. Even at that late hour, Hitler's lieutenants could not stop jockeying for position, each one seeking to become his successor. Göring had done everything he could to avoid his message reaching Bormann first; he sent it to Hitler personally, with duplicates to his own Luftwaffe liaison officer, Colonel von Below, and Keitel. But somehow Bormann got hold of it before anyone else, and persuaded Hitler that in spite of its abject servility it was actually treasonous.

Bormann's case was completed when a second radio message arrived from Göring, this time addressed to Ribbentrop, ordering the foreign minister to go to him on the Obersalzberg if he had heard nothing from Hitler by midnight. There could be only one reason for such a message: Göring intended to start peace talks right away.

With the second message, Hitler was convinced of Göring's guilt. Bormann had orders telegraphed to the Obersalzberg for the SS to arrest him. He was stripped of all his offices and titles, even that of the Reich's chief huntsman.

Unknown to either Hitler or Bormann, it was not Göring who was the traitor among the highest Nazis, but Himmler, '*der treue Heinrich*'. At the very moment when the orders for Göring's arrest were being sent, Himmler and Schellenberg were meeting Count Bernadotte in the Swedish consulate in Lübeck. 'The Führer's great life is drawing to its close,' Himmler told Bernadotte, explaining that he now felt he was released from his oath. He, Himmler, saw himself as the new Führer. He authorized Bernadotte to communicate his offer of surrender to the Western Allies via the Swedish government. The German army would continue fighting the Soviets until the Allies advanced to relieve them. Bernadotte agreed to pass on the offer, and departed at once for Stockholm, leaving Himmler to ponder such vital questions as how he should greet Eisenhower, and what name he should give to his new government.

# 21

ALL THROUGH the day on 23 April, Max Buch had watched from his flat in Meineckestrasse as waves of Russian fighters flew across the clear sky overhead, followed by formations of from four to eight bombers. There was no sign of any German aircraft, only constant flak from the Zoo tower. Since dawn there had been the sound of uninterrupted gunfire getting steadily louder from the north-east, east and south. 'One has the feeling that Berlin is being surrounded,' he wrote in his diary.

On 24 April, the noise of fighting continued from the early morning, punctuated by the sound of shells whistling past in the direction of Charlottenburg. That morning, the last surviving regular newspapers, the *Deutsche Allgemeine Zeitung* and the *Völkischer Beobachter*, failed to appear. It was no great loss, for they had both shrunk to only half a sheet and any news they carried was already out of date. Berliners no longer needed a newspaper to tell them where the Russians were – they only had to use their own ears. However, the newspapers had been replaced by a new sheet, the *Panzerbär* ('Armoured Bear'). Subtitled 'Fighting News for the Defenders of Greater Berlin', it was published by the Wehrmacht, and handed out free by soldiers, to be read and passed on. It covered two days, and reported fighting in Lichtenberg, Niederschönhausen and Fürstenwalde. And in large, bold print it hammered out the same old warning that Goebbels had been shrieking for days: 'Anyone who tries to weaken our resistance or who spreads propaganda is a traitor and will be shot or hanged instantly. Signed: Adolf Hitler.'

WHAT THE *Panzerbär* did not know was that early that morning the Red Army had taken another significant step towards locking off the city. Troops of the XXVIIIth Corps, from Chuikov's Eighth Guards Army, were working their way across Schönefeld airfield to the south-east of the city when they suddenly came upon several Soviet tanks advancing from the opposite direction. The tanks belonged to Rybalko's Third Guards Tank Army, and formed the right wing of Koniev's First Ukrainian Front.

The unexpected meeting took Chuikov by surprise. It also came as a shock to Zhukov, who did not learn of it until later in the day. He had still not been told of the new demarcation line laid down by Stalin, and apparently did not know that his rival was already pushing into the city. When he first heard, he refused to believe it. He telephoned Chuikov and demanded details. How did Chuikov come to hear of the link-up? he wanted to know. Who reported it? Who saw Rybalko's tanks?

'The corps commander, General Ryzhov, reported it to me,' Chuikov told him.

Zhukov was silent for a moment, digesting the news. Then he querulously demanded that Chuikov send out reliable staff officers to make a careful check on precisely what units of the First Ukrainian Front were in the southeastern suburbs, the precise time they had reached the Berlin ring road, and what their objectives were. Chuikov dutifully sent out three officers, but a few hours later Zhukov's doubts were dispelled when Rybalko himself arrived at Chuikov's command post and spoke to him on the telephone.

Chuikov's army, operating in conjunction with the First Guards Tank Army, was ordered to wheel right to face the north-west. During the day of the 24th, his forces moved forward through Rudow, Buckow and Lichtenrade, where the railway line running north into the centre of the city formed the new boundary between the two fronts, into Mariendorf, to the southwest of Tempelhof. By the evening they had closed up to the line of the Teltow canal. There they halted, regrouped and prepared to cross the canal to strike at the centre.


KONIEV'S ASSAULT on his part of the Teltow canal met with mixed fortunes that day. He began as always with a fifty-minute artillery bombardment on German positions at 4.20 am. Great chunks of concrete and masonry were hurled into the air as heavy guns blasted the northern bank, raising a thick obliterating fog of dust. Into this, he launched the three corps forming the left flank of the Third Guards Tank Army. But the defenders had been changed during the night: Weidling had deployed what was left of the 20th Panzergrenadier Division in that sector, to strengthen the Volkssturm units.

The first of Koniev's formations to cross the canal on the right flank at Lankwitz, the IXth Mechanized Corps supplemented by the 61st Guards Division, was driven back by German tanks and infantry. Their bridgehead was eliminated, with heavy losses. On the left flank at Stahnsdorf, meanwhile, the VIIth Guards Tank Corps established a small foothold, but opposition was so fierce that they could not expand it. Again, the defenders took a heavy toll of Soviet troops. In the centre, however, near Teltow itself, the VIth Guards Tank Corps managed to get across and to establish a firm bridgehead. By 11 am they had a bridge over the canal, and could start getting guns and tanks across.

During the day, Koniev funnelled all three corps through the one bridgehead, and they began fanning out on the other side. German troops still fought back stubbornly, and it took Koniev's men the rest of the day to gain another one and a half miles to secure the southern part of Zehlendorf, suffering heavy casualties all the way. It was a stern reminder that taking the city was never going to be a pushover. But the Germans suffered, too, and the 20th Panzergrenadiers were forced back on to Wannsee island, where they were isolated from the remainder of the battle for Berlin.

# 22

KREBS HAD moved into the Führer bunker on 23 April, along with his adjutant, Bernd Freytag von Loringhoven, and his ADC, Gerhard Boldt, when the rest of the army general staff left the city to join Keitel, Jodl and the OKW at Neu Roofen. It was obvious that it would soon be impossible for anyone to travel between the new headquarters and the chancellery, and Hitler wanted his army chief on hand. Boldt and Freytag were not pleased to be given what amounted to a death sentence, but like good soldiers they accepted their orders and continued to do their duty. They were given a room in the upper bunker, divided in half by a curtain hanging from the ceiling. Krebs's bed was on one side, a two-tier bunk bed and two desks on the other for Boldt and Freytag.

Boldt's task was to prepare hourly reports on the situation in Berlin and Potsdam. Freytag dealt with the other battle areas where German troops were still fighting. They were awakened at about 5.30 on the morning of 24 April by five or six heavy shells landing uncomfortably close to the chancellery. By 6 am the shelling had settled down to a regular pattern, with heavy bursts every three minutes.

Boldt and Freytag started compiling their first report of the day. The bunker's only contact with the outside world, apart from messengers and officers arriving in person, was via one underground telephone cable. This was connected to the communications tower alongside the Zoo flak tower, where messages could be relayed by radio, telephone or teleprinter to other centres, including the new combined OKW/OKH headquarters at Neu Roofen. There, the radio depended on one aerial suspended from a barrage balloon. Boldt rang round the defence sectors, and got the same picture everywhere: after one hour's artillery bombardment the Soviets were attacking all around the north, east, and south of the city. Shortly afterwards, he received news that the one remaining main road out of Berlin to the west was under attack at Nauen. Freytag, meanwhile, had discovered that Manteuffel's Third Panzer Army was now completely cut off in the north.

\*

AT 10.30, KREBS and his two aides tramped through the underground passages to the conference room in the deep bunker. There had been so much damage to the roof of the upper tunnels that they had to make a wide detour through the bunker garage and other passageways. In several places the concrete roof had been holed by bombs and shells, and the floor was ankle deep in water, with wobbly planks laid down for walking. Their credentials were checked no fewer than six times, by SS sentries posted in pairs. They entered Hitler's bunker through a scullery and two narrow dining rooms crowded with SS men drinking coffee and brandy and eating big plates of open sandwiches. The SS men scarcely acknowledged the three army officers.

Formal daily conferences were now a thing of the past. In the study with Hitler were only Goebbels, looking gaunt and harried, and Bormann. Burgdorf joined them later. Hitler followed the situation reports on the map, tracing movements and positions with trembling fingers. When they were finished, he sat hunched gloomily in his chair for a moment, then started shouting at Krebs. The news from Manteuffel seemed to have hit him hardest. 'In view of the broad natural barrier formed by the Oder,' he yelled, stabbing shakily at the map, 'the Russian success against the Third Panzer Army can only be attributed to the incompetence of the German military leaders there!'

Krebs tried, albeit half-heartedly, to defend Manteuffel and the other generals, reminding Hitler that they only had mainly untrained and poorly armed emergency and Volkssturm units, while Rokossovsky and Zhukov had whole armies of crack troops. But Hitler would not listen to excuses. When Krebs said that in any case Manteuffel's reserves had been thrown into the battles for the north of Berlin, he stopped him with an irritable wave of his hand, and barked out a new order: 'The attack from the north of Oranienburg must be initiated by tomorrow at the latest. The Third Army will make use of all available forces for this offensive, ruthlessly depleting those sections of our front line that are not under attack. It is imperative that the link with Berlin from the north be restored by tomorrow evening. Have that passed on at once.'

Krebs nodded to Freytag, who left the room at once to issue the order. As he did so, Burgdorf casually mentioned that Steiner would be leading the attack. Hitler flared again, worse than before. Having already attacked the army, he now turned on the Waffen SS. 'Those arrogant, boring indecisive SS leaders are no good to me any more,' he screamed. 'I do no wish Steiner to continue in command there under any circumstances!'

IF STEINER and Manteuffel, two of his former golden boys, were in Hitler's bad books, it seemed that Weidling, the man he had wanted to have shot only the day before, was now being cast as the saviour of Berlin. Having spent the night deploying his corps in the southern and eastern defence sectors to which Krebs had assigned him, he was called back to the Führer bunker at 11 am. He

379

was waiting impatiently in the ante-room when Krebs emerged from the conference. Krebs greeted him affably.

'You made a very good impression on the Führer last night,' he told him. 'He has decided to appoint you commandant of the Berlin Defence Region forthwith.'

Stunned, Weidling could only retort bitterly, 'You might just as well have had me shot.' But then, recovering his composure, he accepted, on condition that he would have sole responsibility for the defence of the city – he did not want Goebbels and his like interfering. Krebs told him this was not possible, but that he would be directly and solely responsible to Hitler.

THE NEWS that Boldt collected in his hourly telephone calls to all the defence sectors grew steadily worse. Towards midday he heard that Soviet pressure had increased considerably from the south. An hour later he was told that Tempelhof airport was under Soviet artillery fire and could no longer be used. At 5 pm he learned that the city's only other functional airfield at Gatow was also under direct fire. Soviet T34 tanks had blocked the last main road to the west at Nauen. By evening, it was reported that the Ninth Army was under fierce attack and there was no longer any possibility of its breaking out of the ring to join up with Wenck's Twelfth Army. And from Twelfth Army itself came the news that it had been unable to make any move towards an assault on Berlin, though its XXth Corps had been organized into assault groups, and was successfully engaging the forward Soviet units.

# 23

THROUGH THE narrow corridor that remained around Nauen that morning, a band of about ninety determined men were making their way east into the city, to help defend Hitler. Led by SS Brigadeführer (Brigadier-General) Dr Gustav Krukenberg, most of them were not German but French, fanatical fighters from the recently disbanded Charlemagne Panzergrenadier Division of the Waffen SS. Krukenberg had received a personal order to report to the Führer bunker in Berlin, and these men had volunteered to accompany him.

At Wustermark, the next village after Nauen, they came under enemy fire. With the main road being raked with machine guns, Krukenberg led his men back through the side roads which he knew well from peacetime rambles in the area, pushing cautiously forward through quiet, wooded countryside. Near Ketzin, they discovered they were sandwiched between Soviet infantry advancing from both the north and south. The two Soviet units both halted and took cover when they saw them, unsure of who they were. Krukenberg and his men held their fire and slipped quietly through the gap – they had made it with only minutes to spare.

Ahead of them, Krukenberg remembered, was a massive sandstone bridge over a canal. To his relief, it was still standing. There was no sign of any defenders, though the local Volkssturm had erected rough barricades. But as the Frenchmen started to dismantle the barriers,, there was a violent explosion and the bridge erupted into thousands of pieces of stone, flying in all directions. Most of Krukenberg's men were badly bruised and battered. One, who had been standing alongside him, had his leg smashed. When the unit doctor had dressed the injury, Krukenberg had the man laid in one of their four vehicles, which he sent driving very slowly back between the Soviet troops, while the rest of the party scrambled across the remains of the bridge, to continue on foot.

On the other side they found three elderly Volkssturm men, who had blown the bridge, mistaking them for Russians – as far as they knew there were no other German troops in the area. They regarded the SS men with astonishment. 'Things being what they were,' Krukenberg wrote in his account of the incident, 'they could not understand how anybody could be foolish enough to try to get *into* the city!'

Krukenberg pressed on towards Berlin. During the whole thirty-mile march, the only German defence forces they saw were three Hitler Youths on bicycles, each carrying one Panzerfaust. The major bridges across the Havel and Lake Stössen on the Heerstrasse, part of the East–West Axis, were blocked but otherwise intact and unmanned. Krukenberg was shocked: 'I wondered what kind of defence we could possibly put up against surprise Russian attacks,' he wrote.

They reached the Olympic stadium at about 10 pm, where they discovered an abandoned Luftwaffe store, from which they obtained food, drink and chocolate. Leaving his men to rest after their long march, Krukenberg and his adjutant commandeered one of the cars parked at the stadium, and drove along the deserted East–West Axis to the Wilhelmstrasse. Again, they saw no troops, and no defence preparations of any kind. No one attempted to stop them. Even at the entrance to the bunker, the sentry simply waved them on when they asked for Krebs, and no one checked them as they made their way into the adjutants' bunker.

After a wait of three hours, Krukenberg finally got to see Krebs and Burgdorf, who were both amazed. 'During the past forty-eight hours,' Krebs told him, 'orders have gone out to a number of officers and units outside Berlin to report here without delay. You are the only one who has actually turned up.'

Krukenberg was to report to Weidling, who had specifically asked for him to take over command of the SS Nordland Panzergrenadier Division from Major-General Jürgen Ziegler. Ziegler, the man who had turned up late at Seelow after allowing his division to run out of fuel, had become a serious disciplinary problem. He resented having to serve under a Wehrmacht general, and was constantly attempting to remove his troops from the LVIth Panzer Corps and take them to join up with Steiner, or even to go to Himmler in Schleswig-Holstein.

As dawn broke on 25 April, Krukenberg left the bunker and drove back through the empty, undefended streets to the Olympic stadium. The sky was clear. In the half-hour before the daily artillery barrage opened up again, he thought west Berlin looked perfectly at peace. But the appearance was cruelly deceptive. Later that morning, at Ketzin, about eight miles north-west of Potsdam, the two outer wings of the First Ukrainian Front and the First Belorussian Front finally met. The encirclement of Berlin was complete.

That same day, sixty-five miles further south, units of Koniev's Fifth Guards Army made contact with men of the 69th Division, part of General Courtney H. Hodges's US First Army, at Torgau on the Elbe. Hitler's Reich was cut in two.

# PART SEVEN

# Götterdämmerung

# 1

As DAWN broke on the morning of 25 April, 464,000 Soviet troops, with 12,700 guns and mortars, 21,000 Katyusha multiple rocket launchers, and 1,500 tanks and self-propelled guns, stood ready and waiting to begin the final assault on the heart of Berlin. To the north, south, east and west, the Soviet spearheads were within four miles of Hitler's chancellery and the Reichstag. Supporting them, two whole Soviet air armies, with thousands of planes, were preparing to make their contribution to the forthcoming holocaust. Having surrounded the entire area of Greater Berlin, cutting off all hope of relief or rescue, the Soviet forces could now concentrate on the job of storming the inner city.

Despite their overwhelming superiority in numbers and arms, the Soviet commanders had no illusions about the magnitude of the task facing them. It is always easier to defend a city than to attack one – no general knew that better than Chuikov, the hero of Stalingrad. At Stalingrad, the Soviets had been defenders. Since then, they had had little experience of street fighting. They had never had to take a huge, well-defended modern city – the long haul across Russia, Belorussia, Ukraine, Poland and Germany had been a war of movement and manoeuvre. They had taken Warsaw, of course, but only after the Germans had withdrawn. They had never been through the hard, bitter slog of wresting a city from enemy hands, especially a city that Hitler promised would be defended street by street, with every house a fortress.

That was precisely the scenario Zhukov planned to avoid. He had no intention of getting trapped into a war of attrition, where his armies were forced to contest the city inch by inch, all the while suffering an arterial flow of casualties. He had seen what happened to Paulus's army in Stalingrad, and he was determined that Berlin was not going to become a Hitlergrad.

Before they crossed the Oder, Zhukov had insisted that all his assault troops should undergo special training in street fighting, so that at least they would know what to expect. Now they were in the city, he had them formed into special tactical assault groups. He and his staff devised a two-shift combat system, which allowed the assault to be continued day and night, maintaining the pressure on the overstretched defenders. The first wave fought from 0700 hours (Moscow time) until 1800 hours, when they stopped to rest for the night; the second wave then took over until next morning, stopping to sleep during the day.

In the event, the round-the-clock system operated more in theory than in practice. The troops and their commanders on the ground soon found that although the open spaces and streets were lit up at night by the flames of countless fires, it was simply not practicable trying to fight inside unlit buildings. They quickly reverted to sleeping at night, and used their vast numbers to enable assault squads to take breaks during the day, too.

These breaks were not universally popular, however. Vladimir Abyzov, the former aeronautical engineering student from Moscow who had watched the first guns firing on Berlin from Müncheberg, agreed with a companion who asked: 'What do we want these respites for? It would be better to move on.' Abyzov hated the breaks. They gave men time to think, time to remember their homes and their loved ones – and time to realize that although the end was near, nobody could be sure he would survive. With victory in sight, this was no time to take unnecessary chances, no time to die.

The troops had got used to street fighting as they advanced through the outer suburbs. For the most part, these consisted of individual houses set in their own gardens, with many parks and open spaces and *Schrebergärten* colonies with their neat little summerhouses and allotments. Closer to the centre, the density of the buildings increased, until by the time the advancing troops hit the old industrial districts like Wedding, they found themselves fighting among the vast five-storey blocks of nineteenth-century rental barracks, with their internal courtyards stretching back one after the other.

Along the way, the troops learned quickly from their mistakes. The tanks, in particular, started off disastrously, moving along city streets in columns. The defenders had only to knock out the leading tank with a well-aimed Panzerfaust, and the others, strung out in line behind it, were trapped, easy prey with their sides exposed to fire from buildings on either side. After a day or two of heavy losses, tank commanders reorganized their battle order, integrating more closely with the infantry, artillery and engineers.


ZHUKOV'S INNER-CITY tactics were simple, brutal and effective. First the artillery would pound any strong point to rubble, with Katyushas firing multiple phosphorus rockets at almost point-blank range, starting huge fires. In particularly difficult situations special siege guns were brought in, huge howitzers firing shells weighing more than half a ton, designed for use against the most powerful fortifications.

'A battle within a city,' wrote Chuikov, 'is a battle of firepower.' Firepower was the Soviet speciality, and they were determined not to be found wanting. Nor were they. 'Our guns sometimes fired a thousand shells on to one small square, a group of houses, or even a tiny garden,' a Soviet war correspondent noted.

Once the German firing positions were silenced, the tanks would go in, smashing down barricades, blowing apart any building, if necessary brick by brick, that might harbour a sniper. And after the artillery and the tanks, the infantry would go in, with hand grenades, sub-machine guns, rifles, and finally knives. For much of the time, street fighting was like jungle fighting – the enemy was usually unseen, hidden in basements, inside buildings. Troops were trained not to move along open streets, but to use holes in walls, back gates, yards and alleys. They soon discovered the cellar escape routes and worked their way through them, past terrified civilians. When they came to an intact dividing wall, they would blow a hole in it with an anti-tank rifle. If they met anything more formidable than mere masonry, they would call in the sappers to blow up the obstacle. With so many Berliners hiding out in cellars and shelters, the potential for civilian casualties was enormous.

## 2

FACING THE Soviet hordes was a largely disorganized and ill-equipped collection of men and a grand total of between fifty and sixty tanks, commanded by a general who had been appointed only a few hours before and knew nothing of the city's defence plans. All told, including the Volkssturm, Hitler Youth and assorted units scraped together from police, SS, factory defence groups and so on, Weidling probably had about 60,000 men. He also had a number of women – on Hitler's orders, women in the central Citadel sector had been drafted into Mohnke's battle group on 24 April. There were also many women volunteers already fighting and dying with the Volkssturm.

The LVIth Panzer Corps, the only cohesive military formation, now numbered no more than 13–15,000 men. They were spread over five nominal divisions: the 18th Panzergrenadier, still more or less intact; the 20th Panzergrenadier, already greatly reduced in size and now being forced back on to Wannsee island; the Müncheberg Panzer, which had just been severely mauled by Katukov's First Tank Army and reduced to about one-third of its previous size; the remains of the 9th Parachute, which had been shredded during the battle for the Seelow Heights; and the SS Nordland Panzergrenadier, still the toughest and most efficient fighting unit, despite its commander's unreliability. The only other effective fighting unit in the city was the Waffen SS group around the chancellery under the command of SS

Gruppenführer (Major-General) Mohnke, amounting to the equivalent of about half a division.

Colonel Wöhlermann, the LVIth Corps artillery commander, was put in charge of the city's artillery. What few guns the corps itself still had were almost useless for lack of ammunition. Apart from these, and the flak batteries on the towers, Wöhlermann found he had only seven light and seven heavy batteries of foreign guns manned by untrained Volkssturm men plus a number of soldiers from other arms of the service, few of them with any experience as gunners. They had an average of about 100 rounds of ammunition per battery. In addition, the existing garrison artillery commander had managed to put together some six batteries of guns reassembled from components used for instruction in local ordnance schools.

Deploying the guns was another problem. 'Had I not been born a Berliner and known the place like the back of my hand,' Wöhlermann noted, 'I should have found it impossible to site the batteries in the very short time I had been given. As it was, I knew where to go without having to bother too much with a map. As most of our guns were low-firing, there were not in fact many places to choose from: the Tiergarten and some of the larger squares, such as Lützowplatz, Belle-Alliance-Platz, the Lustgarten, Alexanderplatz, and so on, and the rail yards between the Potsdamer and Anhalter stations in the centre of the city. We also placed a few mortars on Belle-Alliance-Platz, Lützowplatz and Steinplatz, and guns on the railway tracks. Towards evening [of 24 April] I visited a 15 cm battery in the Botanical Gardens near my Berlin apartment.'

The frantic reorganization of the city's defences during the night of 24–25 April added to the confusion and to the pressure on officers like Wöhlermann. To allow Weidling to concentrate on his overall responsibilities as city commandant, Major-General Hans Mummert, commander of the Müncheberg Division, was ordered to take over the eastern defence sectors A and B, and was given nominal charge of the LVIth Corps. Weidling took with him his chief of staff, Colonel Theodor von Dufving, to look after the military side of his assignment, but kept Reymann's former chief of staff, Colonel Hans Refior, to handle the civil side, including dealing with Goebbels and the party. Wöhlermann was asked to take command of the Müncheberg Division, while still remaining in overall charge of artillery. All through the night, Weidling and his senior officers struggled to make some sort of sense of the shambles that had been forced upon them.

# 3

A T FIRST light on 25 April, Chuikov climbed to his observation post near Johannisthal airfield. This was a bathroom high on the corner of a large five-storey building. Through a jagged hole in the wall he looked out over a sea of roofs, broken by gaps where bombs and mines and shells had done their work. In the distance, factory chimneys and church spires stood out. Parks and public gardens, with the young leaves already out on the trees, seemed to him like spots of green foam. The early morning mist along the streets mingled with dust still hanging in the air from the previous night's artillery fire, overlaid in places with fat trails of greasy black smoke, reminding him of mourning ribbons. In the centre of the city, ragged plumes of yellow smoke and dust rose into the air as bombs exploded – the targets for the forthcoming attack. One hundred heavy bombers made the first strike. Throughout the day a total of 1,368 aircraft, including 569 PE-2 dive bombers, were to attack in continuous waves.

Apart from the 217-foot Kreuzberg, there were no hills in central Berlin. From his vantage point Chuikov had a clear view of the rings of defence works built along the canals and railway lines which curved around the city centre, where every building seemed to have been transformed into a fortress. The most powerful defences appeared to be in the area of the old city walls, built in the eighteenth century by the soldier king, Friedrich Wilhelm I of Prussia. The Landwehr canal and the sharp bend in the Spree with its steep, concrete-lined banks, formed a protective screen around the government buildings, including the chancellery and the Reichstag – the bull's eye in Chuikov's target.

Chuikov suddenly thought of his youngest daughter, Irina, who adored playing in her bath. He bent down to pick a piece of brick out of the battered tub, and suddenly felt a maddening itch, a burning sensation in his forearm as though he had plunged it from fingertips to elbow into burning pitch. He knew exactly what it was – an attack of eczema. It was a familiar condition which flared up from time to time at moments of acute stress, usually when he was in contact with brick dust. It brought a sharp reminder of the first time it had happened – it had been during the battle of Stalingrad.

Suddenly, the floor beneath Chuikov's feet shuddered and rocked as thousands of guns announced the opening of the final assault. As he watched, the full force of the bombardment descended on the buildings ahead: the walls of houses with their windows turned into embrasures suddenly collapsed, road blocks and barricades disintegrated and were sent flying into the air. The city was being pounded into rubble before his eyes.

# 4

THE OPENING bombardment caught Wöhlermann between his divisional command post at Tempelhof airport and Weidling's headquarters in Hohenzollerndamm. With his officers following his staff car in a heavy lorry, he had just crossed Belle-Alliance-Strasse (today known as Mehringdamm), when a strong bomber formation appeared directly overhead. As bombs hurtled down around them, Wöhlermann scrambled out of his car and flung himself full length in the gutter, the only bit of shelter he could find.

There were no houses or cellars nearby. Wöhlermann and his staff were trapped alongside the railway tracks, which were fenced off by high iron railings. Eventually, they found a hole blown in the fence by earlier bombs, and managed to squeeze through and run to a warehouse. When the bombers had passed they hurried back to their vehicles, which had suffered slight damage, and drove on, only to be forced to halt again by more bombs. Then the Soviet guns joined in. 'Large shells kept coming our way,' Wöhlermann wrote, 'and we realized that we had got ourselves right in the middle of a concerted air and artillery bombardment.' Although he was little more than two miles due east of his destination, it took him several hours to get there. When he arrived, he was told to set up his command post in the Zoo flak tower, which he had passed two hours earlier.

WHILE WÖHLERMANN was dodging bombs and shells near the Yorkstrasse railway lines, Brigadeführer Dr Gustav Krukenberg was doing the same two and a half miles further east. He was hunting for the command post of the Nordland Volunteer SS Panzergrenadier Division, which he was to take over, and which had lost contact with Weidling's HQ some time before. On the edge of the Hasenheide, a park just north-east of Tempelhof airport, he found a number of completely unguarded vehicles standing outside a house. 'Although no command flag was flying,' he commented caustically, 'I assumed this to be my divisional HQ, and my assumption turned out to be right. Unfortunately, the Soviet Air Force had gained the same impression, and had just dropped a heavy bomb on the building. All the upper storeys had been destroyed. When I arrived, clouds of dust were still rising. The staff were on the ground floor. They had suffered heavy casualties in the bombing, and wounded men were lying around everywhere. Among them, in the corner of the room, I found the divisional commander.'

Krukenberg was not impressed with Ziegler, the existing commander. The man seemed to have given up hope already. He told Krukenberg that he would not be able to hold the position for more than twenty-four hours, and that in any case the defence of Berlin was an impossible task. Ziegler only had seventy men deployed in the front line, and the rest of his troops were exhausted.

By this time, the area was under artillery fire not just from the long-range guns but also from light field guns only about a mile and a half away in Treptow. Krukenberg found his front manned solely by Volkssturm units, commanded by a district party leader, who admitted they were too weak to offer any serious resistance. As Krukenberg was talking to him in the wrecked Karstadt department store, two Soviet tanks appeared on the other side of the Hermannplatz and opened fire on their position. Coolly, Krukenberg assured the Volkssturm man that he would take care of them. He figured that since there were only two tanks, without infantry support, he and his men could get close to them and destroy them.

He got back to his own command post safely – 'apart from a slight shrapnel wound in the face', he noted nonchalantly – where to his delight his own commando of ninety experienced Frenchmen had now arrived from the Olympic stadium. Swiftly, he deployed an anti-tank squad under Haupt-sturmführer (Captain) Henri Joseph Fernet, a holder of the Knight's Cross for outstanding bravery. They disposed of the two tanks in short order. During the rest of that day and evening, they destroyed another fourteen, holding up the Soviet advance in that sector for the best part of twenty-four hours.

KRUKENBERG GAVE Fernet command of the French squad, which they promptly named the Charlemagne Battalion, after their disbanded SS division. Although they were members of the SS, the Frenchmen formed their own tight-knit community, with its own rules and allegiances. The Nordland Division was made up of several such groups of foreign volunteers – Danish, Norwegian, Swedish, Dutch, Belgian, Estonian, Latvian, Ukrainian and Spanish – Fascist fanatics from all over Europe. Considered outcasts and traitors in their own lands, they saw themselves as members of an exclusive but doomed military order, still fighting a holy crusade against communists, Semites, degenerates and the barbarians from the east. With no families or friends to hide them, they had no alternative but to stand and fight, which made them formidable enemies, a deadly combination of zealot and mercenary.

Their numbers were swelled by equally fanatical youngsters of the Hitler Youth, all eager to demonstrate that they were as brave and as ready to take risks as their elders. Fernet welcomed their presence. 'At this supreme moment of peril,' he declared, 'Berlin demands a supreme sacrifice: the flower of its youth.'

# 5

FEARING THAT Hitler and the other Nazi leaders were preparing to flee the city, the Soviet high command gave special priority to seizing the last two serviceable airfields, Gatow and Tempelhof. According to intelligence gleaned from German prisoners, there were planes standing by in underground hangars with full tanks, ready to take off at a moment's notice.

Gatow, on the western edge of the city, was an important Luftwaffe base, the site of academies for officer cadets and engineers and the air staff college. The remaining staff and students were supplemented by construction troops and Volkssturm, none of whom had any combat experience, armed with the usual assortment of weapons. The guns on the Zoo flak tower gave extra long-range artillery support.

In the evening the Volkssturm troops deserted *en masse*. The Luftwaffe men, however, although not trained as infantry, were disciplined and well organized. They fought bravely and well, holding out against Soviet forces of the CXXVth Corps, part of the Forty-Seventh Army, which were spread too thin to be fully effective after their long dash around the north of the city. Even though the field was under Soviet fire, aircraft continued to land and take off right through the 25th and 26th, but by the end of those two days, all the defenders had been either killed or captured.

TEMPELHOF, ONLY two miles south of the chancellery, was in the direct line of Chuikov's main thrust. The Müncheberg Panzer Division had its command post there, and the field was defended by crack units including anti-aircraft batteries, SS troops and tanks, most of them dug in to create near-impregnable fire points – they had no fuel so could not move. But the approaches were defended by the usual mixture of scratch units.

The sector of the Teltow canal a few hundred yards due south of the airfield was defended by a combat group consisting of the grandly named 2nd Battalion, Fortress Regiment, plus three companies of Volkssturm, all under the command of Major Wolfgang Skorning. A former armaments inspector at Krupps, Skorning had been an instructor at the Army Munitions School at Lichterfelde. A short, lean man with a quick mind, he had served on the eastern front, and was a thoroughly experienced and professional officer. When the Soviet attack began he hurriedly formed the remaining staff and young officer students of the school into an emergency battalion.

The battalion had been deployed between Bukow West and Marienfelde, to help cover the southern approaches to the city. When the Soviet final push began, the three Volkssturm companies were attached to it. They were mostly elderly men equipped with equally elderly Italian rifles and ten rounds of ammunition each; few had ever fired a gun before. They did have one efficient company commander, but unfortunately he was killed by a grenade fragment early in the fighting.

Under fire from Soviet advance units, Skorning's combat group was soon in danger of being surrounded. The regimental commander ordered them to pull back to the northern side of the canal, where Skorning set up his strong point at a narrow bridge, holding back the Soviets with machine guns and light artillery while the bridge was prepared for demolition.

The pioneer sergeant who was supposed to be laying the explosive charges, however, was out of his mind with fright and drink. Trying to fire a Panzerfaust in his drunken state, he burnt off the lower part of one of his legs with the exhaust flame. Skorning knew it was up to him to save the situation. As a trained arms technician, he knew how to rig the charges himself. Scrambling down the steep side of the canal cutting he swung himself under the bridge. Under covering fire from his men, he crawled forward, inserted the detonators, and reeled out the cable until he was safely back on the north bank. He hoped the Soviet tanks would try to cross the bridge, so that he could blow it while they were still on it. But they failed to oblige, so he pressed the plunger. The whole thing went up with a satisfying roar.

Shortly after, the Soviets opened up with guns and rocket launchers, driving Skorning's men back. As they moved, Skorning suddenly realised that he had been hit by shrapnel in the neck, body and hand – he had had his right hand in his tunic, and his thumb had stopped a splinter of metal that would otherwise have penetrated his heart. A first-aid man patched him up as well as he could. He stuck a plaster on the throat wound, then gave him a drink of cognac and watched anxiously to see whether it would go down. It did. 'It's OK,' he shouted with relief, 'Herr Skorning can swallow!'

Soviet troops were soon crossing the canal, and Skorning and his men were forced to retreat under fire, back through the graves of St Luke's and Emmaus churchyards towards the S-Bahn skirting the airport, part of the city's inner defence ring. They sought safety in the courtyard of a clinic – but were ordered to leave by doctors, who rushed out shouting that this was a clinic for women. Skorning led his men over a nearby bridge across the S-Bahn, to find cover and set up new defensive positions on the other side of the tracks.

At the corner of the street was a small flak position, with a single 88 mm gun. Skorning found a telephone and called the Luftwaffe division's chief of staff in the Zoo tower, offering to take over the flak troop and turn it into an infantry unit. He was sent a dozen Luftwaffe men to help.

By evening, Skorning's wounds were troubling him, and he sought treatment at the military hospital in Tempelhof. Promising to return as soon as possible, he left his deputy in command – Rittmeister (Cavalry Captain) Duvbrich, a reserve officer with an artificial leg, who was a famous painter of military scenes.

BY MID-AFTERNOON Soviet troops had broken through the defence lines and were on Tempelhof airfield itself. Vladimir Abyzov was in one of the forward assault squads, sent to secure the runways and prevent any aircraft from landing or taking off. Now, he was crouched by the side of the main runway, desperately wishing he had not thrown away his entrenching shovel – during street fighting, there was no time to dig foxholes, and the shovel was just another encumbrance. 'We were on one side of the runway,' he noted, 'and the German tanks were dug into the ground on the other. They were firing armour-piercing shells, which flopped down in front of us and behind us with a hollow sound, like fat quails in autumn falling on mown grass. We had to use knives and our hands to dig into the ground.'

In the streets and squares all around the airport the fighting grew more and more intense. The divisional war diary kept by an officer of the Müncheberg Panzer Division provides a vivid impression of the scene:

> Our artillery withdraws to new positions. They have very little ammunition left. The howling and explosions of the Stalin organs, the screaming of the wounded, the roar of engines and the rattle of machine guns. Clouds of smoke and the stench of burning. Dead women in the streets, killed while trying to get water. But also, here and there, women with Panzerfausts, Silesian girls thirsting for revenge.

WALTER SCHMID had been ordered to take his flak troop to Kreuzberg, and to take command of another unit from his regiment in an anti-tank role on the north side of the bridge on the Landwehr canal. The unit was in a critical situation, with Soviet troops already closing on the other bank. The canal was about twenty-five yards wide at that point, and Soviet infantry were installed in the houses facing it. The bridge was supposed to have been blown, but the Volkssturm men responsible had botched the job, and part of it was still standing, still connecting the two sides.

Schmid's unit had a 20 mm gun covering the bridge. Chuikov's men on the other bank were using captured Panzerfausts. One rocket hit the gun, knocking it over on to a seventeen-year-old youth and trapping him underneath. They managed to get the boy out alive but injured, but it was clear that the gun would never fire again.

In all the excitement, the Soviets managed to get some of their men over the bridge. There was a cowboy-style shoot-out in a nearby cemetery like something from a surreal Western movie, with Schmid's men and the Soviets firing at each other from behind tombstones only ten to fifteen yards apart. In spite of the close range, neither side caught more than fleeting glimpses of the other, and although a lot of shots were fired, there were few casualties.

# 6

WHILE CHUIKOV was hammering his way to central Berlin from the south and south-east, seven other Soviet armies were blasting in through all the other sectors. Together, they were steadily choking the life out of the city. Diametrically opposite Chuikov, Kuznetsov's Third Shock Army was heading straight for the Reichstag from the north-west. In places, his men met much stiffer opposition than they expected. Major-General S. N. Perevertkin's LXXIXth Corps crossed the Hohenzollern canal at Plötzensee locks with little trouble. Early in the morning, they liberated Plötzensee prison, with its infamous execution shed, releasing all the prisoners who were still inside. But then, trying to move on into Moabit along the southern bank of the canal, they were held up by fierce resistance at the Westhafen, Europe's biggest inland harbour.

The harbour area was a daunting obstacle, with two more wide canals and three huge basins lined with wharves and strongly built warehouses with thick walls. These had been turned into fortresses, well positioned to cover the approaches to the Königsdamm bridge over the Westhafen canal, the only road into Moabit. The bridge had already been partially blown and the wreckage was now mined and obstructed, so that no more than five men at a time could get across. To complete the picture, there was a Tiger tank well dug in behind a solid wall of paving stones and cobbles, its turret commanding the bridge. Immediately beyond the bridge were well-defended rail yards and the S-Bahn line, part of the fortified inner defence ring. Perevertkin's men were held up at Westhafen for the rest of the day. After taking heavy casualties trying to get men over the bridge, they decided they would have to wait till dark, when they could bring up engineers, heavy machine guns, and more artillery.

*

THE XIITH GUARDS Corps, immediately to Perevertkin's left, was making better progress through the tenement blocks of Wedding, one of the workers' districts of the old Red Berlin. They were held up for a time at the S-Bahn station, but the artillery were able to deal with it without too much trouble. Then, however, they came up against the Humboldthain flak tower, which was only slightly smaller than the one at the Zoo. The tower's defenders brought their guns to bear, pinning down the attackers. The tower was protected from the north by deep railway cuttings, and the park all around it provided a good field of fire against attackers who would have to brave the open spaces to get close.

Among the defenders was Wolfgang Karow, an infantry NCO who had, amazingly, been on leave in Berlin when the final attack began. He had been drafted into service at the tower on 23 April, and had fought throughout the 24th in a nearby apartment block. The residents, who had all been in the shelter, had to be fetched out to unlock their apartment doors – even under enemy fire, Karow and his companions balked at the thought of breaking their way in! They kept up a steady exchange of fire with Soviet troops in buildings across the street. Neither side had been eager to take many risks. When things started to get too hot, the Germans pulled out and took shelter in the flak tower.

The tower was already shaking violently as its own eight 125 mm guns fired salvos at the enemy. Soon it was being shaken by Soviet shells, too, crashing against the walls as the Soviet commander, realizing there was no chance of storming it with infantry, followed the usual practice of calling up the heavy artillery. Karow was distressed to see the young gunners on the upper platforms being killed. 'They were nearly all young flak auxiliaries, fourteen to sixteen years old,' he wrote. 'These brave youngsters continued to serve their guns fearlessly, and several of them fell in front of our eyes.'

Although the Soviets were throwing everything they had at it, the tower held out. Its massive concrete walls were simply too thick even for the heavy artillery to break down. The people inside prepared themselves for a siege, but, unlike the Zoo tower, stocks of food were low. Karow was ordered to go with a squad in search of nourishment.

'We were ordered to try to get supplies of sweets from the Hildebrandt chocolate factory in Pankstrasse, which was nearby in no man's land, so we got some big Luftwaffe rucksacks and set off. We got there without any trouble, but then had to seize a Nazi Party official who threatened us at gunpoint and tried to stop us entering. We were able to return without loss and with bulging rucksacks to the flak bunker, where our comrades greeted us with delight.' The chocolate must have helped sustain the defenders: they held out successfully until the rest of the city surrendered.

✳

THE THIRD of the great flak towers, two and a half miles to the south-east in Friedrichshain park, was also besieged from 25 April, after it had shelled troops of Colonel-General Nikolai Erastovitch Berzarin's Fifth Shock Army advancing along Frankfurter Allee, the main road into the Alexanderplatz. Berzarin, who had been nominated the evening before as Soviet commandant of the city and commander of the Berlin garrison, decided to take no chances. When his troops also came under sustained fire from defenders along the broad avenue, he ordered every building on its entire length to be systematically destroyed.

Berzarin's troops were facing even sterner opposition to the south of Frankfurter Allee, around the Schlesicher station, where they had to face withering fire from German defenders across wide open areas of track and sidings.

# 7

IN FROHNAU, the leafy suburb north of Tegel, the end came quickly and quietly. Gerald Rahusen, the young Dutch citizen who had returned from farming near Magdeburg, had been sheltering with his mother in the basement of their house for days, protected by sandbags piled in front of the windows. For the last couple of days, they had had to endure Soviet artillery and Stalin organs firing over their heads into the city from the polo ground about a mile away. Gerald had left the basement to visit the bathroom, when he heard a metallic clanking outside. Opening the window he saw a column of Soviet tanks. In a moment of silence, he could hear a voice shouting: '*Na pravo! Na pravo!* [All right! All right!] The Russians are here!'

The Rahusens had a big Dutch flag hanging from the window in front of the house, and a notice painted on a small board in English, Russian and German, saying 'This house is Dutch property, under the protection of the Swedish embassy.' Passing Soviet officers stopped to ask what it meant. They and their men were courteous and well behaved.

It was a similar story in Babelsberg, on the south-western tip of the city. Maria Milde, the young film starlet, emerged from the Jagdschloss Glienicke, alongside the Glienicke Bridge, to find herself facing a Soviet tank outside the gate in Königstrasse, its commander sitting on the turret like the caterpillar in *Alice in Wonderland*. He and his men greeted her cheerfully and made no attempt to attack her. But having heard all the horror stories about rape in those parts of Germany already occupied by the Red Army, she decided very sensibly that she would find herself a nice Russian officer as a 'friend' and protector, just as quickly as she could.

IN THE more central districts, the noise of battle, of shells and bombs and small-arms fire, was everywhere. Max Buch, alone in his flat in Meinecke-strasse, had been listening all morning to 'the terrible noise of fighting over the city, which is now considerably closer'. Added to the noise of the conventional bombs and shells, there was now the terrifying screech of the Stalin organs with their multiple rockets. But as the morning wore on, he became bolder.

'Although one can hear single shells whistling past, probably aimed too high and off course,' he wrote in his diary, 'I venture out on to the balcony to make my morning coffee.' He had, like so many Berliners, rigged up a small fireplace in the corner of the balcony, using two bricks and a ring from his gas cooker, on which he could boil a pan of water. With so many wrecked buildings all around, there was no shortage of bits of timber for fuel. But as the shells came closer and closer, though still one at a time, his courage faded again. Opposite his flat there was a gap in the buildings, where two apartment blocks had been destroyed by bombs a year earlier, so there was no cover from that direction.

At about 11 am Max was just collecting his hot water from the fire when there was a tremendous bang nearby. He was blown back into the corner of his kitchen and showered with falling plaster, but otherwise unharmed. A small-calibre shell had caught the branch of a tree outside the corner of the building and exploded. He thanked God for protecting him once more – reflecting that a difference of ten to fifteen yards in the firing line would have finished him. Outside, there was uninterrupted firing all day from the Zoo bunker.

IN KREUZBERG, less than half a mile from Walter Schmid's position, Ludwig von Hammerstein and the Kerp family listened anxiously to the noise of battle and wondered, half fearfully, half in hope, what was happening and how long it would be before the end. Hammerstein telephoned friends in the south-eastern district of Zehlendorf, to see if they had any information on Soviet progress. He got his answer without even asking – the telephone was answered by a Russian.

STEGLITZ, WHERE Ruth Andreas-Friedrich lived, was the neighbouring district to Zehlendorf. She and her friends had already been sheltering in their cellar for twenty-four hours. They could have no doubts that the battle was approaching fast: the next-door building had been demolished by a direct hit from a heavy artillery shell. All their own windows and doors had been blown in. And now the howl and bang of shells was joined by the slap of machine-gun bullets hitting the walls of the building. In one corner of the cellar the men had built themselves a secret hiding place out of carpets and boxes, in case the Gestapo and SS came looking for them. So far, however, the only intruder had been a terrified young soldier, Panzergrenadier Fritz Stolzberg, who had burst in looking not for fugitives but for shelter. They had taken pity on him, provided him with civilian clothes and disposed of his uniform. Now he was one of them.

Like Max Buch, they made soup and boiled potatoes on an iron stove on a second-floor balcony during brief lulls in the firing. But water was becoming more and more of a problem. Only the women could go out to the pump, braving the barrage outside. It was a dangerous business even though they had all acquired steel helmets. As if to emphasize the fact that death was lying in wait round every corner, four Volkssturm deserters had been strung up near the well, with the usual cardboard signs around their necks.

Venturing out for a breath of air when the firing seemed to have died down, Ruth and her friend Dr Walter Seitz had a graveyard experience even more surreal than Walter Schmid's. They had just turned into the nearby Bergstrasse cemetery when the Soviet barrage started again. Shells whistled into the earth around them, hurling broken tombstones, wreaths, planks and bodies into the air. Ruth looked up to see the remains of a recently buried corpse hanging from the branches of a willow tree. She and Seitz dashed back to the building, vowing not to go out again until it was all over.

IN PRENZLAUERBERG, three miles north-east of the chancellery, Fred Laabs and his family had other worries. Greifswalderstrasse, on which they lived, was not one of the main routes into the city centre, so it was not an important part of the defence lines. But although there were no artillery and tank duels, there were some infantry skirmishes, and heavily armed German infantry units started using the breakthroughs between the cellars of the blocks to outflank Soviet attackers.

All the civilians were terrified that their cellars could become underground battlefields, in which they would be trapped between the two sides. Even one or two German soldiers shooting at Soviet troops from the cellars could have had appalling consequences for the residents. The Soviet method of dealing with such problems was simple and brutal. They brought up heavy tanks and guns to reduce the building to rubble, then disposed of anyone left in the cellars with grenades and flame-throwers.

Fortunately, the German troops – mostly either Volkssturm or members of the 9th Parachute Division – were too few to make any proper stand, and too concerned with getting out of the way of the Soviets to cause any problem. In a very short time, they had all gone. An uneasy calm settled over everyone.

Greatly daring, and in spite of his mother's pleas, Fred made his way out of the cellar and on to the front doorstep. Filled with youthful bravado, he wanted to see what the Russians were really like. Was the Nazi propaganda on which he had been raised true? Were they really wild beasts, who would cut off his ears and tongue and drag him away to Siberia? Would one of those Russians come and nail him to the wall?

He stood in the open doorway, waiting, with the nervous excitement of a man playing Russian roulette. But nothing happened. He watched as seemingly endless columns of T34 tanks rumbled past. No one took any notice of him. Some of the tanks had their hatch covers open, with soldiers or officers looking out. One of them actually waved to him, and he waved back. Later, one of the tanks stopped. A Soviet soldier climbed out and walked over to him. Reaching into the pocket of his overalls, he pulled out a pack of Makhorka cigarettes, gave one to Fred with a grin, then drove on.

For Fred, the impossible had happened. He walked back inside, and descended to the cellar to tell the frightened people still hiding there that the war was definitely over. There was no joy on the faces of his family or neighbours when they heard his news. They were exhausted, and their relief was tempered by too many doubts about what the future might hold in store.

# 8

THROUGHOUT THE day in the Führer bunker, Boldt and Freytag struggled to keep pace with events, and to compile accurate reports of the deteriorating situation. They were usually able to get through by telephone to the various sectors. The news was universally bad, and Hitler's spirits sank. To make matters worse, the bunker received its first direct hits by heavy shells during the afternoon. The roof held, but showers of concrete particles fell from ceilings. The ventilators had to be turned off for about a quarter of an hour, because they were sucking in sulphurous fumes, smoke and cement dust instead of fresh air. The single telephone cable linking the bunker to the outside world was put out of action temporarily. With no radio links yet established, they were out of contact for some hours.

Around Oranienburg, Steiner was still holding on, and had even managed, somehow, to launch the counter-attack that Hitler had ordered the night before. Using seven battalions, he had caught the Soviet troops facing him by surprise, and had advanced about four miles. But now came news that the attack had been halted, and Steiner's men forced back to the Ruppin canal, with heavy casualties. Hitler did not even fly into one of his rages when he realized that Steiner had led the attack, though he had specifically ordered that he be replaced. Faced with this, he could only comment wearily: 'I told you so. Under Steiner's leadership the whole attack was bound to come to nothing.'

When Boldt phoned around the defence sectors later that evening, all the commanders reported that morale was at rock bottom. Older Volkssturm members, convinced of the futility of fighting on, were deserting their positions everywhere at the first sign of Soviet troops, escaping to join their wives and families in their cellars. Most of them were there only because they had been press-ganged by Goebbels's thugs, and had stayed only because of fear of the Gestapo and the SS – but that had now been overtaken by fear of the Russians. The few regular soldiers still left were fighting hard, but were almost out of ammunition. Even where they had been able to hold out they were constantly being outflanked and then attacked from the rear by Soviet troops who had driven through neighbouring positions with virtually no resistance at all. There were also disquieting reports of German deserters or prisoners of war serving the invaders as guides. Others, officers who had gone over to the enemy cause while in captivity in the Soviet Union, were causing disruption by infiltrating German positions and ordering whole squads away from the front lines.

From every sector, Boldt heard of fires caused by phosphorus rockets roaring uncontrolled through whole blocks and streets. With no water supplies and no fire service to put them out, they were only stopped where already burned-out ruins acted as fire breaks. The one benefit of this was that there were fewer Soviet aircraft bombing and strafing. Huge plumes of smoke, rising as high as 1,000 feet, obscured everything, reducing visibility so much that aircrews could make out very little on the ground. If they dropped bombs they were as likely to hit their own men as the enemy. By the same token, Luftwaffe planes could not be used to attack Soviet troops in the city.

WEIDLING ARRIVED at the bunker at 10 pm, to report on his first day as commander of the city. He found the small conference room packed with people eager to hear what he had to say. In the centre, Goebbels, Bormann, Krebs and Burgdorf sat or stood around Hitler, with adjutants and service representatives standing behind them. To one side were Mohnke, the commander of the Citadel sector, and Axmann, the Hitler Youth leader. Briskly, Weidling summarized the situation with the help of a large sketch map, showing that the Soviet ring was about to close – he apparently did not realize that it had already done so – and that no matter how hard they fought, his forces were being driven back into the city centre.

In response, Hitler started rambling on about why he had to remain in

Berlin, to triumph or to die. Egged on by Goebbels and Bormann, he declared that Berlin must be defended to the last gasp, for its fall would set the seal on Germany's final defeat. If the defenders were running out of ammunition and the airfields were unusable, the conversion of the East–West Axis into a landing strip must be completed, and fresh supplies flown in to it. If the Soviets were threatening to break through in the west of the city at Spandau, then 5,000 of Axmann's boys must be dispatched there with their Panzerfausts and their bicycles, to hold the bridges. Weidling was nauseated by all this. Yet he could not bring himself to puncture Hitler's fantasies, or to condemn the lunacy of it all. Like the good officer he had always been, he continued to obey orders, no matter what the cost.

When Weidling had gone, Hitler turned once more to his armies outside the city. Again ignoring the realities of the size and state of the opposing forces, he sent instructions to Jodl to speed up the relief operations he had outlined the day before. Steiner was to start another attack, south-west towards Spandau. Busse was to hold the Ninth Army fast to the south, so that Field Marshal Schörner's Army Group Centre could drive north to link up with it, while his left wing pushed back to the west to meet Wenck's Twelfth Army, returning from the Elbe. The two armies were to join up south of Potsdam, then advance on Berlin together on a broad front. Jodl, by now sharing and encouraging Hitler's illusions, replied that all the relief operations had either already begun, or were about to do so.

BY THE time the conference was over, word about the universally bad news had spread throughout the bunker. As Boldt and Freytag made their way back towards their own quarters, they found that the SS officers who had previously treated them with such scorn were now friendliness personified. 'When do you think Wenck will get to Berlin?' they asked. 'Can we break out to the west?' 'How much longer can we hold out?'

Boldt and Freytag drew a certain macabre satisfaction from the way that men who had always treated them with supreme arrogance were now seeking comfort from them. Now, it was the turn of the despised army officers to regard the SS men, few of whom had ever faced death at the front, with contempt. Boldt noted with disgust how many of the SS officers sought oblivion through drink. He was not the only one to despise the SS men, wallowing in anguish as they realized the bunker would probably be their grave, but never considering volunteering to die in action. Standing outside the scullery door, he overheard some kitchen maids berating some of the 'bunker soldiers'. The maids were real, down-to-earth Berlin women, and had no time for fancy ways. 'Listen,' Boldt heard one of them say to a bunch of SS men, 'if you lot don't pick up your guns and start fighting soon, you can put our aprons on and we'll go outside and fight. You ought to be thoroughly ashamed of yourselves. Just look at the kids out there smashing Russian tanks. . . .'

LATE THAT evening Boldt and Freytag climbed the concrete steps from the bunker, and stepped out into the garden. The noise of battle had died down; they could hear only the dull thud of occasional shells landing some distance away. The ruins around them were tinged with red from the glow of fires, but the air was surprisingly clean and cool. After so long in the fetid atmosphere below, it was a great relief to fill their lungs with air, however dusty. There were no clouds, only a myriad bright stars filling the sky. For a long time they stood, each lost in his own thoughts, then Freytag spoke.

'In a few days, all this will be over,' he said quietly. 'I don't want to die with that lot down there in the bunker. When it comes to the end, I want my head above ground and free.'

Boldt did not reply. As midnight approached, the two men turned and went back into their underground madhouse again. Professionals to the end, they both had a great deal of work to do.

# 9

AT DAWN on 26 April the battle began again. The day started with the usual hour's artillery bombardment from the Soviet guns, and an air raid on the city centre with 563 heavy bombers. Then the ground attacks began again in all sectors. In the Westhafen, a group of Soviet combat engineers had spent the night defusing the mines on the wrecked bridge, at some cost to themselves. The bridge at least was now safe, but there were still the machine-gun nests in the warehouses, and of course the Tiger tank behind its wall of stones. Following normal practice, Soviet artillery was ordered to deal with them. After a considerable bombardment, which did not seem to damage the warehouses much, the first wave of tanks and infantry went in. They were met by withering fire, which drove them back with heavy casualties. A second bombardment was ordered, but it appeared to cause no more substantial damage than the first.

At this point, Captain Stepan Neustroyev, commander of a Young Communist battalion, agreed to lead the next assault on the bridge. This time, the attack was launched under cover of a dense smoke screen, and Neustroyev and his Young Communists established a bridgehead on the other side. Under their covering fire, a second battalion crossed, and began to fight its way down Beusselstrasse towards the railway station. Yet still the Germans held the warehouses, from which they were able to blanket the bridge with machine-gun fire. They killed a Soviet four-horse team that was pulling a gun carriage across it, blocking all traffic until Soviet troops, under heavy fire, could shove the dead animals and the gun carriage into the canal. It took most of the day for the LXXIXth Corps to eliminate the strong point at Beusselstrasse S-Bahn station and get into Moabit proper. On the way, they released 1,200 Soviet prisoners of war, who were immediately armed and fed and pressed into service as replacements.

MAX BUCH awoke at daybreak, awaiting the day's bombardment. And at 5.30, almost on the dot, it started. Four shells whistled past his window in quick succession, and exploded two or three blocks away. By the time he was up and dressed, the gunfire and aerial activity were the heaviest he had yet experienced. Grabbing a few necessities, he hurried down to the cellar. In the street, columns of vehicles were parked under cover of the trees, much to the annoyance of the residents, who feared that if they were spotted by the Soviet aircraft they would make the street a target for bombs. Their fears were soon justified.

At 11 am Buch slipped back to his flat to fetch something, and was caught in a carpet bombing raid. The whole building rocked and shook. Pieces of plaster fell from walls and ceilings, a door blew off its hinges and crashed into the room, and the sound of breaking glass was everywhere. Then the raid passed. Thanking God for his survival, Buch went down to have a quick look at the street outside. 'Number 24 across the road is in flames,' he recorded in his diary, 'hit by bombs. The inhabitants are searching for their belongings. Then quickly back into the cellar because the artillery has resumed its bombardment with incredible and uninterrupted intensity. Some people fetching water from the Rankeplatz have been hit by shells and killed. A queue outside a butcher's shop in the Augsbergerstrasse received a direct hit, with many killed. One hears about many similar incidents from surrounding areas. Poor innocent victims of a desperate regime.'

AT FIRST light, Walter Schmid left his squad in the graveyard in Kreuzberg and crept forward to the partially wrecked bridge over the Landwehr canal, to see what was happening. Suddenly, an enemy tank appeared, crossing the bridge. He only had time to shout 'Watch out! Save yourselves!' to his men before it opened fire on them. Several were killed. Schmid felt a blow on his chest, as though he had been punched hard with a fist. It was a shell splinter, which penetrated his body. Although he was worried that the wound might be serious, his main reaction was a sense of joy and relief. 'I was happy,' he said, 'because I was freed of my responsibility.' He would no longer be forced to lead youngsters into battles they could not hope to win, to lead them to their certain death.

When he had done what he could for the survivors, Schmid made his way to a nearby first-aid post. The woman doctor who examined him and dressed his wound had no way of telling how serious it was, or if the splinter had pierced his lung. She gave him a chit saying he was no longer fit to fight – an essential protection against SS death squads – and sent him to the rear.

Schmid's one idea was to get away from the Russians. He was not afraid of them – he knew and liked them, having served in the Moscow embassy – but he did not like the idea of becoming a prisoner. He managed to hitch a lift in an ammunition lorry going to the Reichstag. The driver put him down in Potsdamerplatz, and from there he walked painfully along Hermann-Göring-Strasse and Voss-Strasse. As he passed the battered chancellery building, he suddenly heard the unmistakable sound of a sentry presenting arms. Bombs and shells were falling all around, hardly a building was left standing, but such are the stupidities of military etiquette that Schmid felt honour bound to stop and return the Waffen SS guardsman's salute.

The Foreign Office, Schmid's former workplace, was close by. The doorman recognized him immediately. 'Oh,' he said in greeting, 'I'm so glad one of you gentlemen has come in today. The other gentlemen who used to come to work every day have failed to turn up this morning. There must be something wrong with the Underground. . . .' Schmid explained that he had not come to work, but was wounded. Did the doorman know where he could go? he asked. The man suggested the nearby Adlon Hotel.

Schmid knew the Adlon well. It was the favourite Foreign Office watering hole, where in happier days diplomats, senior officials and foreign journalists used to rub shoulders in the famous downstairs bar. The Adlon, at Number 1, Unter den Linden, was the last of Berlin's grand hotels still standing. A couple of shells had wrecked the roof, but otherwise it was remarkably undamaged, though it was smack in the middle of the target area, midway between the chancellery and the Reichstag. There were still guests living in some of the rooms. Since 21 April, when the first Soviet shells had landed nearby, the management had stopped billing them, and even fed them free of charge and without ration coupons. But now, with the dead, dying and wounded lying untended in the streets, the Adlon had been converted into a field hospital, with the barber's shop in the basement serving as an operating theatre. The bodies of those who died were laid out neatly in the Goethe garden at the rear of the hotel, covered with hotel blankets. Schmid, by now bleeding badly, had his wounds dressed and stayed in the officers' ward – a room behind the main bar on the ground floor.

*

MAJOR WOLFGANG SKORNING was released from hospital at Tempelhof first thing that morning. His wounds had been treated and dressed, and were not serious enough to keep him out of the battle, even though his injured hand made it impossible for him to hold a gun. When he got back to his unit, he found the officer he had left in charge, the one-legged painter, Rittmeister Duvbrich, in a state of collapse – he had not eaten or slept for days. Skorning sent him off in his car, in the care of a highly decorated sergeant from the armaments school, to find food and rest. It was the last he ever saw of them. He learned many years later that they had run into a Russian patrol, and been shot.

During the night, Skorning's adjutant had been hit in the shoulder, and put out of action, and the twelve Luftwaffe men sent to help the unit had all disappeared. The position was untenable, but when he made contact with the Müncheberg divisional command post, he could get little help. The division itself was in complete disarray. At 5.30 am they had been ordered to pull out at once and move to Alexanderplatz. At 9 am the order had been cancelled. Now, no one knew what they were supposed to be doing. Skorning was told to hold on, as air support was on its way. Needless to say, the German fighter planes never appeared – but Soviet tanks did. With no more Panzerfausts left, Skorning's men had no chance of holding them off. Under fire from Soviet gun positions, they escaped along the S-Bahn to Tempelhof station, where his regimental command post was situated in a public air-raid shelter.

The scene around the station was chaotic, but to his delight Skorning discovered an army field kitchen behind a nearby house. He and his men had not eaten for four days – as an emergency battalion they had no kitchen of their own, only one sergeant who was supposed to provide them with cold food. Skorning asked a first lieutenant standing there alone to look after his men while he went on foot to his regimental headquarters for new orders. He left them eating ravenously.

In the air-raid shelter there was a mood of resignation and doom. Skorning did his best to get some information but eventually was forced to give up. He had no intention of sitting there just waiting for the Red Army, so he left and went back to the field kitchen. To his astonishment, it was deserted. There was no sign of his battalion. He rushed around, searching for them. Gunners manning a 3.7 mm pack howitzer on the edge of the airfield told him they had seen his men marching off towards the east, under the command of a first lieutenant. Then Skorning realized what had happened: the lone lieutenant had been a renegade, one of the German troops working for the enemy. He had induced the men to go with him, to give themselves up to the Soviets.

Wounded, unable to hold a weapon, and with his battalion gone, Skorning knew he had come to the end. He had done his best, and could do no more. Turning northwards he started walking again, this time heading for Monumentenstrasse, two miles away at the foot of the Kreuzberg hill and

Viktoria Park, where his sister lived. He found her in the cellar with her family and neighbours. They were not pleased to see him – in his uniform he posed a threat to them from both the Soviets and the Gestapo. Too weary to argue, Skorning left them in the cellar and went upstairs to his sister's flat. All he wanted to do was rest. Crashing out on the bed, he fell into a deep sleep, unperturbed by the air raids raging all around.

By MID-MORNING, the Müncheberg Division had no choice but to abandon Tempelhof, as Chuikov's forces finally overwhelmed them. The divisional diarist recorded the events that followed:

> 1000 hours. Russian drive on the airport becoming irresistible. New defence lines Schöneberg Town Hall/Halle Gate/Belle-Alliance-Platz. Heavy street fighting, many civilian casualties, dying animals, women fleeing from cellar to cellar. We are pushed north-west. New orders to go to Alexanderplatz as before. . . . The Führer bunker must have false information; the positions we are supposed to be taking over are already in Russian hands. We withdraw again under heavy Russian air attacks. Inscriptions on the walls of buildings: 'The hour before the dawn is the darkest!' and 'We withdraw but we are winning!' Deserters hanged or shot. What we see on the march is unforgettable.

While the Müncheberg Division was being driven out of Tempelhof, Boldt, Freytag and Krebs were tramping through the corridors to the Führer bunker to present their first report of the day. As they entered the ante-room at 10.30, they found the press officer, Heinz Lorenz, waiting with Bormann. Lorenz was now the Führer's only source of news from the outside world: he spent his time listening to foreign broadcasts – including those of the BBC – on his radio set in the Propaganda Ministry. Both men looked excited.

Before Krebs could begin, Lorenz asked if he could speak first. He could not wait to tell Hitler that he had picked up a broadcast from a neutral country which described differences of opinion between the American and Soviet units that had met the day before at Torgau. There had, it seemed, been some disagreement about the sectors to be occupied, with the Soviets complaining that the Americans had not fully observed the Yalta agreements. The three army officers waited for the point of the story – had there been a bloody end to the argument, or what? But it appeared that was all there was. Why, they wondered, had Lorenz bothered?

Lorenz, however, clearly knew his Führer better than they did. Hitler was electrified by the news and seized upon it eagerly, sitting erect in his chair again, his eyes shining. 'Gentlemen,' he announced, 'here once more is striking evidence of the disunity of our enemies. Would not the German people and posterity brand me a criminal if I were to make peace today, while there is still the possibility of our enemies falling out amongst themselves tomorrow? Is it not possible that on any day, even at any hour, war will break out between the Bolsheviks and the Anglo-Saxons over their prize, Germany?'

# 10

CHUIKOV'S FORCES drove slowly north and west from Tempelhof. There was heavy street fighting, with the Soviet troops smashing their way from street to street, through gaps in walls, over piles of rubble. Inevitably, there were many civilian casualties. Women fled desperately from cellar to cellar trying to keep ahead of the advancing troops. Potsdamerplatz and Leipzigerplatz came under heavy fire. Viktoria Park, topped with the Kreuzberg memorial, fell during the afternoon, giving Chuikov an elevated position for his guns to fire on the centre.

But further west, on the other side of Potsdamerstrasse in Heinrich von Kleist Park, one of Krukenberg's SS units was holed up in a corner building which it had turned into a fortress, commanding an important street junction. The SS men seemed to be a suicide squad, determined to go out in a blaze of Wagnerian glory. From their hide-out in the basement they were shooting at anything that moved, including women, children, medical orderlies and wounded.

So far, Chuikov had tried to avoid using flame-throwers, but now it seemed there was no alternative. He ordered up a team of sappers with portable flame-throwers and grenades. They worked their way right up to the building and poured streams of fire into every basement window. For a moment, the machine-gun fire stopped. Then it started up again. Clearly, the Soviet troops would have to break in.

One man, Private Nikolai Popov, a Siberian, took matters into his own hands. Blowing in the door with a bunch of hand grenades, he leapt inside, incinerating the SS troops in the hallway before they had a chance to shoot. But most of the defenders were in the cellar. Popov hurled several more grenades down the stairs, then charged after them. He found himself in the midst of about thirty SS men, all trying to shoot him. Ducking behind a wall, Popov swept them with a jet of flame, turning them into human torches. Before long, the whole building was ablaze. The surviving SS men fled into the street, where they were met by Soviet troops.

Chuikov had not relished the idea of sending in the flame throwers, and shortly afterwards he suffered another raging attack of eczema. But that was not the most horrific decision he had to make that day. He was already on his second pack of Kazbek cigarettes when he saw a crowd of about 400 Hitler Youths, none aged more than fifteen, marching in formation down Kolonnenstrasse with Panzerfausts on their shoulders, straight towards his lines. They had been sent out to do battle with his tanks.

One of the officers at the front radioed for instructions. 'What are we to do? Let them come on, or open fire?'

Chuikov could not bring himself to order his men to open fire on mere boys. 'Hold your fire. Find some way of disarming them,' he replied.

The Soviet front line sent up yellow flares to show the boys where they were, in the hope of scaring them off. But still they came on. Once they were close enough to see the Soviet positions they broke into a run. They started firing their Panzerfausts, tearing men and horses to pieces. Now Chuikov had to order his troops to open fire. The boys in the front, leading the charge, fell dead or dying. Those at the back turned and fled.

# 11

WEIDLING'S COMMAND structure was changed yet again during the morning of 26 April, on another of Hitler's whims. This time, however, the change was for the good. Hitler had promoted Lieutenant-Colonel Erich Bärenfänger, who had acted briefly as his deputy during the one day he had personal command of the Berlin defences before appointing Weidling. The thirty-year-old Bärenfänger, a holder of the Knight's Cross with Oak Leaves and Swords and a keen member of the SA since 1933, was now a major-general, and was given command of defence sectors A and B. This meant that Mummert could return to the Müncheberg Division, releasing Wöhlermann to concentrate on his job as artillery commander. For Weidling, this was a great improvement. For the men of the Müncheberg Division, experiencing their third change of command in little more than twenty-four hours, it merely added to their total bewilderment.

WÖHLERMANN WAS aghast at what he discovered when he returned to his artillery command post. The only way he could communicate with most of his gun positions was by the public telephone system, and that was likely to be out of action before long. But there was worse to come: when asked about ammunition, he was told that the garrison's entire stocks had been piled up in two enormous dumps in the west of the city. Both had been captured by Soviet troops that morning.

In response to Weidling's pleas of the night before, a squadron of Messerschmitt 109s had started flying over the city centre around 8 am, dropping over a hundred canisters containing ammunition and medical supplies. Their target was the Tiergarten, but inevitably many canisters landed in Soviet-held positions, or simply disappeared into the rubble; less than a fifth were recovered. Weidling was said to have received only six tons of supplies, including just sixteen tank rocket shells.

Krebs sent a radio signal to Jodl at OKW headquarters, ordering more supplies to be flow in on transport planes, which were to land, regardless of the danger, on the East–West Axis. By 9.32 he received confirmation that two Ju-52 aircraft had taken off, laden with tank ammunition. Boldt telephoned the Zoo flak tower to warn them that the planes were on their way, then called the Charité hospital and told the casualty officers to have fifty wounded men ready to be flown out in about two hours' time.

At 10.30 the two aircraft landed safely between the Victory Column and the Brandenburg Gate, to the great excitement of the beleaguered garrison. Within half an hour they had been unloaded, turned round and made ready for take-off, with the fifty wounded men aboard. The first roared down the improvised runway and just made it into the air. The second followed, but as it rose from the ground its left wing caught the front of a ruined building and it crashed, killing most of those on board. There would be no more supply flights.

WITH THIS latest tragedy still fresh in his mind, Weidling went to see Bärenfänger, to assess the position in his sectors. It was not an encouraging experience, as he himself related:

> Potsdamerplatz and Leipzigerstrasse were under heavy artillery fire. The dust from the rubble hung in the air like thick fog. The car taking me to General Bärenfänger made only slow progress. Shells burst all around us. We were covered with bits of broken stone. We had to leave the car near the Schloss and covered the last part of the way on foot. The streets were riddled with shell craters and piles of brick rubble. Street and squares lay deserted. Dodging Russian mortars, we made our way to the U-Bahn station in leaps. The roomy U-Bahn station, two floors deep, was crowded with terrified civilians. It was a shattering sight.
>
> Bärenfänger reported strong Russian attacks near Frankfurterstrasse. . . . He now pressed me for more men and more ammu-

nition, but I could promise him neither. Most of Bärenfänger's men were Volkssturm troops who had been sent into the exceptionally hard fighting with captured weapons, French, Italian, and so on. No ammunition could be found for these weapons in the whole of Berlin. . . .

Weidling's own headquarters was disrupted that day. The building on Hohenzollerndamm was under heavy shelling, and Koniev's troops were closing in fast from the south and west. Units of Rybalko's Third Guards Tank Army had emerged from the woods of the Grunewald and were already fighting through the streets of Schmargendorf, a mere one and a quarter miles to the south-west, while others were in Friedenau, the same distance to the south-east. Colonel von Dufving organized a wholesale move into the OKH buildings in Bendlerstrasse, on the Landwehr canal just south of the Tiergarten, where Stauffenberg had been executed nine months before.

The new command post was set up in cellars underneath the building. Thousands of people, including many civilians, were sheltering in other parts of the cellars. But almost before Dufving had laid out his maps, the building above them was hit by a bomb. A wall collapsed and the huge safes on the second and third storeys crashed down through the floors, crushing those underneath. Dufving and his staff could hear cries for help coming from the cellar. They broke a hole through a wall, and a nursing sister crawled through. Injured survivors were dragged through and laid on Dufving's tables, their blood running on to the maps of Berlin. One of them was a young Red Cross nurse. Colonel Hans Refior, Weidling's second chief of staff, was among those who watched, helplessly, as she lay dying. 'We men,' he recalled later, 'who had all come face to face with death so many times during the war, were strangely touched and moved by this senseless loss of life.'

The cellar was no further use to Weidling and his staff. They moved out again, and into a nearby bunker under the old headquarters of the Abwehr, a hundred yards or so away. It was cramped and crowded, but it would have to do. There was a telephone connection to the Führer bunker, but it was already unreliable. Most contact, including two-hourly reports to Hitler, had to be sent by dispatch riders, who generally took about fifteen minutes to make the one-mile journey.

# 12

Some people in Berlin that day had no difficulty in telephoning the bunker. Victor Boëv, a young lieutenant with the Soviet XXIInd Tank Corps, was resting with his unit in a cellar in Siemensstadt. The residents of the district had all fled, leaving their houses and flats empty. Boëv had gone from house to house, searching for Werewolves or any other form of opposition. He had found none. What he had found in one bedroom were the bodies of an elderly couple lying peacefully side by side in a double bed. The glasses from which they had drunk poison stood neatly on a bedside table, alongside their two wedding rings, placed touching each other, and a framed photograph of their son, who had been killed in battle.

Earlier, Boëv had been visited by two war correspondents, from *Pravda* and *Izvestia*. Finding that the telephone on the ground floor was still connected, they persuaded Boëv, who spoke excellent German, to make a call. He dialled Directory Enquiries – which was still working – and asked for the number of the Propaganda Ministry. With commendable efficiency, the operator supplied the number, and in a moment Boëv was speaking to the ministry switchboard, asking to speak to Dr Goebbels. He was put through to various officials, who all wanted to know what his business was. He told them he was speaking from Siemensstadt, and that he needed to speak to the minister urgently. His persistence paid off. Goebbels was fetched from a conference, and came on the line.

'I am a Russian officer, speaking from Siemensstadt,' Boëv told him. 'I should like to ask you a few questions.'

Goebbels showed no surprise. 'Please go ahead,' he replied in a calm, matter-of-fact voice.

'How long can you hold out in Berlin?' Boëv asked.

Goebbels's reply was distorted by a crackle on the line.

'Several . . .'

'Several what? Weeks?'

'Oh, no. Months. Why not? Your people defended Sevastopol for nine months. Why shouldn't we do the same in our capital?'

'Another question. When and in what direction will you escape from Berlin?'

'That question is far too insulting to deserve an answer.'

'You must remember that we shall find you, even if we have to comb the ends of the earth. And we have prepared a scaffold for you.'

There was a confused jumble of voices at the other end. Boëv shouted: 'Is there anything you would like to ask me?'

'No,' Goebbels said, and hung up.

# 13

THE TELEPHONE operators were not the only government employees still trying to work normally in Berlin at that time. The public library in Ludendorffstrasse, just south of the Tiergarten, had been issuing books until the weekend. On Monday, 23 April, some of the staff struggled through the wrecked streets and the barricades and blown bridges to report for duty – they had received no instructions to stay away. Next day, they were told to go to the local town hall in Turmstrasse, to work as couriers.

Anneliese H. – she did not write her full name on the diary she started keeping on the Sunday, when the staff started burning the town hall files – struggled to work on foot from her flat in Alt Moabit, past burning buildings and mutilated corpses. When she learned that her beloved library had been hit, she felt guilty: 'My heart was heavy at the thought that I was not at work at my post at the library,' she wrote, 'now that there was no real work for me to do at the town hall.'

That afternoon, Anneliese was given a job. It was back in Ludendorffstrasse, which entailed making a terrifying one-hour walk in each direction, across the battlefield of the Tiergarten. She accepted it without question. Her job was to issue ration cards and allocate empty flats to people who had been bombed or shelled out of their own. The fact that there was no food to be obtained with the ration cards, and no one knew where the flats were, or if they were still standing from one hour to the next, seemed unimportant. What mattered was that she had a proper job to do, with forms to be issued, and rubber stamps to make everything official.

On 26 April, as Soviet troops smashed into Moabit from the Westhafen, cutting off her home, Anneliese was still busily occupied in her makeshift office. From then on, she had to stay in the cellar in Ludendorffstrasse, venturing out to fetch water from the nearest pump and to beg for bread from a bakery where a dead German soldier had been lying in the doorway all day, then scurrying back clutching four free loaves, with shells exploding all round her.

\*

THREE MILES to the south-east, Maria von Maltzan was also out searching for food, accompanied by her nephew, Brumm von Reichenau. The Soviets were not in Wilmersdorf yet, but the noise of battle from surrounding districts could be heard everywhere and shells screamed overhead. A horse-drawn ammunition wagon was passing along the street just ahead of them; much of the military supply traffic was pulled by horses now. Suddenly Brumm, with the instinct of a front-line soldier, sensed danger. Diving at Maria, he bundled her down a flight of basement steps just as a shell hit the ammunition wagon and blew it to pieces.

Before the dust had settled, Maria was on her feet again, heading for the wreckage – there would be horse meat for supper that night. Many horses were killed on the streets of Berlin during those times. None stayed there long before people appeared from their cellars armed with hatchets, cleavers and knives to butcher the carcass. Maria had an advantage over most of them – as a veterinary surgeon she had both the skill and the tools to carve up any animal swiftly and efficiently. In a matter of moments, she and Brumm were heading back to her apartment with their prize.

FOR RUTH ANDREAS-FRIEDRICH and her friends, the last two days had become a confused jumble. They lost track of dates as the war arrived on their doorstep. Her daughter Karin chanced the shellfire to queue for two hours for meat at a nearby shop. She came back safely but in a wild rage with the other women outside the shop, who had spent their time cursing not Hitler and the Nazis but the deserters, threatening to string them up.

When a squad of seven Waffen SS soldiers hammered on their door, begging for water, Ruth coldly told them they had none and sent them on their way.

'Where to?' one asked. 'We've lost our squad leader. They'll shoot us if we come without a leader.'

'My heart bleeds for you!' Ruth snapped back.

'Don't rejoice too soon,' the youngest soldier retorted. 'You people are the first ones they'll smash to a pulp.'

'When the relief army gets here from the west – watch yourself,' another joined in. 'Things haven't gone as far as you think!'

Ruth slammed the door. Shortly afterwards, the battle erupted around them, growing fiercer every minute. Soldiers raced past the houses, crouching, taking cover, dying. Somewhere in the distance, a military whistle blew. More soldiers swarmed northwards in a disorderly rabble, Volkssturm men, medics, Luftwaffe gunners, all scrambling to get away. Then, suddenly, the shooting died away. Two or three lone soldiers stumbled across the churned-up cemetery, staggered, fell, and lay still.

For twenty minutes there was an ominous silence. Then something moved beyond the corner of a gutted building. A rifle barrel poked cautiously

414

out. After a few seconds, a soldier's head appeared, ducked back, then appeared again.

'Russians!' Leo Borchard whispered.

As more Soviet soldiers advanced, suspiciously, Karin hurried to strip a sheet from her bed, fastened it to a broom handle, then crawled upstairs to hang it from a window as a white flag. She scrambled back down to the basement as incendiary bullets started a fire in the upper rooms. After half an hour, the fire went out. More agonized waiting, then the friends heard the sound of boots, running towards them, into their building. Ruth and Leo rushed out of the cellar and up the stairs. They were blinded for a moment by the beam of a powerful flashlight, shone in their faces.

'*Drusya!*' Ruth called out in Russian. 'Friends!'

The light moved from her eyes. Behind it she could see a bearded face, two slanting, Tartar eyes, and the turned-up collar of a leather coat. The barrel of a sub-machine gun still pointed at her.

'*Drusya!*' the soldier replied, with a smile.

Leo, who had been born in Moscow and spoke fluent Russian, took over. 'We've been waiting for you,' he said. 'We're glad you're here.'

'Really?' the soldier asked, regarding them suspiciously.

'Really.'

The man nodded, shone his light through the open doors to check the other rooms, then shrugged and went away. Ruth and Leo walked numbly back to the others in the cellar. Everyone was jubilant. Someone had opened the last bottle of red wine. They drank a toast to liberation in tin mugs and teacups.

# 14

WHILE THE Müncheberg Division was being driven out of Tempelhof, Krukenberg's SS Nordland Panzergrenadiers were determined not just to hold on, but to stage counter-attacks in the neighbouring district of Neukölln and the eastern part of Kreuzberg.

The Frenchmen of the Charlemagne Battalion staged a copy-book attack, moving forward from doorway to doorway, from heaps of rubble to shattered walls as coolly as if they had been on an exercise. They caught the Soviet infantrymen off guard, and their tanks followed up fast to strike before the Soviets had the chance to return fire. But they did not have things their own way for long. The first blow came when a reserve section marching up from Neukölln town hall was suddenly hit by a barrage of tank shells. Broken-hearted, the company commander counted fifteen bodies of young soldiers sprawled on a roadway running with their blood.

As the attack started to break down in confusion, with French and Soviet units hopelessly entangled, the battalion received a strange signal from divisional HQ. 'If the attack has not already begun,' it said, 'stop and await further orders. If it has, then do your best.' Krukenberg had decided his young warriors were too good to be wasted on a futile fight. This was not the blaze of glory they all sought. They had to be saved to take part in the heroic last stand in the Citadel. He was already arranging to pull them back into the centre, to prepare for that final battle.

Three hours after the counter-attack had begun, the division was withdrawn, leaving a group of Hitler Youth occupying Neukölln town hall, to make their last stand and delay the Soviet advance for as long as possible.


IN ORANIENSTRASSE, Ludwig von Hammerstein watched the last of the troops creeping out of the courtyard behind the Kerps' store in the late morning. Then there was a long pause, with nothing happening. While they were waiting, Mother Kerp collected all the food supplies that had been saved, bought or looted, and cooked a magnificent celebration meal, which they ate accompanied by a bottle of good red wine.

Shortly after they had finished eating, at about 3 pm, the first Soviet infantry appeared in the street. Hammerstein saw no sign of anyone offering resistance. All the inhabitants stood in their doorways to greet them as liberators, rejoicing that for them the war was over at last.

At first the Soviet troops generally behaved well, apart from taking everyone's jewellery and watches at gunpoint. Refugees from the east had long ago warned that this would happen, and most people had taken care to hide their most precious things. Watches seemed to hold a particular fascination for all Soviet troops, officers as well as other ranks. Wherever they went, they always started by demanding '*Uri*'. Soon, no Berliner was left wearing a watch, while some Soviet soldiers had arms literally covered from wrist to elbow with their trophies, all put forward two hours to show Moscow time, to which the Soviets were still keeping.

Once their desire for timepieces had been satisfied, the Soviet troops raided the tobacco store on the corner of the street, sharing out the cigarettes and cigars not only among themselves but also with the German population. Then they began a thorough and careful search of each house and flat, looking for German soldiers. Hammerstein was questioned more than once, but managed to convince them that he was neither a soldier nor a Fascist – he had hidden the pistol he had kept for protection against the Gestapo in the dustbin. But he almost came to grief when a soldier he was accompanying while he searched the Kerps' place fell down the stairs in the darkened pharmacy. Fortunately, the man was not hurt, but he blamed Hammerstein and threatened to shoot him. Hammerstein raised his hands and smiled frantically; the man contented himself by punching him on the jaw instead. It was, perhaps, a reasonable indicator of the sort of relationship that could be established with the occupying forces.

IN THE French prisoner-of-war hospital in another part of Kreuzberg, conditions were frightful. The water and sewerage systems, of course, had stopped working long ago, and everywhere was overflowing with rubbish and sewage. The stench was unbelievable. The only light or heat came from oil lamps and an iron stove. As well as the sick, the cellar was crammed with civilians sheltering from the fighting. Surgical patients were stretched out on mattresses wherever there was space – soldiers, old men, women, children, French, Russian, Serb and Italian workers, all jumbled together and begging for water. There were already a dozen corpses stacked in an old shelter trench nearby.

Everyone waited anxiously, listening to the sound of tanks and the rattle of machine-gun fire outside. Then a sick man lying on the first landing of a staircase saw a Soviet tank pass by in the street outside. A Soviet infantryman stuck his head through one of the holes in the metal plates covering the porch grille. Seeing nothing in the dark interior, but fearing that there might be enemy soldiers holding out in the building, he fired a burst from his sub-machine gun through the windows.

Afraid that the building might be attacked at any moment with tanks and flame-throwers, the staff quickly assembled a delegation consisting of three Frenchmen, the senior German doctor and an army medical lieutenant who spoke fluent Russian, to go out and parley with the Soviet commander. Everyone else stayed out of sight, while those lying near doors and windows provided a running commentary on what was happening. The delegation made contact, and returned with a group of Soviet officers, who thought their men had been fired on from the south wing of the hospital. The situation was resolved by a Soviet tank, which rolled up and carefully lobbed two shells through the windows from which the shots were thought to have come.

# 15

B Y THE end of the day, Gatow airfield was still holding out. But it was under constant fire, and its runways were so badly holed that they could no longer be used. Before it was finally put out of action, a few more aircraft had managed to land there. The first was a Ju-52, carrying a company of marines sent by Dönitz. They made their way into the city across the Havel bridge, and dug in near the Foreign Ministry before being allocated to Krukenberg's Nordland Division. Krukenberg was favourably impressed by their commander, who seemed a good professional naval officer. But the troops were another matter – they were trainee radar technicians, fresh off a technical course, and had never handled any sort of weapon. The rifles they brought were 1917 Italian models.

Twelve more Ju-52s carrying SS reinforcements were shot down. But one other aircraft made it into Gatow: a Focke-Wolf 190 carrying Colonel-General Robert Ritter von Greim, holder of the Knight's Cross and commander of the Luftwaffe on the eastern front, and Hanna Reitsch, his mistress, Germany's greatest woman pilot. Hitler had commanded Greim to come to the bunker after he had ordered Göring's arrest. He had not said why, but Greim had obeyed without question. Hanna insisted on going with him.

Hanna had piloted Greim to Rechlin air base, some sixty miles north-east of Berlin, hoping to be able to fly into central Berlin from there in an autogiro. But at Rechlin they found the machine had been damaged that morning by US fighters strafing the airfield. A Luftwaffe pilot – the same man who had flown Albert Speer to Berlin for his final visit – offered to fly them to Gatow. The FW-190 had only one passenger seat, but the diminutive Hanna, who stood barely five feet tall, squeezed into the space in the fuselage behind it, and with the three of them on board the plane took off, escorted by twenty fighters.

They reached Gatow safely, with no more damage than a few bullet holes in the wings, but seven of their escort were shot down on the way. There, they switched to a Fieseler Storch, a slow observation plane with fixed under-carriage. While the remains of the escort held off Soviet fighters, they took off and headed across the city at rooftop height, with Greim at the controls and Hanna in the passenger seat behind him. Over Grunewald they were hit by Soviet gunfire. Greim's right foot was shattered, and he passed out. Fuel poured from the damaged wing tanks. But Hanna seized the controls over Greim's shoulders, and touched down safely right by the Brandenburg Gate.

Greim was having his foot dressed in the bunker medical room when Hitler marched in, raging about Göring. 'Nothing is spared me,' he ranted, his face twitching, his breathing fast and shallow. 'No allegiances are kept, no honour lived up to. There are no disappointments I have not had, no betrayals I have not experienced!' He raved on and on, then abruptly informed the astonished Greim that he was promoted to the rank of field marshal and appointed commander-in-chief of the Luftwaffe. This was something Hitler could easily have done by telephone or radio, but it seemed that part of his reason for calling Greim to the bunker was to find out if escape by air was still possible. Clearly it no longer was.

Hanna, a devoted admirer and old friend of Hitler, asked what he planned to do. 'My Führer,' she asked, 'why do you stay? Why do you deprive Germany of your great life?' He replied that he still had hope: 'The army of General Wenck is moving up from the south. He must and will drive the Red Army back.' Manic and sweating profusely, he stumped around the bunker, waving a disintegrating road map in one hand, eager to demonstrate to anyone who would listen his master plan for Wenck's triumphal advance on Berlin. Then his mood would swing to the other extreme and he would be in despair again, speaking of suicide. He even gave Hanna two cyanide capsules, one for herself, one for the injured Greim.

AT THE conference that evening Krebs was able to give Hitler some good news, bolstering his belief in the fantasy of salvation from the west. Wenck had launched his relief attack at dawn that morning with the XXth Corps from about twenty-five miles south east of the city. It was headed for Potsdam, where Koniev's forces appeared to be weakest, and where Reymann was still holding out with his army detachment. The attack had begun magnificently, driving forward with all the flair of the early days of the war. The corps's four divisions had caught the Soviet Thirteenth Army on its exposed flank, and had captured many units, including tank workshops and supply columns. By evening they were only fifteen miles from Berlin at the spa town of Beelitz, where they recaptured a German field hospital complete with all its staff, supplies and equipment, and 3,000 German wounded. The wounded men and hundreds of refugees were ferried back to the Elbe, fifty miles to the west, by train.

Busse's Ninth Army, meanwhile, was grimly fighting west in a desperate effort to link up with Wenck's troops. Their aim, of course, was not to save Berlin but to save themselves, by creating an escape route to the Elbe and the Americans. Nevertheless, they could be seen as offering some hope to the defenders of the city.

To the north there was no sign of hope whatsoever. Steiner was simply refusing to begin his proposed attack, knowing that his troops were too weak and that he would be sending them to certain death. And no one seemed to know what was happening to Manteuffel's Third Panzer Army – in fact it was pulling out as fast as it could go.

Manteuffel had warned Heinrici that his army was on the point of being surrounded and annihilated. Heinrici, deliberately flouting Hitler's and Jodl's direct orders, had told him to withdraw. For the moment, though, Heinrici said nothing about this to Jodl, Keitel or Krebs – he wanted to give Manteuffel's men time to get clear before anyone had a chance to stop them. For the next two days, Hitler and the general staff remained unaware that one of their remaining armies was in full flight.

Communications had become so chaotic that Heinrici had little difficulty in keeping his secret. The last long-distance telephone line out of Berlin was severed on 26 April. Although the city's internal network was still in remarkably good shape, the only two-way contact between the Führer bunker and the outside world was now the unreliable radio link with the OKW. Reception quality was so bad that it was often impossible to make out what was being said at the other end, and every time it rained at Neu Roofen the balloon supporting the aerial sank slowly to the ground, fading out transmissions.

There was little hope on offer in the city itself, either. The various defence sectors were in a state of flux, and it had become almost impossible for Boldt and Freytag to get accurate and up-to-date information from command posts that were constantly being moved. They fell back on the public telephone system. First, they called their own friends and acquaintances in districts where they knew fighting was going on, and asked what was happening. For districts where they knew no one, they thumbed through the telephone directory and picked out names and addresses that looked likely to be near the front line. It was a pretty crude way of obtaining military intelligence, but it worked.

'Excuse me, madam,' they asked, 'have you seen the Russians?'

Only too often the reply was 'Yes. Two of them were here half an hour ago.' Or: 'I saw the tanks from my bedroom window about fifteen minutes ago, driving towards Ringstrasse.'

When they put a number of such conversations together, Boldt and Freytag had a fairly complete picture; it was a great deal clearer than the reports from military units.

# 16

THAT NIGHT, Chuikov moved his command post for the last time, to a large, five-storey building a few hundred yards north of the main entrance to Tempelhof airport. The outside walls were of grey cement, stained and streaked by flames and smoke, and a Reich eagle clutching a swastika spread its cement wings over the doorway. The narrow, high-ceilinged entrance hall was adorned with black marble pillars. It was, said Chuikov, a dark, unpleasant place. But it suited his purpose.

While the signals girls were installing their communications equipment in the hall, they were fired at from the third-floor landing. Grabbing rifles and sub-machine guns, they dashed up the stairs and spotted a man. He fired at them again. They fired back, then chased him up the remaining flights of stairs to the top floor, where he ran into a dark attic room. The girls followed, spraying the place with automatic fire and shouting in German '*Hände hoch!*' ('Hands up!') There was no answer. They started searching. Suddenly, the man ran out from a dark corner. Still holding his pistol, his face contorted with fear, he kicked open a window and dived to his death, shouting '*Hitler kaput!*' They found his body lying in the yard, a Nazi who had lost his faith.

# 17

THE MÜNCHEBERG Division diarist ended the entry for 26 April on a depressingly low note:

Evening. Announcement of a new organization, Freikorps Mohnke: 'Bring your own weapons, equipment, rations. Every German is needed!'

Heavy fighting in Dirckstrasse, Königstrasse, the Central Market and inside the Stock Exchange. First skirmishes in the S-Bahn tunnels, through which the Russians are trying to get behind our lines. The tunnels are packed with civilians.

The skirmishes in the tunnels of the S-Bahn and U-Bahn were with Chuikov's scouts, on reconnaissance missions searching for a route under the Landwehr canal into the city centre. One scout, Alexander Zhamkov, told how he and his small squad groped their way forward in the darkness for about 300 yards, until they saw a light:

> We decided to crawl the rest of the way. There was a niche in the wall with a storage battery in it and a small electric bulb burning. Close by we heard Germans talking, and there was a smell of tobacco smoke and heated-up tinned meat. One of them flashed a torch and pointed it towards us, while the Germans remained in the shadows. We pressed ourselves to the ground and peered ahead. In front, the tunnel was sealed with a brick wall with steel shields set in the middle. We crawled forward another few metres. All of a sudden, bullets began to sing. We hid in the niches. After a while, we attacked, throwing hand grenades and firing Panzerfausts, and broke through. Another 200 metres and another wall. In general, the German defences in the subway are compartmentalized, with tunnels divided into sections by walls.

It was obviously not going to be possible for Chuikov to use the tunnels to get a large force under the canal, but he could and did send stronger squads underground, to engage the defenders and try to drive them out. The squads were then to join other parties on the surface to carry out reconnaissance in force behind the German lines. During the day, three of these squads were involved in heavy fighting around the Potsdamer railway station and the Halle Gate, where two tanks reached the bridge before being knocked out. One group of tanks penetrated as far as the lower part of Wilhelmstrasse before they were stopped.

THE U-BAHN and S-Bahn tunnels were becoming increasingly important to the defenders for underground command posts. Bärenfänger had already established himself in Schillingstrasse U-Bahn station, beneath Frankfurter Allee near Alexanderplatz. Now, Mummerts moved the Müncheberg Division command post into the S-Bahn station underneath the main Anhalter station. Both were within a mile of the chancellery. 'The station looks like an armed camp,' the Müncheberg diarist wrote. 'Women and children huddle in alcoves, some sitting on folding chairs, listening to the sounds of the battle. Shells hit the roof, cement crumbles from the ceiling. Smells of powder and smoke in the tunnels. S-Bahn hospital trains trundle slowly by.'

Later in the day, Krukenberg moved his SS Nordland command post into the U-Bahn at Stadtmitte, less than a quarter of a mile from the Führer bunker. He was decidedly unimpressed with what he found. 'I was deeply disappointed not to find the slightest sign of any of the defence preparations that had allegedly been made over the last three months,' he complained. 'No light, no telephone. An Underground carriage with broken windowpanes was all the so-called Command Post City Centre consisted of in the so-called fortress of Berlin. We stood there and felt completely lost.'

Their food supply was from the grocery shops in the Gendarmenmarkt above them, all of which had been put under guard against looters. But ammunition was a more serious problem. 'Fortunately,' Krukenberg wrote, 'we discovered some Panzerfausts in the chancellery, which we were allowed to take with us. Our needs were so great that not a single Panzerfaust was left behind for the defence of the chancellery itself.'

KRUKENBERG MAY have thought himself hard done by as he moved into his makeshift command post, but there was worse to come. At the conference that morning, Hitler was enraged to hear that Soviet troops had been using the tunnels. Disregarding the danger to troops, the sick and wounded in hospital trains, and the thousands of refugees, he ordered that the watertight bulk-heads keeping out the Landwehr canal should be blown, to flood the tunnels. The Müncheberg diarist describes the result:

> Suddenly, water splashed into our command post. Screams, cries and curses in the tunnel. People are fighting around the ladders leading up the ventilator shafts to the street above. Water comes rushing through the tunnels. The crowds panic, pushing through the rising water, stumbling over rails and sleepers. Children and the wounded are deserted. People are being trampled underfoot. The water covers them. It rises a metre or more, then slowly drains away. The panic lasts for hours. Many are drowned. . . .
>
> Late afternoon, command post moved to Potsdamerplatz station first level, the lower tunnel being still flooded. Direct hit through the roof. Heavy losses among wounded and civilians. Smoke drifts through the hole. Outside, stocks of Panzerfausts explode under heavy Russian fire. Terrible sight at the station entrance, one flight of stairs down, where a heavy shell has penetrated and people – soldiers, women and children – are literally stuck to the walls.

Conditions in the new location were no better than at the Anhalter station. Communications were impossible, with telephone lines shot to pieces as soon as they were laid. There was no regular food, no bread, and the only water was that flooding the lower tunnels. The men filtered it as well as they could before drinking it. Outside on Potsdamerplatz, once reputedly the busiest crossroads in Europe, the scene was equally horrific. The square was littered with damaged vehicles, including partially destroyed ambulances with the wounded still lying in them. Dead bodies were everywhere, many of them appallingly mangled by tanks and trucks.

The Münchebergs, like many other German units, were still clinging to the forlorn hope of rescue, assiduously fostered by Goebbels's declarations that Wenck and the Ninth Army were on their way. Fresh hopes were raised by additional rumours of peace treaties being signed in the west and of American divisions joining the Germans to drive the Soviets back. The divisional staff tried to get confirmation that the rumours were true from the Propaganda Ministry, of all places, but failed to get an answer.

By evening they were subjected to more violent shelling, coinciding with renewed attacks on their positions. At 4 am next morning the divisional command post was forced to move yet again, falling back on Nollendorfplatz through the dark tunnels. In the parallel tunnel, Soviet troops were advancing unopposed to Potsdamerplatz.


WHILE THOSE underground were suffering and dying as a result of his callous order, Hitler was conducting a bizarre little ceremony in the bunker. Freytag and Boldt watched in disbelief as a young boy, 'in a bad state of shock and looking as if he had not slept for days', was led into the Führer's presence. Single-handed, the boy had just knocked out a Soviet tank near the Potsdamerplatz, and was to be decorated for his bravery. 'With a great show of emotion,' Boldt wrote of the scene, 'Hitler pinned an Iron Cross on the puny chest of this little chap, on a mud-spattered coat several sizes too big for him. Then he ran his hand slowly over the boy's head and sent him back out into the hopeless battle in the streets of Berlin.'


IN THE streets, Chuikov's troops were involved in heavy fighting for the Eden Hotel on Budapesterstrasse, at the southern tip of the Tiergarten. A few of his tanks broke into the Zoo and drove right up to the hippo house and the planetarium. From there, they opened fire on the twin flak towers, aiming for the steel shutters over the windows, which soon caved in. The 18th Panzergrenadier Division's command post, and the 1st Flak Division, which were both on that side of the main tower, had to be moved swiftly to the other side.

The city's art treasures from the Kaiser Wilhelm Museum were safely stored in rooms on the north and north-east, so they escaped damage. But there were many human casualties: the tower was packed with an estimated 30,000 civilians, sitting or standing on every floor, every stairway, every landing. After several days the strain had become intolerable for most of them. Some had committed suicide. Two old ladies sitting bolt upright side by side had taken poison, but remained propped up by the jam of bodies. It was days before anyone realized they were dead.

The operating theatre in the tower's hospital had been working flat out for the past five days, trying to cope with the casualties among gunners, troops and civilians brought in from outside. Dr Walter Hagedorn, the chief Luftwaffe surgeon, was at his wits' end trying to dispose of bodies and amputated limbs, since no one wanted to step outside the security of the immense walls to bury them. There were now over 500 dead, and he had 1,500 wounded to care for, as well as uncounted suicides and sick civilians. But there were still an amazing number of people who declared they were prepared to stick it out until either Wenck or the Americans arrived to rescue them.

# 18

CHUIKOV NOW had the ultimate target within his sights. By the end of 27 April his main striking force was drawn up along the Landwehr canal, from the Tiergarten to the Halle Gate, barely a mile from the Reichstag. But the race was by no means won: Chuikov's efforts to cross the canal on the run were brought to an abrupt halt by the fanatical SS defenders of the Citadel. He was forced to order a twelve-hour pause, to allow his men to rest and regroup and to bring up reinforcements and ammunition.

Other Soviet armies were also converging on the Reichstag, each general with his eyes fixed on the prize. Attacking from the east, Berzarin and his Fifth Shock Army were on the Spree opposite Museum Island at the other end of the Linden, having already taken Alexanderplatz. Coming from the north, Perevertkin and his LXXIXth Corps, part of Kuznetsov's Third Shock Army, were in Moabit, only a few hundred yards from the Spree on the northern edge of the Tiergarten. Bogdanov's Second Guards Tank Army was fighting in Charlottenburg, nearly two miles west of the Tiergarten, and was no longer really in the race.

These were all Zhukov's armies, of course. But Koniev had not yet given up all hope: Rybalko and his Third Guards Tank Army had made an incredible dash around the west of the city and were now powering through Wilmersdorf. The forward units had been halted for the moment near Weidling's former headquarters on Hohenzollerndamm, but there was no saying that the army might not achieve another breakthrough, to be in at the finish.

The tightness of the Soviet ring around the city centre brought its own problems. A second reason for the pause before the final assault was the need for the artillery commanders in the various armies to coordinate their actions. They were now within range of each other's guns, and it would be only too easy for any of them to overshoot the target and shell their own men advancing from the opposite direction.

So the Soviet commanders spent the night of 27 April like wolves surrounding their prey, watching, waiting, and gathering their strength before going in for the kill.

# 19

WHILE CHUIKOV was preparing to attack the Citadel, Hitler was concerned with a more personal matter. One of his favourite protégés, SS Gruppenführer Hermann Fegelein, was missing from the bunker. The thirty-seven-year-old Fegelein was Himmler's representative at the Führer's court, where he was a boon drinking companion of Bormann. A born trickster, charming, handsome and totally unscrupulous, he had somehow acquired a Knight's Cross with Oak Leaves and Sword and was therefore seen as a hero – though he himself readily admitted that the award was the result of a lucky fluke, and that he was by nature a devout coward. He had been a prime mover in persuading Hitler to dispose of Canaris and give Himmler sole and undisputed control of all the Reich's espionage services.

Fegelein was also Eva Braun's brother-in-law. Hitler himself had acted as matchmaker with Eva's younger sister, Gretl, in 1944. He had joined Hitler in the bunker, as he was bound to do, but with no great enthusiasm – by then he had no illusions about Germany's chances of winning the war. While Eva carefully prepared to commit suttee like a small girl planning a birthday party, writing farewell letters and arranging for her precious dresses and jewels to be sent to Munich for safe keeping, she looked to Fegelein for moral support. But it was not forthcoming. And now, he had vanished.

On 27 April, Hitler sent for him, but he was nowhere to be found. According to Traudl Junge, Eva told her that he had phoned her that evening and told her: 'Eva, if you can't convince the Führer to get out of Berlin, you must leave without him. Don't be an idiot – it's a question of life and death now!' Eva is said to have replied by warning her brother-in-law against antagonizing Hitler. She also reminded him that he had a pregnant wife in Bavaria, about to give birth to his child. But Fegelein's attitude was crystal clear: the 'Valhalla stuff', as he called it, was strictly for Bayreuth. It had no place in real life.

Telephone calls located him at his apartment in Bleibtreustrasse, just off the Kurfürstendamm, but he showed no inclination to leave it and return to the bunker. Although the Soviet guns were still active, a squad of six men was sent through the Tiergarten to fetch him. They found him with his mistress, unshaven, unkempt and too drunk to move. They told him to clean himself up and sober up, and that they would return for him later. When they did, however, he was still drunk, but he had dressed and shaved and was busily packing a suitcase ready to flee. In the case the SS men found a pouch packed with diamonds and other precious stones, other jewellery including three gold watches, and a collection of Reichsmarks, Swiss francs and false passports. The woman escaped through the kitchen window, but Fegelein was arrested and taken back to the bunker, where he was stripped of his rank and handed over to Gruppenführer Mohnke, to be dealt with when he was sober enough to stand trial.

TWO BLOCKS away from Fegelein's apartment, just across the Kurfürstendamm, Max Buch was preparing for another disturbed night. 'Uninterrupted roar of guns, circling of planes, bellowing of machine-guns like all hell let loose,' he noted in his diary.

> I have turned our cellar into a 'bunker', piling boxes and cases ceiling high against the windows and exterior walls. In the small remaining corner, about two metres wide, I have put a small armchair with some cushions, hoping to spend the worst days still to come in some measure of safety, since the Russian bombs are not of a very heavy calibre, and one is fairly safe against shells, which are more dangerous upstairs. So tonight I remain in the shelter, put a blanket on the camp bed and cover myself with two overcoats – I have not taken my clothes off for days. Unfortunately, it is very cold for April, so the cellar is pretty uncomfortable, but what can one do? One must have some rest. The noise of guns continues until it is almost dark. The silence that ensues is frequently interrupted by intermittent shots from a nearby light gun whose shrill noise constantly interrupts one's sleep.

Boldt and Freytag had their sleep interrupted in the adjutants' bunker that night not by gunfire but by the sound of drunken voices in the middle of the night. Freytag woke first, listened for a moment, then prodded his companion in the upper bunk.

'You're missing something, old chap,' he whispered. 'Listen to this a minute.'

Bormann, Krebs and Burgdorf had been drinking together in the next room all night. Now they were shouting at each other at the tops of their voices. Burgdorf was in full flow, bemoaning the fact that no one appreciated his efforts to bring the army and the party closer, that his old service friends despised him, accusing him of being a traitor to the German officer caste. And now, he declared, he could see that they were right, 'that my work was in vain, my idealism wrong – not only wrong, but naive and stupid!'

The two aides listened as their own chief, Krebs, tried to quieten Burgdorf, reminding him that they were with Bormann. But the army adjutant would have none of it. The drink had loosened his tongue and released his inhibitions, and he went on, gathering momentum and volume all the time, to denounce the party leaders. He accused them of sending hundreds of thousands of young officers to their deaths, not for their Fatherland but for the party leaders' high living and megalomania. 'You have trodden our ideals in the dirt,' he charged, 'and our morality, our faith, our souls. For you, human beings were nothing more than a means of feeding your insatiable lust for power. You have destroyed our culture with its hundreds of years of history. You have destroyed the German people. That is the terrible burden of guilt you bear!'

For a moment, it became very quiet. Burgdorf's remarkable outburst was almost certainly the most impassioned condemnation of Nazism ever heard within the confines of the chancellery. It must certainly have been the most direct attack Bormann had ever heard. Over the previous twelve years, thousands of men and women had been executed for less. But now, when it was too late to matter, it had as little effect as a schoolmarm saying 'tut-tut'.

Bormann, 'cool, deliberate and oily', simply remonstrated: 'There's no need to start getting personal about it, old boy. All the others may have got rich quick, but I'm not guilty. That I swear to you by all that's sacred to me. *Prost*, old boy!' Coming from a man who had gained vast estates through his position, Bormann's statement struck Boldt as staggering.

Next day when Boldt delivered his morning report to Hitler, he found the three drinking comrades stretched out side by side in armchairs in the ante-room, wrapped in blankets and snoring loudly. Across the little room, Hitler, Goebbels and Eva Braun looked on with tolerant amusement.

'When Hitler saw me coming,' Boldt recorded, 'he got up. It was not easy for him or for me to climb over their outstretched legs without waking the trio from their deep sleep. Goebbels, who followed us into the conference room, took particular care not to disturb them, which in view of his limp appeared almost grotesque. Eva Braun could not resist a smile at this sight.'

# 20

THE BOMBARDMENT that began at 5.30 that morning quickly escalated into an unending inferno worse than anything before as the combined guns of at least three Soviet armies concentrated their fire into the shrinking island around the chancellery. The ventilation system in the bunker had to be turned off for hours at a time, to keep out the cordite fumes and dust. The atmosphere became unbearable. Everyone sweated, suffered headaches and shortness of breath. The aerial of the 100-watt radio transmitter was shattered, and the telephone lines destroyed. The only contact now remaining between the bunker and the outside world was Lorenz's Propaganda Ministry radio set and runners carrying messages to and from Weidling's command post.

All the time Boldt was presenting his report to Hitler, the thump and crash of shells reverberated through the bunker. From time to time direct hits brought lumps of concrete crashing down from the top layer on to the floor and ceiling above them. After one particularly heavy bang, Hitler interrupted the report, putting a shaking hand on the young captain's arm and staring intently into his eyes. What do you think?' he asked. 'What calibre gun are they firing out there? Could it penetrate right through to here? You've been a soldier at the front, you must surely know.'

Boldt replied that it was probably 175 mm heavy artillery, and that in his view the shells were not capable of destroying the bunker. Hitler seemed reassured, and asked him to go on.

The information in the report, brought by the runners braving the shells and bombs during the morning, could hardly have been worse. The situation was deteriorating all over the city as badly as it was in the Citadel. The last defenders had been killed or captured at Gatow airfield. The fortress at Spandau was about to surrender. Charlottenburg was almost completely lost and Bogdanov's men were about to cross the Spree at the locks immediately north of the Schloss Charlottenburg gardens.

News from outside was even more scanty, and no more optimistic. It was becoming increasingly clear that Wenck's chances of reaching any part of Berlin were fading fast. His progress had been halted near Beelitz, though some elements were still struggling towards Potsdam, where they would shortly make contact with Reymann's encircled force and open a narrow escape corridor. The survivors of Busse's army were struggling westwards, and were reported to be approaching Zossen. But there was no possibility of their turning north to Berlin: they barely had enough strength to extricate themselves from Koniev's grip and were concerned only with escape.

From the north, there was no news at all of the rest of Heinrici's tattered Army Group Vistula: no one knew what Steiner's army detachment and Manteuffel's Third Panzer Army were doing.

# 21

IN THE early hours of 28 April, Keitel discovered that the Third Panzer Army was in full retreat. He had visited Steiner at 4 am, trying to find out what was happening to the attack that had been ordered. Steiner had fobbed him off by assuring him it would begin just as soon as he was ready. Although it never occurred to Keitel that Steiner could be lying to him, he remained suspicious, and set off to see the state of preparations for himself. He found no sign of any troops on the road designated for the attack. But what he did find, to his astonishment, were squads of infantry and horse-drawn artillery units from Manteuffel's army, all heading away from the front line. 'I nearly had a fit!' he wrote later. 'During our conversation the afternoon before, Heinrici had not breathed a word to me about this orderly retreat – in full sway even then.'

Keitel was not only furious because both his and Hitler's specific orders had been ignored, but also because the withdrawal would leave his own headquarters at Neu Roofen completely unprotected. 'We and our camp,' he wrote indignantly, 'at the very latest by the next day, would have been delivered up unawares and defenceless to the Russians.' Seething with rage, he drove back to headquarters to tell Jodl what he had discovered, then ordered Heinrici and Manteuffel to meet him for a conference at a crossroads in the forest north of Neu Brandenburg.

It was obviously going to be a stormy meeting. Suspecting treachery, Manteuffel's chief of staff organized his officers into a bodyguard. Armed with machine pistols they concealed themselves among the trees before Keitel and his entourage arrived, and stayed on the alert while the three chiefs verbally slugged it out in the clearing.

Keitel began immediately with a storm of abuse against Heinrici, who waited calmly until it abated, then quietly and logically explained the situation. 'I tell you, Field Marshal Keitel,' he concluded, 'that I cannot hold the Oder with the troops I have. I do not intend to sacrifice their lives. What is more, we shall have to withdraw even further.'

Manteuffel added his own assessment, supporting everything Heinrici had said and confirming that he would have to pull his troops back again unless he received reinforcements at once.

'There are no reserves left!' Keitel yelled, pounding his fist with his field marshal's baton. 'This is the Führer's order! You will hold your positions where they are! You will turn your army round right now!'

'Field Marshal,' Heinrici interjected, 'as long as I am in command, I shall not issue that order to Manteuffel.'

'Field Marshal Keitel,' Manteuffel added, 'the Third Panzer Army listens only to General Hasso von Manteuffel.'

Faced with such total intransigence, Keitel blew up. 'He went into such a tantrum,' Manteuffel recalled later, 'that neither Heinrici nor I could understand what he was saying.' He finished by shrieking at them: 'You will have to take the responsibility for this action before history!'

This was too much for Manteuffel. 'The Manteuffels have served Prussia for two hundred years,' he snapped. 'They have always taken the responsibility for their actions. I, Hasso von Manteuffel, accept this responsibility gladly.'

Keitel turned back to Heinrici. If Heinrici had had the guts to shoot a few thousand deserters, he raged, there would have been no retreat. In response, Heinrici took Keitel by the arm and led him to the road, pointing at the columns of exhausted men. 'If you want these men shot,' he said in an even tone, 'why don't you do it yourself?'

Keitel stomped angrily back to his car. 'From now on,' he blustered, 'follow OKW orders to the letter.'

Heinrici glared back at him. 'How can I possibly follow your orders,' he barked, 'when you are so obviously out of touch with the current situation?'

'You have not heard the last of this matter,' Keitel ended, defeated. Stepping into his car, he drove quickly away. Behind him, the retreat continued.


AWAY TO the south of Berlin, Busse's Ninth Army had started its attempt to break out of its pocket during the night. They were travelling light – this was strictly a salvage operation, and they intended to do as little fighting as possible. Everything that was not essential had been dumped. Motor vehicles had been disabled and their fuel drained for use in armoured fighting vehicles. Guns for which there was no ammunition were spiked.

Busse's plan was to try to break out along the demarcation line between Koniev's and Zhukov's fronts, where coordination was likely to be weakest. It was an excellent idea, and within the limits imposed by lack of strength or support it was well executed. But Busse's mobility was hampered by the presence of tens of thousands of refugees, all determined to go along with the troops, and as the Soviet Air Force had spotted some of the preparations, much of the element of surprise was lost. Busse managed to open a breach in the Soviet lines, and got two formations through and away: the XIth SS Panzer Corps, with all the available tanks, and the Vth Corps. The remainder were not so lucky. They were caught as they tried to break out, and were massacred in two days of savage fighting.

Konstantin Simonov, a well-known Soviet novelist serving as a war correspondent, came across part of the result as he was driving into Berlin along the autobahn from Breslau. It was at a point where the autobahn cut through a stretch of forest, which was split into two by what looked like a huge fire break, a wide corridor between the trees that ran for miles. The Germans had been caught trying to reach the autobahn using this corridor. Under heavy fire they had tried to turn back and escape. In their desperation their armoured vehicles had uprooted hundreds of trees, which lay as if hit by a whirlwind, amid a chaos of shattered tanks, cars, trucks and ambulances. 'In this black, charred confusion of steel, timber, guns, cases and papers,' wrote Simonov, 'a bloody mass of mutilated corpses lay strewn along the clearing as far as the eye could see. There were wounded men everywhere, lying on greatcoats or blankets or leaning against tree trunks; some of them bandaged and others covered in blood, with no one to tend them.'

## 22

IT TOOK Chuikov's men virtually the entire day on 28 April to get across the Landwehr canal at the Möckern and Potsdamer bridges. The banks of the canal were lined with sheer concrete, and the bridges and the approaches were heavily mined and covered by heavy machine guns in well-prepared positions on the other side of the deep water. Before the attack began, however, there was a delay caused by an incident that would later be commemorated with a bronze statue. The troops were moving forward in small groups to take up their positions by the Möckern Bridge. Suddenly, in the ominous, tense silence that precedes any major assault, they heard a child crying. The voice seemed to come from somewhere underground, and it was repeating one word over and over again: '*Mutter! Mutter!*' It needed no translation.

Colour-Sergeant Nikolai Masalov, standard bearer of the 220th Guards Rifle Regiment, was closest to the bridge. He listened carefully. 'Seems to be on the opposite bank,' he said.

Handing the regimental colours to his two escorts, he went to his commanding officer and asked permission to rescue the child. 'I know where it is,' he told him. The CO agreed, and Masalov made his way forward, crawling along the ground from one shell crater to the next, sheltering from machine-gun fire, feeling every bump and crack in the asphalt for signs of mines. At the embankment he hid behind the concrete wall of the canal for a moment. The child's voice cried out again, plaintively calling for its mother. Masalov stood up and dashed across the bridge. He leapt over the parapet on the other side, and disappeared. For minutes there was silence, while his comrades watched and waited, fascinated. Just as they were giving up hope, they heard his voice. 'I got the child! Cover me! There's a machine gun on the right, on the balcony of the building with columns. Shut 'em up!'

At that moment, as if by magic, the artillery bombardment opened up, with thousands of guns and mortars pouring fire on the German positions, as though to cover Masalov's return, clutching a three-year-old girl in his arms. The mother had been shot while trying to flee, and had died under the bridge. Handing the child over to the medics, Masalov grabbed the colours again, and took up his position for the attack.

To CHUIKOV, Masalov's heroism was heart-warming, but it did nothing to solve the problem of how to get his tanks across the bridge and through to the Anhalter station and the Wilhelmstrasse. Each time they advanced they were met by fierce enemy gunfire and beaten back. To make matters worse, the bridge itself was mined with two huge charges suspended just below the girders, which could be detonated at any time. Soviet sappers under cover of a dense smoke screen and constant enemy fire worked to try to defuse them. A few infantrymen took advantage of the confusion to get across, but were pinned down on the other side. More tanks were sent in. One that made it to the other bank was immediately Panzerfausted and put out of action. It began to seem as though Chuikov was doomed not to get his armour into the city centre.

Finally, his men came up with an ingenious ploy. They took one of their tanks and hung it about with sandbags, like some steel bag-lady. They then doused the bags with diesel oil, hung smoke canisters all round it, and sent it trundling across the bridge to face the German guns. The moment it was hit, it seemed to burst into flames and thick, dark smoke. The SS men manning the guns were momentarily confused. They did not know whether to fire on the blazing tank, which was still advancing, apparently out of control, or to concentrate on the ones coming behind it. By the time they had made up their minds, it was too late – several Soviet tanks were already in their midst.

ALL ALONG the canal, other units were battling to make their way across in the best way they could think of. Some small groups used the U-Bahn tunnels. Others chose the sewers. Senior Lieutenant Nikolai Balakin of the 39th

Division led his men down into the canal through the wide drainpipes on the southern bank. They swam across and found another drain emptying into the canal on the other side, and climbed into it, sneaking through the German defences to emerge behind them and capture two buildings and about seventy prisoners from a Volkssturm battalion. Senior Lieutenant Alexander Klimushkin also used the sewers and underground conduits to get his men to the Möckern-Brücke U-Bahn station, which they captured, allowing the rest of the battalion to cross and launch a successful attack on the block next to it.

As more and more men forced their way across the canal and into the city, fighting grew more intense. This was real house-to-house stuff, where troops had to advance building by building and block by block. Mohnke's SS men were well established, and were winkled out slowly and with great difficulty. Close-quarter battles, fought mostly with hand grenades and knives, were taking up to six hours. Gunners were faced with the problems of restricted fields of fire along streets. They blasted away most of the barricades across the main streets without too much trouble, but could do little about machine guns hidden in side streets and around corners, which opened up as the attackers tried to pass across the intersections. During the previous four days Chuikov's troops had covered nearly eight miles. Now they had to count their progress in yards, and blasting their way through individual buildings to the Reichstag could take several days.

To his intense fury, Chuikov had had to contend not only with the Germans but also with the First Ukrainian Front. With Stalin already pressing for the Reichstag to be taken in time for the May Day celebrations in Moscow, Koniev was flogging Rybalko and his Third Guards Tank Army mercilessly. During the previous night he had ordered Rybalko to be across the Landwehr canal and into the Tiergarten by nightfall on 28 April. The main thrust was northwards from Wilmersdorf, with the 55th Guards Tank Brigade blasting its way east along Kantstrasse towards the Zoo. The attack was well under way, with the opening artillery barrage completed, before anyone in Rybalko's army realized that most of the area they were advancing on was already occupied by Chuikov's men. The original orders were hurriedly cancelled, and the charge was stopped and redirected to end at Savignyplatz, a little under half a mile from the Zoo station. Koniev had finally been squeezed out of the race, which was now between Chuikov, Berzarin and Perevertkin's LXXIXth Corps of Kuznetsov's Third Shock Army.

THAT AFTERNOON, Perevertkin's advance units, led by Captain Neustroyev's Young Communist Battalion, were battling along the street known as Alt Moabit. On their way, they had bypassed the grim fortress that was Moabit Prison, leaving the main force to storm the building. Neustroyev's regimental commander, Colonel Zinchenko, led the assault personally. Spurred on by a rumour that Goebbels himself was in command of the jail, his men hurled themselves into the attack, freeing 7,000 prisoners. Among them were many prisoners of war, who were pressed into service to replace the heavy losses sustained during the grinding battle through the factories and tenement blocks of Moabit.

Suddenly, through the clouds of smoke and dust ahead of them, Neustroyev's men caught sight of the Reichstag dome across the Moltke Bridge. Amid great excitement, Perevertkin joined them to see for himself. As the corps reached the banks of the Spree, Perevertkin set up his final command post in the tall customs building overlooking the bridge, with a clear view of the Reichstag and its approaches.

This final assault would not be easy. The river was about fifty yards wide at that point, and the only way across it was the Moltke Bridge, a massive stone structure with barricades at either end. The bridge presented serious problems for the attackers: it was mined and wired up ready for demolition, and there were barbed-wire entanglements and other obstacles across the wide, open approaches, where there was little cover against machine-gun and artillery fire from positions in the heavily fortified buildings on the other bank, especially the huge bulk of Himmler's Ministry of the Interior.

Perevertkin estimated that there were some 5,000 troops waiting across the river. They were mostly SS, but included two battalions of Volkssturm, some remnants of the 9th Parachute Division, and the naval radar technicians of the Grossadmiral Dönitz Battalion. Perevertkin also had to contend with German units still holding out on his own bank of the river, on either side and to his rear. Nevertheless, the Reichstag was now only about 600 yards away from his command post.

## 23

RYBALKO'S DRIVE north towards the Tiergarten had left many uncleared pockets in Wilmersdorf, where the remnants of German units were still fighting. Maria von Maltzan's flat in Detmolderstrasse was in one of them. She caught two SS men – blond, good-looking young men in their early twenties – setting up a machine-gun post in a corner room of the building. Pointing her pistol at them, she ordered them to stop. 'I'm not going to have this house shot up,' she told them. 'I won't have it. I'll give you a choice – you can hand over your weapons and your uniforms and stay with us, or you can be shot right now. Which is it to be?'

'You can't give up now!' one of the men shouted. 'You can't win the war if you give up!'

'You stupid fools,' Maria shouted back. 'The war is lost. Now, come on. Make up your minds!'

The SS men hesitated, then gave in, looking relieved. Maria and the hefty, sixteen-year-old son of the Polish family who had moved into the wrecked flat above hers marched them down to the cellar, took their uniforms, then locked them up. The Polish boy carried the uniforms out into the courtyard and burned them.

About an hour later, Maria and her friends saw their first Soviet soldier. He was walking up the street, all alone, carrying a light-coloured summer parasol. A few moments later, a column of tanks appeared. Tamara, the elder of the two young Russian girls taken in by Maria, hurried out to meet them. Maria went with her.

'Hello!' Tamara called out in Russian. 'I'm a Russian child. I've been staying with good German people. They're against Hitler.'

Someone fetched a Soviet officer. Tamara told him her story, and he called out to his men. Suddenly, Maria and the girl were surrounded by beaming Soviet soldiers, holding cans of food and loaves of black bread. One produced a bottle of brandy and offered it to Maria. She drank a tumblerful, straight down. She had waited six years for this moment, and she felt like celebrating.

# 24

WHILE HIS troops were still fighting across the Spree just beyond the old Imperial Palace, Colonel-General Berzarin took up his appointment as Soviet Commandant of Berlin. Notice of this, with his first order to the citizens, was pasted up in Alexanderplatz and then all over the city, printed on brilliant green paper:

ORDER BY THE COMMANDANT OF THE BERLIN GARRISON

April 28 1945                    No. 1                    City of Berlin

I have this day been appointed Chief of Garrison and City Commandant of Berlin.

All administrative and political authority passes into my hands by virtue of the power vested in me by the High Command of the Red Army.

Military district and section commands will be set up in every part of the city along the lines of the existing administrative divisions.

Beneath this came eleven detailed orders regulating life in the city. Some had an ominously familiar ring to them. People were to maintain complete order, and stay in their homes. The Nazi Party and all its affiliated organizations were banned. All members of the armed forces, the SS, the SA, police and fire services were ordered to register within seventy-two hours. Staff and officials of all public utilities were to return to their posts immediately. Food stores were to register with the authorities, and to open up at once. Existing ration cards would be valid for the time being. It was forbidden to print, duplicate, post up or circulate documents of any kind without prior permission from the military commanders, and all typewriters, duplicating machines and printing presses were to be registered immediately. There was to be a curfew between 2200 hours and 0800 hours each day. And so it went on.

In the occupied districts, new local councils were already being set up, with men plucked virtually at random to serve as mayors and officials. The Soviet authorities were anxious to restore order as fast as possible. While the noise of fighting still echoed across the city from the central area, people in other districts were being ordered on to the streets to start clearing rubble and filling in the craters.

Ludwig von Hammerstein decided to leave Oranienstrasse that day and try to get to his sister's house in the south-eastern suburb of Stahnsdorf, on foot, with a rucksack of food on his back. He only got as far as Mariendorf, before he was forced to join a gang repairing a street. After two hours he was allowed to go, but discovered that someone had stolen his rucksack. While he was begging for food from a Soviet rations truck, he was arrested, but slipped away and tried to continue his journey. He was stopped and forced to turn back – and was again arrested and stripped down to his underclothes to see if he was wearing anything that showed he was a German soldier, to be rounded up and shipped east as a prisoner of war. By now, the Soviet authorities had banned movement of civilians between districts, and it was only with the greatest difficulty that he eventually managed to get back to the Kerps' place. There, he found a Soviet colonel had been billeted in the flat, and the family had to live in the store.

WOLFGANG SKORNING awoke in his sister's flat in Monumentenstrasse to find his feet and legs had swollen so much he could not get his boots back on. His wounded hand was extremely painful, and needed a fresh dressing. In his stockinged feet he made his way down to the cellar of the modern block, where one corner was equipped as a first-aid room, with a nursing sister in charge. He took off his uniform jacket, and the nurse prepared new bandages and began dressing his wound. Suddenly his sister dashed into the room, shouting 'The Russians are here!' She grabbed his jacket and rushed through the outside door, just as a Soviet officer came in through the other door, saw her, and gave chase without pausing to look at Skorning himself. She eluded him, and threw the jacket out, with Skorning's driving licence, identification papers and money still in the pockets.

Even without his jacket, it was obvious that Skorning was an army officer in his riding breeches and green officer's shirt. His sister fetched him an old suit of her husband's and an old pair of ski boots to put over his swollen feet. He changed, and hobbled away to another cellar where there was a woman doctor who could look at his hand.

Outside, he was amazed to see no tanks or armoured vehicles but a street filled with men on horseback, and horse-drawn wagons, a scene from fifty or a hundred years before. Staring incredulously, he could only think 'Are these the people who have defeated us?'

Skorning was not the only one to be amazed by such scenes. In Frohnau, Gerald Rahusen watched open-mouthed as troops of cavalry rode past his door, each troop or squadron riding different coloured horses, some all black, some all grey, some all chestnut, all in immaculate order. An anonymous woman diarist saw 'an endless supply column pulling up outside: well-fed mares with foals between their legs; a cow mooing to be milked. In the garage opposite, they were already setting up a field kitchen.' Other observers noted wagonloads of pigs and sheep. The Soviet troops had trekked like this for over 1,000 miles, bringing much of their food with them, on the hoof.


AT FIRST sight, the soldiers outside the woman diarist's house and in the street near Skorning's sister's apartment block seemed pleasant enough. But the illusion did not last long. These were the second-echelon troops, the brutalized survivors of the prison camps, Asiatics with their own ideas about women, Mongols whose attitudes to conquered peoples had been inherited by direct descent from Genghis Khan. These were the men the refugees from the east had warned the Berliners about. But as the fighting ended, and the tensions and the iron discipline were relaxed, front-line troops, too, sought the soldier's traditional rewards. All over Berlin, a new phrase was taking over from '*Uri*'. Now the men were roaming cellars, bunkers and apartments, grunting the dreaded words: '*Frau komm!*' It was worst at night, when men were off duty and found stocks of liquor to plunder and guzzle. But it could happen any time, anywhere, as often as not in broad daylight and in public view. For these were virile young men, many of whom had been away from their own families for up to four years – there was no such thing as home leave in the Red Army.

For two days and nights Skorning was forced to stay in the cellar, watching helplessly as Soviet soldiers dragged away women and girls, raping them time after time. He tried to save the woman doctor by claiming her as his wife, but the only response was *'Komm! Komm!'* As he listened to the screams and cries, he was tormented by the thought of what might be happening to his own wife in their apartment in Lichterfelde.

The woman diarist, meanwhile, was facing her first assailant:

> Behind me the cellar door closes with a soft thud. One man seizes me by the wrists and drags me along the corridor. Now the other one also pulls at the same time, gripping my throat with one hand so that I can no longer scream . . . I'm already on the ground, my head lying on the lowest cellar step. I can feel the coldness of the tiles against my back. Something falls from my coat with a tinkling sound. Must be my house keys, my bunch of keys. One man stands guard at the door upstairs, while the other claws at my underwear. . . .

After that first time, she fled upstairs to seek refuge – it was said that many Russians did not like going to upper floors. But she was found almost at once by a giant Siberian, 'broad as a wardrobe with paws like a lumberjack', who did at least pause long enough to take off his boots and his gun. Next day, she was attacked again by two men who kicked in the door of the apartment and took turns to stand guard while the other raped her. She recounted the horror of that occasion:

> Shut your eyes, clench your teeth, don't utter a sound. Only when the underwear is ripped apart with a tearing sound, the teeth grind involuntarily. The last underwear.
>
> I feel the fingers at my mouth, smell the reek of horses and tobacco. I open my eyes. Adroitly, the fingers force my jaws apart. Eye looks into eye. The man above me slowly lets his spittle dribble into my mouth. . . .
>
> Paralysis. Not disgust, just utter coldness. The spine seems to be frozen. Icy dizziness encircles the back of the head. I find myself floating and sinking deep down through the pillows, through the floor. . . .
>
> Before leaving, he fishes something out of his pocket, throws it without a word on the night table, pushes the chair away and slams the door behind him. What he has left behind turns out to be a crumpled packet of cigarettes. The fee.

Like thousands of Berlin women and girls, some little more than children, others as old as eighty, the anonymous diarist was to endure more sexual attacks, day after day, some singly, some by gangs, some savage, some almost tender. The raping that started in the last few days of April went on for weeks,

439

though the worst of it was over by 8 May. Thousands of women and girls committed suicide – over 200 in Pankow alone. Many husbands and fathers died with them, unable to accept the dishonour. Thousands of other women came to terms with it and made the best of a bad situation by finding themselves individual protectors. 'Better a Russian on the belly, than an American on the head' became their catchphrase, comparing the sexual attacks with the bombing. But the scars were to remain in their minds for many years. Over 90,000 women and girls visited doctors and clinics in Berlin as a result of rape. No one can say how many kept silent.

# 25

THE ONE piece of good news for those in the bunker that day was that the warrant officer pilot who had previously flown Speer in and out of Berlin, and then Greim and Hanna Reitsch into Gatow, had achieved the impossible once again. He had landed an Arado 96 training aircraft on the East–West Axis, and was ready to fly Greim and Reitsch out again. Hanna offered to stay with Hitler to the end, but he refused. In any case, Hitler wanted Greim, as commander-in-chief of the Luftwaffe, at his operational headquarters. Soviet tanks were already reported to be in Potsdamerplatz. Greim must send planes to attack them. Then he must organize further attacks on Soviet positions threatening the chancellery, and provide air support to help Wenck get to Berlin.

At about 7 pm, while Greim and Reitsch were waiting for darkness to cover their take-off, Lorenz hurried into the bunker from his office in the Propaganda Ministry bunker, with a sensational piece of news for Hitler. He had just picked up a broadcast from the BBC in London, quoting a Reuters report that Himmler had offered the Allies an unconditional surrender on behalf of all German troops. Hitler was utterly shocked, far more deeply upset than he had been over the supposed treachery of Göring. He had always regarded Himmler as his most trustworthy and loyal follower, but now he had gone behind his back over the most important issue of all. This, he raged wildly, was the most shameful betrayal in human history.

When he had regained some control, he shut himself away in the conference room with Bormann and Goebbels, leaving everyone else to wait in the ante-room. No doubt his two heirs apparent were delighted to see yet another rival disposed of. And no doubt they were only too happy to suggest a way he could satisfy his thirst for revenge: Himmler was for the moment out of his reach, but his representative was in the bunker, and under arrest. The unfortunate Hermann Fegelein would make an excellent scapegoat for the sins of his master. Although he denied any knowledge of Himmler's treasonable activities, Hitler was determined someone should pay. Fegelein was taken out into the chancellery garden and shot.

In a state of near hysteria, Hitler rushed to the sickroom, to speak to Greim. He ordered him to leave at once for Plön, where he was to put Himmler under arrest. 'A traitor must never succeed me as Führer!' he yelled. 'You must get out to make sure that he doesn't.'

Soon afterwards the two flyers were driven to the airstrip in an armoured car. Hanna was in floods of tears. She carried with her various letters from people in the bunker, including a farewell from the Goebbels to Magda's son by her first marriage, Harald, and one from Eva Braun to her sister Gretl, in which she made no mention of Fegelein and his fate. The little plane was tossed around like a leaf in a gale of shellfire, but finally climbed out of it to 20,000 feet. Below, they could see nothing of the centre of Berlin but a sea of flame. Setting course for Rechlin air base they flew safely on their way.

# 26

WITH THE departure of Greim and Reitsch, Hitler's wild behaviour subsided. All the excitement of the previous two hours drained away completely, and he withdrew to his private quarters without another word, his face an expressionless mask. Clearly, Himmler's defection was the final betrayal. There was nothing left now but to end it all.

Weidling had reported earlier that although he still had an estimated 30,000 men, he had only a handful of tanks and guns, and food and ammunition for no more than forty-eight hours at the most. The area of Berlin still in German hands had been reduced to a strip less than nine miles long and one mile wide, from Alexanderplatz in the east to the Havel in the west. The good news was that part of Wenck's XXth Corps had made contact with Reymann's garrison in Potsdam, creating a possible escape route from the centre. Weidling had prepared a plan for this. With his troops providing a protective shield for Hitler, they would drive west along the East–West Axis and cross the Havel Bridge at Pichelsdorf, which was still being held by Hitler Youths, to fight their way through to the narrow corridor into the main body of the Twelfth Army. Hitler thanked him, but refused. He could not take the risk, he said, of falling into enemy hands.

*

EXHAUSTED BY the constant noise of the Soviet bombardment, not to mention the traumatic events of the day, Traudl Junge found a camp bed in a corner and went to sleep. She was woken after about an hour, and told Hitler wanted her. He had something to dictate. When she arrived in his study, Hitler came over and took her hand. 'Have you had some rest, my dear?' he asked solicitously.

Traudl was puzzled to see that the room appeared to be arranged for a party. The table was covered with a crisp white cloth embroidered with the initials AH, and on it stood the silver dinner service and eight champagne glasses. Hitler winked at Traudl then led her through into the conference room. 'Perhaps we can begin now,' he said.

Standing at the map table, staring down at its bare polished surface, he began to dictate his last political testament, which she took down in shorthand. 'More than thirty years have passed,' he began, 'since I made my modest contribution as a volunteer in the First World War, which was forced upon the Reich. In these three decades, love and loyalty to my people alone guided me in all my thoughts, actions and life. . . .' He covered the old familiar ground in the old familiar manner, claiming yet again that he had never wanted war, but that it had been forced upon the world by the machinations of international Jewry. The sole responsibility for all the subsequent death and horror – including the death of so many Jews – lay with the Jews themselves. But now that the end had come, now that he had decided to remain in Berlin, 'I die with a joyful heart in the knowledge of the immeasurable deeds and achievements of our peasants and workers and of a contribution unique in history by our youth which bears my name.' He reserved some of his bitterest comments for the German officer corps who, unlike himself, 'had failed to set a shining example of faithful devotion to duty, unto death'.

Turning to more practical matters, he officially pronounced anathema upon both Göring and Himmler, expelling them from the party and stripping them of their offices. They had brought, he said, 'irreparable shame on the whole nation by negotiating with the enemy without my knowledge and against my will'. He named the members of the government that was to take over when he was dead. Grand Admiral Dönitz was to become president of the Reich and supreme commander of the Wehrmacht, Goebbels was to be Reich chancellor, Bormann party chancellor. A variety of loyal nonentities were named for the other offices of state. To ensure that the new government was injected with the virus of anti-Semitism, he urged his successors 'to uphold the racial laws to the limit and to resist mercilessly the poisoner of all nations, international Jewry'.

Finally, he came to personal matters. 'During the years of combat,' he declared, 'I was unable to commit myself to a contract of marriage, so I have decided this day before the end of my earthly life to take as my wife the young woman who, after many years of faithful friendship, has of her own free will come to the besieged capital to link her fate with my own. She will, according to her wishes, go to her death as my wife. For us, this will take the place of all that was denied us by my devotion to the service of my people.'

It was the first that Traudl Junge had heard of his intention to marry Eva Braun. She started to look up at him, but he was still dictating. He ended with a typically Wagnerian flourish: 'My wife and I choose to die in order to escape the shame of flight or capitulation. It is our wish that our bodies be burned immediately, here, where I have performed the greater part of my daily work during the twelve years I have served my people.'

Oddly, Traudl did not weep. But Goebbels did. She had returned to her office and was typing out the document when he suddenly appeared, distraught, and with tears streaming down his face. Hitler had ordered him to leave Berlin. 'But I don't want to run away and leave the Führer,' he wailed, like a child being sent away to school. 'I am the Gauleiter of Berlin and my place is here. If the Führer dies, my life has no meaning. He even said to me, "Goebbels, I didn't expect this from you! You refuse to obey my last orders!"' Then, not to be outdone, Goebbels started dictating his own will to Traudl, which he ordered should be attached to Hitler's as an appendix.


INTO THE midst of all the hysteria, a purely practical matter suddenly intruded. No one in the bunker was legally empowered to perform a marriage ceremony. Without some appropriate official to declare them man and wife, Hitler's last act would be nullified. He had chosen to marry Eva because only thus could he demonstrate that, at the end, he rejected Germany – he had divorced her because she was no longer worthy of him. Germany had failed him.

Goebbels had the answer. As Gauleiter of Berlin he knew of someone authorized to act as a registrar of marriages who was still in Berlin, fighting with the Volkssturm. He was a municipal councillor, and his name, appropriately, was Wagner, Walter Wagner. A group of SS men was dispatched across the city, to bring him back alive.

The ceremony took place in the map room. Eva wore a long black silk dress. Hitler, of course, was in his uniform. Because of the exalted nature of the groom, the formalities were reduced to the bare minimum required by law. Normally, the happy couple would have had to answer questions about their Aryan origins and their freedom from hereditary diseases, but in the circumstances, Herr Wagner waived these. In fact, the only questions asked were the ritual ones: 'Do you, Adolf Hitler, take Eva Braun to be your wife?' followed by the reverse for the future Frau Hitler.

After this brief ceremony, the newly-weds signed the standard two-page wedding contract, followed by the witnesses – Bormann and Goebbels – and the registrar. Eva made the same mistake that many brides make – she started to sign her old name. Herr Wagner gently pointed out her error. She smiled and crossed it out, then signed 'Eva Hitler, née Braun'.

Arm in arm, the newly married couple led the way into the study to share the wedding feast of champagne and sandwiches with their guests: the Goebbels, Gerda Christian, now Hitler's senior secretary, Constanze Manziarly, the young Austrian dietitian who prepared his vegetarian meals, Krebs, Bormann, Burgdorf and Axmann. Eva chatted brightly, in her chirpy, pleasant Bavarian accent. She sent for the wind-up gramophone, with its single record, 'Red Roses', to provide a sentimental musical background. She went into the corridor outside the conference room to accept the congratulations of staff not invited to the private party. She was relaxed and smiling, every inch the gracious hostess.

# 27

WHILE HITLER and Eva Braun were celebrating their marriage, Captain Neustroyev's Young Communist Battalion, strengthened by new recruits from Moabit Prison, were spearheading Perevertkin's assault on the Moltke Bridge. Shortly after midnight, they smashed their way through the obstacles and started pouring across the bridge towards the Interior Ministry – 'Himmler's House' as they called it – and the Reichstag. It was a hard and bloody fight which lasted right through the night, with defensive fire and counter-attacks from behind and to the sides as well as the front, since there were still German troops in the Lehrter freight station on Perevertkin's right flank. The Germans blew the bridge, causing further casualties, but they did not have enough explosive to do the job properly. Although it was severely damaged, only part of the central span fell into the river, leaving room for men and vehicles to get across. By morning, the buildings on the opposite corner had been taken, and the first echelons of two divisions were packed tight in a bridgehead on the southern bank.

ALL THROUGH the morning, the men of the four Soviet armies that now had footholds in the Citadel sector – Chuikov's Eighth Guards and the First Guards Tank, Kuznetsov's Third Shock, and Berzarin's Fifth Shock – battered away at the SS defenders. The Citadel was now split into three parts, under separate commanders – Mohnke, Krukenberg, and Colonel Seifert. Their men, so many of them foreigners, were stubbornly defending every room in every building. There was savage hand-to-hand fighting in the Interior Ministry, in the Red Town Hall, in Stettiner railway station, in government buildings at the southern end of the Wilhelmstrasse.

Vladimir Abyzov and his comrades were still in the vanguard of Chuikov's advance, but were finding it increasingly hard going. 'The whole city was in flames,' Abyzov recalled:

> Dense foul smoke curled over the roofs and hung heavily over the injured land. It seeped into the houses and basements through every crack and slot. There was no air to breathe. Despite this, we ran, falling to the ground between blocks and then getting up again to run further through the yards, along and across the streets. There was no clear-cut front line, nor a rear, nor any carefully worked out combat missions. If you are on the first floor, it's your front line, and the ground floor is your rear. But that was ten minutes ago, and now everything was in utter confusion. Where are the front and the rear, as laid down by the Infantry Field Manual? Bursting into a five-storey building, we threw hand grenades into the doorway as a preventive measure. We then 'swept' through the rooms. We had taken the first, second and third floors. Half the house was in our hands and half in the hands of the Germans. It was divided by a very thick wall. We thought of climbing on to the roof, but the top floor on our side was demolished. . . .

Abyzov and his companions were facing the men of Krukenberg's SS Nordland Division, some of the toughest warriors of the war. Krukenberg himself confirmed what Abyzov said about the dangers and difficulties of the battle. Since Chuikov had got pontoon bridges across the Landwehr canal, he wrote, fighting had been going on for every house, ruin and shell crater. Losses on both sides had been high, many of them caused not only by enemy guns but also by damaged buildings collapsing on to the men inside them.

# 28

IN THE bunker at about 8 am on Sunday, 29 April, Burgdorf sent for Major Willi Johannmeier, Hitler's army adjutant, and told him he was to undertake an important secret mission. He was to carry the Führer's last will and political testament out of Berlin and hand it personally to Field Marshal Schörner, who had been chosen to become commander-in-chief of the army. Copies were to be carried by two other couriers: SS Standartenführer

Wilhelm Zander, Bormann's personal assistant, would be taking one to Dönitz as the new head of state; Heinz Lorenz would represent Goebbels, carrying a copy which included Goebbels's own testament – destined eventually for Munich, the cradle of National Socialism, where it was to be preserved for posterity. As a courageous and experienced soldier, Johann-meier was to be in charge of the party. They left through the chancellery garages in Hermann-Göring-Strasse at about noon, accompanied by a corporal named Hummerich. Moving stealthily on foot, they set off through the Tiergarten, heading for the bridge at Pichelsdorf.

WHILE THE three messengers were preparing for their journey, Boldt and Freytag were doing their best to piece together a picture of the situation outside from the sparse and disjointed reports. Until 9 am the thunder of the bombardment over their heads grew steadily more intense. But then it suddenly stopped. Soon afterwards, they discovered why – runners reported that Soviet troops with tanks were advancing towards the Wilhelmplatz. For the next hour, all those in the bunker held their breath and waited in silence, straining their ears for any sign of attack. Then came word that the tanks had stopped, only four or five hundred yards away from the chancellery.

With the end so close, Boldt and Freytag decided there was no time to lose if they were ever to get out. A few minutes later they learned that the link between Reymann's troops and Wenck's XXth Corps at Werder, just beyond Potsdam, was still holding. Briefing Krebs for the morning conference with Hitler, Freytag suggested that in view of the total breakdown in communications it might be a good idea if he and Boldt were to go there, so that they could personally tell Wenck exactly what was going on in Berlin. What was more, he added, they could then act as guides, helping to direct Wenck's attack on the city. Boldt backed his friend, pointing out that there was really nothing more they could do in the bunker now. Krebs was nervous, afraid of getting into trouble with Hitler, but Burgdorf and Bormann were enthusiastic about the idea, and Burgdorf's own adjutant, Lieutenant-Colonel Weiss, decided he would leave with them.

At the end of the midday conference, Krebs told Hitler there were three young officers who wanted to break out of Berlin to give Wenck a full picture of the situation in the city and urge him to speed up his rescue mission. Hitler said nothing for several moments, looking up from the map and staring straight ahead. After what seemed an eternity, he asked, 'Who are these officers?' Krebs told him, and the three stepped forward. Again there was an agonizing silence. Then Hitler asked Freytag: 'How do you think you will get out of Berlin?'

Freytag said there were two possibilities. They could try to get through the Soviet lines in the Grunewald, but it was unlikely they would succeed. The other option was to leave by night, down the Havel, by boat. Hitler pondered this for a moment, then suddenly started to get excited. Yes, he declared. That would be the best way. And in no time, he was starting to plan their journey for them. He knew where there was a boat with an electric motor, he said. That would be silent. They must use that. He began ordering Bormann to arrange for them to have it. Freytag interrupted, cautiously, to say there was really no need – they would be able to find a boat themselves. Hitler nodded, rose to his feet, and shook hands with each of the three, wishing them luck. 'Give my regards to Wenck,' he said wearily. 'Tell him to hurry or it will be too late.'

The three men left the conference room at 12.45 pm in high spirits. At least they now had a fighting chance. They had already had passes made out and signed, to let them through German lines. They rushed around preparing for their journey – packing rations, finding maps, camouflage jackets, steel helmets and sub-machine guns. Finally, Freytag tore the broad red staff officer's stripe from his trousers, and they were ready. At 1.30 pm they slipped out of the bunker and were on their way, free at last from the suffocating atmosphere of doom.

FIVE HUNDRED yards from the bunker, in the candlelit train carriage in Stadtmitte U-Bahn station, a curious ceremony was taking place. The train was Krukenberg's command post, and the occasion was the last presentation of one of the Reich's highest military awards, the Knight's Cross. The proud recipient was not German but French: Unterscharführer (Sergeant) Eugène Vaulot of the Charlemagne Battalion. Vaulot, known as 'the Panzerfaust virtuoso', was the Charlemagne Battalion's star performer. This twenty-year-old former plumber's mate had won his first Iron Cross in Russia. Now, single-handed, he had destroyed eight tanks in the course of two days' fighting, to earn a higher decoration.

By the light of the candles, and in the presence of his staff and some of Vaulot's comrades, Krukenberg made a speech in French. He said that the bearing of this young volunteer was what the SS had come to expect of French soldiers, men who had won their spurs on battlefields throughout the world. He then hung the cross, on its black, white and red ribbon, around the young man's neck and gave the Hitler salute. Everyone followed suit. A few minutes later the latest holder of the Knight's Cross left the station to go back to his company, and to his death.

BACK IN the chancellery a different celebration was taking place. Goebbels was giving a small party for nurses and children, about forty people in all, in one of the cellars under the chancellery building. It was, he said, the last farewell to Berlin for himself, his wife and their children. Everyone sat around a long oak table in one of the cellars of the new chancellery, while a fifteen-year-old Hitler Youth with an accordion entertained them with songs like 'Die Blaue Dragoner' ('The Blue Dragoons').

In the next cellar, Professor Ernst-Günther Schenck, one of Hitler's doctors, had set up his emergency casualty station. As the Hitler Youth sang his cheery songs, Schenck, 'up to my elbows in entrails, arteries and gore', continued with some of the 370 major operations he had carried out over the last week on men and boys seriously wounded in the streets. As well as an acute shortage of bandages, drugs and all but the most basic equipment, Schenck had to cope with two personal problems: he was not a qualified surgeon, but a nutrition expert. Moreover, he was almost insensible for lack of sleep – the nine senior SS officers who shared a room with him were now permanently drunk and noisily enjoying the favours of equally drunken women determined to make the most of their last hours.

IN THE Führer bunker a grim prelude to what was soon to come was being enacted in the toilet at the end of the corridor, by Professor Haase, one of Hitler's doctors, aided by Sergeant Tornow, who looked after the Führer's dogs. A few days earlier, Himmler had provided Hitler with a collection of cyanide capsules, but now that Himmler was no longer to be trusted, Hitler had his doubts about them. Was there cyanide in the capsules? Did they really contain poison, or were they intended to drug him so that he could be handed over alive to the Soviets? The only way to be sure was to test some of them.

Tornow and Haase took Blondi, Hitler's favourite German shepherd dog, into the toilet. While the sergeant held her and forced open her mouth, Haase used a pair of pliers to break a capsule into it. Blondi died almost instantly. Shortly afterwards, Hitler went into the toilet to check on their handiwork, to ensure that his beloved Blondi was really dead. Then he was satisfied. With all his usual consideration, he handed capsules to Traudl Junge and Gerda Christian. He was sorry, he told them, that he had no better parting gift to reward their loyalty and courage.

Tornow went away and started drinking, seeking Dutch courage to help him complete his grisly task of shooting Blondi's four puppies and giving fatal injections to the other dogs in his charge, including Eva Braun's two, Gerda Christian's, and his own pet dachshund.

HANS BAUER, Hitler's personal pilot, was staying sober. He hoped to be flying very shortly, and he would need every scrap of concentration and control. At 7 pm he went to Hitler's room to try to persuade him for the last time of the feasibility of escape. He, Bauer, could still fly him out, even at this late stage. What was more, he knew where he could lay his hands on a new Junkers prototype aircraft, not all that far away, a bomber with a range of 6,000 miles. That meant Bauer could fly Hitler to the Middle East or possibly even to South America. But Hitler refused.

Before they parted, Hitler gave Bauer a very special gift: his portrait of Frederick the Great by Anton Graff, which Bauer had for so long been responsible for carrying to each Führer headquarters. As Bauer left with it under his arm, Hitler told him: 'I want my epitaph to be "He was the victim of his generals."'

Bauer left the bunker soon afterwards. But he did not even get as far as the emergency airstrip. A Soviet shell landed near him and he wound up in a Soviet military hospital minus a leg – and the painting.

IT TOOK Freytag, Boldt and Weiss four hours to get as far as the Zoo station, through scenes of dreadful horror and an increasing smell of decomposing flesh. On the way they passed ten to fifteen gun emplacements, intact but deserted – they had been abandoned when their ammunition ran out. By evening they were in the vast, echoing emptiness of the Olympic stadium, and shortly before midnight they reached the Pichelsdorf bridge. In the darkness a few hundred yards away, Boldt and Freytag could make out the shapes of heavy Soviet tanks, with their guns trained on the bridge, which was guarded by boys of the Hitler Youth, lying singly or in pairs, armed with rifles or Panzerfausts. When the fighting started there five days before, there had been 5,000 boys. Now there were only about 500 fit for combat.

Underneath the bridge the three officers found a collapsible, canvas-covered canoe, slipped it into the water, and climbed quietly aboard. With Boldt in the bow, navigating with his sub-machine gun at the ready, and the others paddling, they pushed off into the darkness. It was a cool, starlit night. By about 2.45 they were passing Schwanenwerder. From Goebbels's villa came the laughter and shouts of Soviet officers, drunk with victory. As the first light of dawn streaked the sky, the canoe touched the bank of Wannsee and the three officers stepped ashore, to be greeted by the men of the German 20th Motorized Infantry Division.

HITLER'S LAST conference took place that evening, his already sombre mood deepened still further by news that Mussolini and his mistress had been executed by Italian partisans. Weidling had no hope whatever to offer. He had no more ammunition, no more Panzerfausts, no means of repairing his last few tanks. Everything would have to end next day. There was a long silence after Weidling had finished speaking. Then Hitler turned to Mohnke, the commandant of the Citadel, and in a tired voice asked what he thought. Mohnke said he could only agree with all that Weidling had said.

Weidling asked what he was to do when the ammunition finally ran out. After a short discussion with Krebs, Hitler replied that troops might try to break out 'in small groups', but that he absolutely forbade the surrender of the city. Sick at heart, Weidling departed. During the night, he received a written order from Hitler, confirming that there was to be no surrender, and that if the ammunition ran out, troops should be organized into small combat units and try to join German forces still fighting outside the city. If they could not do that, then they were to take to the woods and continue fighting from there.

After the conference, like a last despairing cry for a miracle, Hitler sent his final signal to Keitel, who was now at a new headquarters on the former estate of the Dutch oil magnate, Henri Deterding, at Dobbin, near the Baltic coast. The OKW had been forced to evacuate Neu Roofen the night before, shortly after Keitel had dismissed Heinrici from his post as commander of Army Group Vistula for ordering another retreat. The balloon holding up the radio aerial had been shot down by Soviet aircraft, so there was no longer any chance of plain speech communication. The signal was received there at 11 pm. It consisted of five short questions:

1. Where are Wenck's advance units?
2. When are they going to attack?
3. Where is the Ninth Army?
4. Where is it breaking through?
5. Where are Holste's XXXIst Panzer Corps advance units?

Two hours later, at 1 am on Monday, 30 April, Keitel's reply arrived. For once, it was brutally honest. The spearhead of Wenck's Twelfth Army had ground to a halt south of the Schwielowsee lake near Beelitz, and was therefore unable to continue its attack on Berlin. Busse's Ninth Army was completely encircled, apart from the one corps that had escaped, but whose whereabouts were not known. It could not break out of the Red Army's embrace, let alone break through to help the capital. To the north of the city, Holste's corps had also been forced on to the defensive. Hitler was forced to realize that the end had come: the only course left to him was suicide.

# 29

IT TOOK Perevertkin's men until 4.40 am on 30 April to complete the capture of 'Himmler's House'. At the same time, other units of the corps had cleared the western half of the diplomatic quarter in the bend of the river alongside it, and a rifle regiment had occupied the Swiss Legation, overlooking Königsplatz and the Reichstag. The cost had been appalling on both sides – at least one entire Soviet rifle regiment seems to have disappeared completely – but there was to be no let-up. They were ordered to prepare to storm the Reichstag immediately, without a pause.

The army order stated clearly that the man who succeeded in planting the red banner on top of the Reichstag would automatically become a Hero of the Soviet Union. No fewer than nine 'Victory Banners' had been handed out to the various units taking part in the assault. Banner number five was given to Colonel Zinchenko's 767th Rifle Regiment. The colonel passed it to his best battalion, Captain Neustroyev's Young Communists.

Neustroyev and Captain Davydov, a battalion commander from another regiment, who also carried one of the precious banners in his knapsack, peered out of a first-floor window in the Himmler House. They wanted to orientate themselves and plan their next move.

For the moment, all was quiet. Mist from the river covered the ground, but they could still see a network of trenches and several gun emplacements in the park, which was really an extension of the Tiergarten. Among the trees, some of which were still standing and, incredibly, just coming into leaf, they could make out the shapes of several self-propelled guns. Beyond the trenches stood a grey building, crowned with a shattered, four-cornered dome and a tower. But beyond this building lay something which looked larger and more impressive. Neither Neustroyev nor Davydov knew what the Reichstag looked like. Faced with several battered buildings, they presumed that the biggest would be their target. Probably what they had their eyes on was the Brandenburg Gate, the top of which could be seen beyond the Reichstag, looming through the morning mist.

At this point, Colonel Zinchenko, losing patience with the lack of action, came on the telephone link from the customs house across the river. Why the devil hadn't they attacked yet? he wanted to know. Neustroyev explained that there was a grey building in front of what they thought was the Reichstag, and they were trying to figure out a way to get round it.

'Wait a minute,' said Zinchenko. 'What grey building?' They explained. There was a silence at the other end of the line, while he studied the map. Then he roared: 'That *is* the Reichstag!'

Neustroyev was still not convinced. But as far as the colonel was concerned, discussion time was over. He ordered the battalion to attack.

Determined to get a second opinion, Neustroyev told one of his men to fetch one of the German prisoners they had just taken. An elderly Volkssturm man, understandably scared to death and wondering what the Ivans could want with him, was brought in.

'*Was ist das?*' demanded Neustroyev, pointing to the grey building.

'The Reichstag,' stuttered the prisoner.

Still not convinced, Neustroyev ordered a second prisoner to be questioned. He, too, identified the building as the Reichstag. To make absolutely sure, Neustroyev called in an interpreter and through him asked if that was the only Reichstag. The prisoner, a Berliner, was adamant. Battered though it might be, that was the one and only Reichstag.

THE FIRST attack was a failure. As soon as the infantry moved forward they came under a murderous hail of fire, not only from the Tiergarten and from gun ports in the bricked-up windows of the Reichstag itself, but also from the Kroll Opera House, facing it across the broad expanse of the Königsplatz. The ruined Opera House had been turned into a formidable strong point, with heavy machine guns and artillery embedded behind stone and brick. Clearly, it would have to be dealt with either before or at the same time as the Reichstag. It took the rest of the morning, with bloody attacks and counter-attacks, before it was cleared.

# 30

HITLER LUNCHED with his secretaries that day. Eva was not with them; apparently she did not feel up to it. Earlier, however, she had given Traudl Junge a superb silver fox coat, one of her favourites, with her initials, EB, intertwined with a four-leaf clover, embroidered on the lining. Outside, Soviet troops had taken the Tiergarten and others were reported to be in the streets next to the chancellery, but Hitler gave no sign that this was anything other than a normal lunch.

After the meal, Traudl and Gerda Christian went off to a quiet corner for a smoke. Major Otto Günsche, Hitler's SS adjutant and bodyguard, came and routed them out. The Führer, he said, wanted to say goodbye to all his staff. They went to the corridor outside his room, where he shook hands with each of them, and murmured a few words. Traudl could not make out what he was saying, he spoke so softly. Eva was with him, looking her best. Her hair had been carefully done up and she wore Hitler's favourite dress, black with pink roses on either side of a low, square neckline. She embraced Traudl. 'Please try to get out of here,' she said. 'You might make it. Give my love to Bavaria.' Then she turned and followed Hitler into their room.

Günsche took up his post outside the door. His orders were to let no one in until it was all over. But he was unable to stop a distraught Magda Goebbels, who came rushing down the corridor and forced her way in. She emerged again almost immediately, weeping – Hitler had not wanted to speak to her. Artur Axmann also appeared, but this time Günsche was adamant. 'Too late,' he said.

Traudl Junge remembered that in all the drama no one had thought to feed the six Goebbels children. She found them, took them along to the dining room and sat them down at the big round table. She found some fruit and ham and was just making sandwiches when she heard a shot.

Outside Hitler's room, Günsche waited a few moments before entering. He found Hitler on the sofa, his body crumpled over the arm, his head hanging down towards the floor. Blood was dripping on to the carpet. He had taken cyanide and then shot himself in the head to make sure. Eva was curled up at the other end of the sofa, her legs tucked under her. On the small side table lay her own revolver, which had not been fired, and a square of pink silk chiffon. The cyanide capsule, like an empty lipstick tube, lay on the floor. A vase of flowers had been knocked over. Automatically, Günsche picked it up.

After checking that Hitler and Eva were both dead, Günsche called in the guards. Everything was prepared. The bodies were wrapped in blankets and carried up to the surface, where they were laid in a shallow trench which had been scraped out for the purpose. Erich Kempka, Hitler's chauffeur, arrived with three or four soldiers carrying about forty gallons of petrol in jerry cans. They poured it over the bodies and tried to set fire to it. It refused to catch. They tried again, growing more frantic – all the time, shells were hurtling around them, many landing uncomfortably close. Eventually, Kempka wound a piece of paper into a spill, lit it and tossed it into the trench from a safe distance. At last there was a whoosh as it caught light. Flames blazed up and black smoke rose into the foul air, to join the pall lying over the city. Everyone around the pathetic little funeral pyre raised their arms mechanically in a final Nazi salute, then scurried back underground.

# 31

THE MAIN assault on the Reichstag started again at 1 pm with considerably stronger forces, which had been built up steadily through the morning. The Reichstag vanished under a cloud of smoke as eighty-nine Soviet guns, ranging from 152 mm and 203 mm howitzers to Stalin organs, opened fire simultaneously. Shortly afterwards, three battalions of infantry charged across the Königsplatz, only to discover that they faced a deep anti-tank ditch filled with water. The ditch was in fact the abandoned excavations for a new U-Bahn tunnel, running right across the square from the diplomatic quarter to about fifty yards short of the Charlottenburger Chaussee. By now, however, the men were charged up and eager to finish the fight. They did not even hesitate but plunged into the ditch and waded across, ignoring shells and machine-gun fire.

During the delay in the start of the attack, some Soviet gunners had managed to manhandle their lighter guns to the upper floors of the Himmler House, from where they could direct their fire on to the German positions. Tanks and self-propelled guns were brought up to the ditch, to cover the infantrymen, who faced an exposed 200-metre stretch, littered with barbed wire and debris from uncompleted fortifications and all the detritus of war – not to mention mines. Carried on a wave of adrenalin, the infantrymen charged across to the steps of the building, past the huge pillars and up to the doors. But the doors had been bricked up. There was no way in. Two mortars fired simultaneously at point-blank range soon changed that, blowing a four-foot hole in the brickwork. The first man in was Neustroyev, followed by Corporal Piotr Cherbina.

Inside, the place was dark and filled with smoke and dust. There was savage hand-to-hand fighting in the darkness, with men using knives, bayonets and rifle butts. It was like Stalingrad all over again. More and more Red Army men forced their way in. They rushed the central staircase and took the first floor, then fought on up more stairs. Using hand grenades, Sergeants Yegorov and Kantariya forced their way up to the third storey, carrying victory banner number five. They were halted by machine-gun fire and forced to retreat.

At 2.25 pm the banner was waved from a second-floor window. But that was not good enough for Colonel Zinchenko. The SS troops still controlled the basement, which they had turned into a small fortress. They also controlled part of the upper floors. Dealing with them was an arduous and slow business. It was 6 pm when Zinchenko called the two sergeants to him and ordered a second attempt at planting the banner. 'Well, then, off you go, lads,' he told them genially. 'Stick the banner up there.' He pointed to the roof. It took them nearly five hours – it was not until 10.50 pm that Yegorov and Kantariya eventually got out on to the roof. They climbed over to the bronze statue of Germania and her horse, and pushed the flagpole into a hole caused by shell fire near the left front hoof of the horse.

The Red Flag was flying over the Reichstag at last, just seventy minutes before May Day. The only trouble was – no one could see it, or photograph it. In the morning light, the photographers found a more photogenic setting for the flag than the hoof of Germania's horse, as the whole scene was re-enacted for the cameras. But even while the shutters were clicking, there was fighting going on in the basement of the building. It would take another twenty-four hours to clear the last defenders from it.

*

ACROSS THE city centre, at about the same time as the sergeants were planting the victory banner over the Reichstag, Vladimir Abyzov and his battalion were breaking out of the Anhalter railway station, which they had captured during the day. Abyzov had lost several of his closest comrades there, including Yurka the musician. A machine gun was firing at them from somewhere on their left. Someone was firing flares into a sky that was already lit up by all the fires. For a while they were pinned down by enemy fire from a tall building that seemed to be an SS officers' club. Abyzov and his squad broke in and fought their way upstairs to the second and third floors, where they overwhelmed the defenders. In the billiards room there were candles burning. Slumped over the green cloth among the billiard balls was the body of a general, a pistol in his hand. He had shot himself.

Back in the street, Abyzov found himself caught between a German and a Soviet tank, slugging it out. Both ended up in flames. The squad took the ground floor of a corner building and crouched behind its windows to fire on the street. As they broke in they were assailed by a powerful smell of lavender from puddles of liquid among the shattered glass on the floor. They were in a barber's shop.

Outside, another Soviet tank went up in flames. 'We saw the tank men open the hatch and escape through it on to the pavement,' Abyzov wrote. 'One of them was in flames. Rolling on the ground, he tried to extinguish the fire. One of our boys jumped out of the window to help him. An enemy sub-machine-gunner opened fire from the attic. Our boy fell down before he reached the tankman, who was killed in the same burst.'

Abyzov was deafened by the explosion of an anti-tank grenade on the floor behind him. For a while, he could hardly even hear the sound of his own gun firing. Almost the first thing he heard when his hearing began to return, some hours later, was the voice of the regiment's Young Communist League organizer, shouting out from the shop doorway: 'Our troops have taken the Reichstag! Hurrah!' Everyone started to cheer – but for them the war was not yet over. Pushing forward again, they made slow progress under heavy fire, still taking casualties. Abyzov found himself taking cover alongside his friend Vasya Medvedev, a former student at the Moscow Film School. Looking through a hole in the cellar wall they were sheltering behind, he saw a railing with massive spearpoints on top. Beyond it was a huge grey building.

'What's that?' he asked.

'The Reich chancellery,' Medvedev told him.

# 32

'CAN WE expect to clear Berlin completely by May Day?' Zhukov demanded.

'No,' replied Chuikov, on the other end of the telephone line. 'The Germans are still fighting hard. Judging by their stiff resistance, even though it is showing signs of slackening, we can hardly expect an immediate surrender.'

Zhukov sighed. It was no more than he expected to hear. He hung up.

Late that evening, Chuikov sat down to a convivial supper as a guest of the army's political department. The other guests included some important visitors to the front: the war correspondents Vsevolod Vishnevsky and Konstantin Simonov, the poet Yevgeni Dolmatovsky, and the composers Tikhon Khrennikov and Matvei Blanter – who had been given the task of composing a hymn for the victory celebrations. It was a jolly evening, with the composers giving an impromptu concert while the table was being laid.

In the middle of the party, Chuikov was called away to take an important phone call, from Lieutenant-General V. A. Glazunov, commander of the IVth Corps. Glazunov was excited. At his headquarters, he said, was a German lieutenant-colonel named Seifert, who had come across the Landwehr canal by the suspension bridge under the protection of a white flag, bearing a packet addressed to the commander of the Soviet Forces. Seifert was asking for a time and place for General Krebs, chief of the German general staff, to cross the front line in order to start talks with senior Red Army officers.

Chuikov could hardly believe what he was hearing. He had failed to achieve glory by taking the Reichstag – though in the event that did not seem to have settled anything – but now it seemed he could still be recognized as the conqueror of Berlin, if he were the one to accept its surrender.

'I understand,' he said, calmly. 'Tell the lieutenant-colonel that we are ready to receive and parley with envoys. He may bring them across the same sector where he himself crossed, by the suspension bridge.' Then he ordered that firing should cease in that particular sector, and that the envoys should be brought to his forward command post, to which he departed at once. He had no sooner reached it, than the phone rang. It was Vishnevsky, who begged him, 'in the name of all the gods', to let him be present at the parley. Ninety minutes later he arrived, accompanied by the poet, Dolmatovsky, and the composer, Blanter. 'Writers,' Chuikov observed wryly, 'never travel singly.'

IT WAS 3.50 am when Krebs entered, accompanied by Colonel von Dufving, Weidling's chief of staff, and a Captain Nailandis, who had been born in Latvia and spoke fluent Russian. Krebs was himself a Russian-speaker, having been acting military attaché in Moscow, but he had insisted on taking an interpreter, telling Dufving that this would give him a little extra thinking time. Krebs needed all the thinking time he could get – he was hoping to outmanoeuvre the Soviets across the negotiating table. But when it came to interpreters, Chuikov had a trick of his own: determined to rub salt into his enemies' wounds, he chose as his own interpreter a Captain Kleber. Both Krebs and Dufving could hardly help noticing that Kleber was a Jew.

Krebs made the first move before Chuikov could even introduce himself. 'I will tell you something extremely secret,' he began portentously. 'You are the first foreigner to be told that on 30 April Hitler departed this world of his own will. He committed suicide.'

'We know,' said Chuikov, unperturbed. It was not true, of course, but he had no intention of allowing Krebs any advantage. He was pleased to note that Krebs was thrown for a moment. 'When and how did it happen?' he asked.

'At 1500 hours today.' Chuikov glanced at his wristwatch, and Krebs hastily corrected himself: 'That is, yesterday. 30 April, around 1500 hours.'

Krebs immediately went on to read out a message from Goebbels: 'We inform the leader of the Soviet people that today, at 15 hours 30 minutes, the Führer voluntarily quitted this life. Based on his legal right, the Führer in the testament he left behind him transmitted all power to Dönitz, myself and Bormann. I am empowered by Bormann to establish contact with the leader of the Soviet people. This contact is essential for peace talks between the powers that have borne the heaviest losses. Goebbels.'

Krebs then handed over two more documents. The first, carrying the official seal, was his commission to conduct the talks with the Soviet supreme command. This was written on the notepaper of the head of the Reich chancellery, and signed by Martin Bormann. The second document was a copy of Hitler's will, and included the list of the new government and the high command of the German armed forces. It was signed by Hitler, and his witnesses, and was dated and timed at 0400 hours, 29 April.

'Do these documents relate to Berlin alone or to the whole of Germany?' Chuikov asked.

'Goebbels has empowered me to speak in the name of the whole German army,' replied Krebs.

Chuikov could see what Krebs was up to. He was deliberately trying to confuse two totally different issues. On the one hand he was presenting himself as the military representative of the army on the verge of defeat, and at the same time as the ambassador of a government seeking peace talks. The two roles, as Chuikov pointed out, were incompatible. Either Krebs was there to surrender, or he was there for talks. He could not do both. As far as Chuikov was concerned, in order to avoid any further senseless spilling of blood the only sane course of action was for Krebs and Goebbels to give orders for the German army to lay down its arms forthwith.

That, however, would mean surrender, and Krebs had no intention of uttering that word if he could avoid it. His job was to buy time, so that Bormann and Dönitz could open negotiations with the Allies, and play on the mistrust between them and Stalin. He kept emphasizing the importance of the new German government entering into peace talks with the Soviet government. This would mean a temporary cease-fire, and with luck and skill the talks might be prolonged until something else turned up. It was the last desperate throw of the dice for the men in the bunker. Chuikov, perfectly well aware of all this, pointed out that at that moment there simply was no properly constituted German government for the Soviets to negotiate with.

'Who is now – *now* – in Hitler's place?' he asked.

Krebs repeated that Goebbels had been appointed Reich chancellor, and Grand Admiral Dönitz Reich president – the two roles Hitler had combined. Chuikov gave up the argument for the time being, and phoned Zhukov, who said he would report to Moscow while Chuikov stayed on the line. In the meantime, he was sending his chief of staff, Colonel-General Sokolovsky, to interview Krebs.

STALIN HAD left his office for the night, and had gone to bed at his dacha at Kuntsevo, about twenty miles south-west of Moscow. Zhukov insisted that the duty general wake him up: 'The matter is extremely urgent and can't wait till morning.'

After a minute or two Stalin came on the line. Zhukov told him what had happened. 'So that's the end of the bastard!' he replied, always a man of few words. 'Too bad it was impossible to take him alive.' Then, suspicious as ever: 'Where is Hitler's body?' Zhukov explained that Krebs said it had been burnt.

There then followed an extraordinary four-way conversation, with Stalin asking Zhukov questions, which he then passed on to Chuikov, who then asked Krebs, whose replies found their way to Stalin by the same route. Eventually, Stalin asked Krebs, point blank: 'Are we talking about surrender, and is your mission to carry this out?'

'No,' Krebs answered. 'There are other possibilities.'

'What possibilities?'

'Permit and assist us to form our new government, appointed by Hitler in his will, and it will decide this question to your advantage,' Krebs declared.

He asked for a temporary suspension of hostilities, and help in arranging a meeting of the new government in Berlin.

But Stalin had heard enough. He wanted to get back to his bed. 'There can be no negotiations,' he told Zhukov flatly. 'Only unconditional surrender. No talks with Krebs or any other Hitlerites. Unless anything special happens, don't call me till the morning. I want to get a little rest before tomorrow's parade.'

UNAWARE OF what Stalin had said, Krebs kept hammering away in the hope of achieving a cease-fire. The circular argument began all over again. Chuikov tried to inject a note of reality by pointing out that the question of temporary armistice or permanent peace could only be settled on the basis of a general surrender, but got nowhere. Finally he went off to report again to Zhukov, who told him to wait for orders from Moscow.

When he returned, Chuikov asked Krebs what on earth was the point of the Germans continuing to fight. Mustering what dignity he could, Krebs replied simply: 'We will fight on to the last.'

'General,' Chuikov asked, 'what have you got left? How? What forces do you intend to use?' He paused, then went on: 'We are waiting for your unconditional surrender.'

'No!' Krebs exclaimed. 'If we agree to an unconditional surrender we shall cease to exist as a legal government.'

Chuikov was growing weary of all this talk. There was, too, something puzzling about Krebs's manner – he seemed to be in no hurry to leave. It was as though he was waiting for something, expecting something from Chuikov – perhaps, Chuikov wondered, to be told he was already a prisoner of war. As the clock showed 5 am, his patience ran out.

'You are insisting on an armistice,' he said, 'and you want to engage in peace talks, but all the time your troops are surrendering of their own accord.'

'Where?' Krebs snapped back in disbelief.

'Everywhere.'

'Without orders?'

'Our men are advancing, yours are surrendering.'

'Perhaps only in some places?'

In reply, Chuikov picked up a Soviet newspaper, and started to read out the reports of Himmler's peace offer to the Allies. The argument turned to Himmler and Göring and their efforts to achieve a separate peace with the West. Krebs, beginning to be rattled, finally tired of using an interpreter and began talking in Russian himself. With no more word from Moscow, Chuikov was forced to go on waiting and talking. The conversation turned to Guderian, whom Chuikov had met at Brest-Litovsk in 1939, and the 'illness' that had removed him from his position. They talked of Krebs's time in Moscow, and then of Stalingrad.

'That was terrible,' Krebs said. 'That was the start of all our troubles. Were you a corps commander at Stalingrad?'

'No. An army commander.'

Krebs looked surprised. He realized he still did not know who he was talking to. 'And you are . . .?' he asked.

'I am Chuikov.'

THERE WAS still no further word from Moscow, though from time to time there were messages requesting details of the progress of the talks. There was also news of another peace move, this time near the Zoo. German military headquarters – the report was not clear whether this meant Weidling or the divisional headquarters in the Zoo flak tower – had sent a radio signal at 4.30 am, asking for a Soviet officer to be sent to the north-east corner of the Zoo to meet German officers to arrange a truce. Lieutenant-General A. I. Ryzhov, commander of the XXVIIIth Guards Rifle Corps, had dispatched a staff officer, Major Bersenev, who arrived at the appointed spot at 5 am sharp, carrying a white flag. After twenty minutes, two German officers with a white flag came round the corner about 200 yards away. He started walking towards them, when suddenly shots rang out from behind them. They were gunned down by fanatics on their own side. Bersenev was hit in the hip and leg, but was dragged to safety by his driver. Clearly, for many German troops, surrender was still not on the agenda.

BY NOW, it was broad daylight outside and the sun was shining brightly. But still Krebs refused to give in. The word came from Moscow: accept nothing short of unconditional surrender. Krebs complained that only his government had the authority to agree to this. He could no nothing more without direct orders from Goebbels. By this time, Sokolovsky had arrived from Zhukov's headquarters, and had joined in the discussions. At about 9 am he declared that the only way out of the impasse was for him to speak to Goebbels himself. They would lay a telephone line from Chuikov's headquarters right through to the Führer bunker. Pointing to Dufving, he said: 'This German officer will lay this line across no man's land, with Soviet help.' Dufving was put in a car with Nailandis and two Soviet signals officers and driven to the front line in Prinz-Albrecht-Strasse, outside the Gestapo headquarters. From there, he was to lay a cable across to the German lines about 400 yards away.

While they waited, Chuikov took Krebs, Sokolovsky and the other senior Soviet officers into the next room for tea and sandwiches. Noticing that the German general's hands were shaking, Chuikov offered him a cognac, which he accepted gratefully.

*

DUFVING HAD a hair-raising time trying to return to his own lines. He shouted that he was coming over, but as he and his party were moving out into no man's land the Germans opposite opened fire. One of the Soviet officers grabbed Dufving and pulled him back into a doorway. The other Soviet officer was wounded, and a bullet went through Nailandis's coat, just missing his body. Dufving yelled angrily at his own side. The response was three more shots.

'Give me a big white flag!' he told the Red Army men around him. 'I've got to get over!'

A flag was found, and Dufving set off, alone and unarmed, the flag in one hand and a reel of telephone cable in the other. More shots rang out, and he was forced to dive into the nearest slit trench on top of a bunch of Soviet soldiers – fortunately, he was a small, sprightly man, and hurt no one. The Soviet soldiers roared with laughter at his sudden arrival.

'Don't shoot! Don't shoot! I'm an official negotiator!' he shouted over and over. When the firing stopped, the Soviet troops cheerfully boosted him out of their trench, and, with white flag and cable, he made it to the German lines, where he was promptly arrested by a young SS officer.

'You can't arrest me,' he told him. 'I'm on an official mission. I'm laying a telephone line.'

The man refused to believe him when he told him Hitler was dead and he was acting under instructions from Goebbels. Two Dutch SS men, neither of whom could speak much German, appeared on the scene and wanted to shoot Dufving, but he persuaded the officer to take him to a telephone, and got through to Bormann. When he had explained what was going on, Bormann ordered the SS officer to set Dufving free. He refused, saying he only took orders from a senior SS officer. Fortunately, at that moment another young SS officer wearing a Knight's Cross arrived, who confirmed that Hitler was dead. The first officer was shattered – he simply could not believe it. There was nothing left for him.

Dufving looked at him with pity. 'Look,' he told him, 'don't hang about here – run! Get away, as fast as you can! Go on – run for it!'

The young men both hesitated for a moment, then turned and ran down the street like Olympic sprinters.

DUFVING WAS driven to the Führer bunker, where he reported to Goebbels and Bormann. Goebbels was still very calm. Bormann, who gave the impression that he had never been under fire before, was clearly frightened. Dufving explained that the Soviets were demanding unconditional surrender. 'I shall never, never agree to that,' Goebbels declared. He asked if Dufving thought, from what he had seen, that it was still possible to break out of Berlin. Dufving's answer was 'Only singly, and in civilian clothes.' Goebbels said he would not make a final decision on the matter until he had spoken to

Krebs. If the telephone line did not work, then Dufving would have to bring Krebs back.

The telephone link with Chuikov's command post proved to be erratic – the line was constantly being cut by bullets. Three times Dufving ran back and forth under fire, trying to lay new cable, but each time it was quickly broken. He then resorted to running across carrying messages, but this was generally unsatisfactory. For one short period, a connection was established, and Krebs was able to speak to Goebbels. The new chancellor insisted that he return to the bunker for further discussions. Krebs left the Soviet command post at 1.08 pm, after making several excuses to return to the room where Chuikov and Sokolovsky sat. It seemed to Chuikov that Krebs was tempted to surrender and become their prisoner, but could not quite bring himself to do it. It was typical of the whole charade that when he did go he forgot to pick up his gloves, which he had deliberately left on the window ledge as an excuse to go back.

As SOON as Krebs and his party were safely back on the German side of the lines, Chuikov ordered every gun and rocket launcher in his command to open up with maximum-intensity fire. After the fiasco of Krebs's supposed negotiations he wanted to finish the whole thing as quickly as possible. The other armies followed suit, blasting the defenders without mercy once again.

---

# 33

To MAX BUCH it sounded as though hell had been let loose on the Kurfürstendamm, Augsburgerstrasse and the Zoo. But since his street was now behind the front line, he felt the immediate personal danger had passed. But the war was not quite over for him. Taking a quick look around the devastated courtyard and street, he met two worried neighbours. They had discovered a light machine gun in the hallway of the building, presumably left behind by retreating German soldiers, and wanted to get rid of it before Soviet troops found it.

'For God's sake,' Max warned, 'leave it alone. If a Russian patrol should see you they'd take you for partisans, and you'd be done for.'

He went back to the safety of his hideaway in the cellar. A little later he saw the two men going out, and shortly afterwards, peering out through the slats of the cellar door, he noticed some sort of activity. Suddenly, he heard loud yells in Russian, followed by a burst of shots. Some of the bullets kicked up the dust quite close to him, and he dived back into cover. Then everything went quiet.

When, after a while, the wife of one of the two men came and asked Max if he had seen her husband, his worst fears were confirmed. Going outside, he found three bodies – the two men and another neighbour whom they had recruited – lying dead in a pool of blood. They had been trying to carry the gun away, for the safety of the residents, when a Soviet patrol spotted them and opened fire. The gun, in fact, turned out to be a Soviet weapon.

Now THE sounds of battle came almost entirely from the direction of the Zoo and the flak towers, which were under intense bombardment. In the Zoo itself there were few animals left alive: Siam, the male elephant, Suse, the female chimpanzee, Knautschke, a male hippopotamus, a few small monkeys, a few birds. One hippopotamus was dying from blast injuries, another floated in the water of its pool, dead, with the fins of an unexploded shell sticking out of its side. When Soviet troops entered the ape house, they discovered Pongo, the biggest gorilla in Europe, lying dead in his cage, as was a big chimpanzee. Pongo, mysteriously, had died from two stab wounds in the chest. Dark rivers of blood ran from them down the concrete platforms of the enclosure. In front of the platform lay two dead SS men. A third was propped against it, his sub-machine gun across his knees.

## 34

WEIDLING WAS in the bunker when Krebs returned from his talks with Chuikov. He had spent the night there after being called from his command post and forbidden to authorize any more break-out groups. When Krebs reiterated that the Soviets were insisting on unconditional surrender, Goebbels and Bormann both rejected the demand. 'The Führer forbade capitulation,' they declared.

'But the Führer is dead!' Weidling exclaimed in great agitation.

'The Führer always insisted on carrying on the struggle to the end,' Goebbels repeated, 'and I do not want to surrender.'

Weidling, thoroughly exasperated, reminded them that resistance was no longer possible. Then he left, to return to his own headquarters. Taking his leave of Krebs, he invited him to go with him, but Krebs told him: 'I shall stay here until the last minute, then put a bullet through my brain.'

*

OTHERS IN the bunker were looking for ways of saving themselves. Mohnke and Günsche had formulated their own plan. With a group of soldiers they proposed to make their way across the city to the west, and break through to Wenck's lines. Traudl Junge and Gerda Christian begged to be allowed to join them.

The Goebbels, meanwhile, had outstanding business of their own. As evening approached, Magda got her six children ready for bed, in their long white nightgowns. The youngest, Heidi, had a touch of tonsillitis, so she had to wear a scarf wrapped round her throat. Magda brushed each child's hair carefully, then gave each of them a chocolate. She told them they were going to be taken to Berchtesgaden with Uncle Adolf, and the chocolate was to prevent air sickness. In fact, the chocolate had been spiked with a powerful soporific drug called Finodin. In her last letter to her son, Harald, Magda had told him: 'I shall give my darlings sleeping potions and then poison, a soft and painless death.' Once they were deeply asleep, she planned to crush a cyanide capsule into each of their mouths.

As she followed her sisters up the spiral staircase to the upper bunker, little Heidi caught sight of her friend Sergeant Misch, standing at the door of the guard's room. '*Misch, Misch, du bist ein Fisch,*' she sang out in the joke she repeated endlessly to him.

No one knows for sure what took place in the children's rooms. Perhaps everything did work out according to Magda's plan. Certainly, all the children died that night, but when their bodies were found, Helga's had several black and blue bruises on it. Perhaps the dose of Finodin had not proved sufficient to sedate the child, the eldest of the six. Perhaps Magda had had to force the cyanide down her daughter's throat. Either way, it did not look as if Helga had had a soft and painless death.

An hour after murdering her children, Magda was seen playing solitaire in her husband's study, pale, red-eyed, stone-faced and smoking endlessly. Later that evening, Artur Axmann left his command post and came over to the bunker to say goodbye to Goebbels. He found the couple sitting at the long table in the conference room with several of the bunker personnel. Goebbels was pleased to see him, and talked nostalgically about the early days of the movement – street fighting in Wedding, beating up communists and socialists, winning over the workers to National Socialism. That was the real triumph, he declared: to have won the hearts of the German workers. Throughout his monologue, Magda sat like a silent Medea, sipping champagne and smoking. Someone whispered to Axmann not to ask after the children.

Later still, Sergeant Misch, who had been manning the switchboard, went out for a breath of air. It was anything but fresh, being filled with choking yellow dust and smoke, but it was an improvement on the bunker. He found Goebbels in the garden, smoking a cigarette. Knowing that Goebbels was now Reich chancellor, he decided to ask him how long he ought to remain at his post. He had been there all day, and there had been only three or four calls. Understandably, he wanted to try to get away before the Red Army arrived. Goebbels was sympathetic. He advised Misch to try to join General Rauch's troops, who planned to break out towards the west from Charlottenburg.

At 8.15 pm Goebbels informed the SS guards that he and his wife intended to commit suicide out of the bunker in the open air. At least, he joked blackly, it would save the guards the trouble of having to carry the bodies upstairs. He put on his hat, scarf, long uniform greatcoat and kid gloves, then offered his arm to his wife. Together they mounted the stairs to the bunker entrance. They planned to die in the same way as the Führer. Both had cyanide capsules, and Goebbels carried a Walther P-38 revolver. They stood together. Magda bit her capsule and swallowed. She slid to the ground. Her husband delivered the *coup de grâce*, shooting her in the back of the head as she half knelt, half lay on the ground. Then he bit on his own capsule, pressed the Walther's muzzle to his temple and fired.

The SS guards doused the bodies with petrol and set fire to them. They burned through the night, but were only partly destroyed – there had not been enough petrol left.

As SOON as the bodies were alight, the escape parties gathered their things and rushed for the exit, in a mad scramble led by Bormann. Soon there were only three people left: Krebs, Burgdorf and the commander of the SS bodyguard, Hauptsturmführer Schedle. They had all decided to shoot themselves.

In the shelter in Bendlerstrasse, Weidling called all his commanders together for a last meeting at 9.30 pm, to discuss whether they should attempt to break out or surrender. Weidling told them it was useless trying to go on fighting, and that in his opinion trying to break out meant 'jumping out of the frying pan into the fire'. All the officers agreed.

AT ABOUT 10.20 pm Chuikov lay down on a divan, covered his head with a cloak and tried to get some sleep, but it was impossible. Everyone hung about the operations room, waiting for the end. The table was covered with maps, and the plates that had once held sandwiches were piled high with cigarette butts. Out on the streets, many of the Soviet soldiers were holding their own late May Day celebrations. In Pariserplatz, beside the Brandenburg Gate, they sang and danced and roasted an ox, while the poet Dolmatovsky declaimed patriotic verse.

In the command post, the telephone rang. It was from the headquarters of Ryzhov's XXVIIIth Guards Corps. At 12.40 am the radio receivers of the 79th Guards Division had picked up a radio signal in the Russian language, which ran as follows: 'Hello, hello! This is the LVIth German Panzer Corps.

We ask you for a cease-fire. At 0005 Berlin time we are sending envoys to parley with you, to the Potsdamer Bridge. Sign for purposes of recognition – a white flag. We await your reply.' The message had been repeated five times. The 79th Division had replied, acknowledging the message and saying it was being passed on to superior officers. Chuikov ordered a cease-fire in the Potsdamer Bridge sector.

ABYZOV AND his company were sheltering in a cellar, to rest, eat and write letters home while they were waiting for the next artillery bombardment on the chancellery to begin at 2 am; they were due to start their own attack on the building at 5 am. Kiselyov, the company commander, posted sentries, then counted his men in. There were exactly 20 of them left out of the 104 who had started the attack on the central sectors five days before.

Suddenly, there were hurried footsteps coming down the stairs, then one of the sentries appeared.

'Comrade Lieutenant,' he called, 'the Germans want to speak to an officer.'

Kiselyov straightened his tunic and went out, gesturing to Abyzov and another man to follow. Outside, the rain had stopped, and the air was full of acrid brick dust.

'Who was asking for a Soviet officer?' Kiselyov shouted into the darkness.

From the other side of the street someone replied in Russian: 'Truce envoys. We have the text of the statement of the Berlin garrison commander, addressed to Marshal Zhukov.'

'Come over, with your hands up!'

One of the men switched on a flashlight. In its beam, they could see a group of Germans carrying a white flag of truce. There were four of them, three men in their thirties or forties and a Hitler Youth boy in a steel helmet, who had obviously been their guide. One of the men was holding a large brown folder, secured with string. With Abyzov and his comrade covering them with their sub-machine guns, they descended to the cellar, where the radio operator was informing the battalion commander.

Nodding at the folder, Kiselyov asked whether it contained the truce document. The man nodded, and handed it over. Kiselyov undid the string and opened the folder. It contained two sheaves of paper, neatly clipped together, one typed in German, the other handwritten in Russian. Kiselyov tried to read the handwritten copy, but his eyes were not good enough in the dim light. He handed it over to Abyzov, and asked him to read it. The paper said that the German command was prepared to negotiate an immediate cease-fire. As he read it aloud, Abyzov could hardly recognize the sound of his own voice, choked with excitement and emotion. Everyone else was silent. Finally, he came to the signature: 'Weidling'.

As Kiselyov was folding up the papers and putting them neatly back into the folder, the battalion commander and the Young Communist League organizer arrived and took over the envoys, leading them back up the stairs to conduct them to their rendezvous at the Potsdam Bridge. When they had gone, the men in the cellar stood speechless, stunned by what they had just heard. Then someone called for a drink. A friend nudged Abyzov in the ribs. 'Still alive?' he asked with a grin. Together they climbed the stairs and went out into the street. A gentle breeze wafted through the smoke and dust from the Tiergarten. Amid the familiar stench of war, Abyzov thought he caught another, faint smell – the scent of lilac in bloom.


CHUIKOV SENT one of his staff officers, Lieutenant-Colonel Matusov, along with the Jewish interpreter, Captain Kleber, to meet the German envoys at the bridge, who were led by Colonel von Dufving. Colonel Semchenko, acting commander of the 47th Guards Division, was already there with his own staff officers. Dufving, this time carrying the biggest white flag he had been able to find, as well as a reel of cable, told them he now represented General Weidling, who wished to surrender along with his troops.

Semchenko asked how long it would take the LVIth Panzer Corps to lay down their arms and surrender in an orderly fashion. Dufving estimated that it would take at least three or four hours to complete all the necessary preparations. He also pointed out an additional problem. The surrender would have to take place at night, because Goebbels had given orders that anyone seen attempting to cross to the Soviet lines should be shot in the back.

Chuikov told Semchenko to release Dufving. The colonel was to be allowed to return to General Weidling. As far as Chuikov was concerned, the general's surrender was accepted.

Relieved that the end was now truly in sight, Chuikov went back to his couch, lay down, and immediately fell asleep. He was woken by an aide, who told him that there had been a call from Dr Goebbels. A delegation was on its way. The time was 5.50 am. Chuikov leapt to his feet and went and splashed his face with cold water to try to revive himself. He emerged to find three delegates in civilian clothes waiting to see him. They were accompanied by a German soldier, carrying a white flag.

The leader of the delegation introduced himself as Senior Executive Officer Heinersdorf of the Ministry of Propaganda. He handed Chuikov a pink folder, inside which was a letter. It read:

As you have been informed by General Krebs, former Reich chancellor Göring cannot be reached. Dr Goebbels is no longer alive. I, as one of those few remaining alive, request you to take Berlin under your protection. My name is known.

Director of the Ministry of Propaganda, Dr Fritsche

At 6 am on Wednesday, 2 May, Lieutenant-General Helmuth Weidling crossed the front line to surrender in person.

BERLIN HAD FALLEN.

# BIBLIOGRAPHY

The following books have been consulted by the authors in writing this book.
All books are published in London unless otherwise indicated.

ADLON, HEDDA, *Hotel Adlon*. Barrie Books, 1956

ALTNER, HELMUT, *Totentanz Berlin: Tagebuchblätter eines Achtzen-jahriger*. Offenbach-am-Main, Bollwerk, 1947

AMBROSE, STEPHEN E., *Eisenhower and Berlin, 1945: The Decision to Halt at the Elbe*. New York, W. W. Norton, 1967

ANDREAS-FRIEDRICH, RUTH, *Berlin Underground, 1939–1945*. Latimer House, 1949

ANONYMOUS, *A Woman in Berlin*. Secker & Warburg, 1955

BALFOUR, ALAN, *Berlin: the Politics of Order, 1737–1989*. New York, Rizzoli International, 1990

BARRACLOUGH, GEOFFREY, *The Origins of Modern Germany*. Oxford, Basil Blackwell, 1979

BAYLES, WILLIAM D., *Postmarked Berlin*. Jarrold, 1942

BAYNES, N. H. (ed.), *Hitler's Speeches, 1922–39*. OUP, 1942

BEREZHKOV, VALENTIN, *History in the Making*. Moscow, Progress Publishers, 1983

BERGER, JOACHIM, *Berlin, Freiheitlich & Rebellisch*. Berlin, Goebel, 1987

BETHGE, EBERHARD, *Dietrich Bonhoeffer*. Collins, 1970

BETTELHEIM, BRUNO, *Recollections and Reflections*. Thames and Hudson, 1990

BIALER, SEWERIN, *Stalin and his Generals*. Souvenir Press, 1969

BIELENBERG, CHRISTABEL, *The Past is Myself*. Chatto and Windus, 1968

BOHLEN, CHARLES, *Witness to History*. Weidenfeld and Nicolson, 1973

BOLDT, GERHARD, *Die Letzten Tage*. Hamburg, Rowohlt, 1947

BOREE, KARL FRIEDRICH, *Frühling 1945*. Darmstadt, 1954

BOSANQUET, MARY, *The Life and Death of Dietrich Bonhoeffer*. Hodder and Stoughton, 1968

BOTTING, DOUGLAS, *In the Ruins of the Reich*. Grafton Books, 1968

BRADLEY, OMAR N., *A Soldier's Story*. Eyre & Spottiswoode, 1951

BRENDON, PIERS, *Ike: the Life and Times of Dwight D. Eisenhower*. Secker & Warburg, 1987

BULLOCK, ALAN, *Hitler: a Study in Tyranny*. Penguin, 1962
*Hitler and Stalin: Parallel Lives*. Harper Collins, 1991

CHANEY, OTTO PRESTON, Jr, *Zhukov*. Newton Abbott, David and Charles, 1972

CHANNON, SIR HENRY (ed. ROBERT RHODES JAMES), *Chips: The Diaries of Sir Henry Channon*. Weidenfeld and Nicolson, 1976

CHARMAN, TERRY, *The German Home Front*. Barrie and Jenkins, 1989

CHUIKOV, V. I., *The End of the Third Reich*. Moscow, Progress Publishers, 1978

CHURCHILL, WINSTON S., *The Second World War*. Penguin, 1985

CLARK, ALAN, *Barbarossa: The Russo-German Conflict 1941–45*. Hutchinson, 1965

COLVILLE, JOHN, *The Fringes of Power: Downing Street Diaries 1939–1955*. Hodder and Stoughton, 1985

COMET, PAUL, *Sur Berlin avec Dailliers*. Paris, Icare, 1975

CONSTABLE, T. J. and TOLIVER, R. F., *Horrido: Fighter Aces of the Luftwaffe*. Arthur Barker, 1968

COOPER, ALAN W., *Bombers Over Berlin*. Kimber, 1985

CZECH, DANUTA, *Auschwitz Chronicles 1939–45*. I. B. Taurus, 1990

DE GUINGAND, FRANCIS, *Generals at War*. Hodder and Stoughton, 1964, *Operation Victory*. Hodder and Stoughton, 1947.

DE JONGE, ALEX, *Stalin*. Collins, 1986

DEMPS, LAURENCE in *Jahrbuch des Märkischen Museums, 1978, 1980, 1981.*

DODD, WILLIAM, *Ambassador Dodd's Diary, 1933–1938*. Gollancz, 1941

DÖNITZ, KARL, *Memoirs – Ten Years and Twenty Days*. Weidenfeld and Nicolson, 1959

DEUEL, WALLACE, *People Under Hitler*. Lindsay Drummond, 1942

EBAN, ABBA, *My People: The Story of the Jews*. Weidenfeld and Nicolson, 1969

EISENHOWER, DWIGHT D., *Crusade in Europe*. Heinemann, 1949

ELLIS, MAJOR L. F. with WARHURST, LIEUT-COLONEL A. E., *History of the Second World War: Victory in the West, Vol II, The Defeat of Germany*. HMSO, 1968

ENGELMANN, BERNT, *Berlin – eine Stadt wie keine andere*. Munich, Bertelsmann, 1986
*In Hitler's Germany*. Methuen, 1988

ERICKSON, JOHN, *The Soviet High Command*. Macmillan, 1962
*The Road to Stalingrad*. Weidenfeld and Nicolson, 1975
*The Road to Berlin*. Weidenfeld and Nicolson, 1983

ETHELL, JEFFREY and PRICE, ALFRED, *Target Berlin*. Book Club Associates, 1981

EVERETT, SUSANNE, *Lost Berlin*. Bison Books, 1979

FEIS, HERBERT, *Churchill, Roosevelt, Stalin: The War They Waged and the Peace They Sought*. Princeton, Princeton University Press, 1967

FLANNERY, HARRY, *Assignment to Berlin*. Michael Joseph, 1942

FLEISCHHAUER, INGEBORG, *Die Chance des Sonderfriedens: Deutch-sowjetische Geheimgespräche, 1941–1945*. Berlin, Siedler Verlag, 1986

FLENLEY, RALPH, *Modern German History*. Dent, 1968

FREDBORG, ARVID, *Behind the Steel Wall*. Viking, 1944

FRIEDRICH, OTTO, *Before the Deluge*. Michael Joseph, 1974

FROMM, BELLA, *Blood and Banquets*. Geoffrey Bles, 1943

GALANTE, PIERRE and SILIANOFF, EUGENE, *Last Witnesses in the Bunker*. Sidgwick & Jackson, 1989

GILBERT, MARTIN, *Finest Hour, Winston S. Churchill, 1939–1941*. Heinemman, 1983
   *The Holocaust: The Jewish Tragedy*. Collins, 1986

GORALSKI, ROBERT, *World War II Almanac 1931–1945: A Political and Military Record*. Hamish Hamilton, 1981

GORLITZ, WALTER (ed.), *The Memoirs of Field Marshal Keitel*. William Kimber, 1965

GOSZTONY, PETER, *Der Kampf um Berlin 1945 in Augenzeugen Berichten*. Düsseldorf, Karl Rauch, 1970

GREY, IAN, *Stalin*. Weidenfeld and Nicolson, 1979

GROSS, LEONARD, *The Last Jews in Berlin*. Sidgwick & Jackson, 1983

GRUNBERGER, RICHARD, *A Social History of the Third Reich*. Penguin, 1974

GUN, NERIN E., *Eva Braun: Hitler's Mistress*. Coronet, 1976

HAFFNER, SEBASTIAN, *Germany's Self-Destruction: The Reich from Bismarck to Hitler*. Simon & Schuster, 1989

HAMILTON, NIGEL, *Monty. Vol 3: The Field Marshal, 1944–1976*. Hamish Hamilton, 1986

HAMPE, ERICH, *Der Zivile Luftschutz im Zweiten Weltkrieg*. Bernard und Graefe, Frankfurt-am-Main, 1972

HART-DAVIS, DUFF, *Hitler's Games: the 1936 Olympics*. Harper and Row, 1986

HASSELL, ULRICH VON, *Diaries, 1938–44*. Hamish Hamilton, 1948

HASTINGS, MAX, *Bomber Command*. Pan Books, 1981

HAUNER, MILAN, *Hitler: A Chronology of his Life and Time*. Macmillan, 1983

HEIBER, HELMUT, *Goebbels*. Robert Hale, 1973

HENDERSON, SIR NEVILE, *Failure of a Mission: Berlin 1937–1939*. Hodder and Stoughton, 1940

HESTON, LEONARD L. and RENATE, *The Medical Casebook of Adolf Hitler*. Kimber, 1979

HITLER, ADOLF, *The Testament of Adolf Hitler*. Cassell, 1961

HOFFMANN, HEINRICH, *Hitler Was My Friend*. Burke, 1955

HOFFMANN, PETER, *The History of the German Resistance*. Macdonald and Jane's, 1977

*Hitler's Personal Security*. Cambridge, Massachusetts, MIT Press, 1979

HÜRLIMANN, MARTIN, *Berlin: Königresidenz, Reichshauptstadt, Neubeginn*. Zurich, Atlantis, 1981

INFIELD, GLENN B., *Hitler's Secret Life*. Hamlyn, 1980

IRVING, DAVID, *The War Path*. Macmillan, 1983

*Hitler's War*. Macmillan, 1983

JONES, R. V., *Most Secret War: British Scientific Intelligence, 1939-1945*. Hamish Hamilton, 1978

KARDORFF, URSULA VON, *Diary of a Nightmare: Berlin 1942-45*. Hart-Davis, 1965

KASPER, BARBARA, SCHUSTER, LOTHAR, WATKINSON, CHRISTOF, *Arbeiten für den Krieg, Deutsche und Ausländer in der Rüstungsproduktion bei Rheinmetall-Borsig 1943-1945*. Hamburg, VSA-Verlag, 1987

KLIETMANN, K. G., *Die Waffen-SS, Eine Dokumentation*. Osnabrück, 1965

KOEHN, ILSE, *Mischling, Second Degree*. Hamish Hamilton, 1977

KOLLER, KARL, *Der Letzte Monat*. Munich, Bechtle, 1985

KONIEV, I. S., *Year of Victory*. Moscow, Progress Publishers, 1969

KÖNIG, JOEL, *Den Netzen Entronnen*. Göttingen, Vandenhoeck & Ruprecht, 1967

KRONIKA, JACOB, *Der Untergang Berlins*. Flensburg, Christian Wolf, 1946

KUBY, ERICH, *The Russians and Berlin*. Heinemann, 1968

KURTZ, HAROLD, *The Second Reich, Kaiser Wilhelm II and his Germany*. Macdonald, 1970

LAMB, RICHARD, *Montgomery in Europe 1943-1945*. Buchan & Enright, 1983

LANG, JOCHEN VON, *The Secretary*. Ohio University Press, 1981.

LEIBHOLZ-BONHOEFFER, SABINE, *The Bonhoeffers: portrait of a family*. Sidgwick & Jackson, 1971

LE TISSIER, TONY, *The Battle of Berlin, 1945*. Cape, 1988

LEWIN, RONALD, *Montgomery as Military Commander*. Batsford, 1971

LIDDELL HART, B. L., *The Other Side of the Hill*. Cassell, 1948

LOEWENHEIM, FRANCIS L., LANGLEY, HAROLD D., and JONAS, MANFRED (eds.), *Roosevelt and Churchill: Their Secret Wartime Correspondence*. Barrie and Jenkins, 1975

LUCAS, JAMES, *Last Days of the Reich*. Arms and Armour Press, 1986

MABIRE, JEAN, *Mourir à Berlin: Les SS Francais*. Paris, Fayard, 1979

MACKINNON, MARIANNE, *The Naked Years: Growing Up in Nazi Germany*. Chatto and Windus, 1987

MALLORY, KEITH and OTTAR, ARVID, *Architecture of Aggression: Military Architecture in Two World Wars*. Architectural Press, 1973

MALTZAN, MARIA, GRAFIN VON, *Schlage die Trommel und fürchte dich nicht*. Berlin, Ullstein, 1989

MANDER, JOHN, *Berlin: The Eagle and the Bear*. Barrie and Rockliffe, 1959

MERSON, ALLAN, *Communist Resistance in Nazi Germany*. Lawrence and Wishart, 1985

MIDDLEBROOK, MARTIN, *The Berlin Raids: RAF Bomber Command, Winter 1943–44*. Viking, 1988

MIDDLEBROOK, MARTIN and EVERITT, CHRIS, *The Bomber Command War Diaries*. Viking, 1985

MITCHAM, SAMUEL W., Jr, *Hitler's Field Marshals and their Battles*. Grafton, 1989

MOLTKE, HELMUTH JAMES VON, *Letters to Freya: A Witness against Hitler*. Collins Harvill, 1991

MONTGOMERY, BERNARD LAW, VISCOUNT, *Memoirs*. Collins, 1958

MOSSE, GEORGE L., *Nazi Culture: Intellectual, Cultural and Social Life in the Third Reich*. W. H. Allen, 1966

MOYNIHAN, BRIAN, *The Claws of the Bear*. Hutchinson, 1989

NELSON, WALTER H., *The Berliners*. Longman, 1969

NEUSTROYEV, S. A., *Put'k Reikhstagu (The Road to the Reichstag)*. Moscow, Military Publishing House, 1948

NICOLAEVSKY, BORIS I., *Power of the Soviet Elite*. Frederick A. Praeger, 1965

O'DONNELL, JAMES P., *The Berlin Bunker*. Dent, 1979

OECHSNER, FREDERICK (et al.), *This is the Enemy*. Curtis, 1942

OLIVEIRA, A. RAMOS (tr. EILEEN E. BROOKE), *A People's History of Germany*. Gollancz, 1942

OVEN, WILFRED VON, *Mit Goebbels bis zum Ende*, 2 vols. Buenos Aires, Dürer-Verlag, 1949–50

OVERY, R. J., *Göring, the 'Iron' Man*. Routledge and Kegan Paul, 1984

PABST, HELMUT, *The Outermost Frontier*. Kimber, 1957

PAUL, WOLFGANG, *Der Heimatkrieg 1939 bis 1945*. Bechtle-Verlag, Esslingen am Neckar, 1980

PRICE, C. WARD, *I Know These Dictators*. Harrap, 1937

RALEIGH, JOHN McCUTCHEON, *Behind the Nazi Front*. Harrap, 1941

READ, ANTHONY and FISHER, DAVID, *The Deadly Embrace; Hitler, Stalin and the Nazi-Soviet Pact, 1939–1941.* Michael Joseph, 1988
*Kristallnacht: Unleashing the Holocaust.* Michael Joseph, 1989

REIMANN, VIKTOR, *The Man Who Created Hitler: Joseph Goebbels.* Kimber, 1976

RIBBE, WOLFGANG, *Geschichte Berlins.* 2 vols. Munich, C. H. Beck, 1987

ROBERTSON, EDWIN, *The Shame and the Sacrifice.* Hodder and Stoughton, 1987

ROCOLLE, PIERRE, *Götterdämmerung – La Prise de Berlin.* Indo China, 1954.

ROKOSSOVSKY, KONSTANTIN K., *A Soldier's Duty.* Moscow, Progress Publishers, 1969

RUMPF, HANS, *The Bombing of Germany.* Frederick Muller, 1968

RYABOV, VASILI, *The Great Victory.* Moscow, Novosti, 1985

RYAN, CORNELIUS, *The Last Battle.* Collins, 1966

SAJER, GUY, *The Forgotten Soldier.* Weidenfeld and Nicolson, 1975

SALISBURY, HARRISON, *The 900 Days: The Siege of Leningrad.* Pan Books, 1971

SANDVOSS, HANS-RAINER, *Widerstand in Steglitz und Zehlendorf 1933–1945.* Berlin, Gedenkstätte Deutscher Widerstand, 1986

SAWARD, DUDLEY, *'Bomber' Harris, the Authorised Biography.* Cassell/ Buchan & Enright, 1984

SCHÄFER, HANS DIETER, *Berlin im Zweiten Weltkrieg: Der Untergang der Reichshauptstadt in Augenzeugenberichten.* Munich, Piper, 1985

SCHATZ, LUDWIG, *Schüler-Soldaten, die Geschichte der Luftwaffen-helfer im zweiten Weltkrieg.* Frankfurt-am-Main, Thesen-Verlag, 1972

SCHELLENBERG, WALTER, *The Schellenberg Memoirs.* Andre Deutsch, 1956

SCHEURENBERG, KLAUS, *Ich Will Leben.* Berlin, Oberbaumverlag, 1982

SCHLABRENDORFF, FABIAN VON, *Revolt Against Hitler.* Eyre and Spottiswoode, 1948; *Begegnungen in fünf Jahrezehnten.* Tübingen, Rainer Wunderlich, 1979

SCHMIDT, MATTHIAS, *Albert Speer, the End of a Myth.* Harrap, 1985

SCHMIDT, PAUL, *Hitler's Interpreter.* Heinemann, 1951

SCHOENHALS, KAI P., *The Free Germany Movement.* New York, Greenwood Press, 1989

SCHRAMM, PERCY ERNST, *Kriegstagebuch des OKW 1940–1945.* Frankfurt-am-Main, Bernard und Graefe, 1961

SEMMLER, RUDOLF, *Goebbels: The Man Next to Hitler.* Westhouse, 1947

SHARP, TONY, *The Wartime Alliance and the Zonal Division of Germany.* Oxford, Clarendon Press, 1975

SHIRER, WILLIAM L., *Berlin Diary: An inside account of Nazi Germany.*
New York, Bonanza Books, 1984
  *The Nightmare Years, 1930–1940.* New York, Bantam Books, 1985
  *The Rise and Fall of the Third Reich.* Secker & Warburg, 1960
SHTEMENKO, S. M., *The Last Six Months.* New York, Doubleday, 1977
SHULMAN, MILTON, *Defeat in the West.* Secker & Warburg, 1947
SIMMONS, MICHAEL, *Berlin, the Dispossessed City.* Hamish Hamilton,
  1988
SIMONOV, KONSTANTIN, *Aus den Kriegstagebüchern.* Moscow,
  Progress Publishers, 1965
SIPOLS, VILNIS, *The Road to Great Victory.* Moscow, Progress
  Publishers, 1985
SLOWE, PETER and WOODS, RICHARD, *Battlefield Berlin.* Hale, 1988
SMITH, HOWARD K., *Last Train from Berlin.* New York, Knopf, 1942
SOMMER, ERICH F., *Das Memorandum.* Munich, Herbig, 1981
SPEER, ALBERT, *The Slave State.* Weidenfeld and Nicolson, 1981
  *Inside the Third Reich.* Sphere, 1971
STRATENSCHULTE, DR ECKART D., *East Berlin.* Berlin, Berlin
  Information Centre, 1988
STRAWSON, JOHN, *The Battle for Berlin.* Batsford, 1974
STUDNITZ, HANS-GEORG VON, *While Berlin Burns.* Weidenfeld and
  Nicolson, 1964
SUTCLIFFE, ANTHONY (ed.), *Metropolis 1890–1940.* Mansell, 1984
TOLAND, JOHN *The Last 100 Days.* Arthur Barker, 1966
  *Adolf Hitler.* Doubleday, 1976
TREVOR-ROPER, HUGH, *The Last Days of Hitler.* Macmillan, 1987
  (ed.) *The Goebbels Diaries: The Last Days.* Secker & Warburg, 1977
  *Hitler's Table Talk.* Weidenfeld and Nicolson, 1953
VASSILTCHIKOV, MARIE, *The Berlin Diaries, 1940–1945.* Methuen,
  1987
ULAM, ADAM B., *Expansion and Coexistence: Soviet Foreign Policy 1917–
  73.* New York, Holt, Rinehart and Winston, 1974
WAGENER, RAY, *The Soviet Air Forces in World War II.* New York,
  Doubleday, 1973
WEBSTER, SIR CHARLES and FRANKLAND, NOBLE, *History of the
  Second World War: The Strategic Air Offensive Against Germany,
  1939–1945.* HMSO, 1961
WEIGLEY, RUSSELL F., *Eisenhower's Lieutenants.* Sidgwick & Jackson,
  1981
WETZLAUGK, UDO and KOZIOL, CHRISTIAN, *Berlin: Outlook.*
  Berlin, Berlin Information Centre, 1985
WHITING, CHARLES, *The Home Front: Germany.* Alexandria, Virginia,
  Time-Life Books, 1982
WILLEMER, WILLIAM, *The German Defence of Berlin.* Berlin, HQ
  USAREUR, 1953

WILMOT, CHESTER, *The Struggle for Europe*. Collins, 1952

WISTRICH, ROBERT, *Who's Who in Nazi Berlin*. New York, Bonanza Books, 1982

WOLF, MARKUS, *Die Troika*. Düsseldorf, Claassen, 1989

YEREMEYEV, LEONID, *USSR in World War Two*. Moscow, Novosti, 1985

ZIEMKE, EARL F., *Battle for Berlin: Purnell's History of the Second World War, No. 6*. Purnell, 1968

ZHUKOV, GEORGI K., *The Memoirs of Marshal Zhukov*. Cape, 1971


MAGAZINES AND NEWSPAPERS

*Air Force Magazine*, September 1975
*Alte Kamaraden*, No. 5, 1965
*Daily Mail*, 24 April 1945
*New York Times*, 2 August, 14 August, 1936
*Soviet Military Review*, April 1975
*Time*, 4 September, 11 September, 1939
*Voenno-Istoricheskii Zhurnal*, 1960
*Wehrwissenchaftliche Rundschau*, No. 2, 1954; No. 1, 1962
*Zeitschrift für Militärgeschichte*, No. 2, 1965


UNPUBLISHED DIARIES, MEMOIRS AND REPORTS

*Military*
General Theodor Busse
Colonel-General Hans Georg Eismann
General Martin Gareis
Colonel-General Gotthard Heinrici
Colonen-General Alfred Jodl
General Karl Koller
Major-General Gustav Krukenberg
Colonel-General Erhard Raus
Colonel Hans Refior
Colonel Günther Reichhelm
General Hellmuth Reymann
Major Joachim Schultz
Lieutenant-General Karl Weidling
General Walther Wenck
Colonel Hans Oscar Wöhlermann
Müncheberg Panzer Division War Diary
OKH War Diary
OKW War Diary

*Civilian*
Jo van Amelrooij
Karl Friedrich Borée
Margret Boveri
Max Buch
Maria Czerniewski
Margret Diehn
Theo Findahl
Rudolf Gehrig
Emilie Karoline Gerstenberg
Helmuth Grossmann
Heinrich Grüber
Felix Hartlaub
Lutz Heck
Katharina Heinroth
Karla Höcker
Thorolf Hillblad
René Juvet
Ursula von Kardorff
Wolfgang Karow
Jaap Knegtmans
Jacob Kronika
Horst Lange
Jeanne Mammen
Matthias Menzel
Helga Meyer
Tami Oelfken
René Schindler
Eliza Stokowska
Isa Vermehren
Eric Wallin
Konrad Warner

## Personal Interviews and Correspondence

Veronika von Below
Elisabeth Deyhle
Edith Diekmann
Helga Dolinski
Colonel (Retd.) Theodor von Dufving
Lieutenant-General (Retd.) Bernd Freytag von Loringhoven
Freiherr Ludwig & Freifrau Dorothee von Hammerstein
Hans & Elisabeth von Herwarth

Major (Retd.) Arthur Hogben
Albert Klein
Commander (Retd.) Walther Kühtze
Fred Laabs
Maria, Gräfin von Maltzan
Maria Milde
Hans-Dietrich Nicolaisen
Gerhard Räbiger
Gerald Rahusen
Manfred Rauschert
Hans-Jürgen Röber
Klaus Scheurenberg
Dr Walter Schmid
Colonel (Retd.) Wolfgang Skorning
Dr Erich Franz Sommer
Hans-Georg von Studnitz
Klaus Ziegler

# SOURCE NOTES

Detailed information concerning the books referred to in shortened form in these notes will be found in the Bibliography.

*PART ONE*
page

3   Göring 'wreathed in smiles, orders and decorations': Channon, 111.

4   'The proper solution . . .': Trevor-Roper, *Hitler's Table Talk*, 426.
'I can still see . . .': ibid.

5   Via triumphalis and special grants: Hart-Davis, 125.
Berliners' superstition about linden trees; ibid.
'Unter die Lanterne': Max Buch diary.
Removal of *Die Stürmer*, etc: Fromm, 194.

6   Scheurenberg family: Klaus Scheurenberg, interview.

8   Deutschkron family: Deutschkron, Gedenkstätte Deutscher Widerstand.

7   Bonhoeffer information: Bethge, 444; Leibholz-Bonhoeffer, 45–48; Bosanquet, 16–37.

8   'Today, no other city . . .': MacKinnon, 39.

9   'Berlin seemed to click its heels . . .': ibid, 38.
Via triumphalis: Hart-Davis, 139.

10   'Holy flame burn . . .': ibid, 152.

11   Mystery couple: Maria von Maltzan, interview.

12   'to distant lands . . .': *The Blackshirt*, 8 August 1936.
'where I know the Führer is watching . . .': MacKinnon, 41.

13   'an orgiastic frenzy . . .': Fromm, 196.
'Remove yourself immediately . . .': *The New York Times*, 14 August 1936.

15   Shirer interviews: Shirer, *Berlin Diary*, 65–66.

16   'The genial tycoons . . .': Shirer, *The Nightmare Years*, 223.

17   Pitched battles on streets: Shirer, *Rise and Fall*, 209–10.

22   135,000 new homes: Sutcliffe, 308; Berlin Information Centre.

23    'a kind of dirty cellar . . .': Reimann, 69.

27    SA attacks, etc: Stratenschulte, 10–11.

28    Book burning: Albert Klein, interview.

29    Ninety-two of them were murdered . . .: Stratenschulte, 11.

31    Bonhoeffer and Bethge: Bethge, 485.

32    Bonhoeffer family, Dohnanyi, etc: Bethge, 490; Leibholz-Bonhoeffer, 33–34.

34    Kristallnacht in Berlin: Sir Hugh Greene, interview; Read and Fisher, *Kristallnacht*, 74–83.

36    'People like Maria von Maltzan . . .': Maltzan, interview.

37    'I need grand halls . . .': Speer, 157.
Details of building: ibid, 158–69.

39    Details of parade: Irving, *The War Path*, 198–200.
'An advance showing . . .': Andreas-Friedrich, 41.
Herr Deutschkron's journey: Deutschkron, Gedenkstätte Deutscher Widerstand.

41    Celebrations for Nazi–Soviet Pact: *Time*, 4 September 1939.
'seasoning the air . . .': Bayles, 9.

42    'If it comes . . .': *Time*, 4 September 1939.
Hitler's meeting with deputies: Halder diary, Documents on German Foreign Policy, Vol VII, Appendix 1, 546.

43    'How can a country . . .': Shirer, *Berlin Diary*, 191.
Street scene during air raid practice: Raleigh, 18.

44    Converting cellar to shelter: Bayles, 12–14.

45    People's numb apathy: Shirer, *Berlin Diary*, 197.
Hitler's speech: *Time*, 11 September 1939.

46.   Two Polish aircraft: Shirer, *Berlin Diary*, 198–99.
William Bayles in shelter: Bayles, 13.

47    'You are at war . . .': Raleigh, 20.


## PART TWO

52    Casualty figures: Shirer, *Rise and Fall*, 760.

54    Street crime in Berlin: SPD reports, January 1940.
'an effective protection . . .': ibid.
Ration cards: Charman, 47–48; Flannery, 57.

55    Ration details: Charman, 48; Andreas-Friedrich, 46; Vassiltchikov, 4.

56    Effects of petrol rationing: Raleigh, 27.

57    Fred Laabs's experiences: Laabs, interview.

58    Jews banned from shelters: Shirer, *Berlin Diary*, 520–21.

60    'the hysteria is frightful': Jodl diary.

62    'Put out the flags . . .': Andreas-Friedrich, 56–58.

63    Victory parade: Smith, 85.
Moltke details: Moltke, 15–30.

64    Bonhoeffer conversion: Bethge, 585.
66    'it seems very important . . .': PRO, Premier Papers, 3/14/2.
      Sinclair reply: Premier Papers, 4/37/4.
67    British leaflets: Shirer, *Berlin Diary*, 489–90.
      'Berlin is the place to hit them': Colville, 230.
      'If the damage doesn't get any worse . . .': Andreas-Friedrich, 61.
      Hitler speech: *Berlin Diaries*, 496.
68    'We shall pay the English . . .': Goebbels Diaries, 135.
69    Paul Scheurenberg's experiences; Scheurenberg, interview.
70    Molotov's visit: Berezhkov, 20–42; Sommer, 57–74.
73    No more RAF raids: Webster and Frankland, 226.
      State Opera House description: Flannery, 163–4.
75    Dummy town: Rahusen, interview.
      Camouflage in Tiergarten, etc: Flannery, 293–94; Oechsner, 181–82.
77    Hitler's bizarre idea: Trevor-Roper, *Hitler's Table Talk*, 303, 669.
78    'the most beautiful weapons': ibid, 304.
      'when the guns start firing . . .': Vassiltchikov, 48.
      Descriptions of flak towers: Middlebrook, 26–27; Schäfer, 31.
79    'From the flak tower . . .': Speer, *Inside the Third Reich*, 395.
81    Hess jokes: Vassiltchikov, 52.
82    'We have finally put an end . . .': Goebbels Diaries, 408.
83    'Two hundred women . . .': Andreas-Friedrich, 62–63.
      Rumours of invasion: ibid, 67–68.
84    Berezhkov in embassy: Berezhkov, 74.
      Sommer collects Dekanozov: Sommer, interview.
86    Slogans on walls: Smith, 194.
87    Moltke's letter, etc: Moltke, 155–56, 160, 166.
88    Klaus Scheurenberg's experiences: Scheurenberg, interview.
90    Charlotte Friedenthal's experiences: Bethge, 651–53.
91    'If you aren't at home . . .': Andreas-Friedrich, 73.
92    Maria von Maltzan and Hans Hirschel: Maltzan, interview.
94    Evacuation trains: Ziegler, interview.
95    Tom Macleod experiences: Macleod, interview.
96    Bonhoeffer and Moltke in Norway: Moltke, 252; Bethge, 658–59;
      Bosanquet, 234–35.
97    'One thing is certain . . .': Andreas-Friedrich, 88–89.
99    Siege of Stalingrad: Zhukov, 388–424; Erickson, *Road to Stalingrad*,
      430–72.


## PART THREE

103    'Suddenly and absolutely hellish . . .': Kardorff, 27.
104    'Berlin is a city of four million . . .': Cooper, 16.

105    'If the Josefs . . .': Hassell, 253.
Casablanca conference decisions: Ellis, 146; Webster and Frankland, Vol IV, 153; Feis, 109.
107    'He should cut out those provocative speeches . . .': Schäfer, 256.
108    Berliners and posters: Smith, 199.
Total war posters: König, 290.
109    Round-up of Jewish workers: ibid, 308.
110    Deutschkrons' experiences: Deutschkron, Gardenkstätte Deutscher Widerstand.
111    Scheurenbergs' experiences: Scheurenberg, interview.
112    Goebbels's anger: Goebbels Diaries, 261.
'Tonight you go to the Big City': Cooper, 19.
Hassells' and Waldersees' experiences: Hassell, 260.
113    Fred Laabs's experiences: Laabs, interview.
114    Extent of damage and casualties: Schäfer, 36.
Goebbels press conference: ibid.
115    Tram passengers' reactions: König, 319.
Anger at foreigners: Fredborg, 199
116    Dolinskis' experiences: Dolinski, interview.
117    Details of 'Operation Flash': Bethge, 684–86; Schlanbrendorff, *Begegnungen in fünf Jahrezehnten*, 225–31; Hoffmann, *German Resistance*, 281–83.
119    Bonhoeffer arrest: Bethge, 685; Leibholz-Bonhoeffer, 54; Bosanquet, 244.
120    Children wandering the streets: Vassiltchikov, 82.
121    Battle of Kursk Salient: Erickson, *Road to Berlin*, 97–135; Zhukov, 432–76.
122    Allied jamming devices: Jones, 301.
Wild Boar tactics: Middlebrook, *The Berlin Raids*, 14–18.
123    'The so-called nightfighter training unit . . .': Leutnant Günther Wolf, quoted in Middlebrook, 19.
125    Andreas-Friedrich's experiences: Andreas-Friedrich, 100–103.
Studnitz's experiences: Studnitz, 101, and interview.
126    'It wasn't the fascist ideology . . .': Laabs, interview.
127    'It was like running naked . . .': Middlebrook, *The Berlin Raids*, 80.
'I stood outside a hangar . . .': Colville, 453–4.
128    Details of bomb disposal: Hogben, interview; Skorning, interview; Räbiger, interview.
130    'Berlin will be bombed . . .': Cooper, 93.
1,593 tons of bombs: Middlebrook, 79.
'They won't be coming tonight . . .': Warner, 144.
131    'They flew very low . . .'; Vassiltchikov, 106.
132    Speer in flak tower: Speer, 395.
Grossmann's experiences in flak tower: Warner, 145–57.
'one gigantic conflagration': Speer, 394.

133    Vassiltchikovs' experiences: Vassiltchikov, 108.
       Grossmann's experiences: Warner, 147–52.
136    Studnitz's experiences: Studnitz, 141–47, and interview.
137    Grossmann's experiences: Warner, 153–53, 158–59.
138    Details of 22 November raid: Middlebrook, 112–18.
139    Destruction of Zoo: Heinroth, 130–31; Heck, 162–63.
       Dohnanyi and Bonhoeffer experiences: Bethge, 711–712.
140    Destruction of Aquarium: Heinroth, 131–32; Heck, 163–66.
142    'In the city there is no water . . .': Moltke, 367.
143    Goebbels speech and tour: Goebbels diaries, 537.
       'In one of the rubble heaps . . .': Moltke, 369.
144    'Wearily I go to bed . . .' and 'No butter with our eats . . .':
       Charman, 147.
       Teheran Conference details: Churchill, 706; Feis, 272–73.
145    'The old year ended . . .': Andreas-Friedrich, 112–14.
       'Since the air attacks . . .': Studnitz, 154.
146    Moltke's visit to Istanbul: Moltke, 369.
       Meeting with Stauffenberg: ibid, 371.
147    Details of February and March raids: Middlebrook, 263, 276; Ethel
       and Price, 86–102; Hastings, 317–23.
148    'Berlin won . . .': Hastings, 320.

## PART FOUR

151    'Alarms, alarms . . .': Andreas-Friedrich, 115–16.
       Details of Soviet advance: Erickson, *Road to Berlin*, 192.
152    'We burned everything . . .': Pabst, 197.
       Details of destruction in Ukraine: Zhukov, 481.
153    Leningrad details: Salisbury, 608–12.
       Punishment of Soviet prisoners: Sajer, 118–19.
154    Eisenhower's arrival: Weigley, 43.
       Stalin's letter, etc: Sharp, 5.
155    Fred Laabs's experiences: Laabs, interview.
156    Helga Dolinski's experiences: Dolinski, interview.
       Lisa Deyhle's experiences: Deyhle, interview.
157    Foreign workers: Kasper et al, 28–89.
       Irma Diehn, Rudolf Gehrig: ibid.
160    'People disappear . . .': Andreas-Friedrich, 123.
161    Pastor Wachsmann's execution: ibid, 123–24.
       Fred Laabs's experiences: Laabs, interview.
162    Soviet plans: Erickson, *Road to Berlin*, 190; Zhukov, 556.
163    Peter's telephone call: Andreas-Friedrich, 129–30.

164. Stauffenberg and details of assassination plot: Schlabrendorff, *Revolt against Hitler*, 103ff; Hoffmann, *German Resistance*, 317–24.
166. Goebbels actions: Speer, 515–19; Oven diary; Toland, *Adolf Hitler*, 805.
169. Disposal of explosive: Vassiltchikov, 194–209.
170. Schlabrendorff torture: Schlabrendorff, op cit, 113.
Hammerstein family experiences: Hammerstein, correspondence with authors; Deyhle, interview.
171. Trial details: Hoffmann, *German Resistance*, 525–27.
172. Execution details: Gedenkstätte Deutscher Widerstand.
173. Dohnanyis' illnesses and interrogation: Bethge, 713–14; Leibholz-Bonhoeffer, 35.
174. Bonhoeffer's escape plan: Bethge, 730–32; Leibholz-Bonhoeffer, 26–27, 190–91, 196.
175. Moltke prepares defence: Moltke, 21–22, 386.
Bonhoeffer's treatment: Schlabrendorff, op cit, 226–31; Bethge, 810–12; Leibholz-Bonhoeffer, 54–55; Hoffmann, *German Resistance*, 294.
177. Soviet crossing into East Prussia: Erickson, *Road to Berlin*, 308.
179. 'I consider we have now reached a stage . . .': Montgomery, 271–72.
Eisenhower's response: Lamb, 207–10; Montgomery, 272–3; Eisenhower, 335–37.
180. 'Steady, Monty . . .': Wilmot, 489.
'Clearly Berlin is the main prize . . .': Montgomery, 277; Lamb, 210.
181. 'Strategically and politically . . .': Blumentritt, quoted in Liddell Hart, 591.
182. 'If I had received these powers . . .': Semmler, 147.
'We are actually in a position . . .': Reimann, 305.
'The physician in charge . . .': ibid, 306.
184. 'They must have thought . . .': Irma Diehn, quoted in Kasper, 62.
'In the Russians' camp . . .': Eliza Stokowska, quoted in Kapser, 101ff.
186. Zhukov's meeting with Stalin: Zhukov, 551–52.
188. Volkssturm details: Willemer, 40–42.
Walter Seitz 'writing his fingers to the bone': Andreas-Friedrich, 180.
189. Construction of bunker: Hoffmann, *Hitler's Personal Security*, 258–560; O'Donnell, 43–44.
'I am on my way to Berlin . . .': Erickson, *Road to Berlin*, 422.
190. Zhukov details: Zhukov, 11–36; Bialer, 640; Chaney, 3–7.
191. Rokossovsky details: Rokossovsky, 266–67; Bialer, 635.
192. Koniev details: Bialer, 633.
193. Massacre at Korsun: Moynihan, 167; Erickson, *Road to Berlin*, 176–77.
Rokossovsky's meeting with Stalin: Rokossovsky, 267.
Koniev's meeting with Stalin: Koviev, 32–33.

194    Hitler's plans for Ardennes offensive: Jodl diaries.
195    Montgomery relations with Eisenhower: Guingand, 106–112.
196    'What I did not say . . .': Montgomery, 315.
       Churchill-Stalin correspondence: Churchill, Vol VI, 243; Feis, 481.
       Stalin's order to Koniev: Koniev, 14.
197    Guderian's Clash with Hitler: Guderian, 315; Freytag von Loring-
       hoven, interview.
       Fred Laabs's experiences: Laabs, interview.
198    Vassiltchikov and Schönburg leave Berlin: Vassiltchikov, 238–9, 246.
       Maltzan and Hirschel experiences: Maltzan, interview.
201    Freya von Moltke and Ruth Andreas-Friedrich: Andreas-Friedrich,
       181–83, 185–87; Moltke, 388.
202    Freya von Moltke meetings with Müller and Freisler: Moltke, 23.
       Moltke's trial: Moltke, 390ff.


PART FIVE

207    Koniev assault: Koniev, 16–39; Erickson, *Road to Berlin*, 456.
208    Chuikov assault: Chuikov, 84–100; Zhukov, 561; Erickson, *Road to
       Berlin*, 458–59.
209    Rokossovsky assault: Rokossovsky, 296; Erickson *Road to Berlin*,
       459.
211    Capture of Lodz: Chuikov, 89–92.
212    Capture of Auschwitz: Czech, 804; Erickson, *Road to Berlin*, 472;
       Eban, 404.
213    Warnings to leave Breslau: Kardorff, 165–66.
       'They stood in the cold . . .': Andreas-Friedrich, 193.
       Eva and Ilse Braun: Gun, 216–18.
214    Marianne Gärthner's experiences: MacKinnon, 177–87.
217    Zhukov's orders: Chuikov, 120.
       Zhukov and Koniev submit plans: Zhukov, 566.
218    Stalin's decision on race: Erickson, *Road to Berlin*, 472–73.
       Chuikov advances to Küstrin: Chuikov, 147–53.
219    Crossing the Oder: ibid, 153–55.
220    Fred Laabs's experiences: Laabs, interview.
222    Description of bunker: O'Donnell, 22–24; Trevor-Roper, *Last Days*,
       148–51; Boldt, 73, 130–31; Freytag von Loringhoven, interview.
223    Hitler's condition: Freytag von Loringhoven, interview; Boldt, 39–
       40, 82; Guderian, 443.
224    'They deserve to be court-martialled . . .': Guderian, 315.
       'In the future . . .': Speer, 566–67.
225    Guderian's disgust: Guderian, 334; Freytag von Loringhoven,
       interview.

Schörner telephone conversation: Toland, *The Last 100 Days*, 17.
Speer's memorandum and note: Speer, 567–68.

227 Foreign workers locked in camps: Stokowska diary, quoted in Kasper, 102.
Walter Schmid's experiences; Schmid, interview.

229 Rolf Schleicher and Freisler's death: Bethge, 815; Leibholz-Bonhoeffer, 28–30; Schlabrendorff, *Revolt*, 235.

230 Dohnanyi and Bonhoeffer: Bethge, 820; Leibholz-Bonhoeffer, 35.

231 'The cellar tribe . . .': *A Woman in Berlin*, 19.

232 Veronika von Below's experiences: Below, correspondence with authors.

233 Karl-Friedrich Borée experiences: Borée, 47–49.
'Morale wouldn't be so high . . .': MacKinnon, 191.

234 Maria Milde experiences, and state of film industry: Milde, interview.
Berlin Philharmonic concerts: MacKinnon, 192.

235 State of Soviet armies: Chuikov, 100.

236 Stalin's phone call: ibid, 120.
Stalin's orders to Koniev and Rokossovsky: Erickson, *Road to Berlin*, 520–21.

238 Deutschkron experiences: Deutschkron, Gedankstätte Deutscher Widerstand.

241 Guderian conference and row with Hitler: Guderian, 324–44; Freytag von Loringhoven, interview.

243 Marianne Gärtner's experiences: MacKinnon, 198ff.

244 'child soldiers . . .': Studnitz, 245.

246 Vanaman's and Spivey's experiences: Major-General Delmar T. Spivey, with Captain Arthur A. Durand, *Air Force Magazine*, September 1975.

249 Reymann's appointment: Reymann diary.

250 'No game is lost . . .': Hitler, *Testament*, 38–41.
Fundamental order: *Zeitschrift für Militärgeschichte* No 2, 1965, GDR Military Publishing House, Potsdam.

253 Reymann's complicated responsibilities: Reymann diary.
'Taken as a whole . . .': Goebbels, 97.

254 'He is the typical sort of bourgeois . . .': ibid.
Reymann's request for men: Kuby, 88.
Problems of manning defences: Reymann diary; Kuby, 83–88.

255 Heroes' Remembrance Day ceremony: Reymann diary.

256 Goebbels's 'melancholy evening': Goebbels, 125–29.

257 'She sees her future . . .': Semmler, 185.
Morell's drug supplies to Hitler: Heston, 122–23.
Goebbels's scenarios for the end: Semmler, 186.

258 Demand for Jewish stars: Studnitz, 257.
Parties in Berlin: ibid, 259.

259    German losses: Ellis, 284; Shirer, *Rise and Fall*, 1306.
260    Speer's appeal to Hitler, and Nero Order: Speer, 582–88.
261    Raid on Borsig works: Stokowska, quoted in Kasper, 102.
262    Guderian's meeting with Himmler: Guderian, 340.
        Appointment of Heinrici: Heinrici papers.
263    'I understand that your heart . . .': Guderian, 343; Boldt, 195–96;
        Freytag von Loringhoven, interview.
        Heinrici description: Ryan, 65.
264    Heinrici meeting with Guderian: Guderian, 343; Heinrici papers;
        Ryan, 78–80; Toland, *The Last 100 Days*, 260.
265    Soviet difficulties at Küstrin: Chuikov, 135.
        Heinrici meeting with Himmler: Heinrici papers; Ryan, 82–85;
        Toland, *The Last 100 Days*, 260–61.
267    Patton's telephone calls to Bradley: Bradley, 521–22.
268    Montgomery and Churchill: Colville, 578; Churchill, Vol VI, 362–33.
269    Molotov's telegram to Churchill: Churchill, Vol VI, 386–92; Colville,
        575–76; Feis, 579–96.
270    'I hardly like to consider . . .': Churchill, Vol VI, 389; Colville, 578.
        Eisenhower's reaction: Churchill, ibid.
        'I had always put Berlin . . .': Montgomery, 331.
271    'I could see no political advantage . . .': Bradley, 535–56.
        Montgomery's orders to go for the Elbe: Montgomery Papers, quoted
        in Hamilton, 440.
272    Eisenhower's reply: ibid. 'I say quite frankly . . .': Churchill, Vol VI,
        390.
        'If we deliberately leave Berlin . . .': ibid
273    Stalin calls Zhukov to Moscow: Zhukov, 586.
        Malinin's conversation with Chuikov: Chuikov, 132–33.
274    'Did you give it to them hot?': ibid, 136.
        Zhukov's meeting with Stalin: Zhukov, 587–89.
275    Hitler's row with Guderian: Guderian, 356–57; Boldt, 98–100;
        Freytag von Loringhoven, interview.
277    Reymann's row with Goebbels: Reymann diary; Goebbels, 260;
        Refior diary.
279    Gerald Rahusen's experiences: Rahusen, interview.
280    Meeting of State Defence Committee: Zhukov, 587–91; Chaney,
        306–8; Erickson, *Road to Berlin*, 531.
284    Heinrici's meeting with Hitler: Heinrici papers; Eismann diary;
        Boldt, 100–102.
287    Goebbels reads Carlyle: Goebbels, 215.
        Horoscopes: ibid, 270.
288    Goebbels proclamation: ibid, 317.
        'I have decided to take brutal action': ibid, 315.
289    Berger's meeting with Vanaman and Spivey: Spivey, *Air Force
        Magazine*, op. cit.

290  Zhukov's conference with commanders: Chuikov, 142–43; Zhukov, 593.
292  Fred Laabs and Karl-Heinz Freund escape: Laabs, interview.
293  Bonhoeffer's journey and execution: Bethge, 824–31; Leibholz-Bonhoeffer, 54, 198–99; Hoffmann, *German Resistance*, 530.
295  Bradley decides to deal with Ruhr pocket: Bradley, 532; Weigley, 680.
296  Simpson's aim to reach Berlin: Ryan, 222; Weigley, 681.
      Eisenhower's letters to Marshall: Eisenhower papers, IV, 2592.
      'Alex, where are you going next?': Bolling, quoted in Ryan, 229.
297  Bradley's conversations with Simpson: Bradley, 534.
298  Wenck's appointment: Wenck report.
299  Goebbels and Roosevelt's death: Semmler, 192ff; Toland, *The Last 100 Days*, 377–9; Ryan, 250–51.
300  'Germany will be finished . . .': Chuikov. 143.
      Heinrici's preparations: Heinrici papers.
301  'Brad, what do you think . . .': Bradley, 535–36.
302  Eisenhower's decision: Ellis, 326–7.
      'I have something very important . . .': Bradley, 536–37.
303  'We're not going to Berlin . . .': Ryan, 260–61; Toland, *The Last 100 Days*, 385.
      Soviet strength: Erickson, *Road to Berlin*, 538; Chuikov, 140.
304  Speer's plea to save bridges: Speer, 624–25; Reymann diary; Heinrici papers.


## PART SIX

309  Men informed by leaflets: Abyzov, 33–34.
      Guards colours taken to front: Chuikov, 143.
      Abyzov's experiences: Abyzov, 34–39.
310  Gerhard Cordes experiences: Cordes, quoted in Gosztony, 171.
311  Start of offensive, and searchlights: Chuikov, 144–45. Zhukov, 603; Erickson, *Road to Berlin*, 563–64; Vasily Subbotin, *Soviet Military Review*, April 1975.
313  'The spring floods . . .': Chuikov, 146.
      'We hugged the ground . . .': Abyzov, 42–43.
314  Heinrici in his command post: Eismann papers.
      Zhukov's rage: Chuikov, 147–50.
      Koniev's operations: Koniev, 92–104; Erickson, *Road to Berlin*, 564–65.
316  Chuikov halted at Seelow Heights. Zhukov's reactions: Chuikov, 147–50; Zhukov, 605.
317  Life in Berlin: Kuby, 39–40; Ryan, 290–92.
      'If the battle for Berlin . . .': Reymann diary.

318     Reymann's row with Speer over lamp posts: Reymann diary; Refior diary.

319     Hitler's last order of the day: Gosztony, 163–64.

320     Speer and Berlin Philharmonic: Speer, 618–19; Ryan, 142–44, 292–93, 302–3.

322     'They can't last much longer . . .': Heinrici diary.
       Zhukov's conversation with Stalin: Zhukov, 606.

323     Tank crews using wire mattresses: Erickson, *Road to Berlin*, 569.

324     Koniev's advance: Koniev, 103.
       Koniev's conversation with Stalin: ibid, 105.

325     Zhukov's new orders: Zhukov, 565; Chuikov, 150.

326     Weidling's Panzer divisions fail to show: Weidling diary.
       'running away like madmen': Wöhlermann diary.

327     Ribbentrop's and Axmann's visits: ibid.
       30,000 men: Busse, 'Die letzte Schlacht der 9. Armee', *Wehrwissenschaftliche Rundschau*, 1954.
       Slogan painting and sabotage: Andreas-Friedrich, 250–53.

328     Infecting wounds: Maltzan, interview.
       Reymann's forces: Reymann diary; Kuby, 83–84.

329     'He is not for half-measures . . .': Oven, 305.
       Reymann argues against sending four battalions: Reymann diary.
       Goebbels speech: Reimann, 313–15.

330     Text of leaflet: Andreas-Friedrich, 264.

331     Abyzov experiences: Abyzov, 45–56.

332     Firing on Berlin: Abyzov, 46–48.

333     'not a single flag . . .': Max Buch diary.
       Banners: Kuby, 98. 'Tell Goebbels . . .': Oven, 307.

334     Issue of travel permits: Refior diary.
       Deutschkrons leave Berlin: Deutschkron, Gedankstätte Deutscher Widerstand.

335     Artillery fire on city centre: Zhukov, 609, 612.

336     'We were given 180 Danish rifles . . .': quoted in Shulman, 307.
       'There is only victory . . .': Le Tissier, 30.

337     Deployment of Hitler Youth: Wöhlermann diary.
       Koniev's and Zhukov's signals: Erickson, *Road to Berlin*, 577–78.

340     Reymann's telephone call from Krebs: Refior diary.
       'I shall fight as long as the faithful . . .': Frau Luise Jodl diary, quoted in Ryan, 317–18.

341     Hitler with female staff in bunker: O'Donnell, 90–91; Gun, 226–27.

342     Eva Braun and gramaphone: Gun, 227.
       Wöhlermann's experiences: Wöhlermann diary.

343     Last day at Zossen: Boldt, 118–21; Freytag von Loringhoven, interview.

345     Walter Seitz and artillery bombardment: Andreas-Friedrich, 278.

Max Buch experiences: Buch diary.
Radio announcement: Fred Laabs, interview.

346 'Do you know that Berlin . . .': Koller, 43–44.
347 Horses with manes and tails aflame: Ryan, 328.
348 Soviet entry into Zossen: Koniev, 114.
350 Walter Schmid's experiences: Schmid, interview.
351 Dr Grüber's experiences: Dr Heinrich Grüber, *Probst zu Berlin*, unpublished MS quoted in Kuby, 104–5.
352 Hitler and drugs: Heston, 142.
'In view of the improvised nature . . .': Keitel, 200.
353 'Steiner, are you aware . . .': Klietmann, 56.
Koller's conversations with Hitler: Koller, 45–50.
354 'I reject the order . . .': Heinrici papers.
355 Appointment of Trotha: ibid.
356 Walter Schmid's experiences: Schmid, interview.
358 'I believe that these services . . .': Grüber, op cit.
359 Weidling's new headquarters: Wöhlermann diary.
360 Hitler's conference and collapse: Keitel, 200–3; Boldt, 121–24; Koller, 54; Freytag von Loringhoven, interview.
362 Speer's visit to Hitler: Speer, 622.
364 Chuikov's crossing of the Spree: Chuikov, 165–68.
365 'We first saw action . . .': Altner, 123–24.
366 Volkssturm defences: Willemer, 29.
367 Murder of Klaus Bonhoeffer, Schleicher, etc: Bethge, 832; Leibholz-Bonhoeffer, 30; Ryan, 348.
368 Keitel's visit to Wenck: Keitel, 203–4; Wenck report.
369 Radio broadcasts: *Daily Mail*, 24 April 1945.
370 Looting in Kreuzberg: Hammerstein, correspondence with authors.
371 Keitel tries to persuade Hitler: Keitel, 205–10.
372 'this hysterical gentleman': ibid.
373 Weidling's visit to Führer bunker: Weidling diary; Theodor von Dufving, interview.
376 Max Buch experiences: Buch diary.
Chuikov's men meet Rybalkos' tanks: Chuikov, 169–70.
378 Krebs, Freytag and Boldt in bunker: Boldt, 139–40; Freytag von Loringhoven, interview.
380 'You made a very good impression . . .': Weidling diary; Dufving, interview.
News getting steadily worse: Boldt, 144.
Kurkenberg's experiences: Kurkenberg diary.

*PART SEVEN*

385 Soviet strengths: Erickson, *Road to Berlin*, 595.

386 'What do we want these respites for . . .': Abyzov, 56.
Zhukov's inner city tactics: Zhukov, 594; Chuikov, 184.

388 German artillery strength: Wöhlermann diary.
Reorganization of defences: Wöhlermann diary; Weidling diary; Dufving, interview.

389 Chuikov in observation post: Chuikov, 199.
Soviet bombers: Wagener, 357–58.

390 Wöhlermann's experiences: Wöhlermann diary.
Krukenberg takes over Nordland SS Panzer Division: Kurkenberg diary; Mabire, 151.

392 'At this supreme moment . . .': Mabire, ibid.
Battle at Gatow: Willemer, 31.

393 Wolfgang Skorning's experiences: Skorning, interview.

394 'We were on one side of the runway . . .': Abyzov, 50.
'Our artillery withdraws . . .': Müncheberg diary.
Walter Schmid's unit at Kreuzberg: Schmid, interview.

396 Defence of Humbolthain flak tower: Wolfgang Karow, article in *Alte Kameraden* No 5, 1965.

397 The end in Frohnau: Rahusen, interview.
Maria Milde meets Soviet tank: Milde, interview.

398 'the terrible noise of fighting': Buch diary.
Telephone answered by Russian: Hammerstein, correspondence with authors.
Ruth Andreas-Friedrich's experiences in Steglitz; Andreas-Friedrich, 288–93.

399 Fred Laabs's experiences: Laabs, interview.

400 Situation in Führer bunker: Boldt, 146–50; Freytag von Loringhoven, interview.

403 Battle for Westhafen: Erickson, *Road to Berlin*, 599–600; Neustroyev, 'Shturm Reikhstagu' (The Storming of the Reichstag), in *Voenno-sitoricheskii Zhurnal* (Military History Journal), 1960.

404 Max Buch experiences: Buch diary.
Walter Schmid experiences: Schmid, interview.

406 Skorning experiences: Skorning, interview.

407 '1000 hours. Russian drive on the airport . . .': Müncheberg diary.
Lorenz report of Allied disagreement: Boldt, 145–46.

408 Assault on SS men in Potsdamerstrasse: Chuikov, 192.

409 Ammunition stocks: Wöhlermann diary.
Relief flights: Boldt, 150–51.

410 'Potsdamerstrasse and Leipzigerstrasse . . .': Weidling diary.

411 Move to Bendlerstrasse, and bomb damage: Dufving, interview.

412 Boëv telephones Goebbels: Boëv, quoted in Kuby, 57–59.

413 Anneliese H's experiences: diary quoted in Kuby, 220–22.

414 Maria von Maltzan's experiences: Maltzan, interview.
Ruth Andreas-Friedrich's experiences: Andreas-Friedrich, 298–302.

415    Charlemagne Battalion attack: Rocolle, 53; Krukenberg diary.

416    Soviet troops arrive in Oranienstrasse: Hammerstein, correspondence.

417    French prisoner-of-war hospital: Rocolle, 53–54.

418    Reinforcements landed at Gatow: Kurkenberg diary.
Hanna Reitsch and Colonel-General von Greim, arrival and time in bunker: Reitsch interrogation report, Nuremberg Documents.

419    Führer conference details: Boldt, 157–58; Freytag von Loringhoven, interview.

420    Boldt and Freytag use public telephone system: Boldt, 152–53; Freytag von Loringhoven, interview.

421    Chuikov's new command post: Chuikov, 211.
'Evening. Announcement of a new organization . . .': Müncheberg diary.

422    Chuikov's scouts in U-Bahn tunnels: Chuikov, 221–22.
'The station looks like an armed camp . . .': Müchenberg diary.

423    'I was deeply disappointed . . .': Krukenberg diary.
'Suddenly water splashed into . . .': Müchenberg diary.

424    Hitler decorates young boy: Boldt, 159.

425    Scene in flak tower: Ryan, 381–82.

426    Fegelein capture: Reitsch interrogation; Galante and Silianoff, 110–11.

427    'Uninterrupted roar of guns . . .': Buch diary.
Bormann, Krebs and Burgdorf drunken quarrel: Boldt, 161–65; Freytag von Loringhoven, interview.

429    'What calibre gun . . .': Boldt, 167.

430    Keitel discovers retreat: Keitel, 217–18.
Keitel's meeting with Heinrici and Manteuffel: Keitel, 218–19; Heinrici papers; Ryan, 384.

431    Busse's attempted breakout: Busse, 'Die Letzte Schlacht der 9. Armee', *Wehrwissenschaftliche Rundschau*, 1954.

432    Massacre of remainder: Simonov
Rescue of child: Chuikov, 204-6.

433    Assault on canal: ibid, 206.

434    Storming of Moabit Prison, and first sight of Reichstag: Neustroyev, op cit; Vasily Subbotin, 'The Final Phase', in *Soviet Military Review*, April 1975.

435    Maria von Maltzan's experiences: Maltzan, interview.

436    Berzarin's order: Kuby, 146.

437    Hammerstein's experiences: Hammerstein, correspondence with authors.
Skorning's experiences: Skorning, interview.

438    Troops of cavalry: Rahusen, interview.
'an endless supply column': *A Woman in Berlin*, 59.

439  'Behind me the cellar door closes . . .: ibid, 66.

440  Hitler's fury at Himmler's betrayal: Reitsch interrogation; Boldt, 169–70; Freytag von Loringhoven, interview.

441  Weidling's escape plan: Weidling diary; Boldt. 160; Freytag von Loringhoven, interview.

442  Hitler's testament and marriage: Toland, *Adolf Hitler*, 882-86; Trevor-Roper, *Last Days*, 225–26; Shirer, *Rise and Fall*, 1334-38; O'Donnell, 241; Gun, 241–44.

444  Assault on Moltke Bridge: Neustroyev, op cit.

445  'The whole city was in flames . . .': Abyzov, 49–51.
Damaged buildings collapsing: Kurkenberg diary.

446  Boldt, Freytag and Weiss escape from bunker: Boldt, 174–79; Freytag von Loringhoven, interview.

447  Knight's Cross presentation ceremony: Krukenberg diary; Mabire, 273–74.

448  Professor Schenck's experiences: O'Donnell, 172–81.
Poison capsules: Trevor-Roper, *Last Days*, 227; O'Donnell, 181.

449  Bauer and the picture: Toland, *Adolf Hitler*, 888; O'Donnell, 55, 328–29.
Hitler's last conference: Weidling diary.

450  Last signal to Keitel: Keitel, 223.

451  Preparations for assault on the Reichstag: Neustroyev, op cit.

452  Hitler's suicide: Toland, *Adolf Hitler*, 888–90; Trevor-Roper, 228; Shirer, *Rise and Fall*, 1346; O'Donnell, 251–59; Gun, 252–53.

453  Assault on the Reichstag: Neustroyev, op cit.

455  Battle around the Anhalter station: Abyzov, 56–58.

456  'Can we expect to clear Berlin . . .': Chuikov, 212.

457  Surrender negotiations: Chuikov, 213–30; Weidling diary; Dufving, interview; translation of official Soviet transcript of negotiations, courtesy Colonel von Dufving; Zhukov, 621–24.

460  Second peace move at Zoo: Chuikov, 226–27.

461  Dufving's experiences: Dufving, interview.

462  Max Buch experiences: Buch diary.

463  Scene in Zoo: Heinroth diary; Simonov.
Krebs's return to bunker: Weidling diary.

464  Goebbels's suicide etc: Shirer, *Rise and Fall*, 1349; O'Donnell, 291–93; Trevor-Roper, *Last Days*, 228.

465  Weidling calls commanders together: Weidling diary; Dufving, interview.
Chuikov attempts to sleep, etc: Chuikov, 247.

466  German envoys arrive at cellar: Abyzov, 69–72.

467  Final surrender of city: Chuikov, 249; Dufving, interview.

# INDEX

# CONTENTS

# INTRODUCTION

There are few better accounts of the first eight days of the Battle of the Bulge than S.L.A. Marshall's excellent account of the events as viewed from the US perspective. This masterful study was first published in 1946 and appeared in the Infantry Journal Inc, but was rescued from obscurity by the programme of reprints undertaken by the Center For Military History.

Marshall's study is definitely "of its time" and was written when the memories of the events were still fresh. The attitudes expressed by Marshall reflect the prevailing mood of the immediate post-war era. To a modern audience the tone might feel jingoistic, and to an extent even boastful, but in many respects that is what makes them so interesting today. This is an account of the fighting expressed in the language of the day by those who were there on the ground. It reflects their pride in their achievements and provides a modern audience with a unique insight into the attitude towards events which had so recently unfolded.

I hope you enjoy this book and will join us in exploring others in the series.

*Bob Carruthers*

# FOREWORD

The Center of Military History is pleased to present the second volume in the U.S. Army in Action series, a facsimile reprint of Brigadier General S. L. A. Marshall's Bastogne: The First Eight Days. Originally published in 1946, this brief study provides a combat history of a critical battle during the Allied liberation of Europe in World War II. Outnumbered and surrounded for five days, a U.S. Army combined arms force of airborne infantry, armor, engineers, tank destroyers, and artillery conducted a successful defense of the Belgian crossroads town of Bastogne in late December 1944. They separated the German combined arms formations and destroyed the pieces, halting the offensive. The outcome of this battle was critical to the successful Allied defense against the German Ardennes offensive.

Bastogne offers unique insights, capturing the immediate impressions of the soldiers who fought in this harsh winter engagement. The author penetrates the "fog of war" with a coherent narrative that clearly captures the strategy, tactics, and leadership of the battle. This action strangled the German logistical flow to their forward assault divisions, disrupting their offensive tempo and slowing their advance. What emerges is a vivid case study of how decisive leadership and incidents of individual heroism can contribute to overcoming enemy forces and weather.

Historians and professional soldiers will find Bastogne a valuable addition to their reading list. The Center of Military History recommends it highly for use in conjunction with Staff Rides. Although later studies provide more depth of research and detailed analysis concerning the Battle of Bastogne, Marshall's book, with its excellent maps, provides a superb one-volume narrative which can be utilized as a guide for officers and noncommissioned officers when visiting the Ardennes battlefield.

The Center wishes to thank Mrs. S.L.A. Marshall for her kind assistance with our efforts to reprint Bastogne as well as her continued support of the U.S. Army Historical Programs.

*WASHINGTON, D.C.*
*WILLIAM A. STOFFT*
*Brigadier General,. U.S. Army*
*Chief of Military History*

# UNITS, COMMANDERS, STAFF MEMBERS, AND MEMBERS OF UNITS MENTIONED IN THIS NARRATIVE

## HIGHER UNITS

### SHAEF (Supreme Headquarters Allied Expeditionary Forces)
Commanding General: General of the Army Dwight D. Eisenhower
Chief of Staff: Lt. Gen. Walter B. Smith
A. C. of S., G-3: Maj. Gen. J. F. M. Whiteley

### 12TH ARMY GROUP
Commanding General: Gen. Omar N. Bradley

### FIRST ARMY
Commanding General: Gen. Courtney H. Hodges

### THIRD ARMY
Commanding General: Lt. Gen. George S. Patton, Jr.

### VIII CORPS
Commanding General: Maj. Gen. Troy H. Middleton

### XVIII CORPS (Airborne)
Commanding General: Maj. Gen. Matthew B. Ridgway
Acting Commander at the beginning of the Bastogne concentration: Maj. Gen. James M. Gavin
Chief of Staff: Colonel Ralph D. Eaton

## THE BASTOGNE FORCES

### 101st AIRBORNE DIVISION
Commanding General: Maj. Gen. Maxwell D. Taylor
Acting Division Commander during the first phase of Bastogne operations: Brig. Gen. Anthony C. McAuliffe
Assistant Division Commander: Brig. Gen. Gerald J. Higgins
A. C. of S., G-1, and Acting Chief of Staff: Lt. Col. Ned D. Moore

7

A. C. of S., G-2: Lt. Col. Paul A. Danahy
A. C. of S., G-3: Lt. Col. H. W. O. Kinnard
A. C. of S., GA Lt. Col. Carl W. Kohls
Surgeon: Lt. Col. David Gold
Civil Affairs Officer: Capt. Robert S. Smith
Aide to the Commanding General: Lt. Frederic D. Starrett
Division Artillery Commander: Col. Thomas L. Sherburne, Jr.

## 501ST PARACHUTE INFANTRY REGIMENT
Commanding Officer: Lt. Col. Julian J. Ewell
S-4: Maj. William H. Butler
**1ST BATTALION (Companies A, B, C and Hq.)**
Commanding Officer: Major Raymond V. Bottomly, Jr.
**2D BATTALION (Companies D, E, F and Hq.)**
Commanding Officer: Major Sammie N. Homan
**3D BATTALION (Companies G, H, I and Hq.)**
Commanding Officer: Lt. Col. George A Griswold
*Members of this regiment who figure in the narrative:*
Company A Capt. Stanfield A. Stach; Lt. James C. Murphy; Lt. Joseph B.
Schweiker; Sgt. Lyle B. Chamberlain; Pfc. William C. Michel
Company D: Cpl. Frank Lasik; Pvt. Manzi

## 502D PARACHUTE INFANTRY REGIMENT
Commanding Officer: Lt. Col. Steve A. Chappuis
Executive: Lt. Col. Patrick J. Cassidy
S-3: Capt. James J. Hatch
Surgeon: Major Douglas T. Davidson
Commander, Hq. Co.: Capt. James C. Stone
**1ST BATTALION (Companies A, B, C and Hq.)**
Commanding Officer: Major John D. Hanlon
S-2: Lt. Samuel B. Nickels, Jr.
Company A Capt. Wallace A. Swanson
Company C: Capt. George R. Cody.
**2D BATTALION (Companies D, E, F and Hq.)**
Commanding Officer: Lt. Col. Thomas H. Sudiffe
**3D BATTALION (Companies G, H, I and Hq.)**
Commanding Officer: Lt. Col. John P. Stopka

## 506TH PARACHUTE INFANTRY REGIMENT
Commanding Officer: Col. Robert F. Sink
S-4: Capt. Salve H. Matheson
**1ST BATTALION (Companies A, B, C and Hq.)**
Commanding Officer: Lt. Col. James L. LaPrade
Commanding Officer (after Col. LaPrade was killed in action): Major Robert F. Harwick
Commanding Officer (after Major Harwick was wounded in action): Lt. Col. Robert L. Strayer
**2D BATTALION (Companies D, E, F and Hq.)**
Commanding Officer: Lt. Col. Robert L. Strayer
Commanding Officer (after Col. Strayer took over 1st Battalion): Major Lloyd E. Patch
**3D BATTALION (Companies G, H, I and Hq.)**
Commanding Officer: Major Gus M. Heilman

## 327TH GLIDER INFANTRY REGIMENT
Commanding Officer: Col. Joseph H. Harper
Executive: Lt. Col. Thomas J. Rouzie
**1ST BATTALION (Companies A, B, C and Hq.)**
Commanding Officer: Lt. Col. Hartford F. Salee
**2D BATTALION (Companies E, F, G and Hq.)**
Commanding Officer: Lt. Col. Roy L. Inman
Executive (and Commanding Officer, following the wounding of Col. Inman): Major R. B. Galbreaith
**3D BATTALION (Companies A, B, C and Hq.)**
*Note: Though carried as the 3d Battalion, 327th Glider Infantry, in this narrative, and considered such by the command, this battalion was actually the 1st Battalion, 401st Glider Infantry, which accounts for the presence within the one regiment of two battalions with A-B-C letter companies. This battalion had served as the 3d Battalion of the regiment since the Normandy landing.*
Commanding Officer: Lt, Col. Ray C. Allen
*Members of this regiment who figure in the narrative:*
Company F: Capt. James F. Adams; Lt. Leslie E. Smith; Tech. Sgt. Oswald Y. Butler; Staff Sgt. Carl E. Dickinson.
Company G: Capt. Hugh Evans; Lt. Stanley A. Morrison
Company A, 3d Battalion: Lt. Howard G. Bowles
Company B, 3d Battalion: Capt. Robert J. McDonald; Tech. Sgt. Mike

Campano

Company C, 3d Battalion: Capt. Preston E. Towns

**321ST GLIDER FIELD ARTILLERY BATTALION**

Commanding Officer: Lt. Col. Edward L. Carmichael

**907th GLIDER FIELD ARTILLERY BATTALION**

Commanding Officer: Lt. Col. Clarence F. Nelson

**377TH PARACHUTE FIELD ARTILLERY BATTALION**

Commanding Officer: Lt. Col. Harry W. Elkins

**463D PARACHUTE FIELD ARTILLERY BATTALION**

Commanding Officer: Lt. Col. John T. Cooper, Jr.

**81ST AIRBORNE ANTIAIRCRAFT BATTALION**

Commanding Officer: Lt. Col. X. B. Cox, Jr.

**326TH AIRBORNE ENGINEER BATTALION**

Commanding Officer: Lt. Col. Hugh A. Mozley

**426TH AIRBORNE QUARTERMASTER COMPANY**

Commanding Officer: Capt. George W. Horn

**101st AIRBORNE SIGNAL COMPANY**

Commanding Officer: Capt. William J. Johnson

**801ST AIRBORNE ORDNANCE MAINTENANCE COMPANY**

Commanding Officer: Capt. John L. Patterson

**326TH AIRBORNE MEDICAL COMPANY**

Commanding Officer: Major William E. Barfield

## *ATTACHED UNITS*

**COMBAT COMMAND B, 10TH ARMORED DIVISION**

**7015TH TANK DESTROYER BATTALION**

**755TH FIELD ARTILLERY BATTALION**

**COMPANY C, 9TH ARMORED ENGINEERS**

**969TH FIELD ARTILLERY BATTALION**

**COMBAT COMMAND R (37TH BATTALION), 4TH ARMORED DIVISION**

## *COMPOSITION AND COMMAND OF MAJOR ATTACHED UNITS*

**COMBAT COMMAND B, 10TH ARMORED DIVISION.**

This unit operated independently in conjunction with the 101st Airborne Division until December 21, when it was attached to the 101st and came under its command.

Commanding Officer: Col. William L. Roberts

Combat Command B was divided for tactical purposes into four main parts: the units held directly under the commander, and Teams Cherry, Desobry and O'Hara. The following units of Combat Command B were directly under the commander.

**HEADQUARTERS AND HEADQUARTERS COMPANY**
**3D TANK BATTALION** (LESS COMPANY C)
**COMPANY C, 21st TANK BATTALION**
**54TH ARMORED INFANTRY BATTALION** (LESS COMPANIES A AND C)
**20TH ARMORED INFANTRY BATTALION** (LESS COMPANY C)
**COMPANY C, 609TH TANK DESTROYER BATTALION** (LESS PLATOONS WITH TEAMS)
**COMPANY C, 55Th ARMORED ENGINEER BATTALION** (LESS PLATOONS WITH TEAMS)
**420TH ARMORED FIELD ARTILLERY BATTALION**
Commanding Officer: Lt. Col. Barry D. Browne
**BATTERY B, 796TH ANTIAIRCRAFT BATTALION**
**TROOP D, 90TH RECONNAISSANCE (CAVALRY) SQUADRON** (LESS PLATOONS WITH TEAMS)

*TEAM CHERRY*
Commanding Officer: Lt. Col. Henry T. Cherry (also commanding officer of 3d Tank Battalion)
3D TANK BATTALION (LESS COMPANY B AND 2D PLATOON, COMPANY D)
COMPANY A: Lt. Edward P. Hyduke
COMPANY C, 20TH ARMORED INFANTRY BATTALION: Capt. Willis F. Ryerson; Lt. Earl B. Gilligan
3D PLATOON, COMPANY C, 55TH ARMORED ENGINEER BATTALION
ONE PLATOON, COMPANY C, 609TH TANK DESTROYER BATTALION
2D PLATOON, TROOP D, 90TH RECONNAISSANCE SQUADRON

*TEAM DESOBRY*
Commanding Officer: Major William R. Desobry (also commanding officer, 20th Armored Infantry Battalion). Major Charles L. Hustead took command after Major Desobry was wounded.
20TH ARMORED INFANTRY BATTALION (LESS COMPANIES A AND C)
HEADQUARTERS COMPANY: Capt. Gordon Geiger; Lt. Eugene Todd
COMPANY B: Capt. Omar M. Billett

COMPANY B, 3D TANK BATTALION

ONE PLATOON, COMPANY C, 609TH TANK DESTROYER BATTALION

ONE PLATOON, COMPANY D, 3D TANK BATTALION (LIGHT TANKS)

ONE PLATOON, COMPANY C, 55TH ARMORED ENGINEER BATTALION

ONE PLATOON, COMPANY C, 609TH TANK DESTROYER BATTALION

ONE PLATOON, TROOP D, 90TH RECONNAISSANCE SQUADRON

*TEAM O'HARA*

Commanding Officer: Lt. Col. James O'Hara (also commanding officer of 54th Armored Infantry Battalion)

S-2: Capt. Edward A. Carrigo

54TH ARMORED INFANTRY BATTALION (LESS COMPANIES A AND C)

COMPANY B: Lt. John D. Devereaux

COMPANY C, 21st TANK BATTALION

ONE PLATOON, COMPANY C, 55TH ARMORED ENGINEER BATTALION

ONE PLATOON, COMPANY D, 3D TANK BATTALION (LIGHT TANKS): Lt. Sherwood D. Wishart

ONE PLATOON, TROOP D, 90TH RECONNAISSANCE SQUADRON

FORCE CHARLIE 16: Lt. Richard C. Gilliland

*705th Tank Destroyer Battalion.* This unit operated independently in conjunction with the 101st Airborne Division until December 21 when it was attached to the 101st and came under its command.

Commanding Officer: Lt. Col. Clifford D. Templeton

Headquarters Company (less the battalion trains which were ordered to "find a haven in the west")

*Reconnaissance Company*

Company A (less one platoon detached to guard the road junction at Laroche)

Company B: Lt. Robert Andrews; Lt. Frederick Mallon; Sgt. Floyd A. Johnson; Sgt. George N. Schmidt; Sgt. Darrell J. Lindley

Company C

Ninth Air Force (members of liaison group attached to 101st Airborne Division during Bastogne operation): Capt. James E. Parker; Lt. Gorden O. Rothwell; Sgt. Frank B. Hotard

*Map 1 : Total extent of the Bulge*

13

# 1. THE SITUATION

THE SIEGE OF BASTOGNE is one chapter in the history of the battle of the Ardennes. On December 16, 1944, the Germans launched their greatest offensive of the war in the west. Achieving a considerable success in their first attacks, they broke through, penetrated 65 miles into Allied territory, halted the Allied offensive then going on, and threatened the entire front in the west. The failure of this German drive was due in part to the American resistance at St. Vith and Bastogne.

The background of Bastogne dates from the fall of 1944. At that time three American armies, forming the 12th Army Group, were in position on the central part of the western front. The U. S. First and Third Armies were along the Siegfried Line and the U. S. Ninth Army was facing the Roer River in Germany some thirty miles from the Rhine. All three armies were pushing for the Rhine over difficult terrain, across swollen rivers, and against determined enemy resistance. Except in the Aachen sector, where an advance was made to the Roer, the line did not move during October and November. The Third Army fought near Metz; the First and Ninth Armies made their advance farther north, near Aachen. In between these two major efforts the First Army held an extensive line of defense. Of this line the southern and major part was maintained by the U. S. VIII Corps.

On December 16, VIII Corps, under the command of Major General Troy H. Middleton had its headquarters in Bastogne, Belgium. Its area extended from Losheim, Germany, north to a point where the Our River crosses the Franco-German border. Generally parallel to the German frontier along eastern Belgium and Luxembourg, its front was 88 miles wide. The country, the Ardennes, has rugged hills; there are high plateaus, deep-cut valleys and a restricted road net.

The mission that First Army gave VIII Corps was to defend this line in place. New divisions were brought into this part of the front for battle indoctrination, and battle-worn divisions were sent to VIII Corps for re-equipment and rest. As divisions were rotated into the sector, they took over existing wire nets and other facilities.

At the beginning of the German attack in December, the VIII

*1. Major Gemeral Troy H. Middleton, Commanding Gerneral, VIII Corps*

Corps front was held by two battle-weary divisions, a green infantry division, part of a green armored division, and a cavalry group. The battle-tested divisions (they had both seen months of fighting) were the 4th Infantry Division, which in November had fought a costly action through the Hürtgen Forest below Düren, Germany, and the 28th Infantry Division, which had sustained heavy casualties in the First Army drive to the Roer. The 106th Infantry Division, newly arrived on the Continent, entered the Corps line four days before the German offensive began. The 14th Cavalry Group, consisting of the 18th and 32d Cavalry Squadrons, held the north flank of VIII Corps, and the 9th Armored Division, minus Combat Command B which was with V Corps, had the most of its units attached to the divisions.

The enemy facing the VIII Corps was estimated at four divisions. From north to south these were the 18th, 26th, 352d and 212th. Early in December the 28th Division took prisoners and reaffirmed the presence of the 26th and 352d Divisions, but rumors that one or more panzer units were in rear of these infantry divisions were not confirmed. From December 12 on, the American outposts along the VIII Corps front heard sounds of a great volume of vehicular movement behind the enemy lines.

On the morning of December 16, the VIII Corps front, which had been quiet since the latter part of September, suddenly flared up. For more than a month the enemy had been concentrating some 25 divisions. It had been skillfully done and the extent of the concentration was not fully known to our forces. At 0500 heavy artillery concentrations struck along the entire VIII Corps front and these were soon followed by tank and infantry attacks. The strongest attacks were in the north, near the V and VIII Corps boundary.

The infantry-tank attack on the north flank of the VIII Corps began at 0800 on the 16th, and in three hours the enemy had penetrated the position of the 14th Cavalry group three miles.

Group reserves were committed and the 106th Division put out flank protection to the north. Through the right of the 106th Division the enemy advanced rapidly for a mile and a half, but then as reserves were brought up his progress was slowed. The German gains threatened to isolate two regiments of the 106th Division. Captured documents showed that on this day the enemy hoped to take St. Vith. This he did not do.

Against the 28th Division the enemy used two panzer divisions, three infantry divisions and one parachute division in an infantry-tank attack on the "Ridge Road" just west of the Our River. In this operation, two enemy divisions assaulted each regiment of the 28th. In the center and right of the 28th the enemy made advances up to four and a half miles and crossed the north-south highway at several points. In the southern part of the VIII Corps the 9th Armored and the 4th Infantry Divisions were also attacked by the enemy. These attacks were diversionary to prevent our shifting troops to the north.

At the start of the German offensive the VIII Corps reserve consisted of an armored combat command and four battalions of combat engineers. The engineers were assembled during the first morning, and as the seriousness of the enemy thrust became apparent, additional troops were made available. In the north on December 17, Combat Command R of the 9th Armored Division was released from V Corps and the 7th Armored Division was ordered to close into an assembly area near St. Vith. In the south the 10th Armored Division was moved toward an assembly area near the city of Luxembourg. Orders were also issued to move the 101st and 82d Airborne Divisions to the general area threatened.

From captured documents and from the direction of early thrusts it seemed evident to VIII Corps that the objective of the attacks was Liège and possibly Namur. This, however, was a clear case of VIII Corps misunderstanding the enemy's intent, though the same misunderstanding prevailed in the entire Army for months afterward. It was finally found, however, that Hitler had given his commanders in the Bulge attack specific and inflexible orders to stay to the south of Liège. *[This information is from the European Theater of Operations Historical File of interviews with high-ranking German commanders. It comes from interviews with Colonel General Jodl and Field Marshal Keitel, and is confirmed by all subordinate commanders interviewed.]*

On the 17th, the second day of the offensive, the enemy increased his pressure along the whole front especially in the north. The right flank of V Corps was forced back and in the VIII Corps, German infantry and armor had by 0900 cut off two regiments of the 106th Division. To stem the advance on St. Vith the 168th Engineer Combat Battalion fought a delaying action north and east of that town, Combat Command B of the 9th Armored Division was put into the line, and the 7th Armored Division was committed piecemeal to defensive action as it arrived during the evening.

In the 28th Division sector the Germans began their attacks early and made large gains. The left flank of the 28th was forced to withdraw to the west bank of the Our River and the right was pushed back an additional one to four miles. But it was in the center of the division that the enemy made his deepest penetrations, thrusting one salient of eight miles and another of six. Everywhere the American withdrawal had been four to six miles. At some points the enemy was within 11 miles of Bastogne.

On the southern flank of the VIII Corps the 4th Infantry Division defended against strong attacks, but the enemy did not make the heavy effort here that he had made farther to the north. The 10th Armored Division reached the Luxembourg area in time to assure its defense.

On December 18, the third day of the offensive, the enemy increased the momentum of his drive in the center of VIII Corps.

The Corps north flank was bolstered by the arrival of the 7th Armored Division but remained extremely critical because of the deep German penetrations into the V Corps sector. But the weight against the 28th Division was so overwhelming that its thin defenses disintegrated and the enemy achieved a breakthrough. The right Hank of the 28th, which pulled back across the Our River on the upper eastern border of Luxembourg the previous night, was unable to stabilize its lines. In the withdrawal a wide gap was created through which the enemy pushed a great deal of armor. In the center, enemy thrusts between strongpoints encircled companies and destroyed or captured them one by one. To the 28th Division headquarters the picture was obscure throughout the day because of lost communications, but the appearance of many enemy columns behind the regimental sectors and the tragic tales of stragglers indicated a complete disintegration of regimental defenses. The 28th Division command post itself was attacked when the enemy approached Wiltz. The 44th Engineer Combat Battalion, the 447th Antiaircraft Battalion, and miscellaneous headquarters personnel from the division were used to defend the town. The command post had communications left with only one regiment.

Directly behind the 28th Division, on the St. Vith-Bastogne road, were roadblocks established by the Combat Command Reserve of the 9th Armored Division. One block, known as Task Force Rose, was attacked by the enemy in the morning and was overrun by 1400, December 18. A roadblock on the Wiltz-Bastogne road, known as Task Force Hayze, came under heavy attack by 1815. The Germans overran this roadblock during the night of December 18-19 to come within three kilometers of Bastogne. The defense of Bastogne now became the task of airborne infantry and armored units which had been ordered into the sector.

# 2. THE CONCENTRATION ON BASTOGNE

O N THE MORNING of December 17 at SHAEF two members of the Supreme General Staff looked at the map and pondered the question of where best to employ SHAEF Reserve, which at that moment consisted of the two American divisions, the 82d Airborne and the 101st Airborne, recently withdrawn from the lines in Holland.

"I think I should put them there," said Major General J. F. M. Whiteley, the Assistant Chief of Staff, G-3, "the place has the best road net in the area."

Lieutenant General W. B. Smith, General Eisenhower's Chief of Staff nodded and said to go ahead and do it. He based his decision purely on the thought of how advantageous Bastogne's radial highway net appeared on the map. It was his idea at the time that both 101st and 82d Airborne Divisions should be employed in the Bastogne area. It was in this way that the Airborne Corps happened to make its start toward Bastogne.

SHAEF's general concept was subsequently modified by decisions made at lower headquarters although the initial impetus had been given in the required direction. The change in direction for the 82d Division, which was to have some of its greatest days in the fighting around Werbomont on the northern flank of the Bulge, came after the XVIII Airborne Corps (82d and 101st Divisions) had passed from SHAEF Reserve into the command of 12th Army Group, which was already forming other plans both for the defense of Bastogne and the employment of the airborne strength. But out of the difference in the SHAEF concept of how to employ the airborne force and the ideas which

*Colonel (now Brigadier General) William L. Roberts, Commanding Officer, Combat Command B, 10th Armoured Division.*

were already forming at 12th Army Group there came some early confusion to the two Corps commanders directly concerned and to their forces. However (as later reported in this chapter) the situation was clarified before any real harm was done.

On December 17 and 18, three battle-tested organizations, by different routes and under separate authority, began their moves toward the town in the Belgian Ardennes with whose name their own fame was to be thereafter inseparably linked. Orders from 12th Army Group were received on the 16th directing the 10th Armored Division to be temporarily attached to VIII Corps, First Army, to counter the serious German attempt at a breakthrough. At 1320 on December 17, in compliance with the order, Combat

*Major General Maxwell D. Taylor confers with officers of his Division after the Bastogne relief by the 4th Armored Division. They are Major James J. Hatch, 502d Parachute Infantry; Brigadier General Higgins, Assistant Division Commander; and Colonel Robert F. Sink, Commanding Officer, 506th Parachute Infantry.*

Command B, 10th Armored Division, took its first step toward Bastogne when it moved from a rest area at Remeling, France, to the vicinity of Merl in Luxembourg.

That evening at 2030 the 101st Airborne Division, which was then re-outfitting in a training area at Camp Mourmelon (near Reims, France, and roughly 100 miles from Bastogne) received telephone orders from Headquarters XVIII Airborne Corps that it was to move north though at that time Bastogne was not the destination given. On the following night, December 18 at 1800, the 705th Tank Destroyer Battalion, then in position at Kohlscheid, Germany (about 60 miles north of Bastogne) was ordered by the Ninth Army to march to Bastogne and report to VIII Corps.

Bastogne, then the Headquarters of VIII Corps, was the natural place for rendezvous and for stabilizing the defense. The town is the hub of the highway net covering the eastern Ardennes - a countryside that is forbidding to the movement of mechanized forces except when the roads are available. By holding at Bastogne the VIII Corps could unhinge the communications of the Germans who were striking west toward the line of the River Meuse.

Combat Command B closed into the vicinity of Merl at 2155 on the 17th. On the following morning it was ordered to move independently of the 10th Armored Division to join VIII Corps. It took the road through Arlon to Bastogne. On the way Colonel William L. Roberts, the commander, received a request from Major General Norman D. Cota, commanding the 28th Infantry Division, to support his force at Wiltz by putting Combat Command B into position south and southeast of the town. But this Colonel Roberts could not do and comply with his Corps orders, so he took his column on into Bastogne and reported there to Major General Middleton at 1600 on the 18th.

At Camp Mourmelon, the 101st Division was short many of its soldiers who were on leave in Paris. The commander of the

*Brigadier General (now Major General) Anthony C. McAuliffe, who was Acting Commanding General, 101st Airborne Division, during the first phase of the siege of Bastogne.*

XVIII Airborne Corps, Major General Matthew B. Ridgway, was at the rear headquarters of the Corps in England. The 101st Division commander, Major General Maxwell D. Taylor, was in the United States. Upon hearing of the attack and of the fact that the 101st had been committed to battle, he immediately took a plane for Europe. The assistant division commander, Brigadier General Gerald J. Higgins, was giving a lecture in England on the earlier airborne operation in Holland. With him were five of the senior commanders of divisional units and sixteen junior officers. The night would pass before these men were to hear that the division had been alerted for movement to the front and it would be noon of the next day before they were all rounded up and ready to emplane for Mourmelon. So the senior division officer present in France, the artillery commander, Brigadier General Anthony C. McAuliffe, got the division staff together at 2100 on December 17 and outlined the prospect in these words:

"All I know of the situation is that there has been a breakthrough and we have got to get up there."

General McAuliffe directed the Division to move out in combat teams without waiting for the men on pass in Paris or elsewhere to get back. However, the destination of the 101st as given at this time was not Bastogne but Werbomont to the northwest of Bastogne.

At 2030 on the 17th, Lieutenant Colonel Ned D. Moore, Chief of Staff of the 101st, had been called on the telephone by Colonel Ralph D. Eaton, Chief of Staff of the XVIII Corps, and the mission had been outlined in that manner. In moving to Werbomont, the 101st would pass within a short distance of Bastogne and to the westward of it. There was no later modification of this order while 101st remained at Camp Mourmelon.

On the following morning, December 18, the Acting Commander of the XVIII Corps, Major General James M. Gavin, attended a meeting at First Army at which it was decided to attach the 82d Division to the V Corps (since the XVIII Airborne Corps could not move in and become operational until the morning of December 19), and the 101st Division to the VIII Corps. However, no word of this change got down to the 101st Division; throughout that day its staff was unaware either that Bastogne was the destination or that VIII Corps was now their next higher headquarters.

An advance party was then set up to precede the 101st

25

*Brigadier General Gerald J. Higgins, Assistant Division Commander, 101st Airborne Division.*

Division to Bastogne. In the party were a representative from each major unit and a company of Engineers who were to be used as guides to lead the combat teams into their Bastogne assembly areas. During the morning of December 18, there had been no time to brief the advance party. Just as the party was pulling away from Camp Mourmelon during the noon hour Colonel Moore ran out of the division command post and advised them that XVIII Corps was to handle the operation and that they should go to a rendezvous with a part of the XVIII Corps staff. They were to meet them at the crossroads in Werbomont. This they did.

General Ridgway arrived at Mourmelon about an hour later, having flown from England. He went to the command post of the 101st and Colonel Moore gave him the situation as he had given it to the advance party. Then occurred an odd sequence of events in which Fate might have played a stronger hand against 101st Division had it not been for several providential circumstances. Ridgway went into General Taylor's empty office and called a higher headquarters - presumably his own Corps. In this conversation he learned that 101st's destination was Bastogne, not Werbomont. On the heels of this conversation, General Higgins entered the room, having just reported from England. Ridgway told him that 101st Division was to go to Bastogne. Ridgway then left Mourmelon for the front. Higgins

*Paratroopers entrucking at Camp Mourmelon, France, December 18th 1944, to move to Bastogne.*

soon followed. McAuliffe had left an instruction that Higgins was to get forward as rapidly as possible, so he picked a route via Sedan, figuring that it would be less encumbered with traffic. But the word that Bastogne was the Division's destination was not passed to Colonel Moore and the units remained alerted for

*Lieutenant Colonel (now Colonel) H. W. O. Kinnard, G-3, 101st Airborne Division.*

movement to Werbomont.

On reaching Werbomont on the night of December 18 the advance party were told that the operation was being handled by VIII Corps and that they were even then due in Bastogne. In this way the advance party failed in its mission and did not reach the objective until 0300 on the morning of December 19. But others were doing their work for them.

Some few minutes before the advance party had left Mourmelon, General McAuliffe had started for Werbomont taking with him his G-3, Lieutenant Colonel H. W. O. Kinnard and his aide, First Lieutenant Frederic D. Starrett. They drove as fast as they could, passing many elements of the 82d Airborne Division along the route. The 82d had been out of the lines in Holland longer than the 101st and was more fully equipped. The 82d was therefore ordered to move out ahead of the 101st. Come to the road juncture south of the Bois de Herbaimont (nine miles northwest of Bastogne) General McAuliffe turned southeast to Bastogne instead of continuing north along the road leading to Werbomont, which is some 25 miles north of Bastogne. He had decided to go to the VIII Corps headquarters and get briefed on the general situation. It was some time following his arrival at General Middleton's VIII Corps command post that he heard definitely for the first time that the 101st was to fight at Bastogne. General Gavin, who had left Werbomont late in the afternoon of the 18th to hand-carry the message to VIII Corps did not arrive until after dark. The delay caused General Middleton a considerable doubt; be had learned from higher authority that the 101st Division would fight at Bastogne but he did not know that the Division was his to use as he saw fit. General McAuliffe's party arrived at the VIII Corps command post, which was located in a former German barracks at the northwestern edge of Bastogne, at 1600 and from that time forward its members concerned themselves with getting ready to receive the Division. At that same moment Colonel Roberts, who had arrived ahead of his column, presented himself to General Middleton and reported that Combat Command B was on the road and would soon be in Bastogne.

Middleton asked Roberts, "How many teams can you make up?"

Roberts replied, "Three."

The General then said, "You will move without delay in three teams to these positions and counter enemy threats. One team will go to the southeast of Wardin, one team to the vicinity of Longvilly and one team to the vicinity of Noville. Move with the utmost speed. Hold these positions at all costs."

Roberts accepted the order without demur though at that moment he believed that the distribution of his force over so great an area would make it ineffective. But he made the mental reservation that the Corps commander must know the situation much better than he did himself. Middleton's decision was the initial tactical step which led finally to the saving of Bastogne." Combat Command B continued on its way moving north and east to carry out its orders.

The first two teams got through the town during daylight. The lead team, Team Cherry, under Lieutenant Colonel Henry T. Cherry, proceeded toward Longvilly, which was considered to be in the direction of the most immediate danger. The second team under Lieutenant Colonel James O'Hara headed toward the village of Wardin in the southeast. It was dark when the last team began moving through Bastogne. Its youthful commander, Major William R. Desobry, went to see Colonel Roberts with whom he had an especially close relationship. For a number of years Desobry had known the older man well; he was talking now to a man who was not only his commander but whom he regarded as a second father. Roberts pointed northward on the map to the village of Noville and told Desobry that he was to proceed there and hold the village. "It will be a close race to get there before the enemy," Roberts said. "You are young, and by tomorrow

*Map 2*

morning you will probably be nervous. By midmorning the idea will probably come to you that it would be better to withdraw from Noville. When you begin thinking that, remember that I told you that it would be best not to withdraw until I order you to do so."

There were no maps at hand; one of Colonel Roberts' staff officers grabbed a Corps MP and sent him along with Desobry to put the team on the Noville road. A cavalry platoon leader from Desobry's column was sent on ahead to reconnoiter Noville, clear it if there were any enemy present, and then outpost it until the arrival of the main battle group. Desobry then dismounted one platoon of armored infantry, placed them on the backs of the three lead tanks and gave the word for the column to move north. Small groups of stragglers were already passing them, drifting southward. The column paid them no heed. The dark had already slowed the armor to a five-mile-per-hour pace and Desobry figured that he had no time to waste.

While McAuliffe and his party were on the road, at Mourmelon the Division was working on the problems of the move. The few hours before the Division began its march were utilized in preparations for departure and in partly providing those combat supplies which had been lost in Holland. Such things as mortars, rifle ammunition, entrenching tools, arctic overshoes, blankets and gas masks had fallen far below the normal and needed amounts in the tables of basic allowances. In the great emergency, Transportation Corps and Oise Base Section acted with utmost dispatch and rallied truck groups from Rouen and Paris. Many of the truckers had already been long on the road when they were ordered to Camp Mourmelon. They were intercepted, the trucks unloaded on the spot, and the drivers directed to their new destination. The first trucks arrived at 0900, December 18. The last of the 380 trucks needed for the movement of 11,000 men arrived at the camp at 1720 the same day. *[In the Strength Report for December 18, 1944, the Effective Strength of the 101st Division is listed as 805 officers and 11,035 enlisted men, a total of 11,840. The exact number who moved forward is not known as this total includes those not yet returned from pass and those who remained in Mourmelon to maintain the base camp.]* At 2000, eleven hours after the arrival of the first vehicles, the last man was out-loaded. As far as Bouillon, Belgium, the column ran with lights blazing. It was a calculated risk, taken by 101st for the sake of speed. The night was clear and the stars shone brightly. Had the Luftwaffe come on then, the story of Bastogne might have taken a different turn.

In Bastogne, General Middleton sketched the situation to General McAuliffe and Colonel Kinnard very roughly, telling them, "There has been a major penetration and certain of my units, especially the 106th and 28th Divisions, are broken." In the absence of the advance staff party Kinnard tried to function as a whole division staff during the conference. But after discussing matters with both the G-2 and G-3 sections at VIII Corps, he had only the vaguest picture of what was happening and felt altogether uncertain about both the friendly and enemy situations. He gathered that some of our armored elements - the 9th Armored Division and 10th Armored Division were mentioned - were out in front of Bastogne, but he could not pinpoint the spots where their roadblocks were. Because of their own uncertainty, both he and General McAuliffe became acutely concerned over plans for the night bivouac. Further than that, they worried that the column might be hit while it was still on the road or that it might even be caught by the German air while still a long way back.

While there was still light, they took a quick swing out over the area west of town and McAuliffe pointed out to Kinnard where he wanted the Division placed. It was a snap decision, yet it influenced the campaign importantly because it placed the Division in a sheltered forward assembly area until it was ready to strike. In the emergency Kinnard grabbed an MP private from the Corps and sent him to the crossroads at Sprimont to meet the division as it came on. He and General McAuliffe then went to the junction of the Arlon and Neufchateau roads in Bastogne to make another attempt to find the advance party. Colonel Kinnard had with him nine 1:100,000 and six 1:50,000 maps of the area. This was all that the Corps staff could give him with which to fight the operation ahead. When he returned from the reconnaissance, Kinnard searched at Corps headquarters for more maps but found that the map section was already moving out. From Corps he obtained an administrative order giving him the location of ammunition dumps, water points, evacuation hospitals and other installations.

However, despite Colonel Kinnard's best efforts, in the speed of the preparations to receive the Division, a good many points had not been securely pinned down. Trailing the last of the 82d

Division's column through Sprimont, Colonel T. L. Sherburne, acting commander of the 101st Division's artillery, and an assistant, Captain Cecil T. Wilson, arrived at the vital crossroads where one road leads off toward Bastogne and the other toward Bertogne at about 2000, December 18. Along the way leading north the rear elements of the 82d Division were blocking and stopping. Colonel Sherburne then wondered whether he couldn't get north and on to Werbomont more rapidly by veering from the Bertogne road and taking the long way through Bastogne. He asked an MP at the intersection whether any units of the 101st had gone that way; the MP wasn't certain about anything but referred him to an MP sergeant in a near-by house. The sergeant told him that General McAuliffe and his party had come along some hours before and had gone into Bastogne. So Colonel Sherburne returned to the man who was directing traffic and told him to turn all 101st Division parties toward Bastogne when they came to the intersection. He then continued on.

It appears likely that this small incident smoothed the whole path for the 101st Division. Two officers from the 502d Regiment, who were supposed to have gone with the advance party to Werbamont but had missed it, were re-routed by the MP a few minutes behind Sherburne to VIII Corps Headquarters.

They joined Kinnard and Starrett and drove west to Mande-St.-Étienne. Here they met a jeepload of 327th Infantry officers who had also missed the advance party. Kinnard now had enough personnel to set up the assembly area. An officer guide was posted on the Mande-St.Étienne road to direct the incoming column and Starrett went to work setting up a Division command post in a near-by farm house. The other officers reconnoitered their regimental areas and made their plans for the night dispositions. The hour was a little after 1800 on the 18th and there was not yet any sound of combat in the vicinity. A heavy maintenance company from 28th Division was already in Mande-St.Étienne. The company commander told Kinnard this was his area and he could not leave. Kinnard had to return to Bastogne to get an order from the corps commander to clear the area. Around General Middleton in the Corps command post there were now only six or eight officers.

From First Army, General Courtney Hodges, its commander, had called General Middleton and advised moving VIII Corps Headquarters to the rear. This had been done but General Middleton had stayed on in Bastogne with Colonel Stanton, his Deputy Chief of Staff, and several other members of his staff for the purpose, as he thought, of acquainting Major General Matthew B. Ridgway, the commander of XVIII Airborne Corps, with the situation, and of helping General McAuliffe get his situation in hand.

General Ridgway arrived at General Middleton's command post in Bastogne about 2030. He was still acting on the not wholly complete information which he had received from his several sources while at Camp Mourmelon. He understood that the 101st Division was to fight at Bastogne, but he thought that it was to operate under his Corps (the XVIII Airborne) though some 25 miles of distance intervened between the two airborne divisions. His acting corps commander, General Gavin, who had come and gone by this time, had brought the word to the 101st that it was to fight in the VIII Corps under General Middleton. But the situation still had not been clarified by higher authority. From Bastogne, General Ridgway called Headquarters First Army. It was at this time that the two Corps commanders got the new instructions which changed the problem of each and which at last set the lines along which the 82d and 101st Airborne Divisions, late of the SHAEF reserve, would operate in the Ardennes. Bastogne was to remain an VIII Corps problem and the 101st Division would operate under that Corps in that town. General Ridgway's XVIII Airborne Corps, less the 101st Division - so General Ridgway now learned for the first time - was to operate on the other side of the Bulge. On the strength of

35

this new assignment, General Middleton subsequently called General Omar Bradley, Commanding General, 12th Army Group, and gave it as his estimate that the 101st Division and other troops assigned to defend Bastogne would probably be surrounded, since he had no reserve. General Bradley said that would be all right with him - to stand and defend even though it appeared probable that Bastogne would become encircled.

General McAuliffe decided to stay at Corps headquarters to get his mission for the next day. During the conference of the two corps commanders, Brigadier General Gerald J. Higgins, assistant division commander of the 101st, who had been called from England by General McAuliffe, arrived.

General Higgins and Colonel Kinnard went out to the Division assembly area. Lieutenant Starrett had found that the local schoolhouse was a better command post than the dwelling which Kinnard had designated and on his own initiative had made the change. He already had telephone lines strung to VIII Corps Headquarters and to the 501st Parachute Infantry area. An officer from the 506th Parachute Infantry who had missed the advance party reported at the command post and was given his sector.

In general, things were now looking a little more snug although one point of irritation had not been entirely eliminated. That was the captain commanding the heavy maintenance company who had refused to move his people out at Colonel Kinnard's request until Kinnard brought an order direct from General Middleton. General Higgins found him now completely blocking the highway over which 101st Division was coming in. His vehicles were parked three abreast and six or seven rows deep. It was an absolute impasse. General Higgins sought out the captain and made his protest. "I can't do anything about that," said the captain. "I have received an order from the General to move my vehicles out. I've made this block to make sure that none of my vehicles get by and get lost; it's the best

36

way to collect them." Even after the situation was explained to him, he said he'd stay where be was. General Higgins then gave him a direct order to get his vehicles in single file along the road at once and himself set about urging the drivers over to the side of the highway.

This was but one incident in a night-long fight with the outgoing traffic. Every time the column of retreating vehicles came to a halt for a few minutes, some of the drivers fell asleep from exhaustion. When the road was again free for a few minutes and the forward vehicles got in motion, these sleeping drivers formed new traffic blocks back along the column. To keep things moving at all, it was necessary for officers and MPs to continue patrolling up and down the column, ready to rouse any slumberer who had tied things up.

That night in Bastogne was quiet, largely because the 28th Division was holding in place on commanding ground around Wiltz and fighting the enemy off for a few vital hours. Many stragglers were falling back through the town and the roads were jammed to the south and west but no attempt was made to hold any of these men at the time. VIII Corps was busy with its evacuation and Combat Command B of the 10th Armored Division and the 101st Division were engrossed in their own problems. Colonel Roberts, who had set up his command post in Hôtel Lebrun at 1800, December 18, found that it was difficult to persuade other units that were about to withdraw out of the Bastogne area even to give up their motor parks so that he could get his own vehicles off the streets.

The third major part of the Bastogne garrison, the 705th Tank Destroyer Battalion, under Lieutenant Colonel Clifford D. Templeton, got its marching orders at 1800 on December 18. It left Kohlscheid, Germany, at 2240, but could not proceed by the shortest route - Liège, Houffalize, Bastogne - because the enemy was already around Houffalize. The column of the 705th therefore moved by way of Laroche where it went into a defensive position along the heights six miles south of the town at 0915 on December 19. Colonel Templeton looked Laroche over and was thoroughly alarmed at what he found. American units were in confusion along the road. They were making little or no effort to adjust themselves to the situation or to set up a local defense. So in mid-morning Templeton sent two platoons with four tank destroyers to set up a roadblock to the north of the town. Leaving the battalion at Laroche, he then went on to Neufchâteau, where VIII Corps Headquarters was newly established. There General Middleton told him to get on into Bastogne and attach his outfit to the 101st Division. An officer was sent back to Laroche to bring the battalion on but to leave the roadblock force in place.

Colonel Templeton and his command section, after reporting to General McAuliffe, started northwest to meet the oncoming column. At Bertogne the section was ambushed by a German party armed with two machine guns, one self-propelled gun and several small antiaircraft guns. The opening fire wounded three men, destroyed a jeep and forced the abandonment of the armored command vehicle. Templeton's men withdrew along the road for about half a mile with all their weapons engaging the enemy. This action took place about 1500 on the 19th and was over in twenty minutes.

Templeton radioed to his battalion to expect the German roadblock at Bertogne. He then told them, however, that the roadblock could be overwhelmed and the battalion was to "come any way possible to Bastogne, but get there." He did not know that the Bastogne road was impassable because the bridge above the town was out. In the late afternoon the command section returned to Bastogne to establish its command post. Templeton then radioed the commander of the supply train to "find a haven in the west and hook up with some big friends." He felt quite certain that his train would get through safely because the one M18 accompanying it was capable of dealing with any roving enemy tank or infantry group along the way. Colonel Templeton's 705th Tank Destroyer Battalion reached Bastogne at 2030, December 19, by the route Laroche-Champlon-Bastogne.

With the arrival of the 705th Tank Destroyer Battalion, all the major elements which would be present in Bastogne during the siege (the first phase of the defense of the town) were gathered. The 101st Division and Combat Command B had begun the fight that morning and the tank destroyers were now ready to link their power with that of the armor and the infantry. Men of every unit had morale of the highest quality and with their weapons each was capable of stiffening the other. It was a matter of finding the way through courage, resource, and good will.

# 3. TEAM CHERRY

O N THE EVENING of December 18, Roberts ordered Team Cherry of his Combat Command B to move out along the road leading east and go into position near Longvilly. It thereby became the first of the Bastogne reinforcements to move out and engage the enemy. The force under command of Lieutenant Colonel Henry T. Cherry (Commanding Officer, 3d Tank Battalion, 10th Armored Division) included the 3d Tank Battalion, Company C of the 20th Armored Infantry Battalion, the 3d Platoon of Company C of the 55th Engineer Battalion and the 2d Platoon of Troop B of the 90th Cavalry Squadron. *[All the material from which this narrative is produced is based on the interview with the members of Team Cherry. The records of Team Cherry were completely destroyed during the Christmas Eve bombings of Bastogne and consequently there is no official record of the operation of Colonel Cherry's force other than the interview and what Colonel Roberts, commanding officer, Combat Command B, 10th Armored Division, could say of Team Cherry's operation.]*

They went on into the darkness, knowing only this of their situation, that some parts of Combat Command Reserve of the 9th Armored Division were supposed to be in the vicinity of Longvilly and that the enemy was reported advancing toward that town from the east. Their march was uneventful. First Lieutenant Edward P. Hyduke (Commanding Officer, Company A, 3d Tank Battalion), who had the advance guard, came to a halt just short of Longvilly at 1920. The town is on low ground and its streets seemed to be already jammed with the vehicles of Combat Command Reserve. Leaving the main body, Colonel Cherry went forward to the command post of Combat Command

*Map 3*

Reserve to learn their intentions. But they had no plan and did not know whether they would stay or get out. So Cherry returned to his force, which was then refueling on the road, and told Hyduke to make a reconnaissance and occupy ground west of Longvilly before dawn came. The main body was to stay one thousand yards west of the town until there was a change in the situation of the Combat Command Reserve. At 2300 on the 18th Cherry returned to headquarters in Bastogne to tell Colonel Roberts how things were going. As he went through Magéret he noticed that Combat Command Reserves trains were headed for the rear. Roberts told him that he was to cover the main body of the Combat Command Reserve if it withdrew, but in any case he was to hold at Longvilly.

The road was already plagued with stragglers, most of them moving in trucks and half-tracks back toward Bastogne. They

41

knew nothing except they had last seen the enemy about six miles east of Longvilly along the main road. Men asked what the Germans had, they repeated: "Tanks, tanks, tanks," and then moved on to the rear.

Combat Command Reserve set up roadblocks to the north and east of Longvilly, with one battalion of infantry and another of tanks supporting the blocks, and two batteries of artillery helping to cover them from a position next to the town. But there was no close-in defense around the houses. Looking these dispositions over, Lieutenant Hyduke decided there was danger that the enemy might come in from the south. So he sent his platoon of cavalry in that direction with instructions to withdraw quickly if the pressure became heavy. Seven light tanks were placed forward with four medium tanks to the right covering them. Infantry units formed an outpost north of the position. One of the field artillery batteries from Combat Command Reserve tied in with Lieutenant Hyduke's party and shortly thereafter opened fire to the eastward, though Hyduke never learned what they were firing at.

At 2340, Combat Command Reserve, 9th Armored Division, began its withdrawal from Longvilly, though it was not until two hours later, while Colonel Cherry was returning to his team, that he got word by radio from Hyduke that Team Cherry was now holding alone.

The next few minutes brought some more distressing news to the commander. In Neffe he met a wounded enlisted man who said that his vehicle had been shot up near Magéret. Then a sergeant told him that a strong German patrol had entered Magéret just after midnight. This meant that the Germans were across the road between Cherry and his Team. Cherry radioed Captain William F. Ryerson (Commanding Officer of Company C, 20th Armored Infantry Battalion, 10th Armored Division), who had been left in command at Longvilly, to get a patrol to Magéret and reopen the road. Two squads of infantry were sent in a half-track on this mission. They dismounted before reaching the village and approached it stealthily. Within a few minutes they had located three enemy tanks and an infantry force which they guessed to be about one company, in positions around the crossroads at Magéret. They had come in along the one side of the town that was not being covered by an enemy tank, and while they waited there they heard another armored vehicle coming up behind them. For a few seconds they were in a cold sweat, thinking they were about to be trapped by a fourth tank. Instead, it proved to be an American tank destroyer. The infantrymen and the tank destroyer crew discussed their chances and decided they weren't strong enough to attack Magéret. So they returned to Ryerson. By then Captain Ryerson had heard from Colonel Roberts that he was to commandeer any American men or equipment which he could use. So he drafted the tank destroyer into his outfit.

The discovery that the enemy was across the Combat Team's rear, quickly followed by Ryerson's report of the enemy strength which his patrol had found at Magéret, convinced Colonels Roberts and Cherry that the situation was now such that Longvilly could not be held. Colonel Cherry ordered the advance guard under Lieutenant Hyduke to hold its ground at Longvilly while the main body tried to beat its way back through Magéret. These orders, which arrived at 0830, December 19, turned the advance guard into a rear guard. Colonel Cherry went back to his command post which was in a stoutly walled château three hundred yards south of Neffe, and stayed there awaiting developments. The command post force, the rear guard and the main body were each engaged during the entire day in widely separated actions.

By daybreak of the 19th Hyduke was set up on three sides of Longvilly and ready to defend the rear. However, the closing of the road at Magéret by the Germans had kept many of Combat Command Reserve's vehicles from withdrawing, and after taking to the road, they sat there, blocking all traffic. There was a heavy nebelwerfer shelling of Hyduke's lines in the early morning and the area then quieted until 1000. The position was reasonably safe from frontal assault for the ground to the north of the main road was marshy for ten yards and facing toward the marsh was an embankment much too steep for tanks to cross. On the right of the road the ground fell away too sharply for tanks. A large culvert a short distance ahead of the position was set for demolition.

The morning engagement opened with the sighting of two enemy tanks about 1500 yards southeast of Longvilly but the visibility was so poor because of fog that only the vague outlines of the tanks could be seen. A shot from the Germans hit a tank in the Combat Command Reserve group along the road, locking the turret. All of the American armor returned the fire and both enemy tanks went up in flames. After this there was a prolonged shelling of Longvilly.

At 1400 the enemy armor put direct fire on Lieutenant Hyduke's position from front and left flank, disabling two half-tracks and one light tank at the tail of the column. Five minutes later the enemy knocked out two more medium tanks 150 yards in front of the burning half-track. An enemy antitank gun on the enemy's right hit a Combat Command Reserve tank which had remained in position with the lone artillery battery. The battery then promptly took off.

The groups on the road were now almost in a state of panic and when some of the vehicles tried to swing around the column, the road became more jammed than ever. One group of stragglers which had been organized to cover the left flank fled their position, leaving that part of the ground to only 23 infantrymen of Company C, 20th Armored Infantry Battalion.

Lieutenant Hyduke had been given authority to take over any portion of Combat Command Reserve which withdrew but he found that it was impossible to do so. However, despite the

44

panicky state of the stragglers he was able to maintain close control of his own force and continued to engage the enemy until 1430 when Colonel Cherry ordered him to fall back on Captain Ryerson's force.

But that order couldn't be carried out. The road was absolutely blocked. Moreover, he couldn't order his men out of their vehicles because enemy foot troops were now moving in on his flanks and the whole area was under heavy bullet fire. Some of the tanks turned around on the road and tried to get back to the ground they had defended.

In this period of threshing around, five of his seven light tanks and one tankdozer and a tank recovery vehicle were destroyed. The half-tracks at the front of the column had to be abandoned and soon after the men got out of them, two more medium tanks were hit by artillery fire. One medium tank got cut off and when last seen was trying to fight off an attack by German infantry. The last medium tank received a direct hit on its track as it tried to get out. The three remaining light tanks, including one that had belonged to an artillery forward observer, were destroyed by their crews to prevent capture. By 1500 most of the survivors had escaped the scene of all this wreckage and joined Captain Ryerson.

Ryerson had had a tough time carrying out his mission because of the traffic jam along the road, but by 0945, December 19, his column had reached a point 300 yards east of Magéret. As his lead tank came round the last bend in the road a shell from an enemy antitank gun in Magéret hit it frontally, burning up the tank and killing or injuring all members of the crew. The road ran through a cut at this point and the burning tank plugged it completely. The stalled column then became a general target for intense shelling and small-arms fire from the German armor and infantry force in the village.

Captain Ryerson's infantry then dismounted from their vehicles and moved forward to reconnoiter the enemy position.

The high ground on both sides of the burning tank protected them for a little way but they could not go on past the ridge because the down-slope was getting heavy bullet and mortar fire. Two 105mm. assault guns maneuvered up to the ridge and shelled a tree line where they thought the German infantry was holding. The small-arms fire from the village soon slacked off a bit.

From the rear, two antiaircraft half-tracks from the 9th Armored Division came on past Captain Ryerson's force, moving toward Bastogne. Ryerson's men tried to stop them but they drove on heedlessly until they turned the curve and saw the burning tank. The crews then jumped for safety without trying to save their vehicles. The Germans shelled both vehicles and now they blocked the road doubly.

Next the gun crews along the ridge saw an American command car and a Sherman tank, complete with cerise panels, whip out of Magéret and move north. They were quite startled for a moment and held their fire. By the time they had decided these vehicles were being used by the enemy, it was too late to do anything; they had moved out of range.

Two batteries of the 73d Armored Field Artillery came up behind the column and on finding the road blocked moved out north and west and going by way of Bizory got into the line of the main American position (the 501st's lines).

By about 1500 the fire from Magéret had subsided so appreciably that a force composed of 18 infantrymen, two medium tanks and a 105mm. assault gun were sent against the village, moving through the fields on the right flank. One of the Shermans got hung up on an embankment and drew a great deal of fire but was able to return to the column. The rest of the force worked its way into the northeast part of the village, receiving some shellfire from the southeast of the village as they went. At the main crossroads they could see a roadblock with one German tank and an American M4. This armor did not move or fire and the party concluded that it was already destroyed. In the southern part of the village they could see two more German tanks, an American half-track, a jeep and a German ambulance. The heavy guns with the party could not find a position from which to fire and the infantry could do nothing effective.

From the rear of his column Captain Ryerson was called by his antitank officer, 2d Lieutenant Early B. Gilligan, who told him that twenty half-tracks loaded with men forward dismounted and send along any tanks that he might see. The new men consisted of about 200 stragglers from different units who had retreated into the Bastogne area from other actions. They were mostly tankers. Lieutenant Gilligan got them out of the half-tracks, but only forty of them, with three captains and two lieutenants from Combat Command Reserve and a few officers from Hyduke's section, moved up toward the fire fight. The others fled across the fields to the north.

"The forty men who stuck were organized into four squads and at 1600, December 19, this force moved against the southeast part of the village, supported by a section of medium tanks. But the tanks could not get over the ground that lay south of the road and the men were not inclined to go far ahead of the tanks.

Within the village several of the German vehicles which had been to the south stated to move north toward the maw crossing. To the amazement of Ryerson's men, the German tank forming the roadblock, which they had thought to be dead all the time, suddenly started up and moved out of the way. Captain Ryerson's force had been for hours within plain view of this tank at a range of 600 yards without receiving any attention from it. The American tank now put it under fire at once and set the German tank ablaze.

There was still so much shelling from the south of the village however, that the American guns had to stay immobile and the small force of infantry could not get forward. Prisoners they had taken said that the enemy infantry group comprised about 120 men. The 40-man force which had attacked toward the south of Magéret had no communication with Captain Ryerson's main force and later that evening somewhat less than half of them came back. They bad made no real progress.

Since noon Captain Ryerson had been aware that infantry forces were coming to his aid from Bastogne. He didn't know which units were coming but the expectation of relief encouraged his efforts to take Magéret.

Through its various misadventures, Team Cherry as a whole had come to a pass where it could no longer confront the oncoming enemy and where most of its energies would be directed to saving its remaining elements, and covering its own flanks and rear. Whether the German advance into Bastogne from the eastward could be checked and thrown into recoil now depended on the forces of the 101st Division itself.

# 4. FIRST MEETING WITH THE ENEMY

**A**T BASTOGNE, THE 101st Division played in luck from the beginning and the luck began weeks before the siege started. In the early part of November a young lieutenant colonel, Julian Ewell, commanding the 501st Parachute Infantry on the Neder Rijn front in Holland, took a busman's holiday and spent two days of his leave at Bastogne. *[Colonel Ewell told Colonel Marshall about this during their conversation. The two men had a close acquaintanceship extending back to the Normandy campaign. However, Colonel Ewell was rated this way by all of his fellows. He mentioned his visit to Bastogne as a matter only of passing interest. It seems likely that this remarkable coincidence would never have been brought to light except that Ewell had to explain how he knew his own troops were on the wrong road initially. Colonel Ewell was badly wounded a few hours after the interview.]*

It was the luck of war that in giving the march order before leaving Camp Mourmelon, General McAuliffe had put the 501st Parachute Infantry at the head of the column. *[The order of march directed by General McAuliffe was: 501st, 506th, 502d, 327th, with 81st Antiaircraft Battalion following the 501st and 326th Engineers following the 506th.]* It was the luck of war again that Ewell got away well in advance of the column on December 18 and was the first commander to arrive in the vicinity of the bivouac. He ran into a wire-stringing detail there, asked what they were doing, found that they were men from the 101st Division and then followed the wires into the Division command post. Then he got ready to guide his own men in.

All down the route over which he had come Colonel Ewell

49

had found the traffic blocking and stopping, and he didn't expect his 501st to come up to him before 2300 because of this congestion. But it beat that schedule by half an hour and Ewell's unit was closed into its area by 2400. General McAuliffe knew at midnight that by then he had one regiment ready.

*Lieutenant Colonel (now Colonel) Julian J. Ewell, Commanding Officer, 501st Parachute Infantry*

*Bastogne looking north*

*Bastogne looking south*

Earlier in the night (December 18) Ewell had talked to Generals McAuliffe and Higgins. The one thing on which all three commanders agreed was that no one could be sure of anything. Ewell said of himself that he was as much in the dark as any man present. But he told his commander, General McAuliffe, that he thought he should be given a definite assignment. It was a big request, the situation considered.

51

*The main street of Bastogne from the monastery command post of the 501st Parachute Infantry. The cold and snow made movement difficult and living uncomfortable.*

McAuliffe and Middleton conferred on it.

The commander's index finger pointed out along the road running eastward - toward the ridges where Ewell had walked in November - although neither General Middleton nor General McAuliffe ever knew that he had seen the ground.7 The enemy was coming that way. At Corps headquarters the 9th Armored Division was thought to have a roadblock somewhere around Longvilly and the 10th Armored Division a block farther west toward Neffe. The 9th's block was thought to be surrounded; the 10th's block was supposed to be engaged but not yet surrounded. *[This was the situation as Colonel Kinnard understood it to be and as he made note of it at the time. But it was not precisely the situation as it existed.]*

General Middleton had described the situation at these blocks when General McAuliffe had reported to him, and he had said: "There is a battle now going on for Bastogne." He spoke of the block out along the Longvilly road as "surrounded" and indicated the positions of the three blocks which Combat Command B of the 10th Armored was maintaining to the east, northeast and southeast of the city. *[The discrepancy between this and the preceding paragraph is a difference in Kinnard's and McAuliffe's understanding of the situation of the roadblocks. In any case it is inconsequential.]* The Corps commander had no specific plan for the employment of the 101st Division. The news that he was to have that division had come so recently that he had had no time to prepare a plan. At first General McAuliffe could think of nothing. At 2200 he suggested to General Middleton that a combat team be sent east to develop the situation. That idea appealed to General McAuliffe simply as a "good old Leavenworth solution of the problem." It was wholly consistent with General Middleton's concern for the preservation of the other elements of his command. As General Middleton reasoned the problem, so long as the 10th Armored team was already employed in the east, it was not urgent that the 101st

*Bomb damage in Bastogne*

Airborne Division develop the situation there, although it was sound practice to reinforce the armored team's roadblock, since it was becoming evident that the weight of the enemy attack was coming down the Longvilly road.

Middleton and McAuliffe sent for Ewell. He had been spending a part of his time unprofitably at the road intersections trying to get information from men who were straggling in from the north and northeast. All talked vaguely and dispiritedly. Man after man said to him: "We have been wiped out," and then stumbled away through the dark. They did not know where they had been. They had no idea where they were going. Colonel Ewell and his officers tried several times to draw these men out, then gave them up as a bad job and paid no further attention. Ewell reached his separate conclusion that any quest for information concerning the enemy, other than going out bodily after it, was useless.

The exact mission given Ewell was to "seize the road junction at 676614 and hold it." That would put him out the eastern road well beyond Longvilly. Middleton told him that combat Command Reserve of the 9th Armored Division had a roadblock At that point which was supposed to be "isolated" and that the 110th Infantry was supposedly still maintaining a command post at Allerborn. From the assembly area of the 501st Parachute Infantry, it was nine and a half miles to the road junction. However, that distant point did not enter into General McAuliffe's instructions to Ewell or into Ewell's estimate of what the 501st would be able to accomplish. McAuliffe was not sure where the enemy would crowd him first, but he thought it most likely that they would roll on him from the east. That bad as much to do with his assignment of Ewell as did the fact that the armored roadblocks were involved with the enemy.

Then General McAuliffe simply pointed to the map and moved his finger along in the direction of Longvilly. He said: "Ewell, move out along this road at six o'clock, make contact, attack and clear up the situation."

Ewell didn't ask a question. He said: "Yes, Sir," saluted and went on his way."

Recalling that scene some days afterward, General McAuliffe was to remark: "There were many men and commanders in my operation who did outstanding things. But Ewell's was the greatest gamble of all. It was dark. He had no knowledge of the enemy. I could not tell him what he was likely to meet. But he has a fine eye for ground and no man has more courage. He was the right man for the spot I put him in."

Of the few maps which the 101st Division had obtained from VIII Corps headquarters, twenty went with Ewell's combat team as it started to march. It wasn't enough to go around. Lieutenant

Colonel Clarence F. Nelson, commanding the 907th Glider Field Artillery Battalion, had only one map scaled 1:100,000 from which to provide his firing data. So as the movement got under way, he had sketches drawn up for the forward observers. On the sketches all control points and critical features-such as crossroads, bridges, woods and towns-were marked and numbered. The observers knew the locations of the batteries. In this way the artillery operation was co-ordinated.

The offensive mission was limited to the one combat team, Ewell's. McAuliffe bad decided right at the beginning that a

*The underground message center of the 101st Airborne Division in Bastogne.*

*Vehicle in Bastogne camouflaged with sheets from village homes.*

successful defense of Bastogne depended on the utmost harboring of his reserves at every stage of operation, and having sent Ewell forth, he decided to sit on Bastogne with the rest of his Division until something new developed.

That same idea - conservation of force - guided Colonel Ewell in his opening moves. In giving his battalion commanders the march order, he told Major Raymond V. Bottomly, Jr., who was leading out with the 1st Battalion of the 501st, that he was not to put out flank security until he reached Magéret; otherwise, the progress of the column would be much too slow. But in line with the governing principle he added the instruction to all commanders that if they met opposition, they were to "take it slow and easy." Being familiar with his men and their methods in past campaigns, he knew that they tended to throw themselves directly on the target. These methods had worked in Normandy and Holland. But from what he had seen of the Bastogne terrain in November, he had concluded that his main chance lay in "fire

*A column of men marching in the vicinity of Bastogne. The rolling ground and pine forest are typical of the area.*

and maneuver" rather than in shock action. He felt that his whole operation should be guided by this principle. He said to them; "I don't want you to try to beat the enemy to death."

The regiment took off at 0600, December 19, passing its command post on the minute.26 Battery B of the 81st Airborne Antiaircraft Battalion - seven 57mm. guns - moved out behind 1st Battalion. The 101st Airborne Division's Reconnaissance Troop, which bad been attached to Ewell's 501st Parachute Infantry, started through the town ahead of Major Bottomly's men. The observers and the liaison party from the artillery moved out with the lead infantry company. The artillery battalion stayed in the bivouac area two miles west of Bastogne waiting for the infantry to find the enemy.

Ewell went forward at 0700. The light was just beginning to break. Already, he felt vaguely familiar with the terrain and the first thing that happened strengthened his confidence in his memory. At the first intersection past the town, he found the 1st Battalion moving down the wrong road - toward Marvie. He saw from memory of the ground, without looking at the map, that they were going the wrong way. He recalled them and got them pointed toward Longvilly. The Reconnaissance Platoon, having proceeded farthest along the wrong road, thus got behind the battalion column, and raced to catch up.

Ewell's column passed on down the road that follows the line of the creek toward Neffe. To their left the hills rose evenly from the edge of the right-of-way-fairly easy slopes up which an infantryman might run without undue exertion. Ahead, they could see very little. The road dipped and turned around the hill facings of the little valley and the morning fog lay so thick that the visibility toward the south, where the land opens up beyond the line of the creek, was limited to 500 yards.

The 1st Battalion had been on the march for a little more than two hours, and the advance party was being passed through by the Reconnaissance Platoon, when the column was fired on by

*The village of Neffe. Early in the morning of December 19 the enemy captured this crossroads village. During that day the position was held against the 501st Parachute Infantry. The Neffe Chateau is int he clump of trees on the right; the road to the left leads to Bastogne.*

a machine gun from along the road and just westward of Neffe. The first burst of fire did no damage but the battalion hit the dirt. They had need to, for they were looking straight down the groove toward the enemy position; for the last 700 yards the road runs straight and almost level into Neffe. To right of the road, the ground fell off sharply to the creek. To the left were the gently sloping hills, and Bottomly deployed his men that way. Ewell told him to go ahead and develop his situation. Shells began whipping along the road and Bottomly sent word back to Ewell that he thought he was being opposed by two tanks and two platoons of infantry.

Colonel Ewell took himself off, leaving Bottomly to direct his own fight. He had already tasted the shellfire and he didn't want to tempt it, unnecessarily. Back beyond the road's first turning, about 100 yards from Bottomly's skirmish line, there

*Neffe, scene of heavy fighting by the 501st Parachute Infantry and Team Cherry, after it was recaptured.*

*Map 4*

was a pocket in the hillside to left of the road where a stone house fitted snugly. There Colonel Ewell set up his command post.

It soon became clear to him that his 1st Battalion would not be able to overcome the roadblock because of the German tanks. The tanks were firing from a defilade close into the hillside where the road runs down to Neffe from Bizory. Bottomly couldn't bring the 57mms. to bear because the Neffe-Bastogne road ran so straight for the last half mile. About 1000, convinced that his 1st Battalion was stopped, Ewell decided to bring the rest of his regiment out of Bastogne. But this was easier said than done.

The VIII Corps was rushing the evacuation of its last units and their troops were streaming through town across the line of march the rest of the 501st Parachute Infantry would have to take. The 2d Battalion fought its way through this traffic during the next hour and Colonel Ewell ordered them on to an assembly area on the reverse of the gently sloping ridge north of Major Bottomly's position. He figured that he would put them out to the left, closed up so that they could be deployed at the most advantageous moment.

Lieutenant Colonel Nelson, commanding officer of the 907th Glider Field Artillery Battalion, and Captain Gerald J. McGlone, commanding officer of Battery B, 907th, had gone forward to Colonel Ewell the minute the radio flashed word that the 1st Battalion of the 501st had met fire at Neffe. McGlone got his battery into position 500 yards northeast of Bastogne on the left of the Longvilly road, and opened fire as soon as he was in position, which was only a few minutes after 1000, December 19. The fog was still thick and the battery was working under several other handicaps - its radios had never been tested and five of its guns had never been fired. But they spoke now from a distance of only 1,000 yards behind Bottomly's skirmish line. Having weighed the risk that the enemy might flow on around Ewell's narrow front - and accepted it - Nelson decided that one battery was enough in that particular position. He put Battery A, under Captain Lowell B. Bigelow, into the action from a position near the battalion command post, 1,000 yards west of Bastogne. Luck rode with him. The defilade where he had placed Battery B on the spur of the moment was so well chosen that the guns were to work there for almost a month without receiving a single round of German counter-battery fire.

This day, however, the batteries had no need to worry about anything coming in on them. The only heavy support for the German attack was from their tanks and it was all close-up fire directed against Ewell's infantry units. The American artillery fire was turned mainly against the tanks and the small groups of German infantry. There were many such targets.

Colonel Ewell sized up his situation. In 1st Battalion, Companies B and C were in skirmish line, while Company A was collected in reserve. Major Bottomly had deployed most of his strength to the north of the highway but he had managed to find room for one platoon in the ground south of the creek and rail line. The battalion had put two mortars into operation almost immediately and their fire was shaking down the houses around the enemy roadblock in Neffe.

But an attempt to get the 1st Battalion's left flank forward had failed. From Neffe, the north road climbs gradually through a shallow draw to the small farming community of Bizory. The country hereabouts is all uninterrupted grazing land except for the small but thick tree plantations and clusters of farmhouses

*A 105mm M3 howitzer being fired by members of the 907th Glider Field Artillery Battalion during the siege of Bastogne.*

which appear as villages on the map. The dominant terrain features are the long and quite regular ridges which run generally in a north-south line. These hills are gently undulating and the hillsides are quite smooth. From the tops of the commanding ridges one can see great distances on a clear day. The reverse slopes of the hills are smooth and are usually accessible from either end of the hills, making them highly useful to artillery and armor. The roads are close enough together so that vehicles can move to the ridges from either direction. When the country is covered with snow, nothing obtrudes on the landscape except the small black patches of forest. The ridges fall away in gently sloping draws which provide clear fields of fire to the flank and make it easily possible to cover the main lines of communication. The road from Neffe to Bizory rises gradually for a distance, providing a perfect slot for fire from the low ground around Neffe. Bottomly had made one pass in this direction and shells from the enemy armor had fairly blistered the little valley.

Ewell decided that as long as the enemy tanks were in Neffe, his 1st Battalion couldn't move in any direction. He ordered the 2d Battalion to seize Bizory. That hamlet is in the same draw up which the tanks had shot at Bottomly's men, but the ground flattens out at Bizory so that the place can't be seen from Neffe. This detail, however, Ewell couldn't see from the rear, but he was curious to find out about it. The map told him that the ridge adjacent to Bizory was the high ground and would be of use to him. He wanted to see if the enemy force east of there was holding a continuous position and he sent his 2d Battalion forward to find out.

His decision, so casually made, probably contributed as much to the salvation of Bastogne as anything that happened during the first few critical days. Colonel Ewell was still strongly of the opinion that he was being opposed by only a minor roadblock. But when he determined to extend the 501st and sweep forward, he made it a certainty that the oncoming Germans would suddenly collide with Americans who were attacking along a broad front. This was the thing the Germans least expected. Until it happened they had been meeting small or disorganized units, which they quickly encircled and overcame.

The shock of the discovery threw them off stride. They recoiled, hesitated and lost priceless, unreclaimable hours and opportunity because of their own confusion. In that action, a few American platoons hardened the fate of armies. But Ewell thought of none of these things as he ordered his 2d Battalion, 501st Parachute Infantry, to seize Bizory. He reflected on them later in his command post in the Bastogne monastery which the German artillery had made one of the best-ventilated buildings in all of Belgium. *[On the day of the interview the building was hit and shelled repeatedly. In the Nunnery yards that morning a truck loaded with 200 mines was blown up. Not one particle of the bodies of the 12 men who were loading it could be found. Whether the truck had been hit by a shell was never determined.]*

# 5. EAST OF BASTOGNE

THE THIRD BATTALION of the 501st Parachute Infantry had been caught in the traffic snarl west of Bastogne and was at a standstill. Colonel Ewell checked on them at 1200, December 19, and found that they had scarcely moved at all. After trying to get out of town, the battalion had backtracked, only to find that other routes were likewise clogged with outgoing troops. Yet even this delay had its benefits. Some of the infantrymen lacked helmets, rifles and ammunition. They begged them from the armored troops of Combat Command B, 10th Armored Division, who were in the town, and thus in the interval the battalion became somewhat better equipped. Colonel Ewell ordered Lieutenant Colonel George M. Griswold, commanding the 3d Battalion, to march his battalion to Mont, a little hamlet lying south of the Neffe road.

It seemed like the best opportunity to get the battalion out of Bastogne. Ewell also directed that one of Griswold's companies

*The Bastogne road entering the outskirts of Mont.*

be sent down the Wiltz road to cover the 3d Battalion's right flank as it moved. Colonel Griswold was told to send the company to the bend in the road directly east of the village of Marvie. Colonel Ewell planned to send the 3d Battalion against Neffe from the southwest after it had reached Mont, but he issued no orders to the effect at the time. He followed his usual plan of giving his subordinate commanders only a limited objective.

At 1203 the 2d Battalion took Bizory without opposition except for unobserved fire from the German tanks in Neffe. Still convinced that the Neffe roadblock was the only immediate threat to his front, Ewell ordered his 2d Battalion to advance and seize Magéret. By this move he figured he would box the tanks in so that he could then move against them either from front or rear according to the advantages of the ground. But he specified that Major Sammie N. Homan, commander of the 2d Battalion, send one of his companies to seize the patch of woods directly north of Magéret. This wood is a small plantation of very tall spruces. Ewell saw that the long ridge running across to the spruces dominated Magéret in the valley. It seemed to him that putting one company there might cover the approach to Magéret. *[Ewell did not know what had been happening to Team Cherry around Magéret.]*

Major Homan started out by road from Bizory to Magéret, but his route march ended quickly. At the crest of Hill 510 he ran into German infantry in dug-in positions: they were the Reconnaissance Platoon of the 26th Volksgrenadier Division. Homan took this first jolt almost without loss; not so, the enemy. Their line was moving forward from the foxholes and coming over the hill when the 2d Battalion mortars and Nelson's artillery caught them with full blast. The paratroopers saw a number of the enemy fall before the survivors ran back. Deploying the rest of his battalion, Homan sent Company F to the left to seize the coveted wood. When this extension was completed he reported to Colonel Ewell by radio that his hands were full and he was now engaged along his entire front. "For the time being," he said, "I cannot think of taking Magéret."

Colonel Griswold's 3d Battalion reached Mont and found one of the engineer roadblocks outposting that point, but the further operation of the main body of the battalion was compromised by the nature of the ground between Mont and Neffe. The two villages are little more than a mile apart and from Neffe one can look right down the little valley and see Mont clearly. The tanks of Panzer Lehr, which were at Neffe, were shipping a few shells toward Griswold's infantry. It seemed possible that a small party might work its way toward Neffe but the ground was much too naked for the exposure of any large force. Colonel Griswold stopped his 3d Battalion where it was.

Company L which had drawn the assignment on the extreme right flank, was instructed to prowl the three large woods west and northwest of the village of Wardin. At 1330 Company I reported that they had checked the three woods and found no enemy. Colonel Ewell then told Company I to advance to Wardin and make contact with a friendly armored roadblock that was supposed to be there. Ewell had not been told officially of the existence of this force but had heard of it quite casually from someone walking down the road. *[Ewell said he had no prior knowledge of this group. Yet Kinnard and McAuliffe had received the information from Middleton.]*

The company went on to make the contact Ewell had ordered. But for all practical effect, the stranger who had mentioned that there was a friendly roadblock near by might just as well have left his words unsaid.

This was Team O'Hara of Combat Command B, 10th Armored Division, which on the night of December 18 had taken up position on the high ground south of Wardin just short of the woods. The night had been quiet except for the stragglers coming through - mostly rear echelon people from the 28th Division

ACTION AROUND WARDIN
19 DECEMBER

PHASE 1

SCALE IN YARDS

0          500

WARDIN

Patrol fired on, withdrew

PATROL

RCN TO BRAS, 1000
TO WILTZ

A CHINECHA

RCN TO FLANK, 1000

1 ER 54

Hasty Minefield

THOMAS

81 MM MORTARS

OUTPOST

CARRICO PATROL, 1050

TO BASTOGNE

R. J. EOKE

*Map 5*

69

whose idea of the enemy situation was confused. The morning of December 19 opened with fog. About 1000 the trickle of stragglers stopped altogether. This worried Team O'Hara for they figured it must mean that the enemy was coming next. They put out a platoon as a reconnaissance screen to the east which moved slowly along the road to Bras. At 1140 they engaged and destroyed a Volkswagen on the Wiltz-Bastogne highway. Just as they opened fire they saw the head of the enemy column break through the fog a few hundred yards away - two Mark IV tanks and a personnel carrier. The platoon had nothing with which to fight armor and so it cleared out rapidly, reporting its findings by radio. As a result of the message, unobserved fire was put on Bras by the 420th Armored Field Artillery Battalion.

At about the same time Captain Edward A. Carrigo, Team S-2, and First Lieutenant John D. Devereaux, commanding Company B of the 54th Armored Infantry Battalion, were entering Wardin from the southwest and finding it unhealthy The town was wrapped in fog; they could scarcely see anything at fifty yards' range. But they prowled on through the town and just as they got beyond it a projectile of antitank size hit the front bumper of their jeep. Nothing was hurt, but the two officers increased their speed and reported that there were people moving into Wardin who were quite unfriendly.

By noon of the 19th the visibility lengthened to 800 yards. Second Lieutenant Theodore R. Hamer, observer for the 420th Armored Field Artillery Battalion, moved forward to the top of a small hill. There were five tanks of Team O'Hara on the crest when he got there. But before he had a chance to observe for fire, his own tank was hit twice from the left by a high-velocity gun, wounding Hamer and three other crew members. One man was incinerated inside the tank. Another medium tank was bit in the turret by a shell that killed the gunner. The driver backed the tank down the hill wildly, not stopping until his vehicle became bogged; the tank could not be salvaged and later bad to be

ACTION AROUND WARDIN

19 DECEMBER

PHASE 2

SCALE IN YARDS

0                    500

NOTE: TEAM O'HARA WITHDREW
NORTH OF MAGÉRET, 1200

ENEMY INFILTRATES INTO WARDIN, 1230

WARDIN

ENEMY ENTERS WARDIN, 1230

TO WILTZ

A CHINECHA

Volkswagen halts
at minefield,
withdraws,
1300

SOI–X
repulsed,
1400

PATROL RETURNS, 1230

OUTPOST

1200

1200

1200

TM O'HARA

SOI–T, 1230

SOI–T, 1230

TO BASTOGNE

R.J. KOKE

*Map 6*

71

destroyed. The other tanks cleared away from the hill as rapidly as they could. Direct-fire artillery began to hit the force's main position from north across the valley. On the road ahead, the team had hastily set up a minefield. At 1300 a few Germans jumped from a Volkswagen and tried to remove the mines. From only 200 yards away to the west, five of the infantry half-tracks and five medium tanks opened fire on the German party. But they were able to jump in their car and make a clean getaway. Shortly after, an outpost at the south of the position saw another enemy group moving through woods northeast toward Wardin. One of the medium tanks moved up and put them under fire.

These were the things that had happened before the time when Team O'Hara saw men coming toward them from the woods at their rear. These men were in patrol formation and wore an unfamiliar green uniform, which looked tight around the legs. The tankers were just about to fire and then someone in the approaching party yelled. The approaching men were the point of Company I, 501st Parachute Infantry. Their green jump suits had almost been their undoing. The main body of the Company was right behind them in the woods and the company was on its way to Wardin - good news to the tankers. The first infantry support had arrived and they could now withdraw their own patrols which had been reaching out toward the town.

Some fateful minutes passed and nothing was done to unify the action. With the enemy crowding in on them, the forces acted like two ships passing in the night. The paratroopers went on. Two medium tanks were placed so as to cover the exits from Wardin. That was all.

Lieutenant Colonel James O'Hara, commander of the 54th Armored Infantry Battalion, 10th Armored Division, and Team O'Hara of Combat Command B, had thought that the enemy would push west on the Wiltz-Bastogne highway. But he was wrong about it. The Germans bypassed his group - except for a few who squeezed a little too far over to the west and got themselves killed for their pains - and went on to Wardin, moving along a deep gully where O'Hara's tanks couldn't bring their fire to bear. The tankers could see the German infantry infiltrating by twos and threes, moving northwest toward the town, until a hundred or more had passed. They asked that artillery be put on the gully but the Bastogne artillery was occupied with the defense of Noville. Then the enemy began to fret O'Hara's immediate front again: one group came close enough to fire at a tank with a rocket that fell five yards short. Half-tracks sprayed the area with machine-gun fire and the tanks pounded away with their 75mms. Thus preoccupied, Team O'Hara paid no mind to Wardin. They knew there was fighting going on but the situation was "obscure."

At 1415, December 19, Colonel Ewell heard that Company I was being fired on in Wardin. The reports trickling in during the next few minutes indicated that the company was doing pretty well. Armor was now opposing them, but they had already knocked out two tanks and were pushing the enemy infantry from the town. By 1600, Ewell was pretty much content with his general situation. He had three battalions approximately abreast; he was in contact with the enemy all along his front and there was a friendly roadblock - Team O'Hara - on his extreme right flank. But he felt that he had gone as far as he could with his offensive action and that such strength was now being committed against him that he could no longer think about his specific mission (to "seize the road junction at 676614 and hold it.") He therefore ordered his battalions to make plans to break contact at dark and draw back to defend a general line along the high ground to the west of Bizory-Neffe, and in an approximate extension of this line to the southward of the creek. At Division headquarters, General McAulliffe and Colonel Kinnard looked over his plan and approved it.

As he was walking back through Bastogne he met a sergeant from Company I who said to him, "Have you heard about

Company I? We've been wiped out." Ewell got to his radio; he didn't believe the sergeant, but the story was nearer right than he thought. Company I had lost 45 men and 4 officers at Wardin and the survivors had scattered so badly that it was no longer possible to form even a platoon. The news was a shock. When he first heard that Company I was becoming involved in Wardin, Colonel Ewell had ordered it to disengage and withdraw. But before the company could comply, it had come under the full shock of an attack by seven tanks and one infantry battalion from Panzer Lehr. The survivors got out as best they could.

This news simply strengthened Ewell's conviction that he must abandon all further offensive intention and tighten up his position. Colonel O'Hara had reached the same conclusion and for much the same reason. Four of the walking wounded who had gotten out of Wardin had come into his lines and told him the news. He saw his force now in an exposed position with no one on his right, an aggressive enemy on his left and pressure along his whole front, and he asked Combat Command B headquarters for permission to withdraw.

By radio he received his reply, "Contact friends on your left, hold what you have." This told him that headquarters still didn't understand the situation. So he sent his S-3, Captain George A. Renoux, to Bastogne to explain in person what he couldn't with safety discuss over the air, and then went to his rear to reconnoiter a better position. At 1715 he was ordered to withdraw to the high ground north of Marvie - the place he had by then already picked as the best defensive line in the area. The Headquarters Company, Heavy-Weapons Company and engineers were first to start digging into the new slope. When they were in place, the rest of the force came along, except for four medium tanks and one platoon of infantry which covered the withdrawal. Throughout the whole move, the 420th Armored Field Artillery Battalion put a heavy covering fire into, the ground where the enemy had been seen during the day. Not a shot was fired in return.

Because of the loss of Company I and his feeling that the enemy was building up on his right, Colonel Ewell asked Division headquarters to attach one battalion to his regiment for a right flank and reserve. He was given the 1st Battalion of the 327th Glider Infantry under Lieutenant Colonel Hartford F. Salee. They were put in behind Ewell's 3d Battalion which put

*Map 7*

them next to Team O'Hara.

Between 1700 and 1800, December 19, the 501st Parachute Infantry fell back to the new defensive line. Estimating his gains and losses, Ewell didn't give his regiment too much credit. He thought that Company I had probably killed some Germans at Wardin, but since the enemy still held the town he couldn't be sure. His impression was that the execution done by his own right and center had not been very great. The honors of the day belonged to the artillery." Colonel Ewell said, "Any actual killing of the enemy that day was due to the artillery."

Captain Ryerson's force (Company C, 20th Armored Infantry Battalion, 10th Armored Division) of Team Cherry , having spent the day hoping that the infantry would get up to them, clung to three houses in the northwest edge of Magéret after dark. The enemy shot up flares and blazed away at Ryerson's vehicles with antitank guns, destroying three of them. Their infantry then came on but was driven back by the fire of the 420th Armored Field Artillery Battalion.

At 0030, December 20, Combat Command B Headquarters sent orders for Ryerson to withdraw before dawn, and to make contact with Colonel Ewell at Bizory. One line in the special instructions said, "The lead vehicle will inform outpost line of number of vehicles in his column to insure that no Germans follow column into our lines."

Captain Ryerson got ready to move his wounded to a point beyond the crest of the first hill - the first step on the way out.

# 6. HOLDING THE CHATEAU

COLONEL CHERRY HAD been sitting on the hot seat. Having failed to get to his forward elements the night of December 18, he went to his command post, which was set up in the château 300 yards south of Neffe. A signal company from VIII Corps which had hastily pulled out of this building bad scribbled signs on the walls saying, "We'll be back - The Yanks." One of Cherry's men read it and snorted, "We'll be back - Hell! We're here to stay."

At 0600 on December 19 - just as Ewell's men were passing the initial point - Cherry's Reconnaissance Platoon, 3d Tank Battalion, which was outposting the road junction at Neffe, was hit by enemy tanks and infantry from the east. The platoon knocked out one tank with a bazooka but the enemy kept coming, and after taking some losses, the line broke back under a storm of German rifle, machine-gun and direct artillery fire. Most of the outpost fell back along the Bastogne road up which Major Bottomly's men (1st Battalion, 501st Parachute Infantry) were coming. But three of them were able to get through to Cherry in the château and they carried the word that the enemy had come to Neffe with two tanks and two infantry platoons. *[As this is identical with Major Bottomly's estimate to Colonel Ewell it seems probable that men coming through gave Bottomly his information.]*

At 1000, while Colonel Ewell was committing his 2d Battalion of the 501st, Colonel Cherry saw four more German tanks (one was a Tiger Royal), an armored car and 97 more infantrymen enter Neffe from the direction of Magéret. Right after that they hit his force, and they spent the rest of that day trying to crush him with their left while poking at Ewell's troops with their right. The château was stoutly built and this somewhat compensated for Team Cherry's depleted numbers. Cherry bad to see it through with his headquarters personnel who moved from one side of the building to another as the attack shifted. The automatic weapons had been taken from the vehicles and placed in the windows and at other points where they could cover the château yard and walls. From three sides, the enemy infantry pressed in against the building; the west side of the château was raked with 20mm. and machine-gun fire. *[Since the château was west of the German roadblock and the west wall faced toward Major Bottomly, this may have been American fire.]*

But though some died within five yards of the walls, not one German got into the château.

There was only one somber note in the defense. A depleted platoon of engineers, which had arrived from the direction of Mont early in the morning, was ordered to the south of the château at the height of the action. The enemy was moving through woods toward the high ground in that direction. The engineers started on their mission but kept on over the hill and Team Cherry never saw them again. *[There were supposed to be two Engineer roadblocks in the vicinity, one between Bastogne and Neffe and the other at Mont. Colonel Ewell says that he found no engineer group on the Longvilly road. The Mont block was intact when Griswold got there. The group that came to the chateau may have been driven off the Longvilly road by the German fire and after going to the chateau decided to rejoin the other group. The Historian was not able to establish the fact.]*

Some time around mid-afternoon on the 19th a platoon from Ewell's 3d Battalion of the 501st in Mont worked its way carefully forward, taking advantage of the cover afforded by the forest patches and the rise and fall of the ground, and entered the château. *[The work of this party was not known to Colonel Ewell and does not appear in the battalion journal. It appears in the Combat Command B Journal and the Team Cherry interview, and is confirmed in the interview with Colonel Kinnard.]*

It had turned out this way, that whereas the fire of the German tanks had kept Colonel Griswold's 3d Battalion from closing on Neffe, his infantry fire had compelled the Germans to release their tight hold on the château. Too, the enemy must have felt mounting concern for what was occurring on their right. The platoon had come as reinforcements-to help Cherry hold the fort. But by that time the roof was blazing over his head and his men were being smoked out by another fire lighted by German HE shells. *[Such is the confusion of battle that 101st Division command post had the impression that Team Cherry had burned the chateau before withdrawing in order to keep it from falling into enemy hands.]*

He waited until the approach of darkness and then led all hands out of Neffe and back to the infantry lines at Mont.

Before leaving, Colonel Cherry sent Combat Command B this message, "We're not driven out . . . we were burned out. We're not withdrawing . . we are moving."

# 7. TEAM DESOBRY AT NOVILLE

THE CONTEMPORARY ACCOUNTS which attempted to apportion the credit for the saving of Bastogne had much to say about the 101st Airborne Division and relatively little about any other units. There was irony in the fact that a paratroop outfit which had already done equally brilliant work in Normandy and Holland won world recognition for the first time, and in so doing eclipsed the splendid help given by the other victors, at Bastogne. It was the belief of the commanders at Bastogne that the 28th Infantry Division had absorbed much of the shock of the attack before the enemy reached their front on that first day, and that the harassing of the German flank and rear by the armored forces that had gone out the Longvilly road further lightened the burden upon their own men of the 101st Airborne Division. *[Colonel Roberts also expressed this view on the 28th Division to Westover, but it was not placed in the interview.]*

In those critical hours the armor out along the roads leading north and east was to the infantry in Bastogne like a football end throwing himself in the path of interference so that the secondary defense can have a clean chance to get at the man with the ball.

One of the most desperately placed of these small armored forces was Team Desobry which assembled in the Noville area at 2300 on December 18. The town of Noville is on relatively high ground. Yet it is commanded by two ridges from about 800 yards, one in the southeast and the other running from north to northwest. Because the team arrived in the darkness, full advantage of the natural defenses of the area could not be taken immediately. Major William R. Desobry (Commanding Officer of the 20th Armored Infantry Battalion, 10th Armored Division)

set up a perimeter defense of the town under Captain Gordon
Geiger of Battalion Headquarters Company. He sent forward
three outposts, each consisting of a depleted platoon of infantry
and a section of medium tanks. One went east on the Bourcy
road, one went northeast on the Houffalize road and the third set
up its roadblock at some crosstrails on the road to Vaux. This
outpost line was about 800 yards from the main body. The
engineers were instructed to install minefields in support of the
roadblocks but found it impossible to comply with the order
because of the flow of American stragglers back over these same
roads. They came on all through the night-men from scattered
engineer units, from Combat Command Reserve of the 9th
Armored Division and from the 28th Infantry Division. Colonel
Roberts had told Major Desobry to draft into his organization
any men he could use.

Every vehicle that came down the road was searched for
infantry soldiers. Desobry had already decided that he would

*Map 8*

incorporate any infantrymen or engineers into the local defense; he needed engineers to set up obstacles. But be ordered his men to let any armored vehicles pass through the lines and continue on to Bastogne. He figured that additional vehicles would merely clog the streets of Noville and increase his vulnerability to enemy artillery fire. The infantry strays came into the line usually in groups of three or four. Many of them had discarded all fighting equipment; few were able to say where they had been; none had maps and none was able to pinpoint the area where he had last seen the Germans. It became the experience of Team Desobry that these stragglers who came to Noville singly or in small groups were of almost no value to the defense; when the action started, they took to the cellars.

This was not true of a platoon of armored infantry from CCR which fell back into Noville near midnight. Their lieutenant had held them together during a running 36-hour fight with enemy armored forces. He gave Major Desobry a vivid picture of his experience and of the action of the enemy forces moving toward Noville from the east. He volunteered to move his platoon into position at Noville and throughout the defense there, it fought courageously.

On the strength of what the lieutenant had told him about the enemy armor, Desobry decided that his own vehicles were overcrowding the village. He ordered the main streets to be cleared and the vehicles to be parked along the side roads. Detailing one officer to stand watch, he then suggested that the rest of the force within the village try to snatch some sleep.

At 0430 on December 19 the flow of stragglers abruptly ceased and Desobry's men grew tense as they waited for an enemy attack. At 0530 a group of half-tracks could be heard and dimly seen approaching the block on the Bourcy road. In the darkness the outpost could not tell whether they were friend or enemy. The sentry to the front yelled "Halt!" four times. The first vehicle pulled to a grinding halt within a few yards of him.

Someone in the half-track yelled something in German. From a bank on the right of the road, Desobry's men showered the half-track with hand grenades. Several exploded as they landed in the vehicle. There was loud screaming as some of the Germans jumped or fell from the half-track and lay in the road. The rest of the enemy column quickly unloaded and deployed in the ditches along the road. There ensued a 20-minute close-up fight with grenades and automatic weapons and although the roadblock crew was greatly outnumbered, the bullet fire did them no hurt because of the protection of the embankment. Staff Sergeant Leon D. Gantt finally decided that too many German potato-mashers were coming into the position and ordered his men to withdraw about 100 yards. At this the Germans turned their half-track around and ran for safety; they were apparently a reconnaissance element and had completed their mission by finding the American outpost. During the action the two tanks had done nothing although they were within 100 yards of the German column. Sergeant Gantt went to Second Lieutenant Allen L. Johnson and asked him why. Johnson replied that he hadn't been sure what to do. He then fired a couple of Parthian shots down the road but the enemy had already disappeared into the fog and darkness. At dawn the outpost fell back on Noville according to instructions.

Twenty minutes after the fighting had died on the Bourcy road three tanks approached the outpost on the Houffalize road. The sound of their motors seemed familiar to Staff Sergeant Major I. Jones who was out by himself some 75 yards in front of the roadblock. He thought they were American. When the tanks were 75 yards away Jones yelled, "Halt!" and fired a quick burst with his BAR over the turret of the lead tank. It stopped 50 yards from him. He heard the occupants conversing in English. Then fire from the tank's caliber .50 broke around Jones' foxhole in the sloping bank on the side of the road. He flattened quickly and the fire missed his back by inches. The men at the roadblock fired on the tanks. Suddenly a cry of "Cease fire, they're friendly troops!" was heard. Jones was not certain whether the cry came from the force in front of him or behind him. The small-arms fire ceased. But the two medium tanks which were supporting the roadblock and were standing about 100 yards from this new armor were less sanguine. The tank on the right side of the road fired its 75mm. The first round hit the bank 15 yards from Jones and almost blew him out of the hole. The foremost tank confronting Jones fired six quick rounds in reply. The first round knocked out the American tank on the right. The second round knocked out the other one. The succeeding rounds also scored direct hits. Yet none of the tankers was killed though several were hard hit. One man had his right leg blown off and his left badly mangled. Private John J. Garry, an infantryman, moved over to the ditch to help the wounded tankers and was hit in the shoulder by a shell fragment.

Jones and the other men in the advanced positions were pinned to their foxholes by the grazing fire from the enemy guns. The American half-tracks were in line behind the Shermans. The position of the ruined armor not only blocked the enemy from coming down the road but gave the half-tracks partial cover so that they could turn their machine guns against the enemy column. A bazooka team tried to get forward but couldn't find a route by which they could bring their rockets to bear. Under these conditions of deadlock the two forces continued to slug it out toe-to-toe while the fog swirled around them and at last closed in so thick that they could scarcely see the muzzle Hashes of the guns. At 0730 the platoon disengaged and withdrew to Noville, acting on the orders given by Major Desobry the night before. They had held to the last minute and so complied with the order, but they were about through in any case, as enemy infantry was now coming up around the flank. The roadblock on the Vaux road was not attacked. But while that party likewise was withdrawing at 0730 they heard die enemy coming down from the north.

During the night of December 18-19 Captain Geiger had set up roadblocks on all roads entering Noville and had placed a thin screen of infantry in a circle just beyond the buildings. The position was particularly weak on the south and west-the sides which the enemy seemed least likely to approach. One tank was posted on the road leading to Bastogne and two were put on the other main exits from the town. In addition, one 57mm. gun and a 75mm. assault gun were placed to cover each of the roads which had been outposted during the night. The survivors of the two opening skirmishes had just drawn back within this defensive circle when 88mm. fire from the northward ripped out of the fog which by this time completely enveloped the village.

From Noville's main street the north-running road is straight for miles. The defenders figured that German tanks were sitting out there on the road somewhere and firing right down the slot. The fire was very heavy for half an hour. It destroyed three half-tracks and a jeep and blew the machine gun from an M8 car. But miraculously, no one was hurt.

At 0830 on the 19th two Tiger tanks nosed out of the fog and stopped within 20 yards of the machine-gun positions covering the northern sector. The 57mm. gun to the right of the road was within 30 yards of the tanks. A medium tank with a 75mm. gun was looking straight at them. The machine gunners alongside the road picked up their bazookas. All fired at the same time and in a second the two Tiger tanks had become just so much wrecked metal. Later, all hands claimed credit for the kill.

A few Germans jumped out of the tanks and started to flee. Machine gunners and riflemen in the outposts cut loose on them. But they could not be sure whether their fire found the targets because the fog swallowed the running men within 30 or 40 yards. Some German infantry had come along behind the tanks and Desobry's men had caught only a glimpse of their figures. But they turned back the moment the skirmish opened.

About 0930 the enemy began to press against the west sector with a series of small probing actions which lasted until 1030. The officer in charge of this ground, Second Lieutenant Eugene E. Todd, was new to action and began to feel that he was sustaining the weight of a major attack by the whole German Army. When he asked Captain Geiger for permission to withdraw, Geiger replied, "Hell, hold your ground and fight." He did.

The real thing started at 1030. The defenders had heard the rumblings of tanks and the puttering of smaller vehicles out in the fog as if a tremendous build-up were going on. Quite suddenly the fog lifted like a curtain going up and revealing the stage. The countryside was filled with tanks. From the second story of his command post in the Noville schoolhouse, Captain Omar R. Billett (Commanding Officer, Company B, 20th Armored Infantry Battalion, 10th Armored Division), saw at a glance more than 30 tanks. Others saw as many more from different points of vantage. In an extended skirmish line along the ridge short of Vaux were 14 tanks. Desobry's men looked at this scene and knew that they were standing square in the road of an entire panzer division. At that moment they might well have uttered the words of Oliver, "Great are the hosts of these strange people, and we have here a very little company," but instead they picked up their arms. The leading enemy formations were 1,000 yards away. The distance made no difference even to the men working with caliber .50 machine guns; they fired with what they bad. When they bad closed to 800 yards out, the 14 tanks on the ridge halted and shelled the town. Other tanks were swinging around the right flank but on the left the enemy armor was already within 200 yards of the American position when the curtain went up.

The events of the next hour were shaped by the flashes of the heavy guns and the vagaries of the ever-shifting fog. The guns rolled in measure according to a visibility that came and went in the passage of only a few seconds. But it never became an infantryman's battle. Little knots of men on foot were coming up behind the German tanks and the batteries of the 420th Armored Field Artillery Battalion hammered at those afoot. It is doubtful if the American artillery stopped a single tank. About the time that the enemy army became fully revealed, a platoon from the 609th Tank Destroyer Battalion rolled into Noville, and added the gunpower of its four tank destroyers to the guns already shooting. The sudden, sharp focus given to the line of Mark IVs and Mark Vs as the fog cleared along the ridge line made them stand out like ducks in a shooting gallery. Nine were hit straightaway, three exploding in flames. One came charging down the highway and was turned into a flaming wreck 500 yards out. At a range of 600 yards an American cavalryman engaged a Panther tank with his armored car and knocked it out with one shot from his 37mm. gun-the most miraculous hit of the morning.

Two tanks that had been close in the foreground, ahead of the ridge, also charged the town at a speed that brought momentary confusion to Desobry's command post. But at 30 yards' range, a 105mm. assault gun fired its first round, stopping one tank, but not disabling its gun. The German fired but missed, then tried to withdraw, but with a quick round the assault gun finished him off. The other German tank had been stopped by one of Desobry's mediums at a range of 75 yards. Looking in the direction from which they had come, observers in the taller buildings of Noville could see four more tanks lying in a draw-almost concealed. The ground cover was good enough so the Noville guns. couldn't get at them-until one of these tanks made the mistake of pulling out onto the road. It was a shining mark, 300 yards away. A tank destroyer fired and the tank exploded in a blaze. The fog swirled back, screening the draw, and the other three tanks ran off into it.

To the east of town, the run down the flank by the enemy

armor ended with the destruction of three of the tanks. German infantry had appeared on that side in fairly large numbers, but when the lifting of the fog exposed them, they turned and ran, and bullet fire from Noville thinned their ranks while they were running. In Noville, the defending infantry company had lost 13 wounded; four of our vehicles had been wrecked and one tank destroyer smashed-mainly from indirect artillery fire with which the Germans had harassed the town as their tanks came on.

By 1130 the fight had died, though intermittent shelling continued to worry the garrison.3A Its effect on Desobry had been as Colonel Roberts had predicted on the night before. The sudden lifting of the fog and revelation of the enemy position had made him acutely conscious that the conditions of ground imposed an inordinate handicap on his own force. From their positions along the ridges on three sides of Noville, the Germans could put their tanks in hull defilade and keep the village under a close artillery fire until all the walls were leveled. Desobry could see nothing but disaster ahead if be tried to hold the present ground. He figured he had better withdraw, but at the same time he remembered the counsel that Colonel Roberts had given him. In mid-morning, at the height of the German attack, he called Roberts and asked for permission to withdraw to the high ground around the village of Foy.

This was an act of near fatal consequences though in the end it saved the situation. What happened was that at Major Desobry's CP no effort was made to keep the message secret from all save its handlers. The operator spoke loudly and all others in the command post heard what he said. The word spread quickly to the troops out on the fighting line. In the course of the action these vague rumors hardened into a positive report that the command had received permission for a withdrawal to Foy. The wish had fathered the thought; the intensifying of the German fire made it very easy to believe. Groups of armored infantrymen - and nearly all of the stragglers who had been plugging gaps in the line - came drifting back into Noville; they had heard the story and had quit their foxholes. It seemed to Desobry that his line was about to disintegrate. He rallied his command post officers and noncoms and they began working frantically with these groups, bullying them, swearing that the rumor was false and turning them back to the action.

Reluctantly the men faced back toward the enemy but others kept on coming. There was no end to the problem. That one lapse in the CP kept the team off balance during the deadliest part of the day. Yet Desobry noted that his subordinates were accepting even these extra odds cheerfully. From the commander on down, not a man had any idea of the over-all importance of the engagement; it was just another local affair and they had scarcely related it even to the defense of Bastogne. What buoyed their spirits was that the Germans were coming in with their chins down; their own armor was remaining open. The difference was telling clearly in the marksmanship of the two sides and in the comparative losses in fighting vehicles. Every fair hit on an enemy tank produced a lift of enthusiasm for the fight partly offsetting the ill effect of the withdrawal rumor. Not all of those who drifted back to the village were bent on withdrawal; some came for just a moment to boast of what they had done to the enemy in their sector and then to return to their work again. Witnessing this strangely disordered contest and catching its wild notes of dismay and triumph, Major Desobry was reminded of a barroom brawl. His concern, however, was not solely due to the power of the German attack. That morning he had sent patrols out to reconnoiter his rear and the patrols had not returned.

Colonel Roberts sparred with the request from Noville. He still possessed authority to sanction the withdrawal of his own elements but he reckoned that the situation required steadfastness for the time being and until the 101st Division was solidly established in Bastogne. So at first he gave no answer.

He left his own CP and started for General McAuliffe's headquarters to see what could be done. Before he had gone halfway he ran into Brigadier General Higgins, assistant division commander of the 101st. Even as he rapidly sketched the situation to Higgins (the time was 1050) the 1st Battalion of 506th Parachute Infantry, under Lieutenant Colonel James L. LaPrade, passed by in the street. At the head of the regimental column, accompanying LaPrade, was the 506th's commander, Colonel Robert F. Sink. Convinced by Roberts' words that the Noville situation was fully desperate, Higgins on the spot ordered Sink to send a battalion to Noville and LaPrade automatically drew the assignment.

*[McAuliffe likewise says that LaPrade was sent to Noville because of Desobry's predicament.]*

Colonel Sink was further directed that his 2d and 3d Battalions should be put in Division reserve just north of Bastogne on the Noville road. At the same time the 1st Battalion, which had been given the Noville mission, was detached from Regiment and put under Division control. Colonel Roberts returned to his CP and called Major Desobry. "You can use your own judgment about withdrawing," he said, "but I'm sending a battalion of paratroopers to reinforce you."

Desobry replied, "I'll get ready to counterattack as soon as possible."

Colonel LaPrade and his staff got up to Major Desobry at 1130 and told him the battalion was on the way. It was not quite clear to either of the local commanders whether there had been an attachment of one force to the other but they decided that for the time being they would keep it a "mutual affair." Colonel LaPrade and his command had just one 1:100,000 map to serve them for the forthcoming operation.

The commanders agreed that the next order of business was to attack due north and seize the high ground the enemy had tried to use as a springboard during the morning. Infantry and armor would jump off together at 1400. However, Colonel LaPrade's battalion didn't arrive until 1330 and couldn't get ready that soon. So the jumpoff was postponed until 1430, December 19, since meanwhile there was a small matter of supply to be finally adjusted.

The 506th Parachute Infantry had left Mourmelon in such a hurry that many of the men did not have helmets and others were short of weapons and ammunition. Colonel LaPrade told Major Desobry about this embarrassment and the armored force's S-4, Second Lieutenant George C. Rice, was sent packing to Foy to bring up ammunition. On the way he met the upcoming 1st Battalion and asked for their supply officer; but this officer was in Bastogne beating the woods for weapons and ammunition. So Lieutenant Rice asked the company officers what they needed most, and found that rocket launchers, mortars and all types of ammunition were the critical shortages. He then dashed on to Foy and loaded the jeep with cases of hand grenades and M1 ammunition. The jeep was turned around and the stuff was passed out to the paratroopers as they marched. On his next shuttle, Rice got back to the moving, battalion with a jeep and a truck overloaded with weapons and ammunition. The materiel was put alongside the road in five separate piles so that the men could pick up the things they needed as they went by. He made one more trip and caught the head of the column just before it reached the limits of Noville. A load of 81 mm. mortar ammunition came into town after the battalion got there.

These details caused a slight delay in getting the battle under way again.

# 8. ATTACK AND WITHDRAWAL

COLONEL LAPRADE and Major Desobry wanted the high ground and this was their plan-that three tanks would strike northward along the Houffalize road and four tanks would hit east toward the high ground west of Bourcy. With this group of tanks would go one and one-half platoons of infantry for their close-in support. In between these two armored groups moving along the road, LaPrade's paratroopers would spread themselves over the middle ground. One company would advance south over the Bourcy road, another off to the left of it would extend to the Houffalize road and the third company would go toward the high ground at Vaux. In this way, armor and infantry would spread out fanwise as they left Noville and started for the commanding ridges.

However, the preliminaries were not propitious. Noville was already taking a pounding from the enemy artillery. The Germans were firing by the clock and dropping twenty to thirty shells into the defensive position every ten minutes. The houses and several of the vehicles were afire. A proper reconnaissance became impossible; the assembly went off badly. Still, the attack got away at 1430, December 19, though somewhat unsteadily.

The line had scarcely moved out from the houses when an artillery concentration landed in the middle of Company C of the 506th Parachute Infantry, which was on the right flank.3 A number of men were hit but the company kept moving. Bullet fire from enemy positions on the high ground bit into the infantry ranks and slowed their advance. The little groups worked their way along, dashing on to favorable ground, stopping there to fire, then making a rush on to the next point of cover.

But elsewhere along the line, except on the far left where

Company B kept moving, the attack was already flagging. The tanks and armored infantry decided the attack was impossible so moved back to their holes, not even realizing that the paratroopers were continuing to attack in any strength. Company A was blocked by heavy tank fire immediately and after a small advance was forced to return to the village. But on the flanks, B and C went on until they reached the lower slopes of the objective ridges and started to climb. At that moment the enemy tanks came against them, supported by some infantry. A few of the paratroopers kept going; their snow-covered bodies were found on the ridges weeks later. *[Backed by statements made to Westover in an interview with battalion officers on March 13, 1945.]*

But the greater part of the two companies went to earth and sought whatever cover was at hand. Then they continued to slug it out with their small arms as best they could. They could hardly see the enemy at any time. The fog was closing down again and

*Map 9*

it was mixed with the smoke drifting over from the fires of Noville.

They held the ground until dark. Then Colonel LaPrade's men fell back on Noville. The fighting on the slopes had cost the battalion heavily but the men thought they had caused equal losses to the enemy. From the town itself three tank destroyers had exchanged fire at about 1500 yards with the enemy tanks and had kept them from coming on. But whether they had done any real hurt to them could not be seen.

*[506th Parachute Infantry claims that five of these tanks were destroyed but the statement is considered insufficient because proofs were lacking and in view of the conditions already described.]*

For about an hour after the return to Noville the front was deathly quiet. LaPrade's men-had had no chance to dig in prior to the attack so they sought refuge in the houses. Colonel LaPrade improved his command post by moving a heavy clothes closet in front of the window. *[From statement by Harwick to Marshall. This statement was never committed to writing because it was made in answer to a question prior to an interview which was to be held at a later hour. Before the interview could be held Harwick was hit.]*

The Germans resumed their bombardment of the town and in the middle of the shelling a platoon of tank destroyers from the 706th Tank Destroyer Battalion reported for duty. Further tightening the defense, General Higgins, having arrived at Noville just as the American counterattack was fading, took the essential steps toward unifying the local command. Major Desobry and Colonel LaPrade were in agreement that one man should be in control, and LaPrade, being the senior, drew the assignment. LaPrade told General Higgins that he thought he could hold on until dark but that he was convinced that the enemy would attack in strength shortly thereafter. Soon after that, Colonel Sink got up to Noville for a personal reconnaissance. He talked to LaPrade and the latter shortly issued his orders for the combined defense. The plan was for Company B to defend to the northwest and Company A to the northeast and Company C was to cover the southern half of the perimeter while the armored group was held in the center of the town ready to strike out in any direction.14 A few minutes after LaPrade was placed in command, an 88 shell landed in the street outside the command post. The explosion shattered the clothes closet and both commanders were struck down by fragments. Colonel LaPrade was killed and Major Desobry wounded. Major Robert F. Harwick, LaPrade's executive, who had rushed back from a leave in Paris to join his battalion and had arrived in Noville just at the close of the afternoon fighting, took command of the combined force. The armor passed into the hands of Major Charles L. Hustead.

For the men of Combat Command B who were within the town the rest of the night (December 19-20) was comparatively quiet. Their peace was punctured at times by the dropping of a few artillery shells and out beyond the wall of fog they could hear the noise of an enemy build-up. There was little quiet, however, along the infantry perimeter. Enemy tanks in twos and threes, supported by infantry, probed toward them. When warned by small-arms or bazooka fire, they checked and blazed away at the positions from which they had seen the flashes. The accompanying Germany infantry tried to infiltrate through the lines. These small penetrations and the resulting fire were such that it was almost impossible to maintain wire communication with the outposts. For the paratroopers those hours were a nightmare of surprise fire, ominous noise and confusion. But when morning came the light revealed that two of the enemy tanks had been knocked out by bazooka fire.

These opening blows in the first round at Noville had been enough to convince General McAuliffe that the enemy was full of fight. After that first day they would never seem as strong to him again and the impression would deepen that their attacks were coming on in diminishing volume. But on the first day he looked toward his northern sector with increasing concern. In the afternoon of December 19, the 3d Battalion of 506th had been ordered to move up to Foy between Bastogne and Noville and establish a line there, with the 2d Battalion moving to Luzery as a regimental reserve. When this move was made, Company H on the right made contact with the 501st Parachute Infantry by patrol and Company G on the left joined with the 502d Parachute Infantry, maintaining a strong point in Recogne. That night all platoons of Company C of the 705th Tank Destroyer Battalion were attached to the 506th Parachute Infantry and General McAuliffe got ready to employ as much of the strength of 502d along his northern flank as the morrow would prove necessary.

This small, confused action had reverberated all the way back to Corps. On returning to Bastogne, Higgins had reported to McAuliffe as follows: "I think we're way out on a limb. There is too much distance between LaPrade in Noville and Strayer in Foy. It is my judgment that the Noville force had better get out."

Colonel Sink, having carried out his independent reconnaissance, had reached exactly the same conclusion. At around 1820 he called Division and said that it was getting very hot at Noville; he urged that his forward battalion be withdrawn to a point north of Foy. But in view of the fact that General Middleton had ordered that Noville be defended and that the armor which had gone forward in response to that direction was still acting under Roberts's orders, it looked like a matter for decision by the higher headquarters. General McAuliffe called General Middleton and relayed Higgins's and Sink's reports of the situation, adding his personal recommendation that the force be withdrawn. Middleton said, "No; if we are to hold on to Bastogne, you cannot keep falling back." Sink was called and told that the Noville force would have to stick. By then, Major

Desobry had ceased to worry about the local problem. He was unconscious when they removed him from the CP to the nearest field hospital. He was still out, when, a few hours later, the Germans overran the hospital and took him prisoner.

# 9. DOUBTS AND DECISIONS

Y ET ON THE WHOLE, that first night in Bastogne, the situation was good, and it was largely the intuition and hunch and driving energy of the leaders that had made it so. The day of the 19th had proved that in the few minutes allowed him the night before, General McAuliffe had sized up the position properly.

*[Examination of the assembly area overlay alongside of how the battle developed makes this fact self-evident. However there was considerable discussion between General McAuliffe and the Historian which is not included in the notes. General McAuliffe said that when the siege was over he felt that his choice of the assembly area was one of his most fortunate decisions and that he would not have altered it in any way looking at battle retrospectively. He said that he had not given a great deal of thought to the situation before making his decision but that he "felt" that the area selected was the right place.]*

He had been tossed into a battle in which nearly all the major facts about the movement of forces were either unknown or obscure. He had rejected Corps' idea that the 101st Airborne Division be assembled to the southwest of Bastogne. It was a point that didn't give particular concern to General Middleton so long as General McAuliffe got his troops in where they were best placed to defend the town. However, VIII Corps Headquarters' reasoning was based on the long-range thought that after the enemy found he could not get through Bastogne, his next important move would be to the southwest. In his hasty reconnaissance out to the westward with Colonel Kinnard, his G-3, late in the day on the 18th, General McAuliffe had selected the ground for his camp from the short-range point of view. He wanted an assembly area which would place him at maximum advantage with respect to his own immediate deployments and the movements of the enemy in the immediate future. Though he had no way of knowing it at the time, his center of equilibrium was on the ground farthest removed from the early dangers of the encirclement although his two eastward-facing regiments were pointed directly toward the avenues along which the Germans would make their first approaches. The first day's results proved that the angels had been with him as he made his first decisions.

In the opening arrangements one decision was taken which worked out adversely. Lieutenant Colonel David Gold, the surgeon of the 101st Division, and Lieutenant Colonel Carl W. Kohls, the Division supply officer, had picked out a conveniently located crossroads to the westward of the Division assembly area and decided that this must be the rear, if there were such a thing. The Division hospital was set up on the crossroads. Near

*Wounded in the hospitals of Bastogne had to lie on the floors because of a lack of equipment.*

*A trailer is loaded with parachutes for use in the improvised hospitals in Bastogne.*

midnight of December 19 the 327th Glider Infantry was told to send a motorized patrol to crossroads X - the site of this evacuation center. The patrol was to investigate and clear up reports of machine-gun fire in that vicinity. They encountered no fire but the hospital was gone - Colonel Gold and all his officers and the men of the clearing company had been captured by the enemy. The 327th patrol decided that there must have been a fight, for dead Germans dressed in civilian clothes were found strewn over the ground, though there were no bodies of American soldiers. The bulk of the Division medical supplies had been captured or destroyed.

Division then called on VIII Corps for medical help, and all 101st Division units were notified that casualties would be evacuated to the aid station of the 501st Parachute Infantry in Bastogne itself. One platoon of the 429th Medical Collecting Company, then located at Jodenville (about one mile west of Sibret), was made available to the 101st. Until the night of

December 21 the platoon used its five ambulances and two weapons carriers to carry some of the wounded back to the 635th Medical Clearing Company. Then the Germans cut across the road and contact was lost with the clearing unit. An abandoned medical supply dump and the chance discovery of another depot in Bastogne containing blankets, litters, splint baskets and other hospital items helped the situation. Yet there continued to be a critical shortage of bed clothing, litters, penicillin, surgical instruments and surgeons.

The losses of the first day of battle had not, however, put any unusual stress on the medical facilities. But later in the fight when Bastogne became encircled, many of the wounded would have to lie on concrete floors with little or no cover. The blankets of the dead were collected so that there would be a chance for the living, and the shattered homes of Bastogne were searched for any kind of quilting.

Colonel W. L. Roberts, commanding Combat Command B, 10th Armored Division, had been at Château-Thierry in 1918 and he well remembered the things that happen during the rout of an army. In his first conversation with General Middleton in which the VIII Corps commander had outlined the missions that sent the three combat teams of Combat Command B to Wardin, Longvilly and Noville on the night of December 18, Colonel Roberts had foreseen one of the main problems.

General Middleton said to him, "The 28th Infantry Division and the 9th Armored are ahead of us. They are badly cut up. The situation is fluid."

Colonel Roberts replied, "Sir, there will be stragglers. I want authority to use these men."

Middleton agreed orally and later confirmed it with a written message: "Major General Middleton directs that you have authority to take over all or any part of Reserve Command, 9th Armored Division, in case they show the slightest inclination to retire. Anything you do to prevent falling back in that area will be given fullest backing."

Colonel Roberts set his net to catch those drifting back. His Headquarters Company was instructed to keep hot food ready all day at a central point in Bastogne. A detail stood by to get these men from other units into billets around the town square. MPs were stationed at the road crossings in the south of Bastogne with instructions to stop every soldier who was trying to get away from the battle and turn him back to the Combat Command B area. About 250 stragglers were thus reorganized in Bastogne on December 19. Some were men from the 9th Armored; most were from the 28th Division. In this way Team Snafu was born, and within the next week it came to include 600 men, led by casual officers; but this outfit was severely handicapped by the fact that they were short of equipment and transportation as long as the siege lasted. Team Snafu was mainly a reservoir for the defending force. The stragglers went into it, the regular units drew from it as they had need.

Any organized units heading south were also commandeered. At 1400 on December 19 the 73d Armored Field Artillery Battalion of Combat Command Reserve, 9th Armored, moved through Bastogne. Colonel Roberts watched it go by before suddenly realizing that it was his for the taking. He sent a staff officer to bring the battalion back and within a few minutes the battalion commander reported at his command post. Roberts told him to put the battalion in position with the 420th Armored Field Artillery Battalion. The commander returned to his battalion but found that there was insufficient fuel for his vehicles and could not make the return trip. The 58th Armored Field Artillery Battalion was stopped and put into position with the 420th, where its twelve guns fired during the next day. Just before the Germans closed the roads to the southward, this unit heard that it had been cut off from Bastogne so it moved to the west. The 771st Field Artillery Battalion - a Negro unit - was commandeered on December 21 and their 155mm. howitzers

102

gave body to the artillery throughout the siege. Colonel Roberts also found in Bastogne eight new undelivered tanks, complete with their Ordnance crews, and he inducted them forthwith into his organization.

Colonel Roberts had worried a lot about the security of the town itself for he had only part of his Engineer battalion and the Antiaircraft Artillery battalion as reserve. General McAuliffe wanted to keep his own reserve as mobile as possible and couldn't see assigning one of his battalions to garrison the town. A task force from Combat Command B, 9th Armored Division, entered Bastogne to learn the situation but was ordered by higher authority to withdraw to Leglise, six miles southeast of Neufchâteau. A request to 10th Armored for the use of the Reserve Command was turned down. So finally Colonel Roberts committed Team Snafu, under command of Captain Charles Brown of 110th Infantry, to the close-in defense of Bastogne. Team Snafu's complexion was somewhat changed on e following morning, December 20, when Brigadier General George A. Davis of the 28th Division arrived in Bastogne with a request that Combat Command B attack toward Wiltz. It couldn't be done, for by that hour all of Colonel Roberts' forces were fully committed. Not long after General Davis departed, Combat Command B was ordered by Corps to release all 28th Division stragglers to their own command. *[Colonel Roberts said he was very sorry to see these men go.]*

Throughout the first day of battle there had been losses and a few minor gains in the 101st Division's already strained supply situation. In the 907th Glider Field Artillery Battalion, Lieutenant Colonel Nelson, worried because his ammunition supply was rapidly reaching the vanishing point, dispatched searching convoys toward what he thought was the Division rear. They moved westward and had been gone about six hours before Colonel Nelson grew aware that he had actually sent his trucks into enemy ground and that they were cut off. A second convoy of five trucks and trailers was sent toward Neufchâteau under Staff Sergeant Vincent Morgan, a supply sergeant. Sergeant Morgan was told that if he could not get M3 ammunition (standard for the 105mm. M3, a gun especially adapted for glider use) he was to bring back some M2 ammunition which the manual said could be used in an emergency.

*[The substitute ammunition proved quite satisfactory. According to Nelson its close-up position enabled Baker Battery to make more effective use of the M2 ammunition. The observers had remained with the forward platoons and this was true of most of the Bastogne operation with the result that casualties among forward observers ran very high. Nelson lost four observers killed. Many of the missions therefore had to be adjusted by infantry observers and Nelson said that the results were generally excellent. Due to atmospheric conditions the greater part of the adjustments had to be made by sound. When observation permitted time fire was used with good results.]*

The fortitude with which this young noncom carried out his assignment was one of the finest things of the siege. He returned late that night through heavy shelling and small-arms fire about one hour before the Germans cut the road of his inbound journey. He bad first gone to Neufchâteau and on being disappointed there he had driven far to the northwestward, covering in all about 75 miles. On his trucks were 1,500 rounds of M2. It was the only resupply of ammunition received by the 101st Airborne Division before the air resupply came in.

*[Most of the supply points listed in VIII Corps' Administrative Orders Nos. 39 and 40 of December 18 and December 19 were either in enemy hands or had been moved to the rear by the hour the orders were received. VIII Corps radioed G-4 one time that there were 7,000 or more rounds of 75mm. howitzer ammunition in the abandoned ammunition supply point No. 128. G-4 asked where that depot was located but never received a reply. On December 20, Captain Salve H. Matheson, S-4 of the 506th*

*Parachute Infantry, drove to St. Hubert and to Bellauz in a fruitless search for small-arms ammunition. Major William C. Young, 101st Division Artillery S-4, reported that both the ammunition officer and the artillery officer of Corps said that the nearest ammunition supply point which had 105mm. M3 ammunition was Audun le Roman, which is in the south of Luxembourg. The 101st Division also received the slightly ironic information that a train loaded with ammunition of all the types desired by the 101st was being unloaded at Bertrix.]*

That partly compensated for a stroke of bad luck. The two convoys of the Division Quartermaster and Ordnance companies reached the Division rear area late at night and were told to remain at a crossroads in the woods (P448630). Lacking time in which to reconnoiter the area, the two companies left all trucks parked on highway N4 facing west. Shortly after midnight on December 20, Division headquarters was notified that the service area was receiving machine-gun fire, and a few minutes later came the message "Evidence indicates service troops have disappeared."

That alarm was enough; within five minutes a message was on its way to Corps headquarters asking for Quartermaster and Ordnance help.

After being flushed by the fire the two companies had headed west and then south. Most of the trucks got through to the Corps rear and on the next day Captain John L. Patterson of one of the units, the 801st Ordnance Maintenance Company, taking a different route, got into Bastogne with two trucks bringing 500 gallons of gasoline. He then turned south again to bring the rest of the convoy forward. But by that time the Germans had already closed the road.

Such was the shortage of gasoline in Bastogne through most of the siege that vehicles were fueled only just before they went out on a run so that there would be no loss of gasoline if any standing vehicle was hit.

# 10. THE REPULSE

IT WAS A NIGHT FOR DRIFTERS, the night of December 19-20. As the darkness grew, more men from the elements which had been shattered to the east of Bastogne came moving back through the regimental lines of the 101st. Few of them stayed. Colonel Ewell and his officers talked to these men. They could tell very little of what had happened to them. Many of them were inarticulate. Infantrymen from units of the 28th Division still trickled into the area in groups of three or four. They made no attempt to organize themselves and they did not for the most part wish to be organized by anyone else. Some of these straggling infantrymen would ask Ewell's men, "What are you doing?" Upon being told, "We are fighting Germans," they would look at the paratroopers as if they were stark mad.

But not all were like that. Some who seemed utterly wretched and spent when they came to within the lines, upon being handed a K ration, would eat it and look around and ask where they could get a rifle. They were ready to fight again. But to others food and companionship made no difference. They had been shocked so badly that they wanted only to keep on drifting. They were allowed to do so. This disorder had no ill effect on the combat force. The demoralization did not seem to bother the nerves of the men who were still fighting and they accepted it as the natural product of battle it often is.

*[However, the Historian talked to perhaps a dozen of Colonel Ewell's officers to gather their general impression of how the stragglers acted and how the combat force reacted and all statements were to the same point.]*

A battalion of Field Artillery, the 109th of the 28th Division, came through as a unit and attached itself to the 907th Glider

Field Artillery Battalion. Those groups from the 9th Armored Division which had been compelled to withdraw from the advanced ground along the Longvilly road were in good order and high spirits when they reached the lines around Bastogne. One platoon of armored infantry attached itself to Major Homan's battalion (2d Battalion, 501st Parachute Infantry) and helped them carry the fight during the next several days. Seven tanks arrived from the 9th Armored Division and constituted themselves a small task force operating in support of the

*A 75mm M1A1 howitzer being fired by paratroop artillery-men during the siege of Bastogne.*

battalion. At 0200 the 2d Platoon of Company B, 705th Tank Destroyer Battalion arrived with four tank destroyers and took position on the south edge of Bizory.

These reinforcements got there in the nick of time. At 0530, December 20, while the 501st Parachute Infantry was patrolling toward its front, the 2d Battalion got an attack over the same big hill to the east of Bizory where they bad been stopped by the German reconnaissance force the day before. At a range of 3,000 yards, the tank destroyer men saw six enemy tanks rolling toward them from the southeast. Sergeant Floyd A. Johnson led his section to the bill north of Bizory and put the two tank destroyers on either side of the road. First Lieutenant Frederic Mallon led the second section to the higher ground southeast of town and waited for the German tanks in an open field.

The firing opened at 0730, the tank destroyers withholding their fire from the enemy infantry so as not to compromise an engagement with the enemy armor, which by this time comprised one Mark IV, one Mark V and two 75mm. self-propelled guns. [This disagrees with Colonel Ewell's statement of force engaged but Ewell said he was uncertain of the facts.]

These were following the infantry line by 400 yards - it was a full battalion of infantry, the 2d of the 76th Regiment, 26th Volksgrenadier Division . In the first long-range exchange of fire, one tank destroyer was disabled and its loader killed by a direct hit on the turret; it limped away to the rear. The second tank destroyer in this section, after knocking out the Mark IV tanks, pulled back into Bizory where, in taking up another position, it damaged the tube of its gun by running against a building and became incapacitated. The other tank destroyer section opened fire at 600 yards on the Mark IV tank and one self-propelled gun, destroying both.

This was the crux of the engagement: most of the in-fighting of that morning of December 20 was done by the heavy guns. Major Homan's machine guns had opened up on the German

HOUFFALIZE 7½ MI.

Situation 20 Dec 1944

① RYERSON'S FORCE WITHDRAWS FROM MACERET
  0430. 501 HEAVILY ATTACKED DURING DAY & AT 1100.
② TEAM HUSTEAD & 506-I WITHDRAW FROM NOVILLE.
  506 REGT ENGAGED AT FOY.
③ ENEMY ATTACKS MARVIE AT 1125.
④ NEUFCHATEAU ROAD CUT BY ENEMY

Mabompre
Bertogne
MARCHE 18 MI.
SPRIMONT ½ MI.   ST. HUBERT 10 MI.
Vaux   TEAM H   2PGR   2PZ(-)
502   506   B   10
Noville   Bourcy
Longchamps
Champs   Foy
Flamierge   506   304   ST. VITH 21 MI.
501 TEAM C   28 RCN
Mande St Etienne   B   10
101   Longvilly
BASTOGNE   B   10   116 PZ
Senonchamps   Bizory   Mageret
Chenogne   Mont   TEAM D   Neffe
Marvie   B   10   901 PGR
Wardin
Magerotte   Villeroux
ST. HUBERT 10 MI   Sibret   902   WILTZ 7 MI.
Morhet   Assenois   Remoifosse
5   130 PZ LEHR (-)
Clochimont
NEUFCHATEAU 10 MI.   ARLON 20 MI.
1,000
SCALE IN YARDS

*Map 10*

infantry while the tanks were coming on and by so doing bad
kept them at a distance. Within a few minutes of this first body
check to the German battalion, all the artillery that General
McAuliffe could turn eastward from Bastogne blasted them.
Homan's infantry along the ridge was too far distant to do much
bullet damage to the advancing German formations but his men
had a clear view of the German ranks coming on slowly, of the
automatic fire making them hesitate, of the shells falling among
them, of the attack gradually spending itself and of the enemy
that was left then breaking away to the northward to escape the
fire.

Colonel Ewell's own infantry losses were almost nothing, but
two tank destroyers were out of action for the time being and the
defense had also lost two tanks. So ended the first, though not
the most ruinous, of the piecemeal efforts which on this day

presaged the failure of the German battle. This particular fighting had lasted about two hours, the artillery barrage perhaps twenty minutes. *[The 501st Parachute Infantry had no record of when action ended.]*

Prisoners-of-war letters captured from the 76th Regiment said that their losses had been terrible.

There followed a day-long wait along Colonel Ewell's 501st Parachute Infantry front. About 1900 the Germans put a heavy shelling from tanks and self-propelling guns on sensitive points over the ground held by the 501st-Bizory, Mont and the road junctions. The bombardment severed all the telephone wires connecting the battalions with the rear.

As the German artillery slacked off, the 1st Battalion of the 501st radioed to Ewell that the enemy was charging straight down the road from Neffe. Major Raymond V. Bottomly's 1st Battalion could hear the tanks coming on but it was so dark that they could tell little else. All the guns from the eleven artillery battalions in Bastogne dropped a dam of fire across the road one or two hundred yards west of Neffe - the heaviest and most effective American defensive fire during the siege. Three German tanks, two of them Panthers and one a Tiger Royal, were hit and destroyed just as they drew past the last houses in the village. Some German infantry, which had moved down the Bastogne road before the barrage dropped, met their fate from machine guns Company B had posted in a house by the side of the road. That company took the shock without having to yield one yard of ground. Their strongpoint controlled the terrain so well that not one German drew near enough to close on the infantry line. They were killed to the last man, and for weeks later, their grotesque forms along the roadside, heaped over by the Ardennes snows, showed where the German death march ended. The most forward of these bodies was 300 yards ahead of the shattered tanks.

The German thrust from Neffe coincided with an assault on

the 3d Battalion's position at Mont, though here the battle took a quite different form because of Major Templeton's tank destroyers. *[Ewell was convinced that the presence of the tank destroyers made this change.]*

The 1st Platoon of Company B, 705th Tank Destroyer Battalion, under command of First Lieutenant Robert Andrews, had arrived to reinforce Colonel Griswold's 3d Battalion position on the evening of December 19. One tank destroyer was posted at the bend in the road. From here it could cover both the dirt road winding across the valley from Neffe and a draw leading off to the southward. A second tank destroyer took position by the last house, which put it somewhat behind, but in line with, the tank destroyer blocking the Neffe road. The other section was placed on the north side of Mont to check any tank advance from directly across the valley. The tank destroyers held these positions until the hour came when they were most needed, on the night of December 20.

Between 1900 and 1930 on that night the enemy struck through the fields lying between Neffe and Mont, advancing against Colonel Griswold's left. But the presence of the tank destroyers had intimidated the German armor. It took refuge in the little wood lying just west of the Neffe château and from the grove it shelled Mont. The German infantry advanced under this fire. Enemy self-propelled guns moved along the railway line from Neffe a short distance (the rails here ran through a cut) and went to work on the same target. These two lines of fire converged on Griswold's positions at almost a right angle; the men in the forward line had to give ground, falling back on the village. The most forward of the tank destroyers, commanded by Sergeant George N. Schmidt, became their rallying point. Schmidt unloaded most of his crew and told them to join the fight with small arms. He then joined the infantry machine gunners who were already searching the down slopes with every automatic gun the Battalion could bring to bear; in the next few

On the night of December 20, the enemy struck at the left flank of the 3d Battalion, 501st Parachute Infantry. This scene from the outskirts of Neffe shows the enemy preparing for the attack. The American position is on the crest of the hill to the left. The little village of Mont is in the center draw, and the barbed-wire fences, so costly to the enemy, are to the right of the pine grove.

minutes be threw 2,000 rounds of caliber .50 at the enemy. Lieutenant Andrews used a radio-equipped jeep as his command post and central control station, and used his security section as ammunition carriers to feed the stuff up to whichever tank destroyer was calling for it most urgently. The other three tank destroyers, under Sergeant Darrell J. Lindley, were shooting at the railway line. They tried at first to spot the self-propelled guns by firing at muzzle blasts; when that failed, they put flares up over the valley.

The fighting died about 2300. By that time, the three self-propelled guns were out, and lines of German dead littered the hillside. Because of the dark the defenders of Mont had no clear idea of why their automatic fire had made such a clean reaping of the German attack or of where the attack had broken. But in the light of the next morning, December 21, they could see what had happened. The hillside between Neffe and Mont is crossed in both directions by barbed-wire fences spaced between thirty and fifty yards apart, with five or six strands in each fence. In ordinary times they were used, apparently, as feeder pens for cattle. With the tank fire behind them the Germans tried to come right through this fenced area without first destroying the fences in any way or equipping infantry to cut them. On coming to the fences they tried to climb through but the spaces were small and their individual equipment was bulky. Griswold's men bad perfectly clear fields of fire and so did the tank destroyer supporting them. The fences were as effective as any entanglement. The evenly spaced lines of dead told the story. They had charged right into a giant mantrap.

Colonel Ewell had the impression that night that the 901st Panzer Regiment had about expended itself and that it could no longer muster enough men to be an effective offensive force. They bad been somewhat roughly handled before they got to Neffe and his own men furthered the good work.

So on December 19 the Germans, having gained contact with

the 501st Parachute Infantry on a wide front, at first drew back to defensive positions. On December 20 the enemy made three attacks and the infantry, armor and tank destroyers in Colonel Ewell's sector beat them all down. One of these fights was tactically less spectacular but strategically more useful than the others.

During the period of the fighting at Noville and Neffe there had been an action between the flanks of the 501st and 506th Parachute Infantry regiments which, although just a minor affair in itself, was to have an important effect on the general situation. When the two regiments moved out to their positions on December 19, one going east and the other going north, they could not initially form a common front. In theory they were joined somewhere along the railroad track below Lahez (11 miles south of Foy) but in fact there was a considerable gap between their closest elements. Each became so closely engaged in its local situation that the matter of contact was neglected. Colonel Sink was alarmed about the peril to his right flank from the beginning, but it was not until late on the night of December 19 that Colonel Ewell fully shared his apprehension.

Company A of the 501st was in reserve in a small wood just north of the quarry on the Neffe road, which made it the most rearward element in the 501st's general position. Several hundred yards to its rear were the guns of the 907th Glider Field Artillery Battalion's forward battery.

At 2300, December 19, a German patrol of thirty men came in between the company and the battery, moving from out of the northeast. A man on outpost duty for Company A saw the patrol and alerted the company. The patrol was permitted to come on. As it drew near the wood where the company had bivouacked, both the artillery and the infantry opened fire. The enemy dispersed into a nearby wood, though one member of the patrol was taken prisoner. Upon being interrogated he said that the patrol had come forward through the gap between the two infantry regiments and that its mission had been to get in behind and cut the Bastogne road. The incident gave the artillery grave fears about the security of their base and it also called Colonel Ewell's attention to the most vulnerable sector of his front.

Sometime on the morning of December 20, after the Germans had attacked at Bizory and then sideslipped northward, Company A of the 501st was attached to the 2d Battalion with the mission of occupying the woods south of the railroad and making contact with the 506th Parachute Infantry. However, it did not proceed immediately on this assignment and during most of that day the effort to join with the 506th was limited to patrol actions out of Company D, 501st, which was in reserve in the 2d Battalion. Four times during the day patrols from Company D tried to move north along the general line of the road running to Foy. But they were always turned back from the vicinity of Halt, where the enemy bad taken up fire positions.

At the same time Company D, 506th Parachute Infantry, was pushing rightward toward the railroad station at Halt against stubborn resistance. When evening of the 20th came the company had reached the Foy-Bizory road. It stayed there with its right flank some hundreds of yards distant from the railroad station at Halt, which was held by an enemy force. There had been no contact with the 501st. Colonel Sink, commander of the 506th, called both Headquarters, 501st Parachute Infantry, and Headquarters, 101st Division, and urged that the 501st swing leftward to meet him. He said that his force was standing on the railroad line which was supposed to be the regimental boundary - but this overstated the case.

The first three patrols which had gone out from Company D of the 501st to search for the 506th's flank had been turned back by fire from the Bois Jacques. They got no idea of the enemy strength in the forest area for they were beaten back by a scattering small-arms fire at long range whenever they moved to right of the Foy-Bizory road in an attempt to gain the railroad.

Corporal Frank Lasik of Company D, 501st, led out his fourth patrol of the day just as the evening twilight of the 20th came on. There were eight men with him, and instead of beating over the same ground as the earlier patrols they swung around to the westward of the Bizory-Foy road. When within a short distance of the railroad Lasik dropped six of his men and continued on with two others. They reached the rail line and moved east along it to within a hundred yards of the Halt station. At that point they saw a force of seven German tanks supported by a body of infantry moving straight toward them down the railroad track, and only 75 yards away. Private Manzi fired one shot toward the enemy force and then the three men withdrew as rapidly as they could. Lasik knew that Company A had been given an assignment and was supposed to be moving toward the same ground which the Germans were approaching. He rushed to the Battalion command post and told them to get word to Company A, 501st, that tanks were coming down the railway track.

Company A had moved out about 1600 on December 20 and was already engaged in clearing the woods that lay south of the railroad and west of the Foy-Bizory road. They found no enemy in the first wood and so they continued on to the next plantation lying south of the tracks and between them and the station at Halt. In the middle of this journey they met a patrol from the 506th Parachute Infantry. Until that meeting they had believed that the 506th was already on the railroad track. But from the patrol they learned that the actual flank of the 506th was about 600 yards north of the railroad track and that Company D, 506th, had been having a running fight with small groups of the enemy for control of the station at Halt.

From the second woods, Sergeant Lyle B. Chamberlain of Company A, 501st, was sent with a four-man patrol eastward along the tracks to search for the enemy. This was at just about the time that Lasik was getting back to warn the battalion. Sergeant Chamberlain's patrol moved through the swampy ground that lay to the left of the tracks and had gone but a short distance when they sighted a German patrol coming toward them. It looked to Chamberlain like the point of a company. Darkness was already closing around them and the German group did not see Sergeant Chamberlain's patrol. The patrol fell back on the company and reported what they had seen. Hastily, the 3d Platoon of Company A was deployed along the edge of the woods north of the railroad track to lay an ambush, for the enemy group which Sergeant Chamberlain had sighted was all northward of the track. While the platoon was deploying thick fog closed in around the woods and this coupled with the darkness reduced visibility to almost nothing. The Germans were allowed to approach within 10 to 15 yards before Company A opened fire. The surprise volley wholly disorganized the leading German platoon and the men who were not cut down ran to the rear to the swampy ground.

The whole Company A front had by this time become engaged. The enemy bad been advancing with two companies abreast astride the railway track. On Company A's right, the 1st and 2d Platoons did not get the same chance to close with the enemy at short range, and after the dispersion of the German right, mortar, grenade and automatic fire from the German force south of the tracks beat heavily against the two platoons. Because of the darkness and the fog the men of the company could get no idea what losses they were taking themselves and could only judge the progress of the action by the build-up of the enemy fire. They saw little or nothing of the Germans they were engaging. The skirmish went on with both forces firing toward the flashes and sounds in the position of the opposite force. Company A lost fifteen men in the night engagements, three of whom were killed in action. But in the black darkness the men of the Company thought at the time that they were taking much heavier losses. The fog made more vivid their impressions of the opposing fire while keeping them from feeling their own strength. The murk was so thick by this time that it was only by the sounds of fire that a man could tell where his nearest comrade was fighting.

While the fire fight on the south of the tracks continued, the Germans who had fallen back toward the swampy ground on the north of the track gradually collected themselves again. For half an hour or more there was a lull in the action on this side except that both forces tried to carry on at long range with hand grenades. Then the 3d Platoon of Company A heard the enemy moving out through the woods around their left flank.

Apprehensive that they would be outflanked if they maintained themselves in the forward ground, the 3d Platoon pulled back its own left flank to the westward so as to cover the rear of the company position. This change in the form of the enemy attack was also indicated on the right flank. Private First Class William C. Michel, a German-speaking soldier who was with the company executive officer, Lieutenant Joseph B. Schweiker, could hear the enemy shouting commands and telling his men to move out around the left and right of the American force. The order may have been a ruse intended to cover a withdrawal, but as the fire fight began to build up again it seemed to Lieutenant Schweiker that the enemy was actively pushing out around the flanks of Company A and threatening his rear.

At about 2230, December 20, Lieutenant Schweiker ordered the company to fall back to the line of the second woods. Lieutenant James C. Murphy called all of the squad leaders together and told them that the signal for withdrawal would be a long burst of machine-gun fire and that all of the other machine guns were to be kept quiet until this signal came. The withdrawal was made in reasonably good order, the circumstances considered.

When Company A took up its position in the second wood it was deployed to right of the railway line. The company was not pressed there at any time during the night. Apparently the Germans had ordered a withdrawal at about the same time. After staying in the woods for somewhat more than an hour the company withdrew a little to the southward and bivouacked in a third plantation.

The advance of the enemy down the railroad track had put them on the rear of Company D, 506th Parachute Infantry, but it was not until 0400 that Company D, which was somewhat engaged by small groups hitting directly at its front, discovered that its flank had been turned. Lieutenant Colonel Strayer reported to Colonel Sink that he believed an enemy force of about two platoons had penetrated between his battalion of the 506th and the 501st. But he did not know that Company D, 501st, was meeting this force frontally. Colonel Sink ordered Company D, 506th, to face some of its men toward the rear and bold their present ground. This, they did. The 1st Battalion, 506th, then in reserve at Luzery, was ordered to send Companies A and C forward to help contain the penetrating force. Both of these companies were badly depleted from their fight in Noville.

When morning of December 21 came the situation was about as follows: Company A, 501st, which had not been further disturbed during its bivouac, moved back up without opposition to exactly the same positions it bad occupied during the night engagement. Company D, 501st, which had bivouacked just to the south of Company A's bivouac area under the mistaken impression that it bad moved into the woods lying south of the railroad tracks, discovered its error when the light came. It immediately moved farther north, with one platoon going directly toward the objective woods and the others detouring east to clean out another small wood which they thought might contain enemy forces.

Through the accident of these shifts, the 501st Parachute Infantry thus had forces advancing from west, southwest and south as if to bring about a general envelopment of the German force at the Halt station. Coinciding with these movements from the south and west the two reserve companies (A and C) of the 506th reached the area to the northward at about 0815 and were committed in companies abreast to beat through the forests lying south and west of Company D's position. The morning of the 21st was heavy with fog; none of these approaching forces moving in on them from northeast, north, west, southwest and south was visible to the Germans dug in around the Halt station and in some of the plantations to westward of it. They were so completely misled as to their own position that when the platoons that had marched east for Company D, 501st, started their sweep north toward the Halt station, several of the enemy glimpsed them through the fog and came walking up to meet them, thinking they were friendly troops.

The line of the 506th came slowly but methodically on toward the railway tracks. Some of the Germans stayed to fight. Others gave up. Still others, in trying to get away were forced back into the killing ground established by the semicircular advance of the different forces of the 501st. By about 1100, December 2 1, the envelopment was complete and Companies A and C of the 506th had made full contact with units of the 501st along the railway line. The two companies were then ordered to return to Luzery, leaving Company D to solidify the front.

But in moving south and westward through the forest Companies A and C, 506th, discovered that the job was by no means completed. The morning advance had forced many of the enemy into the woods to the westward beyond the lines of Company A, 501st Parachute Infantry. The rat hunting continued throughout the day and it was almost dark before the 506th was convinced that the mop-up operation was complete. By that time it was realized that the original estimate of two platoons of enemy - these were troops of the 77th Volksgrenadier Regiment of the 26th Volksgrenadier Division - had far undershot the mark. The German force was more nearly the size of a battalion. About

100 of the enemy were captured and 55 killed by the units of the 506th Parachute Infantry in an operation that cost them only five or six casualties. About 80 Germans were driven into 501st's sector, where they were either killed or captured. Later, when the whole battle could be reviewed clearly, the senior commanders of 101st reckoned that the enemy missed his finest opportunity on this ground and during these hours. A strongly weighted attack straight down the railroad track could have carried through to Bastogne and turned the flanks of 501st and 506th Regiments.

*[Because of the fog, this action was especially "confused" and neither regiment had any clear idea of what had happened or how the killing ground had been established. To clarify the story, Colonel Marshall held a series of company and patrol after-battle interviews. The story was put together with the aid mainly of the enlisted participants. This episode and the action at the Longvilly block were at first regarded as minor incidents in the general battle. As additional facts came to light - particularly the enemy story - their pivotal nature was revealed. General Higgins was of the opinion that had both regiments seen and exploited this opportunity more promptly and strongly, it would have produced one of the sharpest defeats to the enemy during the Bastogne battle. (Interview with Marshall February 5, 1946.)]*

With the end of this engagement on December 21, re sectors of both the 501st and 506th became relatively quiet until after January 1. But there were other important consequences. Firm contact had been established between the two regiments, and it was never broken or weakened after that time the Germans were served notice that the road to Bastogne from the east and north was not open.

Out of these things also developed a new feeling of confidence among the artillery in the Bastogne area. They were now fully covered on the north and east by a reasonably strong shield and they could more easily direct their attention to the other parts of the defensive circle, wherever the danger mounted.

From December 21 on, the Germans gave over their attack against the 501st Parachute Infantry's part of the Bastogne front. The road to Bastogne did not lie through Colonel Ewell and his 501st.

# 11. RUNNING BATTLE

IN NOVILLE THEY were running short of armor-piercing shell as the morning of December 20 dawned. In Bastogne, General McAuliffe was wondering whether Noville was worth what he might have to pay to hold it, and was about to reach a decision. Deprived of any support from the commanding ridges, Noville is not a military position but just another village on low ground, and a perfect sinkhole for fog. The issue was already hanging in the balance because of the ammunition situation and the miscarriage of the American attack on December 19; only a little more pressure would tip it.

*[The Historian had several discussions with Colonels Sink, Ewell, Kinnard and others concerning the nature of the Noville position at the time when the 101st Division attacked toward it in early January, and this was the estimate which all concerned placed upon it.]*

On left flank of the 506th Parachute Infantry, the 502d had passed a quiet night. In midafternoon of December 19 the 502d had moved to Longchamps and established a perimeter defense there. Its 3d Battalion deployed on a high hill to south of the village. Its 1st Battalion was in the Bois de Niblamont which was southward of the hill. Initially, the 1st Battalion had held half of the front, but at 2400 of the 19th General McAuliffe told Lieutenant Colonel Steve Chappuis, commander of the 502d Parachute Infantry, that inasmuch as his regiment was the Division reserve he could leave one battalion on the northward-facing line. The 2d Battalion drew the assignment. It made no difference in any case, for though the battalion was stretched seven thousand yards, there was no action anywhere along its front that night.

But to the eastward where 506th stood guard, the boys who had prayed for morning soon wondered why. At 0730 two enemy tanks came hell-roaring through the field along the Houffalize road, swung in beside the first building of Noville, wheeled so as to protect each other and then stopped. On their way in they had knocked out a jeep with one shell, and had sprayed forward with their machine guns as they rushed. Unseeing, they came to a halt within ten yards of a bazooka team and the first rocket fired set one of the tanks on fire. Staff Sergeant Michael Lesniak, a tank commander, had heard the German armor roaring along. He dismounted from his tank, walked up the main street for a look, then went back and swung his gun in the right direction and moved to the center of the street. He fired before the enemy realized that he had gone into action and his first round finished the German tank. A third German tank that stayed just north along the road but out of sight in the fog threw a few loose shells into the town and one of them hit Sergeant Lesniak's tank, damaging the turret.

That was the beginning. Almost nothing that followed could be seen as clearly. During the next two hours the defensive perimeter was under constant attack from the German armor and infantry. But the enemy pressure developed quite unevenly as if their forces, too, were groping or were keeping active simply to conceal some larger design. It was battle with the bewildering shifts of a montage; there were momentary exposures and quick shiftings of scene. The enemy came on in groups of a few tanks supported by small parties of infantry and were held off by the armored infantry and paratroopers with their own weapons just long enough to let a friendly tank or tank destroyer get into firing position. Fog mixed with smoke from the burning buildings again mantled the country between the village and the ridges, diffusing the efforts of both forces. It was all but impossible for anyone to get any impression of how the tide was moving; the combatants could tell only what went on right before their eyes.

Curiously enough the tank destroyer men of 2d Platoon, Company C, 705th TD Battalion, who had taken position in the south of Noville, had the impression that in these early morning hours the infantry was standing off a full-fledged attack. They could see only a hundred yards beyond their own guns and they could hear large numbers of enemy tracked vehicles moving toward them through the fog. Their imaginings were further stimulated by a direct hit on one tank destroyer at the outset which killed the gunner, Corporal Stephen Cook, and wounded several of the crew. For two hours they fired in the general direction of where they thought the German armor was massing; they could see no targets but they thought their unobserved fire might have some deterring effect. At 1000, December 20, the fog quite suddenly lifted and the sky became almost clear. In the field within view of the tank destroyer force were 15 German tanks; they were proceeding toward their own lines at about 1,000 yards range. Four of the tanks were hit and disabled and the tank destroyer men were confident that their own shells did it. They had seen their shots hit home and watched Private Steve E. Reed empty seven boxes of caliber .50 ammunition into the German crews as they tried to flee across the fields.

Just before the fog had cleared a Tiger tank had charged right into the heart of Noville. Visibility among the buildings was just about zero. The tank stopped in front of the command post of Company B, 20th Armored Infantry Battalion. The tanker swung his gun uncertainly toward the door. Captain Omar Billett said a quick prayer. A joker beside him remarked, "Don't look now, but there is an 88 pointing at you."

*[Harwick witnessed this incident and gave this detail during his informal interview with Colonel Marshall which was not committed to writing.]*

Sergeant Lesniak's tank was within twenty yards but the German had failed to see him in the fog; by rotating his damaged turret just a short space to the right Lesniak had his gun dead on the Tiger. At twenty yards he fired three rounds of 75mm. at the German tank without doing any apparent damage. The German quickly put his tank into reverse. But the left track ran up and over a jeep. The jeep was completely crushed but at the same time it fouled the track and beached the tank. The German kept on pushing back-the jeep under him. He next collided with a half-track and the tank tipped dangerously over on its right side.

*[Confirmed by Harwick's description to Marshall though Harwick also thought that a tank destroyer came from the other direction and fired on the German tanks. In this he appears to have been mistaken.]*

That was enough for the German crew. They jumped from the tank and ran out of the town, going through the American lines without getting a shot fired at them, such was the thickness of the fog.

The radio inside the Tiger was on a busy channel, and talk flowed on inside the dead tank. It looked like a wide-open opportunity, but before the command post could round up anyone who could understand German, the channel went out. The tankers destroyed this Tiger with thermite and later on they caught hell from Colonel Roberts for not bringing the tank back to Bastogne.

*[Colonel Roberts told Westover about this but Westover did not make note of it at the time.]*

But they had a good excuse. The losses among the tank drivers were already such that they did not have enough men to maneuver their own armor. Two tanks were without drivers and partly without crews. So the tankers asked the paratroopers if there were any men among them who could handle tanks and two of Major Harwick's men of the 1st Battalion, 506th Parachute Infantry, climbed aboard and started out with the Shermans. Later on both men were killed in their tanks during the withdrawal.

*[Harwick reported this to Colonel Marshall and at the same*

*time he was telling Colonel Sink about it and was expressing his regrets that he had lost some good men. He even named the men. However, the tankers did not report to Westover that they used any paratroopers at this time, and therefore the facts are not confirmed by the armored units. It is notable all the way through these reports that both forces minimize the help received from the other group. Often that is not an oversight on their part; they simply lacked the information.]*

They knew now that they would not be able to hold Noville much longer. The clearing of the fog revealed to Major Hustead (now commanding the 20th Armored Infantry Battalion) and his staff a situation they had already suspected. During the night of the 19th the men on the outposts had heard enemy armor moving across their rear, particularly to the southwestward.

*[Members of the armored units reported these impressions to Westover but he did not write them down in his report.]*

In the morning, patrols had gone out, and although they couldn't tell much because of the enveloping fog, they found enough to confirm the fact that enemy forces were between them and Bastogne. Hustead had lost radio contact with Combat Command B Headquarters during the night. So in the morning he sent First Lieutenant Herman C. Jacobs to Foy; he was to get to Headquarters, 3d Battalion, 506th Parachute Infantry, in Foy and use their radio to inform Combat Command B of the situation and request that the Noville garrison either be withdrawn or reinforced. He carried out the mission in a half-track and several times on the way to Foy he blundered into enemy parties and had to shoot his way through. But at Foy he found no one; by this time 3d Battalion was engaging the enemy to the south of the village. Lieutenant Jacobs continued on to Bastogne and found Colonel Roberts who sent his only available reserve - an antiaircraft platoon - forward. But the platoon was blocked by enemy forces before it could get to Foy. The Germans were coming across the road from both sides. When the fog rolled away the men in Noville could look southward and see the circling armor. To make their isolation more complete, they bad lost all contact with the main body of 506th Parachute Infantry and they did not know whether the situation at Foy was developing for or against them.

The Germans had already made their onfall against Colonel Sink's support position. In early morning, December 20, the 3d Battalion of the 506th received light shelling and flat-trajectory fire along its lines at Foy. During the night and through the first hours of daylight the enemy had taken advantage of the heavy fog and moved in very close to the American outposts, though it seems probable that they knew very little about the location of the American lines and were only groping.

At 0800, December 20, a force of about two companies of infantry supported by three tanks attacked toward the ground defended by Companies I and H. By 0900, they had driven in far enough to put direct fire on the American positions with their supporting weapons. The tank destroyers of 3d Platoon, Reconnaissance Company of the 705th Tank Destroyer Battalion were not in position to give the infantry any direct fire support during the engagement. They were in the woods south of Foy when the attack came on, and in the later stages of the action they were established as roadblocks, but during that morning they did not fire on any enemy armor. Company G in Recogne was engaged by another company of German infantry supported by three tanks. The command post of the 3d Battalion in Foy came under direct fire from an enemy tank. Until 1030 the Battalion held its ground in Foy and then withdrew to the high ground south of the village. Here it reformed for the counterattack.

It was about mid-morning when 101st Airborne Division Headquarters called the 502d Parachute Infantry and directed that its 3d Battalion (under Lieutenant Colonel John P. Stopka) attack through Recogne and gain contact with the American

Map 11

force at Noville, thus reestablishing the left flank. The battalion crossed the line of departure at 1130 and then pushed right on, meeting little opposition.

But when the 3d Battalion, 502d, reached Recogne a change in the order came. At somewhere around noon General McAuliffe had decided that Noville wasn't important enough to warrant a last-ditch stand on the inferior ground around the village. Colonel Stopka was accordingly instructed to make a limited attack forward to cover the extrication of Major Harwick's men of the 3d Battalion, 506th. That battalion was to fight the same kind of action on the other flank. It was figured that the Noville force could sideslip into the area of the 502d once Stopka's battalion got up to it. However, his Battalion had fought its way only a short distance past Recogne when the plan was again changed.

Colonel Sink, commanding the 506th, had looked the situation over and decided that the best way out was for Major Harwick's force to retire down the Bastogne road. Colonel Stopka's battalion remained in position on a line running through Recogne with its left flank extended westward to join the 2d Battalion of the 502d. Its advance had been made wholly without artillery support because of the dense fog.

Radio communication between Bastogne and Noville was not reestablished until 1300. The order then came through on the artillery radio net to Harwick and Hustead that their command would withdraw to the Bastogne perimeter of defense. They were told that an attack on Foy was being made immediately to relieve the pressure on Noville. When they saw that the attention of the enemy was diverted to the Foy attack, they were to make a break for the south.

A few local problems had to be solved in Noville preceding the withdrawal. A considerable amount of ammunition had to be destroyed. There were more than fifty wounded men awaiting evacuation. But the shrinkage of manpower in the Noville force through battlefield deaths and casualties already evacuated had totalled so many men that, despite a steady loss in vehicles, there were enough tanks, half-tracks and trucks left to move back all the casualties and permit all the armored units and most of the paratroopers to ride out of Noville.

Company C of the 506th was already south of Noville in a

reserve position, and accordingly, it was nominated as the advance guard to move out on foot. Three tanks would support Company C. The half-tracks and jeeps loaded with the wounded would come next in the column. Then would follow the main body, the personnel carriers and armor. Those of the infantry who couldn't find a ride would move out in file on both sides of the road. Company B of the 506th was to be the rear guard, supported by four tank destroyers. One platoon from that company was detailed to destroy everything useful that could not be evacuated.

At 1315, December 20, Company C took off. At 1325 the first vehicles quit Noville.33 Major Hustead and his engineer officer had prepared the ammunition dump for demolition; the dump was alongside a building and they were hopeful that the blast would lay the building low and block the highway. Hustead waited until the last vehicle had passed the ammunition point. He then gave the engineer the signal to set off the delayed charge. They heard the explosion as they moved on down the road.

The start was good. Until 1300 the air had been crystal clear for most of the noon hour. Then, as if Providence again chose to intervene in their favor, the fog closed around them and screened their departure from the enemy. They knew that they could be, heard and they wondered whether the Germans would try to take them in flank while they were on the move. But the fire which might have been turned against the road was spared them and they moved along quite easily, except for an occasional flurry of bullets.

A little protecting belt of armor - one armored M8, followed by four half-tracks, and five medium tanks - moved in front of the vehicles containing the wounded. Just beyond the village, one of the tanks broke down and bad to be destroyed with thermite. The armored car took off at full speed without waiting for the others, and got to Bastogne without receiving any fire.

The column continued on toward Foy and the half-tracks had come abreast of a farmhouse within 500 yards of the village when occurred one of those chance things which may change the whole course of a battle despite their own intrinsic unimportance.

In the leading half-track the shutter dropped and the driver could not see. The driver raised up and moved his arm to adjust the shutter and Major James B. Duncan mistook the gesture and thought that the man bad been wounded and was holding his eyes. So Duncan quickly pulled the hand brake. That stopped the entire column. The first half-track was rammed from behind by the second half-track which had lost its brakes. The third half-track pulled up close. At that moment bullets and grenades bit into the column from both sides of the road. The men could not see clearly what they were fighting but they knew that some Germans were deployed in the ditches and that they were also drawing fire from the house. Major Duncan figured that he had to fight it out on that ground. The machine gunners in the half-tracks put heavy fire on the ditches; and the dismounted riflemen, after flattening themselves, blazed away with their tommy guns. In ten minutes the skirmish was over. Some of the enemy had been cut down. Others had dispersed into the fog.

*[The S57 report of this whole episode is vague and confused. It is to be noted that both the infantry and the tank destroyer units reported that there was a German roadblock at Foy and that this was what checked the column. These forces were not up front and were not in position to see. The assumption was a natural one in view of the circumstances.]*

The fourth half-track had withdrawn a short distance to keep from jamming the column. Major Duncan had gone back that way. The amount of firing that he could hear from forward among the half-tracks, mingled with the noise of the firing of the 3d Battalion, 506th, which was attacking north toward Foy, gave Duncan an exaggerated idea of the importance of the action. He asked for the tanks to get forward and fire on the house.

Meanwhile the three half-tracks had shoved on. Back through the column all men had dismounted and taken to the ditches. Major Hustead came for-ward to see what was blocking the road and he met Major Duncan near the head of the column. Both officers then tried to get the tanks moving again. The crew of the first tank told Major Hustead they had no ammunition. The second tank couldn't fire either; there was no ammunition for the big gun and the machine gun was jammed. Duncan prodded two of the tanks into carrying out the order and they shelled the house until it caught fire. Thereupon, they backed away. Duncan was still worrying because be could bear small-arms fire, so he ordered them to go in. As they moved away they were caught broadside by fire from three German tanks which had slipped through the fog from the eastward. The first American tank caught fire. In the second American tank the driver was hit and the tank came to a halt.

Because of the murk, men who were only a few yards back in the column could get no true idea of what was happening. Captain William G. Schultz, the tank commander, was in the fifth tank. He walked up to the third tank, which was short of personnel, and drove it on down the road past the two disabled tanks. They were beyond his help and he thought that if he kept moving the rest of the column would follow.

But in this he was mistaken. He drove through Foy alone and about a quarter-mile beyond the village his tank was hit by a shell from an enemy tank and disabled, but Captain Schultz and his men got out alive and walked on into Bastogne. Meanwhile, Major Hustead and Captain Billett were striving to get the column moving. A tank destroyer of the 705th TD Battalion whipped up from the rear of the column to try to get a line on the yet unseen German tanks. A Sherman tank from the forward group backed straight toward the tank destroyer and the tank destroyer, reversing direction to save itself, backed over and crushed a jeep.

*[Duncan was not in the jeep at the time and no one was injured.]*

Then the Sherman moved on up to have another go at the house and it was hit by a shell from a German tank and exploded in flames. The turret blew off into the road and blocked the passage. The driver of the fifth tank, who had been with Schultz, had moved up and taken over the second tank just before it was demolished. This left the fifth tank driverless. As the road was now blocked by the turret, Hustead and Billett moved back and forth among the tankers looking for a driver so they could start the column moving across the field to Foy. There was not a single response. Every tanker replied that he was qualified for some other kind of work but couldn't move a tank. The paratroopers and the armored infantry jumped to the conclusion that the men were dogging it. They walked among the tankers cursing them and calling them "yellow bastards"; they threatened *[sic]* to beat up one man whom they suspected of being a driver. But they were all wrong about it. Most of these men were new replacements. Some were cooks, some were mechanics and some were riflemen. They were tankers only in that they belonged to a tank organization. The impasse at Foy could only be charged to the replacement system.

The paratroopers farther back along the road had picked themselves up and moved out through the fields on both sides. The group on the right swept all the way to Foy, met no organized resistance but bagged a few Germans whom they found wandering around in the fog. The tank destroyer force at the rear also became restive and at 1430 First Lieutenant Tom E. Toms led his vehicles down a little stream line on the right of the road and by way of this defilade entered Foy from the west. He had gotten there in ten minutes. The paratroopers who had swung out to the right reached the village at the same time. The tank destroyers were not quite through for the day.

The foot troops who had swung out to the east of the road were stopped by the line of fire which the unseen German tanks were throwing at the Shermans at the front of the column. They sent word back to the main body. However, the danger was removed by help from an unexpected quarter. Private First Class Thomas E. Gallagher was driving one of the tank destroyers which had gone into Foy and was on his way to an assembly area in a woods south of the village when be was stopped by an officer of the 3d Battalion, 506th Parachute Infantry. He knew the location of the German tanks and told Gallagher to go after them. Gallagher said he had no crew and no one to work the gun. Two paratroopers climbed into the tank destroyer and took over the gun. Gallagher then moved forward and with the infantrymen doing the firing the tank destroyer engaged one tank at 200 yards range and destroyed it. The other German tank escaped over the hill.

Because of the fog Major Hustead and Captain Billett hadn't seen the infantry parties move out to right and left. Billett felt that he ought to clear a route for the tanks and vehicles to advance and he sent back for his outfit, Company B of the 20th Armored Infantry Battalion. One platoon stayed back in the column with the vehicles and he started out with the other two platoons moving through the fields to the right. Major Hustead had the same idea but didn't know that it had already been put into execution twice on this same flank. He gathered about 20 paratroopers together and made an additional hook to the right. The odd part of it was that although this party groped its way forward over the same ground as the others, they did so in time to reap part of the harvest. The enemy groups around Foy were now feeling the heat from both directions. Hustead's sweep toward Foy resulted in the capture of 43 Germans.

In the village Hustead met troops of the 3d Battalion, 506th, who had advanced from the south and he asked them, "Has our armor come through?"

The men had seen the three half-tracks and Captain Schultz's tank go by and they thought this was the armor Major Hustead was talking about. So they reassured him. Hustead borrowed a jeep and drove to Bastogne to report to Colonel Roberts that he had completed his mission. But when he got to town be learned that he was mistaken and could only tell Colonel Roberts that the column was on its way and should soon arrive.

Major Hustead in Bastogne and Captain Billett in Foy were both on the radio urging the column to come around to the right. But Major Duncan and Second Lieutenant Burleigh P. Oxford were already jockeying the column through the fields. The fifth tank was on its way. A crew of paratroopers had climbed aboard after telling the tankers, "We'll learn bow to run the son of a bitch." When the column drew into Foy some of the vehicles got stuck in the soft ground. Lieutenant Oxford dismounted all of the men and got the winches and the manpower working first of all on extricating the vehicles that contained the wounded. At dusk of December 20 the column was finding its way through Foy and past the lines of the 3d Battalion, 506th. The command in Bastogne had intended that the force would go into a defensive position on the high ground south of Foy. But Hustead told Colonel Roberts that the column was dead beat and bad better be brought into Bastogne. The tank destroyers under Lieutenant Toms stayed in Foy supporting the 3d Battalion.

Team Desobry had gone to Noville with fifteen tanks; it limped back with only four. The 1st Battalion of the 506th Parachute Infantry was in full strength when it went to Team Desobry's support. It lost 13 officers and 199 enlisted men at Noville.61 By their combined efforts they bad destroyed or badly crippled somewhere between twenty and thirty known enemy tanks of all types including not less than three Mark VIs.

*[Members of the armored units put a lower estimate on the damage done to enemy armor than the paratroopers did and the*

136

*figures given here are a compromise of the two. It is obvious that the battle was such that an accurate count could not be made.]*

They probably damaged or destroyed many more. Headquarters of the 506th estimated that the assaults of the German infantry had cost the enemy the equivalent of half a regiment.

*[As to the identification of enemy units in the Neville action, the G-2 report shows that by the night of December 20 six prisoners captured in the Foy-Recogne area had been identified as coming from 2d Panzer Division.]*

Yet all of these material measurements of what had been achieved were mean and meager weighed against the fact that the men of Noville had held their ground for a decisive 48 hours during which time the defense of Bastogne had opportunity to organize and grow confident of its own strength.

# 12. FIRST ACTION AT MARVIE

AT 0645 ON DECEMBER 20, the enemy shelled Team O'Hara's roadblock on the Wiltz-Bastogne road about 1,300 yards east of Marvie. The fog was thick and little could be seen of the enemy's movements out along the road. But as the light grew, the tankers could hear enemy armor moving somewhere in the fog up beyond the block. At around 0900 the fog lifted a little and they saw a dozen German soldiers trying to break up the block. A concentration from the 420th Field Artillery Battalion caught this group while they were, tugging away at the felled logs. Two were killed (they were later identified as part of an engineer working party) and the others fled the fire. The enemy then put smoke on the roadblock - enough to conceal the block and the terrain right around it. Figuring that an infantry attack might be coming, Team O'Hara covered the block with fire from mortars and assault guns. It is believed that this fire fended off the thrust toward Colonel

*The village of Marvie, looking north.*

138

*Men waiting in the regimental command post of the 327th Glider Infantry.*

O'Hara's front and deflected it toward Marvie, where five of O'Hara's light tanks had taken up position the night before.

In the meantime Colonel Joseph H. Harper, commanding the 327th Glider Infantry, had been getting acquainted with Colonel O'Hara. The 327th had taken over the command post at Mande-St.-Étienne at 1500 on December 19, and at 1630 its 1st Battalion had been attached to Colonel Ewell's 501st Parachute Infantry to support his right flank. At 0400 on the 20th the 327th command post and the 2d Battalion of that regiment were ordered into Bastogne and at 0600 they marched on into the town. Without a pause, the 2d Battalion, 327th, moved straight on to Marvie and took over that village from the 326th Engineers. The 3d Battalion remained in Flamizoulle (some 2,000 yards east of Flamierge) and established its command post in the woods at (494610).

The 2d Battalion entered Marvie just about as the enemy first opened fire on Team O'Hara's roadblock. *[This entry was made between 0630 and 0700.]*

Colonel Harper had been told by Division that the reconnaissance group of light tanks would be in support of his 2d Battalion. Going straight away to see Colonel O'Hara, he said to him, "I've been told to hold this sector. I understand from Division that you are in support of me and I would like to go on

139

*Map 12*

ACTION AT MARVIE
20 DECEMBER

R. J. KOKE

TO BASTOGNE

HARPER
WATCHES
FIGHT

MARVIE

F

G

E

2
27

Light tanks
withdraw

Medium tanks
which destroyed
enemy armor.

ENEMY INFANTRY
INFILTRATE INTO
BUILDINGS

ENEMY TANKS AND
MARVIE: 1/125

1/125 INFANTRY HIT

O'HARA
3/72

O'HARA
11
O'HARA

501-3
11
O'HARA

B / 20

HASTY MINEFIELD

HASTY MINEFIELD

ROAD BLOCK
ACTION, 0900

TO WILTZ

Scale in Yards
0          500

140

a reconnaissance."

O'Hara said, "Let's get started." With them when they went out was Lieutenant Colonel Roy L. Inman, commanding the 2d Battalion, 327th Glider Infantry. The officers discussed the relationship of their respective forces as they made the reconnaissance. Under the existing arrangement, Colonel O'Hara's force was not under Colonel Harper's command, for the armored force was still not attached to the 101st Division but was in support only. Colonel Inman had moved his 2d Battalion, 327th, in on the right flank of Colonel O'Hara's force with his line so extended as to secure the village and then bending southwestward to the main road just above Remoifosse. This was a distance of about 2,500 yards. The Engineers had three outposts distributed over this southeastern facing arc and none of them had as yet been engaged. It was agreed that Colonel O'Hara would be responsible for the defense of his immediate front and that Colonel Inman, who would take over from the Engineers immediately, would be responsible for the sector to right of O'Hara's. Harper then left Inman and drove down the main road toward Remoifosse. He established the southwestward extension of his line on the forward slope of the hill over which the main road passes a little more than half way from Bastogne to Remoifosse. The position thus chosen was a few hundred yards north of where the original Engineer outpost bad been.

After looking over the situation and making sure that his men were where he wanted them, Colonel Harper drove back to Marvie. The jeep reached the road intersection just west of Marvie. There Harper stopped for a moment and debated with himself whether to go on into the village or take the west-running road and have a quick look at the high ground above the village. He decided in favor of taking a look and the jeep moved on up the hill.

At 1125, December 20, Colonel Inman's command post in

Marvie (2d Battalion, 327th Glider Infantry) reported to Colonel O'Hara that they were receiving a great deal of shelling and that they could see enemy tanks coming toward them.

*[Made from Colonel O'Hara's journal. There was no time entry in the 327th Glider Infantry journal covering this incident. Colonel Harper, commander of the 327th, had the impression that it occurred much earlier in the morning.]*

This movement had already been observed from within O'Hara's sector. Yet Harper, driving up the hill at the very moment of the attack, was unaware that anything untoward was breaking until he got to the crest of the hill. There he turned about and saw the enemy guns blazing from the edge of the woods directly southeast of Marvie and their point-blank fire hitting among the houses of the village.

Harper could see that the fire came from tanks within the wood but he could not be certain how many. The barrage was followed immediately by an advance out of the woods by four enemy tanks and six half-tracks. They were well spread out and they advanced slowly, firing as they came, apparently drawn on by the prospect of an easy success over the light tanks. These tanks kept dodging in and out among the buildings and the enemy fire appeared to follow their movements closely. The light tanks replied futilely with their 37mm. guns and the enemy armor appeared to come on more boldly. Feeling that the presence of his unit, rather than helping Colonel Inman's men, was drawing more high-velocity fire into the town, the light tank commander asked Colonel O'Hara for permission to withdraw. It was granted. By then, one of the light tanks had been set afire by a shell burst; a second had been hit in the suspension system but could make its escape by backing up the hill.

Yet Colonel Harper did not know all of these things. He saw the tanks quit the village and concluded that they had been routed and were deserting his infantry.

Up on the hill behind Marvie, Colonel O'Hara's larger guns

kept silent. In front of the oncoming armor a German self-propelled 75mm. gun was pacing the advance. Its gunner spotted a half-track near O'Hara's command post and fired several quick rounds at it. The shells hit an Engineer jeep, demolished a one-ton trailer and blew through the lower portion of the command post, killing a cow. The command post was in the first floor of the house and this fire was hitting into the basement right under the headquarters.

The tanks were by now almost broadside to Team O'Hara at 700 yards range. Firing at right angles to their own front, two of Team O'Hara's medium tanks opened up on the line of Mark IVs and half-tracks. The Germans never saw what hit them for they were still shooting at the light tanks now pulling out through the end of the village. One Mark IV was blown up by a direct hit from one of the mediums. The other Sherman knocked out a second Mark IV and one of the half-tracks, the fire killing all of the tank crew and most of the men in the personnel carrier. One German tank fled to the rear. The fourth tank dashed for Marvie where the infantry destroyed it with bazooka fire. The self-propelled gun, having gotten almost into the village before the Sherman opened fire, tried to turn about. It was hit from all sides and it went up like a torch.

In the last stage of the German advance, the half-tracks had sped forward and increased their interval so that they were almost closing on the first houses when the tank line was destroyed. They kept going. They got to the streets of the village and the infantry jumped down. With one small exception the glider troops stayed right where they were and met the German on-fall without flinching. The attack had come just as the relief of the Engineer units had been completed, and some of the Engineers were moving out of the north end of Marvie. Men from Inman's heavy mortar section, stationed in an apple orchard, saw the Engineer party leave as the fire began. They could not understand what the movement of troops was about and they thought that part of their own Battalion was withdrawing. And so they followed.

Colonel Harper, watching all of these things from the hill, made the same mistake as his mortar section. He thought that his men had been stampeded and that the village was gone. He called General McAuliffe on the radio, told him what he had seen and said that he was on his way to gather the men and that he would make a counterattack. His car sped back over the route it had come and Harper started to rally his men. Then he learned that most of the party were Engineers and that only the mortar squad from among his command had displaced. He told that squad to get back into the battle and they moved at once. This error in judgment is the only instance during the siege of Bastogne when any American Infantryman is known to have left his position under fire and without orders.

Colonel Harper, still outside the village, called Colonel Inman on his radio. The executive officer of the 2d Battalion, 327th Glider Infantry, Major R. B. Galbreaith, answered the call. He said that both Colonel Inman and Captain Hugh Evans, commanding officer of Company G, which was holding the village, had been hit by a tank shell while making a reconnaissance just as the German onslaught began. He did not know how badly they were wounded. Harper asked him, "Are you still in the village?"

"Yes," Galbreaith answered. "Yes, but the Germans are here also. We expect to drive them out."

The close-in fighting continued into the early afternoon. Inman's men stayed in their foxholes. Some died there, shot at ten yards' range by machine guns as they tried to stop the half-tracks with their rifle and tommy gun fire, their bodies almost cut in half where the machine guns had ripped them through. Their comrades found them later sitting stiffly at their weapons. Colonel Harper himself inspected these positions. He noted that every one of his dead was still facing forward as if trying to engage the enemy. The bazooka men bad likewise met the attack head-on. Some of the German infantry, clearing away from the half-tracks, had ducked into the houses. The glider men went in after them and cleaned them out house by house. Within two hours twenty Germans were prisoners and thirty were dead in Marvie. First Lieutenant Stanley A. Morrison of Company G, who had been captured when the Germans first came into the village, was recaptured by his own men. Colonel Inman bad lost five men killed, each of them killed in a foxhole while resisting the half-tracks. Fifteen men of Company G were wounded in the action.

During all that time, Team O'Hara sat high and dry on the ridge, taking no part in the engagement except during the brief gun duel. On the right flank that force received some small-arms fire but the enemy made no attempt to close on that side and the armored infantry in Team O'Hara's position was too far away to lend any support to the men in Marvie. That village was again clear by about 1300. At 1400 some of Colonel O'Hara's tankers saw an enemy half-track stuck in the mud about 150 yards southeast of Marvie. It had been with the striking force during the morning and had become bogged. In the previous excitement all hands had overlooked it. The tankers quickly knocked it out.

At 1420, December 20, the enemy put smoke on Marvie. Some of the tanks made another sally from the woods but changed their minds. The situation began to ease and Colonel Inman's men went about improving their positions, digging their foxholes narrow and very deep and right next to the foundations of the houses. The day ended fairly quietly but with a definite change in the weather. The Ardennes was cold and frozen. The ground had hardened enough for the tracked vehicles to get about over the hills in almost any direction. Still no snow bad fallen.

Now, as the first skirmish ended around Marvie, the first flurries fell. Soon the ridges were whitening and the snows thickened during the next few days. Increasing cold, light winds and deep drifts changed many of the characteristics of the battle. One of the problems that now pressed most heavily on the commanders was to get their men indoors and keep them from freezing. Villages became places of refuge not only from enemy fire but from the cold. The Belgian villagers, clinging stubbornly to their homes even in the face of the German attack, had to be evacuated to provide shelter and cover for the infantry. In a world of white, the forest plantations were the only other areas of easy concealment for troops. The local actions swirled more and more around these two objectives - to capture a few houses or to take a line of fir trees.

# 13. THE RESPITE

ON DECEMBER 21 and 22 the opposing forces around the northeast sector simply sparred with one another. *[This is perhaps an over-simplification. There were fairly heavy attacks against the north on December 21 and one running engagement in the southwest, but the failure of the enemy to press a general attack against the Bastogne defenses during the two days is conspicuous.]*

The enemy had been stopped cold at Neffe and Mont by Colonel Ewell's 501st Parachute Infantry and supporting units. The effort to slip through the ground held by the forces of Colonels O'Hara and Harper had been equally unsuccessful though less costly. After these futile passes, and following the shock action at Noville, the enemy seemed almost to abandon the effort to break through Bastogne and concerned himself with extending the westward flow of his forces on both sides of it so as to complete the encirclement.

The road to Neufchâteau was cut by the Germans on the night of December 20, isolating Bastogne. General McAuliffe had gone that way just a few hours before to talk to the Corps commander.

*[The precise hours of the cutting of the Neufchâteau road is not known and the statement on which this paragraph is based is taken from the interview with General McAuliffe.]*

It was a pregnant conversation. General McAuliffe said that he was certain he could hold on for at least 48 hours and maybe longer. General Middleton replied that in view of the fact that the hour would probably come when communications could not be maintained, General McAuliffe would have to be prepared to act on his own. He pointed out that the 116th Panzer Division was coming in on General McAuliffe's flank - in addition to the three German divisions already fighting him. McAuliffe said, "I think we can take care of them." Middleton said that he certainly wanted to hold Bastogne but was not sure that it could be done in view of recent developments. It was important, General Middleton added, that the road to the southwestward be kept open as long as possible.

As General McAuliffe walked out the door, Middleton's last comment was: "Now, don't get yourself surrounded." McAuliffe noticed that he said it very lightly and felt that the Corps commander was simply having a little joke in a tense moment.

*[Quoted directly. According to an interview with Colonel Walter C. Stanton, Deputy Chief of Staff, VIII Corps, General Middleton never weakened in his desire to hold Bastogne. On the 19th, however, Lieutenant General George S. Patton, Jr., commanding general, Third Army, ordered a withdrawal. Colonel Stanton believed this order was possibly influenced by the weak showing of First Army. The VIII Corps order appeared on December 20. Interview by Captain L. B. Clark, 3d Information and Historical Service, and Captain K. W. Hechler, 2d Information and Historical Service, January 16, 1945, vicinity Assenois, Belgium.]*

General McAuliffe went on out, jumped in his car and told the driver to make for Bastogne as fast as he could get there. He figured he was already surrounded - or just about so. A half hour after he did come over the road, it was cut by the German armor.

That was not, however, an unmixed evil, for it brought an important change in the relationship of the forces in the defense. During its first two days the infantry and the armor had collaborated well but they had not been a team. On the first night, General McAuliffe had asked that the armor (Combat Command B, 10th Armored Division) be attached to him and its commander Colonel Roberts had said, "What do you know about armor?"

General McAuliffe had replied, "Maybe you want the 101st Division attached to your Combat Command."

*[Confirmed by other members of the staff who were present. This exchange of words, however, does not appear in the Westover interview with Colonel Roberts.]*

It was partly because of this division in the command authority, and partly because the armor and the infantry were units strange and new to each other, that during the first stage there was a lack of cohesion." That lack was felt more as a moral than as a tactical thing. To one staff officer of the Division the armor along the front seemed "like a will o' the wisp."

The armor felt the same way about the infantry. Each force had the feeling those first few days that it was propping up the front pretty much unhelped. In general, neither force was feeling the presence of the other strongly nor having a clear idea bow much support was being received from it. Liaison was fragmentary. Both tankers and infantrymen had bad to come out of their comers fighting and during the first crucial hours they had no choice but to look straight ahead and slug.

But with the cutting of the Neufchâteau road and the isolating of the Bastogne garrison, General Middleton called General McAuliffe and told him that the armor (Combat Command B) and all other troops within the circle were now under his command.

General Middleton also called Colonel Roberts and told him, "Your work has been quite satisfactory but I have so many divisions that I can't take the time to study two sets of reports from the same area." Colonel Roberts reported in person to General McAuliffe to do command liaison and from that time on until the siege was lifted his post was almost exclusively at the 101st Division command post. The result was that the coordination was complete. Roberts, a veteran tank commander, was particularly concerned that the armor be used properly, used to the maximum effect and not wasted. He strongly resisted the attempts of infantry commanders to use tanks as roadblocks. He worked specifically to get his armor quickly released after each engagement so that there would always be a maximum strength in General McAuliffe's mobile reserve for the next emergency. In the middle of the siege he published a mimeographed memorandum to the infantry officers on the right ways to use tanks.

The order to Combat Command B on December 21 from VIII Corps to "hold the Bastogne line at all costs" gives a key to General Middleton's view of the situation during this period. On the evening before, he had talked with McAuliffe and bad expressed a doubt whether the strength at Bastogne was sufficient for the task. All along he bad been willing to make the gamble of an encircled force at Bastogne, and for a few hours he may have felt that the gamble was dubious. Now be had come to believe the gamble would succeed and that the battle must be fought out on that line. There was no longer any doubt or question anywhere in the camp. From this hour the action of all concerned, the VIII Corps commander, the 101st Division commander, and the armored force commander of Combat Command B-Middleton, McAuliffe, and Roberts-became wholly consistent with the resolve that Bastogne could and would be held.

*[This conclusion is supported by the proof that air resupply of the Bastogne position immediately became a foremost concern of VIII Corps, and that VIII Corps Headquarters labored throughout December 21 to make the operation possible.]*

General McAuliffe now had the answer to all of his questions. No situation could have been more clearly defined. During the first two days he had entertained many doubts and bad continued to wonder just what the situation was. He had heard about various groups from the 28th and 106th Divisions which were still out fighting somewhere and might fall back upon him. The 7th Armored Division was supposed to be somewhere up around

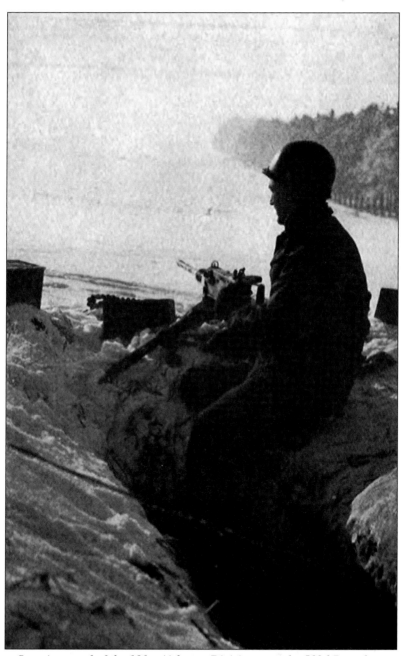

*Security guard of the 101st Airborne Division near the 502d Parachute Infantry Command Post.*

St. Vith. He had also had to worry about the organization of stragglers. At the first, part of the 28th Division had been screening him on the south flank. Its commander, Major General Norman D. Cota, had called him on the morning of December 20 and said, "I'd like to see you," and McAuliffe had replied, "I'm too damned busy." Cota then said, "I'll come up to see you."

Now, on the 21st, McAuliffe knew that General Cota would not be coming to see him, and that the only situation involving American troops about which he would have to worry for a while was the situation right within the two-and-one-half mile circle of German forces closed around Bastogne. The only support he could expect for the time being was just what he had - all within ranging distance of his own 105mm. Batteries. It was a nice, clear-cut position and it had materialized in just about the way that he had expected upon first reaching Bastogne. *[General McAuliffe says specifically that from the moment he reached Bastogne he expected to get cut off because there seemed to be nothing in front of him that would prevent it.]*

But what he had not foreseen, something that came like a gift form the gods, was that after the first hard collision, the enemy would give him a comparative respite in which to reflect on his situation and knit his armor and infantry close together, now that both were his to work with as he saw fit. The Germans had spent two days trying to break on through Bastogne. They had failed to crush it; they would try to choke it. But while they were building up around the west and south, the pressure against the city relaxed. *[It is notable that December 22 was the least active day on the Bastogne front.]*

The flow of bubbles on the G-2 overlays, showing the extension of the enemy to the south and westward, was moving along. Panzer Lehr Division had been the first to break upon the Bastogne rock. But the 26th Volksgrenadier Division had also come in from the east. A captured map showed that it had failed in one of its appointments, for the 26th Volksgrenadier was to have had the honor of capturing Bastogne.

The Germans were traveling light. Their commanders had told them that Bastogne was bursting with American food and that they could eat when they got there. Some had gone hungry for three days while trying to reach the American rations. Too, the enemy fire power manifested a certain weakness. While his heavy mortars and nebelwerfers were shaking down the store fronts in Bastogne and wounding a few soldiers and civilians, his artillery effort was largely limited to the covering fire given by the tanks and the fire of a relatively few self-propelled guns when his infantry charged forward. This, G-2 attributed to a critical shortage of ammunition.

The cutting of the Neufchâteau road, closing the German circle, appears in the 101st Division records as hardly more than an interesting incident. *[This detail is almost overlooked in all the journals.]* Up till then, the Division's intelligence of the enemy strength and movements was more notable for its blanks than for its specific detailed entries. The G-2 section had, of course, moved cold into an unknown situation and was having to build up its picture of the enemy and friendly forces piece by piece. There had been no pretty "estimates of the situation" to take over and build upon. *[Kinnard and Danahy both stated to Marshall that from their examination of Corps' situation maps upon reaching Bastogne they learned practically nothing of the enemy situation and decided they would have to build from the ground up.]* All that Division could know for certain was what it learned from examining the enemy dead or questioning prisoners. That was enough for Lieutenant Colonel Paul A. Danahy's (Division G-2) main purpose and enough also to satisfy his taste for melodramatic utterance.

Eleven dead men had been found on the ground where the hospital was captured. The corpses had civilian clothes - and German military dogtags. Colonel Danahy went out to make the identifications. A few hours after this find, a message from 10th Armored Division came through Combat Command B to 101st Division Headquarters saying, "You can expect attacks from Sherman tanks, civilians and almost anything now." *[This message was received by Colonel Kinnard and appears in the interview with him. The exact reason for it being sent, however, is not known.]*

Reports came into the G-2 office through the first day of Germans killed while wearing American uniforms and of Sherman tanks pouring fire on our lines. Danahy checked up. He found that invariably, where the enemy used American dress, it was mixed with some of their own clothing, so that they could maintain they were in uniform. *[Danahy was convinced that while using every stratagem possible the enemy was trying to keep within the appearance of acting according to the laws of war for the purpose of protecting their men. He said that the prisoners taken in American uniforms said they had put on this extra clothing to keep from freezing.]* What be had seen gave him fresh inspiration for prophecy.

"Their equipment is augmented by captured U. S. equipment which they do not hesitate to use," he wrote to the commander. "Their morale is excellent but will disintegrate as they come in contact with American airborne troops. It is well known that the Germans dislike fighting. The false courage acquired during their recent successes has so far proved insufficient to prevent their becoming road-bound."

While this message was going out to the regiments of the 101st, the enemy was crossing the Neufchâteau road and cutting the last line to the south, closing the circle around Bastogne. Reconnaissance and combat patrols reported strong enemy infiltrations in the areas west and southwest of the town.

In the morning of December 21, a patrol from Troop D of the 90th Reconnaissance Squadron went down the road to see what the Germans had there. The patrol, under First Lieutenant Arthur

*Map 13*

B. Arnsdorf, consisted of one tank destroyer and two squads of infantry. They met a group of 101st Division men near Isle-le-Pré (a mile and a half southwest of Bastogne), then moved on some distance farther until they encountered a well emplaced enemy force which made them turn about.

Another armored patrol under Captain Keith J. Anderson went to Clochimont where it observed a large enemy force-riding in American vehicles and dressed in American uniforms.

Later in the morning of December 21 Team Pyle - 14 medium tanks and 200 infantry, mostly from the 9th Armored - moved to the vicinity of Senonchamps to assist the 420th Armored Field Artillery. Lieutenant Colonel Barry D. Browne, in command of the 420th, had received reports that Sibret and Morhet (see map 13) had fallen into enemy hands. He figured that he was out on a limb and that the enemy might come upon him from either flank. So he turned one of his batteries to fire on Sibret and rushed a forward observer out to adjust on the village. At that moment, he saw the motorized column of the 333d Field Artillery Group as it came speeding up the road out of Sibret. Another column came driving hard behind the 333d - men in American clothes and riding American vehicles. They got fairly close to Senonchamps, then stopped, deployed and opened fire with an M8 assault gun.

Even as Colonel Browne realized they were Germans, they started side-slipping off into the Bois de Fragotte which lies just south of Senonchamps. Team Pyle got there in time to help Browne fill those woods with fire; one battery from the 420th Field Artillery Battalion and one from the 755th Field Artillery Battalion (155mms.) also engaged in this action. The infantry and tanks moved west into the woods. Almost immediately, one

*Map 14*

of the tanks knocked out an enemy 75mm. self-propelled gun. The force then advanced into a large clearing in the center of the forest. While crossing the clearing, one of the tanks was disabled by a shell from a high-velocity gun somewhere in the woods. The tank lost a track. A smoke screen was laid in an attempt to cover its withdrawal, but the tank wouldn't budge and had to be destroyed.

The force then withdrew to a line farther to the east, but within the forest. Additional support kept coming to it until by night Colonel Browne was commanding 300 infantry and 19 tanks, in addition to running two battalions of artillery. His troops were covering a sector more than 4,000 yards long (see map 14) and running from south of Senonchamps to the Bastogne-Neufchâteau road. All of this had been built up during the day of December 21 as forces were shifted to meet the attack from the new direction. *[Westover's estimate of the position covered.]*

But the heavy increase of fire on the left found Danahy ready to meet the emergency. "The cutting of the roads," he wrote in his periodic report to the commanders that evening, "had had no effect upon our present situation except to make travel hazardous."

# 14. "NUTS!"

At 1130 ON DECEMBER 22 four Germans, a major, a captain and two enlisted men, came up the road to Bastogne from Remoifosse carrying a large white flag. They were met on the road by Technical Sergeant Oswald Y. Butler and Staff Sergeant Carl E. Dickinson of Company F, 327th Glider infantry, and Private First Class Ernest D. Premetz of the 327th Medical Detachment.

Premetz could speak German. The captain could speak English. He said to Butler, "We are parliamentaires."

The men took the Germans to the house where Lieutenant Leslie E. Smith of Weapons Platoon, Company F, 327th Infantry, had his command post. Leaving the two German enlisted men at the command post, Smith blindfolded the two officers and led them over the hill to the command post of Captain James F. Adams, commanding officer of Company F. Adams called 2d Battalion headquarters in Marvie, Battalion called Regiment in Bastogne, and the 327th Headquarters called the 101st Division, relaying the word that some Germans had come in with surrender terms. The rumor quickly spread around the front that the enemy had had enough and that a party had arrived to arrange a surrender. Quiet held the front. Many of the American defenders crawled out of their cover and spent the noon hour shaving, washing and going to the straddle trenches.

Major Alvin Jones took the terms to General McAuliffe and Lieutenant Colonel Ned D. Moore who was acting Chief of Staff. The paper called for the surrender of the Bastogne garrison and threatened its complete destruction otherwise. It appealed to the "Well known American humanity" to save the people of Bastogne from further suffering. The Americans were to have

*Command Post of Company F, 327th Glider Infantry, near Remoifosse. Here the German officer demanding the surrender of Bastogne was blindfolded before being taken to the 327th Glider Infantry Command Post. In the center are Colonel Harper and Major Jones exchanging salutes with the German officers as they were returned to their lines.*

two hours in which to consider. The two enemy officers would have to be released by 1400 but another hour would pass before the Germans would resume their attack.

Colonel Harper, commanding the 327th, went with Jones to Division Headquarters. The two German officers were left with Captain Adams. Members of the staff were grouped around General McAuliffe when Harper and Jones arrived. McAuliffe asked someone what the paper contained and was told that it requested a surrender.

He laughed and said, "Aw, nuts!" It really seemed funny to him at the time. He figured he was giving the Germans "one hell of a beating" and that all of his men knew it. The demand was all out of line with the existing situation.

But McAuliffe realized that some kind of reply had to be made and he sat down to think it over. Pencil in hand, he sat there pondering for a few minutes and then he remarked, "Well, I don't know what to tell them." He asked the staff what they thought and Colonel Kinnard, his G-3 replied, "That first remark of yours would be hard to beat."

General McAuliffe didn't understand immediately what Kinnard was referring to. Kinnard reminded him, "You said 'Nuts!'" That drew applause all around. All members of the staff agreed with much enthusiasm and because of their approval McAuliffe decided to send that message back to the Germans.

Then he called Colonel Harper in and asked him how he would reply to the message. Harper thought for a minute but before he could compose anything General McAuliffe gave him the paper on which he had written his one-word reply and asked, "Will you see that it's delivered?" "I will deliver it myself," answered Harper. "It will be a lot of fun." McAuliffe told him not to go into the German lines.

Colonel Harper returned to the command post of Company F. The two Germans were standing in the wood blindfolded and under guard. Harper said, "I have the American commander's reply."

The German captain asked, "Is it written or verbal?"

"It is written," said Harper.

And then be said to the German major, "I will stick it in your hand."

The German captain translated the message. The major then asked, "Is the reply negative or affirmative? If it is the latter I will negotiate further."

All of this time the Germans were acting in an upstage and patronizing manner. Colonel Harper was beginning to lose his temper. He said, "The reply is decidedly not affirmative." Then he added, "If you continue this foolish attack your losses will be tremendous." The major nodded his head.

Harper put the two officers in the jeep and took them back to the main road where the German privates were waiting with the white flag.

He then removed the blindfold and said to them, speaking through the German captain, "If you don't understand what 'Nuts' means, in plain English it is the same as 'Go to hell.' And I will tell you something else - if you continue to attack we will kill every goddam German that tries to break into this city."

The German major and captain saluted very stiffly. The captain said, "We will kill many Americans. This is war." It was then 1350.

"On your way, Bud," said Colonel Harper, "and good luck to you.

The four Germans walked on down the road. Harper returned to the house, regretting that his tongue had slipped and that he had wished them good luck.

The rest of the day was comparatively quiet. The wholesale destruction by artillery that the Germans had promised did not materialize. But, at 1555 there was an attack by some 50 of the enemy against Company F, 327th Glider Infantry, over precisely the same ground where the German mediators had come into our lines. The attack was broken up by small-arms and artillery fire. At 1700 another small attack was again pressed to within 200 yards of Company Fs lines but was beaten back by fire.

The terrain at this spot formed a kind of bowl. The Germans came with their tanks into the bottom of the bowl and fired up against the foxholes along the slope. The men under Sergeant Butler, who had the rifle platoon, and Lieutenant Smith, who had the weapons platoon, held their ground and drove the attackers off with infantry fire alone.

The main event for that day was summed up, though not too neatly, in the G-2 Periodic Report No. 4:

"The Commanding General's answer was, with a sarcastic air of humorous tolerance, emphatically negative. The catastrophic carnage of human lives resulting from the artillery barrage of astronomic proportions which was to be the fate of the defending troops failed to materialize.

"The well known American humanity was considerate of the threatened possible civilian losses by firing artillery concentrations directed at the enemy's impudence."

It was a victory for eloquence at some expense to grammar but in keeping with the other grim humors of the day.

That night, December 22, the Luftwaffe began its bombing attack which was repeated on the next four nights.

# 15. THE SECOND MARVIE ATTACK

THERE WERE TWO relatively quiet days on the Marvie part of the circular Bastogne front after the snows came - December 21 and 22. Bastogne was searched for enough bedsheets to camouflage the patrols. Early in the afternoon of December 21 the Germans came across the main highway directly south of Bastogne and then began working north toward the battalion lines on the hill.

Colonel Harper shifted the 2d Platoon of Company G, 327th Glider Infantry, from the ground immediately west of Marvie to a place west of the highway. Three of Team O'Hara's tanks were already on the hill where Harper had placed them the day before.

The armor and infantry together were able to turn this thrust back before it became any real threat. *[On the afternoon of December 20 a small task force under 1st Lieutenant Richard C. Gilliland was sent to support 327th along the line covering the main highway. It was called Charlie 16 and included three tanks - two 75mm. and one 76mm. It remained away from the main group for a week, lost the 76mm. tank from a rocket, engaged in 15 skirmishes and destroyed much enemy equipment.]* The 1st Battalion, 327th Glider Infantry, was relieved from attachment to the 501st Airborne Infantry, reverting to direct Division control. It was moved to the southwest of Bastogne in the vicinity of the woods there and ordered to establish a roadblock along the main highway, and from this point to patrol westward to make contact with the 326th Engineer Battalion. They were also instructed to patrol to Villeroux and Chenogne and make contact with "friendly troops"

NIGHT BATTLE AT MARVIE
23-24 DECEMBER
PHASE I

SCALE IN YARDS

*Map 15*

164

but before they could do it the enemy had moved through these positions and driven back the 333d Field Artillery Group. The Engineers then set up as small combat groups and covered the ground between Colonel Hartford F. Salee's 1st Battalion, 327th Glider Infantry, which was over the Neufchâteau road and the platoon from Company G, 327th, which was west of the highway leading south from Bastogne.

In Team O'Hara's part of the sector, too, there was a lull. Some time during the night of December 20 the Germans removed the trees from Team O'Hara's roadblock. At 1100 on the next day a combat patrol went forward to investigate. But on approaching the point where the block had been they found that the enemy now had it covered with crossing bands of machinegun fire. They were able to withdraw without casualty and mortar fire was then put all around the road junction.

In the early hours of December 22 one of Team O'Hara's patrols going forward saw an eleven-man patrol enter their own lines. The night was clear and crisp. The small group from the 54th Armored Infantry first heard the crunching of the snow as the other patrol came toward them. They lay quiet, not firing because they were outnumbered. Too, the strangers were moving as if they were wholly familiar with the ground. They had no visible weapons and they did not carry themselves stealthily. They went boldly over the fences and entered the American lines along the ground that lay between the 327th and the 54th. They walked right by the sentries, moved to within 100 yards of the command post of the 327th Glider Infantry and within 200 yards of the command post of the 54th Armored Infantry.

Four different groups reported the patrol later and all four said they had seen eleven men. Yet the patrol was not challenged anywhere simply because it had moved so confidently. They got in and out without provoking any fire or interest. When Headquarters heard casually how this group had been drifting about, they checked to see whether any nearby unit had put out such a patrol and found that none bad done so. Whether the eleven were friend or enemy was never learned. The visitation and its mystery became one of the legends of Bastogne.

At 1725 on December 23, the 2d Battalion, 327th, in Marvie was heavily shelled by enemy tanks concealed in a small plantation of firs within the hollow just above the village of Martaimont. From their position the tanks could shoot directly into Marvie. It was a characteristic enemy action for throughout the siege it was the German practice to use tanks as artillery, perhaps from fear of hitting their own troops if they used field guns from far back. *[This is not the Historian's conclusion but is based on the interview with Colonel Harper and on statements by Major Templeton and Colonel Harper's battalion commanders. Colonel Harper said, "Most of the time when our troops were under shell fire the German gunners were in position to lay directly on the target."]*

At about 1735 the 2d Battalion, 327th, was attacked by tanks and infantry coming from the same general direction (see map 15), though they had debouched from a larger wood lying a little farther away from Marvie. The attack developed very slowly. The German infantry was clad in snow suits and a light snow was falling. They seemed to be waiting until the gloom deepened so they could make the most of their camouflage. The enemy barrage had ignored Team O'Hara's part of the sector but the outposts of the 54th Armored Infantry spotted two enemy machine guns that were firing into Marvie. Flanking fire was placed on them and they were silenced. Heavy automatic fire then searched the position of the 54th. No enemy could be seen and the men of the 54th held their fire except for one heavy machine gun on the left. The enemy spotted that gun. A few minutes later a hand grenade dropped next to the gun killing the gunner and wounding one other man. The rest of the crew quit the position. Next morning a patrol returned to the gun and found the second man still alive but so nearly frozen that he could only nod his head to them. Both he and the dead man had been searched and stripped of their possessions by Germans who had come in fast upon the position after the grenade fire.

Within half an hour the attack was fully developed and soon after 1840, December 23, one platoon of Company G, 327th became surrounded on Hill 500 to the south of Marvie. The enemy had begun a gradual envelopment of the platoon's position by moving into and through houses and yards that were around the base of the hill on all sides. A few members of the platoon were able to withdraw along the flanks of the hill as the encirclement began. The others stayed in their positions and the time quickly came when they could not get out. *[Colonel Harper later had this to say of what happened to Morrison, "I'll never again put infantry on a forward slope unless I have tank destroyers or tanks where I can protect them. I lost two platoons separately in defense of the perimeter by making this mistake. In each case they were overrun when there were no tank destroyers to defend them."]*

Four tanks, which had accompanied the German infantry advance to Hill 500, turned their fire against Marvie, adding to the bombardment that was still coming in from the armored guns in the big wood.

Colonel Harper had worried about this part of the perimeter. Earlier in the day he had asked Colonel O'Hara to put a tank on the hill. O'Hara agreed to station a 57mm. gun on the lower slope of the hill where a 37mm. gun had previously defended it. The half-track carrying the 57mm. gun was just going into position when the German tanks and infantry closed in on Hill 500. The first few German rounds that came his way were enough for the driver; he turned the half-track around and sped north toward Marvie. The troops in the village saw the half-track coming toward them from out of the body of the German attack. They thought it was a German vehicle and they fired at it with everything they had, demolishing the vehicle and killing the crew. Two German tanks that had followed along the same road crossed the stream south of Marvie and got into the village as far as the church. They saw then that the destroyed half-track blocked the road and that they could not advance any farther. So they turned around and withdrew. *[This incident was related during the interview with Colonel Harper and supported by the battalion commander. It was not brought to light, however, during Westover's conversations with Colonel O'Hara's force.]*

Having begun the attack in stealth, the German infantry now came on toward the houses in a frenzy, yelling and firing as they advanced and shooting many flares. To the men in Colonel O'Hara's position it looked as if the tracers were flying in all directions. Bullet fire began to envelop them from the southern edge of the village. A self-propelled gun came charging toward them up the Wiltz road. As it rounded the bend and came abreast the farmhouse there, one of our medium tanks fired and the gun went up in flames. The fire lighted the entire area. The enemy turned their artillery loose on the farmhouse. A loft filled with hay soon blazed like a torch. Because of the intense illumination from these fires, the tanks and infantry of Team O'Hara's line withdrew 100 yards to the west.

Counting an Engineer platoon on the right of Colonel Harper's 327th Glider Infantry, there were 98 men defending Hill 500. Already, a few had been killed or wounded. At the same time that a part of the German force pressed against Marvie from the south, twelve German tanks supported by infantry advanced north along the main road toward the position occupied by Company F, 327th. This body had debouched from the same woods from which the German tanks were firing. Instead of continuing along the Bastogne road, part of the German armor moved rightward toward Hill 500. The infantry were clad in white and were almost imperceptible.

On the slopes of Hill 500 Lieutenant Stanley Morrison and his men of Company G, 327th Glider Infantry, had dug in around the base of the houses. Colonel Harper in his command post got word that the enemy was attacking. He called Lieutenant Morrison and asked, 'What is your situation?"

"Now they are all around me," Morrison replied. "I see tanks just outside my window. We are continuing to fight them back but it looks like they have us." To Colonel Harper's listening ear he seemed perfectly calm and he spoke in a level tone.

Harper called him back in about three minutes. Morrison replied but he said only these words, "We're still holding on." Then the line went dead.

Lieutenant Colonel Thomas J. Rouzie, the executive officer of the 327th Glider Infantry, said to Harper, "I guess that's the end of Morrison."

The men of Hill 500 were never heard from again in the battle. They had been overwhelmed by troops of the 901st Panzergrenadier Regiment of the Panzer Lehr Division. The end came for Lieutenant Morrison's detachment some time after 1900, December 23. *[Morrison's body was not found and it was hoped that he was taken prisoner. Both Harper and Rouzie recalled the words of the conversations.]*

There had been no tanks or tank destroyers in support of Morrison. Force O'Hara had not fired either in defense of the hill positions or against the German front moving into Marvie from the south. Colonel Harper couldn't understand it. He called Colonel O'Hara who said, "They are attacking me also and are trying to come around my north flank."

This flank had a patch of woods lying just north of the bend of the road but not within the American position and the enemy was striking from out of those woods. Now the snow suits no longer helped them for they reflected the light of the blazing house. From 100 yards away O'Hara's men fired. Some of the figures pitched forward in the snow and others sought its concealment.

One of Colonel O'Hara's men had failed to withdraw in time.

Map 16

NIGHT BATTLE AT MARVIE
23–24 DECEMBER
PHASE 2

SCALE IN YARDS
0    500    1000

TO ARLON

TO BASTOGNE

TO BASTOGNE

PLATOON F

BATTERIES D AND E, 81 A.A. BN. AND TEAM HUSTEAD

ROUZIE'S FORCE

LINE ASSUMES "CUP"

SHAPE—HEAVY PRESSURE

MARVIE

E

ENEMY ENTERS MARVIE WITH INFANTRY[2]

PLATOON G DESTROYED 1900–2000

O'Hara sends two tanks, 2030

B / 20

B / 20 WITHDRAWS 100 YARDS TO AVOID LIGHT

Enemy infiltrates north into forest

TO WILTZ

170

He played dead when the Germans came to his foxhole. They said, "Hello, Hello," then kicked him, sat on him, took his BAR and rifled his pockets. But he kept absolutely still. Some time later be heard them bring up two guns on the left, a large one and a small one. They fired the small gun indiscriminately, apparently with the expectation of getting return fire which would provide a target for the large gun. Yet during the night the large gun never did fire. The man in the foxhole also heard the German ambulances make numerous trips into the area for the purpose of taking out their dead and wounded.

Major Galbreaith (executive officer of the 2d Battalion, 327th), reported to Colonel Harper at 2000, December 23, that the German infantry were in the south end of Marvie and were working through the houses. (see Map 16) The tanks which had been on Hill 500 and had shelled Marvie from there were now moving toward the houses. Galbreaith asked Harper, "Can't I get tanks?" Harper replied, "I'll try." But the line to Team O'Hara had gone out. Colonel Harper tried the radio but could only hear Team O'Hara headquarters faintly.

Major Galbreaith called Colonel Harper again, and said, "They are all around us now and I must have tanks."

"You call O'Hara on your radio," replied Harper, "and say 'It is the commanding general's order that two Sherman tanks move into Marvie at once and take up a defensive position.'"

Colonel Harper had no authority for his action but be figured this wasn't the time to stand on ceremony. A few minutes later the two Sherman tanks moved into Marvie on Colonel O'Hara's orders. The infantry of both sides were already locked in a fight for possession of the houses but the destroyed half-track kept the enemy armor from entering the south of the village.

Colonel Harper's force was now totally stripped of reserve. His line was buckled in and from Hill 500 the Germans were in good position to exploit the break in his center, roll back the flanks of his position, and through this breach enter the heart of

Bastogne. But once again in renewing their direct assault on the city the Germans had made the same error of engaging heavily only along one part of the front. The front at Foy bad cooled off and Colonel Ewell's forces along the Longvilly road could even doze a little. *[This general estimate of situation is supported by all the records and interviews.]*

At 2145 a platoon of paratroopers from Company A of the 501st Parachute Infantry under Captain Stanfield A. Stach was sent to reinforce Company F of the 327th Glider Infantry. That company was already in a pretty bad way. One of its squads had been in the small patch of woods just to the southwest of Hill 500 and part of a platoon had been on higher ground to the squad's right rear. These positions had been overrun by the German armored advance from out of the woods around Martaimont.

A few of the men got away. Others had been killed or taken prisoner defending their ground. The bulk of the company, in position along the crest of the hill commanding the main highway into Bastogne from the south, had held like a rock. The German assault had come on with its right closing around Marvie, its center enveloping Hill 500 and its left lunging forward along the main highway. The armor that supported the advance of the German left could be stopped only by bazooka fire from Lieutenant Smith's platoon, for this was no place for tank destroyers. Anything that came over the skyline of the hill moving southward from Bastogne was immediately put under fire by German tanks or self-propelled guns firing from defilade. No tank destroyers could be risked at the position. Three of Colonel O'Hara's tanks, known as Force Charley 16, were in support of our infantry line, but the night attack closed in in such manner that the fate of the line depended on the infantry weapons. There was a respite after Smith's fire beat back the first attack but the enemy tanks withdrew only a short distance.

The ruptured line north of Hill 500 was quickly patched and

*Map 17*

strengthened before the enemy could exploit his opening success. One platoon of Company F, which had been astride the Bastogne road, was put in position to east of it (see Map 17). The 327th Glider Infantry was also given Batteries D and E of the 81st Antiaircraft Battalion and Major Hustead's part of Team Cherry. Twelve guns were put in an arc along the high ground in the road triangle just above Marvie.

Colonel Rouzie picked up twenty-four men of Company F and with the forty men under Captain Stach proceeded through Lieutenant Smith's position and took up a defense line corresponding with the distribution of the 81st's antiaircraft guns. These moves - made between 2400 and 0100 (December 24) - temporarily closed the breach. Colonel Rouzie took personal charge of the defense of the threatened area. Upon reaching the ground he had decided he was in no position to attack. He felt that he would simply waste his strength if he tried to drive the Germans away from Hill 500. The best course open was to establish a defensive line on the "inner part of the cup."41 Captain Adams reorganized the position of Company F so that the line bent back northeastward to join with the position covering the 81st's guns. *[Adams's command post was on the west side of the Bastogne road across from Smith's.]*

Twice again that night the German armor lashed at the left flank and always the fire fell heaviest, not on Colonel Rouzie's scratch force, but on the position held by the platoons of Lieutenant Smith and Technical Sergeant Butler. The regimental officers of the 327th Glider Infantry said later that Sergeant Butler's courage and energy were the mainstay of the defense. In one of the assaults a pair of German tanks got to within fifty yards of the foxholes held by Lieutenant Smith's men before they were turned back by bazooka fire. By then Smith's command post was blazing, for the tanks had fired fifteen rounds into the house as they came on. Smith and his assistants had set up in the basement and they stayed there while the upper structure burned.

Rouzie's force patrolled southward to the small woods from where part of Company F had been driven and found that it was now held by an enemy outpost. A few Company F stragglers were trying to work their way out of the woods. The patrol mistook them for Germans and fired on them. They hit the ground. One member of the patrol, suspecting that they were Americans, crawled forward, identified them and brought them out. The enemy had captured a number of American mortars around Marvie and through the rest of the night American mortar shells dropped on the ground which Smith and Butler were defending. In the early morning the Germans asked and received permission to remove their dead and wounded from in front of Smith's platoon. It was only when the Germans came forward to collect their dead that the pressure slackened and the mortar fire ceased.

Elsewhere along the sector the issue of the fight was still in balance. Two tanks which had ripped through Harper's forward line had gone right into Bastogne and shot up the houses around his command post, without doing any vital damage. In Marvie the arrival of the two Sherman tanks had stabilized the fighting.

Near midnight, December 23, as the Shermans rolled south into the village, they could hear German armor coming north. They could not see the force nor tell its numbers but the muzzle flashes told them they were engaged at very short range. Again the dead half-track helped save the situation. The leading German tank got up to this accidental roadblock and then tried to turn around, but was knocked out by the two Shermans before it could do so. This loss checked the rest of the enemy armor.

Colonel Harper's infantry in Marvie bad dug themselves in very deep right next to the foundations of the houses and they stayed in their holes without flinching. They now had all the best of it because the village was blazing from many fires set by the artillery. Their foxholes were in heavy shadow while the snow-suited German infantry were highlighted as they came across the open spaces. The general assault was quickly checked by bullet fire but enemy parties got a lodgment in the houses at the lower end of the village and pushed slowly northward.

Along Team O'Hara's front things had quieted well before midnight. The enemy advance into the fire-lighted area was checked and then driven back by machine-gun and rifle fire. Later, after the scene bad again darkened, an enemy tank was heard advancing along the road. The artillery forward observer fired the 75mm. gun from his tank and a 105mm. assault gun fired in the direction of the rumble. Second Lieutenant Sherwood D. Wishart, tank platoon leader, reported that night that he was certain his shells had bounced off and the tank bad backed away. But he had scored a bull's-eye in the darkness and in the morning the tank - a Mark IV - was found sitting to the left of the road with a 75mm. hole clear through it. Not a single body was found on the ground which had been held by the enemy infantry, though the snow bore many other marks of death and confusion. The German medical units had done their tasks well. *[Colonel O'Hara made a thorough search in the interests of identification.]*

Soon after dawn of December 24 Colonel Harper went down to look at his lines. He sent a patrol to the hill where Lieutenant Morrison had been and found it was still in enemy bands. His own men still held most of Marvie though the Germans were in some houses in the south of the village. Five men had been killed and seven wounded in the fighting there and one and one-half platoons had been wiped out on the hill. There were no further developments in the situation during the morning.

At 0900 a patrol from Colonel O'Hara's force went to the old roadblock position and found that the enemy bad withdrawn except for two Germans who were sitting fully exposed on a nearby pile of beets. They shot the two beet sitters and this drew machine-gun fire on themselves. So they pulled back.

At 1340 six P-47s bombed Marvie, dropping six 500-pound bombs among the American positions. Then they came in over the housetops and strafed the streets with caliber .50 fire. Colonel Harper was walking through the streets when the first bomb fell. Even as he jumped for a foxhole he saw that there were two cerise-colored panels clearly showing where the front of the position was. He thought he saw one of the bombs bit among a patrol that was working through the south of the village toward Hill 500 and he sent two runners after the patrol to see if any damage had been done. Then he walked in the same direction. A German wearing a dirty snow suit dodged out of one house and into another so that he could get into a position from which he could fire on the patrol. Harper fired his M1 at the house in order to warn the patrol. The patrol, which seemed OK from the bombing, went to work on the house too, but on receiving rifle fire from the south of the village, they came on back.

During their brief reconnaissance they bad seen a German tank completely camouflaged as a haystack except that the Germans had made the error of leaving the gun muzzle sticking out of the hay. Colonel Harper went to the one Sherman tank remaining in the village and gave the gunner the target - just beyond the last houses. He continued on to the tanks of Team O'Hara along the Wiltz road and told them to start pounding the tank and the houses in the lower part of Marvie which concealed the German infantry. With their first fire the Shermans got direct hits on the tank and blew the hay away. They kept on blasting it and the crews thought they knocked it out. Major Galbreaith (2d Battalion Exec, 327th) said, however, that he saw the tank get away under its own power.

At 1645 the P-47 planes returned again and attacked Marvie with bombs and bullets.59 At 1945 Bastogne was bombed and strafed by several enemy planes.

At 1800, December 24, Colonel Harper was told that he was in command of the perimeter all the way from Marvie to northwest of Hemroulle.

Colonel Harper said to General Higgins, "Look at it! This is half of the Division perimeter."

General Higgins replied, "It's all yours. Do what you can with it. There isn't any other solution."

Higgins reasoned that it was a fairly safe gamble. He had studied the map carefully and had gleaned all that he could from firsthand study of the country just outside the Bastogne perimeter. The landscape to the south was heavily wooded and therefore not suitable for armor. He considered that the only place where the enemy was likely to strike Harper's sector in force was at the Wiltz road. But the opening there was a pretty narrow corridor and he felt that Harper had enough strength across the Wiltz road to deal with any fresh threat at that point. What concerned General Higgins most was the position in the northwest sector, a gently rolling hill country, with no natural obstacles and very little tree growth. Thus far it had been the quietest portion of the perimeter but that fact did not lessen Higgins' apprehension; he felt sure that if a real tank stroke was coming, this would be the point of danger. He remarked to General McAuliffe that they could expect to be entertained out there on Christmas Day.

"The Germans are a sentimental people," he said, "and they are probably thinking about giving a present to Hitler."

# 16. LOW EBB OF SUPPLY

DESPITE the deceptively inactive appearance of the front, the defenders of Bastogne had actually reached the lowest ebb of their fortune by the night of December 22. The crisis was a matter of supply. *[General McAuliffe says that December 23 was the day of crisis. In this he appears to be mistaken. The artillery commanders all said that it was on the afternoon of the 22d that they were most worried about their supply. This checks with the fact that resupply began to arrive fairly early the next morning.]*

General McAuliffe's confidence thus far had been well founded. In manpower, he had been able to maintain a very favorable balance between his reserves and his deployments. His infantry losses had been light. The circle of defenses had been scarcely dented. The German forces, which as a whole had been rapidly moving in the Bulge offensive elsewhere, had so signally failed to put on a coordinated attack against his all-around front that he had been able to beat down each of their separate thrusts by massing the fire of his artillery.

The gun pits of all the defending 105mm. batteries were complete circles. At different times during the siege nearly all guns fired around the whole 6,400 mils of the compass. Most of the artillery fired in support of each infantry battalion against every major attack the Germans made. *[From Colonel Marshall's interviews with Lieutenant Colonel John T. Cooper, Jr., and Colonel Nelson, and from General McAuliffe's statement on the employment of his artillery.]*

More than that, however, the artillery could not do. All day long the infantry commanders witnessed the enemy build-up opposite their sectors. Tanks and half-tracks loaded with German infantry moved freely and contemptuously along the lateral roads, making no effort at concealment although they were within easy range of the howitzers. It made the defenders frantic.

For by noon of December 22 the 463d Field Artillery Battalion, which was supporting the 327th Glider Infantry, had only 200 rounds of ammunition left and the other battalions were in a similar plight. During the first three days there bad been shells enough. Now, in the face of the enemy build-up, the pinch was really hurting and General McAuliffe was about at the point where he would have to ration his guns to ten rounds per day.

There was a delightfully ironic touch even to that restriction, for the supply had dropped very low indeed. Checking the battalions on that day, Colonel Sherburne, the artillery commander, found that with the exception of one battalion which had several hundred rounds of short-range 105mm. ammunition which it alone was equipped to fire, the batteries were down to less than ten rounds total per gun. Still, he kept his own counsel, and when men and officers asked him how the general supply of artillery ammunition was faring, he lied cheerfully and skillfully. At times members of the staff became confused between the true figures and the figures which Sherburne was quoting publicly for the sake of morale. The shell shortage continued to be General McAuliffe's worst, in fact, his only real worry. He told his batteries not to fire "until you see the whites of their eyes."

The infantry commanders and the few remaining artillery observers screamed their heads off about it. One commander phoned General McAuliffe, "We are about to be attacked by two regiments. We can see them out there. Please let us fire at least two rounds per gun."

Colonel Kinnard listened to this plea and later recalled General McAuliffe's reply, "If you see 400 Germans in a 100-yard area, and they have their heads up, you can fire artillery at them - but not more than two rounds.

At the same time, the Bastogne defenders were running low on small-arms ammunition. *[General McAuliffe recollected this as happening on December 23. Colonel Kinnard said it happened on December 22. The 22d appears to be correct inasmuch as resupply became assured on the morning of December 23. There is no doubt, however, about the validity of this quotation. Kinnard and Danahy both heard it, and when his memory was refreshed General McAuliffe recalled that he had said it.]*

So with somewhat mixed feelings the word was received among the regiments at 1530 on that evening that a column from the 4th Armored Division was coming up from the southwest to support the 101st Airborne Division and would be able to give the 101st relief in time.

It was still a neat question whether that relief would come before the ammunition ran out.

In the smaller units which were attachments to the 101st perhaps the strain was even greater. *[Westover was impressed by this difference in how the little units looked at the operation as compared with the 101st Division Headquarters viewpoint. The observation was made on the basis of Westover's findings as contrasted with Marshall's.]* Confidence can come of numbers around the headquarters of a large organization. Talking with his staff, General McAuliffe gained the impression that none doubted the outcome. But out on the fire line, friends shook bands as the darkness came, figuring that all might be overwhelmed before morning. They could take no measure of the reserve strength of the position. What they saw was how few rounds per gun they had left and how large were the numbers of the enemy. The paratroopers were somewhat accustomed to being surrounded by enemy, but it was a new experience for the units who stood with them, unwavering.

The first message from the 4th Armored said, "Hugh is coming." When General McAuliffe had visited General Middleton (commander of VIII Corps) in Neufchâteau on the night of December 20, he had been told that General Patton was attacking east of Bastogne. The two commanders then set up a simple code, each town along the route getting a letter. Bastogne was "K." Others were designated A, B, C. Now the word was that "Hugh *[Major General Hugh J. Gaffey, commanding the 4th Armored Division]* is on his way."

On the heels of that assurance came another message equally bright. VIII Corps radioed that pathfinders, would arrive in Bastogne at 1600 and that resupply by air would start coming in at 2000. Colonel Kohls, G-4, 101st Division, had waited all day long for that appointment, for on the day before VIII Corps had told him to prepare for "resupply tomorrow if weather permits."

Directly west of the houses of Bastogne are large, clear fields on a gentle hillside, close to where the 101st Division had made its command post. This was the designated spot.

Under average operating conditions resupply bundles are recovered by Quartermaster and Ordnance companies and their items of matériel are then segregated in Class I, III and V dumps under Division control. At Bastogne, Colonel Kohls had no Division supply forces available either to pick up the resupply or manage the distribution. The regiments were therefore told to send at least five quarter-ton trucks to the field to handle the supplies directly and haul them to unit dumps. The units were told to report what supplies they had each recovered and then to distribute them according to orders which would be given by the G-4 Section.

At 0730 on December 22, the task of recovering the aerial resupply was given to Major William H. Butler, S-4 of the 501st Parachute Infantry, and Captain Matheson, S-4 of the 506th.

They went to the drop zone, got the crews and vehicles alerted, put out the panels to guide the plane and then waited.

Nothing happened during the day. In the late afternoon came the message from VIII Corps. At 1605 Corps said that the pathfinders would be dropped at 1723 and that the flight would be two planes with ten men each. Captain John M. Huffman, Assistant to G-4, went at once to the drop zone to notify Major Butler. However, at 1641 the operation was cancelled because of ice conditions.

Then the Division rear base radioed at 1700 that sixty C-47s would drop supplies on the first flyable day. However, VIII Corps had not yet given up. At 2115, it radioed that an attempt de will be made to drop a portion of the supplies."

Colonel Kohls again alerted Butler who went to the drop zone and put out the fluorescent panels. Nothing happened. Out of great expectation came only great disappointment.

# 17. SUPPLIES ARRIVE

FROM DAYLIGHT ON December 23 all guards stood alerted for the first appearance of the C-47s. At 0935 a military policeman on duty at the entrance to the 101st Division command post carried the word to Colonel Kohls that several large planes were circling the area.

A few minutes later, the pathfinders jumped in the area where the 2d Battalion of Colonel Harper's 327th Glider Infantry was deployed. They were quickly rounded up by his men. One minute later, First Lieutenant Gordon O. Rothwell, commanding the pathfinder team, was on the telephone explaining to Colonel Kohls that the supply planes would arrive in about 90 minutes. Kohls told him how to get to the drop zone and where to put the radar set. Again the regimental supply men were alerted. Again Major Butler displayed the panels. At 1150 on the 23d, men all along the front saw the planes coming in; it was the most

*Medicine, food and ammunition being dropped from C-47s to the defenders of Bastogne.*

*Members of the 101st Airborne Division bring in a supply bundle.*
*Recovery ran as high as 95% and the bundles were utilized immediately.*

heartening spectacle of the entire siege.

Men and vehicles were all set for it. The pathfinder radar had given Captain Huffman and Lieutenant Colonel John T. Cooper, Jr. (Commanding Officer, 463d Parachute Field Artillery Battalion) a half-hour advance warning that the planes were coming in and the supply parties reached the field ten minutes before the flight, in time for Huffman to assign zones of retrieving to each unit so that there would be a uniformly quick pick-up. There was very little enemy fire on any part of the field.

Sixteen planes arrived in the first flight, but these were just the beginning. By 1606 of that day, 241 planes had dropped 1446 bundles weighing 144 tons by parachute into the milesquare drop zone. The drop pattern was excellent and there was about a 95 per cent recovery of the dropped material.

Working against the approaching darkness, the supply crews threw whole bundles, parachute and all, into the jeeps and shuttled between the drop zone and their dumps as fast as they could tear over the ground. All supplies were in the unit dumps by 1700, and even before that time ammunition had been rushed directly to the front lines and the battery positions. The artillery was firing part of the resupply ammunition at the enemy before the drop zone had been cleared.

By the time darkness came on, Colonel Kohls had at hand reports from all the unit supply officers telling what quantities of matériel had reached their unit dumps. It took only a brief checking on his part to see that his supply problem was far from being solved. The contents of the bundles were not in balance with the real needs of the troops. They still desperately lacked certain items and they had received others which they did not need or want. A great amount of caliber .50 ammunition had been sent up but this was not much in demand. The new supply of caliber .30 for the M1, and of 76mm. APC and 75mm. ammunition was insufficient. The Division needed litters and penicillin badly and though it had collected all of the available bed clothing from the Belgian community, many of its men were still miserably cold at night and were asking for blankets.

Colonel Kohls talked to VIII Corps again at 0830 the next morning (December 24) and said he wanted these things. He asked for additional quantities of ammunition for the 75mm. pack howitzer and also of 105mm. M3 shell. He asked VIII Corps to investigate the possibility of using gliders in the further resupply. All the early resupply missions had been done by parachute. As they came in the Germans put up a terrific amount of flak. The troops saw a number of C-47s shot down, but these losses had not made other planes take evasive action. Colonel Harper said of the pilots who flew these missions:

"Their courage was tremendous, and I believe that their example did a great deal to encourage my infantry."

While Kohls was talking, the first resupply planes of the day appeared over the drop zone and more bundles continued to rain down on the field until 1530. About 100 tons of matériel were parachuted out of 160 planes during that second day of resupply. Even so, the Division's stocking was not by any means full as Christmas Eve drew on. The shortages weighed more on Colonel Kohls than what had been accomplished. Only 445 gallons of gasoline were on hand. The 26,406 K rations that had been received were only enough to supply the defenders of Bastogne for a little more than a single day. The troops were instructed, for a second time, to forage for any food supplies in their areas and to report them to G-4 so that they could be distributed where they were needed most.

This bad been done from the beginning and a large part of the subsistence of the defense had come from the ruined stores of Bastogne or from the stocks of the farming community. From an abandoned Corps bakery had come flour, lard, salt and a small quantity of coffee. Colonel Kohls got these things out to the troops and during the first days of the siege the favorite menu item along the firing line was flapjacks. The coffee, however, was saved for the hospital. The farmers had fairly good supplies

*This 155mm M1A1 howitzer has just received ammunition from the glider in the background. This incident occurred during the siege of Bastogne.*

of potatoes, poultry and cattle. These were taken over on requisition, to be paid for later by the United States. In an abandoned Corps warehouse were found another 450 pounds of coffee, 600 pounds of sugar and a large amount of Ovaltine. These things were all hoarded for the wounded. Prowling about Bastogne, the Civil Affairs Officer, Captain Robert S. Smith, found a large store of margarine, jam and flour in a civilian warehouse. This assured flapjacks for several more days. What was equally important, he found 2,000 burlap bags among the groceries and the bags were rushed out to the infantrymen in the foxholes to wrap around their feet where they lacked arctic overshoes.

By Christmas Eve these supplementary stores were pretty well exhausted. Christmas was a K-ration day - for the men who had K rations.

# 18. THE SITUATION IMPROVES

WITHOUT FULLY REALIZING IT, the defenders of Bastogne passed their crisis on December 23. They could not measure the change, nor did they know how many elements were acting in their favor. But quite suddenly everything began to come their way. This was not a matter alone of successful local tactics against the enemy. Nor was it only that the measures taken by the VIII Corps and the larger forces concerned with the relief of the defenders were at last beginning to bear fruit, as evidenced by the arrival of the resupply missions. For one thing, such a vital matter as the weather continued to favor the defense.

In the beginning there had been fog and acute dampness which appeared at first blush to doubly jeopardize the situation of a force that was having to feel its way to the enemy and was suffering from shortages of clothing and blankets. Yet all that happened in the opening encounters during the first two days Bastogne's fate was in the balance proved that the atmosphere served almost as a protecting screen for the defenders and wrought confusion among the oncoming forces.1 Had there not been fog of course there could have been air support. But it is a question whether that support could have been greatly effective during a period when it would have been difficult to distinguish between the retreating remnants of the broken American divisions and the advancing German columns. Again, an early intervention by the air power might have forestalled those concentrations of German armor and other vehicles which were to provide such inviting targets when the opening at last came.

On December 19 Captain James E. Parker, of the Ninth Air Force, reported into Bastogne as air controller for the defense.

*Map 17*

His equipment consisted of a pocket full of radio crystals; what he needed was a high frequency radio that would give him contact with American planes. He searched the whole 101st Division without success, then found that the attached 10th Armored Division units had two radios of the type needed - one in a tank and the other in a jeep. The tank could not be spared but the jeep and a technician from Ninth Air Force, Sergeant Frank B. Hotard, were given to Captain Parker. By December 21 his radio equipment was complete and he was ready to work with supporting planes. But the fog still enveloped Bastogne to keep the planes away. Parker had to wait two more days.

While the fog held, the first snow flurries came and the weather grew increasingly cold. On the night of December 21 came the first heavy snowfall, adding to the hardships of the front-line troops and the hazards of patrolling. The overcast was still thick and the ground fog irregular. On the morning of December 23, for the first time since the Bastogne defenders were committed to action, a day dawned fair and clear though with freezing temperatures. It looked like the hour of opportunity.

By then the defenses of Bastogne had become so closely knit, and there was such complete harmony and mutual confidence among the oddly assorted groups of the defense, that it seemed certain that all of the changes in the natural conditions of the battlefield would work only to the disadvantage of the enemy. The defensive lines were set. The crisp clear air insured that if the Germans came on, their snow-suit camouflage would not be overly helpful; at least their features and their weapons could be seen. *[This conclusion is drawn from numerous conversations the historians had with front line troops.]* The roads from Bastogne to all parts of the perimeter were like the spokes of a wheel. They were generally good roads. But particularly around the northern half of the defense they entered the perimeter over ground where a stout roadblock might well hold up an armored regiment for hours. The German armor and its support had largely held to the roads during the period of build-up; and they were still out there, daring the lightning. Wire communications from Bastogne command post to all parts of the perimeter were working as strongly on behalf of the defense as was the axial highway system. Only a few times had the wire gone out. The 101st's practice of emphasizing a net of lateral wires, which set up several ways of reaching the outfits on the perimeter, had saved a number of situations that might otherwise have been blacked out. And foresightedly, the Signal Company had brought in plenty of extra wire.

Now that there was the sure prospect of air resupply, the artillery situation was looking up. It had suffered thus far only from its fears that the ammunition wouldn't last. By the 22d, General McAuliffe's supply had dropped down to twenty-odd rounds per gun and Colonel Roberts' about as low, and some guns were down to ten rounds. But both commanders were certain that as long as the artillery ammunition lasted, Bastogne would hold.

The opening engagements had reaffirmed the power of an ample artillery properly directed, and by committing their forces piecemeal the Germans had played right into the hands of the defense which had staked its life on the massed fire of its guns. The guns of Combat Command B, 10th Armored Division, were capable of getting 11,000 yards out of their 105mm. ammunition while the same ammunition in the short 105 tubes of the Airborne Artillery units could only reach about 4,500 yards. The Armored Artillery was therefore the real power of the defense together with the twenty 155mm. howitzers of the Artillery battalions that had been caught in the town(the 755th and part of the 333d Field Artillery Group).

During the first stage, the great natural strength of the position and the vast superiority of the American artillery had worked together for the salvation of Bastogne. The German artillery had been little more than a cipher, save for the fire from the tanks and self-propelled guns. At times it seemed to consist of single guns and their shoots were never very long. The town itself had not yet been given any steady shelling by the enemy guns and the command posts were able to maintain their liaison with little difficulty.

This lack of power in the German artillery and the inability of the German foot and armor to coordinate their assaults against different parts of the perimeter-probably because their communication system had broken under the pressures of the advance-minimized the moral strain which would normally afflict a body of troops that found itself surrounded. The command and staff of the defense were not feeling what they had expected to feel from the lessons they had learned at Leavenworth and Benning. They knew they were cut off. The

G-2 reports and the incessant patrol activities against all portions of the defensive circle told them so. But they did not feel cut off. They remained mobile and mentally able to promote all of the tactical advantages of their interior position. The thought that there were Germans all around them brought no particular extra worry. They were confident that help from the outside was just around the corner.

However, the most decisive gains of the period had been in the work of the fighting men themselves and in their feeling about one another. In the beginning the different elements of the defense were almost out of communication one with the other. Things had happened so fast that they had been compelled to engage the enemy before giving a thought to their own liaison. But in the course of battle the infantry, the armored force and the tank destroyer crews had taken full measure of each other and found the measure sufficient. The birth of mutual confidence and respect had produced not only tactical cohesion but comradeship in such a degree that before the siege was over these units were to ask their higher commanders whether it wouldn't be possible for them to be joined permanently in one large force. They had come to believe that together they had become irresistible.

After their first tilt in which each had spoken bluntly and made his point, General McAuliffe and Colonel Roberts tabled their feelings and worked together to perfect the team play of their respective forces. As McAuliffe's advisor on armor, Roberts found himself among "the best and keenest staff" he had ever seen. Not only did they radiate extreme confidence but they proved to be "great bird dogs" in detecting early enemy build-ups. As soon as the first signs of an enemy attack became apparent, Colonel Roberts would alert his Division reserve and get it moving toward the likely area of irruption. He would then concern himself with building another Division reserve. He never bothered General McAuliffe with these details. If it chanced that Colonel Cherry, the Division reserve commander, got cut up, or if the 101st Division troops moved over during an action and drew parts of Team Cherry into the front line, there was always Team O'Hara with 14 tanks which he could get out of line quickly in case of necessity.

Colonel Roberts' force had more than paid for itself during the first two days. He had taken his greatest losses in tanks and men in the opening engagement, but that sacrifice had staved off the Germans and gained the exact amount of time needed for the 101st to establish itself solidly. After the first two days Colonel Roberts' two chopped-up teams were consolidated as one and this part of the force became his Division reserve. The number of tanks available for it varied from day to day between six and ten.

Lieutenant Colonel Templeton, the Tank Destroyer commander (705th Battalion), took hold in the same strong way, an even having his men fight as infantrymen when they could not be employed otherwise. On the other hand he was never loath to make his point strongly any time he thought the higher commanders were planning to make an unwise employment of his forces.3Colonel Templeton's command post was only a hundred yards from the command post of the 101st Division, so coordination was simple. In turn he received from the battalion commanders of the 101st the kind of support that rewarded all of his effort. During relief periods the infantry platoons covering his tank destroyers made the security of Templeton's guns their first concern.

Colonel Roberts, too, was learning from Templeton as they went along. He had reached the conclusion that, properly employed in a defense like Bastogne, some tanks must be up with the infantry and some in reserve in the "socker" role. But what bothered him was the discovery that while his tankers were actually having to work as tank destroyers about 98 per cent of the time, the tank destroyer men seemed so much better trained to get away with it. This was strongly reflected in the ratio of losses in the two forces when compared with the damage done to the enemy armor.

At 1000 on December 23 Captain Parker at his radio heard that supporting planes were on their way. Within a few minutes he was telling them where to strike. The strongest enemy buildups at this time were west and northwest of the town, threatening the sectors held by the 502d Parachute Infantry and the 327th Glider Infantry regiments. The infantry front lines had been hearing and seeing the arrival of these concentrations during the past two days. But because of the shortage of artillery ammunition, there had been no real check against them. The planes dropped low and came in fast against the enemy columns, gaining complete surprise. The German vehicles were on the road facing toward Bastogne when the first bombs fell among them. Such was the execution that one of the pilots later said to General McAuliffe, "This was better hunting than the Falaise pocket and that was the best I ever expected to see." *[As for the extent of the enemy build-up in the northwest, Colonel Chappuis says in the 502d Parachute Infantry interview that the most trying thing in those days on his troops was that they had to look out every day and see enemy trucks and men swarming up and down the roads all around them. He said, "We could have murdered those Germans. The road intersections in front of us looked like 42d and Broadway after a football game. Most of the traffic seemed to be moving to the west. They were in easy reach and were quite contemptuous about it. But we could do nothing about it because we did not have the artillery ammunition."]*

On that first day the Germans did not use their antiaircraft guns against any of the dive bombers. If this reticence was due to a desire to cover up the positions of the guns, it was a view quickly changed because of the damage the Ninth Air Force planes had done during the first day. For thereafter the German flak was intense over the front at all times and the air units had no further hours of unopposed operation.

They made the most of their opening opportunity. The snow was a great aid. Clearly visible tracks pointed to forest positions which were promptly bombed. The fir forests burst into flames from the fire bombs and before the day was out the smoke from these blazing plantations and from the brewed-up enemy columns made a complete circle around the besieged forces until it seemed almost as if the fog was closing in again. The air people hit every nearby town at least once with explosive and fire bombs. Noville was hit ten times.

The entire air operation was carefully systematized and then supervised in detail. As planes were assigned to the 101st Division by VIII Corps, they checked in with Captain Parker by radio. He put them on a clear landmark such as a railroad or highway as they came in toward Bastogne. Several check points were then given to them from the map. When the approaching planes were definitely located, an approach direction was given that would bring them straight in over the target. This procedure eliminated all need for circling and searching and helped them surprise the enemy. When the bombs and gun ammunition were expended, the planes were ordered up to a safe altitude to patrol the perimeter of the defenses or were given specific reconnaissance missions. Their reconnaissance reports were used as the basis for giving targets for succeeding flights and for giving the ground forces advance information on the build-up of enemy strength. After the first flight there were always targets listed ahead. Captain Parker, carefully monitoring the air, also came across flights assigned to other ground forces battling in the Bulge which had no missions for their bombs. He would then call to them and he often succeeded in persuading them to drop their bombs in the Bastogne area. In a few minutes these planes would be back on their assigned missions.

During the first four days of their support, December 23 to 26, the planes averaged more than 250 sorties daily. After that there were two days of bad weather and then the weather came fair again. But it was on December 23 that the air support clanged the bell most loudly and thereby assured decision for the American forces. Colonel Roberts, watching the planes at work, said with enthusiasm that the effect was worth two or three infantry divisions. General McAuliffe bracketed their work with the overwhelming superiority of his artillery and the supreme courage of the men on the ground in his analysis of why Bastogne was saved.

It was not unusual during the siege to have an infantryman call in that five tanks were coming at him and then see six P-47s diving at the tanks within 20 minutes.

# 19. WEST OF BASTOGNE

FOR SIX DAYS the enemy had made only a few swift passes at General McAuliffe's line facing toward the west. That was the way the command and staff had figured the battle was most likely to develop. Colonel Kinnard, who had worked out the tactical plan for the defense of Bastogne, felt that the forces could be spread thinnest toward the southwest.

Between Colonel Harper, commanding the 327th, and Lieutenant Colonel Ray C. Allen, commanding the 3d Battalion which held the attenuated lines covering toward Neufchâteau, there passed a jest typifying the situation. "How are you doing on your left?" "Good! We have two jeeps out there."

In the northwest sector, the Germans accommodated General McAuliffe's plan of saving the 502d Parachute Infantry for his Sunday punch and that regiment had relatively little fighting though it went through a great many motions.

In the beginning Colonel Allen's 3d Battalion, 327th, became engaged because of the enemy penetration which on the night of December 19-20 reached the Bois de Herbaimont from the direction of Houffalize and overran and captured the 326th Medical Company near crossroads "X." Nine men from the 28th Division - remnant of a group of more than 100 men - got back to Colonel Allen's command post at 2030 and told him how this same German force had ambushed and destroyed their company. It was the first information that the Bastogne-St. Hubert road had been cut and it meant the probable end of any possibility that supplies could be brought in from the northwest. The 101st Division Headquarters became alarmed. At 2200 Colonel Allen was told to move a company out against the roadblock which the enemy had established and destroy it.

Company B under Captain Robert J. McDonald was two hours in preparing for the attack, but it moved out at midnight, December 20-21, and was approaching the roadblock after about a 90-minute march. The men moved down the ditches on either side of the St. Hubert road with two guides walking on the road to keep contact in the darkness. Ahead, they could see a number of vehicles burning and they could hear the enemy laughing and talking. The horns on several of the vehicles had become stuck, adding volume to the sounds which guided them toward their target. The company moved to a ridge within 75 yards of the roadblock, and there deployed. The din from the German position was such that they accomplished this movement without

*Men on guard in a pine plantation near Bastogne.*

being detected. They formed up with the 2d Platoon on the left, the 3d Platoon on the right, and the 1st Platoon in the center, supported by the heavier weapons. One squad of the 2d Platoon moved to the Sprimont road and formed a block across it about 100 yards from crossroads "X" On the other flank a squad from the 3d Platoon established a block for the same purpose about 100 yards outside the enemy outposts.

Captain McDonald had figured that the roadblock on the right would take longest to establish, so he directed the squad leader to fire two quick rifle shots when his men were in position. The plan worked perfectly. When the two shots were fired, the center moved forward, the men shooting from the hip as they advanced. The Germans were taken wholly by surprise and most of them fled toward the Bois de Herbaimont just to the north whence they had come originally. So doing, they crossed the killing ground which was covered by the squad on the right under Technical Sergeant Mike Campano. They were in such numbers that Campano's men could hardly shoot fast enough. More than 50 Germans were killed. None was taken prisoner. Company B didn't lose a man.

When the last German had been cleared from the area roadblocks were organized in all directions, with an especially strong block being set up on the highway to Salle (31 miles southwest of Bertogne). In this general position, Company B became the farthest outpost of the division. In their search of the area the company found three Americans who had been prisoners of the Germans. One was a Negro truck driver and the other two were from the Finance Department of the 28th Division. They also found two dead paratroopers whose throats had been slashed; they guessed that these men had been patients when the hospital was overrun. A number of American trucks were recovered, some containing medical supplies, one carrying a load of mail and another loaded with explosives.

On finding an American light tank among the enemy booty,

Company B incorporated it into their defenses along with several caliber .50 machine guns from the recaptured trucks. The noise of the skirmish had drawn an artillery observer from the 333d Field Artillery Group and he attached himself to Company B and stood ready to deliver supporting fire from the 155mm. howitzers when it would be needed.

At 0700 on December 21 an enemy column was seen approaching from the direction of Salle. The men at the roadblock guessed it was an artillery battery for it contained nine half-tracks, seven 75mm. guns and seven light vehicles. Captain McDonald's men were in a cut above the highway and their position was so well screened that the German column came to within 25 yards before the defenders opened fire. Then they let them have it with all weapons-their rifles, machine guns, a 57mm. gun and the guns of the light tank. Only one light vehicle from the column managed to turn and get away. All of the enemy guns were captured intact but they could not be moved to town and they were therefore destroyed with the aid of the recaptured explosives.

Shortly thereafter, two tanks supported by a group of German infantry tried to flank the position from the northwest. Company B crippled one tank with a rocket and the other tank withdrew. The infantry group was driven back by small-arms fire from Company B's position, supported by artillery fire.

At noon the roadblock positions were put under fire by enemy tanks operating to the southward of Salle. The tank fire was silenced by two tank destroyers from the 705th Tank Destroyer Battalion which had just come forward to help Captain McDonald's company. However, by this time it had become clear that the roadblock had little importance. Patrols had been sent out to the northwest and southwest and they returned with information that the highway bridges in both directions had been blown. Since the highway was of no further service as a supply route for the Division, Company B was ordered to return to the battalion sector. It did so in the early evening.

At 0900 on December 22, one German group cut the road to Mont southeast of Flamizoulle. (Near Mande-St.-Étienne.) The outpost which sighted it said that it had set up a roadblock with "two half-tracks, one jeep and a trailer." Just before noon, Colonel Allen put on an attack directly south to clear the road. He took twenty-five prisoners and drove the rest off. The motor vehicles turned out to be ordinary farm carts which the Germans had hooked together for use as a block. A platoon of Colonel Templeton's tank destroyers then reconnoitered the road, the sections covering one another alternately from one terrain feature to the next. They reported to Colonel Allen that the road was open.

In the northwest sector, the 502d Parachute Infantry engaged directly without any long-range sparring with the enemy. That came of the order which initially took Colonel Stopka's 3d Battalion, 502d, to Recogne to help extricate the Noville force (See Chapter 7). Four tank destroyers accompanied the battalion to Recogne and stayed there, backing up the line. They got no action the first day though two men and a jeep from the 705th's Reconnaissance Company set up as an evacuation team and shuttled the wounded out of the 502d area after a heavy shelling by the German tank artillery.

At 0730 on December 21, the 1st Battalion, 502d, moved to the area just east of Grosse-Hez (two miles east of Champs) on Division order, and with this shifting of the line, Company A was ordered back to its own battalion. (It had been attached to the 2d Battalion to fill out the 2d's long front.) One hour later, the 1st Battalion started up the road toward Recogne. Company G of the 506th Parachute Infantry bad been hit at Foy and had pulled back its left flank to high ground. This maneuver exposed Colonel Stopka's (2d Battalion) right flank which was anchored in the first few buildings at the north end of Recogne. Stopka had already swung his reserve, Company G, around to his right and faced it south so as to cover the open flank. He bad been helped a little by one of the tank destroyers. The morning was intensely foggy and enemy armor could be beard roaming around just beyond the murk. Sergeant Lazar Hovland got a clear sight of one enemy tank and set it afire in four rounds. A second German tank fired on Hovland and missed; Hovland crippled it with a quick shot but it pulled back into the fog.

By the new order from 101st Division, the 1st Battalion was to clean out Recogne finally and then fill the gap between the 502d and 506th regiments. The order was changed a few minutes later when Colonel Sink (506th commander) reported to General McAuliffe that despite Company G's difficulty the 506th's position was pretty sound. General McAuliffe decided that it made little difference whether he held Recogne. The 1st Battalion, 502d, which had been sweeping forward with two companies abreast, was told to keep on moving but in column of companies. General McAuliffe asked Colonel Stopka if he could disengage, pull back of Recogne and stand on a line running southeastward to where he could join Colonel Sink's flank. Inasmuch as Company G was already standing on this line which curved crescent-fashion around a reverse slope, Stopka said he would be glad to make the move. At noontime the 1st Battalion was moved back to Grosse-Hez and Company A was moved to the south of Longchamps to stop anything that might come that way. The 377th Field Artillery Battalion had given support to the 502d during the latter stage of this operation and had fired 60 rounds on the highway from Salle to Bertogne. The fire knocked out six vehicles of a German column which was turned back by these losses.

On December 22 the enemy build-up along the Salle-Bertogne road continued at such a pace that at noontime Colonel Chappuis, the 502d's commander, moved Company A to Champs and the rest of the 1st Battalion to Hemroulle (two miles west of Bastogne), which faced them to the westward. A platoon from Company B was set up as a roadblock, where Company A had been, along the Longchamps-Bastogne road.

The 3d Battalion received German probing attacks all day long, but on a limited scale. Two of the tank destroyers which had been with Colonel Stopka's 3d Battalion were switched over to support Company A in Champs. A patrol was sent to Rouette, a mile north of Champs, to check on enemy activities. It encountered a small detachment of Germans in the village, engaged 14 of them in a 20-minute fight, drove them off with machine-gun and rifle fire and withdrew under cover of fire from the 377th Parachute FA Battalion.

On December 23, the positions were unchanged. Another patrol went into Rouette under the leadership of First Lieutenant David E. White. They got close enough to see that the enemy was occupying a line of outposts on high ground which overlooked the roads to Champs and Givry (two miles northwest of Champs). The enemy was feverishly at work setting up roadblocks of farm carts bound together. There was a great deal of digging going on next to the positions.

Farther to the southward the signs were becoming equally ominous. Colonel Allen's 3d Battalion of the 327th Glider Infantry was situated in defense of the area of Flamierge, Flamizoulle and the St. Hubert highway west of Mande-St.-Étienne. This put it well to the west of any other unit, without friendly contact on either its right or left. Feeling that his battalion was overextended, Colonel Allen issued a withdrawal plan to his units on December 21 which was known as Plan A. By this plan, Company C would move through Company B in Flamizoulle and Company B would then follow and go through Company A. It was the responsibility of Company A to hold off the enemy until the two other companies were situated on the high ground west of Champs and Grandes-Fanges (a mile to the south). Company A would then withdraw through Company B and Company C would go into a reserve position.

At noon on December 23, patrols reported enemy tanks approaching from the woods to the south of the St. Hubert road. On drawing nearer, this force revealed itself as twelve tanks accompanied by infantry in snow suits. About 1330 Colonel Allen's outposts began their withdrawal without trying to engage the German armor. Allen was fearful that the Germans would move to his right and cut him off from Bastogne. Instead, they moved to the left and halted on the ridge just south of the main road near Cochleval. From this ground they fired upon Company Cs position, but upon trying to advance, were turned back by the American artillery. In one sortie they lost two tanks to artillery fire and the rest of the German armor then withdrew to turret defilade and continued to fire into Company C for the rest of the afternoon. Six of Colonel Templeton's tank destroyers (of the 705th), along with the reconnaissance platoon, had been in position where with good fortune they might have supported Company C in the first stage of this action. But as they pulled out of the cut just beyond Mande-St.-Étienne, enemy tanks shelled them from the woods off their flank and two tank destroyers were lost immediately. This caused a more cautious attitude on the part of the other tank destroyers and they withdrew slightly while the reconnaissance platoon went forward to screen them on the left flank. The other tank destroyers distributed themselves so as to block the roads leading into Mont and the reconnaissance Platoon dug in along the same line.

As darkness came on, Colonel Allen got word that his roadblock at Flamierge had been overrun by an enemy infantry force wearing snow suits. This German column had come down the St. Hubert highway from out of the northwest. Allen's men had been under the mistaken impression that a friendly force - the 4th Armored Division - would arrive by this same route. They mistook the identity of the group and let it come on until the time had passed for successful resistance.

Four tanks moving along with the road column suddenly opened fire on Company C, hitting a number of men and destroying the company aid station, an antitank gun and a pile of mortar ammunition with the first few rounds. The four tanks pressed on against the company position. At the same time the ten tanks to the southward began coming over the ridge. Company C withdrew as best it could.

Colonel Allen figured that by now his whole battalion position was in jeopardy and he ordered Plan A put into effect, But Company C was in such confusion that it couldn't carry out the withdrawal exactly as planned. One platoon got out to the southeastward by way of the main road to escape being cut off. The other platoons pulled back along the predetermined route. Company B came through Company A as planned and took position on the left flank of the high ground where Colonel Allen had determined to make his stand. Company A moved to the rear in reserve. However, Company C's losses were such that Company A had to come back forward again and take Company C's place in the line. Fortunately, the enemy did not press the attack.

Allen told his men, "This is our last withdrawal. Live or die - this is it."

He had spoken correctly; the battalion was never pushed from that ground though it was still to face its worst ordeal.

The next day was quiet. The men cleaned their weapons and waited for Christmas Eve.

# 20. CHRISTMAS EVE

CHRISTMAS EVE WAS quiet. The commanders and staffs took official notice of the occasion. To all of the command posts within Bastogne went a G-2 reminder from the 101st's chief joker, Colonel Danahy. It was a sitrep overlay in red, white and green, the red outlining the enemy positions completely encircling the town and the green showing only in the words "Merry Christmas" across the position held by the defenders.

General McAuliffe also rose to the occasion with an inspired communiqué in which he told his men about the German demand for surrender and his answer to them. The rest of his Christmas message read as follows:

What's merry about all this, you ask? We're fighting - it's

*Map 18: Christmas Eve at Bastogne*

*German propaganda leaflet (two sides) fired by artillery shell into the American lines on Christmas Eve.*

cold - we aren't home. All true, but what has the proud Eagle Division accomplished with its worthy comrades of the 10th Armored Division, the 705th Tank Destroyer Battalion and all the rest? Just this: We have stopped cold everything that has been thrown at us from the north, east, south and west. We have identifications from four German panzer divisions, two German infantry divisions and one German parachute division. These units, spearheading the last desperate German lunge, were heading straight west for key points when the Eagle Division was hurriedly ordered to stem the advance. How effectively this was done will be written in history; not alone in our Division's glorious history but in world history. The Germans actually did surround us, their radios blared our doom. Allied troops are counterattacking in force. We continue to hold Bastogne. By holding Bastogne we assure the success of the Allied armies. We know that our Division commander, General Taylor, will say: "Well done!" We are giving our country and our loved ones at home a worthy Christmas present and being privileged to take part in this gallant feat of arms are truly making for ourselves a merry Christmas.

Privately, on the phone that night to General Middleton, McAuliffe expressed his true feeling about Christmas in these words: "The finest Christmas present the 101st could get would be a relief tomorrow."

But General McAuliffe's greeting to his troops proved to be in every part a prophetic utterance though the quiet of Christmas Eve did not last for long.

That night the town was bombed twice. During the first raid, in the late evening, a bomb landed on the hospital of the 20th Armored Infantry Battalion near the intersection of the main roads from Arlon and Neufchâteau. It caved in the roof, burying 20 patients and killing a Belgian woman who was serving as a nurse. Another bomb landed on the headquarters of Combat Command B, doing heavy damage and knocking down the Christmas tree in the message center. The men set up the tree

*Map 19*

again, and in an elaborate ceremony, one of the sergeants pinned the Purple Heart on a mangled doll.

Except for those bombings Christmas Eve passed without unusual pressure from the enemy. The journal entries of the different regiments all use the word "quiet" in describing the period. But that is a word that simply does not record the tumult in the thoughts and emotions of the men of Bastogne. Such was their reaction to the Christmas and to the memories surrounding it, that for the first time all around the perimeter men felt fearful. It seemed to them that the end was at hand. That night many of them shook hands with their comrades. They said to one another that it would probably be their last night together. Many of the commanders saw this happening, though they knew it had little relation to the still strong tactical situation. *[Colonel Ewell, among other commanders, commented on this in the second interview. Many of the men spoke of how fearful they felt on Christmas Eve.]*

In the 502d Parachute Infantry the officers heard Christmas Eve Mass in the tenth-century chapel of the beautiful Rolle Château which they were using for a command post." It was a

*The château at Rolle, 502d Parachute Infantry Command Post*

*Map 20*

happy occasion, well attended by the neighboring Belgians who had rounded out the regimental messes with contributions of flour and sides of beef from their own stores.

The regimental officers turned in about 0130 on Christmas morning.

At 0245 there was an intense shelling of the forward area by the German artillery. Lieut. Colonel Patrick J. Cassidy, the 502d's executive officer, called Captain Wallace A. Swanson of Company A who reported that his front had suddenly become active (see map 20). But he added that the situation was obscure; he could not figure out yet what the Germans intended.

At 0330 Colonel Cassidy called Captain Swanson again. Swanson said that the enemy was on top of him. While they were talking, the line went out. Colonel Cassidy awakened Colonel Chappuis, the regimental commander. Then all lines went out.

Chappuis called his 1st Battalion by radio and told them to get ready to move, adding that the commander, Major John D. Hanlon, was to come to Rolle as quickly as possible. By radio Chappuis heard from Swanson that Germans in large numbers were in Champs and that his men were locked in a hand-to-hand and house-to-house fight with them. Major Hanlon reported at the command post and was told by Colonel Chappuis to move Company B to the Champs road just west of Rolle and then get forward into Champs and help Captain Swanson's Company A.

While Swanson was becoming engaged, other German forces had filtered through the woods to the east of Champs on the 2d Battalion's left flank. After reporting this to regiment, Lieut. Colonel Thomas H. Sutliffe, the 2d Battalion commander, shifted part of his force leftward against this threat. Colonel Chappuis supported his move by instructing Major Hanlon to send one platoon of Company B to the right to join hands with Company E. Hanlon called in at 054512 and said the Germans were still fighting in Champs. He did not want to put the rest of his battalion into the village until it became light because the darkness and confusion were so bad that it was almost impossible to distinguish friend from enemy. Colonel Chappuis told him to hold steady.

As Chappuis and Cassidy estimated the situation at 502d Headquarters, Company B was already backing up Company A and would still be effective if Champs were lost, whereas it might lose its reserve value if it pushed on into the village and the Germans came around it. So they waited. They knew that somewhere a real blow was coming but they could not figure where. So far the German pressure had jarred them only at the right and center of the 502d and was coming at them from the north. They looked anxiously to the westward where their sector joined that of the 327th Glider Infantry. Their command post was under heavy artillery fire and was no longer in either telephone or radio communication with Headquarters, 101st

*Bazooka position in the 502d Parachute Infantry area. It was over this terrain on Christmas Day that enemy tanks moved on Rolle. The enemy tank in the foreground was destroyed in that fight.*

Division.

Just as the first light of Christmas morning broke, the S-2 of the 1st Battalion, First Lieutenant Samuel B. Nickels, Jr., came at a dead run into the château where the Headquarters, 502d, was. "There are seven enemy tanks and lots of infantry coming over the hill on your left," he said. He had first sighted them moving along parallel to the ridge southwest of Hemroulle. They were striking toward the ground where the 502d and 327th joined hands.

The Rolle Château was emptied almost before Lieutenant Nickels had finished speaking. Cooks, clerks, radio men and the chaplains collected under Captain James C. Stone, the 502d headquarters commandant, and rushed west to the next hill.18 From the château gate at Rolle, the road dips down through a deep swale then rises onto the ridge where it joins the main road into Hemroulle, about two miles northwest of Bastogne. The road line is on high ground all the way until just before it reaches Hemroulle where it drops down again to the village.19 Captain Stone's scratch headquarters force ran across the swale and took up firing positions close to the road and facing westward. Within a few minutes they were joined by the men of the regiment's wounded who were able to walk. Major Douglas T. Davidson, the regimental surgeon of the 502d, had run to the chateau stable that was serving as a temporary hospital, rallied his patients, handed them rifles and then led them out against the tanks.

They could see the tanks coming on toward them now. From the archway of Rolle Château it was about 600 yards to the first line of German armor. Colonels Chappuis and Cassidy and the radio operator looked westward from the archway and could see just the outline of the enemy movement in the dim light. They were now the only men at the headquarters.

Colonel Cassidy called Major Hanlon and told him to leave Company B where it was but to get the company ready to protect its own rear and then try to get Company C faced to the west to

*After breaking through the position of the 3d Battalion, 327th Glider Infantry, enemy tanks came across the hills to the left on Christmas Day to attack Champs and Rolle. The road leading to the right goes to Champs. Paralleling the second row of trees a road goes to Rolle. Company C, 502d Parachute Infantry was attacked while marching along the center road. It then fell back to join some tank destroyers of the 705th Tank Destroyer Battalion at the trees in the foreground. From this position many enemy tanks were destroyed.*

meet the German tanks as they came on.

The 327th Glider Infantry was already engaged. At 0500 Colonel Harper had heard by phone from Company A of his 3d Battalion that 18 enemy tanks were formed for attack just east of Mande-St.-Étienne. At 0710 the German armor supported by infantry of the 77th Grenadier Regiment smashed through the positions held by Companies A and B. In coming through the companies, the tanks fired all their guns and the German infantrymen riding the tanks blazed away with their rifles. The spearpoint of the German armor had already broken clear through to the battalion command post. At the 327th regimental headquarters Colonel Harper heard by telephone of the breakthrough, and on the heels of that message came word from Lieut. Colonel Cooper that his 463d Parachute Field Artillery Battalion already had the German tanks under fire. At 0715 Colonel Allen, the 3d Battalion (327th) commander, called and said that the tanks were right on him.

Harper asked, "How close?"

"Right here!" answered Allen. "They are firing point-blank at me from 150 yards range. My units are still in position but I've got to run." But Colonel Allen's battalion had not been wholly taken by surprise. "Tanks are coming toward you!" Captain Preston E. Towns, commanding Company C, had telephoned to Allen.

"Where?" Allen had asked.

"If you look out your window now," said Captain Towns, "you'll be looking right down the muzzle of an 88."

Christmas Day was just then breaking. Colonel Allen stayed at his 3d Battalion, 327th, command post only long enough to look out of his window, and prove what Towns had told him, and to call Colonel Harper and tell him he was getting out. Then he ran as fast as he could go and the German tanker fired at him as he sprinted toward the woods. He could see the muzzle blasts over his shoulder in the semidarkness. But all of the shots were

Map 21

leading him. The Germans were giving him credit for more speed than his legs possessed.

Two members of Allen's staff followed him. As they all came out of the other end of the woods, men of Colonel Chappuis' 502d Parachute Infantry along the ridge road saw them and promptly pinned them down with heavy rifle fire. The three then crawled back to the woods, circled south through a little valley and returned to Hemroulle.

As they came out of the woods the second time, they were fired on by artillerymen of Colonel Cooper's 463d Parachute Field Artillery Battalion who had formed a skirmish line in case the enemy broke through the infantry. But Colonel Allen was getting tired of all this and he waved his handkerchief vigorously until finally the gunners lowered their rifles and let the party come in.

217

Colonel Harper, on getting the phone call made by Allen just before Allen had to dash from his headquarters, realized that there was now no control over the 3d Battalion, 327th. So he sent his own S-3, Major Jones, with his radio to Colonel Cooper's artillery command post and Jones got there just as Allen did, and he got through at once to the companies with the radio.

In the meantime the forward line had held (see map 21), partly because of the quick thinking of Captain McDonald of Company B. He had heard Colonel Allen's urgent report to Colonel Harper over his own telephone and he at once called Companies A and C by radio. "The battalion commander has had to get out," he said to them. "I can see you from where I am. Your best bet is to stay where you are. Hold tight to your positions and fight back at them."

That was what they did. The main body of the German armor rolled straight through Company A's lines - 18 white-camouflaged tanks moving in column. The men of Company A, 327th (First Lieutenant Howard G. Bowles was the acting commanding officer), stayed in their foxholes and took it, replying with their rifles and whatever other weapons were at hand. After the tide of German steel had passed over and through them, 4 men of the company were dead and 5 lay wounded. But the 68 survivors were up and fighting, and in the next round of the battle they captured 92 German prisoners.

Having crashed through Colonel Harper's 327th front, the German armor split as it came on toward the ridge and half of it swung north toward Rolle where Lieutenant Nickels saw it and warned Colonel Chappuis, commander of the 502d Parachute Infantry, in time for him to make his last-minute preparation. Companies B and C, 502d, were even then in column of twos moving up the road toward Champs.

Thus far Colonel Templeton's 705th Tank Destroyer Battalion had played only a minor part in the defense of the sector, but their best moments were approaching. Two of the tank destroyers had been of some assistance to Captain Swanson (Company A, 502d) in his fight for Champs. They were already in position there when the German attack got under way, one destroyer in the center of Champs and another slightly to the west of it so placed that it could cover the road to the southwest and the ridge to the north and northwest. Upon setting up, the tank destroyer crews manned four machine guns on the ground around their centrally located guns. This position held when the German infantry closed on Champs and the tank destroyer force even spared a few of its men to go forward and help the paratroopers root the enemy out of the houses.

Too, the heavy guns were used for close-up interdiction fire to keep the enemy from moving any deeper into the village. In this work, the 37mm. guns, firing canister, were especially effective. Captain Swanson got one of the tank destroyers, under Sergeant Lawrence Valletta, to go forward and blast a house where about thirty Germans had taken cover. Sergeant Valletta moved right in next to the building, trained his big gun on the doors and windows and blew the place apart. He then shelled two more houses and returned to his original position. Just about dawn, he made a second sortie of the same kind.

To the southward of Champs where the crisis of the Christmas action was swiftly maturing, the tank destroyers got away to a bad start but then staged a swift recovery.35 Two of them from Company B, 705th Battalion, had been in the 327th Glider Infantry area and were out along the road which runs from Rolle toward Grandes-Fanges, a mile to the southwest (this put them to the southward of Company C, 502d Parachute Infantry), when the German attack came over the hill. The crews had at first put their tank destroyers into concealment behind a haystack and from there had engaged the enemy armor at a distance, knocking out two or three tanks. Yet as the power of the German armor became more obvious, they decided to withdraw. That was how it happened that they were moving back toward Rolle and were directly in line with the German tank fire when Company C of the 502d Parachute Infantry faced toward the enemy.

Both tank destroyers were knocked out almost instantly. The men of Company C saw them reel and stop from the enemy fire and realized that the loss of the tank destroyers had helped spare them the worst part of the blow.

The encounter had had one other powerful effect - two tank destroyers from Company C, 705th, were waiting in the woods behind Colonel Chappuis' 502d infantrymen. The German armor, confident that it was now in full command of the field, came on boldly against the infantry line. Colonel Cassidy (executive of the 502d) had sent a runner sprinting toward the woods to alert the two concealed tank destroyers. The runner had been told to run from the guns on to Captain George R. Cody's Company C, 502d, position and tell him that the tank destroyers would be backing him up. But he didn't get there in time.

The guns of the seven Mark IVs were already firing into Company C. About 15 to 20 German infantrymen were riding on the outside of each tank, some firing their rifles. But the

*Typical Ardennes countryside between Bastogne and Wiltz.*

ground fog was bad and their fire was erratic. Captain Cody turned his men about and told them to fall back to the edge of the forest. Without any part of its line breaking into a general dash for the rear, Company C fell back to the shelter of the trees and there took up positions and opened fire on the tanks with machine guns, bazookas, and rifles. Despite the surprise of the German assault, this movement was carried out with little loss and no disorder.

Then swiftly, there was a complete turning of the situation as Company C's first volleys from its new position took toll of the German infantry clinging to the tanks. Dead and wounded pitched from the vehicles into the snow. As if with the purpose of saving their infantry, the tanks veered left toward Champs and the position held by Company B, 502d.

Until this moment the two tank destroyers in the woods behind Company C had not fired a round. *[Colonels Chappuis and Cassidy were in a position to observe the relationship in time of the tank destroyer fire to the rest of the action.]* But as the tank line pivoted and began to move northward along the top of the ridge, the flank the German armor became completely exposed and the two tank destroyers went into action. *[The tank destroyer account of this episode is not well rounded out but the crew were not in position to see the action clearly.]* So did Company B, which was now firing at the enemy front. Three of the Mark IVs were hit and knocked out by the tank destroyer fire before they completed their turning movement. One was stopped by a bazooka round from Company C. A fifth tank was hit and stopped by a rocket from Captain Stone's scratch group from Headquarters, 502d. *[This is 502d Parachute Infantry's report of the detail. The tank destroyers themselves claim credit for a greater number of hits.]* The infantry riding on the tanks were cut to pieces by bullet fire. As Company C s part of the battle ended there were 67 German dead and 35 prisoners, many of them wounded, in the area around the ruined tanks.

One tank did break through Company B and charge on into Champs. Company A, 502d, fired bazookas at it and it was also shelled by a 57mm. gun which had taken position in the village. The tank was hit by both types of fire but which weapon made the kill is uncertain.

Captain James J. Hatch, S-3 of the 502d, had gone forward to reconnoiter Company A's situation and was in the Company A command post at the time. He heard the fight going on outside, grabbed his pistol and opened the door. He was looking straight into the mouth of the tank's 75mm. gun at a range of 15 yards.

Hatch closed the door and said to the others, "This is no place for my pistol."

The seventh tank in the German group - it was later determined that this was the same tank that had knocked out the two tank destroyers - was captured intact at Hemroulle. By 0900, December 25, the action was cleared up around Rolle. Headquarters of the 502d Parachute Infantry had called 101st Division Headquarters and asked about the situation of 327th Glider Infantry over on its left. Colonel Kinnard (101st Airborne Division G-3) reported that the 327th's lines were generally intact and the situation there well in hand.

In the 327th's sector there had been four tank destroyers behind Captain McDonald's Company B and four behind Lieutenant Bowles' Company A. Captain Towns' Company C was unsupported by tank destroyers but Colonel Harper had sent him two Sherman tanks on hearing that the German attack was coming.

These guns, the bazooka fire of the 327th Glider Infantry outfits and the barrage fire of Colonel Cooper's 463d Parachute Field Artillery Battalion had dealt in detail with that part of the German armor that tried to ride on through toward Hemroulle after breaking Harper's front. The German tanks were fired at from so many directions and with such a mixture of fire that it was not possible to see or say how each tank met its doom. One

BATTLE AT CHAMPS
25 DECEMBER

PHASE 3

SCALE IN YARDS

ROUETTE

LONGCHAMPS

1300

CHAMPS

REMAINDER OF

ROLLE

TEAM CHERRY

1600

HEMROULLE

TO
BASTOGNE

*Map 22*

battery from the 463d stopped two tanks at a range of 600 yards
and then some men ran out from the battery position and
captured the crews. Eighteen German tanks had been seen on
that part of the 327th Glider Infantry's front that morning.
Eighteen tanks had driven on through the infantry. But not one
got away. When the fighting died at last there were eighteen
disabled German tanks, many of them with fire-blackened hulls,
scattered out through the American positions along the ridges
running from Hemroulle to Champs.

In the 502d Parachute Infantry area, the wire maintenance
men had kept on working right through the fire fight and by 0900
the lines were again in solid.58 None of the German infantry had
managed an escape.

The few survivors, upon recoiling, were rounded up by the
members of Colonel Allen's overrun 3d Battalion, 327th. The

*Map 23*

German tankers died inside their tanks.

Although Company C, 502d, had been compelled to engage without artillery support because of the closeness of the action, its losses were negligible. It was put in position along the high ground west of the scene of the skirmish. At about the same time the Company C fight ended, Company A, 502d, was getting Champs under control and was doing the last of its rat hunting through the village houses. Company B was put over to the eastward of Company A to fill out the line as far as the 3d Battalion. In getting to this position, Company B, 502d, took heavy losses from enemy artillery while moving across the high ground north of Champs, but by 1500 the position was complete (see map 22). Company A counted 98 Germans killed and 79 enlisted men and 2 officers captured in the Champs action.

About 0800 on Christmas, 101st Division moved Force

Cherry out through Hemroulle to a position on the high ground along the edge of the woods to the southward of the 502d Parachute Infantry. Colonel Cherry stayed there until after dark to cover the restoration of the 1st Battalion, 327th, position. He then pulled back to Hemroulle. A German field order captured during the morning fight showed that the German tank and infantry mission that came to grief along the ridge south and west of Rolle had been attempted by the 115th Panzergrenadier Regiment of the 15th Panzergrenadier Division (see map 23). Two battalions of the 77th Panzergrenadier Regiment, supported by the division artillery of the 26th Volksgrenadier Division, had implemented the assault against Champs and to the southward which preceded the Panzer advance.

Christmas day closed with Colonel Chappuis and Colonel Cassidy of the 502d sitting down to a table spread with a can of sardines and a box of crackers. *[This was the high tide of the German attack against the 502d Parachute Infantry. The 1st Battalion, 502d, was again attacked and on December 27 was driven off the hill briefly. By that time Division had been joined by the force from the south. During December 26, the 502d continued to maintain an all-around defense of the position. Six prisoners were taken near Champs.]*

General McAuliffe, disappointed that no relief force had come, called General Middleton and said, "We have been let down."

# 21. THE RELIEF

O N THE MORNING of December 26, the German forces renewed their pressure against the western side of the Bastogne perimeter (see map 24). But they did not press their attack in real strength and the American lines held solid. Around the other parts of the defending circle, the day was relatively quiet though both sides intensified their air activity.

The intervention of the air directly hastened the hour when the enemy encirclement of Bastogne was broken through by the arrival of the armored column from the south. Since 0600 on December 22, the three Combat Commands of the 4th Armored Division had been fighting their way steadily toward Bastogne by three separate routes from their assembly areas north of Arlon. They had met intense resistance all the way along the line and had taken heavy losses in men and tanks. By 1500 on December 26, Combat Command Reserve of the 4th had arrived at the high ground overlooking Clochimont and was preparing to attack toward the village of Sibret. This put the command about four miles to the southwestward of Bastogne with their local objective about one mile to their own northwestward. As the attack was about to get under way, the men saw and heard what seemed to be "hundreds" of C-47 planes coming directly over them and bound for Bastogne. The spectacle encouraged Lieutenant Colonel Creighton W. Abrams, Jr., commanding the 37th Tank Battalion, and Lieutenant Colonel George L. Jaques, commanding the 53d Armored Infantry Battalion, to make a break for Bastogne, disregarding their original mission. They believed that Sibret was strongly held. Colonel Abrams' force had been cut down to twenty medium tanks and Colonel Jaques' force was short 230 men. They figured that it might cost less to ignore Sibret and attack straight toward Bastogne.

At 1520, December 26, Colonel Abrams ordered his S-3, Captain William A. Dwight, to take a light team composed of tanks and infantry, break northeast to the village of Assenois and keep moving until he reached the Bastogne lines. The artillery with Combat Command Reserve, 4th Armored Division - three battalions of 105mm. and one battery of 155mm. howitzers - was directed to stand ready to place a concentration on Assenois as the team moved up to it. Such was the plan.

In the execution of it, the commander of the leading tank called for artillery support as soon as he came within sight of the village. The guns poured ten rounds apiece against the target, concentrating their fire against the woods north of town and into an area in the southern edge of town where the enemy was supposed to be strongly fixed with antitank guns. Combat

*Map 24*

Command Reserve's shells were still dropping on Assenois when the first tanks moved in among the houses. There were some infantry losses from our own fire. In the smoke and confusion, the infantry company of Captain Dwight's team dismounted and engaged the enemy in a fight for the village.

But five tanks and one infantry half-track stuck to the letter of their assignment and kept moving toward Bastogne. Three of the tanks had forged several hundred yards to the fore and the enemy strewed Teller mines between them and the rest of the tank force as they were pulling out of Assenois. The half-track hit a mine and was destroyed. Captain Dwight jumped down from his tank to clear the other mines away, so that he could get forward with his two tanks. Meanwhile, the three lead tanks kept going and at 1650 First Lieutenant Charles P. Boggess, commanding officer of Company C, 37th Tank Battalion, drove the first vehicle from the 4th Armored Division to within the lines of the 326th Airborne Engineer Battalion, 101st Division, of the Bastogne forces.

This was the beginning. The German encirclement was now finally broken, though some days would pass before the American lines to the south were again firm and several weeks of fighting would ensue before the siege of Bastogne was finally lifted. Captain Dwight, having followed Lieutenant Boggess on into Bastogne, radioed Colonel Abrams to come up with the rest of the breakthrough team.

With them came Major General Maxwell D. Taylor, commander of the 101st Division, who had flown back from the United States to join his Division. General Taylor had arrived in time to lead his men through their bitterest days of fighting on the Bastogne ground, the days yet to come.

Captain Dwight then continued on to report to General McAuliffe and arrange for the convoys to enter the town that night. Assenois was cleared by 2000, December 26, with the capture of 428 prisoners. Before morning, the woods on both

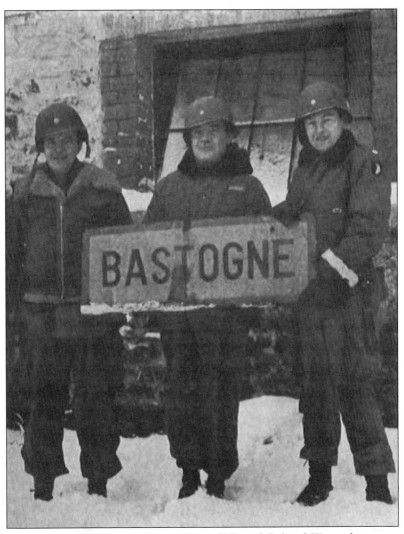

*Colonel Danahy, General McAuliffe and Colonel Kinnard.*

sides of the road running north from Assenois were cleared sufficiently to assure relatively free use of this line of communication.

Much hard fighting still remained for the other two combat commands of 4th Armored Division before they, too, closed to within the Bastogne perimeter. By their drive north, they had opened an avenue to the south which would insure that the victory won by the Bastogne defenders could be fully exploited

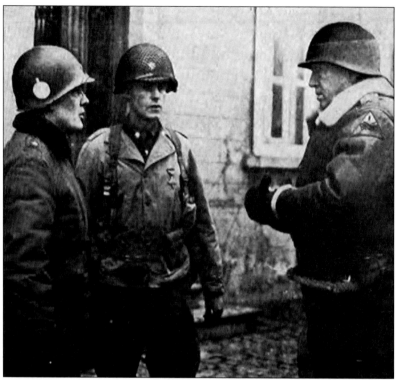

*General George S. Patton, Jr., talking with Brigadier General McAuliffe and Lieutenant Colonel Steve A. Chappuis after awarding these officers the Distinguished Service Cross for their actions int the defense of Bastogne.*

by the United States Army and the forces of its Allies.

The relief of Bastogne signaled the defeat of the German Army in the Ardennes offensive. But it had cost the 4th Armored Division a price comparable to that exacted from the defenders of Bastogne themselves.2 In the seven days during which its forces were moving to the relief of Bastogne the Division lost about 1,000 men. Its total medium tank strength at the end of the period was equal to the full tank strength of a single battalion.3 As for what this victory - won by the defenders of Bastogne and confirmed by the force that relieved them - availed the Allied cause, and as to how it influenced the emergency of December 1944, there is an official estimate from the command of 12th Army Group.

The After Action Report for December 1944 says:

Preoccupation with the key position of Bastogne dominated enemy strategy to such an extent that it cost him the advantage of the initiative. The German High Command evidently considered further extension to the west or north as both logistically and strategically unsound without possession of Bastogne, as that town overlooks the main roads and concentration areas of the spearheads. By the end of the month, the all-out effort in the north had become temporarily. defensive; in the west there was a limited withdrawal, and the array of German forces around Bastogne clearly exposed the enemy's anxiety over that position. Until the Bastogne situation is resolved one way or the other no change in strategy can be expected.

How well those words were sustained by the further passage of events is now history.

# APPENDIX I. THE CASUALTIES

The casualties of the 101st Airborne Division up to January 6, 1945, in the Bastogne operation were as follows:

|  | *Officers* | *Enlisted Men* |
|---|---|---|
| **Killed** | 29 | 312 |
| **Wounded** | 103 | 1,588 |
| **Missing** | 34 | 482 |
|  | 166 | 2,382 |

The Artillery losses were extremely light except among forward observers. The Engineer Battalion lost 26 enlisted men and one officer killed and 84 enlisted men wounded up to January 6. Owing to the capture of the hospital, the 326th Medical Company showed the largest number of missing of any unit at Bastogne with 125 gone. There was a surprisingly even distribution of losses among the Infantry regiments:

|  | 327th | | 501st | | 502d | | 506th | |
|---|---|---|---|---|---|---|---|---|
|  | *Off* | *EM* | *Off* | *EM* | *Off* | *EM* | *Off* | *EM* |
| **Killed** | 2 | 60 | 68 | 8 | 66 | 5 | 67 | |
| **Wounded** | 13 | 279 | 29 | 471 | 22 | 246 | 28 | 359 |

The total of German prisoners taken was 981. The estimated number of enemy killed is 7,000.

MEMORANDUM RECEIPT
VIII CORPS
DATE 18 JAN 1945

RECEIVED FROM THE 101ST AIRBORNE DIVISION
THE TOWN OF BASTOGNE, LUXEMBOURG PROVINCE, BELGIUM.
CONDITION: USED BUT SERVICEABLE, KRAUT DISINFECTED

SIGNED *Troy H. Middleton*

TROY H. MIDDLETON
MAJ GENERAL USA
COMMANDING

*Memorandum receipt given by Major General Troy H. Middleton, Commanding General of the VIII Corps, to the 101st Airborne Division for holding Bastogne.*

# APPENDIX II. THE ENEMY STORY

I N ONE RESPECT, the Bastogne story is complete as told in the preceding chapters. There is the battle as it was seen by the defending forces from within the Bastogne perimeter and as it could be clarified for them by all of the normal and accessible sources of information such as our own official documents, captured enemy documents, interviews with our key personnel at all levels, and interrogation of such of the enemy as fell into our hands in the course of operations. To preserve the integrity of the narrative from the viewpoint of the defenders, it seemed essential that the material be presented in that form. Moreover, since it will be noted in reading this added chapter that the errors caused by so doing were minor indeed, the Bastogne story becomes tangible proof of the competence of our own methods of acquiring intelligence of the enemy and of estimating his capabilities.

There remains, however, the question of exactly what was occurring among the enemy forces while our own forces were defending Bastogne so stoutly. What was their design? How did they view the American action? How did their estimate and judgment of the tactical events modify their own plan and movement?

It has been said in high places that the enemy was not really trying to capture Bastogne. This judgment was taken after a cursory examination of his plan which fell into our hands in the course of the war. But that is not a final truth and if the full importance of all that happened in the first days of the Bastogne defense is to be accurately measured by history, the witnesses must speak from the opposing camp.

In November and December 1945 there took place a series of conferences between the three chief actors in the attack on Bastogne and the author of the Bastogne story. Present were Lieutenant General Heinrich von Lüttwitz, Commanding General of the XXXXVII Panzer Corps, Lieutenant General Fritz Hermann Bayerlein, Commanding General of the Panzer Lehr Division, and Major General Heinz Kokott, Commanding General of the 26th Volksgrenadier Division. Colonel Meinhard von Lauchert, the commander of the 2d Panzer Division, was not present nor was his presence deemed necessary. Of the three divisions, the 2d Panzer had had least to do with the direct attack on Bastogne; and further, the Corps commander, having formerly commanded that division and having a sentimental feeling for it and not too much faith in Von Lauchert, had directly supervised its operation during the German advance. With what at least appeared to be utmost candor, the three enemy commanders proceeded to discuss all that had happened to them.

There were in all ten conferences on these matters, during which the commanders worked with all of the necessary maps and such staff notes as were available to them. Inasmuch as the data on the American operation were already complete, it was easy to provide the check points which would establish the accuracy of their story in all particulars. Colonel H. W. O. Kinnard, who had been G-3 of the 101st Airborne Division during the Bastogne operation, also attended these interrogations. The meeting with Kinnard was a visible shock to the German commanders. It seemed incredible to them that this boyish-faced soldier had been one of their principal antagonists. They asked several times for reassurance on this score. Lüttwitz said, "Are you certain he was chief of operations? Isn't it possible that he was only the chief for one regiment?"

Lüttwitz is an old-time cavalryman. Now past fifty-eight, he is large, gross and paunchy. His monocle and his semi-belligerent manner of speech would suggest that he is the typically arrogant Prussian, but among other German commanders he had the reputation of being especially kind to troops. He would talk only when he had a map before him; then he liked to lay pencils on the map to represent the movements of his regiments. What was most remarkable about him was that in battle he seemed to have concerned himself more with the movements of squads and companies than with the employment of divisions. He was frequently hazy about how his regiments had been disposed but he could invariably say what had been done by a particular patrol or outpost. Once he starts talking, he is extremely windy. He appeared to be chagrined over the fact that he authored the request to Bastogne to surrender; the other commanders concerned all regard that request as a military faux pas. But they believe that Lüttwitz has the "Nuts!" message and that he has hidden it away somewhere as a valuable historical document.

Bayerlein is a short, solidly built man of fifty, sharp-featured and keen of eye. All of his actions are vigorous and his aggressiveness in and out of conversation reminds one of a terrier. This outward seeming hides the fact that he is suffering from a fatal kidney ailment. He prides himself on the fact that in the past ten years he has taught himself to speak English. While working with the American Historical Section, he sat down one evening and wrote as a diversion a fifty-page history of the United States which was quite accurate. His contempt for Lüttwitz is obvious. When Lüttwitz rambles in his conversation, Bayerlein waves a hand in his face and snarls, "Not important! Not important!" He believes that Lüttwitz made the worst fumbles at Bastogne though the record indicates that Bayerlein's individual actions and estimates cost the Corps some of its finest opportunities. About those mistakes and the mistakes of all others, he is brutally frank. They become almost a mania with him. When confronted with his own gross blunders, he puts his head back and laughs with abandon; it seems to be about the one thing that thoroughly amuses him.

Kokott is a shy, scholarly and dignified commander who never raises his voice and appears to be temperate in his actions and judgments. Now past fifty-two, he is doubtless the steadiest man of the three. In his account of battle, he is strictly objective. He shares Bayerlein's opinion of Lüttwitz but is more amused than resentful. Better than any other commander, he saw the true situation at Bastogne though he also made his share of mistakes, as the record shows. He felt, even more strongly than the others, that adherence to the original plan at Bastogne became unwise on December 19 but he is a natural optimist and he expected to win the battle.

The onfall of XXXXVII Panzer Corps against the front held by the American 28th Infantry Division and the general consequences of that onfall have been briefly told in Chapter I of this book. Having made its penetration, the further movements of XXXXVII Corps were intended to be consistent with the overall policy of the Fifth Panzer Army throughout the German Ardennes offensive: The mobile divisions would by-pass points of resistance and remain free to continue the movement; the clearing out of islands of resistance would be done by the slower-moving infantry bodies. The policy of the Army was duly transmitted from Corps down to the divisions. It was believed that the two armored divisions could quickly overrun Bastogne before resistance there could solidify. In their sweep directly westward, the boundary between the 2d Panzer Division on the right and the Panzer Lehr Division on the left, for the attack on Bastogne, was an east-west line about halfway between Bastogne and Noville. The objective of the 2d Panzer Division was the same crossroads X south of the Bois de Herbaimont which figured so prominently in the American story. The purpose of the Panzer Lehr Division was to take Bastogne by attack from the south. This was the original order as established by the initial plan. It was not changed before the battle opened although it was

Map 25: Bastogne envelopment according to the German plan

BASTOGNE

NOVILLE

**Panzer Lehr**
Committed to first effort
to take the town but
ordered to continue west-
ward advance if it failed

**26th Volksgrenadier**
Committed to investment
and capture of town if
armored attack failed
during first phase

**2nd Panzer**
Trying for quick capture
but under orders to continue
westward advance

in a degree modified.

On December 12, Lüttwitz called his division commanders together, and addressing his remarks especially to Bayerlein, the commander of Panzer Lehr, he said to all of them: "Bastogne must be taken. Otherwise it will remain an abscess on our lines of communication. We must clear out the whole of Bastogne and then march on." He added the instruction that if Bastogne was found to be relatively open, it should be attacked directly by the most feasible route, but that if it were defended in strength frontally, the two armored divisions should attempt to envelop and attack the rear or west. These two expedients failing and quick capture of the town appearing impossible, the two armored divisions were to continue their general advance and the 26th Volksgrenadier Division was to undertake the investment and capture of Bastogne. The effect which this conference produced on the minds of the subordinate commanders is to be measured in the story of their separate actions and decisions.

In the attack of December 16 against the general American front, the Corps attacked with 2d Panzer Division on the right flank and 26th Volksgrenadier Division on the left, and Panzer Lehr Division in reserve. Penetrations into our lines having been made, during December 17 the Panzer Lehr Division moved ahead of the 26th Volksgrenadier (see map 25). On the right, the northern bridgeheads across the Clerf and Our rivers had been built by the 2d Panzer Division; these were the bridgeheads enabling the movement of enemy forces along the road to Longvilly. On the left the engineering units of the 26th Volksgrenadier Division had done the necessary bridging to enable Panzer Lehr to cross the Clerf and Our and push on for Bastogne. The two southern bridgeheads opened onto secondary roads by way of which Panzer Lehr could cut the lines of communication South of Bastogne and attack the town initially from that direction.

The 2d Panzer Division advanced rapidly throughout that day

and the next day. Heavy resistance from our 28th Division units in Clervaux slowed its pace on December 17; but after that there was no check to the progress of the 2d Panzer Division until it came almost to the road intersection to the east of Longvilly, where it intended to veer north and proceed toward Noville.

In mid-afternoon of December 17, Lüttwitz, the XXXXVII Corps commander, visited his front lines where his armor was pushing westward from the bridgeheads. He returned late in the day to his CP near Karlshausen on the east bank of the Our River to find a message from his communications officer lying on his desk. It read that he had intercepted an American radio message saying that the American airborne divisions, then near Reims, had been alerted for a fast movement to the battle area. Lüttwitz looked once more at the map and reasoned that they would be sent to Bastogne.

To Lüttwitz, this spoke volumes. In his own words: "Ever since the Arnhem operation our command had feared another attack by airborne forces. When the message came in, we knew not only that there would be no such attack but that the American Army must be extremely short of reserves in the immediate vicinity. Otherwise, it would not commit airborne divisions of such high standing to the battle." But the knowledge that those forces were bound by ground movement for the same objective as his own forces did not change his plan or his instructions. He was already proceeding toward Bastogne with all possible speed and he calculated that he could get there before our airborne units arrived, and he would be opposed by negligible forces in so doing.

During December 18, the advance continued, with both German armored divisions adhering to the boundaries established in the original plan. Through the day there had been no interruption of progress in either lane that dimmed Lüttwitz's hope of beating the opposing forces into Bastogne. As the night drew on, his divisions were promisingly poised: The forward

*Map 26: Opening German movements: December 18-19*

elements of the 2d Panzer were at the point east of Longwilly where the division was to turn north from the main road. The forward elements of Panzer Lehr were at Niederwampach, to the south (see map 26).

It is to be noted that the turning movement of the 2d Panzer Division was taking place at such a distance from the roadblock of our 9th Armored Division in Longvilly (which was in process of being supported and then replaced by the forces under Captain Ryerson of Team Cherry, Combat Command B, 10th Armored Division) that both of these armored bodies could have carried out their assignments without head-on collision. The German force was, of course, turning a shoulder and then exposing a flank toward the American armor in Longvilly; moreover, it was assumed by the German commander that the American armor was in march toward him. He therefore took steps to cover the avenues of approach leading toward his exposed flank. At the same time the Americans in Longvilly, knowing nothing of the turning movement, took it for granted that this German column was coming on down the main road. It was therefore almost inevitable that the two forces would engage but the extent of engagement was limited by the mutually exclusive character of their separate missions.

Panzer Lehr, however, was under no such restriction, since Bastogne lay within its boundary. It was only a question of which was the most opportune road and hour, whether time was left to go directly at the town or whether it was the better part of wisdom to strike first at the lines of communication leading south. To do the former, Bayerlein, then at Niederwampach, would have to get his striking force moved northwest to the Longvilly-Bastogne road - the smoothest route into town.

It seems altogether probable that the soaring ambition of this commander was responsible for his decision. He wanted to take Bastogne in person and the quick thrust was the only way to do it. He talked to some Luxembourg civilians in Niederwampach;

they told him that the side road through Benonchamps to Magéret was in good condition and perfectly feasible for the passage of armor. They said, "It looks bad but will get better and better." In this they misled him but the intelligence was enough to get him started. The road was narrow and deep in mud and became steadily worse. But no resistance was encountered and having started from Niederwampach at 2200, the force crossed the Luxembourg-Belgium border at midnight and reached Benonchamps one hour later. In the force was one battalion of infantry from the 902d Panzergrenadier Regiment, fifteen Mark V tanks and one battery of artillery, all under the command of the 902d Regiment's colonel, although Bayerlein went along in one of the lead tanks and appears to have personally directed the task force.

At 0200 the force reached Magéret on the main road. There a Belgian civilian told Bayerlein that two hours earlier an American force of fifty tanks and forty other armored vehicles under an American ma or general had passed through Magéret going east at about midnight. He was of course referring to Ryerson's scant force of tanks but the degree of exaggeration in the Belgian's statement was enough to offset all the damage that might have been caused by his disclosure. It shook Bayerlein badly and from that point on, the farther he moved forward the more he was constrained to worry about the security of his rear. Because he now knew that there was American armor operating along the Longvilly road between him and the German main body, Bayerlein set up a road block in Magéret composed of three tanks, some supporting infantry and a minefield covering the road from the east - the same roadblock that split Team Cherry and contributed so much to Ryerson's subsequent difficulties. The Germans at Magéret were certain that they could hear American armor moving around in their immediate vicinity but so dark was the night and such the confusion made by the slow movement of the last of their own vehicles into Magéret that they could not be sure where the sounds were coming from and hesitated to open fire for fear of hitting their own. The passage of this armored striking force onto the Longvilly road with the object of capturing Bastogne was regarded by the Americans who partially observed it at the time as only a "strong patrol action." It was so reported to Colonel Cherry and by him to Colonel Roberts. The Americans were still expecting the main enemy thrust to come straight down the main road.

At about 0400 the German force in Magéret began to draw fire from the near-by terrain. Though not greatly harassed, it fought back for about an hour and a half. At 0530 Bayerlein started his tanks on down the road to Neffe. As they worked their way cautiously along toward that hamlet they drew considerable fire from the high ground to right of the road. It is probable that this resistance came from retreating elements of the 9th Armored Division which had taken to the hills at the approach of the German column. The German force kept moving. The lead tank hit a mine at Team Cherry's roadblock just cast of Neffe and blew up; the Germans did not receive any fire from the Americans who had been manning the block and saw no signs of these men. So far not a shot had been fired and they got the impression that Neffe was undefended.

While the remaining mines were being cleared away from the road, one infantry company moved south of the tracks and advanced toward the Neffe Château. The company had no close tank support for the ground was still much too wet for armor.

So in this double-pronged fashion, the advance got under way again at 0550, with the armor (eleven tanks) riding the main highway. At 0700 the head of the armor reached the Neffe station and there it paused for almost an hour-an interlude that cost Bayerlein his one chance to strike Bastogne before Colonel Ewell could get started. All of the dash had gone out of the man by this time. There was no good tactical reason for the pause. But his own doubt about the situation stayed him. When the order to proceed was at last given, the tanks advanced down the Bastogne road about 200 yards. Then they were struck by American fire. A machine gun in one of the leading German tanks had opened fire at about the same time. It was hard to say who had fired first. *[Here note that what Colonel Ewell had considered to be an enemy roadblock was in fact a striking force in motion.]* The German recoil was immediate. The loss to the German infantry from Colonel Ewell's opening fire was insignificant but the reaction among the foot forces was enough to deny the tanks the prospect of immediate support. The infantry wouldn't move and the tanks couldn't go forward alone. This deadlocked the advance for the necessary interlude. Then when Captain McGlone's battery went into action against the Neffe position an hour or so later, the impact was great. About eighty Germans were killed or wounded at Neffe within the first hour or so. Bayerlein, convinced by the sound (there was no observation because of fog and he was misled by the sound of the glider 105mm. gun M3) that he was being opposed by armor, retired to a cave near the Neffe station.

By noon, Bayerlein's mood was one of extreme pessimism. He had felt out the situation on his right and had found Colonel Ewell's left already advancing. Also, he had been impressed by fire that was coming at him from his left - the probable source of which was the small force of men under Colonel Cherry in the Neffe Château. He imagined that infantry battalions were advancing against both his flanks and that the battalion on the north was about ready to close in on Neffe. So he returned to Magéret, where the American tanks rolling back from Longvilly were continuing to hit against his armored roadblock. He passed through the village during the noon hour, some time before Ryerson's force really went to work against the block. His men had captured an American hospital in Magéret and he asked one of the nurses to look after his wounded. His nerve was working better now. He noted that the nurse was "young, blonde and beautiful." He no longer had any thought of pushing forward with his initial task force and he had about concluded that the capture of Bastogne would require the utmost effort on the part of his entire division.

It is now necessary to follow the course of the 2d Panzer Division through these same hours. That division was under orders to capture Noville as soon as possible. Having made the northward turn to the east of Longvilly, the point of the division advanced rapidly toward Bourcy, meeting no resistance en route. The small action at the Bourcy roadblock, although seemingly inconsequential, was sufficient to convince the division commander that he was blocked in that direction and that Noville was probably strongly held. He so advised the Corps commander and the course of the division was turned north so that Noville could be attacked from several sides. The men at the Bourcy block had mistaken this point for a "reconnaissance element" and concluded that they had made off after completing their mission. Instead, the block had changed the course of an entire division. There followed the heavy attacks against Noville on December 19 with the tactical results described earlier in the book. Its road temporarily blocked by this engagement, the 2d Panzer Division on the morning of December 19 was strung out along the road all the way from Noville back to the northwest of Allerborn.

By afternoon of December 19, Bayerlein, commander of the Panzer Lehr Division, had begun to feel himself harassed from every side and was thinking of extricating what he considered to be his "pocketed" forces. In his own words: "As to my own position, I felt that the resistance on my flanks would have to be annihilated before I could again attack. The movement of the infantry regiment which had come out of Bastogne to attack me had reacted decisively on my thinking. Their fire superiority at Neffe was something I had witnessed with my own eyes. I thought and said that we should attack Bastogne with the whole

XXXXVII Corps."

In these calculations, an overstrained imagination undoubtedly played a strong part. During the day, elements of Panzer Lehr (Bayerlein's reconnaissance battalion) covered on their south flank by the third regiment of Kokott's Division - the 39th Fusiliers of 26th Volksgrenadier - had pushed on toward Wardin. As we saw earlier, they had a limited success there and one of Colonel Ewell's companies of the 502d Parachute Infantry - Company I, on his extreme right - had been fragmented. But Bayerlein had eyes and ears only for the signs and sounds of enemy fire on his left, a state of mind aggravated no doubt by the activity of Team O'Hara's guns which had not supported Colonel Ewell's attack on Wardin but which were continuing to punish all enemy forces within sight or hearing.

Bayerlein, by his own account, gained the distinct impression that strong American forces had arrived in Wardin and were about to envelop his left; he could not conceive that the American infantry had been defeated there and that the American armor was preparing to withdraw to ground closer to Bastogne. The time had come, Bayerlein concluded, to direct every energy to the extrication of his force. But this was not easy to do. He felt that retirement by the narrow, winding road on which he had come - the road to Benonchamps - was now out of the question. If he were to make it at all, he would have to completely destroy and clear the American roadblock at Longvilly and move by the main highway. These were his thoughts after he had moved farther rearward from Magéret and he so reported them to his Corps commander, adding his personal urging that the plan be changed and that the entire Corps be thrown against Bastogne.

During these same hours, the XXXXVII Corps commander, Lieutenant General Lüttwitz, had received nothing but bad news from any part of his front. In sum, he had heard that Bayerlein had been stopped at Neffe, that parts of the 77th Regiment of the 26th Volksgrenadier Division had been stopped east of Bizory (by the 501st Parachute Infantry), and that the 78th Regiment of the 26th Division had been stopped at Hill 540, southeast of Foy (by Colonel Sink's forces). General Kokott, too, had expressed the same gloomy views as Bayerlein. He realized that the 101st Airborne Division had beaten him to Bastogne. And feeling that his own division might not be equal to the task of dislodging them, he urged that the entire Corps be committed to the task.

Lüttwitz reported to Fifth Panzer Army that each of his division commanders had gathered the impression that the enemy was in extraordinary strength at Bastogne. He added his recommendation that the original plan be changed and that the XXXXVII Corps be solidly committed to the reduction of Bastogne. Army refused the request, but it added a strange amendment to the previous orders. The Corps as a whole was given permission to renew the attack on a limited scale, since the position of the Panzer Lehr Division had become seriously compromised and so had that of the two northern regiments of the 26th Volksgrenadier Division. This was how matters stood on the highest level at 1600 on December 19.

But on the tactical plane, Corps and all three divisions bad been harassed mainly by thoughts of what might happen unless they destroyed the Longvilly roadblock. They had gone to work on that problem in early afternoon with such results that they should have become convinced they had reduced it to a cipher. The consequences to the American armor of the German attack against the Longvilly position on the afternoon of December 19 have been described earlier in their bare detail. But neither Captain Ryerson nor Lieutenant Hyduke had any idea then what major forces had been arrayed against them. In the course of the forenoon, out of Panzer Lehr, the 901st Panzergrenadier Regiment, one tank destroyer battalion with about twenty TDs, and an artillery battalion, had collected in the area of Benonchamps. Bayerlein, worrying about the Neffe-Magéret forces and the probable involvement of his reconnaissance battalion - the Panzer Lehr Division's reconnaissance training battalion - which had been shaken out farther to the south, seized on the Benonchamps forces to break the grip of the Longvilly block. Bayerlein did not realize at the time that a body of American armor was collected at the position which he was about to attack, for he had received principally mortar and small-arms fire from that direction. He bad already begun to discount the story told him by the Belgian the night before and was now swinging around to the idea that there was no American armor on his rear. This is the reason why he weighted his attack heavily with infantry. He ordered the force to attack from Benonchamps through the woods toward Longvilly, going east. Fifteen of the TDs were to give strong preliminary and supporting fires; the other five TDs were directed to accompany the two companies of infantry to the high ground. It was a trick, he said, that he had learned from opposing our 4th Armored Division in Normandy.

This assault force reached the top of Hill 490 a little time after 1400. From there, they saw the welter of American armor and motionless combat vehicles strung out along the Longvilly road, the tanks trying vainly to break away from their own trap. It was a target they had not expected at all, and it lay fully vulnerable at range of 1,500 to 2,000 yards. The other tank destroyers came forward. The twenty heavy guns of the TDs opened fire and so did all other weapons. (see map 27)

Nor was that all. To support Bayerlein's Neffe position on the right, Lüttwitz had ordered one regiment from the 26th Volksgrenadier Division to move to Bizory via the most direct side road. The advance elements of that regiment, the 77th, had already taken the road from Oberwampach going through Niederwampach. The rear elements were still within convenient reach to the southeast of the Longvilly block. Lüttwitz, not knowing of Bayerlein's action, met the commander of the regiment on the road between Oberwampach and Niederwampach and directed him to collect all artillery and

Map 27: Destruction of the Longvilly Block, December 19

heavy weapons in the general area and attack Longvilly from the southeast. He did so, and the force which went forward was heavy in antitank guns. By accident rather than from design it arrived at the high ground south of Longvilly simultaneously with the opening of Bayerlein's attack and its gunpower was added to the impact of the TDs.

Colonel Meinhard von Lauchert, commanding the 2d Panzer Division, had talked with Lüttwitz about the Longvilly block, but since his own people were turning north some distance short of the American armor, it hadn't concerned him overly in the beginning. But when he drew fire from the Longvilly direction (the action taken by the batteries supporting Hyduke) during the morning of December 19 and the shells threatened to interdict his turning movement, he directed that five or six 88-mm. guns be set up at the road junction below Chilfontaine to counter the American fire. This battery had been in operation for perhaps two hours when the two attacks were launched against Longvilly from the southeast and southwest. Its guns continued to fire and do great execution upon the stalled American column during the hours when the guns along the southern line were raking the armor point-blank. Here was surely the strangest passage in the whole enemy attack on Bastogne - all three divisions engaged at one time, bringing together the greatest fire concentration produced during the first phase of the siege. And their luckless target was a force which already felt itself defeated and was simply looking for a way out!

The bombardment lasted for about two hours, but even after that the German infantry did not close in. After Hyduke and his group fell back on Ryerson, who was trying to break through Magéret and so open a road of escape for what remained of the American force, some few American riflemen remained hidden amid the wreckage of the American armor and kept the enemy at bay with rifle fire - or at least that is the explanation of the German commanders. Dark was almost at hand when the

Germans moved out onto the road. Lüttwitz, fascinated by the spot, strolled among the riven hulls and noted that it was a strange place for a battle. This portion of the road was a kind of sacred way, lined on both sides with large stone crucifixes and a dozen or more heroic figures of saints. The burning armor was jammed in among these objects; the sacred images had served to block the way out. But Lüttwitz looked the tanks over carefully and concluded that Von Lauchert's guns had done most of the damage.

It was a melancholy night for Lüttwitz. He was under the impression that a strong American force had arrived at Wardin. And if that were true, it was a serious impingement on any effort to attack Bastogne from the south. His immediate problem was a kind of tactical monstrosity. He could use his entire corps against Bastogne and yet he had to commit it in such a way that there would be no chance of an involvement that would militate against the accomplishment of his basic mission to keep on advancing. He was dropping infiltration for the moment but he was not undertaking siege: there was no time to coördinate a general plan.

In the morning he felt a little better. Word came that Bayerlein's reconnaissance battalion (Panzer Lehr Division) had taken Wardin. Lüttwitz felt that this eased his situation, though no one bothered to tell him that Wardin had fallen into his hands without struggle because there were no Americans there. On the right the 2d Panzer Division took Noville somewhere near the middle of the afternoon, and again the Corps commander grew confident that the Americans were yielding to his superior force. He thought that an outflanking movement directed at Noville by the 2d Panzer Division from the northwest had brought off the capture of the village. He didn't know that the pressure on the American right rear had anything to do with it - a pressure coming from one of Kokott's regiments. Kokott's men had come through the woods and were pressing on Foy. It was this pressure that persuaded Colonel Sink to ask for permission to withdraw. So during most of that day Lüttwitz entertained an illusion that his hit-and-run effort was succeeding.

His hopes were again dashed by what happened to his center. The 901st Regiment, Panzer Lehr Division, tried for Marvie in the hours of the late morning and was repulsed. However, to Lüttwitz that was no more than an incident in the battle; he hadn't expected much. But when Bayerlein hit again from Neffe just after dark fell, and his attack was stopped cold, the whole command reacted gloomily. Again Bayerlein got a slightly exaggerated idea of the forces opposing him. "I was stopped by a tremendous artillery *[true enough]* and I also found myself opposing a great number of tanks *[not accurate]*. The effect was overpowering. We were stopped before we could begin." Again, to General Bayerlein the shock at Neffe was decisive. It also spelled failure for the Corps as a whole.

The Corps, meanwhile, had been extending westward to the south of Bastogne. When Lüttwitz heard that units of the Panzer Lehr Division had taken Wardin, he told General Kokott to take his reconnaissance battalion and the 39th Regiment, and swinging on a wide arc toward Sibret, make ready to attack Bastogne from the south. The advance followed the general line through Lutremange to Villera-la-Bonne-Eau to Hompré to Sibret but the roads on this line were so difficult for the armored cars that they had to advance well to the southward of the forest. Sibret was captured about 2000. The 39th Regiment reached high ground one kilometer north of Remoifosse and the wood one kilometer north of Assenois and there was brought in check, chiefly through the efforts of Colonel Harper's 327th Glider Infantry and the engineers. Having taken Sibret, Kokott's reconnaissance battalion went on to Chenogne, where it was brought in check temporarily.

Thus the Corps stood on the night of December 20, with Bastogne almost solidly in its embrace. On the south was

Kokott's 39th Regiment (26th Volksgrenadier Division). To the southeast, near Marvie, was Bayerlein's 901st Regiment (Panzer Lehr Division). And next to it, confronting Neffe, was his 902d. The 77th and 78th Regiments of Kokott were on each side of the railway running northeast out of Bastogne. Across the north, blocking all roads, were the elements of the 2d Panzer Division. That division was advancing to the west, and the extension of the general line, in so far as it was concerned, consisted only of roadblock elements whose mission was to protect the flank of the marching column.

Yet despite this apparently excellent situation of the Corps, Lüttwitz felt that night that so far as Bastogne was concerned, he was temporarily defeated. His chief subordinates, too, with the exception of Kokott, believed that the enforced continuation of the advance of the mechanized divisions to the westward, leaving the Bastogne assignment to Kokott's division, dimmed the prospect for a final victory. They had been impressed by the strength of the Bastogne forces and they felt that the task required unremitting pressure from the entire Corps.

In the course of December 21, Kokott's reconnaissance battalion got almost to the highway near Mande-St.-Étienne before being stopped by Colonel Harper's forces. The day was given over largely to the shifting of regiments as Kokott's division took over the general assignment which the day previous had been a Corps responsibility. Panzer Lehr was bound for Morhet. Bayerlein's 902d Regiment was replaced on the Bastogne line by Kokott's 77th, and his 78th Regiment took over the sector which had been held by the 2d Panzer Division. One regiment, the 901st, and some of the special elements of the Panzer Lehr Division were left behind, passing into Kokott's command.

On that day, also, the reconnaissance group of the 2d Panzer Division got only as far as Tenneville. Lüttwitz by now was devoting his entire attention to the progress of the 2d Panzer. He had wanted the reconnaissance group to move fast through the Bois de Bande and reach Bande by nightfall, but for some reason he couldn't get his lead forces rolling and the division strung out all the way from Tenneville to Bourcy. He found out later that the head of his column had been stopped by "strong enemy forces" maintaining a roadblock at a crossing southeast of Tenneville. This was, of course, the block maintained by Company B of Allen's battalion of the 327th Glider Infantry. It held up the progress of the 2d Panzer Division for one whole day, and of this delay much resulted subsequently. On December 22 and 23 the division pushed on only a little way; it was for the 2d Panzer Division a day of endless stopping, starting and turning, the sounds of which gave the defending forces within the Bastogne perimeter the impression that a tremendous enemy build-up was taking place to the north of them. *[The patrols into Rouette led by Lieutenant David E. White of 502d Parachute Infantry were in fact hitting against the outposts covering the flank of this withdrawing division.]* Again word came to Lüttwitz that the 2d Panzer Division's road was blocked by a stoutly held enemy roadblock. The report came from the same regimental commander who had engaged Company B, 327th, on December 21.

On the night of December 23-24, Lüttwitz went forward in person to examine the block. He received no fire as he came within range of it, so be rode on to the block and began taking the logs down. The block had been undefended throughout the entire time and the division had lost two days because of the hesitancy of this regimental commander who was subsequently court-martialed for cowardice. It cost the division dear, and not alone in time, for its vehicles were still strung out over these roads when the skies lifted and the American air strike came. Haltingly, and with other similar bad experiences, the division continued on its way toward Marche, Lüttwitz accompanying them.

Kokott, on taking over the main burden of reducing Bastogne, was at first flushed with optimism. On the morning of December 20 he had been at Wardin, where an American shell hit his CP truck, killed the other occupants and propelled Kokott against the wall of the village church. He was badly stunned; it was his closest call of the war. But he had been encouraged by the taking over of the position. After briefing the 39th Regiment and the reconnaissance battalion for the move westward toward Sibret, he went with them, to make certain that they moved as he wanted. So doing, he gained a first-hand impression that Bastogne was wide open on the south and west. He saw certain of the American elements which, either in moral or physical dissolution, were attempting to move south away from Bastogne. But what he saw he mistakenly interpreted. He thought these retreating fractions signified that the Bastogne defense was now disintegrating. This suspicion became a conviction when at Sibret he talked to a Belgian who assured him that the Bastogne garrison was falling apart. Arriving at his CP at Bras at 0200 on the morning of December 21, he was further cheered by the news that the 5th Parachute Division on his left flank (to the south) was making good progress. Kokott had found the roads very muddy, greatly choked by disabled vehicles left behind by both armies and frequently disturbed by artillery fire from within Bastogne.

The next two days were largely given over to maneuver, as Kokott's 26th Volksgrenadier Division extended westward in an attempt to complete the envelopment. The 77th Regiment was shifted to confront Bastogne from the northwest quarter; the 78th was to the 77th's left in the northeast sector; the 901st of Panzer Lehr Division still confronted the Marvie sector; the 39th Regiment was astride all roads leading into Bastogne from the southeast; the reconnaissance battalion had almost closed the circle on the west side and was moving toward the town from the southwest. On the west side between the reconnaissance battalion and the 77th Regiment, there was a small armored force from Panzer Lehr Division. But even so, where the road ran from Bastogne to Champlon, the line had not been rounded out. The American fire upon this artery was so intense that Kokott's forces could not gain the road, though they had it under such fair observation that they could interdict it effectively against American traffic.

For the time being, the 26th Volksgrenadier Division was sufficiently supplied with gasoline, having taken over some American stores during the swing through to Sibret. Mortar and artillery shells, however, were running short and this had become a drag upon operations. General Kokott didn't have the slightest suspicion that the opposing camp was plagued by the same problem. He noted that whenever the American artillery spoke, it did so in heavy concentrations. It was seldom that a single gun fired for in the interest of conserving ammunition there was little use of harassing fires. To Kokott's mind this suggested that the American artillery was being used with confidence and he reasoned that it must be amply supplied with ammunition. Heavy concentrations equal heavy supply: that was how he reasoned it.

Matters worsened on December 23. To the southward there was a near crisis when Kokott's rear began to feel pressure from the American thrusts northward to relieve Bastogne. Kokott's forces first became aware of the pressure when elements of the 5th Parachute Division fell back into their area. There were five newly arrived Tiger tanks near Kokott's CP. He didn't know where they had come from and he didn't stop to inquire. He sent them on down the Clochimont road in an effort to restore the situation. Soon after the German tanks departed, Kokott saw the first American troop-carrier planes come over on the Bastogne re-supply mission. He and his officers saw the parachutes dropping; they thought that additional paratroops were arriving to swell the ranks of the defenders. The effect was, as he expressed it, "to increase the disorder in the ranks of the attackers."

That night, on Corps order, he attacked Marvie, intending to smash through to Bastogne. The 901st Regiment was sent against Marvie, while the 39th Regiment, on its left, moved along the main road from Assenois. In an extension of this same line, forming roughly a half circle, the reconnaissance battalion, 26th Volksgrenadier Division, also moved to the attack and for the first time was able to close its grip on the Bastogne-Champlon road. The attack failed, as related earlier in the book. Kokott received early reports that his forces had "captured" Marvie *[an exaggeration]* but he never knew that the Panzer Lehr Division had broken the line at Hill 500 that night or that some of its tanks had entered Bastogne. *[Kokott's comment on this was: "They took only the first few houses and then reported to me that they had captured the village. I acted on the assumption that they were telling the truth. This is a very common type of error in our operations."]*

On the same night, while the Marvie attack was flickering, Kokott was visited at his CP by General Hasso-Eccard Manteuffel, Commanding General of the Fifth Panzer Army. An order had come down from XXXXVII Corps that Bastogne would be attacked again on Christmas Day and Manteuffel had come in person to give his instructions. By this time the German high command was thoroughly alarmed. The continued resistance at Bastogne and the southern action in support of it were holding up the advance of their entire Seventh Army. Manteuffel said it was necessary to hurry the conquest of the town because resistance from the south against the 5th Parachute Division was increasing hour by hour. He added, "Bastogne must be taken at all costs."

Manteuffel asked Kokott what he proposed and Kokott said that inasmuch as he had tried from every other direction and had taken heavy losses, he would now attack from out of the northwest. The 77th, which was the freshest of his regiments and had taken the least losses, was holding this sector. He reasoned, too, that the Americans would be looking primarily to the east and south and that their strength would be deployed in these directions, with weakness in the northwest. *[He was all wrong about this. The forces were strongest and freshest in the area he proposed to attack.]* His final argument was that the terrain in the northwest was the most favorable for the employment of armor, being relatively open and firm, so that the tanks would not have to be bound by the roads.

Manteuffel then agreed to put the 15th Panzergrenadier Division at Kokott's disposal and directly under his command for this attack. The division was only then moving up, a veteran division with considerable experience on the Italian front, and it would arrive in good condition.

The forward elements of the 15th Panzergrenadier Division reached the sector confronting Champs and Hemroulle about 2200 on December 24. There were immediately available two artillery battalions, one tank battalion (with about thirty medium tanks and tank destroyers) and the spearheads (two battalions) of the first two infantry regiments. For the troops of that division, it was simply a question of how many could get forward to the assembly area before jump-off time. Kokott bad decided that he had to attack in the dark because of American air superiority and be had set the hour at 0300 on Christmas morning. He reasoned further that his troops would have to be in Bastogne by 0800, for he felt that he would not be able to continue the attack advantageously after daylight.

The greater part of the first two regiments of 15th Panzergrenadier Division got forward in time to be fed into the attack, along with the tank battalion. Some of these men rode the tanks; others followed in an infantry line that wavered from the beginning, because its members had had little chance to catch breath or get their bearings after arrival at the front. Kokott's 77th Regiment attacked on the left against Champs, and he had the impression that this was the only part of the attack that got off strongly. His reconnaissance battalion, to the southward of the sector where the elements of the 15th Panzer Division struck against Colonel Harper's position, was also supposed to have joined in the attack, although this demonstration made almost no impression on the defenders. The troops confronting the eastern and southern parts of the perimeter were ordered to support the attack with continuing fires to prevent reinforcement of the westward-facing positions.

Thus the plans and intentions of the enemy in the Christmas Day fight. The results were as described in an earlier chapter. By 1000 Kokott knew that his plan was irretrievably lost. At 1200 he asked XXXXVII Corps for permission to stop the attack and reorganize. Corps refused, saying that it had become absolutely necessary to capture Bastogne, since the pressure on the south was becoming uncontainable. But the fight *[at the hinge of our 327th Glider Infantry-502d Parachute Infantry front]* had run its own course and was already dying. Kokott reluctantly renewed the attack, knowing now that the only effect would be to increase his losses.

# MORE FROM THE SAME SERIES

Most books from the 'World War II from Original Sources' series are edited and endorsed by Emmy Award winning film maker and military historian Bob Carruthers, producer of Discovery Channel's Line of Fire and Weapons of War and BBC's Both Sides of the Line. Long experience and strong editorial control gives the military history enthusiast the ability to buy with confidence.

The series advisor is David McWhinnie, producer of the acclaimed Battlefield series for Discovery Channel. David and Bob have co-produced books and films with a wide variety of the UK's leading historians including Professor John Erickson and Dr David Chandler.

Where possible the books draw on rare primary sources to give the military enthusiast new insights into a fascinating subject.

*For more information visit www.pen-and-sword.co.uk*